The Interactive and Direct Marketing Guide

Volume 2

The Interactive and Direct Marketing Guide

Published by

The Institute of Direct Marketing

1 Park Road, Teddington, Middlesex TW11 0AR

Tel: +44 (0) 208-977 5705
Fax: +44 (0) 208-943 2535

The IDM has made every effort to ensure that all the information contained in The Interactive and Direct Marketing Guide is as accurate and as up-to-date as possible. However, readers will appreciate that the data is only as recent as its availability, compilation and printing schedules will allow, and is subject to change during the natural course of events. If critical, please check.

ISBN 0 9518692 9 9

Typeset by C&H Prototype, Teddington, Middlesex and printed and bound in Great Britain by Imperial Printers UK Limited.

CD-ROM produced by Chameleon, e-mail: chameleon@chameleonhh.co.uk
Proofreading by LF Proofreading Services at www.lfproofreading.co.uk, e-mail: Linda@lfproofreading.co.uk.
Index by Angela Cottingham, e-mail: angela.cottingham@btinternet.com.

Foreword

How things have changed since we published the last (2nd) edition of this guide, as recently as 1998.

New millennium marketing is a tense cocktail of customer empowerment, information management and brands *sans frontiers*. Mass markets have been usurped by mass customisation. Supply chains are replaced by demand chains, and selling agents are giving way to buying agents. The sum of all this change is perhaps best observed in CRM's rise up the corporate agenda, to the very highest levels of business decision-making.

Within this new context, the everyday business of finding and keeping customers continues. It too has moved on – on to the desktop and in to real time. Campaigns can be planned, implemented and evaluated with lightning speed. But the complexity of taking your products or services to market has increased in equal measure. New media, new channels, greater customer choice and convenience are fuelled by insatiable demand and the opportunities of evolving technologies.

Managing all of this is not an easy task!

To give you a head start, this completely rewritten and revised edition of the unique IDM practitioner's guide captures the essential, practical know-how to modern – interactive and direct – marketing. Long-proven direct marketing techniques that are as effective today as ever (and even more relevant) can be found alongside the emerging techniques of interactive, electronic marketing.

When the very first edition of this guide was published in 1992, the acronym CRM had not yet been coined, direct marketing was only just established as a recognised marketing discipline, and interactive marketing was still a dream. Today, whether in whole or part, every successful marketing plan is now underpinned with the accountable, measurable performance of direct marketing and the new techniques of interactive marketing. This guide gives you access to both. And like the technology that now gives you access to your markets, this guide should be kept close at hand – on your desktop.

Professor Derek Holder
Managing Director
The Institute of Direct Marketing

A new Guide for new challenges

■■■■■■■■■■■■■■■■■■■■■■■■■■■■■■■■■■■

 hrough two editions, and more years than some of us care to remember, the IDM's Direct Marketing Guide has been the bible of the direct marketing industry. Now it has come time for not just a new Guide, but a new title.

Why? Well, part of the answer is obvious enough: as the years go by, new methods, new ideas, add to, or replace, or at least modify previously accepted wisdom. Sometimes these changes can seem to be more about terminology than reality: data marts and data warehouses are no different in principle from the databases which have been part of our vocabulary and our practice for years past. What *is* new is the number of players in the data acquisition and analysis game, the amount of data that technology makes available to them and the sophistication of the analytical systems in the marketplace.

Year on year, the number of companies turning to direct marketing has grown. That great guru, David Ogilvy, is alleged to have said years ago that, in time, all marketing would become direct. This Nirvana may seem some way off yet, but the way that banks, building societies, insurance companies, supermarkets, car manufacturers - newspapers even - have embraced direct marketing in recent years makes a wild prophecy seem more and more like a coming reality.

But there is more yet. Comes the Internet; comes e-mail; comes the World Wide Web; comes text messaging and iTV. It is possible, of course to regard the web as just another advertising medium - to be used principally to enhance brand awareness - or as a channel for passing information to consumers. Just as it is possible to use Crown Derby china at a children's tea party. But the power of the web, as some at least have been quick to recognise, is as a direct marketing medium *par excellence*, while e-mail is neither more nor less than a variant - with relative advantages and disadvantages - of direct mail.

These new media, of course, have their own imperatives, and their proper use demands new knowledge, new skills. Something of these it is our aim to impart. But we aim also to ground these new skills firmly on the solid base that direct marketers have laid down over generations. It would be tragic if web users, or e-mail practitioners, were to spend years learning the hard way lessons already familiar to direct marketers.

Not all of those who have come to the web or to e-mail marketing straight from a retail or a manufacturing environment have recognised that these are simply new media offering new scope for the exercise of direct marketing skills. Hence the coining of the expression 'interactive marketing' to describe the marketing use of the new technologies. Of course, *all* forms of direct marketing, from direct mail to telemarketing to direct response advertising to door-to-door, have always been interactive – how could it be otherwise? But to make it abundantly clear to our new, technophile colleagues just what we are about, we have called ourselves – at the risk, perhaps, of tautology – the *Interactive and Direct Marketing Guide*.

We hope that long-established direct marketers will find here an appropriate introduction to the new technologies whose arrival marks the apotheosis of their trade, and that the new virtual marketers can find in these pages a proper grounding in past practice for the exercise of their skills.

To our many contributors we offer, on behalf of the IDM, and you, our reader, our heartfelt thanks. We hope that when it next becomes necessary to update, or rewrite this Guide, there will be those in the industry equally willing to give of their time and experience for the benefit of future generations.

Robin Fairlie
Editor-in-Chief

Acknowledgements

A word from The IDM

■■

ulling together a publication like the new Interactive and Direct Marketing Guide is very much a team effort. The transition from initial concept to the volume you hold in your hands now has required much energy and dedication. It could not have been achieved without the help of many people who have given freely of their time and considerable expertise.

So, like an Academy Award winner, I'd like to offer some thanks:

✔   Derek Way for designing the cover and the CD-ROM

✔   Mike Hughes, Mick Upton and Ian Alexander of Mail Marketing International for their invaluable advice on production, packaging and fulfillment

✔   Robin Fairlie's calm and authoritative help as Editor-in-Chief

✔   Graeme McCorkell and Peter Mouncey for reviewing the content and writing introductions

✔   Robin Cross and Marion Hasseldine for their help developing the CD-ROM

✔   Proof-reader Linda Ferguson and indexer Angela Cottingham

✔   Paul Palmer at Mailcraft and Juliette Parsons in the M&CS department for coordinating the fulfillment which ensures that it gets to you in one piece

✔   And last, but most importantly, my writers, who I have cajoled, implored – pleaded with! And who, as I hope you will agree, have not let me down!

You can read these volumes – I don't recommend cover-to-cover in one sitting – safe in the knowledge that there is no other place where you can pick the brains of so many experts. And no one should feel disillusioned at not knowing everything already. However senior or experienced – no one individual could hold all that is contained within these covers in their head.

Lastly, I must mention my editorial assistant, Anna Witham, without whose help we would still be sitting with a pile of raw manuscripts. Anna has done a sterling job chasing progress on each of the 51 individual chapters – as well as the index, contents, introductions and cover. Anna was seconded to the IDM for her work placement during a Business Studies degree, but I foresee a fine future in Account Management for her.

Happy reading!

Liz Bryant-Heron
Commissioning Editor

Explanation of icons used throughout this Guide

 Case study

 Definition

 Example

 Further reading

 Money saver

 Note / Checklist

 Quotation

 Remember

 Talking point

 Tip

 Warning

Contents

i

Contents ───

Section 2 — Customer management tools and technologies

Section 3 – Understanding your customer information

Contents

Section 4 — Communications media

Contents

Volume 2

Section 5 — Acquiring customers

Chapter 5.2 — Success Factors *Graeme McCorkell*

Chapter 5.3 — Offline and online acquisition media *Graeme McCorkell*

Chapter 5.4 — Recording and analysing the results *Graeme McCorkell*

Section 6 — Managing and retaining customers

Chapter 6.1 — Creating customer loyalty and relationships *Angus Jenkinson*

Section 7 – Designing your communications

Section 8 — Production and fulfilment

Chapter 8.5 — Using mailing shops *Mike Hughes*

Chapter 8.6 — Fulfilment — delivering the promise *Stephanie Rouse*

Chapter 8.7 — Interactive and direct marketing and the mail *Tim Rivett*

Chapter 8.8 — Contact Centres *Steven Pink*

Volume 3

Chapter 10.1 — Trade and professional organisations, other useful addresses and further information

Chapter 10.2 — The interactive and direct marketing bookshop/bibliography

Chapter 10.3 — A glossary of direct marketing terms

Chapter 4.12

Mobile marketing in the 21st Century

This chapter includes:

- ❏ **Understanding today's mobile landscape**
- ❏ **Mobile technologies, devices and portals**
- ❏ **Building the brand**
- ❏ **Building a mobile user database**
- ❏ **Six mobile marketing campaign scenarios**
- ❏ **Measuring mobile marketing**
- ❏ **Campaign planning – the ten rules of mobile marketing**
- ❏ **The future of the mobile Internet**

About this chapter

The growth of the mobile phone market has been one of the most extraordinary phenomena of the late 20th Century. What it has achieved for marketers is to give them, for the very first time, potential access via an interactive channel to a huge youth market. This chapter explains some of the new terminology which goes with this territory, and the various methodologies that are already being employed by the early adopters seeking to establish a position in this fast-moving marketplace.

James A Matthewson
Managing Director, shrinking earth.net

As well as developing and implementing 'e' strategies for his clients, including brands such as Britannic Money, Corgi, Direct Debit and Filofax, James A Matthewson lectures for the IDM in e-Marketing, e-Business and mobile marketing.

He would like to thank his contributors for supporting the production of this chapter. In particular, Chris Wilton – CEO of mobile communications company Red Tower and Anne de Kerckhove – MD of 12snap.

James A Matthewson M IDM
e: james@shrinkingearth.net
w: www.shrinkingearth.net
t: 0700 2 74 74 65

Chapter 4.12

Mobile marketing in the 21st Century

Understanding today's mobile landscape

Why mobile phones?

obile marketing could be as much as 15 times more effective than traditional forms of direct marketing.

SMS is considered to be about the purest form of viral marketing.

Source: Mobile Transactions Report, May 2001 'SMS marketing trial shows viral potential'

The mobile phone is the new mass marketing medium.

Today more than 240 million people use mobile phones in Europe. 7 out of 10 households in the UK own a mobile phone and 73% use SMS. In the UK alone, the number of text messages increased dramatically from 25 million a month in 1999 to over 109 billion chargeable messages in September 2001, according to the Mobile Data Association. This massive surge in mobile phone ownership creates a unique communication channel which is direct, personal, interactive, targeted and accessible 24 hours a day, 7 days a week.

Facts and figures – the mobile scene

- There will be over 1 billion mobile phone users worldwide by 2003 – Yankee Group.

- Japan has more mobile phones than fixed phones.

- Italy has more mobile phones than credit cards.

- Approximately one third of mobile phones will be WAP enabled by 2003.

- In the UK, mobile phone penetration has now reached 73% of the population.

- Ovum predict that by 2005, over 500 million mobile device users will engage in m-Commerce.

- According to Durlacher, European mobile commerce will be worth an estimated 24 billion euros by 2003, led by Italy, Germany and the UK.

- Worldwide device sales of mobile phones will exceed $22.2 billion by 2005.

Mobile marketing

Mobile marketing offers direct marketers a new way to communicate with their target audience providing fun, interactivity and entertainment. Mobile marketing successfully enables consumers to enjoy a host of interactive entertainment and shopping services, available through 98% of today's mobile phones.

By combining text messaging, voice/sound, web and WAP capabilities, pioneering marketers can turn the mobile phone into a powerful and wholly interactive mass medium.

To ensure that standards are set and adhered to for the wireless advertising market, the Wireless Advertising Association (WAA) and the Wireless Marketing Association (WMA) have been formed.

What are the benefits of mobile marketing?

- It complements offline and online marketing campaigns by ensuring direct customer contact and integration with traditional marketing activities.

- It's exciting and fun and creates the right image among young target groups.

- Customer response rates can be as much as 15 times higher than traditional direct marketing methods, with 30% of responses made within an hour.

- It's the only medium that allows direct interaction with the customer on a personalised basis.

- It gives unique opportunities to develop a mobile customer database.

- Customers are retained by the use of an exciting and innovative service.

- Services can be designed to suit regional needs and offers can be tailored accordingly.

- All services can be monetised to meet business objectives.

How do you attract consumer interest using mobile marketing?

Mobile-based campaigns must offer consumers what they want, when they want it and wherever they are. The mobile marketing mix includes:

- Mobile betting

- Interactive games

- Live text votes

- Teaser voice mail

- Mobile game cards (eg match and win)

- Competitions and instant wins

- Vouchers and coupons for shopping

- Ring tones and logos

- Alerts – news and horoscopes

Quick case study – American Pie II

When film company United International Pictures launched American Pie II, they wanted to find a more creative and hip approach to their primary market. An outbound SMS campaign was devised, supported by banner advertising and poster campaigns.

Recipients were asked to enter their selection and text it back to UIP, who then text back a comical statement from one of the movie's characters.

By pulling response from recipients, UIP was able to collect 'opt-in' based mobile phones. The objectives of the mobile campaign were to:

1. Drive awareness of the cinema release date
2. Drive traffic to the United International Pictures website
3. Target males (70:30) aged 16-35

A sequence of different messages was developed using extracts from the film, each encouraging a choice of answer to be selected by the recipient. Using a text-back feature, the recipient numbers provide text alerts to confirm the local launch date to the phone users.

The campaign targeted 35,000 mobile phone users across the UK and received a 14% response. In addition, the viral nature of the campaign delivered an uplift of 2.3% and recall research conducted post campaign showed an impressive 95% recall, with nearly 60% of those surveyed saying that the campaign had a positive impact on their opinion about American Pie II and their interest in seeing the film.

But does this prove mobile marketing works? Not entirely; there are a whole range of key challenges faced by marketers when using mobile channels.

What are the key challenges faced by direct marketers intending to use mobile channels as part of marketing campaigns?

One of the key challenges direct marketers face is gaining consumer acceptance of the medium and a willingness to volunteer personal information to enable personalised and directed marketing. Although mobile marketing activity is increasing month on month, it is difficult to predict accurately what consumers will agree to accept on their phones and palm tops and how involved they will want to get with brands using this channel.

Studies, conducted both in the US and Europe, have measured consumer response to, and the effectiveness of, basic mobile marketing, primarily in the form of SMS and WAP alerts. The studies found that as long as subscribers were offered something of value in exchange for receiving the advertisements, such as credit for free SMS, the response rates were favourable, with click-through rates up to 52% and 15 -18% of participants actively seeking more information after receiving the advertisements and alerts. These results are indicative of good consumer willingness to receive and participate in wireless campaigns.

Therefore, the key notable points for direct marketers to observe when developing mobile marketing campaigns are:

- Consumers must retain control over the extent of their involvement with the campaign.

- The campaign must be permission-based.

- The recipient's personal information must be protected at all times.

Who's doing it?

Towards the end of 2001, mobile marketing activity stepped up a gear, with more and more brands testing out wireless marketing. However, these campaigns were implemented by the early adopters, those willing to take risks in their existing and new markets.

There is an inherent trade-off between risk and capturing early market share, and the companies that are experimenting with mobile marketing recognise the benefits that can be gained by getting in early. Is mobile marketing risky? To a certain extent, yes. Currently, marketing to mobile devices is unregulated and unproven as a medium. Brands could risk alienating consumers if the campaigns they execute are not well received. Additionally, mobile marketing is new, and therefore campaigns currently attach a novelty factor to them, in the same way viral had when the first viral campaigns were launched.

The companies and brands that are experimenting with mobile marketing campaigns are either technology companies that are already active in the wireless space, such as network providers like Orange and Vodafone, or popular consumer/youth brands looking to reach the huge wireless subscriber market.

In the UK, approximately thirty-five organisations, including Cadbury's, Carlsberg, Coca-Cola, First Direct, Dell, McDonald's and Walkers Crisps have been involved in mobile marketing trials. Response rates vary (between 10% and 28% were recorded within the first two weeks of the trials), which is indicative of a very high percentage of recipients viewing the advertisements and acting on them.

For more information on who's using mobile marketing, see Table 4.12.1 at the end of this chapter.

Mobile technologies, devices and portals

Mobile technology is evolving at a rapid pace and new devices come to the market each day. SMS, WAP, GPRS, iMode and 3G are all buzz-words you are likely to hear in connection with the mobile channel. But what do they mean?

SMS

Short **M**essage **S**ervice (SMS) is part of the Global System for Mobile communications (GSM) network and was actually an add-on feature to phone, originating in network maintenance and diagnostics. However, it was discovered that SMS offered mobile users the ability to send and receive text messages between mobile phones. Messages can comprise words, numbers or alphanumeric combinations, but not graphics, sounds, animations or movies — yet!

The first SMS was believed to have been sent in late 1992 from a PC to a mobile phone on the Vodafone network.

GSM

The **G**lobal **S**ystem for **M**obile communication — the first truly international digital mobile communications standard, of which there are 373 network providers operating across 161 countries. Global subscribers to GSM stood at 655 million at the end of December 2000.

Each SMS message offers up to a maximum of 160 characters including spaces and punctuation, meaning messages need to be crisp. For the creative marketer, SMS can be great for **location-based** initiatives, such as promotions that offer customers a discount if they take their mobile phone into your shop and show the SMS message received to the checkout using **e-tokens**.

Location-based marketing is the method of targeting customers at a specific location and point in time using the mobile communications network as the delivery vehicle.

e-tokens are a simple but effective way of sending a promotion to a mobile phone using text messages.

Advantages of SMS:

- It's ubiquitous – over 95% of mobile phone users can send and receive 'text' messages.

- It's new, simple and an effective method of communications.

- It's popular, particularly with the youth sector.

Disadvantages of SMS:

- It's limited to text only (160 characters including spaces).

- It lacks interactivity.

- It's not transactional.

- It offers limited measurability.

But SMS does not stop there. For more interactive text messaging, there are two other services available: EMS and MMS.

EMS

The Enhanced Messaging Service (EMS) is the ability to send ring tones and operator logos and other simple visual messages to EMS capable handsets and additionally the ability to send and receive a combination of simple media such as melodies, pictures, sounds, animations, modified text and standard text as an integrated message for display on an EMS compliant handset.

There are many different potential combinations of these media. For example, when an exclamation mark appears in the enhanced message, a melody could be played. A simple black and white image could be displayed along with some text and this sound effect. As such, EMS has two main applications: person to person messaging and phone personalisation.

New phones supporting EMS are needed. Support for EMS is widespread among terminal manufacturers such as Ericsson, Alcatel, Siemens and Motorola.

MMS

The Multimedia Messaging Service (MMS) is, as its name suggests, the ability to send and receive rich media messages comprising a combination of text, sounds, images and video to and from MMS capable handsets. The Multimedia Messaging Service (MMS) offers users the ability to send still images such as mobile postcards, pictures, screensavers, greeting cards, maps and business cards. Additionally, moving images, cartoons and interactive video will also be supported by Multimedia Messaging (MMS).

A new mobile network infrastructure is needed for Multimedia Messaging (MMS). MMS services will run over Internet Protocol (IP) based mobile networks, initially GPRS networks and later EDGE and 3G networks.

WAP

By the end of 2001, most mobile phones sold in the UK were capable of accessing the Internet using Wireless Application Protocol (WAP).

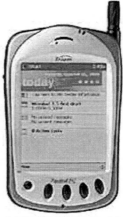

Mitsubishi's Trium Mondo

WAP – Wireless Application Protocol – is a new communications protocol that enables a mobile phone user to access 'Internet style' content while on the move. WAP-enabled phones have become more widespread as both business users and consumers become increasingly attracted to these devices for their portability. Predictions by leading Internet research firm Forrester states that by 2005 there will be 41 million mobile users in the UK.

Yankee Group suggest that there will be over 1 billion mobile phone users worldwide by 2003.

These users will be split into two groups: multi-device users and single-device users. Multi-device users will have other means of going online apart from their phones, such as via their PCs, while single-device users will use the Internet only on their phones. It is predicted there will be 28 million multi-device users and 13 million single-device users in the UK by 2005.

WAP is the standard designed to allow Internet style content to be displayed on mobile devices, such as cell phones, personal organisers (Personal Digital Assistants) and pagers. The information is predominantly text-based to ensure rapid loading to the phone, but does include some small graphics.

WAP provides the first building blocks to mobile marketing and is the logical next step from SMS and the Internet evolution. WAP will become important to marketers, as it's the first technology that liberates the web from the desktop and allows customers to surf using 'pocket' browsers in hand-held devices and cell phones.

The population of WAP users is growing, with more and more coming into the market now that WAP handsets are low cost. WAP is now a standard handset feature.

Additionally, demand for greater integration between PDAs and mobile phones has generated a new breed of mobile devices, called 'Smart Phones'. These include the functionality of PDAs, such as calendars, e-mail, contacts database, word processors, spreadsheets and multimedia, plus WAP. Smart Phones are getting smaller, quicker and cheaper!

Advantages of WAP:

- It's a new channel to market.

- It's truly independent of time and space.

- It's measurable.

- It's popular, primarily among information seekers and business users.

Disadvantages of WAP:

- It has limited penetration among mobile users currently.

- It offers limited content delivery.

- It lacks interactivity.

- It's currently insecure, making it non-viable for financial transactions.

GPRS

Currently in its rollout stages, General Purpose Radio System (GPRS) is designed to change the way mobile Internet users interact with the web. For a start, the mobile Internet device will be *permanently* connected to the Internet, removing the need to connect to the Internet to perform functions, and concerns over cost. Secondly, GPRS is 'high bandwidth', meaning that web-style content accessed through mobile devices will be more like the web content accessed via your desktop computer, using a browser (eg pictures, videos, audio, animations and more).

The introduction of GPRS will offer brands significant opportunities, such as being able to deliver highly targeted, rich-media advertising messages to customers while they are on the move.

Advantages of GPRS:

- **Increases data rates** by about 3-4 times – offering speeds of around 20-24Kbps.

- **Permanently connected** to the network, so information flows to and from the handset almost instantaneously.

- **Integrates e-mail** and other online applications.

- Introduces **location-based** marketing.

Location-based marketing will become a key targeted element of mobile marketing with customers requiring more versatile content, such as streaming video, audio and animations. There are no definitive cost guidelines currently for GPRS marketing, but as the technology moves on, this will become clear.

Mobile internet portals

In the United Kingdom there are currently four mobile network operators – BT Cellnet – now known as O2 as the company has been split from BT, One2One, Orange and Vodafone. For legal reasons, to do with fair competition, O2 and Vodafone have to sell their network services via third party service providers – middlemen who sell the networks air time – while Orange and One2One can sell their services direct to the market.

Sitting on top of the mobile networks are **Mobile Internet Portals**. Similar to traditional Internet portals, the Mobile Internet Portal offers users access to a website that enables them to organise and present content, services and products to suit their needs. However, unlike traditional Internet portals, the Mobile Internet Portals are geared to mobile devices as well as the Internet.

Several Mobile Internet Portals exist, including Genie from O2 and Vizzavi, a joint venture between Vodafone and Vivendi. These are network owned portals, designed to drive revenues from network usage, increase tariff sales and build customer loyalty. However, some independent Mobile Internet Portals also exist, such as BoltBlue who compete with the network operators and offer a mixture of free or paid-for content and services to their user base.

Revenue generation

Mobile marketing doesn't simply represent an opportunity to deliver advertising messages to consumers and customers while they're on the move; it also represents an opportunity to increase revenue earning capabilities. Messages can be sent by the brand that are charged to the recipient. For premium rate or chargeable information, this charge to the recipient can be anything from 10p to £1 per message. A share of this revenue is then passed on to the brand, as the sender, by the network operator. This type of charging is often seen in SMS games – for example the recent SMS version of 'Who Wants to be a Millionaire'.

Examples of Who Wants to be a Millionaire SMS game from Telstra

Mobile marketing solutions

Mobile marketing solutions, such as those provided by companies like Red Tower (www.red-tower.com) are slowly gaining popularity, as marketers and their agencies distance themselves from the 'enabling' technology. A mobile marketing solution generally takes the form of a dedicated software solution hosted at an SMS centre (SMSC). Complete control over multiple mobile marketing campaigns is accomplished through a simple, web-based user interface.

The benefits of this are:

- No additional IT deployment costs.

- Multiple campaigns can be set up, controlled and measured from remote locations.

- Your solution provider will manage the SMS delivery.

- Agencies can be left to concentrate on the creative execution.

Building the brand

Ring tones, graphics and voice mail

An effective marketing technique, used primarily to support brand communications is the delivery of branded ring tones, such as a corporate theme tune; and graphics such as logos, which can be sent to (*some) mobile phones. The mechanism for doing this is precisely the same as for a normal text message, so requires no additional technology.

This kind of SMS is known as OTA (Over The Air) and is also often referred to as provisioning.

(*Note: not all mobile devices can accept ring tones and logos.)

In addition to ring tones, SMS can also be used to send WAP site bookmarks, together with WAP configuration information.

Case study – Bango

Bango Numbers and Mobile Internet help ADHOC Guides build customer loyalty and increase advertising revenues.

In print and on the world wide web AdHoc is the market leader producing free, unique, valued information for people living in and visiting some of Britain's great cities. Put simply, AdHoc helps people make the most of life in their city. One of the key aspects of AdHoc is timeliness of information, whether editorial or advertising. Information on the site changes 24 hours a day, 7 days a week. What's more, AdHoc magazines are read in locations and at times when a PC with Internet connection is simply not available. That's what made access to the wealth of AdHoc information through WAP so important.

According to AdHoc Managing Director, Alistair Wayne, "One of AdHoc's founding values is accessibility. With each of our traditional and new media formats, including WAP, we are ensuring that everyone can access our up to the minute free information in the manner best suited to each individual user."

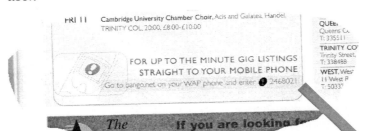

Although it is possible to navigate from the WAP home page on AdHoc to reach content in the extensive site, the need for information is often triggered by reading a review in the magazine. Advertising off the page, in particular, is a frequent cause of a reaction by the reader. By assigning Bango Numbers to 'deep link' into specific content within the site, the Bango Number in the magazine is used by the reader with a phone to link straight to relevant online content. For advertisers, the content can be interactive – enabling booking of a table, ticket purchase or travel bookings.

"By working with Bango we are cutting new ground and thereby further enhancing our customer bond by providing the best WAP service possible. Bango Numbers enable our users to key in a simple number, which allows them to drill directly to the information they desire and will help to ensure a satisfying experience. Without doubt Bango is helping to put further distance between our brand and our competitors in pretty competitive markets," said Alistair Wayne.

The system was extremely easy to implement for AdHoc, who simply block purchased a set of numbers to use across the various publications. Numbers are under the management of AdHoc through a comprehensive online interface to Bango.net. AdHoc reuse numbers from week to week, and the company sells the online service to advertisers. The status of a limited offer, house for sale or sell-out concert can be discovered by a reader through their phone at any time of the day or night.

Building the mobile user database

Another key challenge for the direct marketer wishing to exploit mobile channels to reach their target market is acquiring mobile user data, be it mobile phone numbers or the profile of the mobile user.

So how do you collect mobile numbers?

When a mobile phone number is issued in the UK, the number is made known to three parties: the owner of the mobile phone (or SIM card), the service provider (if applicable) and the network operator. Here in the UK, the mobile phone number is considered private, personal data. However, in other parts of Europe, such as Belgium, personal phone numbers are published in directories. The Data Protection Act prevents the mobile network operators and service providers from publishing mobile phone numbers, yet many still use these numbers to promote and sell their own products and services.

As a direct marketer, you have two choices for gathering mobile numbers. Firstly, you can collect mobile numbers and build your own database, or secondly, you can use a third party's such as 12Snap, who own a mobile database of approximately 8 million mobile numbers. Naturally, option two may be more expedient and more expensive, but it is important to ensure that the third party has the consent of the mobile number owner to send solicitations by SMS.

If option one is the route for you, then building your mobile user database will take time and effort, ensuring that the mobile phone number field appears in all the relevant data collection places whether done online, by post, by phone or face to face. To make the process more efficient, consider offering incentives in exchange for mobile phone numbers, or for switching communications to this channel from another one. Always be sure to check that the mobile owner consents to be contacted via his or her personal mobile phone.

If you collect mobile phone numbers with the intention of conducting mobile marketing campaigns, it is likely that the first type of campaign you will engage in will be SMS based. To facilitate that, you will need an SMS broadcast provider capable of delivering anything from hundreds to thousands to millions of SMS messages. This will not be a service you can buy direct from the network operators, but via companies such as Mobile Internet Portals (BoltBlue), SMS Aggregators (mBlox) and SMS service providers (eg Iobox).

When selecting an SMS broadcast partner, consider important issues such as:

- Will you receive confirmation of delivery?

- Are there managed reply functions in place?

- Can the service provider also manage the database?

Fundamentally, SMS service providers are the mobile world's equivalent to a direct marketing agency, responsible for creating and sending the message out, measuring response rates and maintaining communications with customers (users) if appropriate.

Currently, not many lists of permission based mobile phone numbers exist or databases that include good lifestyle data, socio-demographic data and mobile phone numbers all together. The best are likely to be available from Mobile Internet Portals, such as BoltBlue, which gathers data on gender, age, postcode, mobile phone number and network etc.

Six mobile marketing scenarios

The breadth of possibilities that exist in utilising the mobile channel are limited only by the imaginations of the brands using them. While technology plays a factor in the delivery of mobile marketing, innovative and interesting ideas will fuel the adoption of mobile channels as part of the direct marketing mix.

Scenario 1 – Simple message broadcast

Objective	To target specific marketing related messages to mobile phone users via Short Message Service (SMS).
Other channels	None.
Description	A specific message needs to be targeted to individuals with certain profiles. A list of mobile phone numbers is used and messages are despatched at specific times in the day or week relevant to the promotion. For example, High Street shops may require messages to be sent on a Saturday during late morning to females whose partners generally go to football in the afternoon.
Technology	No reply path is required, therefore volume alone dictates the way in which SMS messages are sent. Anything up to 10,000 messages per month can be achieved through a GSM modem terminal; greater than this can be achieved through direct connection to the network operators.
Future possibilities	At some time in the future the networks will be providing location information, thus enabling individuals to be targeted by profile and location.
Measurement	Market research.
Response	Proven to be greater than offline advertising due to the positive effect of receiving an SMS message. Novelty factor must be considered here.
Advantages	Bulk transmission of SMS messages is straightforward particularly with a solution that allows the scheduling of messages to pre-defined groups. Virtually maintenance free and therefore low running costs.
Disadvantages	Overuse could result in SMS spamming accusations. The youth sectors are more tolerant to receiving promotional SMS messages. Best practice guidelines advise a means for the recipient to unsubscribe via the delivery channel. Therefore a reply path should be considered.
Cost	Cost of running a campaign comes from the cost of the target list and the cost per SMS transmission (4p to 7p per message dependent on volume). Pricing on bulk SMS delivery is tariffed up to 1 million per month before specific deals with network operators are beneficial.

Scenario 2 – Information alerts

Objective	To provide a value added service to opt-in target lists and new subscribers by delivering requested information.
Other channels	Web – can be used to set up preferences. Offline print – to promote service.
Description	This is purely an opt-in service accomplished through a profiled opt-in list or by request of the user. On seeing a promotion a user can send a 'subscribe' message to the advertised mobile number.

On receipt an acknowledge message is returned. At a pre-defined time information messages are despatched to all subscribers. If a subscriber wishes to stop using the service a message containing *'unsubscribe'* can be sent. As an example a cinema complex wishes to advertise films being screened at their complex. They wish to send out an SMS every Friday detailing the screenings for that week. They have an opt-in list but wish to expand this further. Through offline postcard hand-outs, newspaper advertisements and web-based advertising they promote the new service. Users subscribe by texting SUBSCRIBE to the advertised number.

Technology

A return path is required here and the information must be sent out in bulk; therefore a direct connection with shared network short code or multiple GSM modem terminals must be used. We would advise starting the service with multiple GSM terminals.

Future possibilities

Web page allowing subscribers to set up preferences such as film genre etc. That can then determine specific information that can be sent. Revenue can be earned by selling spare SMS message space for advertising.

Measurement

Churn rate can be measured and correlated with market research. Driving users to a related website can result in data collection and profiling.

Response

30%+ responses have been measured from this kind of marketing.

Advantages

As with scenario 1, bulk transmission is straightforward, content of messages can be entered through a web based user interface and despatch can be accomplished through scheduling. Highly youth orientated with consequently low churn.

Disadvantages

None.

Cost

Cost of running this service comes from the cost per SMS transmission, (4p to 7p per message dependent on volume). Pricing on bulk SMS delivery is tariffed up to 1 million per month before specific deals with network operators are beneficial.

Scenario 3 – Competitions

Objective

To raise awareness of a particular brand by way of an incentive based competition.

Other channels

Offline print – to promote service.

Description

A manufacturer is releasing a new retail brand that they wish to promote. Displays are printed and erected in retail outlets promoting an SMS text competition. Purchasers are invited to text a PLAY message; on reply they are sent back a message containing a multi-choice question. The user sends an answer back, which if correct enters them into a draw. A message will be sent back indicating if their answer is correct or not. There is no limit to the number of times someone can enter but each subsequent time they will be given a new question. The prize will be goods relating to the brand being promoted. A real case example comes with a leading confectionery manufacturer. On the inside wrapper of some 50 million chocolate bars was a general knowledge question, the answer to which was to be sent via SMS. This proved hugely popular and produced interesting data: the assumption can be made that the competition was entered at the time the chocolate bar was consumed; therefore an accurate profile was built up of the exact times during the day these chocolate bars were eaten.

Technology	This campaign is initiated by the user; therefore SMS delivery will be spread over time. A GSM modem terminal will be ideal for this solution.
Future possibilities	This is a simple campaign with a single purpose.
Measurement	Multiple entries can be monitored but there is no direct correlation between entering the game and buying the product. Market research. SMS market research is also possible and frequently conducted.
Performance	These competitions are well received and regarded with a high degree of novelty. The simplicity and immediacy of entering is extremely appealing (no sending off postcards etc).
Advantages	Once set up this will run itself, producing reports at key times on request. The simplicity and cost of running is a key factor. Provides a means of collecting mobile phone numbers for future campaigns.
Disadvantages	Limited measurement capability, but can be overcome by the design of the competition, eg the chocolate bar campaign.
Cost	SMS costs (4-7p per message).

Scenario 4 – Text back information

Objective	To provide an information-based service through user initiation.
Other channels	Offline print – to promote service, web and WAP to select and change user preferences. WAP to provide a more detailed information service. Viral to promote the use and simplicity of receiving timely relevant information.
Description	Similar to the alert service but is user initiated. No subscription is required so the service can have a viral effect particularly among the youth. On sending a specific keyword, information, ring tones and pictures can be sent to the initiator's phone. For example sending a text containing 'Dog & Duck' to the service may result in information being sent by reply indicating the gigs or events that are taking place at the Dog & Duck pub. Similarly by sending a song title by text, a ring tone will be sent in reply.
Technology	This service will almost certainly benefit from a reverse charge model and a cross network short code. This will provide sufficient revenue to support the service.
Future possibilities	Again location-based information will be available in the future. Selling spare message capacity for advertising.
Measurement	This service is particularly relevant to entertainment information and would benefit from tokens as a form of tracking, eg request information about gigs in the D&D and receive a free entrance token (see scenario 5).

Performance	These services, if planned effectively and simply, are becoming increasingly popular among youth and young professional sectors. The key is to keep it simple and relevant and to utilise offline and viral channels effectively.
Advantages	Hugely popular particularly if associated with a substantial brand.
Disadvantages	Requires content management overhead to keep information up to date. Requires a popular and substantial brand to be effective.
Cost	Reverse charge revenue share is advised in order to cover operational costs.

Scenario 5 – Event promotion

Objective	To raise awareness of an event and provide information and utility during the event.
Other channels	Offline print – to promote service e-mail, web, WAP
Description	A typical example would be a promotion for a sporting event taking place over a number of days; for example a five-day test match. By way of a simple competition promoted in newspapers users register interest in the event. Promotional text messages are then sent to them in the run up to the event, possibly including money off vouchers. Users are directed to the event website on the incentive of entrance discounts. Information is collected by the website and tickets can be purchased. If the user opts in to receiving SMS alerts then they will receive match updates (including promotions) throughout the course of the event. By utilising a text-back service (see scenario 4), users can gain information on player statistics etc. This facility will also be available on the associated WAP site.
Technology	SMS delivery can be simply achieved through GSM modem terminals; however if revenue is required direct connections will be required. The WAP site can be administered through the same user interface.
Future possibilities	Location information would again be a future enhancement.
Measurement	Measurement can be achieved from first contact through to attendance.
Performance	Reaction to these services is extremely positive particularly in a B2B model. Positive response rates of 40% are achievable.
Advantages	If targeted correctly this service can add an extra element to an event that is both useful for the end user and beneficial to the organiser.
Disadvantages	Can become over-complicated if not managed effectively.
Cost	SMS costs (4-7p per message), WAP hosting costs (£100 per month), website build and hosting (£5,000 to 20,000).

Scenario 6 – Incentivisation – tokens and vouchers

Objective	To promote a brand or product by way of incentivised response using mobile tokens or vouchers.
Other channels	Press, direct marketing and online (banners, e-mail) – to promote service.
Description	Tokens and vouchers are proving to be a powerful means of promotion in the mobile marketing channel. Many large brands, including McDonalds, have used this form of mobile marketing with great success. This is as a result of the use of a low cost incentive, the ability to track the performance of the campaign and the significant viral uplift it can generate. Tokens and vouchers are normal SMS messages that contain a promotional incentive. Technically, they are no different from a normal SMS message. There are two approaches that are generally adopted: the first is to send the SMS to an opt-in list, with the token allowing, for example, 20% off a certain brand or product type or free entry to an entertainment venue. These tokens are generic and the redemption will be logged at the point of sale. Vouchers are the same but generally contain a unique alphanumeric reference (logged at the point of sale). There is a significant viral effect from token and voucher based campaigns. Incentives are often forwarded to friends, family and colleagues. However, tracking viral activity can only be achieved with unique reference codes per voucher. If a 'one use only' system is required, then unique reference codes must be used and logged at point of sale. These are not so popular as it results in squashing the viral effect, but it does increase the level of control over the cost of the incentive.
Technology	There are no time critical delivery restraints. Therefore, GSM terminals are ideal until volume requires a direct connection. A mobile marketing solution must be capable of automatically issuing SMS messages that contain unique reference numbers. Once the content of the message(s) and the send schedule have been determined, the campaign would effectively run automatically. Logs are continually kept from which reports can be generated. On observing offline promotions, consumers should be able to opt-in to receive vouchers by texting a 'send voucher' message. This is particularly relevant for campaigns run in shopping malls, outlet villages etc, where on arrival consumers can opt in to receive vouchers for one day only.
Future possibilities	Probably the most powerful mobile marketing model for the B2C retail brands. In the future, Bluetooth enabled phones will be able to redeem vouchers directly to Bluetooth enabled point of sale terminals, ticketing systems or turnstile systems.
Measurement	Use of tokens can be logged at the point of sale, giving direct measure of performance. Vouchers allow an extra level of tracking by relating a purchase to a mobile number and assessing the viral effect from each original recipient.
Performance	Performance figures vary and are broad. Well known High Street brands can achieve typically 20-25% response. Outlet centres and shopping mall based campaigns achieve similar response levels.
Advantages	Low running costs – once set-up, the solution will automatically run the campaign. Hugely popular among recipients – spamming

	complaints are very low. Excellent means of tracking and measurement.
Disadvantages	As with all campaigns that create a viral effect, this effect must be measured. All offers must be on an 'Offer to Treat' basis and outlets must possess the right to decline a voucher at their discretion.
Cost	SMS costs (4-7p per message, depending on volume).

Measuring mobile marketing

How do we measure the success of a mobile marketing campaign?

Measurements of success/impact of mobile marketing campaigns are entirely dependent on the actual marketing objectives of the campaign.

The following are broad direct marketing objectives:

- Increase in brand awareness.

- Increase in campaign awareness.

- Improving customer loyalty and retention.

- Improving direct response/call to action/sales.

Measurements for brand awareness

Example of campaign: "Coke brings you the first ever mobile world cup game"

Measuring brand impact:

- Brand recall (aided and unaided awareness):
  - Via survey SMS or phone.
  - Surveys must be done to sample of entire base, not only people who responded to campaign.

- Brand attributes.

Measurements for campaign awareness

Example of campaign: Promotion communicated via a mobile channel. Nightfly promoting a specific beer brand and promotion via its channel.

Measuring benefits of campaign

Measuring the channel:

- Need to measure value of media channel:
    - Size of audience
    - Quality of audience

Measuring the advertisement:

- Advertisement/message recall.

- Brand recall (aided and unaided awareness).

- Impact on purchasing intent.

- Impact.

Factors impacting campaign results:

- Creative.

- Brand fit with target audience.

- Incentive.

- Timing of campaign.

- Clutter.

Measurements for customer loyalty

Measuring the effectiveness of the mobile channel to enhance customer loyalty through better service/customer communication can include:

- Reminders and alerts.

- Notifications of notification.

Measurements for direct response/sales promotion

Example of campaign: Promoting 2 for 1 tickets to American Pie 2. "Win a ticket to xxx, by sending a txt into … txt in to win".

Measuring benefits of campaign

- Response rate/interactions with campaign based on messages sent.

- Viral impact.

- Conversion rates from:
    - Number of people contacted to number of people who participated.
    - Interaction to redeeming voucher/promotion.
    - Redeeming voucher to purchase.

Measuring benefits of mobile marketing

Short-term measurements:

- Cost savings of text messages compared to other communication means.

Long-term measurements:

- Increased sales/customers acquired.

- Reduction in customer churn.

- Customer satisfaction index/lifetime value.

- Attrition/Growth of the mobile base (unsubscribe)/repeat or extended permission.

- Customer knowledge and targeting capabilities for future service launch.

- Increased loyalty of brand advocates.

Campaign planning – the ten rules of mobile marketing

If you are planning a direct marketing campaign with a mobile element, remember the following ten rules to ensure it delivers the results you need:

1. Give your communication context.

2. Time specify your offer – this will ensure you capitalise on the immediacy of the medium.

3. Keep it simple – don't over-complicate the message or the process.

4. Make your campaign two-way – avoid SMS 'spam' – mobile devices are about two-way communication.

5. Reinforce and lift existing marketing campaigns and use mobile to make them interactive.

6. If you're targeting under 14 year olds, remember you must seek parental permission first.

7. Blend your brand values with entertainment and a clear call to action.

8. Make your mobile campaign fun and interactive.

9. Think viral – develop your creative execution so that recipients will want to pass it on.

10. Build your database – gain permission and always capture mobile phone numbers to capitalise on ongoing communications.

The future of the mobile Internet

While SMS is the primary application used in mobile marketing today and WAP is becoming more and more useful for business users, the mobile Internet will evolve over the next few years in key areas such as speed, hardware (such as screen quality and battery life) and applications.

In 2002-2003, new systems will arrive like Universal Mobile Telecommunication System (UMTS) which, like GPRS, will move data around in packets, giving an 'Always On' functionality, but at higher speed.

On the future of mobile marketing

Technology does not create new business models or consumer services: people do! Operators, service providers and handset manufacturers need to work together in a more collaborative way to create new services. Dr Michael Birkel, CEO, 12snap

Table 4.12.1   **Mobile marketing UK campaigns – 2001 to 2002**

Brand	Date	Campaign	Duration
Mobile operator	October 2001-March 2002	Football League table SMS game supported with bonus trivia and role play games.	24 weeks
Fast food chain and radio station	November 2001	Mobile coupons for food chain, and build up database.	3 weeks
Soft drinks brand	October 2001	Two campaigns: Premiership: Interactive poster and SMS campaign. Free air time: Interactive poster and SMS campaign.	Two months starting October 2001 One month starting October 2001
United International Pictures (UIP) American Pie 2	October 2001	Text message launched campaign with interactive SMS quiz. Messages based on Jim's dad answering questions and offering advice on participant's problems.	One month, intensive 24 hours
Online music Awards (Music Week Music Group)	September 2001	Facilitating and co-ordinating live votes from the attendees on the evening and SMS gossip line.	One evening (live event)
Large retailer	September 2001	Store launch campaign	2 days
Planet of the Apes (20th Century Fox and Vodafone)	September 2001	1 x text competition 2x Interactive voice response competitions Supported by point-of-sale campaign. Prizes included VIP tickets to the premiere, t-shirts, caps and posters.	2 weeks

Brand	Date	Campaign	Duration
KitKat (Nestlé)	July 2001	Text campaign developed to support new TV ad. Separate messages were sent to males and females to provide data on the different impact of mobile advertising on both sexes. The text was sent to participants announcing the coming of the TV advertisement both on the previous day and 30 minutes before the ad broke.	One day
Kiss, key 103 (Emap radio)	June 2001	A database of opt-in callers by station. Logo campaigns. Text used to drive traffic to the station's shows around specific promotional drives. Radio/club joint campaign to create 'mobile phone' guest list promotions – for free entry/free drinks (text coupons). Text voting.	3 weeks
McDonald's		Largest mobile marketing deal in Europe designed to target young target group (16-29 years). Build McDonald's 500,000+ database and ongoing promotions.	One year
Nestlé		Nestlé KitKat Chunky SMS/voice based game and on-pack promotion.	Spring 2001
Wella		Mobile Kiss campaign to 200,000 users.	September 2001
Cosmopolitan		Text quiz sent to 65,000 Cosmo readers in Italy.	July 2001
Esprit		Campaign supporting launch of new perfume.	July 2001

Chapter 4.13

The rest of the media scene – 'other' media

This chapter includes:

■■■■■■■■■■■■■■■■■■■■■■■■■■■■■■■■■■■

- ❑ **Outdoor – posters and billboards**
- ❑ **Planning poster campaigns**
- ❑ **Buying posters**
- ❑ **Ambient media**
- ❑ **Cinema advertising**

■■■■■■■■■■■■■■■■■■■■■■■■■■■■■■■■■■■

About this chapter

 part from the mainstream, volume direct response media, there are a whole host of alternative media options that exist for direct marketers. Some are transient, some have been around for ever, but as with all media if they catch the attention of your target audience and can deliver your message effectively, then they could be on your test schedule.

The following chapter is intended to spark interest and provide direction to help you open up potential new avenues. Many of these 'media' could not strictly speaking be defined as either responsive or interactive, but could still have a place in an integrated communications strategy.

Beverly Barker author and consultant

Beverly's biography appears in chapter 4.3

Chapter 4.13

The rest of the media scene – 'other' media

Outdoor – posters and billboards

The outdoor market

utdoor has shown constant growth over the past ten years, and during 2000 was the fastest growing medium, being up 18% year-on-year and representing 7.6% of all advertising revenues.

This growth is the result of a number of factors:

- Substantial investment by the media owners to revitalise the sites that are available and increased efforts by site owners to limit the damage caused by vandalism and poor weather.

- A growing 'outdoor' audience as we lead more active lives and a continued growth in the number of cars on the road.

- A general increase in popularity among advertisers since it combines greater value, impact and creative flexibility.

- Heightened accountability from the research.

Figure 4.13.1   **Outdoor revenue growth 1991-2001(turnover (£m))**

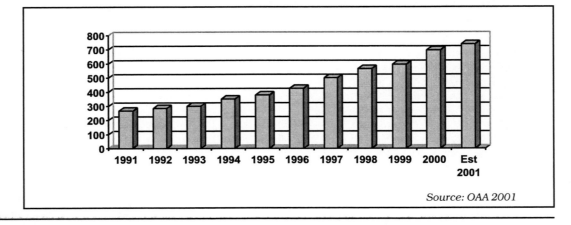

Source: OAA 2001

Product innovations such as large formats, scrolling backlit panels and LDC panels have kept the medium fresh and in demand, and dramatically reduced its unpopularity in the winter months. Historically advertisers have felt that their campaigns were only effective during the daylight hours and illumination has added 30% more Opportunities to See (OTS) to a panel in December.

Figure 4.13.2   **Outdoor seasonality – driven by market demand and daylight hours**

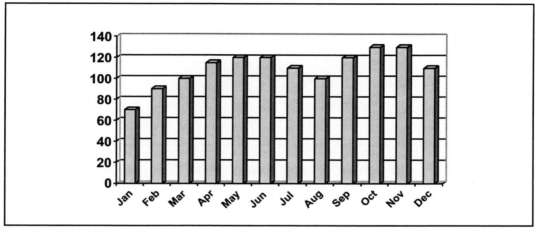

However, the outdoor market does still show a degree of seasonality.

In addition, prices vary for the different sizes and locations in line with the market demand.

Panel classifications

Panels are categorised into four main groups:

- **Roadside** – consists of all panels by the side of major roads – predominantly 6-sheets, 48-sheets and 96-sheets.

- **Transport** – all panels at airport terminals, underground and railway stations, bus/tram exteriors and interiors and taxi advertising.

- **Point of sale** – encompassing advertising in supermarkets and shopping malls.

- **Ambient** – including the more 'off-the-wall' opportunities such as floor media, banners, petrol pumps, washrooms, takeaway lids and beer mats etc. Currently representing about 6% of revenue – but definitely the fastest growing sector.

Figure 4.13.3   **Share of outdoor revenue by sector**

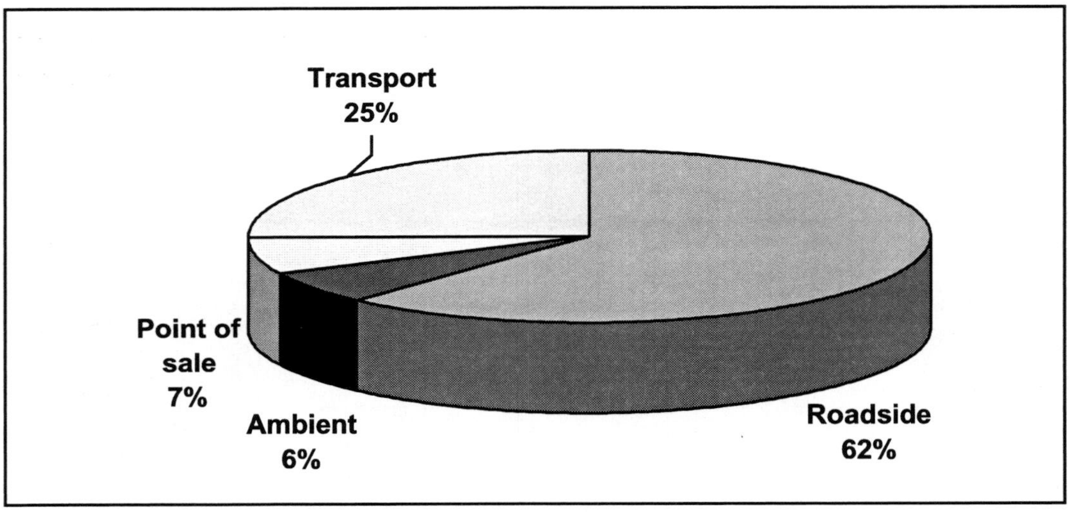

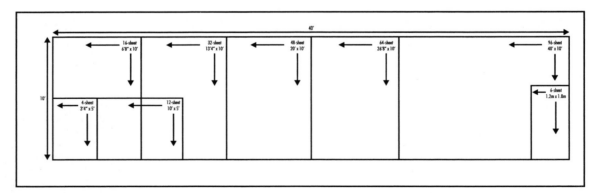

The number of panels has grown over the last five years, bringing the total number up to more than 130,000, the majority of which are in the roadside category.

Roadside

Within the roadside sector there are three main sizes of poster that are utilised, 96-sheet, 48-sheet and 6-sheet, of which the 6-sheet is the most numerous and invariably to be seen loitering at bus-stops under the name of Adshel.

The following shows the variety of sheet sizes used:

Figure 4.13.4

Figure 4.13.5   **Roadside 48-sheets used by Lancashire Constabulary for recruitment**

Recruitment advertising is often consigned to the hard-to-find pages somewhere at the back of the second or third section in a newspaper. But why should it be? Lancashire Constabulary wanted to create a more visible invitation to suitable candidates, so they chose outdoor to do the job. A campaign using 48 sheets and bus-sides has already proved effective in reaching the 16 to 28-year-old target audience they were after.

The poster audience research 'POSTAR' calculates a weighted impact score for the larger panel sizes, reflecting their greater domination of a site and the extended viewing time that they receive. This is indicated by the visibility adjusted impact score, (VAI).

Roadside panel sizes and numbers

Panel sizes are subject to fluctuations in popularity – the 4-sheet has been completely overtaken by the 6-sheet.

Table 4.13.1   **Roadside panels**

Size	Dimensions	Impact score VAI index*	1994 Volume	2001 Volume
96 – sheet and superlites	40' wide x 10' high	320	2,989	4,378
48 – sheet	20' wide x 10' high	183	30,555	32,234
32 – sheet			439	-
16 – sheet			1,477	1,112
6 – sheet	1.2m wide x 1.8m high	100	30,707	56,502
4 – sheet			20,991	4,968
			87,564	99,194

Source: POSTAR 50/POSTAR 26 (*VAI's Visibility Adjusted Impact (ie net reach). Roadside 6-sheet indexed at 100 to serve as base)

While location is classified as roadside etc. it must be remembered that posters are getting everywhere, and often there are associated promotional or distribution opportunities that are available alongside the basic site that can make the activity work twice as hard.

Transport

Transport sizes are obviously much more dependent upon the location:

- London Underground has a large number of escalator panels, smaller 6- and 4-sheet poster sites along the corridors and larger 48-sheet style 'cross tracks' – with a total of over 131,000 panels of one shape or another throughout their network, including 102,472 tube cards.

- Buses vary in shape but generally sites can be 'T' sides, full-length sides, bus backs, rear panels and interior panels – totalling 168,676 panels and sides in total, with 105,313 of those being interior panels.

Audiences

More people are out and about, and there is more traffic – all of which means that outdoor audiences are increasing. The DOT certainly expects this trend to continue. The car population was at around 28 million in 1999 – and anticipated to rise by at least 10% over the following five years.

Figure 4.13.6   **Index of overall rise in traffic volumes in the UK – (1998 =100 million)**

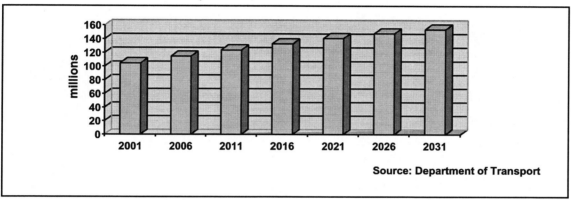

Source: Department of Transport

- There has also been an increase in urbanisation with nearly 90% of the UK population living in cities – exactly where posters are most concentrated.

- But it is not just the increasing numbers that is of interest, but the variety of audiences that are being delivered – from up-market professionals to young shoppers.

- Roadside audiences, the primary audience for large format posters (48- and 96-sheets) has grown by 25% in the past five years.

The audiences are researched by POSTAR

POSTAR, the outdoor industry's research company measures 'likelihood-to-see' and provides accountability through a detailed description of the audience so that the advertisers know whom they are reaching. The methodology uses:

- Local authority, traffic vehicle and pedestrian counts to assess the volume of traffic past each site.

- Gross coverage is calculated from the evaluation of the site traffic and the frequency with which the same people make up the traffic.

- Passages past the site are reviewed to ensure that the direction of the panel orientation is taken into account.

- Likelihood-to-see is factored in, measuring the quality of the site and applying the VAI score – the higher it is the more people will see the site.

- Modelling is then used to predict the impact of the poster sites.

- POSTAR can also measure the quality of panels bought against the universe. Figures relate to the thousands of people passing each site, each week.

It is estimated that of the 46m + adults in the population, 99% are exposed to posters at some time. The heaviest exposure, according to TGI, is found among young men living in London and the South East, who are working, have high-income, and read the Guardian, Independent and Golf Monthly. (Nov 2001.)

Planning poster campaigns

The general principles for planning are the same as for all other media:

- Establish the campaign objectives

- Review targeting and site audience delivery information

- Review creative and opportunities for innovation

- Assess regionality and timing issues

- Assess weight of campaign versus objectives and budget constraints (weight includes number of sites and length of posting)

Strengths of outdoor

- Stand out

- Quality

- Impact

- Coverage

- Out of home

- Variety of sizes, illuminations and environment

- Targeted packages ie HW – bus-stops etc.

- Innovation potential
    - Painted buses, taxis etc.
    - 3D creative

- Audience bias – male/younger/light TV

Downside and drawbacks of outdoor

- Six Seconds to communicate

- Passive communication

- Limited research

- Inconsistent quality of sites

- Reliant on creative solution

- Inconsistency of regional packages

Major uses of outdoor include launches, branding, direct response, sales promotion and sales support. Among the leading users are car manufacturers and financial services advertisers.

Used on its own, outdoor can provide quality, cost-effective impacts, but within a mixed media campaign it can extend the life of a TV campaign, up-weight regions of strength, make a final impact close to the point of sale, or reach light TV viewers.

A very versatile medium.

Buying posters

In practice there is an extra link in the chain for poster buying – the poster specialist advertiser ➔ agency/media independent ➔ poster specialist ➔ outdoor media owner.

Posters can be bought in a number of package formats:

- Line-by-Line – individually selected sites

- Campaign packages arranged by poster specialists or contractor-selected packages, either nationally or by TV region

- By target audience – delivering reach (percentage of audience contact) and frequency (number of viewing occasions)

Costs vary dramatically by the site type, size, location and seasonal demand, but the following is a guide:

- Average cost of a 48-sheet for two weeks = £300
- Average cost of a 6-sheet for two weeks = £150

So, for example, £600,000 would buy you:

- 4,000 x 6-sheets nationally for two weeks
- 2,000 x 48-sheets nationally for two weeks
- These costs exclude agency commission (20%) and production (estimated 10%)

Ambient media

The outdoor market has developed an entire area of oddball opportunities that have become incorporated into the catch-all of 'ambient media'.

Campaigns can be investigated through a number of poster specialists and some specific 'ambient' independents. They will help to ensure that the opportunities are explored and used in a way that delivers your business objectives.

There follows a list – by no means exhaustive, of the major opportunities that exist within the 'ambient'. Many offer the potential for getting close to prospects.

Airports and aeroplanes

Aeroplanes – sky banners

- Advertising banner trailed behind an aeroplane – available all across the UK.

- Banners can be up to 100 feet long and over 30 feet high and can be hand-painted or computer-generated.

- Rates are charged by the aeroplane, by the hour – circa £1,500 for first two hours, reducing to £5,000 to 6,000 for 10 hours.

Aeroplanes – sky writing

- Aeroplanes use smoke to draw logos or messages in the sky – usually at outdoor events for about £1,500 for two hours.

- It is also possible to paint aeroplanes – either your own or someone else's. This is a much longer contract – in general one to two years.

The flying direct response advertisement

While other airlines worried about their image and their livery, easyJet decorated their aeroplanes with their phone number. Then, when they wanted to switch enquirers and bookers to the Internet, they replaced the phone number with www.easyjet.com. Now 91%* of bookings are received by the website.

*As at September 2001

Airport opportunities

- Passengers can be targeted in a number of areas across the average airport, such as executive lounges and check-in areas.

- The earliest related opportunity is the airline ticket wallet, used successfully by many financial services and holiday product advertisers. Business passengers can be identified independently through a number of travel agents for about £250 per thousand. Wallet print runs number in excess of 30 thousand and a campaign usually runs for six months. Companies such as

Chemical Bank, Deutsche Morgan Grenfell and Prudential have used ticket wallets to reach their business-based target groups.

- There are about 11 executive lounges across the UK being used by about half a million business people a year. Opportunities exist for product sampling, demonstration and placement, and sponsorship of services, including the available computers and free phone calls.

- At check-in, boarding cards can take advertising on the reverse side and check-in staff can distribute promotional leaflets and vouchers. These could be used to drive people to purchase specific products available within the airport – (currency, duty-free produce), on arrival at their destination (car hire, accommodation, fast food, international calls) or on return.

- Around airports, stair-risers, escalator panels, electric carts etc. can take panels and posters or can take sponsorship ideas that could convert an entire terminal into a themed advertising experience.

- Carrier bags: prices vary dependent upon the size of the bags, and whether they are paper or polythene materials – but generally they are between £6 and £12 per thousand.

Petrol forecourts

Petrol pump nozzles

- Available at most petrol stations – including those in supermarkets and motorway service areas.

- Packages are generally sold nationally by the petrol companies.

Forecourt TV

- Available in and around London and the South, 52-inch screens with sound – either at the pumps or along the front of the petrol station 'shop'.

- Adverts usually in 30-second slots on a five-minute repeat.

- Satellite delivery system extends flexibility and targeting.

Royal Mail/private post boxes on forecourts

- Post boxes at garage forecourts; panels measure 51 x 76 centimetres and available through all major forecourt chains.

Entertainment/Leisure venues

Toilet media

- One of the most successful ambient media to become available – now well-established with national and regional distribution,

- Can target specific audiences through the venue – motorists at service stations, youth in pubs and clubs and at football matches etc. And of course, males or females.

- Already many of the major motor direct insurance companies are using wash-room advertising at motorway service stations to take their message close to the driving public.

Beer mats

- Full advertising on both sides and getting distributed in pubs and clubs; run by breweries such as Bass, Allied Domecq, Scottish and Newcastle etc.

- Good for that hard-to-reach younger audience – plenty of frequency between drinks and good 'street-cred' if done properly.

Cinema cards

- Can be audience-related and linked to a specific film or the type of film.

- Excellent way to apply the call-to-action to the impact of on-screen cinema advertising.

Rock boxes and festival advertising

- Opportunities exist in many places for sponsorship, co-branding or straightforward display advertising. Most deliver specific types of consumers depending upon the event. Poster and ambient specialists will identify up-and-coming events and help maximize the opportunities to interact with the audiences.

Leisure centres, gyms and clubs

- Traditional 4- and 6-sheet opportunities but ideal for targeting the young, family, up-market or health audience. Different packages reach different audiences – eg swimming pool packages being more family and youth-orientated.

Retail – shops – supermarkets

Store sites

- A3- and A4-sheet sized panels in shop windows, including newsagents and chemists.

- Leaflets can be incorporated into the campaign to be given away at the point-of-sale/till area with customer purchases.

Pharmsites

- Opportunity for window panels and leaflets but specifically situated in chemists – illuminated panels ensure good presentation and impact. Counter leaflets are distributed with customer purchases. Good for sampling, vouchers and information.

Illuminated shop front

- Point-of-sale – eye catching – good quality – illuminated – can be linked to in-store promotions.

Trolley advertisements

- Described as the last point-of-sale reminder – second only to a shelf wobbler etc. but available across all supermarket chains nationally.

- Great for housewives with children.

Baby changing and toilet media

- Baby changing can deliver an estimated 2.8 million highly targeted impacts a year through shopping centres and service stations.

Floor panels

- High-impact – still unusual – available in supermarkets and a range of other venues.

- Can be used in a business' own retail stores – such as in a building society to support new product introductions etc.

Receipts

- Direct to consumers, voucher and information opportunity – can be targeted to specific retails.

Bag advertising

- Advertising on the bags that are given out in a variety of stores across the UK. The ultimate product despatch.

- Sandwich bags have proved to be very popular, but among those taking part are fish and chip shops, chemists, CTNs, bakers, butchers, and specifically – Blockbuster.

Advertisement lids

- The top of any takeaway container is now also up for grabs.

At school

Sponsored school books, school litter bins etc.

- Exercise books are now available across the UK, in both junior and senior school.

- Advertising categories subject to CPA and ASA approval.

School postcards

- Postcard racks located in over 1,000 secondary schools nationally, in common-rooms and libraries.

- Also available in universities, along with sample bags, radio, beer mats and a host of opportunities for targeting students.

Along the pavement

Phonesites

- As seen for Bob the Builder – panels in the windows of phone boxes and panels inside the phone box – very good for 12 to 19-year-olds – and proximity to retail.

- Potential for BT hot-link button.

Postcards

- Opportunities for promotions and sampling, generally the more novel the better the uptake.

- Found in restaurants, schools, shopping centres, clubs etc. can be a good call-to-action or quasi-consumer-get-member device.

Ticket advertising

- Generally available on anything from airline, bus and tube tickets to events and shows and anything else that wants to amortise the cost of its ticket.

On the road

Truck advertisements

- Many retailers have woken up to the opportunity presented by their fleet of trucks; now most of the High Street supermarket trucks are well-liveried in corporate colours.

- Some trucks remain available for sponsoring and are the equivalent of a 96-sheet poster – and theoretically – the only advertisements that would get onto a motorway.

Painted cars and taxis

- Painted cars and taxis are available. They tend to be high-impact and quite stunt-orientated but give very good exposure.

- Taxis can be run in combination with Take-ones from seat dispensers.

Adbikes

- Panelled and available to demonstrate items or distribute samples, leaflets, ice creams, music or anything else suitable.

- Reaches people at point-of-sale or unusual venues – at the beach for instance.

Adpeople

- Potential for your audience to be followed anywhere. Luminous panel jackets etc. improve evening visibility.

And back to the air

Lasers

- Projected images, very high-impact, often linked to well-staged PR support; campaigns have beamed their images onto many venues, including the towers of Battersea Power Station and the House of Commons.

- Being on the edge of 'stunt' the activity is usually run over quite a short period of time.

Cinema advertising

Cinema is a wonderfully impacting medium, bringing images to life with a captive and attentive audience. The creative work can be strong and predominantly brand-orientated. To date there haven't been many direct-response case stories but as marketers move towards more integration of their brand advertising and direct response activity, the opportunities to exploit this medium should be taken seriously.

Now the impact of full-screen advertising can be combined with:

- A local range text messaging to the audience's mobile phones to create the call-to-action.

- Leaflets distributed in person, in poster-panel dispensers or with the ticket by the cashier.

- Messages can be written onto the hot dog bag, the back of the cinema ticket etc.

- Panels can be bought in the washrooms, down the corridors, on the floors and probably on the seat backs.

The increase in popularity of the cinema experience has led to a sustained increase in cinema advertising revenues.

Figure 4.13.7   **Cinema advertising revenue growth (£ millions) – 1990 to 2001**

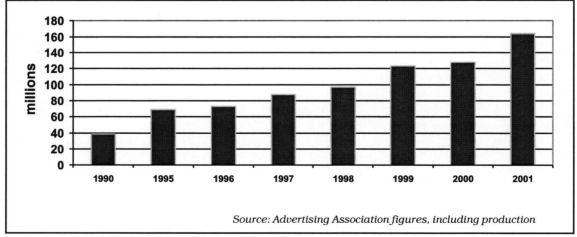

Source: Advertising Association figures, including production

Motor advertisers continue to be the biggest advertisers, spending more than £26 million on cinema in 2001. ACNielsen/MMS track the advertising revenue figures and can provide competitive data, tracking the scale and regionality of cinema campaigns.

Figure 4.13.8   **Cinema ad revenue £ millions by advertising category January to December 2001**

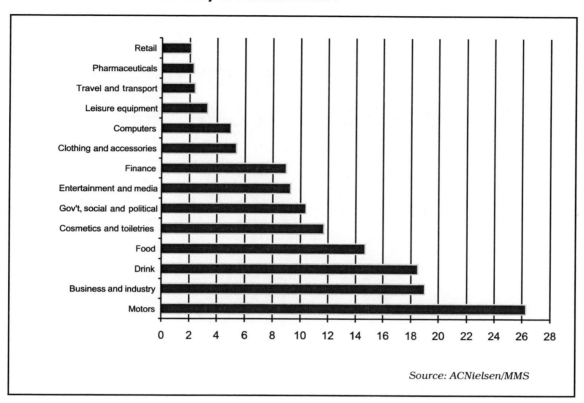

Source: ACNielsen/MMS

Strengths and weaknesses of cinema

Strengths of cinema
- Accessible
- Cost efficient for young, difficult-to-reach audience – light TV viewers
- High recall (impact – 5:1/ cinema: TV)
- Attentive audience
- Programme quality – advertising environment
- Buying flexibility
- High concentration within urban areas

Weaknesses of cinema
- 'Slow burn'
- Poor coverage of older age groups
- High CPT vs. TV for 'all adults'
- Fierce creative competition
- Limited cover outside urban areas
- Production costs exceed that of TV
- Long lead time for implementation of campaigns

Audiences

Figure 4.13.9   **Admission figures 1990 to 2001 (millions)**

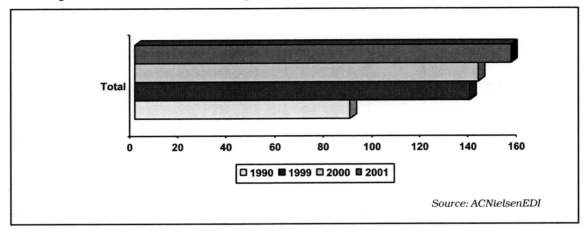

Source: ACNielsenEDI

Cinema Audience Profile:
15-24 years 40%
25-34 years 27%
35-44 years 17%
45+ years 16%

In terms of audience growth, the cinema is certainly a major success story with audiences increasing from around 90 million in 1990 to nearly 160 million in 2001. The whole experience has changed and the multiplex entertainment centre has become well-established.

The profile remains young and up-market with the vast majority of cinema-goers being under 34 years.

Cinema is primarily described as being:

- Young
- Impactful
- Involving
- Up-market

ACNielsen EDI (Entertainment Data International) conduct a continuous cinema admissions audit, collecting *actual* cinema admissions from virtually all UK cinemas on a weekly basis (less than 3% are estimated).

Figure 4.13.10   **Admission figures by month 1999 to 2001 (millions)**

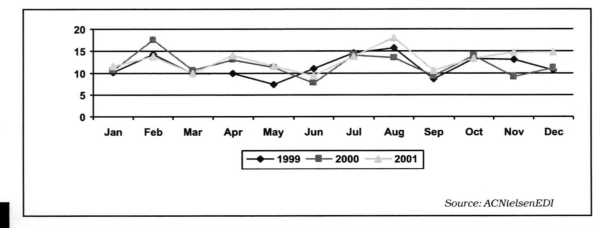

Source: ACNielsenEDI

Cinema is seasonal, but generally the main peaks and troughs reflect the movie releases, the end of 2001 being particularly strong:

- Cinema admissions in December 2001 reached 14.8 million, averaging 3.35 million cinema admissions a week. This is an increase of 32% on the same month last year, and is the biggest December for 33 years.

- *The Lord Of The Rings* released on 19 December, achieved the second highest opening of the year, taking £7.3 million. Also, it has taken a staggering £25 million in its first 2 weeks of release and is the 4th largest film of the year.

- *Harry Potter and The Philosopher's Stone* continued its phenomenal success, taking just over £20 million in December. It finished the year on £54.4 million making it the biggest film of 2001 and 2nd in the UK box office records of all time.

Cinema admissions data is available for individual weeks, by region and by cinema advertising contractor.

Cinema planning and buying

Buying cinema is easy and flexible. Screen time is available in weekly blocks from Friday through to Thursday. A variety of buying options cater for any advertiser requirements, allowing you to target locally via a specific cinema site: regionally, nationally, by film or by demographic.

Example cinema packages include:

- **Guaranteed audience package**
  This sales package provides cost-effective mass coverage of the core cinema audience – up-market and young with a high disposable income, and light users of other traditional media.

- **Line-by-line**

- **Screen-by-screen**
  Where and when you want to appeal.

- **Film package**

  Recommended for precise targeting of niche audiences. Relatively low capital cost with a national presence. Can be bought by title or by week. The film package is highly flexible – titles can be bought on a national, regional or nominated town basis, Benefits include complete control over film environment; specific targeted campaigns; opportunity for creative links; low capital cost and flexibility.

  - **Alcohol advertising**

  - **Art screens**

  - **Bollywood**

  - **Targeting students**

  - **Disney package**

  - **Premier films package** – Recommended for advertisers who need to target more specific audiences. Enables tighter targeting and minimises wastage. Specific audiences include: *Premier Youth* or *Teens Package*, *Male/Female Premier* and *Premier Plus*.

Carlton Screen Advertising represents approximately 70% of cinema admissions in the UK and sells the advertising for 2,175 cinema screens.

Customer incentives

This chapter includes:

- [ ] **Applications for incentives**
- [ ] **The three kinds of incentive**
- [ ] **Loyalty and collect promotions**
- [ ] **More about free gifts**
- [ ] **What makes a good premium?**
- [ ] **The cost of premia**
- [ ] **The negative effects of premia**
- [ ] **Where to source premia**
- [ ] **Choosing a specialist supplier**
- [ ] **Questions to ask incentive suppliers**

About this chapter

ncentives play a major role in both incentivising prospects to make contact, place a first order, exceed a given order value etc. and as a reward for confirmed custom as featured in a customer-loyalty programme.

A well-chosen incentive results in an 'everybody wins' situation whereby customers enjoy added value to their basic purchases, and advertisers reap higher volumes, lower unit selling costs and longer customer life cycles.

Graeme McCorkell consultant and author

Graeme founded MSW, one of the first UK direct marketing agencies. It grew from three to 103 people between 1976 and 1987 and introduced clients such as Volvo, Abbey National and P&O to direct marketing as well as serving past masters such as the AA, IBM and GUS. In 1983, MSW became the first UK direct marketing agency to be acquired by an American advertising group and was renamed MSW Rapp & Collins. After Graeme left it was merged by new owners, Omnicom, with WWAV to form WWAV Rapp Collins.

Working as a consultant and occasional copywriter since 1988, his clients have included The AA, Alliance & Leicester, Barnardos, Boots, The Consumers' Association, GE Capital, GUS, Holiday Property Bond, National Savings, Royal Mail and many more.

Graeme served as a director of the Institute of Direct Marketing, of which he is also a Fellow, until May 2000. From 1990 to 1995 he acted as chairman. Between these years, the IDM grew by over 300 per cent, opened its doors to membership and was awarded institute status by the DTI. Graeme also acted as non-executive chairman of Australia's fastest growing direct marketing agency, Lavender Direct, from its formation in 1997 to 2000.

In 1990, his first book *Advertising That Pulls Response* was published by McGraw-Hill, selling all over the world. This was followed by the standard Institute of Direct Marketing work, *Direct and Database Marketing,* published by Kogan Page in 1997.

Graeme McCorkell F IDM, The Gables, Wistanstow, Craven Arms, Shropshire SY7 8DG, England. Telephone 01588 672900.

Chapter 4.14

Customer incentives

Applications for incentives

ny desired kind of customer behaviour can be incentivised:

✔ **Response to mailing or ad**
✔ **First order**
✔ **Order by specified date**
✔ **Order over specified value**
✔ **Multiple order**
✔ **Payment by specified method, eg direct debit**
✔ **Opening of account**
✔ **Recommending a friend (Member-Get-Member)**
✔ **Answering a questionnaire**

Incentives are invaluable for overcoming inertia. Most people are on the brink of responding to many more mailings or ads than they actually get round to responding to. The incentive is there to ' tip them over the edge' and will work all the better if it requires an early or immediate response.

Incentives work. That is why sales promotion is a £10 billion business. Incentives work in supermarkets, petrol stations and direct marketing. They work for consumables, white goods, computer software, holidays, book clubs, magazines and cars.

Not surprisingly, the most important role for incentives in direct marketing is to help begin new customer relationships. An essential point to keep in mind is that:

> People respond to advertisements only when the immediate gain in responding exceeds the risk or cost of responding by an acceptable margin...
>
> Advertising that pulls Response, Graeme McCorkell (1990)

The purpose of the incentive is to adjust the risk/cost to reward ratio. Incentives work best when the behaviour they are designed to produce is **exceptional** behaviour, not **expected** behaviour. Otherwise we will reward too many people for doing what they would have done anyway.

Since we do not **expect** our cold mailing recipients to respond (that is, we expect a minority of them to respond) then it may pay good dividends to incentivise response. By contrast, it seldom makes sense to incentivise people to pay their bills, since we expect the great majority to do so anyway.

Optimise, not maximise

In two-stage selling, our aim is to strike a balance between quantity and quality of response. We do not want too much inconvertible response if our fulfilment cost is high. So we must be wary of over-incentivising **response** as opposed to **purchase.**

On the other hand we will try to avoid incentivising our regular customers too much – except when they do something exceptional – such as recommend a friend or buy two shirts to get a third one free.

The three kinds of incentive

Not all types of incentive are applicable to inducing every kind of desirable behaviour. For example, prize draw entries cannot be restricted to customers making a purchase. By law, a prize draw must offer free entry. That means it must be made clear that 'no purchase is necessary'.

According to sales promotion expert, **Lesley Tadgell-Foster** of Shelfline, there are three main kinds of promotional incentive:

☐ **FREE**   ☐ **SAVE**   ☐ **WIN**

In addition we will refer to **loyalty** promotions as a separate category because, although they are primarily SAVE promotions, they are also COLLECT promotions, designed to influence longer term behaviour.

Lesley Tadgell-Foster subdivides the three main kinds of promotion into nine types:

FREE
- Free extra value
- Free in/on/with purchase
- Free mail-in
- Free sampling

SAVE
- Money-Off
- Self-Liquidating Promotions
- Charity Promotions

WIN
- Competitions
- Prize Draws

FREE extra value

This means more of the same for your money. Examples are:

Buy one, get one free
Three for the price of two
20% extra

This type of offer, popular with multiple retailers, is frequently seen in one-stage mail order ads, inserts and mailings.

There are two big advantages: first, **the perceived value is greater than the cost**. For example, giving away a shirt costs only half its retail value.

Second, if you like the first shirt enough to consider buying it, there's no risk you won't like the second shirt. If we give away a tie instead, there is a slight risk that you may not want it.

FREE with purchase

This can be any gift or voucher supplied with the purchase. For example:

Free tie with every shirt
Free software with each PC
Choose any two of these 12 free gifts

For direct marketers, this is by far the most important category of purchase incentive and we will examine it in more detail later. It is important because it is almost infinitely flexible. A free gift can have any value from a few pence to £50 or more and be used for a wide variety of purposes in B2C and B2B marketing.

FREE mail-in

It is not always practicable to supply the free gift with the product. For example, the product may come in a bottle that you buy from the supermarket or off-licence. Alternatively, you may not want to reward a single purchase, but want to reward repeated purchases. The answer can be a free mail-in. The customer sends the required number of PoPs (proofs-of-purchase) – such as bottleneck foils or pack tops – and claims the gift. Examples:

Free pocket wine guide with three PoPs
Choice of 3 free CDs with completed guarantee form
Free English Heritage admission tickets with returned direct debit mandate

The last example illustrates a partnership marketing deal. It could be for, say, the AA, RAC or Direct Line. This type of promotion can be effective when the customer profiles of the two participants match closely.

Getting the numbers right

Forecasting redemption rates for free mail-ins can be difficult. That is because there is no direct link between sales and redemptions. The more PoPs the customer needs to collect, the more difficult it is to get the forecast right.

For direct marketers the general advice is to **keep it simple and TEST**. But if your promotion is in-store or requires several PoPs, testing is often not an option. Then underredemption may leave you with redundant gift stocks. Much worse, overredemption can have a catastrophic effect on the budget and leave customers frustrated while you order more of the desired trinkets from Taiwan.

Overredemption insurance may be the answer. Specialist brokers advise in this area. You have to balance the risk of overredemption against the cost of the insurance premium – around 10-15% of the sum covered.

FREE sampling

Free sampling can be restricted by quantity (eg a miniature of whisky) or time (eg a weekend in a timeshare apartment). A sample restricted by time is referred to as a **FREE TRIAL** by direct marketers. A free trial is not the same as a money-back guarantee. No money has changed hands at the time of the free trial. Examples include:

Free language course CD (see how easy it is before ordering full course)
3 months' free subscription (postdated direct debit mandate)
Sample-size dishwasher liquid (delivered door-to-door)

All three examples are classic direct marketing initiatives. The first has been used by Linguaphone, the second by *Which?* and the third is one of the staple database builders used by Lever Brothers and other FMCG manufacturers.

The Bounty Box provides sample products to new mothers. Contact is continued from birth through the various stages of child development by offering a range of age-related products for mothers to try.

The incentivised test drive

One type of free trial is a test drive. This is usually very restricted and needs to be sold. That is why the trial itself often carries an incentive.

The duration of such a trial needs to be considered. Being overly generous could attract the wrong kind of respondent. To maintain quality control, Land Rover, for example, have restricted an extremely generous offer to carefully selected people. By mail they have offered trialists a free hotel break to go with their weekend test drive.

Renault have incentivised test drives by inserting door keys into Sunday magazines. Readers take the key to their local dealer – if it fits they win a car. Clearly, the salespeople would encourage those visiting the showrooms to move towards a test drive – providing of course that they fit the customer profile.

SAVE – money-off

The least imaginative and most used of all promotions is money-off. But money talks and discounts are almost invariably effective. Examples are:

Money-off coupons for in-store redemption
Seasonal catalogue and retail store SALES
Bulk purchase discounts
Online order discounts

Money-off coupons come in two varieties. Firstly, there are those which are redeemed direct with the issuer – through their own outlets/distribution channels. These offer the very best chance of control. **Sketchley** and **Beefeater** both issue coupons – door-to-door and via direct mail to customers. Coupons are only valid in their outlets, and cannot obviously be used elsewhere.

Both types are exchangeable for a specified discount against the nominated product. Sampling and couponing are natural partners. Having provided the customer with a small amount of the product to try out, couponing moves the prospect along the acquisition trail to eventual full-price purchase.

Online offers

Check out the www.persil.com site. You may get a £1 voucher (mailed) when you answer a questionnaire on your laundry habits! Likely that online voucher is not available because of security/handling problems in-store. So direct mail still has a place for this type of promotional delivery. But a 28-day wait is rather disappointing.

SAVE – self-liquidating promotions

Traditional self-liquidators are a form of mail order. In return for both proof-of - purchase and some money the customer receives merchandise. To be truly self-liquidating, all costs should be covered – the item itself, postage, packing and handling and marketing. This type of promotion is the weakest of all when the customer has to redeem with PoPs, but it can work well within a catalogue (home shopping, office supplies and so on). Examples include:

Yours for £2 with 3 pack tops (traditional on-pack offer)
Buy one, get another half-price (website, catalogue, in-store)
40% off when purchased with any full-price product (catalogue etc.)

The second and third examples are often used in catalogues. The third example is promoted as an 'insider deal' in the **Expert Verdict** catalogue.

SAVE – charity promotions

These are generally similar to mail-in promotions except that the benefit is received by the participating charity or charities. They tend to work most effectively on a 'collect PoP' basis and have a limited application to direct marketing. They appeal to marketers because they offer the chance to link a brand with a popular cause and, often, a big name charity. However, charities are aware of the value of their own brands and may charge £100,000 or more as an up-front guaranteed return from the promotion. Examples are:

Computers for schools (Tesco and Sainsbury's)
Save the whale

The *Consumers' Association* (January 2002) investigated these promotions and concluded that they did not offer customers good value in return for their purchase.

WIN – competitions and prize draws

Competitions and prize draws are prize schemes. Prize schemes differ from all other promotions in two crucial fashions:

1. Not every respondent is rewarded.
2. The cost of the prize fund is fixed, irrespective of the number of entries.

Lesley Tadgell-Foster recognises two types of prize scheme: competitions (also called contests) and prize draws (sometimes call sweepstakes). Strictly and legally speaking, this is correct. However, in terms of presentation, there are three distinct types:

Three types of prize scheme

Prize draw
(eg lucky numbers)

Requires no skill. Entry must not be conditional on purchase. Free entries cannot be presented as reward for custom.

Competition
(eg spot-the-ball)

Entry can be conditional on purchase or other form of response or performance **provided that** an element of skill is required.

Game
(eg bingo)

Rules depend on whether the game involves skill (eg fantasy football) or is really just a draw.

Games are usually a form of prize draw in the guise of bingo or some other game format.

Competitions attract many fewer entrants than prize draws. However, an imaginatively designed competition can attract a great deal of interest and, unlike a prize draw, entries can be conditional on purchase.

For a competition, you can ask as few or as many questions as you like but, if contestants have had to purchase, or to make any financial outlay in order to gain entry, the winner(s) must be selected as being the best – not the luckiest.

Hence the use of the tie-breaker or slogan – ' I love xxxx because ... (in twelve words or less). The winner(s) will be those who have devised the most apt and original answer in the opinion of the judges. Tie-breakers are unpopular because they demand effort.

The **Lotteries & Amusements Act 1976** (see Chapter 9.1) determines the conditions under which both competitions and prize draws are run. Both statute law and case law are involved in determining the legality of particular schemes, so you should certainly read the appropriate part of Chapter 9.1 before embarking on one, and, unless you are following very precisely in the steps of a reputable and established operator, you should consider taking legal advice.

Competitions or games are often associated with **advertorials.** These use paid-for space in magazines or newspapers but are presented in the guise of an editorial feature. In effect, they are co-operative promotions between the media owner and advertiser. A reader competition helps to generate prospect names and addresses which the advertiser will follow up.

Prize draws (and prize draw games) are by far the most important type of prize scheme to the direct marketer. We will examine this type in more depth.

Prize draws

Prize draws (and games depending purely on chance) attract much higher entry levels than all but the most appealing contests.

They have taken a knock since the introduction of the National Lottery but are essentially a cheap and effective way of increasing response to larger-scale promotions. This is because one prize fund, of say £500,000, may be used to incentivise two million entries at a cost of just 25p each. It would be hard to find a truly appealing gift for 25p.

By the same token, they are impossible to test on a small scale. The number of entries you would get from a test in which you cut the prize fund to £50,000 might bear little relation to what you would expect from a £500,000 prize fund.

There are two main types of prize draw:

- **Pre-drawn** – draw takes place in advance of entry distribution
- **Post-drawn** – draw takes place from entries returned

A pre-draw usually awards the prize to an adjacent or reserve number if the winning number is not returned. However, it has been known for some promoters to use a pre-draw to save the cost of prizes that are not claimed.

Direct marketers use pre- or post-draws as devices for increasing catalogue requests or send-no-money (free trial) orders. In the former case, a 'no' option (the chance to refuse the catalogue) is not usually offered. In the second case, because the goods are not free (merely on free approval), the chance to enter the draw without requesting the goods must be offered. The number of 'no responses' will usually be around four or five for every 'yes'.

'No' entries and catalogue non-converts are not wasted but are remailed (usually with another offer) with the object of converting them later on.

If you use a prize draw to increase catalogue requests it is vital to follow up with a powerful conversion incentive. That is because your prize draw will have provoked many marginal requests that will be hard to convert. In practice, prize draws are rarely an alternative to other promotions, but must be used in combination with gifts or discounts.

The psychology of lucky numbers

Prize draws work far more powerfully when the entry piece carries unique numbers. That is why prize draws are more likely to be featured in inserts or door-to-door leaflets than press ads. Prize draws work better still in mailings, the combination of unique numbers and personalisation being especially powerful.

It is a common mistake to soft-pedal with prize draws. They work because they are dramatic and succeed when the recipient feels fortunate to receive the entry or entries.

Nearly all the prize fund should go on the first prize. The best high-value prize is cash. However, cars are better than holidays. Bonus prizes for prompt entries work well (the entire bonus prize fund goes to the outright winner).

The declining appeal of prize draws

Apart from the negative effect of the Lottery, another trend that has adversely affected draws is the near abandonment of postal response in favour of response by phone. So far, no one has thought of a way to make prize draw entries seem as exciting (or safe, perhaps) over the phone. Possibly, this is one case when people would prefer to talk to an IVR (interactive voice response) computer or key in their entry numbers, using the tone pad on their home phone.

But prize draws may have lost some of their appeal for another reason. **Stuart McKibbin**, the renowned former Head of Copy at *Reader's Digest*, believes the old style presentation of prize draws has had its day:

The archetypal sweepstakes package is familiar enough: a portentous-looking document that resembles nothing so much as a share certificate in a defunct South African mining company, replete with the cartouches, scrolls and watermarks one finds on obsolete bank notes ... tacky, contrived and unconvincing, the whole thing has come to look like an exhibit in a museum of direct mail in its least scrupulous days.
Stuart McKibbin, The Business of Persuasion, 2000

The challenge is to devise sweepstakes that are exciting but fun, that encourage response through more channels and that appeal to more than the most credulous.

Clearly there is potential to develop e-mail prize draws and games. Interactive marketing lends itself to the currently popular instant-win game formats more than the long-delayed prize distributions favoured by traditional sweepstakes promoters. Whatever the design of the prize scheme, a strong purchase incentive will be needed to turn site visits into business.

Codes of practice

It is essential that you have a clear set of rules for entrants. The ASA Code of Advertising and Sales Promotion Practice lays down the type of information you should include. A copy of this is freely available from the Advertising Standards Authority.

Ensure that you show the closing date of the contest prominently, together with details of how and when the winners will be chosen and announced. All entrants have a right to ask for a list of the winners' names/counties and (in the case of a contest) details of the winning answer.

Clarifying the exact nature of the prizes/to whom the contest is open, with any restrictions, will help ease any pain of winners 'pushing their luck' in trying to improve the prize offer. Expressions such as 'an all expenses paid holiday' should be avoided for obvious reasons- unless of course you really do mean everything that implies!

Loyalty and collect promotions

There are two main types:

Proprietary schemes (eg Air Miles, mypoints, ipoints)
Tailor-made schemes (eg Tesco, Sainsbury's, Boots)

The distinction between these two types has become somewhat blurred. Proprietary schemes such as Air Miles have been incorporated into tailor-made schemes such as Sainsbury's Reward Card. In fact Air Miles has now been dropped by Reward Card (2001) and picked up by Tesco's Clubcard (2002).

Furthermore, tailor-made schemes may be shared by non-competing retailers in partnership marketing deals.

Both types of scheme reward behaviour over a period, ie the reward for a single action is small, but the cumulative reward gained over a period may be valuable.

Mum's precious gift

Procter and Gamble have operated a highly successful loyalty programme for mothers in over a hundred countries. Direct marketing techniques are used to enlist new mothers and to communicate regularly with them. (Purchases, however, are made through the usual retail outlets.) Mothers can exchange tokens from retail packs for a wide variety of household and children's goods displayed in a special catalogue mailed to them direct.

Online schemes

Beenz was the first online specific promotional programme and was an attempt to establish an online currency, in which surfers could be paid for visiting websites, registering to receive 'permission' e-mail and so on. It was wound up in October 2001.

However, **ipoints** and **mypoints** have survived and are building up customer credibility. As with all sales promotions, the best way to understand the mechanics and appeal of the incentives is to try them out personally – and online nothing could be easier.

www.ipoints.co.uk
www.mypoints.co.uk

Both schemes are similar in that they reward you for viewing and purchasing online products provided by specified sites. In addition, they also offer points for answering surveys and just checking out various sites.

The major improvement enabled by interactive media is the ability to offer an instant dialogue. Add in all the data collection opportunities and you can see that, from small beginnings, online sales promotion could be a very significant element in building customer loyalty to partner brands.

Tailoring a scheme

Any long-term promotion represents a big commitment. What seems like a good idea in 2002 can become a millstone by 2005. Loyalty schemes can't be picked up and dropped without considering the customers who are halfway to redeeming their points, possibly against an eagerly anticipated flight to Rome or Istanbul.

Although retail and packaged goods loyalty programmes are steeped in history, the modern version – permitting customer segmentation or even one-to-one treatment – originates from travel and credit card incentive programmes, of which American Airlines' **AAdvantage** scheme (1981) was by far the most influential.

There is clearly a limit to the number of such schemes the customer will take the trouble to join. The greater the proliferation of loyalty schemes, the less they act like loyalty schemes, appealing more to those customers who are especially susceptible to promotions. In this context the truly successful scheme needs a number of key ingredients **(Table 4.14.1):**

Table 4.14.1 **Key features of successful programmes**

1. Enrol a critical mass of committed customers

Enabling recruitment offers to be targeted to non-customers.

2. Pay back on increasing share of customer

Do not depend on extending customer life cycle.

3. Offer opportunity to improve customer service

Do not depend solely on rewards of a monetary value but use data collected to bring customer benefits of special relevance.

4. Recognise individuality of customer

Include rewards, benefits and courtesies that recognise the customer as a person.

5. Provide absolute continuity

A scheme that forces customers to start from scratch again each year or after each redemption is sowing the seeds of its own extinction.

6. Offer added-value benefits

For example, a scheme operated by several non-competing retailers collectively permits faster qualification for rewards. A scheme that offers new types of reward provides fresh stimulation. A scheme that allows the utility of the membership card to be increased (eg to draw cash or save up air miles) is more valued.

7. Use data collected for intelligent marketing

Schemes can be used to provide data that drive communications recognising customer shopping patterns, preferences, breaks in continuity and so on. They can also provide useful area data to retailers, improving catchment area definition and permitting accurate targeting of competitive customers.

Direct and Database Marketing, *Graeme McCorkell (1997)*

A good loyalty programme is one that is skilfully designed to meet a specific objective. The best advice is to avoid starting any loyalty programme unless it represents the best chance of building a customer database – a database that enables *true loyalty* to be won: through more relevant offerings, services and two-way communications.

Banks, public utilities and others with complete lists of customers (and the ability to retrieve their transactional history) should not even think about starting loyalty schemes. They could never benefit to the extent that Tesco has benefited by using **Clubcard** to build a sophisticated customer database from scratch.

More about free gifts

What is a premium?

A premium (short for premium gift) is sales promotion jargon for a free gift incentive. The simple definition of a premium is a bonus – a small extra reward to the customer for agreeing to take a purchasing step. Premia are also known by some users as 'kickers', a clear indication of how they are intended to influence a wavering prospect.

Premia differ from prizes in that there is no element of chance or doubt: if customers take the required step they can be sure the bonus gift will be theirs.

Premia differ from discounts and other financial inducements primarily because they cost less yet have a high perceived value. Premia are also more fun, making for livelier copy and art, providing a good association with the product on offer.

Although there is no absolute certainty as to how premia work – it varies according to markets, products, customers and the gift itself – the *Direct Marketing Association of America* defines the function of a premium as follows:

> *The function of a premium ... is to move the consumer who is already predisposed to the product – but reluctant to make a purchase commitment – into taking purchasing action as a result of the bonus which the premium represents. – DMA, New York*

True, and a good start point, but the DMA definition is nevertheless restrictive: it refers only to purchase commitments, assuming the customer's predisposition to buy.

In practice, premia may be offered for actions other than purchase commitment. Nevertheless, the primary role of a premium is to overcome inertia and bring about a response.

Specific applications of premia

The simplest and most obvious effect of including a premium is to add value – or more accurately 'perceived value' – to goods or services.

A good premium can also have the effect of rendering an offer unique, ie the only means by which a prospect can obtain both product X and premium Y may be through a banded premium offer.

Coupled to a time limit, the uplifting effect of a good premium can be large. Hence premia have long since been the cornerstone of sales promotion practice.

But in more recent years creative marketers, spearheaded by an array of innovative direct marketers, have devised scores of new ways to use premia to improve overall performance, among them:

- To add perceived value
- To render an offer unique
- For a prompt reply
- To increase order values
  - by worth
  - by number of items ordered
- To drive renewals
- To boost enquiries
- To elicit names, eg of friends
- To reward information, eg questionnaires
- To encourage trials
- To welcome new members/subscribers
- For repeat orders
- To build loyalty
- To say, "Thank you"

Testing

As with all elements of direct marketing, the testing of incentives can significantly improve your response levels and reduce expenditure. So, test the use of incentives at different stages of the buying process – trial, first purchase, repeat purchase etc.

Consider one- and two-stage incentives. Think about the range of different incentives that can be used to meet different objectives and actually test various ones against your 'banker' or best ever incentive.

Reply gifts

A peculiarity of direct marketing is the reply gift. That is the reward just for requesting a catalogue or other information, registering at a website or taking a test drive. The reply gift is a great device for overcoming inertia in responding to two-stage ads, inserts or mailings. A reply gift is not the same as a free sample. It may not even be related to the item on sale.

A reply gift is often best used when:

- There is also a strong purchase incentive
- There is a close-date or other device to speed response

A strong purchase incentive may be needed to ensure that the conversion rate is maintained; reply gifts inevitably generate more casual or impulse enquiries.

A close-date is essential if you don't want to be committed to supplying the gift indefinitely (or until the replies have dried up). In any case it will increase response.

Cost must be controlled. If the conversion rate is 10% you will use 10 reply gifts per sale. That's why a purchase incentive is likely to pay for itself.

Pre-reply gifts

Many years ago it was discovered that enclosing a pen with a postal survey questionnaire produced far more response than offering a pen to reply to the questionnaire (about 33% more on average). Later, the idea of mailing an unsolicited gift was adopted by mass mailers, such as *Which?*, and is now used by every other charity. It will continue to be used until it stops working.

Other pre-reply gift ideas have included defunct bank notes, small coins, stamps, Christmas gift tags, greetings cards and postcards. The theory is that the gift makes the recipient feel under a slight obligation. Overuse of a particular gift (a pen) is bound to erode this feeling.

What makes a good premium?

Experience and careful testing indicate certain denominators which may be common to all good premia. These include:

? **Trouble-free**. For example, mechanical and electrical goods can be problematic. Make sure they are covered by a manufacturer's warranty, or else have sufficient replacement stocks available.

Beware of complicated products, eg electronic equipment, when your database consists mainly of older people.

Luggage, on the other hand, is especially trouble-free.

? **Easy to mail**. Try to source premia that come ready-packed in mail cartons. Jiffy bags and extra protective packaging can be prohibitively costly relative to the price of the item being shipped.

? **Low cost.** Not simply a question of reducing outlay. Customers often prefer gifts that are not excessive. Perhaps modest gifts are more credible. Likewise, do not offer too many premia at once – one is usually enough.

? **High perceived value.** Quite inexpensive items can often have extraordinarily high perceived values. This is especially true if a premium is unique and its true value therefore difficult to calculate.

Books, maps, guides etc. have often proved exceedingly popular, their value being in their editorial content while actual production costs are minimal.

Bags, for instance cosmetic bags, tote bags and sports bags, are consistently successful for a wide variety of products, from cosmetics to insurance. One reason: their retail value is high whereas the price you pay is low (from £3-£5). Bags are an ideal vehicle for logos and purchasers are prepared to carry them with pride; a source of free advertising.

? **Family appeal.** The most successful premia often appeal to men and women of all ages and all social strata. Household items are always a favourite.

Household premia may end up as gifts to other members of the purchaser's family – or are considered family assets – thereby helping the purchaser to justify the original purchase.

? **The toy effect.** Successful premia often replicate many of the qualities of toys; they serve as gifts that one would like but not necessarily buy for oneself.

In this category fall small clocks, calculators, key-rings, torches, diaries, miniature Swiss Army knives etc. In the case of high-ticket purchases, 'toy' premia may be affordable simply to boost enquiries.

Luxury premia have been particularly successful for financial products, are also used extensively in credit home shopping and may be used as self-liquidating premia as in the two cases you see below:

Elevenses for six

Amazing £6 offer

Six mugs, teapot, milk jug and sugar bowl, all for just £6 when you order any other item from this catalogue. (Less than half price – La Maison.)

Pick up a piqué

Our piqué polo won't cost you a mint. Just make any other order and it's yours for only £5. (Half-price – Hawkshead.)

? **Product linked**. Notice that the two items shown above are product linked. If you can find a premium that is linked favourably to your product, and which works, so much the better for your overall image and credibility.

However, the crucial factor is the link between the premium and the lifestyle, interests or taste your catalogue represents.

A half-price visit to England's heritage

English Heritage are offering you a wonderful opportunity ... everyone who places an order will receive one free ticket to any English Heritage site, when accompanied by a fully paying adult visitor. (Scotts of Stow.)

Other gift ideas

Despite the success of the types of item already mentioned, the search for new ideas continues. In recent years the following have all enjoyed success in both consumer and business situations:

? **Magazine subscriptions.** Very high perceived value, and a long-lasting effect.

? **Weekend breaks.** Hotel accommodation is an effective gift, but be sure to spell out exactly what the recipients receive (or have to pay for themselves). Beware the word ' Free' except to describe that part of the offer which is truly free.

The cost of premia

Whatever your business, the amount you spend on a premium should relate directly to the additional revenue it is expected to produce. It must, of course, not only pay for itself but show an increased profit as well.

Table 4.14.2   **Incentive test example: one-stage mailing**

Gift cost £2 each						
Mailing	Quantity mailed	Cost of mailing	No.orders	Order value	Cost of premium	Cost per £100 sales
A) Control	10,000	£5,000	250	£10,000	–	£50.00
B) Test	10,000	£5,000	300	£12,000	£600	£46.67
C) Incremental sales (B minus A)			50	£2,000	£600	£30.00

In this simple example (**Table 4.14.2**) we see a £3.33 reduction in the marketing cost is achieved by introducing a premium (the difference between £50 and £46.67 in the right hand column). However, when we isolate the effect of the premium, we see that the extra £2,000 sales it has added cost only £30 per £100 (30%) compared with £50 (50%) from an unincentivised mailing.

It is important to isolate the effect of premia as shown in Table 4.14.2. Even if the cost per £100 sales had risen slightly in (B) the test, it might have been considered worthwhile (good mailing lists are not in unlimited supply). However, the only way to be sure is to isolate the effect of the premium (C), showing the cost of incremental sales. A premium offered for any order (irrespective of order value) may depress the value of the incremental orders it brings in.

Clearly, in a successful promotion the premium effectively costs nothing. Increased conversion rates or sales lead to lower marketing costs, which in turn may be reflected in keener selling prices and even bigger volumes. An 'everybody wins' situation.

The bottom line for premia is simply this: The function of the premium is to make **extra profit** and, if you can demonstrate that, you have succeeded. However, extra profit does not necessarily mean short-term gain – today we are more often concerned with longer term customer values.

Looking back at our test example, we might be prepared to pay a little more per £100 orders on the basis that extra customers gained could become extra profit later on. Having proved that a £2 premium worked, we might test the effect of a higher value premium.

The negative effects of premia

So much for the good news. There is a downside to premia, especially if the whole issue is not handled with experience and caution.

The potential problem with premia is that they affect the characteristics of buyers/enquirers.

Premia, especially if too generous, can attract people who are more interested in the free gift than the product. For example, they may return goods in greater numbers (all legal and above-board, but frustrating and costly). Or they may exhibit poorer performance when it comes to renewals or future purchases.

Customer recycling

If premia offered to new recruits are too powerful, you may lose regular customers, only to find they re-enter your system some months later having collected yet another gift (in their eyes, quite legitimately).

A further problem of overtly offering overgenerous recruitment premia to new prospects is that you can upset loyal customers. However, most customers are quite tolerant of new customer inducements.

Clearly the choice and use of premia is an extremely skilled aspect of direct marketing, and one where there is no substitute for testing and experience.

The trend to somewhat humbler premia is in part driven by a realisation that *over-gilding the lily* can be ultimately counter-productive.

A final point concerning the negative aspects of premia: do not expect a premium (however well chosen) to overcome the effects of product, targeting or timing deficiencies.

A choice of premium?

The question is frequently asked: should customers be offered a choice of premium? The answer is **not if you can avoid it**. The effect on logistics is nightmarish. One of the major difficulties with premia is knowing how much stock to order in advance.

If you need to know which of several premia is the more popular, it is better to test them separately and in advance of your main promotion. Alternatively, keep multi-premium tests to very small quantities.

However, you may well make additional premia work for different aspects of the customer's response, eg an extra premium for a prompt reply. Be careful not to appear to be simply stacking up bribes in desperation to make a sale – the customer will smell a rat.

Do not discard old premia

Remember, new prospects, or customers who have recently joined your database, are probably not familiar with your earlier offers. Just because a premium is familiar to you is not a reason to discard it.

Discard a previously successful premium only when it fails on test.

Even then, be prepared to rediscover it in a year or so. And never discard a successful premium until you have found a replacement that proves better on test.

Remember: there is no special magic about the latest gadget. The golden oldies are often the best.

Where to source premia

To source and buy premia you have basically two options: either go to the manufacturers direct or use a specialist sourcing company.

If you are making an occasional one-off purchase, you may prefer to go direct to the maker. If buying regularly, or in large volumes (and if premia are a serious component of your marketing strategy), you are advised to consult a specialist.

There are three clear-cut advantages to buying premia from a sourcing specialist:

- **Lower prices.** The result of the specialist's bulk-buying arrangements.

- **Help and advice.** A good premium sourcing company knows what has worked best for particular industries, and in which situations.

- **Avoiding hassle**. There are a great many pitfalls for the unwary in sourcing, buying, packing and shipping premia, most of which can be avoided by the right choice of supplier. This is especially relevant when buying overseas.

The overseas minefield

The danger when buying overseas is in the legal implications. It is very easy for an overseas manufacturer to copy a product. The unsuspecting buyer then imports it and finds himself in a legal battle over patent infringements. There is no easy way round this, other than asking the supplier to indemnify you against any legal wrangles. If you ask for this at the outset and the manufacturer refuses, suspect trouble and avoid that particular supplier.

A big advantage of using a sourcing company is its regular dealings with overseas suppliers. In their travels to the various factories its specialists become aware of each supplier's capabilities, as well as of customs and import regulations. Most big buyers use a sourcing company to locate overseas products for these reasons.

Choosing a specialist supplier

Fortunately in the UK we have a good trade association: the British Promotional Merchandising Association (BPMA). They and the various trade magazines offer extensive information about premium suppliers.

Alternatively, act on word-of-mouth recommendation. Phone someone you trust in a similar line of business, and ask them who they use for premia. They will put you in touch with a reliable source.

A golden rule when dealing with any supplier is never to pay up-front. Companies who ask for money in advance are probably weak financially and therefore best avoided. A good, well-founded company will be able to deal with all payments and letters of credit and settle with you in the normal way.

One exception to the never pay up-front rule, however, is when buying products which have been purchased overseas. In this case you may be asked to settle a little in advance, say on a strict 10-day basis, because the supplier has had to open a letter of credit some 60 days previously. In this situation a supplier is justified in asking for quick settlement once the goods have been delivered.

Questions to ask your incentives supplier

Table 4.14.3

- Are samples chargeable?
- Are small quantities available for testing and will the price remain the same on rollout if successful?
- Will the supplier buy back any unused merchandise?
- Do all prices quoted include origination, packaging, duty, delivery and any overprinting that might be necessary?
- On what rate of exchange is the supplier basing his quotation and how long will it remain in force?
- What is the delivery time and how is the item being despatched if it is coming from overseas, ie is he going to use air freight, sea freight etc?
- If you require any warehousing, storage etc. can the supplier do this?
- Are regular/monthly/weekly reporting schedules available? Remember, if you are using premia in a large way, at some point an auditor is going to ask you to justify the costs incurred and to say where all the product has gone.
- Are product warranty guarantees included in all the products that you wish to buy from the supplier?

Finally, before placing your order, make sure you have seen and agreed terms and conditions.

Section 5: Acquiring customers

 hy just make a sale when you could acquire a customer?

There is a difference, of course. And it's the difference between profit and loss in all but a few markets today.

Despite the recent focus on customer retention, customer acquisition remains the biggest challenge in direct marketing. In fact, customer retention really begins with recruiting enough of the right customers in the right way. This is rarely as simple as it may appear. Successful campaigns are continuously monitored, reconsidered and revised as results suggest.

In this section we examine every aspect of profitable customer acquisition:

In Chapter 1: **ROI-driven customer acquisition** we look at the acquisition plan. How – and why – does it differ from a non-direct marketing communications plan?

This is where you will find explanations and examples of the alternative ways of measuring return on customer acquisition investment: Allowable Marketing Cost (AMC), Yield and Return on Investment (ROI).

We show how forecasts are used in **setting acquisition priorities and targets**. To help us do this we work through a case study of a home shopping company. Finally, we provide an **example of a 3-year forecast** showing the ongoing value of customers acquired in year 1.

Chapter 2: **Success factors** begins by defining a 'direct response' and looking at **why people respond** and then examines each of the elements of success in turn.

In Chapter 3: **Offline and online media**, you will find a number of **useful inter-media comparisons**. Some media work for customer acquisition and some don't. Chapter 3 begins with the **four key selection factors** you should consider before even testing a new medium and then considers the **8 types of response** and how these can affect your media selection.

After a brief overview of each of the acquisition media, you will find tables comparing the media.

Finally, in Chapter 4: **Recording and analysing the results**, we highlight the crucial importance of monitoring campaigns as they are running – not waiting until it's too late to make changes. There you will find out **what you should record along with the results**, so that you can analyse them later and also what your **recording of results should include**.

We look at the special data gathering opportunities of the web, how to track and convert prospects, how to use back data as an aid to forecasting and how to use results to negotiate better media deals.

Chapter 5.1

ROI-driven customer acquisition

This chapter includes

- ❏ **Acquisition and retention**
- ❏ **The direct marketing acquisition plan**
- ❏ **Allowable costs, yield and return on investment**
- ❏ **Setting targeting priorities by expected return**
- ❏ **Case One: an established home shopping business**
- ❏ **Projecting payback on customer acquisition**
- ❏ **Case Two: projecting the ongoing value of new customers**

About this chapter

his chapter introduces the exciting business of customer acquisition by placing it in the context of the marketing plan. To the less mathematically inclined, this chapter is the most challenging of the four in section 5 but your patience is requested. It is important to grasp the concepts of **allowable costs, yield** and **return on investment.** This chapter paves the way for the remaining chapters in this section, when we will discuss what makes people respond, which media work best and how we monitor the results.

We begin the first chapter with a reminder of why and how direct marketing focuses on the acquisition-retention cycle. We follow by showing what is different about the direct marketing acquisition plan and the measurements that are commonly used in direct marketing acquisition forecasts and results analysis.

In this chapter we see that it is not necessarily a good idea to place acquisition and retention in separate compartments. It may be more profitable to save a customer than to replace a customer.

The chapter concludes with two case studies. The first, which is simplified, shows how priorities are decided. The second, which includes all the detail required to make a business case, shows how future customer values are projected in direct marketing.

Author/Consultant: Graeme McCorkell

Graeme McCorkell consultant and writer

Graeme founded MSW, one of the first UK direct marketing agencies. It grew from three to 103 people between 1976 and 1987 and introduced clients such as Volvo, Abbey National and P&O to direct marketing as well as serving past masters such as the AA, IBM and GUS. In 1983, MSW became the first UK direct marketing agency to be acquired by an American advertising group and was renamed MSW Rapp & Collins. After Graeme left it was merged by new owners, Omnicom, with WWAV to form WWAV Rapp Collins.

Working as a consultant and occasional copywriter since 1988, his clients have included The AA, Alliance & Leicester, Barnardos, Boots, The Consumers' Association, GE Capital, GUS, Holiday Property Bond, National Savings, Royal Mail and many more.

Graeme served as a director of the Institute of Direct Marketing, of which he is also a Fellow, until May 2000. From 1990 to 1995 he acted as chairman. Between these years, the IDM grew by over 300%, opened its doors to membership and was awarded institute status by the DTI. Graeme also acted as non-executive chairman of Australia's fastest growing direct marketing agency, Lavender Direct, from its formation in 1997 to 2000.

In 1990, his first book *Advertising That Pulls Response* was published by McGraw-Hill, selling all over the world. This was followed by the standard Institute of Direct Marketing work, *Direct and Database Marketing,* published by Kogan Page in 1997.

Graeme McCorkell F IDM,
The Gables, Wistanstow, Craven Arms, Shropshire
SY7 8DG England. Telephone 01588 672900.

Chapter 5.1

ROI-driven customer acquisition

Acquisition and retention

n some product categories, most notably FMCG, users maintain a portfolio of preferred brands, readily switching from one to the other as money-off promotions and availability dictate. Yet, even in consumable goods markets, most of us have a first choice brand and can remember when another brand occupied that position.

At some point in time the lion's share of our business was **acquired** by our favourite brand and at another point the brand will lose (fail to **retain**) this preferred status.

In most markets, things are simpler. The majority of us will use only one home computer or dishwasher and will drive only one car. Our brand loyalty is not tested until a replacement is required. Similarly, our earnings are paid into only one bank account and we will book our next holiday through only one travel agency or operator. In B2B markets, customers generally set up an account with a new supplier and close the account when the supplier has lost their business. Thus, in most markets, it is not very difficult to identify the moment when customers are *acquired* and to record the customers' activity while their business is *retained*.

Of course, to record the moment of acquisition and the period of retention, we need a customer marketing database that incorporates transactional history:

Customer's transactional record

- Date acquired
- Source (eg offline – direct mail, online – affiliate network)
- First transaction value (£)
- Number of transactions
- Average transaction value
- Cumulative transaction value
- Date of last transaction

If we also know the **cost of acquisition**, we can measure how long it takes for the new customer's business to repay that cost. To do this we will also need to know our profit margin on the transactions and the cost of further marketing to retain the customer's business.

Knowing these facts and figures enables us to bring scientific method to customer acquisition. This is one of direct marketing's major contributions to the business of marketing.

Acquisition media: above-the-line and below-the-line

With three exceptions, acquisition involves trawling for customers outside the database. The three exceptions are:

1. Conversion of previously unconverted prospects

2. Recovery of lapsed customers

3. Referrals (of new customers) from established customers

All other sources of new business lie outside the database. So what are they?

First let us dispense with the mythical, or imaginary 'line' that is still used by some marketers to distinguish between advertising in press, on TV, radio etc. – and sales promotion and direct marketing.

The line came about historically between media which automatically paid advertising agencies 15% commission, and 'sundries'. A line was drawn below 15% ('above-the-line' media) and everything else had to fight for the contingencies budget.

The 'line' in media has long been obsolete. Marketing people in other countries don't confuse themselves with it. The fact is that direct marketing uses all media, whether above or below the defunct line. The Internet and its associated interactive media have now changed the media map completely in any event. **All media that can be used cost-effectively to generate response are sources of new business.**

The 'line' does not sensibly distinguish between activities. There are only two jobs to be done by all marketing communications:

1.   Acquire (or help to acquire) new business

2.   Maximise (or help to maximise) net earnings from existing business

The distinctions between advertising, sales promotion and direct marketing communications are in any case often so vague as to be meaningless. Direct marketing is better distinguished by the way it is planned and the information it uses for planning.

Sales promotion or direct marketing?

For example, a money-off coupon that lands on the doormat is a sales promotion device. But what if it is personalised or asks the prospects to fill in their name and address? What if it asks for details of which brand they buy now and how much of it they use? What if the information they supply is used to decide how often to send them direct mail or e-mail and which offers to make to them?

In this example we have crossed any boundary that may be thought to exist between sales promotion and direct marketing.

The direct marketer's dividing line

Direct marketers draw a line in their marketing communications plans, too, just as the old media planners used to do between commissionable media and the rest. Only for direct marketers the line is turned through 90 degrees to represent the clear distinction between:

Customer	Customer
Acquisition	**Retention**
(includes recovery)	(includes development)

This distinction has the merit of being entirely objective-related. It is not influenced by how media are bought or paid for. It accords absolutely no special importance to one or other activity.

Customer acquisition includes the recovery of lapsed customers, as we have noted, and retention includes development, that is, maximising the value of current customers.

A point to understand is that even this line can easily be crossed. For example, established customers may respond to a direct response advertisement designed to acquire new customers. A transactional website can be visited by customers who are directed there and by surfers who discovered it.

Corporate image building

Many marketing communications tasks appear to have little connection with customer acquisition or retention. For, example, **British Airways** spent a reported £60 million on an attempted repositioning as a 'world' airline. **BP** has since undertaken a similar exercise. Arthur Andersen rebranded its consultancy empire as **Accenture**. The business case for such initiatives may include consideration of the short-term effects on staff morale, distribution channels or the City, but unless they can also be justified as paving the way for more effective *customer acquisition* or *retention*, they are a waste of management time and shareholders' money. BA later decided to reverse its decision when the 'world' positioning failed to win or keep business.

The fact that direct marketing communications invariably carry a response mechanism makes it simple for direct marketers to focus on acquisition and retention in a disciplined way. However, other advertising should also be accountable for its contribution even when this is less direct.

Direct marketing may operate anywhere in the buying process

Direct marketing can be applied successfully at all the stages of the customer's buying cycle, from generating awareness to clinching the sale.

Direct marketing often undertakes the whole of the acquisition activity. For example, in the case of **Britannia Music**, there is no pure awareness or image building activity. Britannia's advertising and direct mail establishes awareness at the same time as it makes direct offers of cassettes or CDs.

However, direct response is not the primary task of most advertising. Nevertheless, advertising these days typically carries a direct response device (eg a brochure hot line or invitation to visit a website), even when response may not be the primary objective.

In cases like this, direct marketing must dovetail with advertising to help ensure the prospect receives the information needed to make a purchase. An example is a car advertisement bearing an 0800 phone response number. Responders receive a brochure and an invitation to take a test drive with a named dealer. The prospects' names may also be passed on to the dealer to fix a convenient time.

For the remainder of this section, we will assume that direct marketing is playing the leading role.

The direct marketing acquisition plan

Why it's different

Because direct marketing communications produce direct responses, the direct marketing planner has a continuous stream of data to inform planning.

By its very nature, the data is back data. It provides a record of what has already happened. Although the data may be refined in analysis, it is broadly true that the direct marketer assumes that **what has happened will be repeated** in the future unless some change is made. Alternatively, the direct marketer assumes that the **current trend will continue**. Except when the marketing environment changes suddenly or unexpected competitive action causes discontinuity, these assumptions are usually correct, plus or minus a few percentage points.

The reason for such accuracy is that the supply of data is immediate and continuous so that changes are spotted very quickly. To enable changes to be acted upon immediately, the planner tries to avoid committing all the available funds far in advance.

Table 5.1.1 points up the basic difference between general and direct marketing campaign analysis.

Table 5.1.1   **Marketing analysis: how two disciplines compare**

General Marketing	Direct Marketing
Whole campaign	Each event
Whole effect	Contribution per event
Tracking studies	Response analysis
Qualitative research	Testing
Market behaviour	Individual behaviour

General marketing

General marketers tend to measure the results of **whole campaigns** and look at the overall effect.

Tracking studies are used to reveal the awareness of advertising among the target audience as well as changes in perception caused by the advertising.

Qualitative research is used to check out the content and presentation of the advertising.

Market behaviour, ie sales and/or brand shares, will generally be the measure of success or otherwise — after attempting to isolate the variables within and without the marketing mix (eg changes in distribution levels).

Direct marketing

By event — the direct marketer (who may also use the above methods) generally prefers to 'take a campaign apart' event-by-event.

Contribution per event — the contribution of each component is then looked at. This will usually be the response or revenue stream created by an individual advertisement or mailshot to a specific list.

(Individual events are not viewed as contributors to a campaign; individual events can only be justified by their own return on investment.)

Response analysis — direct marketing is concerned with measuring *response*. However, the analysis will not end with immediate response.

Testing is used to compare the response effectiveness of various communications (although these may also be subjected to qualitative research before testing).

Individual behaviour — the behaviour of each customer is tracked.
Analysis at the direct marketing level depends utterly on computer power: the analysis of one large direct marketing campaign can involve sifting through literally millions of data items. The point of going to all this trouble is, of course, to optimise the return on future marketing expenditure.

Figure 5.1.1 shows the loop that is followed for planning both acquisition and retention activity. (*Analyse - plan - implement - control - analyse - plan etc.*)

Although direct marketers often refer to '*campaigns*,' the business of acquiring and trying to avoid losing individual customers is most often continuous. Even when it is not (as in the case of a seasonal business), the planning loop is a continuum.

Figure 5.1.1   **The direct marketer's planning loop**

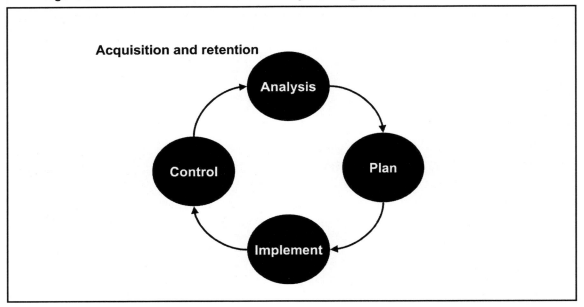

Using the loop in **Figure 5.1.1** enables the direct marketer to exercise the direct marketing principle of **control**, which is one of the four principles on which direct marketing depends. Control depends utterly on recording interactions.

It follows that the close examination of each result is an essential part of planning the next advertisement, mailing, campaign and so on.

While it may appear simplistic, and is indeed simple in concept, the idea of a continuous loop is fundamental to the direct marketing method.

In practice the analysis of simultaneous events does not all necessarily take place at the same time. There are three situations:

1. **Results of events that could have a bearing on immediate plans. Daily reviews.** For example, the first of a planned series of advertisements in a daily newspaper produces an unexpectedly low or high response. We might want to cancel our plans, renegotiate the space cost, increase the size of our spaces and order more fulfilment materials etc.

2. **Results that are immediate but not immediately actionable. Regular review.** For example, a seasonal e-mailed invitation to prospects produced more or less business than expected.

3. **Results that will take time to mature. Repeated reviews.** For example, the profitability of customers acquired from a new source.

Allowable costs, yield and return on investment

Measurement

Measurement of direct response effectiveness depends on attaching a source code to each advertisement or mailing. This is not difficult in the case of online advertising or offline advertising when the response is received by mail.

When response is received by phone, it is possible to dedicate different DDI (Direct Dial-In) lines to different advertisements. Sometimes this is impracticable and the agent must then ask the caller where he or she saw the offer or ad.

One-stage and two-stage response

When the advertisement or mailing makes a direct offer for sale, measurement is simplified. When it merely invites an enquiry (eg a request for a catalogue), it is more complex. It is now necessary not just to measure the response but the **conversion rate** as well.

In some circumstances this is difficult. If a new customer came straight from an offline source to a website, there is no record of what prompted the visit. The only way to find out is to ask (either every new customer or a sample).

Results recording and analysis

The question of how responses, orders and sales are recorded and analysed will be covered thoroughly in chapter 5.4. For now, we can observe that any activity designed to provoke a direct response will generate a stream of data capable of analysis:

✔   Click-through and click-stream data

✔   Responses/enquiries/leads

✔   Further information requests

✔   Orders and order values

✔ Order:enquiry ratios

✔ Sales and sales values

✔ Sale:order ratios

✔ Returns and bad debts

This stream of information is monitored, allowing immediate comparisons to be made between one medium and another, one offer and another and so on. Adjustments to planned expenditure are likely to be made as a result.

A major benefit is that controlled testing of new media and offers can take place *before* too much money is put at risk.

However, none of this information takes us to the bottom line, to answer the question, "Was it profitable?" or the equally important question, "Will it be profitable?" To answer these questions, we need to track newly acquired customers' transactional behaviour.

There are three useful measures of the efficiency of marketing investments, all of which can be applied more easily and accurately in direct and interactive marketing. They are:

1. **Allowable Marketing Cost** (AMC)

2. **Yield**

3. **Return on Investment** (ROI)

What is the 'marketing allowable'?

The concept of the marketing allowable or **AMC** (allowable marketing cost) is familiar to nearly every marketer. It is usually expressed as a formula, as shown in **Table 5.1.2** below:

Table 5.1.2   **The AMC formula**

£	Sales value		eg £50	(100%)
less	£ cost of goods		-30	(60%)
less	£ cost of distribution		- 5	(10%)
less	£ required profit margin		- 5	(10%)
=	£ AMC		£10	(20%)

This simplified formula works quite well when we expect to make a profit on each transaction. But what if the first sale to a new customer is made at a loss? It usually is. For example:

✔ Book and music clubs 'subsidise' the new member's first purchase to tempt people to respond.

✔ In the automotive market it has often been quoted that it costs five times as much to make a 'conquest' sale (a sale to a new customer) as it does to make a repeat sale.

In such cases what is the marketing allowable to capture a new customer?

A feature that distinguishes the direct marketing professional from ordinary marketers is that the direct marketer knows the answer.

Many marketers work to an overall AMC. They tot up the sales they expect to make in any period and the AMC is simply a percentage of that. Not very scientific. It is as if marketing expenditure were caused by sales instead of the other way round.

The direct marketer calculates what can be *invested* to acquire a new customer by estimating what the customer is likely to be worth over time. The estimate will be based on what previously recruited customers of the same type and from the source are proving to be worth.

Customer acquisition and 'cash burn'

The reason dot-coms were once so overvalued is because the investors did not understand how to estimate future customer values. A high marketing spend was thought to guarantee success. For example, at one point **Freeserve** was valued at £700 per 'customer' even though the customers had paid nothing to join. No direct marketer would have believed that the average lifetime value of Freeserve's customers, in direct and indirect revenues, could reach even one tenth of this figure, yet customers were Freeserve's main asset.

The concept of yield

To calculate Return on Customer Investment (Customer ROI), we need to estimate the future profitability or LTV (Lifetime Value) of customers. This can be difficult. When it is too difficult, a sensible measure to use is **yield.**

Yield is a measure that is used to compare the rate of payback from customers acquired from different media or with different offers, as shown in **Table 5.1.3**.

Table 5.1.3 **Measuring rate of payback – yield**

$$\frac{\text{£ contribution over 12 months}}{\text{£ acquisition cost}} = \text{yield} \qquad eg \quad \frac{\text{£300}}{\text{£60}} = 5:1$$

	Daily Mirror			Sun	
Sales per customer	£320			£275	
	$\frac{}{}$ = 5:1			$\frac{}{}$ = 5.5:1	
Cost per customer	£64			£50	

In **Table 5.1.3** yield is measured over a 12-month period. The value of sales over the period is divided by the acquisition cost. The longer the period is extended, the higher the yield will be.

In the lower half of **Table 5.1.3**, we see the main application of yield – to compare the performance of media that are competing for a share of the acquisition advertising budget. Yield can be used to compare media at a **macro** level – eg direct mail versus press advertising or at a **micro** level, eg *The Sun* versus *The Daily Mirror* as in the table. In this example, *The Sun* produces a better yield than *The Daily Mirror* because it costs less to acquire a customer from *The Sun.* If yield were to be measured over a longer period, the positions might be reversed – because the sales to *The Daily Mirror* customers are currently higher.

Yield comparisons can be made at different intervals, for example three months, six months and 12 months. The more experience we have of using yield, the more meaningful measuring yield early on will be. The yield over three months should enable an accurate forecast of 12 months' yield to be made.

Yield is, of course, a crude measure. It does not show profit and does not take into account any ongoing costs of maintaining customer relationships. This does not militate against its usefulness as a basis of comparison between alternative acquisition sources or offers.

Yield reflects loyalty, too

In **Table 5.1.3** it may appear that *The Daily Mirror* customers are higher spenders than *The Sun* customers. This is not necessarily the case. The lower sales to *The Sun* customers may be due to fewer of them making repeat purchases. The *loss rate* of *The Sun* customers may be higher. It is important to continue measuring yield over a sufficient period for a clear pattern to emerge.

Return on investment (ROI)

Return on investment (ROI) is one of the most commonly used performance measures in business. Therefore it provides a useful yardstick, not only enabling marketing investments to be compared with each other but also with any other investment the business might make.

ROI answers the question: *"How well did we use this money?"*

The way ROI answers the question is by showing *the eventual return* on the money that has been spent. Unfortunately, business moves too fast to allow the whole return to be achieved before making a judgement on the investment.

Therefore, the *rate of return* is plotted at different intervals from the investment and the trend is used to forecast the eventual ROI:

$$\text{ROI} = \frac{\text{£ future contribution}}{\text{£ expenditure}}$$

The *contribution* figure in future contribution is the net margin on sales (or profit before operating). The net margin on sales will take account of the costs involved in making the sales and providing customer service.

Table 5.1.4   **Measuring rate of payback - ROI**

$$\frac{\text{£ contribution over 12 months}}{\text{£ acquisition cost}} = \text{ROI} \qquad eg \quad \frac{\text{£45}}{\text{£60}} = 75\%$$

	Daily Mirror		Sun	
£ contribution per customer	£48		£41	

$$\frac{£48}{£64} = 75\% \qquad \frac{£41}{£50} = 82\%$$

The contribution figure of £45 in **Table 5.1.4** is derived from the sales figure of £300 in **Table 5.1.3**. If the company in the example were supplying goods to home shoppers, the net margin might be calculated like this:

Sales (£)	300	
Gross margin	120	(40%)
Less distribution	30	(10%)
Less returns	30	(10%)
Less handling	15	(5%)
Net margin	45	(15%)

In the example used for **Tables 5.1.3** and **5.1.4**, we can see that the net margin is 15% of sales. If this remains constant (or nearly constant) for all sources of new business, then *yield* will provide the only measure needed to compare one source with another.

However, if *The Sun* customers are twice as likely to return goods as *The Daily Mirror* customers, then looking only at yield would present a false picture. In such a scenario *The Daily Mirror* customers would be considerably more profitable than *The Sun* customers because the cost of handling returned goods would be much less.

Profit and loss statements

Where do P & L statements fit in? In many business situations, it is more appropriate to use P & L **forecasts** when planning campaigns and P & L **statements** when all the results are in. That is because the object of the campaign may be to sell a specific quantity of a product at the lowest possible cost. Customer acquisition will then be seen as a by-product.

Examples might include:

✔   The event organiser staging a business conference

✔   The collectibles producer marketing a commemorative plate

✔   The specialist tour operator marketing a new holiday

In all of these cases, the marketer will want to measure the success of the venture by its overall contribution. Many of the sales may be made to established customers (because that will help to reduce marketing expense). The ongoing value of new customers who book conference places, buy plates or take holidays is excluded from the P & L calculation.

In general, the aim in these situations is to avoid making a loss on any of the sources of business that are tapped. However, the marketer may be prepared to take a small loss on sources that add new customers to the database. To justify this, a calculation of the likely future value of new customers *must be made*, although it will not appear in the P & L statement.

The value of reactivation

Sales made to established customers are said to *reactivate* them. They may prevent defections and may be almost as valuable in maintaining customer strength as sales made to new customers.

Note that the P & L forecast sets the AMC for the product. The AMC may be exceeded in the case of new business sources, but sales made to established customers will be (or be expected to be) made at less than the AMC.

The P & L statement will show the **product** ROI. It will not usually show the **customer** ROI.

Setting targeting priorities by expected return

Whether the object is to meet a product sales target or a customer acquisition target, best direct marketing practice involves prioritising target groups by potential responsiveness (or potential ROI if we can project this).

If the object is to meet a sales target, the aim will be to maximise those sales that can be made at little or no cost (inevitably sales to established customers) before giving consideration to other target groups.

If the object is to meet a customer acquisition target, the aim will be to maximise intake from the most responsive target groups before focusing on the less responsive.

In either case, the most responsive target groups of all will be those with whom some sort of business relationship exists or has existed. Earlier in this section we noted that, with three exceptions, acquisition involves trawling for customers outside the database. The three exceptions were:

1.   Conversion of previously unconverted prospects

2.   Recovery of lapsed customers

3.   Referrals (of new customers) from established customers, eg viral marketing

99 times out of 100 these three sources of new customers will be cheaper than all others. It therefore makes sense to do what we can to maximise return from these sources and reduce our dependence on more expensive external media.

Targeting by value, not responsiveness

Sometimes the targeting priority is determined by **potential value** as opposed to responsiveness. For example, FMCG marketers may prioritise those who use competitive brands *only*. Although members of this target group will be expensive to convert, return on investment can be improved by selecting only those who are **heavy users.** Data from lifestyle surveys or field marketing exercises will be used to select target group members.

Once priorities among broad target groups have been established, selection continues at a micro level *within* target groups, eg *The Sun* versus *The Daily Mirror* or even taking a fourth ad in *The Sun* versus a third ad in *The Daily Mirror.*

Case one: an established home shopping business

For this example, we take a fairly small home shopping company trading from seasonal catalogues and a website. About 80% of the business is offline.

In the home shopping business, marketing costs depend on the required rate of growth. That is because it is much cheaper to market to identified and established customers than to secure the initial order from new customers. When the enterprise starts trading, all the customers are new and so marketing costs are very high. As the enterprise matures, more and more business comes from established customers and marketing costs reduce. Eventually, however, the business may reach saturation level and it will again become expensive to acquire new customers at a greater rate than old customers are being lost.

Table 5.1.5 **Case one: established home shopping company**

Target groups in order of responsiveness/profitability

1. Active customers   purchased in one of last two seasons

2. Lapsed customers   not purchased in either of last two seasons

3. Unconverted prospects   requested last catalogue but made no purchase

4. External media

The definitions of active and lapsed customers used in **Table 5.1.5** are fairly typical. Target groups are prioritised in order of potential profitability (in making the next sale) and this will equate to responsiveness adjusted by sales value.

The more recently a customer has ordered, the more responsive the customer is likely to be. Therefore, lapsed customers will be mailed or e-mailed for as long as it is profitable to do so. Eventually, they will be removed from the mailing file.

Unconverted prospects are likely to remain on file for a much shorter period because they are, in general, less profitable as a target group. They will include people who requested a catalogue but did not order, people who abandoned an online order and others who ordered but then returned the goods. (The behaviour of these subgroups will be analysed separately in case they are very different – for the sake of simplicity we are assuming they will behave similarly.)

Table 5.1.6 **Case one: home shopping company – full year (two seasons) sales forecast**

Target group	Sales forecast	Marketing cost	Cost to sale (%)	Gross profit	Net contribution
Active customers	£5,000K	£400K	8.0	£1,500K	£1,100K
Lapsed customers	£750K	£150K	20.0	£225K	+ £75K
Unconverted prospects	£350K	£105K	30.0	£105K	Nil
New business	£1,000K	£400K	40.0	£300K	- £100K
TOTAL	£7.1m	£1.055m	14.9	£2.13m	£1.075m

In this example in **Table 5.1.6**, the gross profit is profit *before* marketing and is taken as being 30% of sales value. In order to grow the business (or stop it shrinking), we are prepared to make a loss on new business and break even on converting previously unconverted prospects. We do this in the expectation of making a profit once these new customers join our profitable 'active customer' target group. In effect, all the profit comes from active customers. However, we are bound to lose some of these active customers.

In the next table, **5.1.7**, we see the population within each target group. This shows how the less profitable target groups are used to repopulate the most profitable target group. The anticipated loss of 30,000 active customers is replaced by 37,000 new or reactivated customers, producing an overall projected gain of 7,000 active customers; this amounting to a 7% increase.

Table 5.1.7 **Case one: home shopping company – customer strength forecast**

Target group	Total population	Number of enquiries	Number of buyers	Gain/loss
Active customers	100,000	-	70,000	(-30,000)
Lapsed customers	90,000	36,000	12,000	+12,000
Unconverted prospects	60,000	24,000	5,000	+5,000
New business	7,000,000	80,000	20,000	+20,000
TOTAL CUSTOMERS			107,000	+7,000

The active customers are not shown as enquirers because they all receive catalogues without requesting them.

Who are the seven million people who are in the *new business* target group? They are the potential customers who receive cold mailings, see ads and inserts in the media we use to acquire customers, or visit the website, either prompted or unprompted.

These population statistics say more about the dynamics of the business than the cash contribution figures. Now we can see that our active customer loss rate is 30% (let's say over a year). Assuming the enterprise is fairly stable in size, we can see that we are targeting about three years' worth of lost customers in our lapsed customer mailings. (90,000 = 30,000 losses x 3.)

But we are only targeting about a year's worth of unconverted enquiries. (**Table 5.1.7** shows that it takes 80,000 new business enquiries to create 20,000 customers – therefore there must be 60,000 unconverted enquiries.) Looking at the conversion rate, we see that this group is just as responsive as the lapsed customer group, but that they are less likely to buy. This is what one would expect – our unconverted prospects failed to buy before.

If you had just bought the home shopping company in this example and wanted to accelerate its expansion rate, what would you do?

Judging by the forecast, the least productive action to consider is spending more on external media, because this is the most expensive source. So what are the alternatives?

Table 5.1.8 **Case one: home shopping company – alternative marketing tactics**

Target group	Objective	Proposed action
Active customers	Reduce loss rate	Identify non-buyers and incentivise
Lapsed customers	Increase orders	Send catalogue unrequested
Unconverted prospects	Increase conversion	Offer incentive for first order

Before proceeding you would set objectives for each action and cost it out. You might then test in one season before rolling the action out against the whole target group in the next season. For example, you might send unrequested catalogues to all of the most recent lapsed offline customers but not to the older lapsed customers. Then you might *test* sending unrequested catalogues to a *sample* of the older lapsed customers and ask the remaining offline lapsed customers (**the control group**) to request a catalogue. Finally, you might e-mail all lapsed online customers with a personalised offer available only on the website.

Lessons from this case

✔ The case illustrates that **customer acquisition** is not easily separable from **customer retention.** We need to do both, but saving old customers reduces the need for new customers. However, we must take care to avoid giving away too many incentives to customers who would order anyway at full-price.

✔ Simple **P & L projections** are an excellent way of illustrating the effects of alternative tactics. However, they do not show the ongoing value of increased customer strength. We need to bear in mind that adding to customer strength is likely to reduce short-term profit but increase longer-term profit.

✔ It is crucial to project differences in **customer strength** arising from alternative tactics. It is an important refinement to project the different potential values of customers derived from different sources; eg lapsed customers who are recovered may be worth less or more than new customers.

Projecting payback on customer acquisition

The launch situation

In case one we reiterated the need to project the potential value of newly acquired customers. Doing so is crucial for a new business – and much more difficult.

Also in case one (**Table 5.1.6**), we see that it costs five times as much to sell to unidentified prospects as to established customers. This is fairly typical of a mature operation and poses a problem to anyone starting a new business.

A degree of compensation exists in two respects:

1. Every market includes early adopters who are more responsive to whatever is new.

2. The fact is that some new business sources prove to be very much more productive than others. A new business can begin by tapping the best media sources.

By following the **test philosophy** described in chapter 4.2 it should be possible to contain customer acquisition costs. However, the established business with a portfolio of satisfied customers will always enjoy an advantage.

Case two: projecting the ongoing value of new customers

In Case two, using real-life projected sales and costs, we shall track the forecast achievement of another home shopping catalogue business over 18 catalogue issues (say three years) from its inception. The forecast is from the original business plan and has not been modified in the light of trading experience. The business plan proposes that the company acquires customers through one-stage activity, using ads and preview catalogues, and sends more substantial catalogues to the customers.

In this projection, no online trading is included, the presumption being that a website will be built once offline trading justifies the additional investment.

Table 5.1.9 shows the projection for the first year.

Table 5.1.9 **Case two: three-year projection of customer values (using one-stage customer acquisition) – year one**

Year 1	Issue 1	Issue 2	Issue 3	Issue 4	Issue 5	Issue 6	Total
Active customers (000s)							
At start of period	-	78	146	190	199	233	-
New customers	78	68	44	51	71	58	370
Customers lost	-	-	-	42	37	24	103
At end of period	78	146	190	199	233	267	267 = catalogues
Acquisition costs							
Per customer	£13.24	£11.72	£15.48	£12.63	£10.80	£12.98	£12.64 =£1.09
Total (000s)	£1,033	£797	£681	£644	£767	£753	£4,675 each
Retention costs (000s)							
Catalogue production and postage	£84	£85	£55	£64	£88	£72	£461
Origination, incentives, other print	£97	£159	£207	£217	£254	£290	£1,211
Total marketing costs (000s)	£1,215	£1,040	£943	£924	£1,109	£1,116	£6,347
Sales (number 000s)							
New customers	78	68	44	51	71	58	370
Repeat sales	24	46	56	63	75	82	345
Total	102	114	100	114	146	140	715
Sales (value 000s)							
New customers	£1,950	£1,700	£1,100	£1,275	£1,775	£1,450	£9,250 = £25 av value
Repeat sales (catalogue)	£607	£958	£1,172	£1,317	£1,571	£1,714	£7,339 = £25 av value
Add-on sales (from other stationery)	-	£146	£190	£199	£233	£267	£1,035 = £25 av x 5% response
Postage and packing	£72	£135	£166	£185	£220	£242	£1,020 = £2.95 per order
Total sales	£2,629	£2,939	£2,628	£2,976	£3,799	£3,673	£18,644
Marketing cost:sales	46.2%	35.4%	35.9%	31.0%	29.2%	30.4%	34.0%

Table 5.1.9 The first year

In this model, active customers are defined as (a) new customers who have bought from a one-stage ad or preview leaflet or (b) repeat buyers who have bought from the catalogue mailings not more than six months ago. If you look at the 'customers lost' line (line 3) you will see that no customers have been lost during the currency of the first three catalogues. That is because customers are defined as active if they have ordered within the last six months. Since the business is less than six months old, no customers can have been lost.

The customers who will be defined as lost at Issue 4 will never have ordered from the catalogue – they will only have ordered from an ad or a preview leaflet. Once customers are lost they will go back into the customer acquisition pond and some will be enticed back by lapsed customer mailings.

By the end of year one, there are 267,000 customers defined as 'active'. This is the number to whom Issue 7 of the catalogue will be mailed.

Looking down to acquisition costs, we can see these are expressed as *cost per customer* as well as being shown as totals. Alternatively, it would have been possible to show the costs as a marketing ratio. Expressing the cost as 'per customer' is very typical of direct marketing. The fact of winning a new customer is seen as being more important than the value of the first sale.

Note, too, that in the next section of **Table 5.1.9** ongoing customer communications costs are captioned *retention costs*. Here we see that retention costs start very low compared with acquisition costs but gradually increase in line with the growth in the number of active customers.

Along lines 9 and 10 we see the *number of sales*. Number of sales appears in the table because each one represents an active customer. The more customers who remain active, the healthier future prospects will be. Repeat sales overtake new business sales with the third catalogue issue. The exact balance of acquisition to repeat activity is affected by seasonal factors and so the growth of the repeat business share of sales is not on a straight-line basis.

In the *sales value* section of the table we can see that more than half the total sales value arises from new business. This causes the marketing cost ratio to remain quite high throughout the first year. For the sake of simplicity, the sales shown are net sales, not orders. The difference between value of orders and value of sales can be considerable.

More demand than sales

Orders are always higher than sales for three reasons:

1.   Some credit orders may be refused.

2.   Some orders cannot be met because goods are out-of-stock.

3.   Some goods are returned unwanted within a free approval period or for a refund.

Table 5.1.10   **Case two: three-year projection of customer values (customer acquisition stripped out) – year two**

Year 1	Issue 7	Issue 8	Issue 9	Issue 10	Issue 11	Issue 12	Total
Active customers (000s)							
At start of period	267	221	167	125	105	82	-
New customers	-	-	-	-	-	-	-
Customers lost	46	54	42	20	23	18	203
At end of period	203	167	125	105	82	64	64 = catalogues
Acquisition costs Total (000's)	-	-	-	-	-	-	-
Retention costs (000s)							
Catalogue production and postage	£241	£182	£136	£115	£89	£70	£832
Origination, incentives, other print	£91	£68	£51	£43	£34	£26	£313 = £1.09 each
Total marketing costs (000s)	£331	£250	£188	£158	£123	£96	£1,145
Sales (number 000s)							
New customers	-	-	-	-	-	-	-
Repeat sales	67	54	42	36	28	23	251
Sales (value £ 000s)							
Repeat sales (catalogue)	£1,395	£1,135	£898	£776	£609	£499	£5,311 = £25 av value.
Add-on sales (from other stationery)	£221	£167	£125	£105	£82	£64	£764 = £20 av x 5% response
Postage and packing	£197	£158	£124	£107	£84	£68	£739 = £2.95 per order
Total sales	£1,813	£1,460	£1,147	£988	£775	£631	£6,814
Marketing cost:sales	18.3%	17.1%	16.4%	16.0%	15.9%	15.2%	16.8%

Table 5.1.10 The second year

Looking now at the second year in **Table 5.1.10** you will notice that 'customer acquisition' appears to have been cancelled. It seems the business is being bled for profit and is being allowed to go into rapid decline.

This is not the case at all. The reason for stripping out 'customer acquisition' is to show the **ongoing value** of the customers who were recruited in the first year. By showing only the costs and value associated with their repeat purchases, the company can see the rate at which it is paying back the 'customer acquisition' cost.

To determine the effect of continuing customer acquisition at the same rate as in the first year, it is simply necessary to add the two years together. This produces sales of £25.458 million with marketing costs of £7.492 million, a ratio of 29.4%. In practice a slightly better position could be expected because the pool of lapsed customers could be fished to produce cheaper new business than would be available from outside media and lists.

Without any new business, the second year would begin with 267,000 customers and end with just 64,000. Meanwhile, the marketing cost ratio falls to about 15% by the end of the year.

Table 5.1.11   **Three-year projection of customer values (customer acquisition stripped out) – year three**

Year 1	Issue 13	Issue 14	Issue 15	Issue 16	Issue 17	Issue 18	Total
Active customers (000s)							
At start of period	64	54	44	35	32	29	
New customers	-	-	-	-	-	-	-
Customers lost	10	10	9	3	4	3	39
At end of period	54	44	35	32	29	25	25 = catalogues
Acquisition costs Total (000s)	-	-	-	-	-	-	-
Retention costs (000s)							
Catalogue production and postage	£59	£47	£38	£35	£31	£28	£239 = £1.09 each
Origination, incentives and other print	£22	£18	£14	£13	£12	£10	£90
Total marketing costs (000s)	£82	£65	£53	£48	£43	£38	£329
Sales (number 000s)							
New customers	-	-	-	-	-	-	-
Repeat sales	22	18	15	16	15	15	101
Sales (value 000s)							
Repeat sales (catalogue)	£565	£485	£407	£433	£417	£402	£2,710 = £30 av value
Add-on sales (from other stationery)	£68	£54	£44	£41	£36	£32	£274 = £25 av x 5% response
Postage and packing	£64	£54	£45	£47	£45	£43	£299 = £2.95 per order
Total sales	£697	£593	£496	£521	£498	£477	£3,238
Marketing cost:sales	11.8%	11.0%	10.7%	9.2%	8.6%	8.0%	10.0%

Table 5.1.11 The third year

In **Table 5.1.11** we see the third year position, still showing only the business that arises from the year one recruits. The decline now starts to taper off as the most active customers tend to remain on board. The projection allows for this by increasing the number of sales per customer by about a third and the value of sales by about 20%. To arrive at a view of year three with customer acquisition, it is just a matter of adding the three tables together. Sales are now £28.741 million with marketing costs of £7.821 million, a ratio of 27.2%.

Points to note

> The marketing costs look very high early on because the required growth rate is very rapid, forcing the level of new business activity up.
>
> The plan shows a consistently high response rate to catalogue mailings and the company may be planning to withhold distribution from non-buyers prematurely. At a cost of £1.09 per catalogue, mailing any database segment that responds at a rate of 10% or more will be cheaper than replacing lost customers with new ones. That is because the cost per sale will be £10.90 compared with an average of £12.64 from new business.
>
> Thus, the company might do well to consider ways of keeping customers on board for somewhat longer. This would not make a large difference to the marketing ratio, but it could have a significant impact on the bottom line.
>
> Clearly, there would be benefit in adding online trading, because this would enable some customers to be reactivated without incurring the expense of additional catalogue distribution.

Applying the case two model

Case two shows all except one of the figures needed to show the ROI on new customer acquisition over a three-year period. The missing figure is **contribution**. By making an assumption on gross profit (say it is 40%), it is simple to add a bottom line to the tables showing contribution. This will be 40% of sales, less the percentage on marketing.

The value of this model is that it illustrates how ongoing customers values are projected. The model can be applied to most situations but the marketing cost ratios are peculiar to the case and not realistic for other types of business. To discover the true cost ratios, industry research is needed to set a benchmark and this needs to be followed by live testing.

Chapter 5.2

Success factors

This chapter includes:

- ❑ **What is a direct response?**
- ❑ **Why do people respond?**
- ❑ **The elements of success**
- ❑ **Product – the whole package**
- ❑ **Promotional offers**
- ❑ **Targeting – effectiveness and efficiency**
- ❑ **Formats – sizes, colours, shapes, animation, lengths**
- ❑ **Creative – copy and design**
- ❑ **Timing – seasons, days, time-of-day**
- ❑ **Summary – the elements of success**

About this chapter

 n this chapter we define a direct response as being the action that turns a 'suspect' into a prospect or a customer. Suspects are potential customers who have not yet volunteered their identities. (Although cookies enable us to deliver personalised content, they are not enough to turn suspects into prospects.)

Direct responses are categorised as one-stage or two-stage. Each of these categories is subdivided into four types.

We look at what makes people respond or not respond. We then examine the six main elements of success in creating direct response and sales. Although these elements are tackled more or less in order of their presumed influence, each one can be crucially important. The six elements are, in fact, so closely interrelated as to be most usefully considered collectively as the essential components of direct response.

Graeme McCorkell consultant and writer

Graeme's biography appears at the beginning of the previous chapter

Chapter 5.2

Success factors

What is a direct response?

The answer to this question may seem obvious. However, there is more than one type of response and each type has a different value.

The lowest grade of response is a click-through to a website from an online ad – or a visit to the site from some other source. In either case, responders have yet to volunteer their identities. If a phoned request for a catalogue has a 10% chance of maturing into a sale, then a visit to the website probably has no better than a 1% chance. (NB This is not to suggest that all sources of website visits are equal. Visitors who arrived in response to an iTV ad, from an affiliated site, from a search engine or from an offline referral may all have differing values.)

The moment of response

For all practical purposes, **a response occurs when the potential customer trades their contact data for some kind of benefit.**

Until website visitors tell us who they are, they are just window-shopping. Until they identify themselves, they are 'suspects' in direct marketing jargon. **Suspects** are potential prospects. **Prospects** are potential customers who have told us where we can find them.

While it is important to track website visitors, the main reason for doing so is to improve our performance in getting them to register as prospects or, better still, customers.

One-stage and two-stage response

In a minority of cases, the first response is to order or buy something. This is called **one-stage** (sometimes one-step) response. Response which does not result in an immediate purchase is usually called **two-stage** response. In practice, it may be multi-stage. There may be a number of communications between buyer and seller before the transaction is completed.

One-stage responses

These are not always purchases. The four main types of one-stage transaction are:

✔   **Purchases:** usually accompanied by immediate payment unless B2B.

✔   **Trial orders:** invoice or direct debit payable after expiry of free approval period.

✔   **Enrolments/subscriptions:** responder takes out renewable membership or subscription, eg book club.

✔   **Applications:** responder applies for product, eg a credit card, usually without guarantee of acceptance.

Two-stage responses

The vast majority of responses are two-stage but they are not all the same:

✔   **Information requests:** usually requests for brochures or catalogues.

✔   **Volunteered information:** responder provides personal information in exchange for a benefit, eg website registrations and lifestyle survey responses.

✔   **Enquiries:** responder requires specific details prior to purchase, eg insurance quotes.

✔   **Sales leads:** enquirer requests information to be supplied by salesperson, often fixing appointment.

In two-stage response, the second stage is as important as the first. The sale will depend on the effectiveness of the catalogue, the website, the call centre, the store, the dealer or the sales team. This in turn will depend very largely on the information technology and logistical support underpinning the sales process.

Why do people respond?

The barriers to buying direct

The biggest hurdle direct marketers and their customers face is the perceived risk of buying 'at a distance'. This, of course, is most pronounced at the time of the first purchase, ie during the customer acquisition phase.

> People respond to advertisements only when the immediate gain in responding exceeds the risk or cost of responding by an acceptable margin ... and it appears easy to respond.
>
> Advertising That Pulls Response *Graeme McCorkell*

This is an important difference between direct and interactive marketing and other marketing disciplines. It merits exploration.

Obviously, reasons for non-response include those causing a 'no sale' in any other situation, ie wrong product, wrong price or wrong audience etc. But with direct marketing there are additional obstacles resulting entirely from the remoteness between seller and buyer, for example:

✗ Prospects may not be able to see or handle the product, or sample the service, until after it has been ordered.

✗ Prospects cannot easily assess the integrity of the seller or the seller's organisation. Bricks seem safer than clicks.

✗ Prospects may not be able to interpret the literature. Questions thus remain unanswered, which is highly destructive.

✗ There may be fears in relation to payment: is it safe to order online by credit card? Will I be able to secure a refund if the goods are returned?

✗ There may be worries about delivery: when will the goods arrive? Will I be at home to receive them?

✗ There may be concerns about data protection and privacy.

✗ There may be specific fears about becoming more involved, eg: will I be expected to buy more books or CDs than I can afford? Will I be pursued for further orders or donations?

All of the above negative perceptions must be overcome before a prospect becomes a first-time buyer. A large part of customer acquisition communication is directed towards overcoming objections.

Why prospects DO respond

Fortunately, to counter the negative associations, direct marketing offers prospects several distinct advantages.

Prospects may choose to deal direct in order to:

✔   Acquire a unique product or a personally specified version of a product.

✔   Acquire an everyday product in a unique configuration, eg with different accessories or, perhaps, personalised with their initials.

✔   Acquire a product at a lower price or with better payment terms or incentives.

✔   Save on procurement through online exchanges, reduced transaction costs and superior supply chain management (B2B only).

✔   Enjoy bargain hunting and comparison shopping on the Internet.

✔   Enjoy better guarantees, eg pay nothing if not satisfied.

✔   Enjoy a wider product selection, eg from a catalogue or website.

✔   Shop without consuming valued leisure time, without car parking hassle, with an option to try out goods at home etc.

✔   Preserve privacy; avoid embarrassment.

✔   Be better informed: direct marketing offers can be accompanied by more expansive information than is available from other channels.

✔   Enjoy an ongoing dialogue: many prospects enjoy 'belonging', whether to a club or a less clearly defined community; they enjoy receiving correspondence and engaging in feedback. This is a special advantage of interactive marketing.

Thus the communications task facing direct marketers at the recruitment stage – and at later stages in the customer dialogue – is to overcome negative associations whilst stressing the positive benefits of the direct route. Clearly the trust factor – which may be implicit in the brand or may need to be delivered by specific guarantees – is important.

How people react to advertising

Having suggested why prospects respond, this is a good opportunity to consider how and when they react to direct response advertising.

The graphic below, based on research commissioned by a large London advertising agency, demonstrates who sees a particular category of advertising, in this case financial ads in national newspapers. Who reads these ads and who acts on them? How individuals react will depend very largely on their stage in the buying cycle, ie where they sit in the 'target' in **Figure 5.2.1:**

Figure 5.2.1 **Reactions to press advertising**

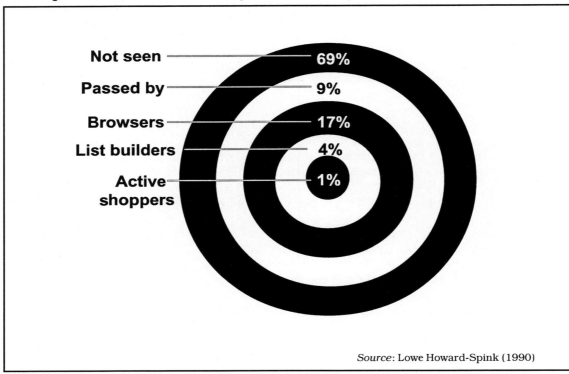

Not seen ———— 69%

Passed by ———— 9%

Browsers ———— 17%

List builders ———— 4%

Active shoppers ———— 1%

Source: Lowe Howard-Spink (1990)

Lowe's research suggests:

✔ 69% do not notice financial ads in their newspaper.

✔ 9% notice but have no prior interest and move on.

✔ 17% browse financial ads with no active reason or interest.

✔ 4% are actively collecting information.

✔ 1% or less are in a buying frame of mind.

Thus, if we are running a two-stage ad, our realistic target would be the 4% information gatherers. Running a one-stage offer our target shrinks to 1% or less.

Any attempt to attract attention among the 'outer ring' would not only be wasteful; successful direct response creative work targets true prospects. The 17% browsers may simply not yet be ready to take action, although a few might respond when noticing an unusually interesting proposition with a strong offer to act now.

Fortunately, 1% is more than enough to repay the cost of our advertising, although we might need a better qualified list for direct mail (because of its higher cost per thousand readers); for example, a list of people known to have an interest in the product category or known to be active home shoppers within a related category.

Active and comparison shoppers

Direct response advertising targets people who are in **active shopping mode** and people who are in **comparison shopping mode.** Despite this narrow targeting, many direct marketing-only brands are well-known, eg **Amazon**, **First Direct**, **Egg**, **Direct Line**, **Linguaphone**, and **easyJet**.

Possibly because ads that make offers are more interesting than brand-building ads, they gain more attention, despite their narrow targeting. This has been demonstrated repeatedly by press ad readership surveys, more popular in the US than in the UK. Be that as it may, it is a side benefit, not the object of direct response advertising in any medium. The object is to gain response.

A conventional advertisement, designed to influence the greatest number of people, has to be aimed at as many people as possible. A direct marketing advertisement, designed to achieve sales as cost-efficiently as possible, has to appeal more strongly to only those people most likely to purchase.

John Watson, Successful Creativity in Direct Marketing

The elements of success

We now move to consider the major success factors in acquisition. The direct marketer sees the first sale as the beginning. To the customer, the first purchase is an end in itself. The customer is buying a product. There is not necessarily (or usually) any intention of forging an ongoing business relationship. But to forge a customer relationship, the direct marketer must first make a sale.

The elements of a successful acquisition programme shown below are the success factors referred to widely in direct marketing texts, namely:

- ✔ **The product** (the whole package, including price, terms, delivery channel)

- ✔ **Promotional offer** (a reason to buy now)

- ✔ **Targeting** (media, lists, segments)

- ✔ **Format** (eg size and shape of ad, length of commercial)

- ✔ **Creative** (including response mechanism)

- ✔ **Timing** (season, day of week, time of day)

These elements are frequently inextricably linked so it is the whole which the customer finds desirable. Especially closely linked are product, price and offer; in combination these can be tuned to suit the available media, market and economics. Similarly, targeting and timing are closely related: timing can be an important aspect of targeting. Naturally, format and creative content are also inextricably linked.

Most direct marketers would agree that the combined elements of product/price/offer outweigh all others. They are followed by targeting or the combination of targeting and timing. Format and creative follow some way behind. Fulfilment seldom creates sales but fulfilment failures kill sales.

We will now take a look at these success factors one-by-one.

Product – the whole package

Direct marketing is used to help win customers for every kind of product or service, B2C and B2B. However, not every product lends itself to direct distribution.

Nevertheless, it has been demonstrated that – if the incentive to buy is strong enough – almost anything can be sold direct.

Surfers save £6,000

To save £6,000 or more on a new car, British car buyers have scoured the web for Belgian car dealers and placed deposits against cars for delivery in six months' time. Such trusting behaviour is induced more by the saving than any prior knowledge of the dealership. A £6,000 saving is, of course, an exceptional incentive. Furthermore, the car itself is not an unknown quantity. The surfer would already be seeking a *specific* model, being presold on it by road test reports, advertising and direct mail. But the dealer must be trusted to deliver the car as promised in a UK specification. This is a classic case for *viral* marketing.

The product defined

We shall concentrate on products whose sales are completed via direct marketing, although it would be true to say that the product would generally appear at the top of the list of success factors in any case. Obviously, if a salesperson is involved, that person will also be a critical success factor.

✔ **Product means product or service** eg **Marbles** credit card

✔ **Product means the whole package** eg *subscription* to **The Economist**

✔ **Package includes terms and channel** (but not short-term incentives)

✔ **Package includes customer service and fulfilment**

✔ **Product might be a collection** eg a home shopping inventory

NB The product might be sold one- or two-stage.

✔ **Product means product or service:** as is standard marketing practice, product is taken to mean a physical product, for example a laptop computer, or an intangible service, for example **Direct Line Breakdown Service**.

✔ **Product means the whole package:** by this we mean the complete proposition, not just the product as an entity. What many marketers call the 'total product' or 'marketing offering'.

Thus, to potential **Economist** subscribers, we are not selling the magazine (which they already know), we are selling a regular subscription on special terms (eg cancellable at any time with a refund), at a price below news-stand price for a particular subscription period (eg six or 12 months).

Package includes terms and channel: (but not short term incentives). Again, taking **The Economist** as an example, the product includes the discount on the news-stand price (because it is a permanent feature in any subscription offer) but not the free gift we are offering for prompt response. The latter will be considered on its own merits and dropped if it does not pay its way.

The product also includes the channel (direct via the postal service or the Internet instead of via the news-stand).

Package includes customer service and fulfilment: here we mean the whole customer experience from navigating the website, through the ordering process, to delivery and response to queries. Good service is likely to be essential, certainly if we intend to develop an ongoing business relationship.

Product might be a collection: although not every item offered within a collection may be exclusive, the collection will still be unique in exact content, presentation and terms. The collection or range might include office products for SMEs or casual clothing for thirty-somethings. It might be available from a website, a printed catalogue or, more likely, both.

The product might be sold one-stage or in two stages.

Successful products

In the pioneering days of mail order, the definition of the ideal product was quite prescriptive. For example, it was either unique, difficult to find in shops or embarrassing to buy face-to-face. Furthermore, it needed to be light in relation to its value, not fragile and be perceived as a bargain even though the mark-up needed to be at least 200%. Incontinence pads, left-handed scissors and courses in English grammar met the criteria and helped fill the bargain pages in the weekend newspapers.

Today's direct marketers are less prescriptive, at least in describing the physical attributes and margin requirements of the winning product. However, the attributes listed below are still useful as checklist items. To be successfully sold and distributed by direct marketing, a product will need at least some of these attributes:

?	Is it unique or does it feature an added unique benefit?
?	Can it be personalised or configured to meet the buyer's specification?
?	Is it a niche product that is difficult to find or embarrassing to buy in shops?
?	Can it be successfully described in marketing communications?
?	Can it be satisfactorily delivered?
?	Does it carry sufficient margins to support direct promotion/distribution?

Advances in logistics and information technology have changed the face of marketing. Today, almost any non-FMCG product can be distributed direct.

Successful products include services such as motor insurance and travel, durables such as collectibles and leisurewear and consumables such as magazine subscriptions and office supplies. Even fragile products such as wine. Wine would be disqualified on any checklist of product attributes from the pioneering days of mail order: the bottles are fragile, the margin on wine is low and the product is heavy in relation to its value. Today's direct marketer, able to forecast the potential LTV (Lifetime Value) of the wine buyer, takes a different view.

From these examples of successful categories, we can now look at two more closely – **motor insurance** and **leisurewear** – to see what makes them work so well.

At first, motor insurance may not seem an attractive proposition to the direct marketer. There is little customer loyalty in the market; it is hard to project any unique benefit for a particular brand and, unless we know their renewal dates, impossible to target many more than one in 12 motorists in the right month, let alone the optimum week. Nevertheless, direct motor insurers came to dominate the market very rapidly. Why?

Successful products – (1) motor insurance

Commodity market – bargain hunters: privately insuring motorists are prepared to act as their own brokers and shop around to save money.

Expert systems – tailor-made quotes: guided by expert systems, the call centre or website can craft the perfect product for the prospect from millions of permutations. No two callers will receive the same quote. The entire process is automated.

Transaction completion at call centre or website: although (under current rules) policy documentation and confirmation must be completed by post, the transaction can be effectively completed at the call centre or website in about six minutes.

Only paperwork to send out: there are no goods to despatch or reorder, just documents to confirm the agreed details.

Annually renewable: 95% of motorists stay in the market annually. In bad years for claims, premiums shoot up and it is cheap to source new customers. In good years, premiums stay down and policyholders renew instead of shopping around.

Cross-selling opportunity: customer contact may give the opportunity to discover household insurance renewal dates. Alternatively, breakdown insurance and credit products might be offered.

Staple 12-month media: motorists are attuned to the idea of looking in Yellow Pages or Thomson's directories to find insurance ads. Furthermore, websites are permanent, open all hours and easy to find through search engines.

As more privately insuring motorists switch to online buying, so costs of direct sales and service reduce, while cross-selling opportunities increase.

Clothing has been another successful home shopping category, the largest in the UK market. With average mark-ups of around 100% but high potential returns through fit and colour problems, the market may seem unattractive. However, fit problems can be minimised by avoiding the more formal, tailored items and this is one reason for the growth of leisurewear catalogues.

Successful products – (2) leisurewear

Growth market – lifestyle targeting: growth was stimulated by a trend for dressing down at work, but possibly more by keep-fit, outdoor pursuits and activity holidays. Targeting by lifestyle through lists and media is simple, while the user profile lends itself to online trading.

Unisex and related women's and men's casuals: possible to create unisex catalogue, thus enhancing its earning potential and adding to customer LTV.

Growth of high income, time poor households: better-off people still young enough to buy clothes frequently are time-poor, often living in dual full-time income households. They are prime targets for home shopping.

Catalogues provide entertainment: stylish, informative catalogues receive as much attention as paid-for magazines. Websites can be designed to add value through personalisation (eg cyber fittings) and to sell off redundant stock.

Call centres and websites offer tailored service: using intelligent software development it is possible to offer one-to-one service by 'remembering' the customer's tastes, interests, requests and dates of previous gift purchases.

Price and value comparisons difficult: because clothes are exclusive, it is possible to avoid excessive commoditisation of the market, adding value through good design and service.

High customer values: clothes are expensive and need replacing as wear and fashion dictate. People with similar incomes spend vastly different amounts, making the application of Pareto's Principle possible.

Low returns and redundant stocks: fit problems are reduced by concentrating on leisurewear. Redundant stock problems are also reduced as garments are less sharply seasonal and fashionable than more formal wear. Despatches and returns are relatively cheap to handle.

One-stage sales possible: using sell-off-the-page ads, mini-catalogue inserts and full catalogue mailings, it is possible to acquire customers on a one-stage basis as well as using smaller two-stage ads. This adds versatility to customer acquisition tactics.

Terms are part of the package, too

Remember this quote?

People respond to advertisements only when the immediate gain in responding exceeds the risk or cost of responding by an acceptable margin ...

Terms can be used to elevate the perceived gain or reduce the perceived risk:

✔ **Sample** product, eg send for a sample of the product before committing to a purchase. Examples: demonstration cassette for language course, free first issue of magazine and sample size consumable product.

✔ **Free trial**, eg try the product at home for 10 to 30 days; return undamaged if not satisfied. Often expressed as "send no money." Another form of free trial is the **deferred direct debit.** For example, the subscriber receives a monthly magazine free for three months before the direct debit mandate takes effect. The subscriber can cancel during the free trial, paying nothing. To cancel, the subscriber must contact the bank.

✔ **Money-back** guarantee: "If at any time you are not satisfied, return the product for a full refund." Usually an enhanced version of statutory rights, featuring elements such as "no questions asked" or with no time limit on returns.

✔ **Invoice**: "Send no money now, we will invoice you with delivery." Example: magazine subscription (often allied to "cancel at any time" option, offering refund of unexpired portion of subscription payment).

All these offers can help to lift orders substantially but will not necessarily lift net sales *proportionately*. Asking for payment up-front will bring in fewer orders than sending an invoice with the goods, but will offer some compensation by eliminating bad debt, speeding cash flow and reducing administration expense.

Features of successful products – a summary:

✔ **Most products can be sold direct:** for example, speciality foods and complete gourmet meals were sold successfully by **Scotland Direct** long before superstores offered home delivery. The marketing idea is more important than the product category. In direct marketing, as in other marketing, the product is the whole added-value package.

Nevertheless, we can update the list of mail order success attributes and identify features that make some products REAL HOT.

Most products can be sold direct. But some are REAL HOT

Relationship potential
Easy targeting   **H**igh customer values
Adequate margin   **O**pportunity to add value
Logistics simple   **T**rue customer benefit

Relationship potential: Our object in making the first sale is to *acquire a customer*. What are the chances of making repeat sales to that customer?

Easy targeting: Can we find and identify potential new customers easily? For example, gardeners, small businesses, investors, walkers, dentists or theatre-goers.

Adequate margin: Is it feasible to sell direct? In some cases, for example in commoditised travel and financial markets, it may *only* be feasible to sell online.

Logistics simple: Can we manage the potential stocking and distribution problems and account management problems?

High customer values: What is the potential lifetime value of a customer? Can we achieve a satisfactory Customer RoI?

Opportunity to add value: Can we add value so that direct distribution is more attractive than other channels? For instance, personalised products.

True customer benefit: Is there an obvious customer benefit, preferably other than price, in buying direct?

Promotional offers

Premia, incentives, and other inducements

However good the product, an added incentive to purchase will usually prove effective. It will help to overcome the inertia which otherwise characterises the direct response process.

Incentives, other than those already included under the heading of *terms* above, include:

✔ Premia (gifts)

✔ Prize draw or competition entry

✔ Promotional discounts

The extra costs of premia and gifts should be offset by an increased response. The cost of the premium we can afford will depend on the price of the product and the level of risk. If we are offering goods on approval or free trial, we may make the premium available only on payment. If the premium is available whether or not those who order keep and pay for the product, we can obviously afford less per order than if we make the premium conditional upon payment.

Two-stage premia

A small gift may be offered just for responding to an ad or mailing, for example to request a catalogue. This will increase response at the expense of increasing catalogue wastage. Such a gift is often teamed with another, larger gift that is conditional on purchase. In combination, the two offers can increase both response and conversion rate. The first gift is often time-restricted and is then called a 'speed premium' or 'early bird offer'.

Generally speaking, more generous offers produce better returns even after the cost of the premium has been taken into account. **Table 5.2.1** demonstrates the effect of a low-cost premium.

Table 5.2.1   **One-stage home shopping offer**

(Direct mail or e-mail)	Without incentive		With incentive	
Mailing quantity	400,000		400,000	
Net sales	24,000	(6%)	28,000	(7%)
Selling price	£12.95		£12.95	
Total revenue	£310,800		£362,600	
Extra revenue			+ £51,800	
Less premium			- £14,000	@ 50p each
Net extra revenue			+ £37,800	

Table 5.2.1 shows an example of an 'everybody wins' situation. The direct marketer sells more and makes more profit; the purchaser receives an extra item free.

Successful marketers offer premia tactically to achieve specific objectives, eg for higher order values, for orders from specific ranges of goods. 'Early bird' or 'speed' premia are offered for response within a reasonable, but short, period of time.

More on offers. What makes a good premium?

The ideal premium has a **high perceived value** and **low actual cost**. Information is often a very effective premium, eg booklets and videos. 'Hard' premia (jewellery and watches) will give higher response but at a higher cost; and it is best to avoid mechanical or electrical premia because of their potentially high failure rate.

Choosing the right premium is important. A premium linked to the product (eg a tape measure with a DIY product) will often work well but, as long as the premium has a perceived value much greater than its cost, the 'fit' between it and the product does not have to be precise. If the product and the marketing have wide appeal, the premium must also have wide appeal.

We need to beware of 'freeloaders' – not all response is good. Conversion rates need to be measured carefully when rewarding people to respond.

Discount offers – powerful but dangerous

The most powerful incentive of all is often a lower price, or, more precisely, a reduced price. However, discounts are also the most expensive incentive: a discount of £5 means £5 less profit unless the discount is linked to an increased order, in which case it may pay for itself, much as a premium.

Many catalogue marketers successfully use volume discounts to increase profitability per sale, for instance:

✔ Buy two, get one free

✔ Postage and packing free on orders over £20

✔ 5% discount on orders over £10, 10% discount on orders over £20

Discounts can be counter-productive, especially when used with quality products. A unique product should sell on its excellence or rarity value. A discount may signal that we are having difficulty in disposing of the stock unless a logical explanation is offered. The most convincing and enticing explanations add exclusivity to the offer, eg "We pass on the savings of selling direct/on the Internet to you".

Special deals for members of affinity groups or customers of affiliates are among the most convincing and effective, eg "Offer exclusive to Members of the Institute of Direct Marketing". Needless to say, exclusive offers must be genuinely exclusive, although they need not always be discounts. Such offers are invariably close-dated and so may be made to another affinity group at another time.

A (book) case of exclusivity

One of the most successful affinity group offers ever to **American Express** cardmembers was one of the most unlikely. It was the complete set of *The Great Books of the Western World* in a limited edition reproduction of a unique revolving Victorian bookcase. A discount would never have sold this scholarly collection to such a status conscious affinity group. But the addition of the exclusive bookcase at a combined price of over £1,000 sold the books like hot cakes. The offer was repeated after an interval of six years with equal success.

The lowest cost offers: prize draws and competitions

For the larger scale marketer, prize draws can prove to be highly cost-effective as response boosters. A £50,000 prize fund spread over 500,000 entries costs only 10p an entry. If it has boosted the response from 250,000 to 500,000 the cost per incremental response is still only 20p. The downside is that prize draws can be used to attract response only, not paid orders. Entry cannot be conditional on purchase.

Briefly, the crucial distinction between prize draws and competitions is:

A prize draw:
✔ Calls for no skill on the part of participants and must not be conditional on the purchase of a product or ticket.
✔ The cost of a phone call or stamp to enter the draw does not count as a purchase.
✔ Lucky numbers may be pre-drawn or post-drawn, ie before or after entry.
✔ The number will normally be drawn by computer.

Competitions:
✔ Competitions (contests) are games of skill where there must be a significant application of skill and judgement.
✔ Competitions can be linked to purchase; entries may be charged for.
✔ They are most often relatively ineffective compared with prize draws.

Prize draws are best used in direct mail and inserts, where pre-drawn numbers can be printed on documents. Although prize draws normally involve pre-issued numbers, this is not a requirement, and it is possible to offer a prize draw entry through other media.

Table 5.2.2 **Prize draw economics**

	Model based on 25% increase in order rate	
	Non-prize draw	Prize draw
Mailing quantity	400,000	400,000
Order rate	5.00%	6.25%
Mailing cost per '000	£750	£750
Total mailing cost	£300,000	£300,000
Prize fund		£ 40,000
Total promotional cost	£300,000	£340,000
Orders	20,000	25,000
Cost per order	£15.00	£13.60

Prize draws have lost much of their former popularity due to the impact of the National Lottery and, more significantly, to the replacement of the post as the chief response medium. Nevertheless, they can sometimes lift initial response by 100% or more. A draw can run for many months, so amortising its costs over a number of promotions. The terms of entry must be made clear to entrants.

Prize draw entries – 'yes' and 'no' options

Generally speaking it is permissible to run a prize draw without a 'no' option if the entrant is asked only to send for a free catalogue. If the offer is made good on the acceptance of a free trial, it must be clear that entries will be accepted from readers refusing to take up the offer.

The most popular prizes are cash. But a prize draw can be run with a relatively small prize, or by offering products as prizes.

Prize draws boost initial response at the expense of poorer conversion to sales. Therefore their use demands a strong *conditional-on-purchase* offer. For example, major home shopping companies may ally a prize draw to a choice of free gifts that can be claimed against the new customer's first purchase.

Users of prize draws or contests are advised to take legal advice and ensure they are set up correctly.

Figure 5.2.2　　**RSPB mailing**

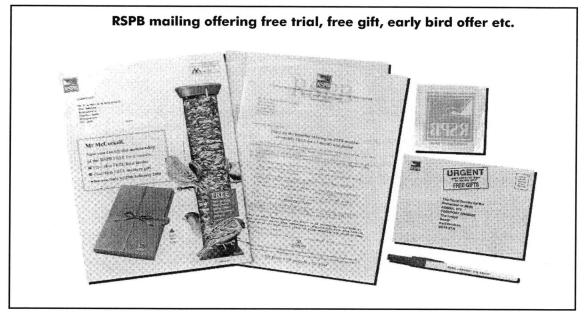

RSPB mailing offering free trial, free gift, early bird offer etc.

Charities are held to account publicly for their expenses, so their donor and member acquisition must be efficient.

When a membership offer is as generous as this one, you can be sure that it must be justified, because hard questions will have been asked.

Here we see a classic membership recruitment offer:

Free 'sample'
Try out membership of the RSPB free for three months.

Free gift
The garden bird feeder is free to keep 'in any case' – ie whether the member cancels during the three month trial or not.

'Early bird'
What could be more appropriate? An 'early bird' gift from the Royal Society for the Protection of Birds. The mystery gift is a useful device for shifting stocks of incentives that were unsuccessful in testing. (This is not to assert that the RSPB were using an unsuccessful gift in this mailing.)

Notice how much more of an imperative it seems to 'reply by 29 February 2000' than to reply 'within 15 days'.

Notice also how personalisation is used to draw attention to the offers.

Plus – a free pen enclosed
Clearly visible through the transparent wrapper enclosing this mailing are a disposable ballpoint pen to sign your acceptance and a small windscreen sticker to signify your support for the RSPB.

The idea of enclosing a no-obligation gift is very old but it was probably pioneered in postal surveys. Researchers found that, if offering a pen generated 30% response, they could expect about 40% when they enclosed the pen, thus putting the recipient under a small obligation. Fundraisers have exploited enclosed gifts mercilessly in recent years but, at the time of writing, the idea still appears to work.

Targeting – effectiveness and efficiency

Acquisition media: if it works, use it

Almost every medium in the media repository can be used for new customer acquisition, with varying degrees of effectiveness. Bought at the right price, the most surprising media can be made to work.

There is no intrinsic merit in accurate targeting. A TV ad or an ad in a national newspaper that pulls one response from every 5,000 people with an opportunity to see the message, may allow us to acquire customers more cheaply than a mailing that pulls one response from every 50 people who receive it. That is because the cost of newspaper space and TV air time is much cheaper (per thousand audience) and it is negotiable, at least up to a point.

Online, our most cleverly targeted banner ads might be twice as **effective** as our ads served on affiliate sites. That is to say, they may pull in twice as many customers per thousand people who see them. But we may pay our affiliates only on results. If our banner advertising costs twice as much per new customer recruited, it will only be half as **efficient** as our affiliate network.

	Response rate	Cost per response
A is more effective	5%	£10
B is more efficient	1%	£5

Unless the quality of customers proves to be very different when we compare one source with another, what matters most is the **cost per customer**.

The best media bargains are often found in unfashionable media; the media that non-direct response advertisers ignore. It is harder to sell space in unfashionable media, so they represent a buyer's market. Similarly, it is easier to make DRTV (direct response TV) work on satellite channels than terrestrial channels. On terrestrial channels, it is easier to make DRTV work in unfashionable daytime slots.

Acquisition media: some rules of thumb

The most effective media are also:

- ✔ The most expensive (per thousand audience)
- ✔ The most intrusive and personal
- ✔ The least popular
- ✔ The most selective
- ✔ The so-called below-the-line media

The biggest volume media are also:

- ✔ The least expensive (per thousand audience)
- ✔ The least intrusive; the most public
- ✔ The most popular
- ✔ The least selective
- ✔ The so-called above-the-line media

Selecting the right audience

Experienced direct marketers use what is known about their existing customers to attract new customers. One of the benefits of a customer database which tracks individuals by their personal details, transactions and promotional history, is its value in forming acquisition strategies, especially in respect of targeting.

Knowledge of current customers can be used to aid media decisions. While many media can be made to work at the right price, they may not all be available at a price that is affordable. Some media, such as door-to-door distribution and direct mail, are more or less non-negotiable. Distribution and postage costs are constants. Thus targeting decisions become critically important.

The technique used for identifying the characteristics that differentiate all customers (or best customers) from the population at large is known as profiling. Key **profiling** tools include:

- ✔ Socio-economics

- ✔ Geodemographics

- ✔ Lifestyle, psychographics

- ✔ Source analysis (acquisition media usage)

- ✔ Offer analysis (acquisition offer usage)

The 'identikit' profiles of known customers, built up from the above, are compared with the profiles of media readerships, lists and geographic areas (postcodes) etc. in search of a close match. The closer the match the more likely it is that the matching suspects will behave like our established customers. In this way, we can pick our target audience with some precision.

The last two items shown in the profiling tool kit above are used when attempting to match suspects with the *best* customers. A disproportionate number of the best customers may have been acquired through particular media or particular offers.

A risk involved in profiling is that the profile of current customers may have been distorted by biases in the targeting of previous acquisition activity. In direct mail acquisition, responders are often profiled against the entire mailing base (which naturally is composed mostly of non-responders) and this gives a very precise picture of which characteristics are associated with response.

Targeting by customers – Member-Get-Member

Customer referrals are an interesting extension of the profiling principle. Suspects identified and recommended by customers (eg friends, neighbours, relatives and colleagues) by means of a 'Member-Get-Member' scheme (MGM) usually share many similarities with the people who put forward their names. Hence referrals are a vital part of any successful direct marketer's repertoire.

A more informal (and potentially effective) version of the MGM is **viral marketing**.

The Internet amplifies the power and accelerates the speed of feedback from customers to potential users. Feedback sources include:

Viral marketing outlets

✔ E-mail to friends, business associates, even lists

✔ Usenet groups

✔ Online forums

✔ Industry portal discussion areas

Bad news travels even faster than good news and so-called viral marketing can be a two-edged sword.

Targeting: more of the same

One of the most important pieces of advice that can be given to new direct marketers is to remember the principle of profiling: what you are generally looking for is not new and different types of customer, but more of the same.

Exceptions to the 'more-of-the-same' rule

An important exception to the more-of-the-same rule is when introducing a product or service which may attract a different type of user. For example, if a manufacturer of soil-based fertilisers introduces a liquid version, will buyers of the new product be people who swear by his soil-based products – or will they be a different sort of gardener?

Another exception is when the pool of matching suspects dries up. The best media and best lists get tired with overuse and there is no choice but to widen the target market. Now it may be necessary to identify and target secondary characteristics that could discriminate between good customers and others. This may even involve modifying the augmented product (the complete product package) and changing the offer. When more than one change is proposed, each variation must be tested separately.

Targeting for start-ups. What if there are no customers to profile?

Even when the enterprise is new, we can still use the techniques of profiling to match the anticipated profile of our likely customers (drawn up from research and observation etc.) with the known profiles of media readerships, geographic areas and so on.

Targeting – let's be realistic

Targeting is vital to modern direct marketing, and so much a factor in its success that the term is often overused. In practice, there is targeting and targeting – ranging from very specific (eg direct mail to known individuals), to very loose (eg newspaper advertising directed at a broad readership which shows only a slight bias towards the customer profile), to almost non-existent (eg TV bought cheaply to reach as wide an audience as possible).

It is a common error to assume that all targeting is precise – direct marketing has not yet reached that Utopian goal. In fact, it pays not to assume too much personal knowledge of a prospect or even a customer, because getting it wrong can cause offence.

Don't assume too much

A supplier was forced to sue its client for non-payment covering the costs of a direct mail campaign. The client counter-claimed on the grounds that the list it had been supplied was not wholly made up of retired people as it had hoped, being based solely on geodemographic codes. The court, having read submissions by advertising experts, decreed that it was unreasonable to expect any form of targeting to be 100% accurate.

Never assume, therefore, that because a list comprises a higher than average percentage of people of one or other characteristic, that all its members will fit that description. Don't make the mistake, as another marketer did, of opening your letter 'Dear Retired Person' simply because it was being targeted to a geodemographic area with a high retired population. 60 percent of recipients were not retired.

In fact, the 'loose' targeting of newspapers, television, radio and the Internet can serve acquisition programmes very well, for three reasons:

1.   We may not always know exactly who is attracted to our product, or why. In the early stages of a product's life, we may be relying on new users to tell us things we will employ later, in more closely targeted media.

2.   Our best prospects may not yet appear on a close targeted list, for example if they have just taken up a pastime, or started a business, or entered a new life stage.

3.   Our loosely targeted advertising reaches many people cheaply – including those who are interested in our proposition but not yet ready to respond.

These advantages cannot easily be quantified. Therefore, we rely on the hard evidence of response. If loosely targeted media help us to acquire customers at an acceptable cost, then we consider them to be **efficient** and we continue to use them.

Formats – sizes, colours, shapes, animation, lengths

Should our banner ad be animated? Should our radio commercial be 60 seconds or 40 seconds? Should our page ad be full-colour or black and white?

We use the word 'format' to cover everything from the size or length of an advertisement to the number of pieces in a mailing pack. It includes the use of **involvement devices** such as stamps, peel-off stickers and scratch cards.

Often, the format of an ad or mailing will outweigh the copy and surface design in its importance. Naturally, however, the format and creative treatment are almost inextricably linked. In both cases the winning formula will have to be discovered through experimentation.

We can offer only one general rule about formats. This is it:

> Fairly short and simple messages work to generate two-stage enquiries and longer, more detailed messages are required to complete a one-stage sale. Since direct response advertising does not thrive on overindulgent space sizes and use of colour etc. for impact, **two-stage formats are usually small**, short or simple and **one-stage formats tend to be larger**, longer or more complex.

Why are smaller ads more efficient?

We filter out what doesn't interest us more or less unconsciously. Ads that are relevant to an immediate interest or need will probably be noticed, however small they may be. Ads that are not relevant will probably not be noticed or recalled, however large they may be.

> Unless we buy a big (or long) ad for much less per column centimetre or per second, it is not usually going to be as efficient as a smaller ad. That is, unless we need the extra size or length to tell our story. We are more likely to need the size or length when we have a lot of convincing to do – that is, when we are selling one-stage.

We will return to the influence of format on results in section 3.

Creative – copy and design

The next element in the success of customer acquisition is the creative treatment given to the ads, mailings and so on, used to attract and convert suspects into customers. While this element is widely regarded by experts as less important than the targeting or even the promotional offer, it still plays a crucial role. It is the creative execution that will attract the suspect's attention and communicate the benefits of the product and the excitement of the incentives and offers.

To become a customer, the suspect must buy the product. The product is not just an entity but is augmented by features that add value. The creative proposition turns the features into benefits – and benefits turn suspects into customers.

The secret of persuading readers to buy can be summed up in one simple equation:

$$\frac{\text{Benefits}}{\text{Price}} = \text{Value}$$

What readers unconsciously do is divide benefits by price. The result is the value they place on the product you are selling ... If ... the benefits outweigh the price you have probably made a sale. It's as simple as that.

The Business of Persuasion, Stuart McKibbin

The creative treatment should identify the key benefits of the product and the offer and express them in a way that will attract, excite and convince the suspect. In a one-stage advertisement, copy will usually be long. The ad has to take the customer from knowing little and being wary about the product, through the benefits, phoning overcoming objections, all the way to phoning, posting, faxing or e-mailing the order.

The creative process is highly disciplined and starts from a clearly defined proposition. The most important single benefit will be included in the proposition.

A proposition is a short statement that gives a clear reason, backed up by some brief arguments, why the target audience will respond.

It is therefore a 'why' statement. 'Why' should someone respond?

John Watson, Successful Creativity in Direct Marketing

John Watson, a founding partner and long time chairman of WWAV Rapp Collins, says there are three things required before writing the proposition:

1.   **Past response data** – what has worked before, what has not

2.   **Competitive ads –** what appears to be working for them

3.   **What your own marketing requirements demand**

The most important of these three things is the first one. Nothing teaches like results.

The proposition is *not* copy. But it may well be adapted to make a headline and provide the bedrock for the selling argument.

> **One-stage** ads and mailings are usually structured to the well-tried **AIDCA** formula. AIDCA stands for **A**ttention, **I**nterest, **D**esire, **C**onviction, **A**ction. **Two-stage** ads need to devote less effort to supplying Conviction and that is why they can often work with short copy. Detailed description and evidence are highly reassuring and are, therefore, critical components of one-stage creative work. In two-stage response, the burden of supplying Conviction may be left until the second stage.

Earlier we quoted from Graeme McCorkell:

> *People respond to advertisements only when the immediate gain in responding exceeds the risk or cost of responding by an acceptable margin ... and it appears easy to respond.*

Since there is a low perceived risk in responding to most two-stage ads, less Conviction is needed. However, it must still appear 'easy to respond'.

Figure 5.2.3   **One-stage advertisement**

Figure 5.2.4   **Two-stage advertisement**

The subject of creativity (including AIDCA) is covered fully in Section 7 but a few words about response mechanisms are appropriate here:

" ... and it appears easy to respond"

Although the majority of *print media* response may come in by **phone**, including a well-designed **coupon** with lots of room for information will usually boost response. It emphasises that the advertisement is soliciting response (an attraction to readers) and allows those readers who prefer not to phone to respond. Furthermore, the information we request from the enquirer in the coupon alerts the phone enquirer to the questions he or she will be asked.

Our postal coupon may also double up as a **fax-back form** if we are dealing with people who are likely to have home faxes or are likely to respond from their office. On the whole, the soft option of visiting the website should receive second featuring only. That is because the conversion rate from website visitors will usually be lower. There are exceptions, however.

For example, potential computer customers or travel customers often *expect* to order from a website.

If experience shows that postal response proves more attractive than phone response (or vice versa) we will adjust the relative prominence of the alternative reply devices so that the recommended method is clear.

Broadcast media response devices need even greater prominence. A phone response mechanism should occupy 15 seconds of air time if possible, although 10 seconds can work. Longer commercials should alert the viewer or listener (at the beginning of the ad) that a direct response can be made.

Interactive TV viewers and *web browsers* need to be clearly alerted as to what to expect when clicking through to a website. This will affect the quality of visitors (as measured by conversion rate) and their experience of the site when they arrive.

Timing – seasons, days, time-of-day

Timing is closely linked to targeting. A message is not well targeted unless it is also timely. Unfortunately, it is often impossible to get the timing right so we may need to employ a device to induce the order when *we* want it.

The three aspects of timing

The product can be right, the targeting can be right and the offer can be right, yet an acquisition initiative may fail. The most likely reason is not poor creative treatment, although that might well be the explanation, but that the timing is completely wrong.

There are three aspects of timing: **inertial, individual** and **external.**

1. Inertial: close-dated offers and prize draw bonus prizes for prompt entry are examples of how crucial it is to inject urgency into offers so that the **threat of withdrawal** can be used to overcome inertia. The threat of withdrawal of a good offer is almost as powerful an incentive to act as the offer itself. "While stocks last" and "First come, first served" must be two of the oldest phrases in copywriting. What the direct marketer is doing is supplying a reason to accept his timing.

Close-dated offers always work better than "reply within seven days" but are more rarely used for practical reasons, such as uncertainty of mailing touchdown dates and the need to replace effective offers after close-dates.

2. Individual: getting the timing right for an individual is an aspect of targeting. At first it may seem that this could only be achieved with communications to current customers. How else could we know enough about the recipients of our messages?

Yet there are opportunities even in customer acquisition. For example, we know when prospects first enquired about our product and we know when ex-customers last bought something. Such information can be used to reopen dialogue in a personal and pertinent manner.

A less obvious example is annually renewable insurance. Most people obtain more than one quote before settling for one insurer. The other insurers now know the renewal date of the policy and they will undertake resolicitation mailings next year. Any list that can be mailed at the right time is worth a lot more than any other list.

Likewise, any defecting policyholder's renewal date will be known.

Smart life assurance salespeople are notorious for scanning the trade press for news of promotions and new appointments. However, the same targeting is used on a more industrial scale by business-to-business marketers of many kinds.

New movers are also a much sought after market segment and there are various ways of targeting them.

Most excitingly, the advent of IT-driven call centres and online marketing has opened up the possibility of reacting in real time to customer orders and preferences, either as they fill their shopping baskets, to provoke add-on purchases, or through providing personalised information as they revisit the site.

3. External: timing is, of course, critical for many products and services — winter holidays provide an example. But some holidaymakers will book a year ahead, while others leave it to a week before departure. In matters of timing, as in most other areas, the customer is becoming ever more individual.

When products are clearly non-seasonal, the direct marketing planner can play the field, buying at times which are the best value and avoiding times of poorest response.

Figure 5.2.5 chart sets out a rough guide to the best and worst value periods for media buying and response when there are no other seasonal factors present. January generally offers sensational TV value and August is good value because air time is generally relatively cheap. (Some media, direct mail for example, are unaffected by fluctuating media rates and are best executed during the good response periods shown.)

Figure 5.2.5 **The best and worst media months**

High response	**Best value**
January – March	Early January
Mid August – October	August
June – July	April – May
Late November – December	November – December
Lower response	**Worst value**

Short seasons: for some products demand is seasonal. Tutorial products, for example, peak late August and early January. Such brief sales periods present the direct marketer with a dilemma: advertise too frequently and risk diminishing returns; advertise infrequently and risk the season ending before the sales target has been met.

Day-of-week: for some reason, people respond more readily to direct response advertising early in the week. This applies directly to press media planning and, to some extent, direct mail, but cannot easily be applied to broadcast media because of the need for repetition.

Time-of-day: audiences are more responsive at off-peak times and most TV advertisers find some dayparts more productive than others. Afternoon slots tend to work well on TV and radio but much depends on the desired audience profile. 'Boring' TV programmes are said to attract best responses.

E-mailed menus

Unlike postal service mail, e-mail can use time-of-day targeting when addressed to people at work. For example, local office workers have been targeted by a fast food restaurant with a new menu in the hour before lunch.

Summary – the elements of success

✔ **Product – the whole package** – a regular subscription I can cancel at any time, at a discount price for 12 months with free delivery to my door

✔ **Promotional offers** – the reason (or reasons) to respond or buy now

✔ **Targeting – effectiveness and efficiency** – reducing acquisition costs through higher response (effectiveness) or lower media costs (efficiency)

✔ **Formats – sizes, colours, shapes, animation, lengths –** using the space or time it takes to deliver the message persuasively – not more

✔ **Creative – copy and design** – turning product features into benefits, leading with the key reason to respond (the proposition) and making it easy to respond. Using AIDCA for one-stage response (invariably), not necessarily for two-stage response

✔ **Timing – seasons, days, time-of-day** – inertial, individual and external

Chapter 5.3

Offline and online acquisition media

This chapter includes:

- ❏ **The media marketspace**
- ❏ **Media roles and selection**
- ❏ **How response data helps**
- ❏ **Acquisition media – an overview**
- ❏ **Which media pull the most response?**
- ❏ **How costs compare – cost per thousand measures**
- ❏ **Media testing costs and lead times**
- ❏ **Acquisition media summary**

About this chapter

 n this chapter we consider the four factors that *invariably* come into play when making media selections. They include **cost**, **targeting**, **message** and **ease of response**.

Is the medium the right vehicle to carry the message? Most media are suitable for generating simple enquiries but some media do not lend themselves to one-stage direct response advertising. It is also a fact that some media facilitate response better than others. Judgement on the suitability of the medium must be exercised before considerations of comparative costs and targeting efficiency become decisive.

Unlike other media planners, the direct marketing planner selects media on the basis of **past results** whenever possible. New media are **tested** before they can claim a large share of the budget. However, not all media are equally cheap to test and some produce results much more rapidly than others. All these considerations affect planning and we need to take them into account.

Tables in this chapter allow quick comparisons to be made between different types of media across various dimensions, including cost per '000 audience and the lead time required to get a test up and running.

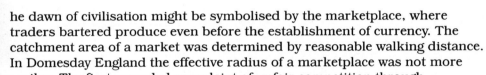

Graeme McCorkell consultant and writer

Graeme's biography appears at the beginning of this section

Chapter 5.3

Offline and online acquisition media

The media marketspace

The dawn of civilisation might be symbolised by the marketplace, where traders bartered produce even before the establishment of currency. The catchment area of a market was determined by reasonable walking distance. In Domesday England the effective radius of a marketplace was not more than five miles. The first recorded complaint of unfair competition through establishing a new market too close to an existing one appears in the Domesday record for Suffolk (Little Domesday, 1085).

The purpose of interactive and direct marketing is to facilitate exchange without the need for a fixed location marketplace. As the Internet gained ground as a marketplace, the term **'marketspace'** was coined to describe a virtual marketplace in which no direct contact occurs between buyers and sellers. However, all direct marketing takes place in a marketspace, whether online or offline media are used.

The enabling facility for exchange (the marketspace) is provided by the media that are used by marketers to promote their wares and by buyers to source potential purchases.

The world wide web as marketspace

Unlike printed catalogues or ads in national newspapers, a website enables diligent search engine and directory users from all over the world to find it. In fact, it is the low cost of the electronic market stall–combined with the power of the web as a research tool–that allows bargain-hunting customers to take over the marketing function of connecting sellers to buyers. **Exchanges** and **reverse auctions** are examples of buyers combining to assume this function.

Initially, there is an exchange of information. When direct marketing is used **in support** of other channels of distribution, the direct marketing exchange may consist solely of swapped information. To obtain further product information by requesting a catalogue or interrogating a website, you may be required to identify yourself and even volunteer additional personal or corporate information.

When direct marketing is used **on a standalone basis**, the transaction may take place on the phone, through a website, by mail, by e-mail or fax, or through any one of a number of digital media, from iTV to kiosks.

The benefits of the direct marketspace

What is the primary economic benefit of direct marketing channels? Is it the saving of customers' time? Is it the reduction in vendors' transaction costs? Is it freedom from the constraints of opening hours and catchment areas? Is it increased competition through improved access to product information? All of these are significant benefits brought by direct and interactive marketing.

Media roles and selection

Woody Allen has made some great films. But you would not cast him to play Hercules even if he were willing to accept the part. It is equally self-evident that not all media lend themselves to performing the same communications roles. However cheaply you might be able to buy advertising space on bus backs, you would not use bus back panels to generate direct orders for laptop computers – or direct orders for anything else.

Why not?

4 key selection factors

In media selection decisions for direct marketing, four factors always come into play:

- **Cost**
  What is the cost of advertising to reach each person who sees or hears it? How will this impact on our cost per response and cost per sale?

- **Targeting**
  How many in the audience will find our offer irrelevant? How many cannot afford the products we want to sell? How will such 'audience wastage' affect our response, conversion and customer quality?

- **Message**
  Can we convey our message effectively in the media we are considering? Will there be enough time or enough space? How will these factors affect the quantity and quality of response?

- **Ease of response**
  Will it be easy to respond or order from our advertisement? Or will would-be responders need to run behind the bus as they take down our phone number?

These are not the only factors that influence planning decisions. Others include **timing**, **capital outlay**, **ambience** and **market coverage**. However, these four factors are invariably present – at least until actual results are available to prove or disprove the value of each medium.

Clearly, judgement plays a part in these selection decisions. Not everything in direct marketing can be easily quantified before the results are in. A factor in our judgement is the nature of the role we are asking a medium to play. Is it just to create awareness? Is it to generate enquiries? Or is it to complete sales? For the purposes of this session, we will concentrate on direct response roles.

What types of response-generating messages might we have to consider?

Types of outbound messages

In the previous section we introduced eight types of response, grouped under one-stage and two-stage. These types of response are generated by advertising that is designed for that purpose–eight types of advertising, in fact–although a few ads invite more than one type of response.

One-stage

1.   *Direct sale offers*: eg enter your credit card number and we will send the goods.

2.   *Free trial orders*: eg order on 15-days free trial – invoice enclosed with goods.

3.   *Enrolment and subscription offers*: eg subscribe to magazine, join roadside rescue service, join book or music club.

4.   *Invitations to apply*: eg apply for credit card, loan or home shopping account.

How one-stage affects media selection

One-stage advertising needs to answer more questions and deal with more potential sales objections than two-stage advertising. This affects the choice of medium. For example, the air time cost of TV is based on 30 seconds as the standard unit. All longer spots are pro rata. So a 120-second commercial is four times as expensive as a 30-second commercial. Furthermore, responders may need to see the ad more than once to recall the essential details and how to respond. On the other hand, the postage cost of a direct mailing will remain the same whether the message is long or short. The recipient can refer back to any points of detail in the mailing – and show it to his or her partner – before responding.

Two-stage

1. *Information offers*: eg request our free brochure or catalogue.

2. *Volunteered requests*: eg tell us about your present car and when you intend to trade it in and we'll give you full details of our latest models.

3. *Enquiry generation*: eg ask for a free insurance quote.

4. *Lead generation*: eg ask us to quote for your office refurbishment.

Types 1 and 3 are most often intended to **maximise responses** while 2 and 4 are frequently intended to **qualify responders**. For example, the pick of responders to 2 might receive a video and invitation to take a test drive while others might just receive a brochure and a list of dealers. NB Lifestyle survey questionnaires are an exceptional, but very important, vehicle for type 2.

The message dictates the medium

A simple information request may be generated by a simple advertisement. But a qualified lead or lifestyle survey response may demand a multi-page loose insert, a direct mail package or an e-mail with an attached file.

Shopper's buying stages and media usage

So far we have looked at media suitability from the advertiser's viewpoint. But what of the potential customer?

The potential customer's choice of medium may reflect his or her interest level in the product that we are offering. Clearly a reader of a gardening magazine is more likely to be interested in gardening products than a reader of a current affairs magazine.

Media usage can also be affected by purchase stage as we will see in a moment. Some purchase decisions are long drawn out. For example, **Figure 5.3.1** shows a research-based view of car purchase decision stages:

Figure 5.3.1 **Purchase decision stages**

Advertising to create **awareness** of the brand will also aim to assist **image-matching**, a dreaming process in which we match the brand image to our desired self-image. This process works even in B2B decision-making. For example, advertising agencies and consultancy firms are often short listed on the basis of image-match. Advertising to assist image-matching will rarely be tightly targeted or include more than a token response device, such as a reference to a website address.

Fact-matching is a stage in the short listing process when practical considerations come into play. Now, usually within six months of purchase, the potential car buyer has become a list builder, short listing the potentially suitable buys. List building may actually be an elimination process in markets where the candidate brands are already known to the potential buyer (as is usual in the case of cars).

Dealer-matching occurs when the retailer and the manufacturer are different companies. The dealer has a separate identity and presents a different image and a different set of considerations. The dealer may foster the sale or put the potential customer off. The more consistent the dealer presentation is with the brand image of the car, the more likely the dealer is to make the sale. However, if successful, the dealer will persuade the customer to take a **test drive** and, if this goes well and the terms are right, the **purchase** is made.

The number of arrows in **Figure 5.3.1** reduces as potential buyers descend towards purchase. This is because the number of people within later purchase stages is much smaller than the number at early stages.

Advertising to assist image-matching will not be tightly targeted and media will be selected for their ability to evoke imagery that will sell the concept of the car. **TV** and weekend **magazines** come to mind. Advertising at this stage will offer few facts. Facts come later.

When the potential buyer reaches fact-matching stage, he will be more likely to turn to **specialist media**, such as *What Car*, and possibly product review websites such as *Ciao*. Increasingly, the dealer-matching stage is becoming a process conducted on

the Internet as the potential buyer seeks out suppliers who will supply at the right price.

A role in the fact-match stage and beyond will be played by **mailed brochures** and manufacturer **websites.** These offer the opportunity to present facts or answer questions in a style that matches the desirable image that first attracted the would-be buyer. That is why car manufacturers use direct marketing – to identify prospects, find out when they plan to buy and enter into a dialogue.

Generally speaking, direct marketing communications work best (even in newspapers or on TV) when they target people who are close to a purchase decision. Having said that, direct marketing can also accelerate the buyer towards a purchase from a point much earlier in the cycle.

Image-matching and fact-matching may occur more or less simultaneously in a low interest product field where we have little prior brand awareness.

Even awareness and purchase may occur almost simultaneously. This is truncated decision-making and often occurs when **trial purchase** involves little or no perceived risk. Trial purchase may not be on offer in every case and, when it is not, the equivalent will be a test drive, a demonstration or a presentation.

Truncated decision-making

There are many examples of truncated decision-making in fast moving consumer goods (FMCG), as our own shopping experience tells us. For example, the decision to purchase a new salad dressing may be made on the basis of a glance at the label.

Table 5.3.1 also shows examples drawn from other product categories:

Table 5.3.1 **Examples of truncated decision-making**

Product	Approximate cost	Medium/channel
Confectionery count line	40p	Retail display unit
Douro Valley river cruise	£1,200	One-stage magazine advertisement
Facsimile of Domesday Book	£6,750	One-stage direct mail
Subscription to new magazine	£48	One-stage insert

NB For high cost purchases, ads or mailings must move prospects from awareness or image-match to trial or purchase in one communication.

Truncated decision making occurs frequently in direct marketing. Expensive goods are often purchased on the basis of a single direct marketing communication.

Looking at the examples above, we can see that a new confectionery count line (a count line is confectionery sold as a unit rather than by weight, **Snickers** being an example) might appeal *because* of its novelty and 40 pence is not much to put at risk.

On the other hand, customers take considerable risks in buying holidays (risking precious leisure time as well as money) or expensive collectibles.

Are the buyers of **Douro Valley** cruises or facsimiles of **Domesday** likely to be natural gamblers? If not, how does the direct marketer secure trust? How would the direct marketer add trust-inspiring factors? Testimonials, third party endorsements, very detailed explanatory copy and guarantees come to mind. Clearly, media that can be studied at leisure are at an advantage over media where the message is transient.

The suggested media are chosen as being suitable for each of the products. They are not the only possibilities, of course. A holiday may be sold two-stage through a requested brochure. A magazine may be sold from the publisher's website and may be available online to subscribers. Domesday facsimiles have been sold successfully through press advertising – but only on a two-stage basis.

Scratch, sniff and order

A novel way of taking consumers through the whole process of image matching, fact matching, trial and purchase was devised in the US by **Giorgio** fragrances. They used loose leaflets in magazines carrying scent-strips to allow readers to scratch and sniff the perfume before ordering.

Giorgio used this method because they were unable to gain sufficient retail distribution. Within a short period, stores were besieged by consumers wanting to buy Giorgio fragrances even though they were then available only by mail order. Giorgio became the brand leader in the premium quality sector and the company was eventually sold for $187 million, thanks largely to this clever innovation.

How response data helps

Obviously, all marketers seek to distribute marketing expenditure so as to optimise their return on investment. But without the ability to monitor each customer interaction, the process is pretty crude.

Without response data – conventional media planning

Without response data, the indirect marketer depends on profiling to achieve a reasonable match between a media audience and product category or brand users.

To do this, a combination of media research and product category research data is available. For example, Target Group Index (TGI) data from the annual British Market Research Bureau survey might be used to discover the profile of product users and to see how efficiently the main media penetrate the assumed target market.

The target market might be described as, say, B/C1 women, aged 25 to 44, living in the South East. Alternatively, geodemographic profiling might be preferred. Or the target group might be the 3.5 million SMEs (Small and Medium Sized Enterprises). That may be as close as one can get when planning cannot call on any response data.

Without response data the marketer cannot discover how effective each medium or each advertisement is in helping to reach the sales target.

With response data – direct marketing

On the other hand, if we have response data, we are altogether better informed. We can measure the relative cost-effectiveness of allocating our marketing budget in alternative ways. At a macro level we will look at dividing our budget between new business prospecting and repeat business.

On a micro level we could be measuring the relative profitability of spending £5,000 on two small advertisements as opposed to one larger one.

Remembering Pareto, we will see from our customer data which 20% of the customers account for 80% or more of sales or profit. We can profile these customers. This may enable us to cut our 3.5 million SME target to the 500,000 potentially worthwhile suspects, although it won't necessarily guarantee we can reach them all without any waste coverage.

Media planning: a comparison

It follows that since general and direct marketers are armed with different data, and frequently have different objectives, their methods are also likely to be different. It is the media planner in each case who must allocate expenditure for customer acquisition.

Traditional media planning

The general aim of the media planner, without response data, is to cover the whole of the target market (eg B/C1 women aged 25 to 44, South East) whilst achieving optimum frequency. In practice, 100% coverage is not realistic, but 80% might well be. 'Optimum' frequency is a best guess.

The planner may attempt some form of refinement, for example based upon the editorial content of a magazine, but will usually be forced to purchase space in large circulation national or regional media, in order to secure best value for money.

Direct marketing media planning

Here the planner does not start with any idea of covering 100% (or 80%) of the target market. Neither does the planner have any theoretical notion of optimum frequency. The starting point is a sales target, a customer acquisition target or a combination of such 'achievement' targets. The direct marketing plan will include a forecast, medium-by-medium, that adds up to the target.

The planner attaches different values to sectors within the target market, giving priority to expenditures predicted to deliver the best ROI. If responsible for an overall sales target, the planner may decide to spend a large part of the budget on securing repeat purchases from previous buyers through direct mail, e-mail and telemarketing.

Suspects (ie people not yet identified as prospects), however, will only be reachable through more public media.

3 fundamental differences in direct response planning

- Whenever possible direct response planning is based on extrapolation from past results.

- No attempt is made to achieve optimum coverage or frequency – the aim is to maximise return on acquisition investment.

- Each press insertion, TV transmission or banner is an event in its own right, not merely part of a campaign, and is required to justify its cost by direct results.

Acquisition media – an overview

Media can be classified by form and function. A convenient classification for the direct marketer appears in **Table 5.3.2**:

Table 5.3.2   **Acquisition media**

Broadscale	National newspapers – space and inserts Popular magazines – space and inserts TV and radio – air time and teletext Door-to-door
Selective	Special interest magazines – space and inserts Business press – vertical – space and inserts Business press – horizontal – space and inserts
Addressable	Direct mail E-mail / SMS text messaging Phone
Online	Paid ads Affiliates Others

The list of media in **Table 5.3.2** is not comprehensive (for example, it excludes regional press and outdoor advertising), but it includes all the media which attract heavy direct marketing expenditure. Websites are not listed because they would be categorised as fulfilment media.

Broadscale media

Most media can be used for customer recruitment, although the costs and volumes of response generated will vary enormously.

Press advertising (newspapers and magazines) can be used to sell direct (off the page) or by generating leads (enquiries) for follow-up and conversion. This broad media group includes business and professional journals (these are categorised as selective media in **Table 5.3.2**) and also includes directories, such as **Yellow Pages**.

Direct response space advertising in **newspapers** is mostly in national titles and most often in black and white. Rates are quoted for standard sizes as well as per column centimetre and vary by page and position.

Although they are categorised as broadscale media, the direct response advertising that appears in national newspapers is often addressed to niche markets within the readership. This is particularly true of upscale nationals (the broadsheets as opposed to the tabloids). Why is this?

✔ National newspaper advertising is comparatively inexpensive. Waste coverage is therefore more affordable.

✔ People very interested in a topic will see even a small ad that features their interest.

✔ Newspapers are organised into separate marketspaces, making it easy to find ads of special interest – eg holiday features, gardening, motoring and personal finance.

Leafing through any broadsheet, you will find examples of niche market advertising, including B2B advertising. It is often cheaper to reach a specific business readership through national newspapers than through business magazines.

The markets for general interest and women's interest **magazines** has been in decline for many years and a high proportion of direct response advertising is achieved by the free magazines, such as *You* and *The Sunday Times Magazine*, that are distributed with newspapers.

Magazines are extremely important vehicles for carrying **inserts.** Unlike space ads, inserts are used almost exclusively for direct response, again on a one-stage or two-stage basis. They are printed separately from the medium in which they are carried (**host medium**). They may be loose, bound-in or tipped on (spot gummed) to a space advertisement. By far the majority of inserts are loose and may appear in a whole variety of formats from single sheet to roll-fold multi-page leaflets and even small stapled catalogues.

Door-to-door leaflet distribution is an alternative to inserts that is particularly appropriate, if targeting by neighbourhood type or region makes more sense than targeting by the magazine readership profile. Door-to-door also offers the advantage of eliminating duplication (providing only one copy of the leaflet is dropped through each letterbox). Duplication inevitably occurs in inserting and space advertising because readerships overlap. Distribution is often with local freesheets but may be solus or shared with other leaflets. Door-to-door is an important medium for car and household insurance, postcode geography being a factor in determining risk and premium levels.

Radio may be used nationally, regionally or locally and has attracted an increasing, though small, share of DR advertising. Direct response television (**DRTV**) is far more important, specially in targeting the non-working population through daytime satellite and cable TV. Direct marketing brands such as **Admiral** car insurance and **Claims Direct** have been built on daytime TV. The introduction of paperless direct debits has also allowed DRTV to take a share of the charity donor acquisition market. Because audience ratings are so low in non-terrestrial TV channels during the day, audience research is of little help to the advertiser. It is a question of learning what works by trial and error.

Interactive television (**iTV**) will become an enormously important direct response medium as digital television supplants analogue TV. As in the case of **mobile phone** Internet links, iTV requires to be linked to a purpose-designed website, as the TV screen resolution is less good than a PC monitor and the distance between the viewer and the screen is greater.

Teletext is used for direct response, especially in the travel market to generate enquiries for low cost flights and holidays.

Selective media

Thousands of **special interest magazine** titles offer the planner a vast array of niche markets. **Inserts** often provide the most cost-effective way of using these titles although they are not accepted by all publishers. Inserts can work well in special interest magazines, including professional journals, even when the subject is not obviously relevant to the editorial appeal of the magazine.

Third-party endorsed inserts

If a **third-party** (affinity group) endorsement can be negotiated, the response will be enhanced considerably. The advertiser makes a close-dated concessionary offer to the readership of the publication, usually a discount, in exchange for the endorsement. Such offers can work particularly well when the circulation of the magazine is confined to members of a *bona fide* affinity group, eg members of a club, a union or professional institute.

Business magazines and journals are usually categorised as **horizontal** or **vertical** media. Horizontal titles are read by people working in more than one industry. They cover general management topics, eg *The Director*, or specific functions, eg *Marketing.* Vertical titles cover the interests of a variety of job functions within a single industry. Again, **inserts** often provide the most cost-effective vehicle for direct response.

Readership survey data is not available for small circulation titles but the amount at risk is smaller than for broadscale media. Once the first ad or insert has appeared, the evidence of response outweighs research data in any case.

Addressable media

Direct mail has long been the most important customer communication vehicle but, through rented lists, is also a very important acquisition medium in both B2C and B2B markets. Like inserts, direct mail is an excellent medium for testing alternative offers and creative treatments on a split-run basis. Unlike inserts, different formats can be tested as well (inserts used for a split-run must all be the same size, shape and weight). The discrete and discreet nature of direct mail makes it ideal for testing.

✔ Direct mail can be *discrete*: an offer can be restricted to selected recipients.

✔ Direct mail can be *discreet*: those not receiving the offer will not know of it.

✔ Direct mail is potentially *duplication-free*: lists can be deduplicated against each other and against the customer base.

✔ Direct mail is a *personal* medium: letters are a very powerful communication device.

✔ Direct mail is *flexible* and *tactile*: almost anything can be sent by mail.

Direct mail plays a part in acquisition both in generating enquiries or direct orders (**cold mailings**) and in supplying information to prospects generated by other media (**conversion mailings**). Direct mail can also be sent out to members of **affinity groups**, often endorsed by the groups' organisers and making an exclusive offer to members. The same roles that are performed by direct mail can be performed by **e-mail**, a medium that offers most of the advantages of direct mail but with three added advantages:

● E-mailings are much cheaper.

● E-mailings can be prepared, released and delivered faster.

● E-mailings generate instant response.

The downside is that (because e-mail is so cheap) recipients can be swamped by unwanted messages (**spam**). For this reason, e-mail is best used for mailing prospects or others who have clearly given permission. The same applies to **SMS** text-messaging and will soon apply to **3G video promotion**. Because e-mail responders can reply instantly, this sets up an expectation of instant service and it is important to cater for this. Most online/e-mail **newsletters** accept advertising and this is an alternative, acceptable use of cold e-mail. SMS news services also accept ads.

News from the home of spam

Notorious US spammer, Rob Cosgrove, defends his untargeted e-mailing by pointing out that spam is 100% biodegradable. "It never hurt a tree and can be recycled at a keystroke", he says. Cosgrove's company, **Quantum Tech**, uses 50,000 e-mails to generate 70 responses and 30 orders for their remote back-up software (it protects your machines across the Internet). The cost of e-mail is so low, Cosgrove can get away with one order per 1,667 spams, assuming he doesn't suffer from the damage to his company's image that may result. (Not that we are suggesting it is time to flame his website, of course.)

American interactive marketing expert, Jim Sterne, points out that if every one of America's 12 million businesses sent him just one spam a year, that would work out at 1,370 per hour. The International Computer Security Association believes that 80% of computer viruses are spread by e-mail.

The **phone** is also a medium that can be used **cold** or for contacting **prospects**. The phone is one of the most powerful and intrusive of all media.

The intrusive phone

As a brilliant telemarketing pioneer, the late Robert Leiderman pointed out:

No one ever got out of the bath to answer a mailing.

The telemarketer should offer a good reason for making the call.

B2B telemarketing is widely accepted, but its use for cold B2C contact should be tempered with discretion. Successful users include charity fundraisers, both to recruit volunteer collectors and to secure pledges of support. **Fax** communications can also be effective in B2B marketing but should be used only when the communication is likely to be relevant and urgent. 'Junk' faxes are deeply unpopular, especially among SME recipients. As with e-mails, receiving faxes costs money.

Online media

Paid ads include **banners, intersticials** and **supersticials**. They can be enhanced by using rich media. For example, a banner ad can allow the potential loan customer to type in the amount required and provide an instant illustration of the repayment cost. Intersticials and supersticials are 'pop-ups' that are generally less relevant to DR applications than banners.

Banners can be served to people with particular interests, insofar as their previous surfing behaviour indicates this. Of course, if the same PC is shared by more than one user, the selection will not be accurate.

Banners can also be targeted by placing on relevant pages and by buying **keywords** on search engines. When the surfer types in the keywords, eg 'bamboo fly rods', your banner ad appears.

Affiliate networks are the online equivalent of **affinity group** mailings ad inserts. Affiliate programmes work even better because the affiliate website is just a click away from the direct marketer's fulfilment system. The affiliate receives a percentage of the sales value and may also make a non-results-based charge if in a strong enough negotiating position.

Others include registering with search engines, announcing the site in newsgroups and swapping links with other websites, without going as far as forming an affiliate network. Another method is to **sponsor** an entertainment or information site.

Which media pull the most response?

Response rates from alternative media or mailing list segments are important insofar as they measure *effectiveness*. The effectiveness they measure is the number of people who respond, compared with the number of people who have an opportunity to see or hear the message. The relative effectiveness of one medium (say, a national newspaper) compared with another (say, a terrestrial TV channel) will differ between advertisers. For example, if your most effective newspaper is *The Times* you will probably find it hard to get the targeting right on TV. Then again, if your most effective mailing format includes a four-page letter, it isn't very likely that a short radio or TV commercial will work for you.

Having stated these limitations it is still useful to have a rough inter-media comparison in mind. In **Table 5.3.3** we assume that the purpose of each communication is the same – to gain an enquiry about a new product.

Table 5.3.3 **Hierarchy of response rates**

Medium	Size/format	Response rate per 1000*
Daily newspaper	20cms x 2 cols.	0.2
Satellite TV	20 secs.	0.4
Search engine	Banner ad, general rotation	0.5
Weekend magazine	Full colour page	1.0
Weekend magazine	Page with tipped-on card	2.5
Daily newspaper	Loose insert	5.0
Cold mailing	Multi-piece format	25.0
Lapsed customer mailing	Multi-piece format	40.0
Lapsed customer e-mail	File attached	50.0
Lapsed customer mailing + telemarketing follow-up	Multi-piece + outbound	125.0

* Direct response rates are usually expressed as a percentage of *circulation*. The TV figure has been converted from adult viewers to homes (sets switched on) to facilitate comparison. Banner ad response represents real enquiries, not click-throughs.

While the relative differences shown in **Table 5.3.3** will not hold good for any single product, they–where possible being acquired from a wide variety of cases–broadly reflect the relative pulling power of alternative media.

What really matters – the hierarchy of efficiency

> The hierarchy of responses shows that mailing lapsed customers and then phoning them is likely to pull about 675 times as much response (per thousand circulation) as taking a 20 x 2 column ad in a newspaper. It would therefore be 675 times as **effective** if only there were as many lapsed customers as newspaper readers.

But, if it were also to cost 675 times as much per thousand as the newspaper ad, it would be no more **efficient** than the newspaper ad. What will concern you more is the relative **cost per enquiry** produced by the two alternative actions. The relative efficiency of the two actions will be harder to work out in advance because the least effective media are also the cheapest. The performance gap closes once costs enter the equation and the results are never exactly the same for any two products. That is why it is important to test media.

How costs compare – cost per thousand measures

The cost of media space and air time is typically compared on a **cost per thousand circulation** or audience basis. This is often shortened just to CPT (cost per thousand) or £'000. However, in recent years the term CPM (cost per mille) has been introduced for online purposes, reflecting the international nature of the world the buyers and sellers are working in; *mille* being both the French and American term for the UK thousand.

For direct response advertisers the term most commonly refers to the **primary contact,** made by the advertising. For print this would be the actual number distributed, be it the number of names targeted for a mailing piece, or the purchaser/first recipient of a publication (ie those that make up the circulation). In the main, these figures can be confirmed, thereby making planning and evaluation as accurate as possible. Secondary (pass-on) readership may be very valuable for generating response but the numbers are not statistically robust, often being based upon averaged estimates and sample group surveys.

In **Table 5.3.4** we see a very rough guide to media costs. All costs shown are per '000 circulation or audience and include production costs. Production costs are included because, while they are a small element in space advertising, they are the major element in direct mail, for example, and leaving out production costs would give a false impression. Naturally, we have had to use an average figure because production costs can vary greatly between alternative formats.

Table 5.3.4 **Comparative costs**

Medium	Size/format	Cost per 1000*
Daily newspaper	25cms x 4 cols.	5.50
Radio	30 secs	4.50
Satellite TV	30 secs	10.00
Search engine	Banner ad, general rotation	18.00
Weekend magazine	Full colour page	10.00
Daily newspaper	Loose insert	40.00
Business magazine	Loose insert	50.00
Direct mail (cold)	Multi-piece	500.00
E-mail (prospects)		250.00
Telemarketing (prospects)		3000.00

Notes to Table 5.3.4:

✔ TV and radio audiences are expressed in terms of 'All Adults' – ie everyone over the age of 15 who watches. Targeting may be used to identify stations and programmers with specific audience profiles, but respondents are self-selecting and may be any one of the viewers. Therefore accuracy is increased if the measurement figures used include 'All Adults'.

✔ Newspaper audiences here are measured in terms of primary readers, equivalent to circulation, not total readership. Also direct mail audiences are measured on a circulation basis, perhaps because only one person is likely to respond. If newspaper costs were measured in terms of adults reading each copy, the costs would be even lower than we see here. The rate shown here is for a mono 25 cm x 4-column advertisement, a fairly common size for direct response.

✔ Newspaper cost will vary widely depending upon the profile of the readers, and the demand for advertising space. Consequently the quality press tends to achieve a higher CPT than the popular titles, and similarly, business titles are more expensive than consumer titles.

✔ Production costs can influence costs greatly:

● TV production can range from under £10,000 to over £500,0000, and usage will also vary dramatically. Some products will only be relevant over one season, whereas some DRTV commercials having been repeated daily across multiple channels for 2-3 years. In the latter instance, the costs of production is negligible when amortised across the entire campaign. The example above assumes a budget split 50:50 between air time and production.

● Inserts, DM packs and all similar print vehicles may range from single page leaflets to 36-page catalogues, and may be in small print quantities or large – all of which affects the cost.

✔ Direct mail costs vary according to the mailing quantity, required delivery time and degree of presorting of the mail by the marketer. Most mailings qualify for the lowest cost by weight and delivery speed.

✔ B2B direct mail, on average, costs at least 25% more than figures shown, because list rental charges are higher, while print runs are shorter.

✔ Online costs will vary dependent upon the style of the advertising, whether text or HTML, whether links are to existing sites or specific campaign micro sites and the degree of analysis that is undertaken on the click and impressions traffic data.

Using cost comparisons

While it is interesting to make these broad comparisons, direct marketers are more concerned with the **cost per response** or the **cost per sale**. The direct marketer is less interested in how the cost per thousand audience compares. After all, how can one compare the value of a 30-second commercial with a 25 x 4 advertisement, unless by the quantity and quality of the response?

The use of measures like cost per response, cost per sale and **cost per £100 sales** helps to facilitate inter-media performance comparisons. Furthermore, it does so in a meaningful way, a way that relates to eventual profit.

In the comparison between the newspaper advertisement and the mailing with telemarketing follow-up, we stopped at cost per response. However, success will depend more on cost per sale or cost per £100 sales (marketing ratio). Ultimately, it will depend on the return achieved from new business investment.

However, media costs are significant as absolute sums. For example, we can either afford to risk testing TV or we cannot. The total outlay on a test campaign will be more important than the cost of a single transmission or insertion. This cost will depend on the **origination cost** (eg the cost of making a TV commercial) and the minimum media cost to give it an adequate test.

Media testing costs and lead times

Moving towards establishing the cost of testing a new medium (or a new product, treatment or offer within a medium) we must now consider **production cost**. The costs quoted are for one version, although two or more would usually be tested.

In **Table 5.3.5** we see a comparison of typical origination costs: that is the cost of creating the advertisement or mailing, not the cost of copies.

Table 5.3.5 **Origination cost ranges**

TV	£3,000 - £300,000
Radio	£300 - £5,000
Newspapers	£300 - £4,000
Magazines/colour	£600 - £5,000
Banner ads	£300 - £2,000
Door-to-door/inserts	£600 - £6,000
Direct mail	£600 - £16,000
Telemarketing (outbound)	£200 - £3,000
Telemarketing (inbound)	£200 - £10,000
Website (transactional)	£500 - £500,000

TV – £3,000-£300,000
A TV commercial can cost over £1million to produce, but no direct marketer would contemplate such an expense. In practice it is possible to create a professional-looking commercial for as little as £3,000 by using simple computer animation, but a live action commercial will cost nearer to £30,000.

Radio – £300-£5,000
Depends on use of music or sound effects, but the actual recording cost can be negligible.

Newspapers – £300-£4,000
A newspaper test could feature a 20cms x 2 column ad costing £300 to produce or a full page ad using new photography at a cost of £4,000.

Magazines/colour – £600-£5,000
A colour ad might use, for example, existing catalogue photography but could easily require high quality original work.

Banner ads – £300-£2,000
A banner ad capable of data entry would cost closer to £2,000. Java banners cost much more, but are not recommended.

Door-to-door/inserts – £600-£6,000
An insert or door drop could be anything from a single sheet piece to, say, a 36-page mini catalogue.

Direct mail – £600-£16,000
A mailing might consist of a letter and one other piece within the outer envelope, or it might be very elaborate.

Telemarketing (outbound) – £200-£3,000
A professional script might not be considered deliverable until it has been tested and corrected. This could take the cost up to the higher figure.

Telemarketing (inbound) – £200-£10,000

Your test may require setting up a response handling facility. An inbound script or series of prompts may require linking software to other systems, for example, to produce a quote, check price or check stock availability. In fact, if system design is involved, the cost could be very much higher.

Website (transactional) – £500-£500,000

Much the same applies to a website with e-commerce functionality. An off-the-peg site design can be purchased for very little but a tailor-made site, dovetailing with existing systems, can cost a great deal.

The costs quoted are rough guides and cover **origination** only. There are additional costs, for example, use fees or royalties, copies etc. In the case of inserts, door drops and direct mail, print costs can easily exceed origination costs, even in test quantities. Websites and inbound phone calls involve maintenance costs as the information given out and received is constantly changing.

Naturally there is a relationship between origination cost and minimum test cost. However, it is not a direct one, because other factors must be taken into account. Apart from origination cost, the other variables that determine the minimum cost of a test include:

? Media cost

? Running cost (eg printing, postage)

? Number of variables (ie are two or more ads being tested?)

? Number of responses needed to provide confidence in the test result

Table 5.3.6 **Minimum test costs**

TV	£60,000
Radio	£25,000
Newspapers	£12,000
Magazines/colour	£12,000
Banner ads	£10,000
Door-to-door/inserts	£10,000 - £30,000
Direct mail	£10,000 - £40,000
Telemarketing (outbound)	£2,000
Telemarketing (inbound)	origination cost
Website (transactional)	origination cost

The costs in **Table 5.3.6** assume each test is kept as simple as possible and that expected response rates are high. If response rates are low, or if factors such as average order value must be tested reliably, then the scale of testing may need to be increased.

Lead times for media testing

Another important consideration is the time required to mount a test in any medium that may be selected. In **Table 5.3.7** we see some example lead times, all incorporating production and media booking time.

Table 5.3.7 **Typical lead times**

TV	3 months
Radio	2 months
Newspapers	1 month
Magazines/colour	3 months
Banners	2 months
Door-to-door/inserts	3 months
Direct mail	3-4 months
Telemarketing (outbound)	2 months

To be fair, most of the typical lead times appearing in Table 5.3.7 can be cut quite drastically. However, the less time allowed, the greater the risk that compromises will have to be made or that mistakes will not be corrected.

There are many exceptions to the above generalised lead times and it is important to be aware of these. For example:

✔   In the case of print media advertising, bookings may be deliberately withheld until the last possible moment as an aid to rate (price) negotiation, or to take heed of test results. However, advertisements will have been prepared in advance, ready for immediate insertion.

✔   In some cases, lead times will be even greater than those shown. That is because certain media (or positions/slots within media) may enjoy a sellers' market and competition may advance book available space, air time or distribution many months ahead.

✔   If tests are to be conducted before 'rolling out' a campaign, lead times for the rollout must allow for the results of tests to be received and analysed. Response to direct mail and monthly magazine advertising can take months to mature. A radio or TV test might continue over four weeks or more. On the other hand e-mail response floods in immediately, while daily newspaper response tends to dry up within 10 days or so.

Acquisition media summary

✔ Ever-present considerations in media planning are **cost**, **targeting**, suitability for **message** and ease of **response**.

✔ Media selection depends on the direct marketing acquisition task – most importantly to recruit customers in one stage or in two or more stages.

✔ Customer acquisition may be long drawn out or truncated and direct marketing communications may need to be integrated with other media activity.

✔ Direct marketing media selection is guided by past results when these are available.

✔ The plan may require broadscale, selective, addressable and online media.

✔ Media types are intrinsically different – offering different communication benefits and having different shortcomings.

✔ Media types differ in selectivity, intrusiveness, cost per thousand audience, lead time and downside risk to test.

Chapter 5.4

Recording and analysing the results

This chapter includes:

- ❏ **Continuous monitoring: making discoveries from results**
- ❏ **Offline media results reporting**
- ❏ **Special opportunities of addressable media**
- ❏ **Website data collection and application**
- ❏ **Tracking and converting prospects**
- ❏ **Data analysis: using back data for forecasting**
- ❏ **Using results data in negotiation**
- ❏ **Summing up**

About this chapter

 e begin this chapter by highlighting the crucial role of monitoring campaigns as they are running and recording the results in meticulous detail. In fact, best direct marketing practice goes beyond just recording the results of each ad. The circumstances, too, must be recorded: such as day-of-week, time-of-day, level of competitive advertising and so on.

For addressable media campaigns, the best practitioners do not just record results list by list. In this chapter we see how response analysis can reveal the profile variables that are associated with responsiveness. This enables us to specify selections within lists.

We see, too, how prospects are tracked until they become customers (or rule themselves out) so that the appropriate and timely steps can be taken to convert them.

We discover how each of the variables on which results depend is analysed, so that forecasts can be made more accurate. The role of forecast data in negotiating advertising rates (the DR media buyer's unfair advantage) is also discussed. Finally, we remind ourselves of the three ways in which DM customer acquisition planning differs from conventional advertising media planning.

Author/Consultant: Graeme McCorkell

Graeme McCorkell consultant and writer

Graeme's biography appears at the beginning of this section

Chapter 5.4

Recording and analysing the results

Continuous monitoring: making discoveries from results

he direct marketing manager may delegate planning and buying to any or all of the following:

✔   A direct marketing agency

✔   A new media agency

✔   A media independent

✔   A list broker or e-mail marketing specialist

However the process of planning and buying media is organised; the performance of current advertising must be monitored more or less continuously, usually on a daily basis.

Although all media expenditures will (or should) have a forecast result, the actual result will never be quite the same. Nothing goes completely according to plan. The forecast will often be soundly based on previous results but history never repeats itself precisely. Sometimes a well-established trend goes into reverse. Sometimes a competitive initiative or external event turns the best laid plan upside down.

This means that adjustments continually have to be made to a current programme. As far as possible, the planner leaves money unallocated so that last minute media buys can be made and commitments that cannot be cancelled are kept to a minimum. However, not all media are equally flexible and the plan has to strike a balance. For example, a large scale door-to-door leaflet distribution programme requires a long lead time while a daily newspaper advertising schedule can (at least in off-peak months) be run on day-before buys. The best planners never bet everything on one media type and always leave some money for testing new media (say, 10% or more) and some money unallocated (say, 20% or more).

In addition to new media tests, there may be creative, format and offer tests that could produce exceptional results, requiring revisions to plans and forecasts.

Intelligent monitoring is critical

This is the key to successful planning and buying. It may be carried out in-house or it may be done by the media independent. Better by both. Both organisations will be the source of some of the data that will be recorded. The information will be accumulated over time and provide the back data on which future planning decisions can be based. It will help answer questions such as:

? Which of our advertisements work best in which newspapers?

? What are the trends in response – by medium, media group, period, size, copy, offer?

? Which days of the week are best for daily newspaper advertisements?

? How much extra is it worth paying for guaranteed front-page or back-page positions?

? How do competitive ads affect our results?

? What is the most efficient newspaper space size or TV spot length?

? Is it more efficient to use colour pages or loose inserts?

? What effect does Freepost or an 0800 number have on response and conversion rates?

? Is it worth paying more to specify pages instead of using general rotation for our banners?

Because each single advertisement is an event in its own right, producing evidence of its relative effect, a large body of information can be accumulated quite quickly. This depends on the meticulous recording of information, both of the results achieved and the circumstances leading to those results.

Offline media results reporting

An example of good practice in results reporting is provided by **Table 5.4.1** taken from *Direct and Database Marketing* by Graeme McCorkell.

Table 5.4.1 **Results recording captions**

Product	Offer	Copy/creative treatment
Medium/station	Date	Circulation/audience
Size/length/colours	Position/time	Rate card cost
Cost paid	Production cost	Total cost
Identifying code	Response total	Response by phone
Response by fax	Response by post	Response by e-mail
Cost per response	Conversions (total and %)	Conv % (by response type)
Forecast response	Forecast conversions	Forecast conversion %
Sales value	Ad: Sales cost ratio	Variance vs. forecast %
Competitors (number)	Competitors (who)	Weather

The level of detail shown in **Table 5.4.1** may be greater than would appear on paper or online report forms. Some of the data is required for making immediate decisions on bookings and cancellations (eg response and cost per response) while other data needs to be analysed over a longer period for a large number of ads (eg response and conversion by phone, fax, post and e-mail).

Product The advertised product will be recorded. In some cases the 'product' may be a catalogue. The catalogue might be inserted in magazines or mailed cold; alternatively it might be the fulfilment piece in a two-stage campaign.

Offer This is the promotional offer, if any, and it will also be recorded.

Copy/creative treatment The copy, too, will be recorded. Together with the product, offer and date, it will be linked to the ad by an identifying code (see below).

Medium/station and **date** The publication, TV channel etc. and the appearance, touchdown or broadcast date.

Circulation/audience For press media, the current six-month average is usually used but, unless broadcast ads have been bought as part of a guaranteed audience package, the number of TVRs will have to be entered when the audience research data is in.

Size/length/colours This refers to the space size and number of colours for a press ad (ie mono, spot colour or full colour) and the length of a radio or TV spot. In the case of inserts or door-drops, this part of the record is used to indicate the format (eg single sheet, roll-fold, mini catalogue).

Position/time This shows the actual position achieved (eg page four, top of column, outside edge) and whether or not a special position was booked. For TV it shows the time of transmission, not just the daypart.

Ratecard cost The published rate for the space, inserts or air time, not the actual rate paid. The rate paid is often less, particularly in the case of newspaper advertising.

Cost paid, production cost and **total cost** The production cost of the ad is included because it is the total cost that is important when comparing one cost per response with another. For example, the production cost of loose inserts may represent as much as 50% of the total cost while the production cost of a space ad may be as little as 5% of the total.

Identifying code The numeric or alphanumeric code given to the individual ad, such as 'DT3'. The code will be printed on coupons and reply cards. Most response will quote this code but some will not. TV and radio ads are not usually coded, although they may be coded by a direct dial (DDI) phone number. If no code is quoted, contact centres and websites will need to ask where the responder saw or heard the offer if the information is to be complete. TV and radio response is attributed to the last ad broadcast before the phone call.

Response: total and by phone, fax, post, e-mail Response is the most useful measure of success or failure for day-to-day monitoring. For one-stage advertising it is equivalent to orders or sales. For two-stage advertising it is a more immediate measure than conversion, so more useful when considering day-to-day adjustments to the customer acquisition plan. The most meticulous direct marketers record the response channel used when a choice of response media is available. It usually pays to highlight the most popular response medium.

Some of the larger DR advertisers forecast the rate at which response will come in. This enables them to see if an ad is likely to reach its response target while replies are still coming in. NB This is the first piece of information that must be supplied by the client (the advertiser) as opposed to the agency.

Cost per response The total cost of the ad, including production, divided by the number of responses.

Conversions (total and %) and **conversion % (by response type)** Conversions usually equate to sales or number of new customers acquired. In some businesses this is not quite true – conversions may equate to *orders*. Since goods ordered might be out of stock or be returned unwanted, or invoices might be unpaid, results might include both **gross orders** and **net sales.** Conversion ratio (%) can be very important when the cost of fulfilment is high. Conversion ratio by response type (eg phone vs. post) may be important if there is a significant variation.

Forecast response, conversion and **conversion %** It is essential to show the forecast achievement against the actual. Sometimes shortfalls in the number of inserts or the number of mailings despatched are discovered through unexpectedly low response. More commonly, an adverse result can confirm a trend that suggests cancellation of future bookings; or a favourable result can indicate that more money should be invested in the medium.

Sales value Order value may be shown instead of sales value or as well as sales value. Sales value is not always the *number of sales multiplied by the price* of the product. Some people may order more than one. Alternatively, sales may be the *total* value of goods or services initially purchased from a catalogue or website, not just a single item.

Ad: sales cost ratio and **variance vs. forecast %** This is the total cost of the ad expressed as a percentage of the sales value. Again, any variance against the forecast is shown. Longer-term measures, such as yield or ROI, will not appear in continuous monitoring reports. They will not usually be recorded for every single ad but will be shown for campaigns, media categories and so on.

Variations to headings

There may be variations to these items depending on the circumstances of the advertiser and the media used. For example, some phone response to broadcast media can be lost because blips cause the call volume to exceed the call centre's handling capacity. If the number of lost calls is not recorded, management may base future decisions on specious information, being unaware of the true problem.

Displaying results for analysis

Results analysis may use classification data to help identify patterns and to make results easier to understand. For example, press media will usually be classified by type, such as 'daily newspapers', 'Women's Weeklies' and so on. Broadcast media analysis will use daypart, and door-to-door distribution analysis will use postal regions or postcode sectors. Classifications of this sort may reveal patterns that would otherwise be obscured by detail.

Results will often be assembled in user-friendly formats, for example showing rank order of efficiency. This may be expressed as advertising cost:sales ratio as in **Table 5.4.2.** If we were more interested in the cost per customer acquired, we could show a rank order headed by the ad recruiting customers at the lowest cost.

Table 5.4.2   **Displaying results**

Publication	Size	Date	Total cost (£)	Sales (£)	Advertising : Sales ratio (%)
1 Daily Mirror	25x4	30.04.01	10,600	28,980	36.6
2 The Sun	25x4	01.05.01	14,600	32,860	44.4
3 Daily Mirror	25x4	15.05.01	10,600	23,670	44.8
4 The Sun	20x2	14.05.01	6,000	12,960	46.3
5 The Sun	20x2	08.05.01	6,000	12,120	49.5

At the end of a campaign or specific period, results may be tabulated showing a rank order by media, by space size, by offer and so on.

The importance of conversion ratio

The cost of fulfilment in two-stage advertising can be more than the cost of the advertising. It may cost more to produce and ship out holiday brochures or catalogues than to generate requests for them. It will certainly cost more to send a salesperson to see a prospective customer than to generate an enquiry.

On the face of it, these two ads might seem equally efficient:

The Director   CPR (cost per response) £10   Conversion rate 10%
The Economist   CPR (cost per response) £20   Conversion rate 20%

Just taking the advertising cost into the equation, the cost per sale is exactly the same. But suppose the fulfilment cost is £10 per response:

The Director   CPR (including £10 fulfilment) £20 Conversion rate 10%
The Economist   CPR (including £10 fulfilment) £30 Conversion rate 20%

The Director requires 10 replies to achieve a sale, so the total cost per sale is £200. *The Economist* needs only 5 replies, so the total cost is £30 x 5 or £150.

For this reason, the cost of fulfilment should be included in the total cost per response.

Response to catalogues

Catalogues are like very complex and expensive DR advertisements. Their results are therefore analysed in some detail.

The performance of each item in a catalogue is assessed through its **sales:space ratio.** If an item occupies 2% of the space allocated to products, yet pulls 4% of the business (by £ value), then its sales:space ratio is 2. This good result may be explained by the pulling power of the product or by its placing in a favourable position within the catalogue.

The performance of each page and each double-page spread is also recorded. Over a series of issues it becomes clear how valuable each position is, because items are rotated and changed between issues, ie the same item does not remain in the same place. The analysis of page and position is called **pagination analysis.**

Commonly, the following types of analysis are undertaken:

✔   Individual items (sales value, margin and number of sales)

✔   Product category (eg woollen sweaters, Greek island holidays)

✔   Price band (eg £11-£20, £21-£30)

✔   Page and position (pagination analysis)

✔   Size of space

Over a number of issues, this analysis helps to determine the optimum size and design of the catalogue, as well as assisting judgements about which types of product to feature in the best positions (which are called 'hot spots').

Special opportunities of addressable media

A record of the files assembled for **direct mail, e-mail** and **telemarketing** should be retained until after the results are in. That is because the **responders** can be profiled against the whole file to see how they differ. We shall discuss how and why this is done very shortly.

Meanwhile, we can record the results of each list used in just the same way as we would record the results of individual press media or radio stations. Typically, a direct mail campaign may use all the names available from previously tested lists (**rollouts**) and a test sample from each of a few new lists (**tests**). (For more on **Testing**, see Section 4, Chapter 2.) An example appears in **Table 5.4.3.** For the sake of simplicity, this shows only a couple of rollouts and three tests, although there would usually be more. There is no significance in the list sizes. They might be 10 times as large or 10 times as small (particularly in a B2B mailing). The mailing cost:order value ratio in the right-hand column allows mailing performance to be compared for each list in financial terms. Equally importantly, it allows overall mailing performance to be compared with the performance of any other media that might be used.

Table 5.4.3   **Typical one-stage mailing (excluding offer, format and creative tests)**

List	Quantity	Response (number)	Response (%)	Orders (£)	Mailing cost:order value (%)
Rollout 1	43,500	896	2.1	43,904	59.4
Rollout 2	26,850	594	2.2	33,858	47.6
Test 1	5,000	94	1.9	4,418	67.9
Test 2	5,000	145	2.9	7,250	41.4
Test 3	5,000	71	1.4	3,564	84.2

Other columns could be added to show, for example, cost per customer acquired and, of course, the cost of mailing to each list.

From the results shown in **Table 5.4.3**, we may assume that tests 1 and 3 are failures and test 2 is a success. This may well be the case, but there could be a chance of improving the results from *all* the lists if we have had the foresight to record the profile of all who have been mailed. The explanation of how the results could be improved begins immediately below.

List deduplication and profiling

To assemble the mailing file for the mailing in **Table 5.4.3**, the names on each list would have been deduplicated against:

✔   The database of established customers, lapsed customers and prospects; and space

✔   Each of the other rollout and test lists.

Deduplication is necessary to save the expense of mailing the same people twice or more, sparing them the irritation of receiving duplicated mailings and preventing established customers from being annoyed by receiving misdirected solicitations for their business.

During deduplication processing, significant features of the names and addresses are compared by 'intelligent' software to detect duplicates. This needs to be done because names and addresses are not always written in exactly the same way. This processing leads to the creation of a mailing file which is an edited version of all the lists used.

The deduplication report will show the profile of **the mailing file** in terms of:

✔ Title (Mr, Mrs, Miss, Ms, Dr, Military etc.)

✔ Gender

✔ Address type (street number, flat, house name, farm etc.)

✔ Postal area

✔ Area demographic or lifestyle type

In B2B mailing files, the profile may include:

✔ Job title

✔ Company/organisation suffix (Ltd, plc, Partners, Associates etc.)

✔ SIC (Standard Industrial Classification) or type of business

When the results of the mailing are in, the profile of those who responded can be compared with the profile of the entire mailing base. These profiles can vary significantly as the following true examples from *Direct and Database Marketing* show. The product was computer software with academic and commercial users:

Best company type was four times as good as worst:

Group	Response index
School	163
Engineering company	154
University	134
Bank	30

Best job title was 15 times as good as worst!

Job title	Response index
Professor	300
Manager	39
Computer job title	20

The computer software example is from a European-wide mailing programme. Simple profiling of this type is particularly valuable for international campaigns, when there is often a shortage of ready-made profiling data.

By comparing the profile of responders against the profile of the mailing base, we can see how all of the lists used could be edited during future deduplication runs to improve their performance. In the example from *Direct and Database Marketing*, the profile variables were combined into a **response score model** that produced a score range from 42 to 200. This is less than the variation in job title scores because the combined score model eliminates double counting, eg the title 'professor' is academic and academic addresses already scored highly.

Net names deals

Direct mail users negotiate net names deals with list owners. This allows them to edit out duplicated and other unwanted names without paying for them all. Usually, a minimum price is agreed and this can be as high as 85% of the price for all the names.

However, it is worth editing out the worst names even if the rental cost is not waived – because list rental usually represents 20% or less of the cost of mailing.

The list user can also specify simple selections at the time of rental. Profile selections by title (eg Mr and Mrs, but not Ms or Miss) and postal area are commonplace.

Application to telemarketing and other addressable media

The similar methods of list selection and within-list refinement can be applied to the other addressable media with the proviso that telemarketing, e-mailing, text messaging and facsimile are media that must be used with discretion for B2C marketing purposes. A special factor that has influenced e-mailing in the US has been its low cost. There is a strong temptation to use every e-mail address that can be obtained. Thus 'spam' was born.

Because of the high cost of B2B telemarketing, lists are often prequalified. The usual method is to discover or confirm the identity of specific decision-makers by phoning the company switchboard and asking. It is quite usual to make at least three attempts to speak to a B2B contact and it is important to ensure that the time and cost is being devoted to contacting the right person. Thus, in B2B telemarketing, selection within a list or segment is likely to be based on the quality of contact data.

Website data collection and application

Websites suck in data like industrial-strength vacuum cleaners. Not all of the data is worth keeping but nearly all of it is useful for diagnostic purposes. For example, if there are 200 unique visits for every order, it is not worth using the clickstream data for each visitor to personalise the site for a possible return visit. It is more sensible to analyse the clickstream data for a sample of visitors periodically, using the results to guide redesigning the site – so that most visitors find it easier to get to the point of logging in or ordering.

Evidence from websites that successfully track the source of visitors shows that most business comes from the (often comparatively few) purposeful visitors, not the many Internet surfers.

Server log file data

Lines in the server file log record *'hits'*. A **hit** is recorded for every piece of information downloaded from a web page and served to the visitor's computer. It is therefore possible to track the progress of a visitor within pages as well as between pages. The data in what is called an *'extended log'* identifies:

✔   The visiting computer

✔   The date and time

✔   The referrer (ie the URL of the referring location)

In addition, a good deal of technical information is included.

Analytical software is needed to make sense of the mass of data recorded in the log file. This enables analyses such as:

Total unique visitors	Length of visits	Document trails
Total page impressions	Most popular pages	Time spent on site
Page impressions by day and time	Exit pages	Referring site details

Total unique visitors is the number of computers recording one or more hits.

Total page impressions is *visitors x pages* seen.

Page impressions by day and time shows the most popular days and dayparts. **Length of visits** shows the average time spent on site.

Most popular pages shows which parts of the site were most used.

Exit pages shows the last page to be used.

Document trails reveal how visitors progressed through the site.

Time spent on site records the average length of visit.

Referring site details can both identify referring locations and even the search engine keywords used to find the site. This information is only available when an extended log (as opposed to the 'common log format') is used.

It will be clear that **exit pages** and **document trails** are particularly useful pieces of information in guiding site design improvements. As suggested earlier, the data is more useful in aggregate than on a user-by-user basis. However, for visitors who are identified customers, the data may be used for personalisation of the site. Visitor analysis can be undertaken at intervals (eg once a week) or continuously with the use of sophisticated software.

Identifying 'hot' keywords

Ward Hanson quotes the case of **VitaNet,** an online health product store, in his book *Principles of Internet Marketing* (South-Western College Publishing, 2000. ISBN 0-538-87573-9). For VitaNet, search engine queries are related to health and vitamin supplements. According analysis of the extended log files, the top 10 search terms were as follows:

Top 10 search terms for VitaNet

1. Free sample
2. Creatine
3. Ripped fuel
4. Hmb
5. Protein
6. Dhea
7. Sex
8. Chrysin
9. Melatonin
10. Glucosamine

This information enables VitaNet to ensure that it gives prominence to the most effective keywords for each search engine.

Evaluating sources of traffic

From the same case, Ward Hanson shows a sample from a monthly website traffic report (**Table 5.4.4**). This shows the value of identified referring locations. They are ranked in order of conversion rate. The first three locations in the table are specialised websites which are alliance partners of VitaNet. Visitors from these sources are relatively few in number but much more valuable than visitors from search engines or directories.

The column on the extreme right records whether a banner ad on the referring site could be potentially profitable.

Table 5.4.4 **VitaNet: Referring sites ranked by visitor conversion rate**

Location	Type	Visits	Orders	Income $	Convers-ion rate	$ per order	$ per visit	Banner ad?
Mentor-merc	Mall	77	5	221.75	6.49%	44.35	2.88	Yes
IPF	Weight-lifting	56	3	239.49	5.36%	79.83	4.28	Yes
ValueNu-trition	Health	754	25	1364.20	3.32%	54.57	1.81	Maybe
Web-crawler	Search	641	5	185.75	0.78%	37.15	0.29	No
Altavista	Search	2,145	15	853.97	0.70%	56.93	0.40	No
Infoseek	Search	336	2	78.90	0.60%	39.45	0.23	No
Excite	Search	3,986	19	800.00	0.48%	42.11	0.20	No
Yahoo!	Directory	4,594	21	1480.12	0.46%	70.48	0.32	No
Lycos	Search	1,932	6	315.15	0.31%	52.53	0.16	No
AOL	Search	4,259	11	672.90	0.26%	61.17	0.16	N

In **Table 5.4.4**, the 887 visitors from the three specialised referring sites (shown in the top three rows) produced $1,825.44 of business at an average conversion rate of 3.72%. The major search engines and portals generated 17,893 visitors, producing $4,386.79 of business at an average conversion rate of only 0.44%. The average value of search engine site visitors can be equated to that of loose insert recipients.

Identifying prospects

A visitor to a website is still just a computer until that visitor has logged in or, better still, ordered something. There is no certainty that a repeat visitor is one and the same person or two people sharing the same machine. A person with both a PC and a laptop will count as two different people. Furthermore, the log file will not record repeat visits to the same page if the web browser has cached the page. Each individual's browser caches pages and corporate sites also cache pages. These pages may be revisited repeatedly or printed out and circulated.

To turn visitors into prospects, it is essential to encourage them to log in to receive a newsletter, a special offer, a competition entry, a free sample or some other benefit.

Measuring sessions

In *World Wide Web Marketing*, Jim Sterne recalls that Mark Gibbs (www.gibbs.com) asks his clients to consider the following scenario for an online catalogue: a visitor begins at the home page, looks at the index, finds a particular product page and then looks at the guarantee. In nine cases out of 10, people who have looked at the guarantee do not buy the product. What's wrong with the guarantee? You need to address the basic question of the quality of your marketing materials. To *really* know what's happening on your site, you need to track individuals, says Sterne. That means getting visitors to log in.

Jim Sterne, Target Marketing, US. www.targeting.com

Tracking and converting prospects

Once a website visitor has logged in to the website, that person becomes a *bona fide* prospect just the same as a press ad or direct mail responder. Usually, prospects will have given permission to contact them in order to provide them with requested information or notify them of offers, events and so on. This sets up a conversion process, which may be very brief or quite lengthy.

The conversion process may involve:

✔   One or more sales calls (usually but not always a B2B scenario)

✔   Introduction to a dealer or retailer

✔   Outbound telemarketing

✔   Mailed or e-mailed information

✔   A combination of media and channels

The conversion effort expended will depend on two primary considerations:

•   How quickly the prospect converts; and

•   How valuable the prospect's business is likely to prove.

Clearly, more effort should be expended to sell a luxury car than would be expended to generate an order from a gardening catalogue. In some cases there may also be a time constraint, eg a cruise departure date or a motor insurance renewal date. Nevertheless, the cruise operator will still attempt to sell a later cruise even when it is too late to sell the specific cruise that prompted the enquiry. Similarly, the motor insurer will recontact the prospect one year later, when his insurance comes up for renewal.

In all cases, **it is essential to track the status of prospects** so that new customers are not mistaken for prospects, so that prospects are contacted at appropriate times and so that ex-prospects are recognised as such.

Tracking prospects in real time

Interactive marketing has brought a new dimension to tracking prospect status. The simplest kind of two-stage transaction occurs when a prospect requests a catalogue or visits a website with a view to making a purchase. When prospects request a catalogue, there is no way of knowing how long they will spend looking at it, or which pages will interest them and which they will skip. They may not even bother to look at the catalogue at all. All we shall know is that some people ordered and some did not. But when prospects log in to our website, we can trace their progress from home page to checkout.

Many (in fact the majority) of would-be buyers abandon their shopping carts before reaching checkout. Tracing their progress may supply clues as to why they discontinued the shop and suggest changes to website design, guarantee wording and security reassurances that can be tested. However, striking a correct balance between simplicity and reassurance is not easy.

One-click shopping

If a customer wants to give **Amazon** a repeat order, they do not need to key in their credit card and address details each time they shop. The Amazon '1-click' button is said to be the easiest online shopping experience of all. But when Amazon first introduced one-click shopping it seemed too good to be true. Many customers thought something had gone wrong. So Amazon received e-mails from customers querying the automation. The answer? They changed the next screen that comes up to say, "Thank You". It was all they had to do.

Unfortunately, one-click shopping is impossible until all the necessary customer payment and delivery details have been captured. But prospects who have abandoned their shopping carts can still be contacted by e-mail. Online consultancy, **Digital Impact**, has reported that, in a test for one client, prefilling the basket with the same goods that were left in the abandoned basket outperformed an offer of a 10% discount on the goods. The e-mail follow-ups were sent some days later.

The use of click-through e-mails making personalised offers (based on the known behaviour of each prospect) is potentially a cheap and powerful conversion formula once the necessary software is in place.

Typical offline home shopping conversion procedures

Smaller home shopping catalogues, holiday brochures and so on are not usually followed by any conversion programme. Without e-mail addresses, the cost would not be justified. Instead, the next issue will usually be sent to the unconverted prospect and further issues may also be sent, depending on the economic viability of doing so.

Major catalogues or fulfilment packages for major purchases (eg language courses) will be followed by a conversion series of mailings and, often, telemarketing calls. Typically, a conversion series might consist of:

✔ First follow-up mailing – three weeks from catalogue delivery

✔ Second follow-up mailing – five weeks from catalogue delivery

✔ Third follow-up mailing – seven weeks from catalogue delivery

✔ Telemarketing call – between three and seven weeks from catalogue delivery

A variety of offers can be made during the conversion series. The offers, timing and content of the follow-ups will be tested, making the accurate reporting of prospect behaviour crucial. Telemarketing calls will generally be spread over a period of one or more weeks, depending on the number of calls to be made and the available outbound calling capacity.

If all conversion attempts fail during the conversion series, the unconverted prospect will remain on a prospect file and seasonal attempts will be made to reactivate people on this file. It may be economically viable to continue these attempts over years rather than just months.

NB Direct mail follow-up inevitably entails some wastage as the prospect mailings have to be assembled at least a week ahead of touch down. Meanwhile, some orders will be received from people who are about to receive a mailing. The immediacy of e-mail is particularly advantageous for time-sensitive mailings.

Typical sales lead follow-up procedures

Most sales lead follow-up situations occur in B2B marketing. Typically, leads will be qualified before it is decided how to continue the follow-up. Leads may leave sufficient qualifying information at the website or contact centre but will usually need to be contacted by 'phone. An initial telemarketing call will establish the prospect's potential value and willingness to receive sales force contact. Appointments will be made with qualifying prospects. Other prospects will be invited to deal through the contact centre and website. They will then receive a telemarketing call and e-mailed prompts in a conversion series.

The meticulous recording of prospects' product interests, channel preferences, profiles and status is essential. This information must be available online to all who need it.

The importance of testing and monitoring

An unconverted enquiry or sales lead may add a name to the database but represents a cost, not an asset. In catalogue and website trading, a good follow-up programme can add 20% or more to conversion rates, often at very little cost. When leads are to be distributed to dealers or a sales team, the entire fulfilment process is crucial. More than anything else, it determines whether the campaign will succeed or fail.

Yet all but the most experienced direct marketers usually fail to **test** alternative follow-up methods, offers and timings. Many even fail to **monitor** their follow-up to ensure that timings or content are not being allowed to slip. Monitoring involves planting 'seed names' in the prospect file and listening in to contact centre inbound and outbound calls. It is axiomatic that, without continuous monitoring and management, any conversion programme will deteriorate over time.

Some prospects may phone or e-mail queries prior to making a purchase. Monitoring involves checking that these queries are handled in a helpful and timely fashion.

Best direct marketing practice involves regular 'road-testing' of competitive fulfilment and follow-up with a view to importing or bettering good ideas.

Data analysis: using back data for forecasting

In chapter 5.3 we referred to three ways in which direct response planning differs fundamentally from conventional advertising media planning:

- It includes results forecasts that are based on extrapolations from past results.

- It prioritises actions by projected return on investment.

- It treats each advertisement in each medium as a separate event that must be justified by its individual contribution.

We must now return to the topic of forecasting. We have said that "forecasts are based on extrapolations from past results". This is quite true, of course, yet it is not the whole truth. If we are trying out a new medium, a new space size, a new spot length or a new offer, there is no back data. Furthermore, some past results look out of character to the experienced planner. Thus the elements of experience and judgement come into play.

Analysing the data: unscrambling the variables

The first step in exploiting back data to forecast the future is to record past results and the surrounding circumstances in considerable detail, as in **Table 5.4.1**.

The second step is to use the detail to ensure that the results are not misinterpreted. This means analysing the data and extracting variables that may have distorted the results. Here is an example:

Media	Size	Day	Position	Copy	Response
Daily Mail	25x4	Monday	Early LHP	A	464
Daily Express	25x4	Wednesday	Late RHP	B	321

The ad in the *Daily Mail* pulled 143 more enquiries than the ad in the *Daily Express*. Can we expect this difference to be repeated? Certainly the spaces in both newspapers were the same size, but we have still recorded three variables, posing three questions:

? Is Monday a better response day than Wednesday?

? Are early left-hand pages better than late right-hand pages?

? Does copy A outperform copy B?

We have no way of knowing unless we analyse each of these variables separately. Providing that we have enough examples in our media schedule of each variable, we should be able to attach a value to each of them. (We may even have a split-run copy test result, suggesting that copy A is or is not likely to obtain better response than copy B.)

Results data analysis takes the recorded results apart, variable by variable, and presents an analysis of the contribution of each variable. Now the forecast can use an adjusted version of the past result to predict a future result. This will be more accurate than assuming that the result will be repeated. It follows that the more complete the detail, the better the data available for analysis and the more accurate the forecast is likely to be.

Often, there may not be enough data in any one campaign to provide for reliable analysis. This makes it all the more important to keep back data from previous campaigns. Some variables, for example page and position, are unlikely to change in value from one campaign to the next.

We have used press advertising for this example, but the principle applies to all media, although the number of variables may differ from one to another. For example, the variables in TV include **channel**, **day**, **daypart**, **programme**, **size of audience** and **spot length**.

When there is no back data

The best planning is knowledge-based and most of this knowledge is derived from the back data. When there is no back data, there are usually clues. For example, how can we replace the queries with response forecasts in **Table 5.4.5**?

Table 5.4.5   **What response should we expect?**

Media	Circulation	Space	Response 1	Response 2	Response 3	Response 4
Daily News	1.80m	25x4 cols	180	170	125	?
Daily News	1.80m	33x6 cols	?			
Daily Comet	1.50m	25x4 cols	?	?	?	
News Mag	1.2m	Page colour	240			
News Mag	1.2m	Loose inserts	?			

In **Table 5.4.5** we see the response from a series of three advertisements in *The Daily News*. We can see that the response to ad 3 appears to have dipped. Will we see a recovery with ad 4, assuming the intervals between the four ads are constant?

The experienced DM planner will say not. Experience has shown that direct response ads generally show a diminishing return with repetition, particularly if the intervals between the ads are short. The response curve usually starts level, descends quite steeply, then flattens out – like an inverted and lazy S. The expected response to ad 4 would be slightly less than ad 3, because the curve would be expected to plateau. A reasonable forecast would be somewhere between 100 and 125, say 112. Before settling on this, the planner will check to ensure that nothing unusual happened to explain the ad 3 result (eg a bad position).

But what if we would like to try an ad twice as big as our regular 25 cms x 4-column space? If we have no back data from other media, we can still call on well-documented direct marketing experience. By doubling the size of space (33x6 is twice as big as 25x4), we do not expect to double the response. On average we would expect to increase the response by the *square root* of the increase in size. That would be an increase of about 41%. However, we would not be testing the new size unless we thought we could use the additional space effectively, so 50% more response might be a fair forecast. Incidentally, we would do better to test the larger size early on, before diminishing returns have set in.

Readership research data suggests that the profile of *The Daily Comet* readership is very similar to that of *The Daily News*. So we can easily forecast the results of a test ad in *The Daily Comet* and also forecast what to expect from later ads assuming the test were successful. You can work these forecasts out yourself.

In the *News Mag*, also in **Table 5.4.5**, we have run a colour page and received 240 replies. What response could we expect from a 4-page loose insert? If we have no back data to rely on, we must again resort to general DM experience. In general, a loose insert may be expected to pull about five times as much response as a colour page. That would be 1,200.

Insurance against the uncertain future

These general rules are by no means entirely reliable. We therefore protect ourselves against the uncertain future in three ways:

- We deliberately marginally underestimate the results from new media, sizes and formats. However, in providing for fulfilment materials, such as brochures, we overestimate slightly.

- We test. For example, we test one ad in **The Daily Comet** before committing to any more.

- We limit test expenditure to whatever we consider it is reasonable to risk. Usually not more than 20% of the total budget in the case of a maturing product or company.

Allowing for diminishing returns

Diminishing returns from increased size or frequency are not unique to press advertising. All media are affected, although TV and radio appear to require a certain minimum frequency to work. This is believed to be because the viewing or listening audience is not alerted to the fact that they can respond the first time they see or hear the ad. In any case, this minimum frequency is very low – much lower than a non-DR planner would contemplate using. In the case of high response media, such as direct mail, a frequency of two mailings in six months may be one too many.

There is no rule of thumb because the tolerable frequency depends on the size of the market and how fast it renews itself. For example, people are only in the market for motor insurance for about two to three weeks a year. Therefore, every two or three weeks, the market renews itself. Motor insurance will stand a high frequency. On the other hand, not all that many people will take a holiday in the Chinese Republic. Of those who do, most will go only once. Chinese holidays will not stand a high advertising frequency.

Response forecasts will usually allow for response attrition over a series of ads unless the frequency is low enough to prevent this occurring.

Diminishing returns from increased size or more complex mailing or insert formats occur as soon as the optimum size or format is reached. Anything over the optimum size will be less efficient.

Finally, diminishing returns also occur due to the readership or audience overlaps between media.

Combating diminishing returns

There are various ways of offsetting response attrition. None of them are entirely effective but all may sometimes help:

- ✔ Widen the media coverage.

- ✔ Change the offer.

- ✔ Use inserts as well as space ads.

- ✔ Change the proposition.

- ✔ Change the copy and design.

- ✔ Change the size, colours or format.

- ✔ Add an early-bird offer.

- ✔ Find more affinity groups or affiliates.

- ✔ Try out new media categories (eg door-to-door or radio).

Experimentation combined with **controlled testing** of reasonable alternatives is needed. Meanwhile, the response forecast may well have to be revised as a campaign proceeds. This may lead to the cancellation or renegotiation of some advertising and the addition of new media.

Forecasting conversion and yield

Two-stage response forecasts will include conversion as well as response. Forecasts of the ongoing value of converted customers (eg sales value and yield) will not usually be produced on an ad-by-ad basis, but will be completed for media categories such as press, direct mail and so on. These forecasts will be subject to less frequent revision than response forecasts.

Using results data in negotiation

Advertising media owners publish advertising rates for the space and time they want to sell. These rates may not coincide with what the space and time is actually worth to the direct marketer.

Unlike non-direct response advertisers, direct marketers know what advertising space and time is worth. Or, to be more accurate, they know what it was worth last time and what the forecast says it will be worth next time. This knowledge places media buyers at a negotiating advantage, providing that they have the trust of those who are selling the space or time.

Unless there is a sellers' market for the required media, there is scope for negotiation. Two types of deal may be agreed:

- A straight reduction in the price

- Payment by results

The former is more common by far because it is much simpler to negotiate. On the whole, media owners are unwilling to take on the risks of the advertiser's business as well as their own. However, there are exceptions and we shall look at these now. The following payment models are used:

✔ Cost per Click (CPC)

✔ Cost per Inquiry or Cost per Lead (CPI or CPL)

✔ Cost per Sale (CPS)

All of these models have been used online but CPI and CPS deals predate digital media. CPI deals have mainly been used on TV but a minimum level of guaranteed payment has always been required. CPS deals are primarily associated with **affinity group** mailings and **affiliate networks.** In the former case, a percentage of sales value is often paid over and above a list rental price.

Negotiating discounts

In direct mail, the main scope for negotiation is in **net names** deals. In any case, list rental rarely exceeds 20% of the total cost of a mailing.

The scope for negotiating discounts in other media is limited by the actual cost of carrying the ad. This is relatively high for media such as door-to-door and inserts. It is low for broadcast media and press space. Terrestrial broadcast media deals generally have to fit within a set of obscure rules, but the law of supply and demand operates to a degree.

Press advertising is a media buyer's paradise, except when space is very heavily demanded. However, the best discounts are obtained by leaving buying decisions until the last possible moment. The most successful media buyers have preagreed prices with their clients, allowing them to make instant decisions on their clients' behalf. This involves close liaison, as prices need to be revised as latest results suggest and, even more importantly, the client must be in a position to fulfil the response from the advertising. This means checking stock levels of brochures, merchandise and so on.

Summing up

> The business of planning and buying is essentially pragmatic. Value for money is what counts. **Only through the meticulous recording and analysis of results can future acquisition advertising be planned and bought successfully.**

Most customer acquisition campaigns have an optimum level. This is set by the optimum format, the optimum frequency and the number of media that can be relied upon to produce good results. Beyond this, optimum level results begin to suffer. Ideas for new offers, media, formats and creative treatments are tested in an effort to counteract diminishing returns.

Analysis of addressable media adds a further dimension. As we have seen, the selection of lists may be only one of several selection criteria for addressable media targeting. Thus results analysis will, ideally at least, compare responders with the mailing or telemarketing base, using such factors as job title, company suffix (plc, Ltd, Partners etc), postal area and so on. Or, for consumer lists, factors such as gender, title and address type could provide good information. Careful analysis will permit accurate selection within lists for future campaigns, not simply selection of lists.

> Our results will give a good general impression of what is working most efficiently. However, it is unlikely that it contains no biases. For example, *The Daily Globe* may appear to be the best medium simply because we placed our most effective ad in *The Daily Globe* more often than we did in *The Daily Comet*. Perhaps *The Daily Globe* ads appeared on Mondays and Tuesdays (our most responsive days) more often than *The Daily Comet* ads. To be absolutely sure we know what is working best, we must either adjust our forecasts to remove such biases or, when we can, test each critical variable independently.

Although the wheeling and dealing is generally best left to those who specialise in it, the process of direct response planning is inextricably linked to marketing. It is about acquiring customers and selling products.

There are three ways in which planning for direct response differs fundamentally from conventional advertising media planning:

- It includes results forecasts that are based on extrapolations from past results.

- It prioritises actions by projected return on investment.

- It treats each advertisement in each medium as a separate event that must be justified by its individual contribution.

Section 6: Managing and retaining customers

██

I n the previous section we considered strategies for acquiring customers. Since no business can retain all of its customers for ever, customer acquisition is an essential process, if only to deal with the natural wastage caused by death. But it is an expensive process, and the longer we can retain customers expensively acquired, the less we will be obliged to spend on acquiring new ones. Hence the great efforts made in recent years by a wide variety of businesses to create and nurture customer loyalty.

In this section we look at the nature of customer loyalty – what it is, and what it is not. We consider the differences between emotional loyalty and behavioural loyalty. We look at the triggers of loyalty, at customer lifetime value, at how to segment the customer base according to the potential value that can be ascribed to each customer, and at developing communication packages around value-defined segments, from the moment of acquisition, through a programme of up-selling, cross-selling and dialogue marketing. The importance of the service element in creating and cementing loyalty is stressed.

In the final chapter we deal with the development and implementation of a customer relationship management (CRM) programme which recognises the different needs and aspirations of different customers, and aims to provide for these at each of the 'touchpoints' that make up a customer relationship, through a programme of integrated marketing communications.

Chapter 6.1

Creating customer loyalty and relationships

This chapter includes:

- ❑ **What customer loyalty is, and is not**
- ❑ **The value of loyalty and customer lifetime value**
- ❑ **Integrating acquisition and retention, long-term and short-term business strategies**
- ❑ **Everything communicates to the customer**
- ❑ **How attitudes affect behavioural loyalty**
- ❑ **Value, rewards and loyalty**
- ❑ **The triggers of loyalty**
- ❑ **The importance of the brand**
- ❑ **Conclusions and learning**

About this chapter

his chapter explains what customer loyalty is and what it is not by reviewing customer behaviours and psychology. Without *understanding* customer loyalty, and the relationships customers have with a brand, it is hard to create it.

Direct and interactive marketing has huge potential to develop customer loyalty, changing customer attitudes through the quality of care and communication that they receive and thereby radically improving the fortunes of the brand without neglecting short-term sales.

Author/Consultant: Angus Jenkinson

Angus Jenkinson author and consultant

Angus Jenkinson is Professor of Integrated Marketing at Luton Business School, Luton University, where he researches strategy and best practice, and Chairman of Stepping Stones Consultancy Ltd, a consultancy firm specialising in getting close to customers. He has led major strategy and change assignments with blue chip companies such as OgilvyOne, Vodafone, Olympus, IBM, Novartis, Thomson Tours Group and The National Trust. He is the author of two books and is a former CEO/Sales and Marketing Director of leading IT firms.

Angus Jenkinson M IDM
Tel: 07767 347532
E-mail: angus.jenkinson@luton.ac.uk

Chapter 6.1

Creating customer loyalty and relationships

What customer loyalty is and is not

irst let us understand what customer loyalty is and is not by reviewing customer behaviours and psychology. In the process, we need to put right some of the misunderstandings that are prevalent among marketers:

- Some people talk about customer relationships and loyalty as if you could create something akin to the passion of red-hot Italian lovers, while others deny the possibility of brands forming a relationship at all.

- For some people, loyalty strategy means the creation of a points-means-prizes sales promotion; for others it means buying and implementing CRM technology.

- For some it is a matter of investing in larger television brand advertising schedules, while for yet others it means creating an organisational service culture.

So what is the truth?

Your own experience is the starting point for understanding customer loyalty: because your own attitudes constitute both your bias and your best opportunity for understanding. So try this exercise:

Consider one brand or service–Dyson vacuum cleaners or your hairdresser, IBM or Coca-Cola–that you are loyal to. Ask yourself why you are loyal. What does (or did) the brand or service actually do to create this loyalty? What emotions (such as anger, concern, happiness, trust) do you feel? What type of loyalty is it: 'Unconditional'? 'Partial'? 'More-attracted-to-this-brand-than-others'?

In the majority of cases, it is unrealistic to expect customers to want to form a commercial relationship and loyalty as they would with someone genuinely close to them. Perhaps some spouses have to worry about whether the pub, the hairdresser or the computer might be a genuine rival, but on the whole customers do not put brands on a par with people and the majority would claim that they don't even want a relationship with many of the brands that they buy.

Before we give up in despair though, it is very important to remember that customers often do not know what they really feel, and when they do they don't always tell you. This is because customer loyalty and relationships take us into the territory of the emotions, an area in which most people are less conscious and more sensitive about disclosure. As we shall see below, most customers, and especially the most valuable ones, really do value the advantage of brands that they can trust and appreciate.

And remember: brands normally don't need that level of relationship or loyalty. Suppose your customers spend on average just 20% of their category expenditure with you and as a result of the marketing efforts that you make, you manage to increase that by a mere 5 percentage points to 25%. You are most likely going to increase your profits by anything from 40 to 100 percent. If you manage to lose just 5% less of your customers each year, the evidence is that you will probably increase profitability by 25 to 125 percent.

This is why many marketers aim to increase their customers' behavioural loyalty:

Behavioural loyalty is the name given to the share of behaviour that demonstrates loyalty to the brand. It means that the customer behaves in the way that the brand wants, eg by spending money. Measures of behavioural loyalty include response rates to direct marketing, share of wallet and market share.

Do we want behavioural loyalty? You bet we do. Behavioural loyalty generates transactions, revenue and in due course, profit.

Loyalty scenarios

Let us compare some different scenarios and attitudes, each of which generates what *might* be called behavioural loyalty, with brief comments on each, and then consider what we can learn from them about the nature of loyalty. While most of these are manufactured examples, they are based on good evidence.

1. *The customer grudgingly commutes by train each day, spending his entire commuting budget on rail, resenting the quality of service and the need to use it, but used to the exercise.*

    Here is 'behavioural loyalty' of a sort, with 100% share of wallet, and to those counting the revenue it might be very welcome. But, it is in fact only behavioural necessity, not behavioural loyalty. It is like this notorious case: in the middle of 1989 the East German car maker Brabant had a 19 year waiting list. Within three months of the Berlin Wall falling at the end of that year and the opening of the market for East Germans, Brabant was bankrupt. Behavioural necessity is **ersatz loyalty**: it looks like loyalty to the bean counters, but it doesn't feel like loyalty to the customers and it doesn't last like loyalty when the customer gets a genuine choice.

2. *The customer insures his house through an insurance broker, and each year gets a recommendation, normally to continue with the same insurance company, which he routinely approves. In fact he doesn't even think about it, because he assumes that the insurance broker is doing a better job then he could, and that even if he could get a better deal it would not be worth the trouble.*

    This is a customer who is fairly satisfied and demonstrates behavioural loyalty by most measures; and from a commercial point of view, such habits are very desirable. Indeed, many insurance companies depend on customers who cannot be bothered to change. But, this is hardly active loyalty to the insurance company. Here, the loyalty to the broker is the primary factor and is likely to continue until or unless something turns up to disturb his assumptions. Consider the next scenario.

3. *On the way home from work on Friday evenings the customer takes a little detour to a supermarket where he prefers to do the weekly shopping. He likes it because he knows where everything is, because it has a range of merchandise that suits his and his family's lifestyle preferences, it is easy to park and not too far away, the queues aren't too long and the service is reasonably pleasant.*

    This is an example of active loyalty, but as you can see it is a much weaker emotion than the customer probably has for his wife and family. Nevertheless, depending on the customer's budget, this loyalty may be worth a lifetime revenue value of anything from £30,000 to £70,000.

4. *The customer loves going with his wife to their favourite Indian restaurant. Of course, in the nature of things they often choose to eat another cuisine, particularly an Italian pizza restaurant and a French pub-bistro, but they recommend 'their Indian' to friends, go there perhaps half the times they eat out and banter with the owner and staff who always recognise and acknowledge them as among their regulars.*

Again, this is an example of active loyalty, but the Indian restaurant is only the most important member of their consideration set; the range of brands that they will normally take into account when making a purchase decision.

5. *The customer had loved her Golf Gti, which she had bought three years before; it felt like the height of chic, and as the first new car she had bought she had been very proud of it. It had been great to drive and she was totally satisfied. However, now that she was buying a new car, the new Mini from BMW just seemed to be the Golf GTi de jour, so she bought it instead of another Golf (for the change).*

Here is a typical example of how satisfaction does not always lead to loyalty and purchase commitment. However, over the course of a lifetime of car buying, depending on movements in the size of her wallet, Golf or VW could expect to get further business.

6. *This customer had once been in a terrible accident driving his Saab 900. A lorry had jack-knifed in front of him, and as he had hit it another had collided into him from behind. He stepped out of the accident virtually unhurt, and had never driven anything other than a Saab from that day.*

Here gratefulness and appreciation have generated total commitment and emotional loyalty. Other real examples of this include the millionaire customer who is willing to fly all the way from Italy to go to a particular dentist in England; the customer who goes to a particular health food store to buy his preferred brand of breakfast cereal; and the fan who travels to Manchester for every home game of Manchester United.

What they show

As these examples show, loyalty is a complex affair, and not always synonymous with satisfaction levels. An analysis of these examples shows that you need to take into account two factors:

- **Emotional attitudes**

- **Behavioural practice**

A transactional view of loyalty is vital when it comes to making a business case, but it can overlook the perceptions and emotions that drive behaviour. At the same time, repeated behaviour has two main effects upon attitudes:

- Sometimes creating a wear-out factor

- At other times generating positive familiarity and trust

…. depending on the category, creativity, communication and experience.

So ...

Perceptions and emotions drive behaviour. Loyalty **involves** customer behaviour and **depends** on customer attitudes: what they think and feel and do in relationship to your brand or service.

That is why the focus of marketers is increasingly on the development of **emotional loyalty and attitudes**. We can see many examples where **bonded customers** believe that the management of the brand has taken the brand off course. Perhaps the best example of this in recent memory is the attitude of customers of Apple. At a less emotive level, many software providers (and similar brands) will routinely work with their major customers on an annual basis reviewing their products to identify where improvements need to be made. Loyal customers, who are willing to come forward and communicate what they are dissatisfied with, group 2 in the chart below, are of real value when listened to.

Figure 6.1.1   **Loyalty spectrum**

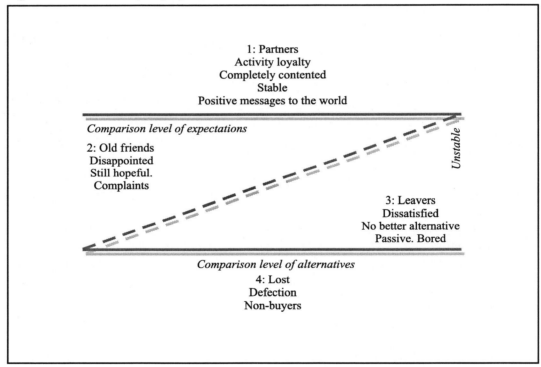

The loyalty spectrum chart illustrates four types of customer attitude based on whether the customer thinks that the experience they are having is better or worse than their expectations and/or better or worse than the alternatives. Groups 1, 2 and 3 all demonstrate behavioural loyalty, but they are likely to have different lifetime values and impact.

The difference between cases 2 and 3 (the insurance and supermarket customers) is that in one case there was only a **passive habit**, while in the second there was some **active loyalty**. However, even a passive habit should not be overlooked as an aspect of loyalty.

In the supermarket case (3), however, familiarity has developed into the basis of a simple relationship and a set of active and positive attitudes. Here we have the first real case of normal emotional loyalty among the examples given.

Emotional loyalty or bonding is extremely important in creating sustainable relationships. Without this you have no true loyalty.

> The value of the *bonded* customer at the average UK supermarket is eight times more than the customer at *presence*, the lowest level of emotional loyalty.
> BrandZ study by Millward Brown.

> Suppose two supermarkets provide identical quality. Supermarket A provides positive experiences to customer A and supermarket B provides positive experiences to customer B. A is likely to become loyal to supermarket A and become expert in its layout, and likewise B to supermarket B. The same, of course, applies to negative experiences. The customer is affected by his or her own experience, not directly by what other people are experiencing elsewhere.

A similar situation exists with the relationship between the restaurant management and the husband and wife in case 4. Familiarity is built up between people who interact, and not between people who don't. Only where the customer interacts is there a significant opportunity to **create social bonding through recognition, acknowledgement and appreciation**, a major route to customer loyalty. It is also a key route to developing **trust** (see *key factors in creating loyalty*). This is also why in many studies around two-thirds of customers who defect say that their reason is that the brand has not shown that it cared.

> Research shows that customers are typically five times more likely to defect because they have been ignored, pushed around or badly treated than because the product was unsatisfactory. Stop thinking you're servicing the product, and serve the customer.

Of course, what customers can do is listen to the **word of mouth reports** of others and use this to form impressions of a brand image or reputation. For example, in cases 1 (the disgruntled railway traveller), 4 (the diners at the Indian restaurant) and 6 (the Saab owner) there are clear examples of negative, positive and very positive word of mouth communication.

In case 5, where the Golf owner buys a new Mini, we can assume that she was influenced by the comments of others and her beliefs about peer and target group approval. She wanted to buy what she thought was chic, and that will normally be heavily influenced by word on the street. Hence the importance of PR, design and ethics in an integrated communication mix.

The aim in loyalty marketing is to get happy customers to tell other potential consumers and get unhappy customers to tell the brand rather than damaging the brand reputation.

> Angry and disappointed customers are likely to tell two to five times more people about their experience than pleased customers do.

However, customers who are recruited from positive word of mouth recommendation are more likely to be loyal: they already have a start in building up trust, as well as some of the social bonding that comes from the feeling of belonging to a community, in this case of customers.

Case 4 also illustrates the concept of the **consideration set**: there are three restaurants that the couple regularly use. In many markets, customers choose between a range of products.

The consideration set refers to the range of brands a customer will *consider* when making a purchase decision.

Sometimes, especially in FMCG or packaged goods markets, loyalty might mean that customers include you in their consideration set. Brands included in the consideration set get a **share of spend**, and this represents the level of behavioural loyalty that the customer gives.

Advertising is often concerned with achieving enough positive awareness for customers to include the brand within their consideration set. The experience that the customer then has in use or service is likely to be more influential in deciding the relative position, or indeed whether the brand remains within the consideration set. Here, the relationship between attitudes and behaviour is explicit: advertising is used to create attitudes that put the brand into the consideration set; being in the consideration set converts into levels of behavioural loyalty (the experience of which will further influence attitudes).

In B2B there is an equivalent concept that is usually called 'preferred suppliers'. Large organisations will create a list of preferred or accepted suppliers for their buyers and executives to choose from. Many also have a policy of having a first and second string supplier. Frequently, it is the job of the sales force to open doors and achieve this level of status.

Commercial loyalty doesn't always have to mean a monogamous relationship, although of course it might be an objective to achieve this.

Whereas the consideration set is most important in packaged goods and low value items, in capital goods what might matter is the **share of time** the customer allocates to the brand. For example, over the course of 40 years of car buying, does the customer allocate 5 years, 20 years or 35 years to your brand?

In case 5 (the Golf owner who ends up buying a Mini), we see a very common example of customers being satisfied but wanting variety.

Research shows that there is no strong correlation between satisfaction and repeat business. For example, many customers indicate that they are satisfied with the hotel, car, restaurant or shop, but when it comes to the next purchase they go somewhere else. If you think about it, if the customer says that they are satisfied, it does not imply a high level of appreciation. On the other hand, if they say they are pleased, delighted or enthusiastic, there is more likely to be appreciation, one of the necessary conditions for loyalty. Satisfaction is generally a *poor* indicator of loyalty.

Some research shows that only in the upper quartile of the *very satisfied* group is there a good relationship with loyalty!

Rank Xerox discovered that customers who were *very* satisfied were six times more likely to repeat purchase than those who were merely satisfied.

Affection is therefore a better guide to use when conducting research and a better goal than satisfaction.

Customers with genuine affection for an institution are loyal customers. Others may be quite satisfied but unless there is an emotional bond, such satisfaction does not necessarily translate into future sales.

R. Peterson, University of Texas

However case 6 (the Saab owner) shows how customers who have had a very strong emotional experience can build extraordinary commitment.

Satisfaction is the scale that is applied to customer expectations: to be very satisfied means that your expectations have been very or extremely well met, whereas an extraordinary experience goes off the satisfaction scale.

The most important time to provide extraordinary experience is when the customer is in crisis. This generates a heightened level of emotional involvement and your help to the customer will be rewarded by huge appreciation. When the brand saves your life, you never forget.

The fact that such high levels of bonded loyalty are possible and even that some brands are very successful at generating them, is one of the reasons why loyalty is often so talked up. At the other end of the scale, the fact that so many customers seem to buy out of a kind of routine, and have a low level of interest in further brand communication (and in a world of increasing volume of marketing communication, they sometimes want less), generates evidence for those who don't believe in loyalty and customer relationships as valid marketing concepts.

Figure 6.1.2   **The loyalty map**

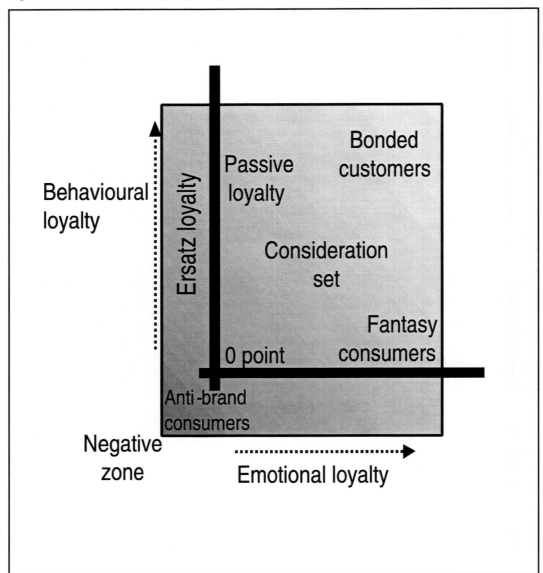

Learning checklist

1. Behavioural loyalty generates transactions, revenue and in due course, profit.

2. Behavioural necessity generates ersatz loyalty and customers who want to defect.

3. The consideration set is the range of brands that a consumer will normally take into account when making a purchase decision.

4. In FMCG or packaged goods markets, loyalty might mean that customers include you in their consideration set.

5. Perceptions and emotions drive behaviour.

6. Gratefulness or appreciation, along with trust, generates commitment and emotional loyalty.

7. Consumers upgrade their perception of their favourite brand.

8. People want to be proud of their brands.

9. Familiarity is built up by interaction.

10. Familiarity can lead to trust and expertise or boredom.

11. Around two-thirds of customers who defect say that their reason is that the brand has not shown that it cared.

12. Customers that feel satisfied don't always buy.

13. Very, very satisfied customers are more likely to be loyal: the higher costs are rewarded by higher loyalty.

14. Make *affection* not *satisfaction* your goal.

15. Create social bonding through recognition, acknowledgement and appreciation.

16. The most important time to provide extraordinary experience is when the customer is in crisis.

17. Customers who are recruited from positive word of mouth recommendation are more likely to be loyal.

18. Angry and disappointed customers are likely to tell two to five times more people about their experience than pleased customers do.

19. Aim to get happy customers to tell other potential consumers and to get unhappy customers to tell you, rather than damaging your brand reputation.

The value of loyalty and customer lifetime value

> **The three primary customer equity dimensions.**
>
> Customer category value
> Share of wallet (S.O.W.)
> Share of heart and mind (a.k.a. share of affection)

Studies by Millward-Brown using their proprietary BrandZ methodology have produced exciting results confirming the impact of emotional bonding and brand equity on customer equity. They found that bonded customers are worth an average 6 times the value of aware customers – and that in a study of 10,000 brand/market combinations!

Table 6.1.1 **Loyalty value**

Customer loyalty level	Toothpaste US	Ice cream UK	Cat food Germany	Coffee France
Bonded	1042	1124	710	1307
Attracted	303	532	272	336
Basic level	154	307	158	156
Latent index	100	100	100	100

Now consider: if the value of the customer in a given time period, for example a year, is 6 times more when bonded, what happens when you add in the effect of keeping the customer longer? Bonded customers are likely to be retained for considerably longer, increasing their lifetime value, perhaps by 20 times or more! What a thought!

- In the next chapter, we also focus on the importance of high-value customers. In UK supermarkets, the average high-value bonded customer is about five times more valuable than the average low value bonded customer.

- Add this factor and the high value bonded customer may be worth 100 times the low value customer with only basic loyalty.

Studies of retention show that the effect of a 5% increase in customer retention leads to significant increases in profitability; anything from 25 to 125% is typical depending on the category. In addition to a greater **share of wallet**, and **more lifetime value**, companies who succeed in creating customer loyalty also enjoy these benefits:

1.   The ability to charge more for products/services
2.   Lower administration costs
3.   Reduced marketing expense
4.   More leverage on fixed costs
5.   More referrals
6.   Faster growth

Integrating acquisition and retention, long-term and short-term business strategies

Later chapters in this section will describe in more detail how to manage the entire customer relationship, focusing on the three key opportunity areas shown in the Relationship Cycle diagram:

Figure 6.1.3 **The relationship cycle**

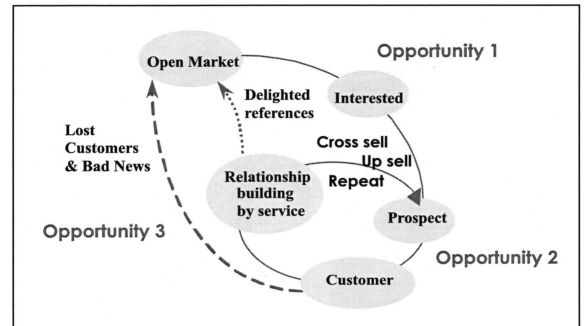

- From acquisition

- To repeated and increased purchases (repeat sell, cross-sell and up-sell)

- And in retention strategies

Your aim should be to focus equally on both long-term and short-term business goals. With good marketing practice these do not have to be in conflict. Repeated purchase experience should be a loyalty generator, provided the experience is not degraded. In later chapters, we will be exploring both the implications of this and how to achieve it.

Everything communicates to the customer

Everything communicates: communication is not just something that happens by direct mail or on TV. If you think of the traditional and new marketing communications media as the advertising voice of the brand, then what often really counts is the **body language of the brand**.

Things also communicate both positively and negatively: one major marketing company spent millions of pounds on a TV campaign that eventually generated several million unanswered calls at their call centre. Clearly the TV campaign communicated, and communicated effectively. So did the follow-up.

get into the ka

bold, elegant and highly individual. Ka is the perfect example of a simple thing done well

Products and services both communicate. They communicate speed, style, reliability, status, comfort and so on. The VW Passat was redesigned in the late 1990s in order to recapture a declining interest among its target market – and won a design award in the process. Ford created the Ka with the specific brief of reaching a group of customers previously disinterested in cars. And on a more mundane level, the heft and balance of a good hammer communicates its workmanship.

When Costa Coffee approached the agency Mother and asked it to develop a campaign to build the brand, the agency decided that it would be insufficient just to develop ads and commercials. What was necessary was to redesign in-store, including the in-store literature. They used the walls of the store and service frontage as communication media. This tactic generated a 9-point increase in customers who said that Costa Coffee made the best coffee, and a higher prompted awareness than Starbucks. This shows how product and communication can seamlessly blend.

Figure 6.1.4: **The image service cycle**

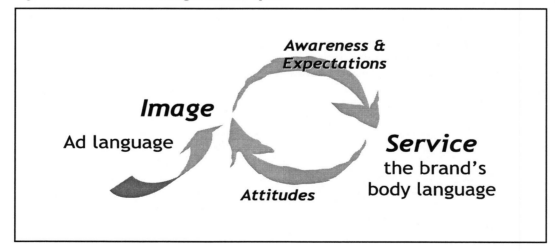

The diagram of the image-service cycle illustrates these principles and also sums up some of the points that were made during the review of the six scenarios. Customer experiences of advertising generate an initial image that forms awareness, and expectations that influence perception of service. But the service experience, in all its forms, then goes on to reinforce and change attitudes. A customer's experience of interacting with the brand is generally rated more important than advertising.

Communication is part of the value package

Communication is also part of the value package. Communication adds value, is of no value, or is a nuisance. When communication is of value it builds the brand and potentially generates sales. In other cases it is either neutral or negative. Research shows that customers fail to repeat purchase because they see no 'brand reason', nor do they feel the brand takes any interest in them.

An example is the American Express monthly statement and annual summary. The statement has been designed to give clear information about transactions, as well as supplementary information about current offers. In practice, various stores, restaurants and travel companies provide a range of offers to the American Express cardmember base. These offers are selected and shown on individual statements, according to the buying habits and apparent interests of the card members.

As part of the American Express service, members get a summary of all their annual transactions broken down into different categories of expenditure. Finally, there is an option of hassle-free bill paying, using the card to automatically pay by direct debit.

The different effects of communication before and after purchasing

Table 6.1.2   **The importance of sources of information to customers**

The Source of information	Before purchasing a product/service		After purchasing a product/service	
• The reputation of the company		20%		11% **20%**
• What friends and associates say about the product or brand	31	25% **45%**	17	9%
• Claims and promises made in advertising		11%		6%
• The imagined/experienced* quality of the product or brand		30% **44%**		54% **73%**
• The imagined/experienced* level of the company's servicing and support		14%		19%

Source: Marketing Metrics survey, 1995 (see Great Customer Service, Customer Retention and Growth, Vavra + Pruden)

* 'Imagined' was used in the before purchasing scenario; 'experienced' in the after purchasing scenario.

This chart illustrates the important difference between what customers respond to and how they respond before and after purchasing. Before customers have bought, they have to imagine the experience of the company's product, servicing and support. Hence these factors are 70% more important after purchase than they are before. Before purchase, customers have to rely on other factors such as brand reputation and comments of friends and associates, along with advertising and promotion: these factors are over twice as important (115%) during the customer acquisition phase.

The customer is the integrator of all your communication

Integrated marketing communications is one of the most important ideas in modern marketing. But it would be a mistake to believe that integration is something fundamentally achieved by marketers and their agencies. The customers themselves, of course, achieve the integration.
What marketers aim to do is to make it easy for consumers to integrate the message and that means ...

• Harmonising messages around the brand promise.

• Achieving consistency of brand values and message.

• Avoiding dissonance, especially any gap between the brand's advertising promise and the brand delivery (and the common B2B equivalent, the front-office/salesperson's service and the back-office/service department service).

This requires managing all interactions with customers, commonly known as Touchpoints, the most important of which are the moments of truth that determine the future of the brand.

Managing touchpoints and moments of truth

As we have already said, consumers have mental pictures of the brand derived from their experiences. Such experiences, also known as 'moments of truth' when they are significant, occur when the customer engages with the brand – whether as a purchase or as part of an advertising/marketing campaign, by visiting a website or simply by walking into a shop.

A moment of truth is each and every moment a customer could or does assess the quality of the brand (or service).

The term **moment of truth** was popularised by Jan Carlzon, then Chief Executive of SAS (Scandinavian Airlines). The concept however, was developed by Richard Normann, a leading consultant in the service industry. Moments of truth were specifically developed and popularised within a service industry, as a way of helping people responsible for service to develop quality.

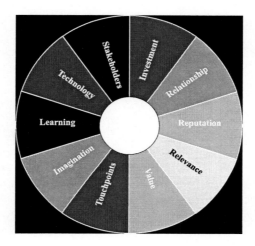

The next chapter focuses on a ten-point framework for designing, executing and evaluating moments of truth that create loyalty. This is based on identifying and then redesigning the sequence of touchpoints or moments of truth, between the customer and the brand in order to increase value for less cost. Obviously, the design needs to be modified for changing customer states (eg stages in a customer' life such as marriage and retirement in consumers, or departmental reorganisation in businesses) and also for changes for different customer types.

We will also explore in the next and subsequent chapters the four key aspects of each moment of truth, aspects that have already emerged in the scenarios, using this cloverleaf model:

- **Knowledge**: Here, knowledge means both the knowledge of the customer demonstrated by the brand and also the knowledge required by the customer or gained by the customer.

- **Customer activity**: what the customer actually is doing or has to do during the process of the touchpoint, and how it is for the customer.

- **Tangibles and functional outcomes**: what the customer actually physically gets, such as a new appearance after a haircut, a working computer after a repair.

- **Relationship**: the social and relationship experience of the customer, recognition, a smile, friendliness, fun.

These moments of truth are strongest at heightened moments and most effective when the customer perceives the brand has earned loyalty, eg

- First welcome.

- Gratitude for a rescue from a crisis.

- Consistent high quality performance and/or occasional stunning performance.

- Moments of intimacy or pleasure.

Transactional, consultative and partnership relationship preferences

The design of interaction with the customer, ie moment of truth design, needs to be based around customer preferences. As we shall see in more detail in the next chapter, there are many very different kinds of needs, but as one example relevant to understanding loyalty, it seems that there are three kinds of loyalty relationship commonly requested by customers that determine very different interfaces between the brand and consumers:

- Some customers want a transactional experience. This is most common among expert buyers who want a simple, quick and effective way to transact with the brand. Many retailers and websites are based on this principle. For example Amazon is a very good place to buy if you know what you want. Many B2B buyers want access to an efficient way of knowing what the supplier has available and at what price, so that they can make purchases. There is usually a premium on quality of information and efficiency of process among such customers.

- Some customers want consultative selling. A typical example of this might be a marketing manager working with an advertising agency. Here, social relationship is much more important than in the transactional customer.

- Some customers want full partnership. An example of this is the electronics and audio firm Bose, who partner with a small range of suppliers on a win-win commitment basis. Here, the relationships of trust have to be very strong, and they are used to improve the quality of social interaction, process, information and functional performance.

How attitudes affect behavioural loyalty

So you want to send out a mailing (or whatever is the medium of choice) and get a really high response! Naturally! But what is going to make that happen? And how do you make a difference also to the next mailing?

When a business spends time, money and effort in developing communication strategies and advertising campaigns, what they are fundamentally attempting to do is affect how people think and feel – and therefore what they do in regards to a particular product, service or brand.

Loyalty develops in response to multiple perceptions, experiences and questions that go through a customer's consciousness.

For example, our consumer in scenario 5, when thinking about purchasing a car, probably asked these kinds of questions:

What will people think?
Which is my image? Can I see myself in that?
Which do I like? (How long? How much?)
What personal relationships do I have?
What do you get for your money (functions, experiences, use)?
How much can I trust it (reliability, meeting expectations)?
How good will the service be?
What does it cost? (Can I afford it? Is it too cheap? Running costs? Resale?)
Is it safe? Will it protect me?
How will I be changed by it?
Is there a brand I want to help (eg, local, my club, friends, buy British)?

When customers ask questions like these, what they end up thinking and feeling about the brand, conditions their purchase action.

Ideas, imagery and associations affect consumers through the twin paths of rational and emotional argument, before creating a potential arousal to action.

Marketing communication aims to alter the customer's perception of the value exchange, ie what they are getting from the brand in exchange for their financial, time and energy costs.

The effect of the emotions on decisions

All decisions are powered by emotions.

The root of the word *emotion* is *motion*: emotions move us. The most important way that they do this is in our decisions. Decisions are actually made not by reason but by emotion. We use reason to create the argument and then we make the decision by judging how we feel about the argument: for example, do we feel comfortable with it?

This is a largely overlooked fact, but it explains why trust is so important in decision-making and loyalty.

Emotions have another way of influencing how we think. Most of the time, in order to think, we have to rely on memories. For example, customers will remember past experiences, advertising and other communication. Psychologists have shown that the way we feel influences our memories. For example, ever been in an argument? When someone is angry with you, they remember all the bad things you have done, whereas in a romantic mood good times are remembered.

The perception-experience cycle

The experiences we have form our attitudes and these change our very perceptions, thus tending to reinforce attitudes.

> For example, in a test of beer drinkers, it made a huge difference to the evaluation of the beer, whether the drinker thought that he was drinking his favourite brand or whether it was a blind taste test. Consumers consistently rated their favourite brand above the same drink unlabelled. It is this principle that is behind the famous Pepsi challenge, in which consumers try unlabelled Pepsi and Coke drinks. The majority choose Pepsi even though Coke enjoys brand leadership.

British Airways found that customers were slightly more forgiving of the product if the service was good. One measure of loyalty is the willingness to forgive. Here, existing attitudes are shifting attitudes to new experience and therefore to behaviour.

By contrast, a customer who has had a bad experience will always look through the filter of the bad experience. At a basic level, by avoiding the brand they will deny themselves future positive experiences. And if they do try the brand, they are more likely to take a critical attitude.

ServiceMaster, a leading home cleaning firm, identifies customer hot spots, the key things that they want cleaned and how, and prioritise these parts of the job. Then when the owner returns to review the work, they are more likely to be impressed and more quickly learn to trust the work of the cleaners.

First impressions count

This is an old truism, but you can easily see how the first impressions lay down the pattern of customer perceptions and brand attitudes.

So what happens if the first major communication and purchase transaction between a brand and customer is based on a high-value deal, such as 0% interest on a credit card? An advertisement like this positions the brand.

It is therefore not surprising that promotions of this kind generate highly upfront transactions and acquisition levels of relatively low retention and lifetime value levels. This is one of the reasons why divorcing the acquisition and retention faces of customer marketing can be very bad practice. The highly successful acquisition manager may be costing the company a long-term fortune!

What to do

The customer's 'inner world' conditions how they experience your product or service, and everything you do becomes your product or service, whether on TV or face-to-face or in a factory-manufactured SKU. Brand management (whether one to one or mass communication) aims to manage these perceptions – powerful advertising and/or service experience can radically change attitudes and perceptions.

So, to return to our opening question in the section, the direct marketer will want to:

- Select customers who have a positive attitude. One way of choosing them is to select customers who have a prior record of purchase without making returns (the behavioural history signposts customer attitude).

- Try to recruit customers with a similar profile to your existing good customers, especially those already primed by their brand-loyal friends.

- Design a creative format, offer and copy to try and influence attitudes towards both an immediate transaction and long-term relationships.

- Try to build positive brand relationships that influence experience of service.

- In the case of acquisition, make an offer that reinforces future loyalty too.

- In the case of ongoing sales, make it easy and friendly, recognise the relationship in an appropriate way, show your appreciation and acknowledgement, try to increase customer expertise in your product/service, make an offer that the customer will value and …

- Integrate your management of the customer experience across the whole range of touchpoints or moments of truth.

- Always make the communication itself of value.

Value, rewards and loyalty

Repeat behaviour is for sale, but brand loyalty has to be earned.

The next three chapters will explore how to create greater value for customers by responding to their value triggers. But it is important to recognise that extrinsic rewards have a tendency to devalue core experience.

For example, some rewards generate the subtle message that the product isn't worth buying on its own merits.

> Rewards do not buy loyalty – because loyalty cannot be bought!
>
> However, like fine wines, service lays down value you will enjoy for years to come.

Customers will buy a product in preference to another if it is otherwise equal and has an **extrinsic** bonus. But they will develop loyalty only when the value is **intrinsic**.

Air Miles have provided one of the most successful of the reward *currencies*. A currency that customers value is excellent - providing you can make it intrinsic to the brand/service/product offer, or ensure that it has strong brand affinity.

Intrinsic value is generated by service content: whatever has value to the customer is the value contained in the product or service. There is nothing else. Communication can increase customers' perceived value, but this simply reinforces the fact that the customer's perception ultimately rules.

And what has value to the customer is what provides service to the customer. A TV entertains, a mobile phone provides status and communication, a restaurant provides a sociable dining experience. The value proposition is always a service proposition.

Concerns about extrinsic rewards are very different from recognising the importance of customers and responding in socially appropriate ways. Customers certainly appreciate recognition of their loyalty. Indeed, many customers indicate that they appreciate a Loyalty dividend in return for their commitment, often, but not always, in the form of financial benefits. For example, better pricing for loyal customers or guaranteed service levels are good ways of demonstrating loyalty to customers in return for their loyalty.

The triggers of loyalty

So what **does** create loyalty? My research shows that the three primary drivers of loyalty are:

- Trust

- Appreciation (a form of gratefulness)

- Need - an ongoing requirement

Think about these. Can you think of any brand or service you are loyal to, where you don't experience these three things? It is hard to be loyal to a brand you don't trust. There is little reason to be loyal to a brand for which you have no appreciation. You might like to be loyal to a brand for which you have no ongoing needs, but this is unlikely to convert into a revenue stream.

- In each transaction the buyer anticipates that the purchase will create inner appreciation (ie a liking for its use or consumption) in meeting a present (or currently perceived) need. This anticipation is based on trust.

- The more risky or important the product/service is, the more the ante is raised. Hence the need grows to find trusted suppliers, and to engage in a process of consultative selling and to feel a sense of participating in the brand.

- The more frequent the purchase the more customers want to be able to be loyal. The corollary of this is that the more customers are forced to buy what they don't want the more they either become resentful or convince themselves it's OK.

Trust and appreciation are feelings, need is a want. Since you can want many different kinds of things (eg safety or adventure, entertainment or learning) what people trust and appreciate is very varied. Hence there are opportunities for different brands in the marketplace, and each brand needs to treat its different customers differently (see chapter 2 in this section).

Bernard Guidon, head of Hewlett-Packard's Bose team:
You need to understand very deeply where the value is to the customer. And it's absolutely true that you have to make sure they get a solution that will bring value. That solution may involve business you don't get. You have to have the courage to recommend a competitive product if that's what the customer needs. This is how you get the level of respect for what you do, and the trust you need to win a customer's confidence forever.

The importance of the brand: creating brand and customer equity

The brand is the psychological nexus of the customer's experience of appreciation and trust.

Direct marketers have not historically given enormous emphasis to the brand, mainly because it was so heavily aligned with creative advertising agencies. That is a mistake that is now rapidly being rectified. All direct and interactive marketing affects the brand to some extent and therefore the aim of direct and interactive marketing must be to integrate emotional and behavioural objectives: ie emotional and behavioural loyalty.

We need to think holistically about what we provide to customers, because they experience it holistically.

Loyalty depends on this whole experience of the brand because people create a network of associations and perceptions, a series of linked concepts that have emotional value. It is out of this network of memories that brand attitudes are formed.

Customers draw on their total experience of advertising, purchase and use - not just a cut down shred that we want them to remember.

Marketing words **must** therefore be backed up by their deeds. Are they synergistic or contradictory? Are you **really** 'The Listening Bank', (or your equivalent)? They indicate the step-by-step process by which ideas and competencies among leaders translate into the experiences that customers value (or don't).

- Your business/brand depends on the experience of potential/actual customers.

- Their experiences depend on what they, your competitors and you are doing in the market environment.

- What you do depends on how good your organisation is - ie your organisational effectiveness measured against critical success factors.

- This in turn depends on company-wide leadership, ie the imagination, beliefs, inter-personal and business skills, initiative and so on, in practice at the top and throughout the company.

Figure 6.1.5 **How leadership creates loyalty**

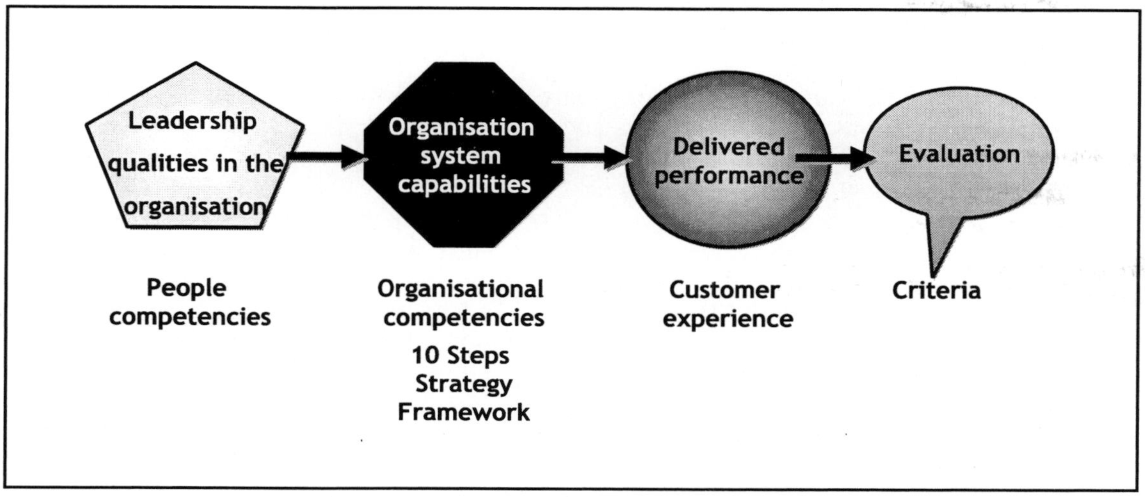

```
  Leadership          Organisation         Delivered
 qualities in the      system             performance        Evaluation
  organisation       capabilities

    People          Organisational         Customer           Criteria
 competencies        competencies         experience

                       10 Steps
                       Strategy
                       Framework
```

Brands also need to **be consistent across the full range of media**. A brand that has one personality and quality on TV, another on the radio, another on the phone, another one at the service point and yet another on the website is likely to be a brand that is in trouble. It is for this reason that many marketers are embracing the need for integrated marketing communications (IMC).

This also shows why it is important that employees are motivated by the brand, aligned, committed, enthusiastic and informed in their service and communication. Loyal employees create loyal customers; demotivated, disenchanted employees create frustrated and disenchanted customers. It is very important to create a win-win-win situation throughout the brand interactions with customers.

- The brand wants to gain financial equity, brand equity and knowledge equity.

- Employees want to get well-paid, develop their career and grow and learn.

- Customers want to get value, feel good and develop their potential.

Where marketing initiates a virtuous cycle that includes benefits for customers, employees and organisations, the loyalty of all stakeholders, customers, employees and shareholders, is usually much greater.

Conclusions and learning

In looking at the various drivers of loyalty it soon becomes clear that there is a mixed set of motivations that drives any customer's actions. If we were to list the underlying truths that need to be taken into account when looking at customer loyalty, these might be summarised as:

1. Loyalty is a mystery. We've all experienced it, and its absence, but it's hard to pin down. You can't buy it. Not even with points! Sometimes you can't even explain it. There are wives who are loyal to the most outrageously behaved husbands, and husbands to disagreeable wives. Likewise, some consumers will put up with bad service. But these are exceptions. The trend, confirmed by research in almost every category, and almost everywhere on the globe, is that customer expectations of care and service are increasing. Which is why marketing during this millennium means absorbing and applying basic home truths: most importantly if you want the customer to be loyal to you, you need to be loyal to the customer.

2. For customers, a loyalty depends on their experiences and this in turn depends on the performance of the brand in all its various interactions with the customer. This is equally important in both consumer and business-to-business markets.

3. Loyalty has both emotional and behavioural factors. High share of wallet and emotional loyalty are not the same thing. Emotional loyalty is needed for enduring commitment.

4. The buying decision is always emotionally powered. Even the most rational decision is finally evaluated by the emotions, eg whether you are comfortable with the decision.

5. Loyalty derives from trust and appreciation, along with an ongoing need for the brand's services.

6. Every act of the brand, through every communication product and service medium, includes a social and values message that creates or disturbs trust and appreciation. Is the brand fair, good, does it keep its promises; is it my sort of brand?

7. Individuals look for different things in the world and in the brand and therefore what causes their trust and appreciation may vary. It will also depend on their personal experience: his letter, her arrival at the website, your telephone call.

8. The brand needs to manage the full range of its interfaces to maintain consistent messages about the brand value and quality, while providing relevant and personalised experiences to customers.

9. Customers have 'archetypal moments of truth' - or mental representations of brands in action. These are often unconscious until called into memory but influence attitudes and decisions. They are woven out of the customer's experience of various moments of truth. Our job is to manage these effectively to win the hearts, minds and actions of our customers, so that they in turn think of us as their brand or supplier.

10. Initial brand awareness is generally needed to get into the consideration set. Advertising is an important way of achieving this.

11. Advertising serves to emphasise preferred aspects of reality, thereby affecting the initial and ongoing perception of the brand.

12. Customers weigh up perceived costs against imagined needs/benefits. That is why convenience and value are essential for creating commitment.

13. Service experience is generally much more significant than advertising or financial rewards in forming ongoing brand loyalty.

14. The most effective communication to existing customers appears to them as service, not advertising.

Chapter 6.2

Strategic thinking for loyalty

This chapter includes:

- ❏ **Creating experiences that create loyalty**
- ❏ **Overview of the loyalty framework**
- ❏ **Focusing on the high value customers**
- ❏ **Integrated management through the customer relationship**
- ❏ **Brand management and integrated marketing communications**
- ❏ **Segment and community marketing strategies**
- ❏ **Designing tailored value that excites loyalty and sales**
- ❏ **Integrated touchpoint management: managing the relationship across channels and media**
- ❏ **The vital importance of imagination**
- ❏ **Planning to learn and improve, and ROI**
- ❏ **Technology strategies for customer relationship management**
- ❏ **Stakeholder strategies and internal marketing**

About this chapter

 he first chapter in this section outlined the core ideas in direct and interactive marketing relating to customer relationships and loyalty:

- The vital importance of building customer trust and appreciation by developing and recognising their needs.
- The need to develop both emotional and behavioural loyalty attitudes and patterns.
- Crucial skills in understanding the nature of customer loyalty to avoid pitfalls and build the bridges that lead to greater profits and stakeholder fulfilment.

In this chapter, the aim is to develop a comprehensive framework to achieve these objectives.

Doing this requires:

- leadership values
- strategy
- and organisation
- focused on creating experiences that bring profitable customers back again and again with ever-enhanced loyalty.

Angus Jenkinson, author and consultant

Angus' biography appears at the beginning of this section

Chapter 6.2

Strategic thinking for loyalty

Introduction

 he aim of this chapter is to outline a comprehensive marketing strategy, a framework for success followed by loyalty leaders. The core argument of this chapter is ...

Whether you know it or not your marketing efforts will be succeeding or failing based on how you manage and integrate your performance across the 10-Step framework explained here.

Each and every moment of truth can be analysed after the event according to this framework or checklist. Equally each and every moment of communication or service that you design or implement will implicitly contain the 10 elements of the framework. However, if you are not following good practice, the results are likely to be reduced performance, profits and loyalty. Fortunately, it is possible to prioritise a step by step improvement in your marketing towards your goal of best in class performance.

Creating experiences that create loyalty

How loyalty depends on leadership:

Figure 6.2.1

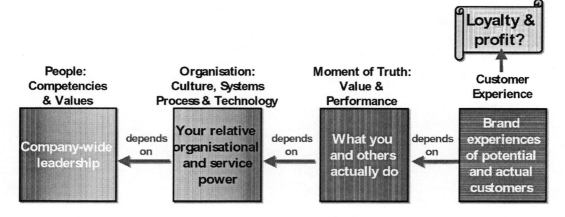

Source: *Leadership Creates Loyalty*, Angus Jenkinson, Journal of Database Marketing, Vol. 7, number 4, June 2000, Henry Stewart.

As the figure above indicates, the loyalty and profits that a company achieves depend on the customer's experience of the brand's performance.

1. Customers evaluate their experience and, depending on the outcome, form attitudes that either lead to loyalty and commitment, or brand switching.

2. The experiences that customers have in turn depend on the performance of the organisation or firm, in particular, on the brand's performance whenever customers interact with it, through any medium and in any situation.

3. The performance of the organisation and therefore the customer's experience depends in turn on the organisation's relative effectiveness in harnessing its technology, ideas, people and so on, to deliver that performance.

Customer loyalty therefore depends on the organisation's quality. That is why leadership is so important: having company leadership that is attuned to building relationships inside and outside the company and harnessing this to deliver totally customer centric performance.

Being totally customer centric means being aware of the potential full value of a customer from the moment of acquisition. Many brands measure acquisition costs without looking at the full value of a customer. Instead of recruiting cheap customers, with low return on investment, why not focus better resources on recruiting valuable ones!

Such is the following lesson learned by American Express Canada and quoted by OgilvyOne director Guy Stevenson:

> Coax, bribe or cajole an individual into purchasing a product or service that's irrelevant or inappropriate to their needs, and chances are they're not going to turn into one of your most valuable customers ...
>
> *Guy Stevenson*, Agency head, OgilvyOne Toronto

They found that their recruitment strategies that led to the highest initial response and conversion into new customers led to the lowest level of retention and customer value.

It follows that marketers need leadership strategies that will produce the performance that creates the loyalty. That is what this strategic framework does. The *10 Steps for Customer Loyalty* is a strategic framework for marketing success based on careful research. Each can be implemented individually. For example, focusing on your high value customers will be extremely beneficial. But build on this by optimising the whole customer relationship with these high value customers and you really build something powerful.

Overview of the loyalty framework

Companies and brands are supremely successful with customers to the extent that they implement these 10 strategic steps:

The 10-Steps loyalty framework

1. **Investment**: Invest according to customer value

2. **Relationship**: Optimise the whole customer relationship

3. **Reputation**: Be trustworthy in ethics and brand values

4. **Relevance**: Serve each customer community appropriately

5. **Value**: Create enduring value first, tactical worth second

6. **Touchpoints**: Manage the relationship at all appropriate *touchpoints*

7. **Imagination**: Bring imagination to the customer experience

8. **Learning**: Measure and learn

9. **Technology**: Use technology like an artist

10. **Stakeholders**: Make it good for everyone

A large body of evidence has been developed to show that companies and brands are supremely successful with customers to the extent that they implement this strategic framework. Each of the 10 steps is shown as an individual item and motto, and can be individually implemented according to priority, for each is a strategic concept and customer-facing methodology proven by best practice in the field. Indeed, a number of the strategies may be familiar to you because they are widely recognised. However, they are even more powerful when combined into integrated communication, product and service solutions.

What is special about this strategic framework is its comprehensive, intelligent and integrated approach.

Each and every interaction with a customer can be evaluated based on a 10-point checklist. For example, has your communication been designed to reflect the full value of the customer, does it demonstrate targeted investment and is it designed to enhance a long-term relationship as well as a specific short-term business objective?

The 10 steps are not abstract or just theory – they are practices and principles to implement. Truly successful companies ensure that every moment of truth or key interaction with the customer reflects these principles.

The balance of the chapter explains the framework in more detail.

A quick example: a bank or credit card statement

Let's take one quick example. Take a bank or credit card statement, which banks are required by law to provide to customers. Usually, bank statements are the responsibility of the administration department, although in recent years as a result of suggestions (like this one) marketing departments have been getting more involved. However let's take a typical bank statement. This is a key moment of truth in the relationship between the bank and the customer and one that in principle the customer is keenly interested in, if sometimes with anxiety. In fact the emotional anticipation is one of the key reasons why this is indeed a real moment of truth. Let's look at it from the point of view of the 10-Steps framework.

10-Steps framework example

1. *Investment:*

    Do bank or credit card statements generally take into account the relative value of the customer? Obviously they include information about the customer's finances, but this is not the same as recognising the relative importance of the customer. One of the ways that a statement might reflect this is by the inclusion of the customer in a specific product or service category that is only for high value customers (gold current account, platinum card). Another might be in specific content.

2. *Relationship:*

    Does the statement communicate that the bank wants to maintain a relationship? The mere fact of sending a communication about movements on the account is a positive step. However, it could certainly go further. The point is that each statement potentially reflects a new customer, a cross-sell opportunity, an up sell opportunity or a retention requirement. When is the last time that you felt that you got a meaningful piece of advice, acknowledgement or appreciation related specifically to the state of your account? Can computer systems be designed to achieve this? Absolutely.

3. *Reputation:*

    Then the bank statement should absolutely reflect the brand values, not just at the level of basics like logo and font, but also in more meaningful ways. The American Express relationship statement is a good example. Most brands are also quite recognisable even from the outside envelope.

4. *Relevance:*

    The communication ought to be customised to reflect different kinds of customers, for example business to business (SME and large account), consumer, student and so on. The point is that the communication should look as if it is targeted for the kind of person you are. Of course, one way that this might happen is by giving the customer choice in how they want their statement to look, what kind of data they want in it and how they want it sorted.

5. *Vaule:*

    A bank statement needs to be a value generating communication. The administration department role reflects the fact that it is frequently seen as part of the product. That's good thinking, but then all communication should be seen as part of the product. Very frequently, the envelope contains a product related service document (the statement) and a bunch of other materials that usually go in the bin. The whole of what goes in the envelope should be seen as adding value, or at least demonstrating that the bank cares and is the province of marketing and in particular direct marketing. Specifically, the bank statement should provide information, knowledge or know-how (which at a basic level, but only a basic level, it usually does); it should be designed to make the customer experience of using it easy and friendly, which I can tell you is not always the case; it should provide something of good tangible and performance quality, and it should contribute to a warm and friendly professional relationship for social bonding.

6. *Touchpoints:*

    This level of quality needs to be applied not only to a bank statement but each and every contact point, with the statement being seen as part of an ongoing dialogue rather than an isolated event.

7. *Imagination:*

    Making all this work requires real imagination: the imagination to really understand customers (backed up by research) and the imagination to do something significant with that know-how. You want customers to say, 'The XYZ brand gives you such great monthly communication about your finances'.

8. *Learning:*

    The organisation needs to be geared to learning, so that with every statement run they aim to improve, with systems and technology and culture geared to achieving this.

9.   *Technology:*

This takes terrific technology, well used. But it certainly doesn't require anything outside the bounds of reasonable possibility. The technology needs to know about the customer and be able to send out personalised communication based on sensible and imaginative rules.

10.   *Stakeholders:*

None of this is going to happen really effectively, unless employees of the bank or credit card company are proud of the bank and the work they do, feel inspired to do a good job and feel that the organisation and its leadership care about quality, service and employees and not just short-term results, ego trips and the like.

These ten points illustrate the model that I will now develop in more detail. Later chapters will further develop the principles.

Focusing on the high value customers

1: Investment: Invest according to customer value

One of the most powerful of all marketing principles is the so-called Pareto principle, or 80/20 rule. This theory suggests that everywhere in nature and the human environment as a result of typical statistical variation, there are relatively small populations that are responsible for relatively large outcomes.

When applied to businesses, this means that most companies find that a relatively small number of customers are responsible for a relatively large amount of their business. These are the so-called high value buyers.

Differential value in the holiday market

A UK holiday company found that a mere 6% of the UK population was generating at least 44% of their annual income.

Within the Pareto principle, there are 4 important points to note:

1.   There are very different levels of spend by customers.

2.   Mass communication techniques are very crude relative to this dispersal.

3.   Mass promotion techniques most often incentivise already heavy buyers.

4.   Much marketing thinking encourages fickle customers, not good relationships.

Take the example of this household product, the sort of product you might expect distributed fairly evenly across households.

Figure 6.2.2   **Household Product Concentration of Profit**

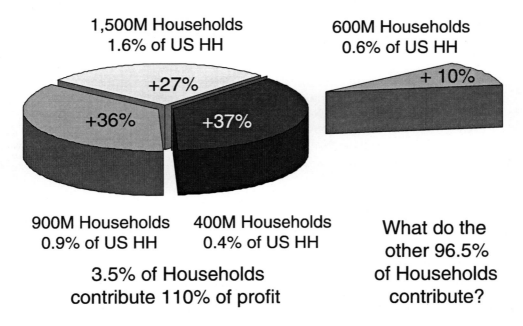

1,500M Households
1.6% of US HH

600M Households
0.6% of US HH

+27%

+ 10%

+36%   +37%

900M Households   400M Households
0.9% of US HH   0.4% of US HH

What do the
other 96.5%
of Households
contribute?

3.5% of Households
contribute 110% of profit

Source: Garth Hallberg, All customers are NOT created equal

In the diagram above we can see that a mere 3.5% of US households generate 110% of profits for a major household brand. The rest contribute only to costs, through sales promotions, advertising and so on. This is a brand that believed in mass communication – TV – as the solution to growing market share. How wrong could they get!

This is an extreme case. Less extreme are the 18% of yoghurt consumers generating 79% of their brand sales volume, yet receiving only 18% of the brand's communication and value creating elements, while consuming a vast 71% of sales promotion spend; spend devoted to winning new customers according to their theory, but actually only promoting promotion-led rather than emotion-led buying. Notice, the sales figures will show that these sales promotions are generating market share, and it will be true. And they will show that when the sales promotion is reduced, so are sales. That is because many consumers trained to be fickle will be off enjoying this week's brand promotion from the competitor, or using up the stock they bought when on promotion.

Still extreme? Well the lowest you are likely to find in conventional markets is one third of customers generating two-thirds of sales. The strategic implication of this is that the marketer needs to focus investment resources where it is most appropriate. If you spend your money equally on all customers, households or businesses then the probability is that it is going to be very wasteful. The wise marketer therefore tailors the investment according to the level of opportunity that exists.

Research by Garth Hallberg has shown that when a brand is losing marketing share, the most likely cause is the loss of high value customers.

Furthermore, as we noted in the previous chapter, the value of high value customers is still further increased when you gain their higher loyalty, as shown in the chart below.

Table 6.2.1

Value of a customer in UK supermarkets by category value segment				
	Average buyer	High value	Medium value	Low value
Bonding	806	1360	699	376
Advantage	300	499	264	152
Relevance and performance	188	299	179	83
Presence	100	149	101	46
			Source: Millward Brown BrandZ research	

Thus the first strategic priority is to invest according to customer value.

Integrated management through the customer relationship

2: Relationship: Optimise the whole customer relationship

The second step is to increase that value by optimising the mix and performance of:

1.   acquisition,

2.   sales

3.   and retention strategies

by taking a lifetime relationship approach.

Marketers need to develop a marketing strategy that will reduce defections and obtain the highest possible lifetime value of a customer. From the point of view of strategic priority that means that investment cannot just focus on *acquiring* customers, the most expensive period and often one that leads to an initial net loss. Instead marketers have to create a strategic plan to maintain the profitable relationship with a customer over a period.

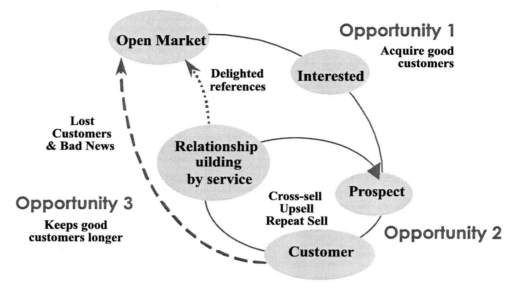

Figure 6.2.3   **Opportunities through the relationship cycle**

Source: Jenkinson, Valuing Your Customers

Often when times are good or in industries that have rapid growth like the mobile phone industry, it is not noticed how many customers they are losing, because of the rate that new ones are joining. It is only at the point of market saturation or when times generally get harsh, such as recession, that companies realise just how many customers they are losing.

Optimising the whole customer relationship means that when you have identified your high value customers, you create opportunities to dialogue with them. Asking them what they want – listening – responding.

Huggies

Huggies was so successful because they created a dialogue with customers around points that the customers were interested in. They made sure that they knew when their customers might be tempted back into the marketplace and put into action a series of events that kept them. Research had shown them that when babies reached certain weights the nappies would leak and the babies would need to go into the next size. At this point the mother would be tempted to look around at other kinds of nappies. It was important that the mothers were reassured of the reason for the leakage and given incentives to stay. In this case, a free trial nappy and a coupon off their next pack.

It is important that however and whenever the customer contacts you, the service and brand experience live up to or exceed their expectations. Whether it's by mail, phone, or Internet – they should be recognised and respected. Once trust has been established through the brand it is vitally important to maintain this experience with the customer.

Brand management and integrated marketing communications

3: Reputation: Be trustworthy in ethics and brand values

An essential part of successful loyalty marketing is to be trustworthy in ethics and brand values. Very considerable research evidence shows that customer loyalty is highly related to the experience of trust – the brand delivers on its promise.

This means that the brand needs to maintain consistency and reliability, factors that have been frequently noted in communication science as well as service marketing.

Brands also have to be seen to be fair and of ethical high quality in the way that they deal with customers. Companies that have a strong brand name and a strong physical presence with a high degree of trust and integrity have found it easier to cross into the interactive virtual market. People are more at ease to give their credit card numbers and trust on delivery in an interactive world if they feel they can trust the brand.

Beyond these basics, it is important that the brand establishes a distinctive personality, positioning and promise that the customer can rely on and expect at all points of contact and service.

Customers turn to brands because they meet pschological needs that they have. The success of a brand is based on the power and significance of the needs in customers and how well the the brand fulfils them.

Brand values therefore mean not only items such as fairness and integrity, they also relate to the distinctive qualities of the brand, whether they be adventurism, conservatism, fun or seriousness, qualities that they bring to the way they meet consumer needs.

The Pepsi Challenge

A classic example of perception affecting brand experience was the blind taste tests carried out between Pepsi and Coke. On hundreds of occasions Pepsi ran trials with consumers that asked them to blind taste two sets of drinks (which actually were Pepsi and Coca-Cola); 51% of customers preferred Pepsi over Coke. In open tests, ie when they knew what they were tasting, only 23% preferred Pepsi. This highly significant difference can be put down to the fact that customers who were loyal to Coke 'knew' that Coke tasted better then Pepsi. Therefore they didn't really need to taste their own experience. Nor did they recognise how their experience was actually subtly modified.

From the point of view of one to one marketing it is important that the organisation is able to manage all of its touchpoints, from TV spots to customer service desks, in such a way as to consistently maintain and enhance its reputation.

So, when ordering from a catalogue or website the goods and service should equal and match the service and goods that one would get if one went into the store – and vice versa. Regular customers expect to be recognised when visiting a store; they should also be recognised when calling by phone or ordering through the web. The only difference should be the convenience of not having to leave your home to order.

This also means, of course, that services should be integrated, so that if you want to take back to the shop something that you bought online or through a catalogue – you can!

Brands that give one message at the point of sale and another in service delivery, or one message on TV and another in direct mail, or differentiate between website and call centre, end up confusing customers and damaging the brand.

Communications theory long ago proved that consistency was key to developing the brand.

For a brand to express the true essence of a company it requires:

1. Knowing your identity and what you stand for, what must not be abandoned and what needs to be enhanced.

2. Communicating that effectively.

3. Being able to evaluate ads and marketing campaigns, services (and products), staff, culture – ensuring that they are on-brand.

4. Having the means to encourage transformational leadership, raising the vision of people around the company and giving them the means to act.

Organisations are most effective when their culture, beliefs, plans, commitments and objectives are aligned behind what they say and do. This creates more energy, synergy, continuity and effect.

Case Example: ASDA

Archie Norman, former Chairman of ASDA describes the way ASDA was turned around through the accelerated repositioning of its brand. At first, it involved going back to the roots of the brand and understanding the core values, making sure that they were championed across the organisation. These were made visible through a range of communications and through the leadership, including Norman himself, exemplifying and modelling those values. This was followed by a powerful advertising campaign that affirmed the brand's values, backed up by a range of activities, including in-store events

The people in the company also needed to be turned round – their motivations re-engaged and their commitment re-inspired. To do that Archie Norman went from store to store and personally retold the story of what he was trying to do and why. Fundamental changes at head office were taken in order to make the organisation more lean, accountable and effective. For example they created an open plan environment. And when the Chief Executive turned up at a store, instead of making an imperial cavalcade, he talked to people and wrote down what they said – and even more amazingly, followed up with actions.

ASDA created a fundamental promise about value, and made it memorable by recreating their once famous tap on the pocket, 'pocket the difference' imagery. The entire branding process was linked into a number of interlocking activities. For example, when visiting a store, you'd find a shopping trolley full of items comparing the price that you'd pay in a local Tesco compared with the same items in ASDA.

Norman's argument is that you can't reposition the brand without repositioning the business.

Segment and community marketing strategies

4: Relevance: Serve each customer community appropriately

Loyalty is more likely to be created when the brand ensures that it serves each of its customer communities relevantly.

Clearly it is important to be able to deliver value that will be relevant and appropriate to customers. Unless this is achieved there would be no reason for them to be loyal.

Thus, the brand needs to think in terms of three levels of communication:

1.   What is universal in the brand.

2.   What is tailored to different communities, including the values that belong to the individual community or segment – for example B2B and B2C customers, interest groups and personality lifetime groups.

3.   Personalising to the particular wants and needs and timing of individual customers.

Figure 6.2.4   **The brand community individual model**

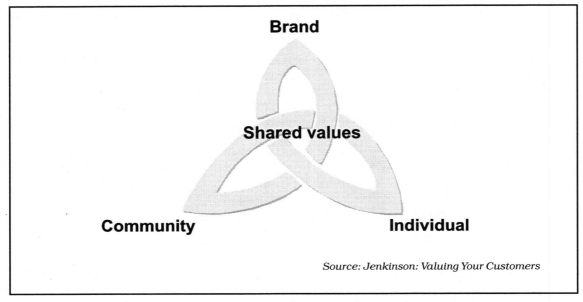

Source: Jenkinson: Valuing Your Customers

Recognising these three levels can help shift us away from reliance on the 'scatter-gun approach' into a more manageable community or segment based marketing proposition.

Seeking to focus the brand on being relevant to different customers in no way denies the universal qualities that belong to the brand that all consumers find a basic affinity with.

The advantage of knowing this kind of information is that you can recruit the customers you want using appropriate, relevant messages. This allows you to:

●   Design more appropriate services and goods.

●   Talk in more relevant, interesting, enjoyable ways at the right time and in the right tone and language.

●   Sell more to the customers you want and keep them longer.

While the brand needs to stand for something consistent for everyone, one of the basics of direct marketing is to recognise different groups or segments of people, as well as individuals with different general and time specific needs.

Harley Davidson communities

For example, while many people value Harley Davidson as a supplier, some do so because it encourages their sense of thrill and adventure while others enjoy a Harley Davidson as a means to go on long distance, getting away from it all, travel. Those two sets of needs translate into two different kinds of motorcycle and two different kinds of marketing strategy and communication content. So, all Harley Davidson customers relate to the 'American Dream – freedom to live' overall brand image, but within that some communities relate to the long distance riding; others for the status and image of just owning a Harley. Harley identified 6 communities in all.

It is important to remember that the overall brand message must be the same for all customers. But you can fine tune to individual customer clusters. So above the line advertising and material that might be seen by all customers should always be brand true. Material sent to individual customer clusters should be brand true and then finely tuned to recognise the specific needs and values of that group.

One of the biggest gripes from mortgage customers is the fact that the mortgage companies sent out so much promotion material attracting new customers with very attractive offers, but never acknowledged the loyalty of its existing customers. Finally, customers went to court to demand what should have been good business practice. It is important to remember all segments of your customer base when putting out media in any form.

There are research and modelling tools that enable you to cluster customers according to their different interests, needs and behaviours and which enable you to focus marketing efforts and communication more effectively, including better selection of media, timing and so on.

A powerful technique is to develop community signatures – word portraits that capture the essence of different communities through describing archetypal customers interacting with the brand in their mental and physical world. This can be used for creative briefing when an image comes alive, there is much more likelihood of being able to live into that experience. A feeling relationship develops between the company and customer. Empathy is one of the most powerful of all marketing tools.

Designing tailored value that excites loyalty and sales

5: Value: Create enduring value first, tactical worth second

If you want to create customer loyalty, create a consistent range of customer experiences, high in quality and true to the brand's values. The brand has a winning recipe when it ...

1. Communicates in ways that customers value (as a service).

2. Communicates that it cares.

3. Creates relevant and personal value.

As you saw in Chapter 6.1, the three main drivers of customer loyalty are **trust, appreciation and ongoing need**.

- **Need**: Customers who do not have a need for the product or service may retain emotional loyalty, but that may not translate into behavioural loyalty.

- **Appreciation**: Emotional and behavioural loyalty exists where such need is married to a feeling of appreciation for past services; in other words, customers feel that they have received value in the past that they like and are glad to have got.

- **Trust**: A traditional name for a logo is a trust mark, indicating the connection between a brand and trust. Indeed the whole value of a brand lies in its ability to generate expectations in customers that they can trust the brand to deliver certain qualities of product or service.

The ability to consistently deliver a higher quality of service than the customer feels is necessary or would expect, or believes that they will be able to get from other competitive brands, is therefore very powerful in creating customer loyalty.

The question is, how do you create such value?

Loyalty creation depends on effective ad language but it also depends on the brand's body language.

What differentiates the potency of a brand is the degree to which consumers:

- care about the category: feel involved.

- believe that different brands provide genuine choice.

- are happy with the brand, feeling that it gives them what they really need.

The job of creating value is therefore to achieve these objectives. Otherwise you will be a commodity at best.

Case study: Tesco: One in front

Brand promise: Any time there is more than one person in front we will open another checkout.

Tesco spent over £5 million on communicating their new service: educating, inspiring and training their staff to recognise the importance of what they were trying to achieve and going on national TV, web and in-store. They spent many millions more on recruiting thousands of staff to deliver the service. Success required the synergy of advertising and service delivery as two halves of the communication task:

- *Giving customers a feeling of being valued and noticed.*

- *Giving employees a feeling of being of value to customers and providing a real service.*

- *Giving the organisation an edge on its competitors.*

Communication is important in drawing the attention of the customer to the added value and qualities of the product or service, as well as to the invisible or less visible benefits, such as product assurance. Communication can also add an emotional resonance to a product by, for example indicating factors such as unique appeal, exclusivity and so on. But in addition to communication, the brand also needs to deliver a range of real and relevant benefits to the customer. These are not just external benefits – like tasty food – but also meeting core needs such as safety, belonging and ease.

Communicating with the customer well is actually one of the greatest benefits for customers. For example, good information has a value. Furthermore, research shows that one of the reasons why customers feel a lack of loyalty to brands is because they do not feel communicated with, cared about or listened to. These are all areas in which direct marketing skills can be very important.

Customer loyalty is not about how customers demonstrate their loyalty to us, it is about how we demonstrate our loyalty to them.

Ian MacLaurin, Chairman of Tesco

A law of loyalty: *loyalty to customers creates loyalty from customers.*

Customer performance value can be created in a variety of ways that direct and interactive marketers can influence. Some key ways to achieve this are as follows:

- Enhanced design, aesthetic and performance functions in tangibles.

- Making life a lot easier or a lot more enjoyable for the customer.

- Good personalised relationships.

- Providing know-how and brand-related expertise.

These constitute the Cloverleaf Value Model that will be further touched on shortly and expanded in the next section.

The three bonds

Three bonds also play a vital part in creating relationship marketing:

1. By creating financial bonds, ie ways in which increased customer purchasing or ongoing customer purchasing leads to improved value propositions, such as discounts or points. These are the weakest.

2. Social and relationship bonds.

3. Structural bonds, such as computer-to-computer links or automated supply processes.

Financial: Financial bonds are often in the form of price discounts for higher spending customers, or points rewards etc. often in exchange for information. Financial incentives for good customers operate as an effective entry-level strategy for loyalty marketing. By themselves, they are not enough.

Social: Social bonds are based on the human need for recognition and a sense of belonging, such as being asked if you want your 'usual' when you visit your local pub. Airlines recognising this have created their VIP lounges to recognise their valued customers. It is about creating relationships based on trust and appreciation, and meeting a customer's real needs.

Structural: Structural bonds are systematised connectors to the customer. They don't need people to make them work. They can be in the form of a direct debit; a physical presence such as a vending, computer or tracking device installed into the customer's premises; a software and data investment like Amazon's One-Click; a contract; or even a guarantee. All of these are forms of structure. Once the customer feels positive about the financial package provided and feels a level of affinity, they are more likely to invest in structural commitments with the brand. Then, committed or systemic solutions that automate services to the client or ensure higher levels of service can be further attractive to customers.

The three levels of relationship marketing they form are therefore:

1. Financial bonds: weak.

2. Financial and social bonds: strong.

3. Financial, social and structural bonds: very strong.

Integrated touchpoint management: managing the relationship across channels and media

6: Touchpoints: Manage the relationship at all appropriate touchpoints

It is in individual touchpoints that everything that has been designed and planned comes into fruition. It is in the touchpoint that we realise the work we have done in understanding what kind of customer we are dealing with, developing an understanding of the brand, and focusing strategic importance on key customers across the whole relationship, and it is in touchpoints that customers experience the value that has been designed into communication, services and solutions for them.

The need for integrated marketing

The classic organisation plans its communication to customers through its various line and organisational functions. As a result of this, one group is designing call centre processes, another group is deciding service delivery processes, and another is creating TV ads, while yet another is designing direct mail. By contrast, the customer stands in the centre of his or her own world. Each and every significant interaction or touchpoint that they have with the brand, whether it is a TV commercial, something they read about in the press, direct mail, a service delivery or indeed a product usage. Together they are integrated and transformed into the customer's attitudes to and experience of the brand.

The most important touchpoints are called moments of truth, when the customer decides what their future attitudes will be to the brand, for example whether they feel appreciation and trust.

Case Study: Waitrose, partners with Ocado to go online

The supermarket store brand recognised the importance of critical interactions when they sent out direct mail packages introducing their customers to their new online service in partnership with Ocado, a service that has been created from scratch to produce a revolutionary new online supermarket service, built entirely around the needs of busy people.

From Waitrose/Ocado

How could they communicate their new service to all their different customer segments, delivering a message of convenience and quality and not one of 'we don't want you to visit the store any more?' It was clear that any new service had a lot to live up to – putting that kind of customer care into online shopping – and communicating it – was a challenge. Waitrose know that their customers expect certain things: quality of information, of service and in the product. Employees at Waitrose stores are trained to be aware of their customer's needs. In peak Christmas periods when parking spaces are notoriously difficult to find, employees can be found in the car park guiding customers to the empty spaces. The mailing had to communicate that these standards could be expected: above all the assurance that the products would be the same quality as in the store. (Obviously the mailing only went to postcodes they could serve).

Waitrose/Ocado sent a small cardboard box by mail to appropriate neighbourhoods and customers detailing the principles and benefits of the new service. Backup support was offered and an apron included.

Notice: this is not primarily a customer acquisition campaign, although you can bet that most people will think so. This is communication to existing customers inviting them to shop in a new way: its retention, win-back, cross-selling or up-selling depending on the customer. Of course it will also pull in some new customers, but that is not what this is about.

Understanding Waitrose launch: Using the cloverleaf touchpoint model

We can use the four dimensions of the Cloverleaf Touchpoint Model (knowledge/know-how; customer process or activity; tangibles and performance; relationship) to analyse this communication. The cloverleaf is a primary tool for analysing overall value of each service incident.

The Cloverleaf Model: a tool for service development

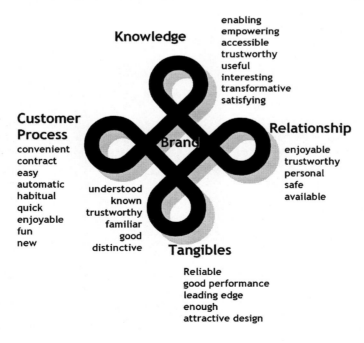

1. **Knowledge**: *Here knowledge means both the knowledge of the customer demonstrated by the brand and also the knowledge required or gained by the customer.*

   Waitrose had to communicate attractively that the service was available and make sure that customers went smoothly and quickly through the learning curve. That's what this communication is all about, but it must do so in ways that add value in other dimensions too. So it had to give knowledge effortlessly. Of essential importance was to get the URL across: on a leaflet and then again on an enclosed apron, in case the leaflet got thrown away. They knew that some would be computer savvy and could just log on and go. Some they knew would be worried about shopping online and they offered varying degrees of help according to their need, by phone or in person, showing that they really did want people to take up their offer of help. They even recognised that some people would feel that it was Waitrose's duty to set up the system and call them, so as not to waste their time until it was all sorted out!

Their leaflet talked you through the 'four easy ways to start':

- *Go straight to the website at www.ocado.com. (This is maybe the weak link in this proposition: it's not branded Waitrose and that creates a communication, knowledge and trust barrier.)*

- *If you are not sure about using the Internet, call us on 0845 399 1122 for a quick-start lesson, where we can guide you through the site.*

- *If you have never shopped online before, you can call us on 0845 399 1122 to arrange a home visit from a member of our customer services team, who will help you with your first order.*

- *Alternatively, pop the receipt for your weekly shop from any supermarket (or the printout of your online order) into the freepost envelope enclosed and we'll call you when we've set up your shopping list online.*

2. **Customer activity**: *What the customer actually does or has to do during the touchpoint; how it is for the customer.*

Waitrose had to make the online shopping experience look attractive and easy. Why would a customer log on to shop instead of going to the store, and how would they encourage them to do so? The key to anything of course is to make the first interaction a positive one, easy to understand and carry out. The pack had to both communicate and be that! Hence, an attractive and easy to enjoy mailpack, with attention to inspiring information, and some goodies inside. The site itself had to follow up with its own ease of use.

3. **Tangibles and functional outcomes:** *What the customer actually physically gets, such as a new appearance after a haircut or a working computer after a repair.*

The mailpack came nicely presented in a smart green box. In it Waitrose gave an opening financial offer of money off (£50 first shop) and free delivery on orders over £75; a social bonding gesture in the form of an apron and an invitation to enhanced service.

Inside the box was:

- *A nice quality cooks apron that had the website address on it.*

- *A well laid out leaflet telling you about the service and assuring you of the quality, value, convenience, reliability etc. and how to save the £50 off your shopping. Also free delivery for orders over £75.*

- *A first class freepost return envelope.*

Thus they reinforced their quality brand message:

- *In the package.*

- *In the quality of the apron.*

- *Having a first class freepost envelope enclosed.*

- *Four ways to start – Waitrose are known for being helpful.*

4. **Relationship:** *The social and relationship experience of the customer: recognition, a smile, friendliness, fun.*

Waitrose recognised the importance of building the relationship around the customer's needs. The mailpack aims to communicate that Waitrose cares and provides personal and relevant service: features of the new service that also have to be expressed in the mailpack. For example, willingness to guide you online or even set up your account for you. The mailing recognised the need for quality in everything – 'Waitrose customers expect quality'. A free apron to cook with Four easy ways to start, meeting everyone's different needs around online shopping and the fears attached to it. And most importantly, empathetically showing how the service has been built entirely around our busy needs.

We can also note that this communication expresses all the elements of the 10-Steps loyalty framework:

- *Investment in the service is focused on core customer areas.*

- *It aims to maximise relationship value.*

- *It is brand true (maybe the Ocado link needs to be evaluated).*

- *It offers solutions for different kinds of customers (pity it couldn't guess their types).*

- *It provides a distinctive value offering and service extension.*

- *It is solidly rather than flashily imaginative.*

- *The communication is low tech but the service is high tech.*

- *There are built in learning mechanisms (who responded?).*

- *It demonstrates partnership between customer/brand/service provider.*

The decisive impact of imagination

7: Imagination: Bring creative imagination to the customer experience

Imagination is an ability to visualise something not actually in front of you. As such you use imagination to decide what clothes to wear for the day ahead or to figure out how to get across town. In both cases, you 'imagine' yourself somewhere you're not, and use that 'picture' to make decisions about what to do now and along the way. We also use imagination to make sense of the present, as when we imaginatively 'step into somebody else's shoes'. And finally, we use our creative abilities to see problems or opportunities — and then come up with innovative methods and solutions.

It takes intelligence rather than creativity to recognise that if you acquire customers on the promise of a cheap deal, you will acquire customers interested in cheap deals. Likewise, if you acquire customers on the basis of high added value, then they will be customers who expect high added value. It takes intelligence and imagination to see the likely impact such thinking makes to future lifetime value and longevity of your customers.

American Express

The famous American Express letter that opened, "Quite frankly, the American Express card is not for everyone", implied the recipient was someone special for whom the American Express card was especially intended. This increased the likelihood that the recipient would find affinity and value in the mailing. Advertisers of all kinds routinely set about trying to establish this. When customer attitudes later changed, so did the Amex mailings. At this point though, they followed rather than led their customers.

A great deal of bad marketing happens because people don't exercise their imagination. They fail to look imaginatively into the future and see the consequences of what they're doing.

Social imagination is what builds relationships between people.

For a communication to be welcomed, a customer must believe there's a reason they should expect that communication. This is what we mean by an **imaginative social platform for interaction**. The customer imagines, "Yes of course I should get a communication".

Often it is the job of the creative to establish this social foundation through visuals or copy.

Felix cat food

Instead of writing to the owner of the cats, the creative director used 'Felix the cat' to write not to the owners, but to the cats in the household. His letters often started 'Dear Friends'. An imaginative way to get people to read and respond to their mail.

Source: Ogilvy One/Felix Netherlands

A good example of social imagination in business to business is the consultative selling process: building a shared imagination between the customer and sales person. The client brings the situation, problems, needs, business knowledge and cash – while the consultant brings experience, problem solving skills, professional competence and organisational solutions. Together they build an understanding of the what and why – and jointly create an agreement on how to go forward. This meeting of minds builds mutual trust; in particular, the trust of the client in the solution provider's ability to deliver.

Loyalty depends on trust. Trust is the feeling that in the future the other party will do what you expect of them.

Creative imagination enables you to think what was unthinkable – until thought – and then it's obvious. It's creative imagination that produces award-winning campaigns.

Media imagination

One way is to be imaginative about the media you use. We'll pick this up again in the next chapter. But the evidence is that too many marketers use old assumptions and prejudices in their choice of media. Integrated Marketing Communications (IMC) requires media neutral planning, which is paradoxically about being excitedly imaginative as well as merit-based:

- Understanding what the different media can do.

- An unbiased and creative stance with respect to the full range of media options.

- An unbiased stance with reference to the capabilities of any particular media solution.

- Ideally, understanding of the preferences of different customers at different touchpoints.

- Optimising media through a time sequence of touchpoints – a contact strategy geared to each customer community.

Virgin Atlantic

One of the most powerful acts that Virgin Atlantic created was handing out ice-creams in their aircraft when the movie began. This highly resonant gesture was good fun, appreciated and different. It invited passengers to relax and enjoy the movie. In doing this, Virgin Atlantic created a new moment of truth, and also a new advertisement. It said something about itself as a creative, caring, entertaining service. We need to recognise that many of the most important brand adverts occur in and around personal encounters. Think of it as live programming.

Planning to learn and improve, and ROI

8: Learning: Measure and learn

Loyalty is a discipline that depends on learning. Customers are always learning about the brand and steadily improving or rather increasing their expectations. In exchange, brands need to be continually learning about their customers and about what is working and not working and how to improve it. Measurement is one of the supports to this process.

Without measurement it is often difficult to tell what has been successful and what has not. On the face of it the following case shows a successful attraction of new clients: a great campaign probably leading to job promotion. However, on closer measurement, all was not quite what they had wanted.

Devaluing the brand while acquiring transactions

A major American bank launched a UK credit card offering 6 months' interest free credit on transfers from other credit cards or bank accounts. This produced substantial response from new customers. The acquisition mailing, with the offer printed boldly on the envelope, amounted to the first major touchpoint and a significant moment of truth for customers. How would they respond? What attitudes would this engender?

Research suggests that although the offer was extremely attractive and generated a large response in terms of new customers, most of them were attracted to the idea of interest free credit for 6 months. The customers most interested in this were those with financial needs. They were potentially interesting customers in that they had large debts, but this also carries the risk of default. Other interested customers included those who were flexible and sophisticated and capable of switching from one best account to another. This was such a brilliant offer; it was worth borrowing money from elsewhere, transferring the debt to this account and using the short-term cash for other purposes. Thus, the attitudinal set that was created was not to do with building loyalty but to exploit a short-term offer.

The bank's objective was to generate a high volume of customers who would remain loyal primarily through inertia. Unfortunately, the very customers who did transfer were exactly those least influenced by inertia.

It is often worth asking existing customers by the way of surveys, as shown in the Nat West Groups pre-tax profits below, as *long as one acts upon the answers!*

National Westminster customer satisfaction surveys

National Westminster carries out customer satisfaction surveys, and has employed 'mystery shoppers' to find out how National Westminster's customers are treated. Up to 120,000 customers are surveyed every month, and a high proportion of them have said they were satisfied with the service they received from their branch. The mystery shoppers visited each branch every quarter up to 1998. The programme was very successful and led to significant improvements in levels of customer satisfaction. National Westminster Group member Coutts introduced customer satisfaction surveys in 1995, and as a result made 252 service improvements. National Westminster Group's pre-tax profits rose 120% from 1997 to 1998.

Measurement for all marketing campaigns should be designed upfront and then progressively improved. Ideally, the learning should address these three levels:

1. What did we actually do and what were the results?

2. How did everybody feel about this; was it a quality experience?

3. What have we learnt, how do we think and plan differently now?

It's a case of wanting to go from doing things better to doing better things.

This suggests that in addition to formal quantitative measurement methodologies, organisations also need to develop social skills in learning together, often called action-learning techniques. The marketing team needs to be able to discuss how things were done and consider alternatives, all as part of an ongoing creative conversation.

Technology strategies for customer relationship management

9: Technology: Use technology like an artist

If you want to achieve customer loyalty, it is important to use technology like an artist: creatively and to help with communicating ideas and experiences of value.

Technology is often the vital way to give customers a special experience. Whether this means ways of making life easier for the customer or communication that is more personalised, the loyalty marketer is smart in understanding how technology can help and in defining and implementing requirements.

The technology should be a means to:

- Understand which customers are more valuable.

- Ensure that the brand experience is consistent and brand true.

- Collect information that enables you to identify different kinds of customers and then treat them differently.

- Deliver personalised value that creates loyalty.

- Manage each moment of truth with the highest quality.

- Implement with imagination, ie practice what you *want* to do rather than what you *can* do.

- Collect the information that is needed for measurement and then put it through processes that deliver easily and quickly the learning that is required.

Technology can support loyalty by working with the 3 bonds we discussed earlier, financial, social and structural bonds, add value to the whole loyalty process.

Technology for financial, social and structural bonds

Financial bonds: Technology is used to support many loyalty programmes that provide customers with points or equivalent. It is the technology that recognises the customer transactions, records the points and is used to drive communications and awards programmes to the customer.

Social bonds: Can be used to enable people to recognise who the customer is and information about the past business relationship. For example, it enables British Airways to recognise its frequent flyers and greet them by name. Websites use technology in order to recognise returning customers and give them tailored services.

Technology can also be used to provide personalised communication, for example in direct mail or over the phone. All of these are ways of creating social bonding.

Structural bonds: Technology is also frequently used in creating structural bonding. For example, automatic services that are based on knowledge about the customer and recognition of their needs. For instance, Amazon will advise customers about their friends' and families' birthdays (once the customer has recorded that information) and Olympus will restock a hospital's reagent supply.

Cloverleaf

In addition to financial, social and structural bonding, technology can also be used to add value to the customer through the cloverleaf model. Here we said that customer value and touchpoints can be identified in terms of knowledge, customer activity, tangibles (including functional performance) and relationships. The Bernard Matthews case history below illustrates this.

Case study: Bernard Matthews: a prime example of the cloverleaf value model

As long ago as 1984, Bernard Matthews, the UK's No.1 supplier of turkeys, installed one of the first CRM systems in the UK. At the heart of the integrated business management system was a telemarketing and order processing system to be operated by its call centre, in order to enable tele-agents to contact supermarket operators across the country. The system helped in these ways:

- *To provide knowledge about customers and aid them with recommendations. Each morning, every agent received a call list generated by a diary system. The agent would call the supermarket manager at a preferred time and the system would provide summary purchase history. In effect, there was an electronic order form with purchase history reference guides. The system also recommended new and promotional products.*

- *To make ordering easier and more accurate for the supermarket customers. The tele-agent could speak to the supermarket operator or designated buyer and check whether they wished to take the same order as usual or a different one. This service maintained the flow of orders, facilitated regular and continuous contact and provided a high level of service.*

- *Enhanced personal relationship. People were fully taken into account during planning and implementation and this helped to create staff motivation and better service. For example, there was careful consultation with the call centre staff about how the system needed to work in order to be effective from the customer point of view, while providing a good operational experience for the staff. The system then organised the same people to call the same customers automatically. Behind the concept was the recognition that each phone call represented a key moment of truth in the relationship, that the mere act of making a regular phone call in this way was value-generating for the relationship as well as for Bernard Matthews and the relevant supermarket. One of the reasons for focusing on the quality of experience for the call centre staff was to ensure that each phone conversation could become an effective performance, an effective delivery of a brand message tailored precisely and individually. The database including key data about the contact existed to improve the quality of the social interaction.*

- *And of course provided the customers with stock on time. Although there was a standard set of products, the service was based on a pure one-to-one relationship, down to the individual store wherever appropriate. There was a total focus on a streamlined set of value-adding processes that integrated every value step from customer contact to delivery, including manufacturing and warehouse operations. These were designed to reduce costs and hassle, as well as improve serviceability to the customer.*

Technology should enable the whole organisation to interact in real time. Allowing communication to flow through easily and hold the customer 'front of mind' the entire time.

Stakeholder strategies and internal marketing

10 stakeholders: Make it good for everyone

The process of creating loyalty in customers depends also on creating loyalty in employees. Not only that, but it also requires loyal shareholders and managers.

1.   When it is good for the customer, it will create appreciation, trust and encourage the need for further purchasers.

2.   When it is good for the employee, it will also create appreciation and trust as well as motivation to continue.

3.   When it is good for the company, it will create brand equity, mileage equity and financial equity.

There is either a vicious or a virtuous circle involved in these three sets of partners or stakeholders. For example, shareholders invest in creating value. This helps employees to do a better job and feel better about what they are doing. This in turn translates into better experiences for customers who reward employees with their positive attitudes and shareholders with their profits.

Focus on your team

Wise marketing managers who want to create customer loyalty also focus on their teams as far as possible to ensure their motivation and morale are positive.

When employees who have a powerful bond of trust and expectation with customers leave, the brand bond is also disturbed.

Toyota dominance at home

Toyota remained the dominant player in Japan because of its strong dealer sales force. Because their salespeople stayed over 10 years on average they got to know customers well. This enduring bond gave them leadership over Honda. But in the US, where car salespeople turn over quickly (60% to 100% annually) and customers have no relationship with the sales force, Honda's product advantage was enough to give it driving leadership: the relationship: factor in the service product. (While the first step must be to retain employees, a database can at least help to retain information.)

When employees who interact with customers lose their loyalty and motivation, the brand bond is also disturbed.

Sears Canada

For example, a study of Sears Canada found that for every 5% increase in associate loyalty there was a 1% increase in customer loyalty, which in turn is associated with a 3.4% increase in earnings before interest and taxes.[1]

The four characteristics of great close-to-customers companies

The very best companies (at getting close to customers and earning their loyalty) demonstrate this principle through four outstanding characteristics, and will excel in at least one of them:

1.   A strong company-wide sense of purpose and alignment, with a widespread vigour to do something considered good and valuable and transforming for the world ...

2.   An employee friendly culture, valuing the dignity and worth and potential of all employees ...

3.   Good systems, processes that sweetly sing ...

4.   Integrated into *theatre*, a commitment and love of performance, beauty, passion, drama and quality in all its visible facets.

How to be a world-beater

- Identify the relative value of customers and use this to target investments appropriately.

- Understand the complete cycle of the customer relationship in order to manage points in that relationship that will significantly increase lifetime value.

- Ensure that everyone who is involved in customer contact is really clear about what the brand stands for and implements communications and solutions that are brand true.

- Tailor to the particular needs of different customer communities.

- Personalise imaginatively and creatively across the full spectrum of an individual customers touchpoints with the brand.

- Measure those results and learn from them and put that into even better practice on the next round.

- Use technology to make that all low cost and easy to implement.

- Ensure your organisation and policies mean that this is not only good for the customer but also good for the employee and management and shareholders.

[1] *A Great Place to Shop, Work and Invest*, Roy King, Melanie Gilbert, Jim Graham and Rick Brown, Published Employee Marketing/Organisational Studies, Inc, A Division of Carlson Marketing Group, 2000.

Chapter 6.3

Interactive and direct techniques for retaining customers

This chapter includes:

- ❏ **Acquire customers with a view to keeping them**
- ❏ **Develop the customer through service-driven up-selling, cross-selling and renewals**
- ❏ **Media neutral planning – the essential efficiency**
- ❏ **Showing you care – why it matters**
- ❏ **Service recovery and loyalty generation**
- ❏ **Dialogue marketing**
- ❏ **Loyalty clubs – making them work**
- ❏ **Be relevant: How it works better to be relevant**
- ❏ **Designing value that builds loyalty**

About this chapter

 n this chapter, we will be exploring a number of tools and techniques and ideas that can equip you to be more effective in managing customer relationships and earning their profitable loyalty. The topics that we will be covering include:

- Using the power of communication and language of loyalty.

- Up-selling, repeat selling, cross-selling, renewals.

- Showing you care.

- Designing loyalty-generating offers.

- Creating bonds and especially social bonds.

- Loyalty cards and clubs.

- Adding the surprise service factor.

- Member-get-member and viral marketing as loyalty strategies.

- Lapsed customer recovery.

- Dialogue marketing.

- Creativity and imagination.

- Media neutral planning.

- Using the phone, web, mail, people for high touch personalised interactions.

- E-marketing – eg viral marketing, permission marketing, e-mail, ezines, affiliate programmes

- Data mining, clustering and event triggers; retention/SOW etc. segmentation

- Automated programmes and event triggers.

Angus Jenkinson author and consultant

Angus' biography appears at the beginning of this section.

Chapter 6.3

Interactive and direct techniques for retaining customers

Introduction

esearch published in November 1996 by the Henley Centre suggests that poor customer service was costing companies hundreds of millions of pounds annually. The Henley study suggested that around 17% of a company's customers are affected each quarter by service deficiencies, including goods out of stock, disinterested and impolite staff, inefficient phone response, and poor quality information.

Nothing much has changed. The effect is cumulative: customers who have complaints are likely to spread the word to their family, friends and neighbours – the typical complainer tells up to nine other people about the experience, the opposite of Member Get Member – and unless determined efforts are made to improve service, customers who do not have an active complaint will stay away because of the company's negative reputation. According to the Henley Centre, two years of less than good service would reduce sales by a third. This is probably a conservative estimate. Poor reputation is likely to account for around 25% of the 'gap', sales lost from customers who have previously defected for 33%, and sales lost because of poor service in the current three-month period for the remaining 42%. Thus, there is a lasting legacy from poor service.

Lost sales generally have disproportionately severe effects on profits, and while it is not possible to make a realistic universal estimate, it is clear that companies cannot afford to ignore issues of customer satisfaction, and that they should take satisfaction a stage further to encourage loyalty.

Acquire customers with a view to keeping them

In acquisition you can't simply look at response rates and cost per new customer; you need to consider customer equity. Direct marketing acquisition should be a brand-building exercise by investing in customer attitudes alongside a sale. Many direct marketers have ignored brands, and many brands measure acquisition costs without looking at the full value of a customer. Which means they end up (cheaply) acquiring less valuable customers as OgilvyOne director Guy Stevenson comments:

> Coax, bribe or cajole an individual into purchasing a product or service that's irrelevant or inappropriate to their needs, and chances are they're not going to turn into one of your most valuable customers ...

An acquisition programme for American Express Canada that targeted affluent business travellers (ABTs) with a charge card offer confirmed this lesson. The strategy was to develop a customised ABT package that addressed the specific needs of frequent business travellers and test it against the broad scale control pack. Additionally, a series of offers were tested within the ABT direct mail pack. As the chart shows, the upfront response rates and the net present value calculations 12 months down the line are diametrically opposed. The best solution actually has the lowest initial response.

Table 6.3.1

Creative/offer test	Response rate	Cost per card	Net present value at 12 months
Broad based control	100	100	100
ABT creative with 5000 point bonus	103	98	211
ABT creative with 400 points/month offer	99	108	306
ABT creative	77	121	568

Take, for example, Cantel AT&T – Canada's largest mobile phone network. In the first 3 quarters of 1998, the acquisition team acquired 340,700 customers at an average cost approaching $400 each. Not bad. At the same time, however, 259,600 customers walked out the door. Research revealed that over two-thirds of defectors left because of lack of perceived need for the service. They'd signed up in the first place because of a free phone offer, low monthly service fees, and free air time in the evenings and weekends.

Unfortunately, very few of these customers stuck around for long enough to pay back the cost of acquiring them. A 'one size fits all' approach was applied to closing the acquisition gap.

The best direct marketers have always believed in direct marketing as a brand building discipline. For example, David Ogilvy, who founded one of the world's leading direct marketing agencies, saw no difference in the cultivation of the brand between the two disciplines and media that they used. Indeed, some of his most memorable direct marketing campaigns involved brand building. He described direct mail as his first love and a remarkably effective 'secret weapon'.

Ogilvy tells the story that when he was just a young office boy, a man who had bought a country house, walked into a London agency with $500 and wanted to open the house as a hotel.

The homeowner wanted to see the agency boss and find out if the agency could help him to get customers. The head of the agency turned the project over to David – who promptly invested his client's money in penny postcards and mailed them to well healed people living in the hotelier's neighbourhood. Six weeks later the hotel opened to a full house and David Ogilvy knew he was on to something.

The postcard campaign above had done more than generate sales: it had promoted the brand.

Years later, over 150 million letters were sent out to potential American Express card members with the opening line, "Quite frankly the American Express is not for everyone." This memorable sentence, possibly the most widely used in direct marketing, was significant in its day, not only as a powerful attention getter but also as an evocation of the essence of the American Express brand.

This is a clear demonstration that direct marketing can also be extremely creative and employ a huge variety of methods in the process of building brand image.

David Ogilvy quotes a further example of the time when prospects for a new Cessna Citation business jet were sent live carrier pigeons with an invitation to take a free ride in a Citation. Recipients of this rather unusual piece of 'direct mail' were asked to release the carrier pigeon with the recipient's address tied to its leg. At least one Citation was sold, for $600,000, from the returning pigeons. Frankly, if direct marketing is not building the brand it is probably destroying it.

All too often, when we look at the history of direct marketing, it is sadly clear that many pieces of work have actually been counter-productive in terms of brand building. While they may have generated responses, the means used were very unlikely to have actually encouraged the brand values that the brand owner wanted to promote. Nor did they optimise sales.

Gimmicks and offers such as prize draws may generate response, but do they inculcate the values of the brand? Thousands of marketers have been told something like: let's introduce a prize draw, it will increase response by 30% or more, and this may well have happened. But what it has meant is that instead of receiving a response of say 2%, there has been a response of 2.6%. Meanwhile 95% of the recipients wondered what a prize draw had to do with this brand.

The point is, direct marketing can be extraordinarily powerful in its impact, especially when we bear in mind the wide range of media that are involved – which include mail, phone, face to face contact, the web and so on. All contacts with customers affect the brand – making it important to ensure that this powerful medium and discipline is used to the best effect.

Develop the customer through service-driven up-selling, repeat selling, cross-selling and renewals

As we noted in the previous chapter, a vital part of good relationship marketing is strategic step number 2: Optimise the whole customer relationship

The cycle of relationship development outlined in the previous chapter shows how the relationship with the customer develops. Once someone has become a customer there is then a continuing process of managing the relationship in order to convert customers into repeat customers. This is the realm of *service* – service being defined as the creation of relationship value between two parties. Service can be used to create cross-sell, up-sell and repeat sell opportunities, as well as to trigger customer attitudes that build bonded loyalty.

When you first enter a restaurant and the waiter comes and asks you promptly what you would like to drink, that is an act of service that is usually appreciated. If you are left sitting in the chair for ten minutes with no attention, this can be a major demotivator and discouragement to ever returning to the restaurant. Not only that, but from a restaurant's point of view it is likely to add up to a significant loss of income during that period when you might be buying drinks.

This simple illustration applies to the whole of the customer relationship. Indeed the metaphor of a waiter is an extremely good one for understanding the relationship. A good waiter is prompt and alert and attentive without in the least bit being pushy, obtrusive or a salesperson. The waiter is there to guide and advise guests in the best way to get the most out of the restaurant experience, taking into account the guests' preferences and experience of the restaurant.

Customers who have bought multiple products, or who have multiple accounts are more likely to be loyal, so good cross-selling, up-selling and repeat selling are ways to build loyalty. Loyalty and sales development should go arm in arm. It is only greedy and bad practice where this is not so.

So what can you do?

- Identify the right time to remind the customer to buy again.

- Identify the single most valuable additional product for the customer and make a brand-enhancing offer.

- Identify the single most valuable improvement to or enhancement of the product/service for the customer and make a brand-enhancing offer.

- Share information across your group: who has the best solution? Introduce the customer or the service/product.

- Use community filtering to identify what the customer would like, as Amazon does, and offer it (what others in that community of interest are buying and rating).

- Show them how others have benefited from these, eg by case histories or M-G-M.

- Make a great offer with a deadline that makes sense.

- Phone, visit or (e)mail the customer to find out how things are. Solve any problems/needs with a solution.

- Design automated systems to renew, eg by direct debit or computerisation of replenishment.

- Make the work of buying as easy as possible: research the right solution, present it and fill in the details for a single signature (eg a good way to sell a credit card). Make sure you invest in good enough data to make this possible.

Have you noticed anything about these? They are all services when done well.

Media neutral planning – the essential efficiency

Media neutral planning is a customer-centric, inclusive and merit based review of media options during marketing communications planning.

Don't get stuck in a media rut. Take a wide-media approach to communication planning, acknowledging the full spectrum of possibility, from face-to-face and viral marketing to product placement and TV, focusing on media in combinations rather than singly. Remember that all media can achieve any objective but with varying strengths and weaknesses moderated by customer preferences, business objectives and market context.

Yet the evidence is that one problem is the single major barrier to the effectiveness of communication spend by large brands. In today's competitive marketplace, when it is more important than ever to select the optimum mix of media, this is rarely achieved. The problem is bias and habit.

Adopting media neutral planning (MNP) is potentially the single most important opportunity for larger brands. The benefits that would arise for those who best make intelligent changes could turn market leaders into followers and followers into leaders.

As the name implies MNP is a specialist cross-functional discipline driven by research, analysis and insight, not by biased habit and preference.

Past	MNP future
Single flavours	Cocktails
Prejudices	Creative openness
Divided skills	Inclusive skills
The answer is preordained	The answer is creatively or systematically discovered

Some of the lessons of MNP include gains to be had from focus and synergies, for example:

- Some media communicate better to some consumers.

- Some customers are worth significantly more than others and therefore need more intensive treatment, while many consumers have no financial value.

- Customers need different messages at different times and this needs diverse messaging and media.

- Some media are more effective at specific times or for specific objectives (sell the car on TV and the deal in the mail).

- Repetition becomes boring, so variety gives advantage. As media strategist Erwin Ephron put it: "Just as a second beer never tastes as good, a second dollar (in the same medium) never buys as much response. That's why the idea of mixing media has always been attractive. It's in the physics of a flattening sales-response curve."[1]

- Finally, research shows that harmonised, mixed exposures seem to have a greater summed effect, the so-called *media multiplier effect*. Meeting the brand in two places is more powerful than meeting in the same place twice.

Consumers have holistic minds, different sized wallets and varying propensities to spend on the brand. They do not conveniently decide that they will receive all their brand impressions from 30-second TV commercials (or mail or web or whatever is your medium of choice). Instead, as described above, they gather their impressions of brands from multiple encounters and snapshots, giving different weight at different times and to different sources. MNP models and plans around this fact.

Media neutral planning is therefore the way to better performance and the only way to make integration work.

Segmenting customers and modelling products

16% of the British population positively dislike the phone. Another 22% prefer suppliers not to use it and 15% will use it only grudgingly. So one way to segment relationships is by attitude to the phone.

Using customer attitudes to the relative importance of the service product elements (based on a trade off matrix) can cluster customers. One questionnaire could both cluster the customers and identify the changes needed to the product.

Be consistent across media and channels and campaigns

Communications theory long ago proved that consistency was key to developing brand loyalty.

A few years ago, some research was done with rats. The rats were put in a cage and given a feeding source. When they went to the feeding source, sometimes they got food and other times they got an electric shock. The two different types of outcome happened at random. Other rats were put in cages where they always got electric shocks. They very rapidly stopped going to the feeding source. A third group were put in cages where they always got food. They learned to go to the feeding source when they were hungry. The rats that were in the random cage ended up going mad, simply curling up in a corner in a neurotic breakdown.

This is obviously a cruel experiment and one that hopefully will not be repeated. Its message however, could be adapted – don't give inconsistent messages to customers.

Brands that give one message at the point of sale and another in service delivery, or one message on TV and another in direct mail, or differentiate between website and call centre, end up confusing customers and damaging the brand.

Case example: Neiman Marcus online

When you provide a service to high value customers as Neiman Marcus does, you need to provide special products and special service ambience. What happens to that when you go online?

Neiman Marcus hopes to build a strong Internet presence with technology that is as fashionable as the $1,000-plus articles of clothing it peddles. The New York retailer is following up a $24 million website investment with new multimedia applications that promise to make the online shopping experience more realistic.

Rather than rely on promotions like most retailers, Neiman Marcus sells goods at full price, whether through the web, in conventional stores or at Bergdorf Goodman, the company's two-store chain in New York. Most of the clothing, jewellery, shoes and other accessories sell to consumers with incomes of more than $100,000.

The challenge for Neiman Marcus was to extend that merchandising success online. Neiman Marcus was the first website to use RichFX Environments, which features a streaming 3-D shopping interface to display Neiman Marcus's line of Manolo Blahnik shoes. The software enabled Neiman Marcus to provide an interactive 'boutique,' where shoppers look at shoe displays almost as if they're strolling into a store on Fifth Avenue.

Showing you care – why it matters

You can't buy loyalty. Not even with points! Sometimes you can't even explain it. There are wives who are loyal to the most outrageously behaved husbands, and husbands to disagreeable wives. Likewise, some consumers will put up with bad service. But these are exceptions. The trend, confirmed by research in almost every category, and almost everywhere on the globe, is that customer expectations of care and service are increasing. Which is why marketing during this millennium with any degree of optimism means absorbing and applying some basic home truths:

1. Service is *the interactive component between supplier and customer that creates relationship value*. Service is therefore to customer loyalty as the goose to the golden egg. But that means optimally designing the service package or bonds, the key moments of truth and the ongoing interactive dialogues that form the relationship.

2. Service is always taken personally, as is lack of service. "He was helpful … to **me**". "Afterwards, they cleaned up … **my** office". Feeling recognised and valued is the basis of the social bond that is at the heart of committed loyalty and all good one to one marketing. It is the emotional tie that leads people to say, "That's *my* brand". Hence, all one to one dialogue must also have a social bridge, the imaginative foundation which is the basis for why the customer would want to hear from you at all. So service design should account for the uniqueness of customers and the communities they form to create relevance.

3. You have to **feel real** to customers. They are expert at observing the body language of the brand and they trust its truth more than words in adland. Up to 85% of consumer disaffection has been linked to the gap between promise and reality. You create trust by *guaranteeing* promises and responding to anything that goes wrong.

Finally, pleasure counts. Great moments are memorable. They create collateral and bring the relationship to life. When you bore people, it rarely makes them love you.

Rescuing customers from problems is a powerful way to create loyalty

Procrit, a drug to help cancer sufferers recover from chemotherapy, intercepts worried new patients online at a critical moment of truth: when they go searching the Internet for information. The trigger is the news that you've been diagnosed with cancer, followed by going online to the web to see what you can find. A Procrit banner responds to the search and takes you to an informational site that links to the Procrit home page, to find out how to make the process less unpleasant.

Loyalty cards are just a way to recognise customers

The purpose of a loyalty card is to show the customer that he or she matters to you, so you want to know who they are and do something meaningful with the information. Anything else is a waste of money.

Only what has value has value

Only that part of the goods and services you provide that has value to the customer has value. For example, if you sell a lawnmower that is capable of dealing with rough terrain, this is of no value to a customer who has a flat lawn. So if you say to them, "We sell a lawnmower that will cut on a rough lawn", their response is likely to be, "Why would I want that?"

This is an old point, but let us examine its significance.

1. **Communicate what has genuine value.** Avoid cluttering up the communication with anything else. This is one of the reasons why understanding different types of customer is important. Their needs create different expectations and wants. A good salesperson will always spend time trying to understand a customer's real needs before proposing a solution.

2. **Add more value.** When a customer buys a television they are not buying it solely for the obvious things that a television can do for them. Everything that the customer buys has a service value. Clearly the television can provide a stream of entertainment in the form of images and sound. But it can also contribute as a piece of furniture in the home or function as a status symbol.

Garden centres sell more than just plants.

A garden centre is selling:

- A lifestyle

- An aspiration for a better life

- A bit of the country

- Freedom

- Good times, fun

- Escape from stress

- Health

- Fulfilment

- A family haven

3. **Products and services communicate.** As we have seen they communicate speed, style, reliability, status, comfort and so on. The job of advertising is to emphasise and enhance that communication. The VW Passat was redesigned in the late 1990s in order to recapture a declining interest amongst its target market – and won a design award in the process. Ford created the Ka with the specific brief of reaching a group of customers previously disinterested in cars. And on a more mundane level, the heft and balance of a good hammer communicates its workmanship.

get into the ka

bold, elegant and highly individual. Ka is the perfect example of a simple thing done well

When Costa Coffee approached the agency Mother and asked it to develop a campaign to build the brand, the agency decided that it would be insufficient just to develop ads and commercials. What was necessary was to redesign in-store, including the in-store literature. They used the walls of the store and service frontage as communication media. This tactic generated a 9-point increase in customers who said that Costa Coffee made the best coffee, and a higher prompted awareness than Starbucks. This example shows how product and communication can seamlessly blend.

5. Finally, communication is also part of the value package. Communication adds value, is of no value, or is a nuisance. When communication is of value it builds the brand and potentially generates sales. In other cases it is either neutral or negative. Research shows that customers fail to repeat purchase because they see no 'brand reason', nor do they feel the brand takes any interest in them.

An example is the American Express monthly statement and annual summary. The statement has been designed to give clear information about transactions, as well as supplementary information about current offers. In practice, various stores, restaurants and travel companies provide a range of offers to the American Express cardmember base. These offers are selected and shown on individual statements, according to the buying habits and apparent interests of the card members.

As part of the American Express service, members get a summary of all their annual transactions broken down into different categories of expenditure. Finally, there is an option of hassle-free bill paying, using the card to automatically pay by direct debit. The question is: whose responsibility is it to design such communication and service opportunities – product development or marketing? When you buy a Lexus or a Harley Davidson the 'relationship package' isn't a frill or added extra, its part of the product. How much use you make of it depends on its relevance to you, ie *its value as a service.*

In summary, what we can say is that value *is* service, and that both product and communication elements can contribute to it. From the customers' point of view the offer is an holistic experience, and they assess this in terms of elements that are positive, negative or neutral. Obviously some elements have more importance than others, and this will vary from person to person and from group to group.

It is only the service element that is of value. It is the service value that creates loyalty. Everything can be represented in terms of high or low service value.

Creativity and imagination

Listening is not enough. Imagination and empathy is what makes your culture of care possible. Its effects apply to both customers and employees. While imagination creates large returns for small costs, brands without imagination are in trouble. They become soulless commodities that generate apathy and price fixation.

Take Novartis. Research among their US Estraderm customer community found that these menopausal women taking oestrogen replacement therapy often felt isolated. They also didn't like some of the normal side effects and thought something must be wrong. Empathising with this knowledge formed the foundation for a more intimate relationship. After *Women's Health Exchange* was created for them, 97% of members said they found it helpful during a turbulent time in their lives. It led to a 25% increase in ongoing active use of Estraderm. Why? Because *Women's Health Exchange* wrapped Estraderm in soul, the soul of the brand.

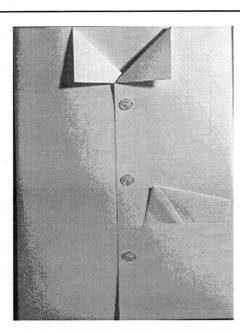

Lufthansa found a way to get through to a key community of senior people in the fashion industry. Following Goethe's advice (be bold and the universe will flow to you) their mail pack looked like a tailored wing collar shirt with the Lufthansa label stitched in and a reply device slipped into the pocket. Five contracts worth around $1 million each followed. Creative acquisition messages instantly establish an altogether different social bond compared with the tired formula of a discount.

Recovery is the priceless opportunity

Of all the events in the ongoing relationship, one is decisive: the customer crisis. At that moment, the brand is under the emotional searchlight. The gap between a positive and negative experience of the brand cannot be larger.

Problems make people vulnerable and therefore perhaps angry. Unless something decisive and effective is done to rescue the situation, the relationship may well be lost.

Yet we have also found that effective and caring rescue is a moment that customers treasure. Research shows that these occasions are highly significant in future loyalty. It therefore makes great sense to put the key potential moments of crisis in a customer's life under the same kind of searchlight as they will, but in advance. In this way crises may be anticipated and prevented, or ways can be found to respond more effectively, for example by training call centre agents.

It is also important to ensure that in the event of a problem, the brand gets a chance to respond. Most crises never get reported to the brand, only to friends. A concrete guarantee, such as those offered by the insurance and vaccine brands, makes the brand a friend too and helps to ensure that customers contact you first when they need help, instead of complaining to the world.

The crisis doesn't have to be with the brand, because of something the brand has done wrong. It may just be helping the consumer or business through a problem, like the accident care of the insurance company or Estraderm's *Women's Exchange* programme. Such contributions demonstrate care and win friends.

Integrate prevention and recovery routines

Some of the most successful brands have developed ways to integrate prevention and recovery by including interactive routines that check out customer priorities and attitudes. Manpower built a great business in calling every customer on the first day of a new temporary employee placement to ask how he was doing. That's now the benchmark for the industry. This technique meant that they found out about their service, the person they had, and any problems early and could fix it (with the help of their guarantee).

The firm *ServiceMaster* exploits this principle in the way that it sets up new contracts for domestic cleaning. When they first visit a household they take details of the kind of cleaning services that are required. They carefully note what appear to be the 'hot points', ie important places around the house that the customer really wants cleaned or tidied; for example, a picture of a loved one that should have the glass cleaned. The cleaning team are given a list of these hot points and these are attended to first and checked last before the team leaves the property. The thinking behind this behaviour is that when the customer goes back, they will check these hot points first and most importantly. If they are well done, then the chances are that the customer will assume that other places have been done well also. (Obviously it is important also to do the rest of the house to a good standard!)

Customers are encouraged to phone up and complain if there is anything they are not satisfied with. Any complaints then go into the hot points list. This means that the team is always paying attention to what matters most to the customer. Thus, the customer is most likely to form a positive image of the *whole* of the job.

Showing appreciation can richly reward both parties

Air France recognises that past experiences of the brand create the gestalt that filters all future experience. Building on this marketing wisdom, they try to show signs of appreciation to frequent flyers with unconditional gifts that create positive experiences. For example, in one campaign, a small white box was sent to regular customers with a video copy of Cocteau's masterpiece *la Belle et la Bête* timed to coincide with the premier of Disney's animated Beauty and the Beast. Not only do such gifts help to make the relationship tangible, they help to bring Air France to front of mind on the next international flight.

Member-get-member (M-G-M) and viral marketing as loyalty strategies

Felix is just one of many brands that have used viral marketing to great success. Viral marketing is the creation of an Internet/e-mail communication that subtly emphasises the brand, often amusingly, and encourages consumers (B2B and B2C) to pass them on by e-mail. Felix created a cute cat that dances around the desktop and plays with objects it finds. It travelled to hundreds of thousands of computers after being distributed around the agency (OgilvyOne).

M-G-M is the old direct marketing tool from which this idea came. For example, I first got an American Express card nearly twenty years ago when my boss got a small crate of champagne for signing up three members. It was a great Amex investment.

Service recovery as a loyalty generation

The average company will lose 10% to 30% of it customers each year, mostly through bad service. Yet, companies can boost profits by 20% to 100% by retaining just 5% more of their customers from one year to the next. One study showed a 25% profit improvement in credit insurance and 85% in bank branch deposits.

What do you do when things go wrong?

While we all know that consistency and completeness of the brand experience creates loyalty, and so try to ensure that each and every moment of truth is brand-true and worthy, 'things can go wrong'.

Air France demonstrated with their Frequence Plus customers the six steps that manage such a crisis, keep friends and even build strong social bonds. An all out strike had delayed cabin renovations (as well as damaging schedules). Customers were paying for upgrades they were simply not getting.

Air France (1) took the first bold and involving step when they acted promptly and proactively to break the silence with a letter from the CEO, (2) apologising and explaining what had happened as well as (3) their future plans. Then they (4) made a personal call to each customer (5) responding sympathetically to the inconvenience and (6) offering individual, symbolic atonement (like Air Miles, upgrades or free tickets).

While most financial organisations have a complaints procedure, it can be intimidating for a customer to feel he is one against a whole company. The Halifax's complaints procedure is a good example of what to do. Customers are given a leaflet called *A Problem? We Can Help*, which sets out, in clear language, the steps to take. If credit is refused, customers are told they can appeal, and how to do so. The leaflet's style is reassuring, and indicates the society's commitment to customer service.

Several organisations send questionnaires to customers, to assess satisfaction levels. The Halifax compiles customer opinion surveys by phone, normally quarterly, to help formulate business strategy. Lloyds Bank's customer service department is another with a regular survey programme.

TARP discovered that in two of every three cases in which the customer had a complaint about a product, the problem had nothing to do with the product itself. The problem was caused by the user not understanding how to use the product for the purpose it was designed to serve. Here is an example of how database marketing can serve, overcome problems, and possibly build opportunities for further sales. Why not call to check, or at least make it easy for customers to call you?

It can also help to identify real needs of customers. We expect the supplier to be an expert in his products and to be able to bring that expertise to bear to anticipate and remove problems in advance. But, many organisations labour under assumptions about what is critical to customers, which prove quite wrong. An Austrian shirt manufacturer discovered that their retail customers' priorities were finish, delivery and image, not full order fulfilment, flexibility and meeting the specification, as they thought. Some hospitals in Britain's National Health Service have been accused of failing to take the customer seriously. Doctors thought that the clinical quality of their work was all that mattered, while patients worried about delays, beds, comfort, food and privacy.

Proactive service recovery means making use of information about problems in order to enhance the service and communication provided to customers. The diagram, below indicates how to do this.

Figure 6.3.1

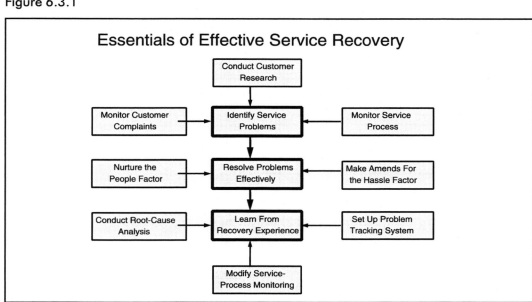

As the diagram shows, at the heart of service recovery is the ability to identify problems – which usually entails a process of customer research. Here guarantees can be a big help in getting customers to talk.

Create a strong guarantee

Follow the example of "Bugs" Burger Bug Killers (BBBK), a Miami based pest - extermination company owned by SC Johnson & Co which built its business around cast iron, 100% commitments to its hotel and restaurant customers. Most BBBK competitors claim to reduce pests to 'acceptable' levels. BBBK promises elimination!

"You don't owe a penny until all the pests on your premises have been eradicated. If you are ever dissatisfied with BBBK's service you will receive a refund for up to 12 month's services, plus fees for another exterminator of your choice for the next year. If a guest spots a pest on your premises, BBBK will pay for the guest's meal or room, send a letter of apology and pay for a future meal or stay. If your facility is closed due to pests, BBBK will pay any fines, as well as all lost profits, plus $5000". (It's worth reading twice.)

This is great direct mail copy, a business philosophy and commitment to customers, product description, corporate strategy, operational goals and definitions for processes all wrapped up in one. Such a guarantee builds trust and keeps the supplier front of mind. It's a perfect illustration of the direct marketing philosophy and the result is that BBBK charges 100% more than rivals, is closer to its community (it's a regional player) and has disproportionate market share. Given end-to-end commitment and processes designed to match, it ends up paying out under 0.4% of turnover.

A guarantee is a direct marketing device that is targeted, communicates and invites response. Link it to a database and you have great analytical and targeting power, eg for follow up. When The Firework Company got its delivery wrong to one large customer, it called back the next year immediately after delivery to check whether everything was right (after having double-checked anyway before delivery).

A good guarantee

- Promises what customers want: relevancy

- Doesn't conceal conditions: it achieves simplicity and clarity

- Makes tailored, meaningful offers; not mild or insulting ones

- Doesn't make itself risk free: or a joke to everyone

- Creates easy response methods, easy to invoke without guilt

- Measures long term effects: lifetime value

Dialogue marketing

Automated programmes and event triggers

CRM systems can provide a **complete** contact management system. This can take into account multiple contacts by multiple business functions such as sales, research, customer service and accounts. It also enables data-driven activity with triggers and diary joggers, so that personalised contact management can be attained. These can be used to create more relevant and timely communication. Most brands are pretty hopeless at using the potential of this technology.

The marketing database should be a central resource to help with the planning of sales force activities, whether or not there is also a specialised sales force or contact management system. For example, it can be used to help with lead generation and lead management, as well as applications such as territory allocation.

First Direct are highly rated by customers. In addition to being the first British bank serious about remote banking, they achieved technical leadership with implementation of an event management or event trigger system. This enabled them to predefine a series of possible customer events and to program a desired response.

An **Event Trigger** is defined by OgilvyOne as: "The configuration of a system to recognise particular customers and their relationship at a moment of truth, and thereby stimulate an appropriate action according to a predetermined and evolving policy."

Marketing management define 'rules' and customers are subsequently selected by the CRM/database system for communication, promotion or service based on their event or behaviour history. For example, depending on a customer's status and the last or current event, or the last series of events and their timing, a customer could get no action, a personal letter or a call.

Like telemarketing scripting and sales contact management systems, these functions in a marketing database therefore enable the computer to be programmed to action reminders or communications based on project rules. Marketing, sales and service people can work out how they want the business to respond to different customer scenarios. This enables marketers to think through corporate policies for service and communication, without ruling out initiative and ad hoc activity. What do they want to have happen, when and under what circumstances, to whom?

KLM's European Customer Support Centre in Amsterdam has been providing Europe wide 24-hour phone service cover since the mid 90s now supplemented by the web. Phone systems are linked to the computer to capture performance data and improve service. Every type of call is coded and according to the call, a personalised response is triggered. This response can be built out of a menu of text components with personalised insertions. Further calls may also be triggered.

The danger, of course, is that just like the dangers of over-automating service or Tele-service, so marketers may rush like lemmings into turning their companies into machines.

Boring automation can seriously damage your wealth.

Such **event triggers** are based on 3 ideas:

1. The recency/frequency/value behaviour thinking which has driven mail order for decades: *Who should we be communicating with?*

2. The moment of truth concept: *When should we communicate?*

3. Contact management techniques developed for sales force management systems and telemarketing scripting, with emphasis on process management: *What should we communicate?*

American Express, using the monthly statement cycle, respond to each individual customer's profile over the last month and generate, using their Relationship Billing facility, a unique statement with a range of offers. The offers are provided jointly with their service establishment base and target individuals based on types of activity, location, usage of card in specific establishments and desired changes.

All sophisticated continuity mail-order companies have developed sophisticated, statistically driven, systems based on **scorecards** to drive a programme of communications to customers designed to maximise retention. Scorecards are statistical models that predict the likelihood of a particular customer reaction and therefore determine contact action. Time Life developed such a scoring system for its worldwide operations in the 1980s, as did Reader's Digest.

Use these enormously powerful tools to specify, trigger and control corporate actions responsibly and wisely. (It is said that to err is human, but to muck it up completely takes a computer.)

E-marketing for loyalty

Websites need to provide value to their customers to be successful. According to Jupiter Communications, 71% of online ad revenue is concentrated within the top 15 websites. This means that the destination site that makes its money out of advertising revenue is effectively dead as a marketing model, except for the super portals. As George Wiedemann describes it, "Marketers must customise and deliver the company's website to its customers, not the other way around"[2].

The Henley Centre's finding that people are visiting an average of two sites per day, spending around 15 minutes on each, indicates that users are giving their chosen sites the kind of attention that companies crave. But the report draws the conclusion that, for business sites to be the subject of this attention, companies need to understand what drives consumers' differing needs–as people–and how this translates into buying preferences. The mistake is to address them as consumers first, rather than individuals with individual interests.

George Wiedemann makes the point as follows: It is no longer 'Hey, please come see me! I think I have some items that you may be interested in.' It is, 'Please take a look at these items that I have selected especially for you because I know they suit your tastes and needs'.

Take Flukx.com, an online store offering *objets d'art* and contemporary furniture and home products. It was because of the type of goods he was selling that entrepreneur, Mark Britton, was keen to get a really smart web presence: "The customers I wanted to attract are discerning and I wanted to give them the site they'd expect."

His award-winning site works because it includes:

A contemporary, clean, elegant design, with sidebars that follow through the pages and provide clearly labelled categories

Small images that enable quick scroll through

Enough text to gain your interest

Clear pricing

Simple click through to shopping basket

That also means that the quality of information about the customer needs to be richer than simply an analysis of site traffic movement. As the Henley Centre points out, the 1st Internet age's preoccupation with the web as a data-collecting tool is losing its appeal. Downloading weekly site logs does not provide practically useful knowledge about people's behaviour or likelihood to purchase – indeed, such data may only be relevant to the computer used, not its users.

The frequently used solution of making registration a condition of access is emerging as not only ineffective, but often damaging. The Henley Centre reports that requesting information has put 41% of Internet users off registering with sites.

Instead, websites need to be based on quality information about customers and their needs and wants, just as good marketing has always done. Most leading thinkers suggest that success on the web depends on a more relational approach to marketing, an approach that is fundamental to retention. This is sometimes called permission marketing.

According to Jerry Shereshewsky, permission marketing is based on six key assumptions[3]:

1. The more you know about the prospect the greater the likelihood that you can find points of interconnectivity between your product/service and that prospect.

2. Prospects are loath to tell strangers too much about themselves.

3. Friends are willing to tell friends about themselves.

4. People prefer to buy things, especially expensive or risk laden things, from friends rather than strangers.

5. Friendship takes time to develop.

6. You cannot sell something to someone who does not want to be sold.

Porter suggests that the key to using the Internet effectively is integrating its position so that it complements – not cannibalises – established competitive approaches, and creates advantages that competitors cannot copy.

The Henley Centre is more specific: trust is a must. Trust is still a core driver toward consumers' willingness to engage in a commercial exchange with companies.

When an existing customer comes online, Amazon practices the direct marketing principle of recognising the customer by using a 'cookie' previously placed on their computer. As a result, Amazon personalises what the customer sees. For example, each customer will get tailored recommendations. These recommendations are generated using sophisticated statistical software that profiles the kinds of interests of each customer and also compares them with other customers, profiling them into similar groups. Each of the books and other products that Amazon carries also has category information about it, and of course there is the buying history of which customers are buying it. As a result, Amazon is more able to recommend books or other products that are likely to be relevant to that particular individual.

Here we can see in action how the website is designed as a sophisticated communication tool, that automates the process of creating value for the customer by recognising his interests.

It is an interactive, direct marketing tool that facilitates a stream of dialogue between the customer and the brand. As the customer buys or does not buy products, knowledge about the customer increases as does the ability to serve their interests and needs.

The Amazon Internet system can also provide other related services that complement this. For example, customers are able to register their interests, which are used in profiling, and can also register to receive information in the form of newsletters. On the Amazon.com site services provided include prompts and advice about birthday presents. This is an example of permission marketing. To add to customer involvement, there is a facility to set up information about yourself for others to read.

Amazon makes use of one of the characteristics of the web that is regarded as its particular strength. This is the ability to allow people to dialogue with each other. The way it does this is by allowing customers to review books and other products. Direct marketing has always aimed to involve the customer and this is a very powerful technique for doing so. Customers trust each other, often more than they trust what they know to be advertising material. So one of the functions on the website is a system to allow customers to record their reviews, which are then scored according to how much they are appreciated by other customers. Amazon, however, goes beyond providing this function; it adds a classic direct marketing technique of recognising and rewarding its best customers – those who provide many valued reviews. Readers can even review the reviewers and find out about their interests.

Amazon's offer of newsletters (e-zines) on various topics is another added value. (But note here how their solution is a series of silo communications rather than an integrated e-zine that carries 'my special interests', a perfectly doable proposition. Since they all come out on the same day this is not smart.)

The Amazon website is designed as a way of selling. Hence it is brilliant at the art of service. Amazon focused step-by-step on the whole process of selling to customers online, streamlining the process to make it as fast as possible while adding in as many hooks as it could to sell additional products in the process (for example, by telling you what other customers who have bought the book you have just bought have also found worth buying). From the moment of clicking on the Amazon site in *My Favourites*, it takes 15 seconds or less to complete the ordering of a book, including paying for it. Its patented one click technology gives unique advantage in creating customer convenience. This is also a very practical use of knowledge of the customer, designed to service the customer.

Using the phone, web, mail, people for high touch personalised interactions

Look how important people are: the top six aspects of customer service in financial companies according to a recent NOP survey, are:

1. well-informed staff who give advice

2. easy-to-understand information and literature

3. rapid response to queries

4. courteous staff

5. fair recompense for mistakes

6. convenient location

Amazon doesn't talk to people, it writes. That's a low cost solution, but it's also relatively low touch. When the face-to-face solution works well (or phone) then great customer service is possible.

The way to success though, is to tailor your use of all the media according to cost, need and customer value. IBM uses individual sales people to look after each of its top accounts, with phone sales/service people buddying with on the ground salespeople looking after groups of smaller customers.

Having someone accessible who knows your situation and deals with it pleasantly, efficiently and quickly is a great loyalty builder.

Consider also how important a personalised letter or e-mail is in managing customer relationships. In fact, most of the greatest direct mail isn't even classified as direct mail because it's so personal it doesn't go through Mailsort. This is just billions of pieces of personal B2B and B2C mail confirming agreements, making proposals, and saying thank you.

Loyalty clubs – making them work

Figure 6.3.2

	Promotion scheme	Loyalty programme
Time	Conceived for a period	Conceived as evolving over time
Rewards	Extrinsic, hard	Intrinsic, firm and soft
Branding	Loose	Woven through
Communication	Infrequent, transactional	Appropriate, relational
Aim	Sales	Profitable relationships
Posture	Defensive	Optimistic
Customer attitude	What is in it for me?	It is for me
Employee role	None; give the rewards, trained, know the rules	Intrinsic to the total conception feel good, empowered
Process status	Outsourced? customer collects and receives	Multiple processes link to achieve, objectives, involving organisation change
System status	POS-driven	Organisation system integration

Promotion schemes are no longer as fashionable as they were a few years ago. There was a time when many marketers seemed to believe that by creating and grafting a promotion scheme on to their basic product and service offer, their customer base would be transformed. Many of these were 'me too' schemes and probably did little more than reduce margins.

The problem with reward schemes is that over time they are often likely to degrade the brand. Customers, for example, might become loyal to the rewards and not to the petrol or the service station.

By contrast, a good loyalty programme is always seen as a means to an end – not an end in itself. The programme is carefully designed to integrate with the brand and other core elements of the service and communication. Sir Ian MacLaurin, the Chairman of Tesco once said:

Customer loyalty is not about how customers demonstrate their loyalty to us, it is about how we demonstrate our loyalty to them.

Sir Ian's argument about *brands demonstrating loyalty* is reinforced by two quotes from individuals involved in qualitative research about what consumers value. One said, "If you are not getting good service from whatever company it is, then you are not going to stay with them". Another consumer added, "I think you should get something for being a valued customer. They should value you because of your ongoing commitment to them".

In the next chapter there is a brief description of how to use the Tesco Club as an example of good practice.

Be relevant: How it works better to be relevant

Many brands claim to be doing one to one marketing when they are only doing mass communication by mail or e-mail. In order to reach the widest possible audience, a brand needs to be universally consistent. On the other hand, in order to reach a particular market or segment, a brand needs to be tailored to individual customer groups and individuals within them.

Thus, the brand needs to think in terms of three levels of performance:

1. What is universal in the brand.

2. What is tailored to different communities, including the values that belong to the individual community or segment.

3. The personal wants and needs of individual customers.

The rule of thumb here is: the brand should always be as consistent as a single person, but should express itself according to different people it meets.

Take ARTISTdirect, a brand that needs to make sure that its communication takes note of the special interests of its customers. Listening to music in the privacy of their own homes, in their car, or on their Walkman, fans develop an intensely personal, one-to-one relationship with their favourite recording artists. With the help of ARTISTdirect, more than 120 artists–from Aerosmith to the Backstreet Boys to ZZ Top – now have the opportunity to actively nurture these relationships.

The company's mission is to develop a direct connection between artists and their fans – and a key component of that strategy is delivering customised communication in the form of e-mails to the fans from the artists. Currently there are over 10 million e-mails a month. These offer fans information of specific interest – upcoming tours and concerts, the release of a new CD, availability of exclusive merchandise or news bulletins about upcoming schedules. ARTISTdirect can also collect customer profile information on each fan, then use that data to send relevant offers and communication.

Says Mark Geiger, CEO of ARTISTdirect, "Customers become more loyal when their personal interests are being acknowledged and their individual needs are being met. For our artists, the big benefit of this system is that they can now give their fans exactly the news and information they're looking for, and keep their all important relationships strong."

By relating to different customer communities the brand becomes more relevant. While it is likely that all consumers using ARTISTdirect's service would appreciate aspects of the brand – the service allows them to differentiate on an individual level.

British Telecom have demonstrated some marvellous examples of the value of recognising the unique characteristics of the community or individual that you are communicating with. One programme involved sending out a questionnaire and sending each of the very large percentage of responders a completely personalised set of offers, gaining a near 100% conversion.

While sales people can know their best customers individually, and service people deal with customers on a case-by-case basis, successful relationship marketing needs systems to collect data and turn it into actionable programmes.

Creating social bonds

Through a strong brand with clear, differentiated values and personality, services and communications tailored to the community and personalised to the individual, people feel more affinity and connection to the service provider.

Add to this the three fundamental principles of social bonding:

1. Recognise the customer as a person who is an individual.

2. Acknowledge to the customers their importance.

3. Show appreciation for their business.

Identifying your customer communities is a primary goal for loyalty marketing

Each strong brand has a tribe of people who share affinity with the brand's values, but this universe typically divides into a number of different communities within which there are the same or very similar buying behaviours, and whose personality and characteristics towards the brand (product or service) can be understood in terms of common values, attitudes and assumptions.

It is much easier to imagine a relationship with a *group* (of people) than a segment. How many *segments* do you personally have a relationship with? Do you even want to be in one? As Professor Walsink observes: *"No consumer sees her or himself as a bundle of mere statistics."* For example, customers would typically not describe themselves as ... *a 40-to-60 year old with high school education and 3.5 children with my own flat. I like to think of myself as a heavy user of wholemeal* ... A group is individuals who share something in common: a community of individuals.

Segmentation frequently begins with recency, frequency and value. This is normally purely behavioural segmentation using a database. Mail-order buyers are routinely segmented as follows:

*   How often the business or consumer customer purchases different products, and what products they buy.

*   How much the customer spends with each purchase.

*   When the customer last bought each of the products.

Segmentation like this can be very useful in developing shall we/shall we not mail to this customer decisions. However, it is not very useful in understanding the characteristics of customers other than at the mechanical level of their behaviour. It is therefore less potent as a tool for creating relationships.

Take the case below, a very good example of segmentation that increases profitability and can improve customer perceptions. But as you can see, it is focused primarily on the brand's needs to be more profitable rather than on understanding the preferences that motivate particular customers and how to make them more loyal. This is good practice, but it's only kindergarten.

CoreStates Financial Corporation is the $24 billion US holding company for three banks in Pennsylvania and New Jersey. They carried out a project to analyse the profitability of individual customers and discovered some surprising results. They had always analysed profitability at product or business line level and as a consequence were able to identify the average profitability for account line. With the new systems they were able to do this by customer and household across product lines.

A desktop decision support system brings together all the information affecting profitability, and this is updated on a monthly basis in order to indicate trends.

CoreStates identified 174 different profitability formulae for their 58 different products, in each of their three banks. As a result, they identified that some of their most successful packages were unprofitable for certain customer segments. For example, the blue riband package for customers with substantial balances, Certificates of Deposit, was considered a marketing success until they found that 25% of households owning this product were in fact unprofitable. Certain market segments were much larger profit contributors than expected. In one branch, 37% of customers generated 59% of the branch's total profit.

Here is where they got smarter, even though they have a way to go:

CoreStates went on to redevelop products and marketing that was more effective. Product packages were adapted to meet key market groups. Branches with similar market potential and customers were clustered with micro marketing campaigns focused on developing the potential. By rolling out the best marketing practices of the most successful branches, they could benefit the least profitable branches. By changing distribution channels and type of service offered to unprofitable households, they were able to make progress towards achieving profitability for all groups.[4]

Community marketing is routinely used, for example to distinguish between B2B and consumer divisions in a company, or those providing services for different kinds of customers. As the diagram below shows, a company like Olympus has a wide franchise of customer communities it serves. Here is where B2B companies with the sophistication of a sales force often achieve levels of focus that eludes B2C, even if it shouldn't. Remember, a good salesperson is the best interactive medium there is.

Figure 6.3.3

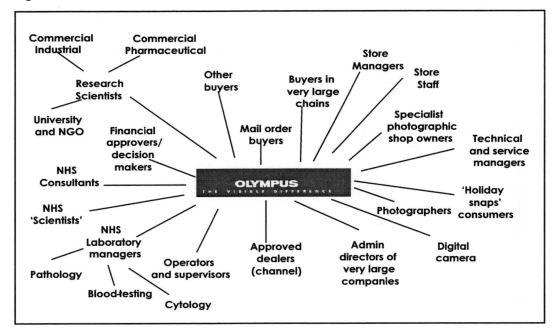

Marketers who understand the feelings and rationale of communities have a very powerful way of communicating to their customers. Interaction with the group/community provides the generalised base for investment and for the tailoring of product and service set to meet a broad base of individual needs. It also gives better opportunities to look for affinity marketing and partners and more steer on media spend and selection.

The customer groups that emerge when using good qualitative data effectively are more than statistical comparisons; they seem to have recognisable personalities and characteristics.

When the United States Postal Service wanted to broaden its base of stamp collectors by appealing to a new, younger and more casual saver segment, they turned to the Elvis Community of Supporters. *First*, they designed and produced Elvis related products, especially stamps. *Then* they mailed 700,000 people who had already either purchased an Elvis stamp or registered an interest in so doing: developing, not initiating relationship. The programme was designed to promote additional Elvis related commemoratives and stamps in the Elvis series and *to enhance the value of saving Elvis stamps*. It received a 22.65% response rate at a cost $1.84 each. More than 3.6 million take-ones were placed in lobbies and pulled a 3% response, and a 3.13% response was obtained from the 25,000 information request forms used. In total the revenue generated was 25 times promotion costs.

Communities are not just something you dream up: they are the result of research and knowledge, not hypothesis.

Designing value that builds loyalty

Avoid trivial offers, discounts and gimmicks – they don't develop enduring relationships

Reducing prices is easy; maintaining the brand's values when you reduce the price is not always so easy. Acquiring customers because you've reduced the price, may not really be recruiting the customers attracted to the brand: you may be attracting customers who like the reduced price. You might be lucky, and their experience might lead them to return to the full price later on. Or it might just be that they move to somewhere else offering a price discount.

In fact, the evidence is that a large and increasing number of customers tend to follow the promotional discount trail.

Tens of billions of dollars of promotional activity spent on alluring new customers is actually wasted. In a major international research project, the effects of large scale price promotions on the acquisition and retention of new customers were found to be effectively zero[5]. According to the study, of 175 sales promotion peaks across 25 leading grocery products in four countries (US, UK, West Germany, Japan), the average before/after repeat level was virtually identical. Basically the effect was as if the promotion had not occurred. In another study, Abraham and Lodish also found that 'the increase in' new customers due to a promotion was small or non-existent for most situations[6].

Research by OgilvyOne found that converting customers whose behaviour is fickle to behaviours that are loyal is harder than getting loyal purchasers of one brand to switch to another trustworthy brand. Loyal customers may be hard to win over but once you do they are worth the investment.

The point is, brands can be destroyed by behaviour that might superficially be attracting customers, but fails to look after the long term future of the brand by creating a belief in its core values of quality, affinity and relevance.

Loyalty-generating offers

Direct marketing has traditionally seen the offer as one of the most powerful, if not the most powerful element of a direct marketing campaign. An offer might be:

- Respond within 30 days to get a free tote bag

- Get three months' free membership

Most such offers are transactionally focused: they are designed to generate an immediate response.

Offers can be positive, neutral or negative in terms of generating long term loyalty.

The National Trust offers three months' free membership and a tote bag to people who respond to their invitation to join the National Trust. They can afford to do this, not only because the offer immediately increases response, but because they know new members typically remain as members for a number of years, and therefore have a significant lifetime value. The offer of free membership is a positive attractor to the National Trust, not only transactionally, but with positive effects on brand attitudes. The offer is also seen as reasonable by the National Trust, stimulating membership without wasting the National Trust's funds. The free membership does not amount to a significant out of pocket expense and the tote bag is seen as a modest 'thank you'. These offers are also brand true. Free membership is obviously completely intrinsic to the brand, and the branded tote bag is something to use while visiting a National Trust property. So this is an offer that uplifts response, does no damage to the brand – and potentially enhances it.

Other brand offers are likely to be more neutral. For example, a credit card company that offers 6 months' interest free balance transfers to new customers may indeed attract many new customers. Unfortunately, these customers are more likely to be attracted by the offer than by the brand itself. Of course, during those six months there are opportunities for the brand to do other things that generate customer trust and loyalty. For some customers no doubt, the six months' free interest will be received with appreciation, which is brand building. The downside is that many consumers take up the offer because they see it as an opportunity to exploit a large financial services firm before moving on somewhere else. In such a case, this is unlikely to be a brand-building offer.

Other offers are likely to promote negative results. As we saw in **chapter 6.1** rewards can have the effect of damaging the intrinsic attractiveness of a product or service.

Create bonds

Bonds are a strategic way to think about offers. Get it right, and your service seems to sell itself.

American Express are now developing the new art of bonds. **Gold Card** for **Frequent Business Travellers** is such an example. Statistical study and research showed a special group of frequent business travellers who would probably appreciate a special tailoring of the service. A new package of services, such as cards for personal assistants and family, travel service and insurance benefits was carefully designed. The approach to the prospect community was relaxed and welcoming, as if the service might have existed for some time and was remarkably successful. Why? Hype was not needed because the design and contact was relevant and right. Each and every experience of the upgraded service now has the effect of strengthening the emotional ties.

As we have already said, unless you are communicating distinctive value, you end up looking like a commodity: hence the proliferation of loyalty schemes designed to manufacture value in the absence of intrinsic value. The oldest killer-apps in the world are well communicated, differentiated solutions that meet real needs. Intrinsic value needs to be expressed to the customer in meaningful ways. For example, a superior petrol fuel is intrinsic, while the opportunity to collect coffee mugs as a result of purchasing petrol is extrinsic. Other intrinsic benefits might be:

- Having your car windscreen washed while you are getting petrol

- Having someone fill the car for you

- Having a petrol account so that you can pay all bills at the end of the month on a single invoice

- Being greeted personally and in a friendly manner by the cashier

All of these are examples of value that are built into the basic service package. Creating loyalty implies building a form of relationship, and if you want to build better relationships you need to **design and deliver better value throughout the relationship.**

The difference between offers and bonds

According to the communication agency, OgilvyOne, offers are less enduring than bonds in attracting customer loyalty. Offers are transactional in the sense that they are designed to produce an immediate response. Bonds are a package of measures designed to change customer attitudes and behaviour over time.

Bonds may include a series of offers, the overall design of the product or service, and the design of a relationship management programme or process.

Bonds need to be based round three kinds of insights:

1.   Insights into the customers. Who they are, how they think, feel and behave, as well as their relationship with the brand, including attitudes to it and its solutions.

2.   Insights into the financial dynamics. The impact of closing the various revenue gaps, such as increasing the lifetime value of the customer by selling more to them or retaining them longer. Also important is the mean lifetime value of customers, segment by segment. Customers with higher value need higher investment.

3.   Insights into the company's positioning and capacity to deliver. Clearly, it is only worth promising things that you are capable of delivering effectively.

Virgin One

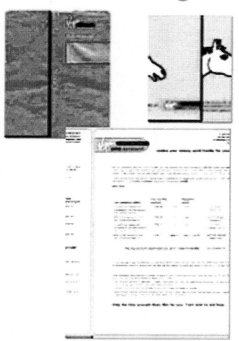

Case example

The Virgin One account is an excellent example of designing a package of differentiated values for the customer and then effectively communicating it. Virgin One adopted the innovative, iconoclastic, value generating approach that belongs to the Virgin positioning to come up with a new kind of solution in UK financial services

The Virgin One solution integrates saving, loans and current accounts in a single package. This provides an advantage to the customer as well as a means to attract a large share of the customer's financial needs in a highly efficient format. The product itself is geared around the communication to the customer of the status of their various financial elements, laid out in a single document. An integrated marketing communication plan promoted the product and its unique benefits. The quality and intelligence of this campaign was reflected as much in its advertising as in the experience that consumers got when making an application to join.

Adding the surprise service factor

The evidence is that the service that really counts is twofold:

1.   That when you really expect something it is there for you without fail.

2.   That you get very pleasant surprises from things you don't expect.

Put these together and you have a winning combination.

[1]   *Media-mix optimizers*, Erwin Ephron, Admap, March 2000.

[2]   George Wiedemann, *Optimised marketing in the Internet age*, The Journal of Interactive Marketing, Vol 3 No 1.

[3]   Jerry Shereshewsky, *Permission versus permissive marketing*, Journal of Interactive Marketing, Vol. 3 No 1.

[4]   Information provided by Kingdom of Marketing Dynamics Ltd.

[5]   Ehrenberg, ASC, Hammond, K and Goodhardt, GJ, *'The after effects of price related consumer promotions"* Journal of Targeting, Measurement and Analysis for marketing (1994).

[6]   Abraham, MM and Lodish, LM, *'Getting the most out of advertising and promotion'*, Harvard Business Review (May/June 1990).

Chapter 6.4

Developing and implementing your CRM programme

This chapter includes:

- ❑ **Introduction**
- ❑ **Creating the strategic business case, plan and time frame**
- ❑ **Profiling and segmenting the base**
- ❑ **Designing the programme**
- ❑ **Identifying defectors and managing complaints**
- ❑ **Planning integrated marketing communications**
- ❑ **Operationalising the programme**
- ❑ **Apply technology**
- ❑ **Conclusion**

About this chapter

n this chapter we are concerned with the practicalities of building systems that will help you to create and maintain long-lasting two-way loyalty relationships with your customers. We look at different levels of company/ customer bonding – financial, financial and social, financial, social and structural, and we consider examples of sophisticated customer segmentation which allows companies to recognise, and thence to serve, the different aspirations of different customers.

6.4 — 1

Angus Jenkinson author and consultant

Angus' biography appears at the beginning of this section

Chapter 6.4

Developing and implementing your CRM programme

Introduction

Loyalty and CRM require leadership for successful implementation, because it is leadership that provides the imagination, purpose, teamwork, values, organisation, commitment and consistency of purpose that transforms companies, brands and business units in ways that customers value. It is leadership that sees the potential of technology and harnesses it to human ends in humanly accessible ways.

Figure 6.4.1

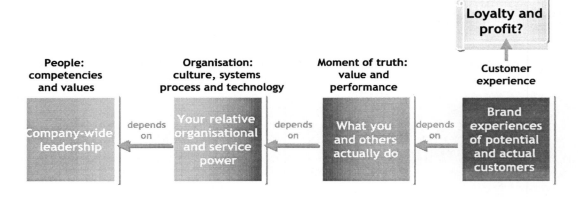

Profitable loyalty is achieved by managing the lifetime relationship of the right customers, focusing on their critical moments of truth. CRM enables greater customisation of service and personal relationships, including relevant, personal communication into the home or business. However, the ability to imagine, design, co-ordinate, develop, deliver, operate, measure, value and improve these moments of truth, customised to different customer communities and then individuals, demands principled leadership by individuals and across the organisation. Buying a database, call centre or even the services of an agency do not by themselves achieve this.

In this chapter you will be learning about this leadership challenge and how to create a customer relationship marketing programme that builds loyalty.

Creating the strategy, business case, plan and time frame

You need to integrate your CRM/loyalty programme through the organisation and across the disciplines, channels and media, as shown in the accompanying diagram.

The vertical axis shows the integration from strategy through to individual touchpoint. Your challenge is to create alignment. Leaders are responsible for formulating strategy and for personally demonstrating core organisational values, ensuring the organisation is equipped, empowered and directed to deliver the highest performance to customers across the full range of touchpoints.

You need an organisational and communication strategy that integrates the full range of communication with customers from PR to point of sale, taking in all media (eg TV, ambient media, mail media, posters, press, websites etc.)

Figure 6.4.2 **Integrated marketing and IMC**

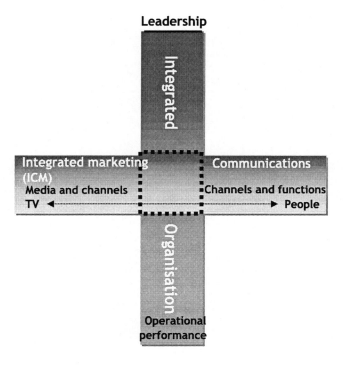

The checklist below is based on applying the strategic 10-steps framework described in previous chapters to developing your channel, product, pricing and IMC strategies.

Table 6.4.1

	Channel	Product	Pricing	IMC
Investment	Use your channels in relationship to the value of customers. High-value customers should get an increased level of direct attention, for example the use of sales force. Mixed channel options may also be appropriate. Lower-value customers need low-cost channels, such as the web or retail.	Optimise products for the high-value customer. Consider exclusive for high-value customers.	Price attractively for the attractive customer and disincentivise the unattractive customer. In B2B provide joint venture pricing options (share in profits) with selected customers.	Invest in communication according to the value of the customer segment. Avoid sales promotion that cannibalises on existing custom or trade.
Relationship	Use channels to manage the entire relationship. For example a salesperson is a powerful channel at the moment of truth when a customer is thinking of buying a car, but mail and web are more effective and lower-cost options for much of the time until the next purchase.	Design new products and services that extend the relationship or increase customer use and access. Design line extensions increase cross-to sell and up-sell opportunities. Test alternative acquisition offers for longer term ROI as well as immediate response.	Maximise investment in new customers to increase overall customer equity. Price to make it attractive to stay a customer. Reward loyal customers with loyalty dividends.	Invest in communication across the entire customer life cycle and to optimise retention value. Use media according to their relative power eg TV during awareness stage and direct and interactive communications with the customer base.
Reputation	Every channel should remain consistently true to the brand. Obviously the brand should be experienced consistently across offline and online. The customer experience should be seamless. Similarly channel outlets should be chosen as far as possible for their affinity with the brand.	Ensure core products and services enhance the brand. Use design, packaging and guarantees to communicate the brand values. Remember that ultimately everything that you do is the product.	Don't degrade the brand with price led propositions and marketing. Try to increase the added value premium.	Ensure that communication is integrated, aligned and consistent with the brand, and that media are chosen on merit to reinforce campaign goals. Remember that all media affect the brand:don't destroy in the call centre what you have created on TV or Internet website. Make sure the brand promise is compelling and clear and that the positioning, promise, core customer needs and values of the brand are reflected in all communication.

	Channel	Product	Pricing	IMC
Relevance	Use different channels to treat different communities or segments appropriately.	Design tailored products and services to meet the needs of different customer communities. Increase the level of appropriate product and service customisation. Find ways to let customers auto-customise.	Create price point positioning of products and services for different customer sets. As far as possible create customised pricing, especially for best customers. Make sure this is perceived as fair across all customers. Where appropriate, provide transactional, consultative and partnership pricing strategies.	Tune your media combinations and messages according to the needs, interests and propensities of different customer communities. Select media according to their potential for different customer types.
Value	Each channel has different strengths and weaknesses. Channel strategy can be used to leverage practice such as convenience and relationship.	Avoid the trap of using financial incentives as the core competitive advantage. Create social and structural bonds. Audit the service to enhance strategic value for customers, using eg the clover leaf tool (see ch 6.2).	Maximise value for money, tailoring the value proposition for different customer groups. Prune unwanted cost in elements in order to maximise value based competitive advantage. Use communication to make customers aware of their value proposition.	Every piece of communication should create value for customers and prospects. If it doesn't, remove it. Remember that the cost of acquiring information is a major influencer on purchase decisions. Create rational and emotional value for customers through experiences.
Touchpoints	Use different channels to address the full range of customer touchpoints ensuring that at all moments of interest and purchase they have a high quality and accessible experience of the brand.	Remember that every interaction with a product or service is a touchpoint. Identify key moments of truth, audit and improve, using clover leaf. Identify and enhance the core customer life cycle for each product or service.	Lower the cost to the customer and to the brand of the customer accessing you. Review bundling versus unbundling pricing strategies to make service touchpoints attractive. Create alternative touchpoint scenarios for different pricing strategies: ie create different experiences for customers.	Every touchpoint communicates: this is the body language of the brand. Strategically review all moments of truth in order to optimise customer communication. Select media and media combinations on merit and not on prejudice. Use media optimisation tools but remember the creativity of the heart. Eliminate negative communication and use communication to prevent lapsing and recover from disappointment or defection.

	Channel	Product	Pricing	IMCI
Imagination	Channels provide creative opportunities to meet the needs of different customers or to provide different customer experiences. The strategy is to use this creative opportunity.	How can you radically alter the product design in order to make it more attractive and differentiate it for different customers?	What is the single most radical thing you can do with your pricing? What are your pricing assumptions? Assume they're not actually true. How would the customer like things to be priced? What can you do to make that happen?	Develop the big creative ideas across all media. Eliminate prejudice and fragmentation while leveraging discipline expertise. Start from the customer view and ask what communication they want and need. Make that priority one. Think about alternative media. Do you want a TV campaign or service people? Look for the electrifying new moment of truth that will transform customer attitudes to the whole service package.
Learning	Put in place learning strategies to be able to choose between channels and to transfer knowledge among channels. Analyse the value of customers acquired through different channels.	Analyse customer satisfaction weighting product and service elements and importance to the customer. Enhance accordingly. Make sure that you are measuring actual performance against desired and identify the frequency and occurrence of surprise value.	Systematically analyse the effectiveness of different pricing strategies for different customer communities or segments.	Evaluate communication not just on transactional results but on fundamental shifts in brand equity, market share and business performance and customer attitudes. Make sure your learning system embraces all your media from sales promotion and packaging to web site, call centre and TV. Use statistical techniques to learn about different customer types in order to provide them with more personalised and relevant communication.
Technology	Implement hybrid and blended channels, remembering that more touchpoints increase customer loyalty and ensure that customer information and service is seamless among the channels.	Ensure customer history includes product and service purchase history including preference differentiating data. Use this to drive customised communication offers.	Provide technology to deliver pricing strategies. Use technology to analyse the results. Ensure that data exists in a convenient form to enable these. Provide data seamlessly across all touchpoints.	Not answering the phone or answering it with boring options is a powerful brand communication. So integrate your technology into your IMC programmes. Use event triggers and automated communication programmes to maintain contact with customers and provide them with added value, personalised communication.

	Channel	Product	Pricing	IMCI
Stakeholders	Ensure that channels are in co-operative rather than competitive mode. Create value for customer, intermediary and brand. Use internal marketing to ensure alignment. Listen to the experience of channel partners and channel executives.	Make it attractive to employees and partners to deliver the product and service value to customers.	Reward associate teams for the delivery of customer value. Communicate the cost and values of different customers in order to create a service and quality culture. Involve all stakeholders in stripping out of waste, costs and increase of value for all parties. Customise value for all key stakeholders.	Include internal marketing in your IMC communication campaigns. Ensure that internal communication is brand enhancing and consistent with external communication. Keep your promises to all stakeholders. Make sure that you have promises that they will all value and that are mutually supporting.

Gaining senior management commitment

Marketing and marketing communications are most effective when the senior team is passionately committed to the projects. So time and effort spent winning this – including all the relevant leaders (eg in sales, service, operations as well as top marketing management) can be well spent.

They need to know what the overall benefit is, how they will gain, what exactly is needed from them and why this will ensure success.

Creating and communicating alignment

There are two levels of alignment to manage: the brand/organisation's general vision and alignment, and campaign alignment. Campaign alignment is achieved through a clear/big creative idea that then drives the briefs for different agencies and operations. This is described in more detail below.

This works best when the brand is already aligned. Andy Law, Chief Executive of the innovative London Advertising Agency, St Luke's, described in his book, 'Open Minds', the formation of their company and the basis of its success. Central to that success was the process by which the core values and mission were formulated as an inspiration for the organisation. St Luke's managed to create a culture and organisation structure, including ownership principles, that reflects and empowers their vision, and values.

So if a client turned up and found a really boring place, this would fail to express qualities like exploring and creating fascination. St Luke's met this challenge by creating different spaces, including rooms dedicated to particular clients, where they could actually come and work with the team. More importantly, they created an overall environment that looked and felt creative and organised around their creative activities.

Values, of course, aren't enough – the work also has to produce results. The proof of the pudding is that St Luke's is one of the most successful of all advertising agencies – largely because of the power of its creative work. By giving ownership (literally in their case) to all the people in the organisation and creating a clear structure of empowerment, it attracted some of the hottest talent in the advertising world. Employ talented, motivated, inspired people and unsurprisingly, results will follow.

Just as a client choosing an advertising agency looks at values, organisation, people *and* results, searching for an agency 'in the groove', so do consumers with consumer products. You expect to be able to buy a can of Coca Cola anywhere in the world, with the same taste and values, or get an American Express rescue if you lose your cards, with the same perfect commitment from Chicago to the Isle of Skye or Bali.

Profiling and segmenting the base

Your campaigns must be based on whom you are communicating with. Research and database segmentation help. If you have a database, segment your customers first on value and share of wallet, identifying any key characteristics that profile the resulting segments.

1. Analyse and profile the current base using the database.
2. Analyse key priority segments using customer questionnaire data.
3. Develop a contact strategy using the findings from stages 1 and 2.

Key data to use:
Recency and frequency of purchase
Share of wallet and value
Cost of acquisition
Propensity to buy

Consider more sophisticated value and behaviour segmentation like these nine key customer segments identified by Garth Hallberg as prime candidates for one-to-one efforts:

- *Nuggets* An extremely small and valuable group of super-heavy category users and highly loyal brand customers – both behaviourally and emotionally – that can account for as much as half of brand volume.

- *Backbone* A much larger group who are also relatively loyal to the brand but buy substantially less per capita than nuggets.

- *Junior Nuggets* A group of medium value users, similar in behaviour to nuggets except for their lower buying rate, whose emotional loyalty to the brand can border on the fanatical.

- *Visitors* The mirror image of nuggets and backbones, these are super-heavy and heavy category users, for whom the brand is part of the considered set, but not the first choice.

- *Switchers* Super-heavy and heavy category users who include the brand in their considered set, but who demonstrate no primary loyalty – especially emotional loyalty – to any brand.

- *Lost Sheep* Super-heavy and heavy category users who once included the brand in their considered set, but who have defected from the franchise.

- *Future Nuggets* Lighter category buying brand buyers who are loyal to the brand and who, because of their particular demographic or attitudinal characteristics, or lifestyle, are likely to grow over time into nuggets or backbones.

- *Suspects* Super-heavy or heavy category users who do not currently buy the brand but who display one or more key 'genetic markers' that make them prime candidates for acquisition efforts.

- *Dark Horse* Non-category buyers who, because of some particular demographic, attitudinal or behavioural characteristic, exhibit the potential to become high-value customers.

Depending on time and budget, as well as the complexity of the marketing situation, research can be as simple and directional as focus groups, or as exhaustive and precise as in-depth quantitative surveys fused with the database to develop segment models. Or a mixture. We can use outside sources to help us - such as Acorn, Mosaic, NDL etc. We can also use telemarketing, shop floor staff, sales, coupons and a variety of other methods to source the information we need to understand our customers. Aim to identify the customer characteristics and drivers to go into the creative brief and strategy development, eg:

Values and image aspirations
Needs and challenges/issues
Lifestyle and interests
Potential lifetime value

You can analyse a CRM database into even more useful **clusters** or **communities of interest** with actionable profiles determined by attitudinal and lifestyle issues by integrating qualitative and quantitative data, as demonstrated by Harley.

Case example: Harley-Davidson

A study identified six groupings of Harley-Davidson owners. Each group has a high degree of internal homogeneity, that is, members of any identified grouping tend to respond to the product in very similar ways and therefore are a prime opportunity for a community marketing strategy.

'Tour Gliders'
This group likes to use its bikes for long-distance riding, are more interested in comfort than speed, prefer riding with a passenger, and wear helmets. Compared to other Harley-Davidson owners, they are traditionally religious, have traditional tastes and habits, are disciplinarians with their children, like reading, and feel they live a full and interesting life.

'Dream Riders'
Represent the largest group, nearly 40% of the sample. They seem to like the idea of motorcycling better than motorcycling itself. They are more likely to have bought their Harley-Davidson new, yet they ride them the least and spend about the least accessorising them. They tend to be conservative in their moral values, marital roles, and daily behaviour.

'The Hard Core'
Are the stereotypical 'bikers.' They associate with other bikers and are more likely to feel themselves as 'outlaws.' They like to be outrageous, like danger, favour legalising marijuana, and embrace the ethic of "eat, drink and be merry, for tomorrow we die."

'Hog Heaven'
Feel better about themselves simply by owning a Harley-Davidson. They experience themselves in the mould of 'old Wild West cowboys' and feel closer to nature when they ride. This group is more mechanically minded and likes to work on their motorcycles, have old-fashioned tastes and habits, read relatively little, and are less likely than others to believe in a life after death.

'Zen Riders'
Consider motorcycling as a spiritual experience. They are more impulsive and report more ambition than other groups. They like to 'party' and have trouble relaxing in everyday life. They also have the highest household income of any group.

'Live to Ride'
Believe in the motto "live to ride and ride to live." This is motorcycling as a total lifestyle. They are more likely than any group to have bought their motorcycle new, and they ride it the most by a wide margin. A higher percentage of them say that, were it not for their family, they would quit their jobs and take off. They have owned almost 10 motorcycles and for most, this is their second Harley Davidson.

The significant difference in this research methodology was that the customer groups (customer segments) were not predefined or anticipated by management, but were assembled on the basis of market data. This data was collected by sending out 2,500 surveys to current Harley-Davidson owners, with a return rate of just over 30%. The questionnaire focused on customer lifestyle statements, both in connection with the specific product (motorcycle lifestyle) and more general lifestyle attributes. An example of a product statement might be, "To me, motorcycles are a symbol of freedom." General lifestyle statements were phrased as, "I like to be outrageous" or "I would rather stay home and watch television than go out."

Figure 6.4.3

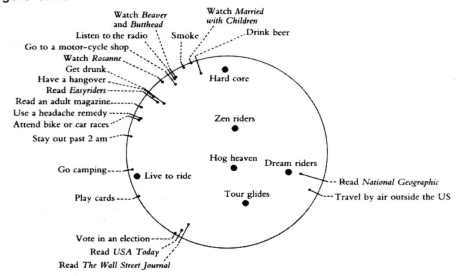

The surveys were analysed by 'clustering' the responses to the motorcycle lifestyle statements. This meant that the final groupings were not based simply on abstract measures, nor did they rely solely on management judgement or intuition. The study attempted to discover whether it was possible to discern 'natural' customer groupings without imposing pre-set criteria. The study concluded that "market defined segmentation can more precisely reveal natural segment boundaries." The move away from predefined customer groupings towards a more individualised or community depiction carries significant advantages. The first is that reality is often more fantastic and surprising than we might logically suppose. Who would have expected the existence of the 'Dream Riders,' a group which composes nearly 40% of Harley-Davidson customers, who purchase bikes and then rarely ride them? Allowing customer groups to emerge from the data is to recognise that fact is truly stranger than fiction. It is vital that marketing strategy should not pre-empt the unexpected.

Clearly, the most important aspect of the research design process was in devising lifestyle statements (both product and general) so that they reflected significant values/beliefs on the part of Harley-Davidson owners. Researchers have to be confident that they are collecting relevant information. Once collected, it is imperative that any data analysis is done outside the framework of preconceived patterns. Only if the researcher is free of habitual responses will there be room for the 'unexpected' to emerge.

It's clear that just because two people buy the same product, the product doesn't necessarily have the same meaning for them both. Any given product, in this case a motorcycle, can serve a range of customer needs. The needs the product serves may be concrete and functional, as in the case of using a motorcycle as the means to go from one place to another. Needs can also be social or symbolic, so that owning a Harley-Davidson might mean having the right image or social credentials.

Figure 6.4.4

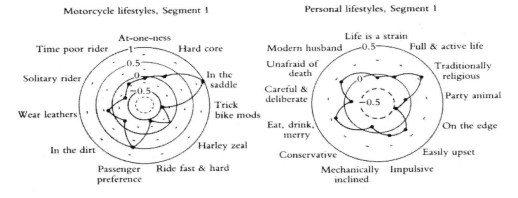

A product's meaning develops as a relationship between product and customer needs. The relationship not only reflects thoughts and feelings about the product, but will influence how any given customer actually uses the product. For some, the mere fact of buying a Harley-Davidson motorcycle fulfilled their need. Riding the thing was very much a secondary consideration. The needs we bring to any purchase influence how we will use, look after, and invest in that product.

Community signatures

Once the research is done and you understand the characteristics of the different groups' profiles, then develop the **community signature** describing the characteristic hallmark of each community in qualitative descriptions that invoke the imagination. Not just a list of abstract characteristics but a description of a person in action with the brand.

Having a sense of how a customer thinks and feels is essential, both in terms of product development and in strategic marketing. The line between knowing about your customers and understanding your customers is a thin one - it is also a crucial one. That is why some consultancies and agencies are now developing new tools for communicating the essence of the different communities. The descriptions above of Harley-Davidson groups represent the typical profiles that would be given by a planner profiling customer clusters. However, when creatives are developing their solutions, they routinely try to imagine the customers they are working with as real people. New techniques replicate that principle as a method of communicating customer characteristics.

The sample *excerpt* that follows is taken from full community signatures developed from the Harley-Davidson study. The aim is to bring an archetypal member of the community to life and use that to design and deliver more creative and relevant solutions and communication.

Zen Riders: Riding as a 'spiritual experience'

Geoff was 37 and had already been riding motorcycles for nearly 15 years before he bought his first Harley-Davidson. He and Linda had discussed it for weeks. After twelve years of marriage, and with both of them working, they were doing all right financially – pushing $60,000 combined last year, and Geoff was intent on getting a raise in the next couple of months. He figured that if he didn't get more money, he'd probably quit working for the firm and try it on his own.

Anyway, he and Linda had finally agreed about the Harley. He'd gone down to pick it up last week. He'd seen an ad in the local paper, and though of course he'd have loved a new bike, this one was in beautiful condition. When he started it up for the first time, it seemed to him the engine sounded like some great gospel chorus. It sang sweet, deep and low. If he wasn't already a happily married man, he'd have said that he fell in love with the thing.

Riding home he couldn't resist finding out what the bike could do. He hit 90 as he crossed the little humpback bridge ...

Identifying specific customer groups enables both supermarkets and Harley-Davidson to personalise their communications. This means they can carefully shape both the language and product emphasis to fit in with the particular needs of the Struggling Idealist or the Zen Riders or any other recognisable grouping.

Designing the programme

Steps in this include designing 'acquisition for loyalty', loyalty and retention programmes: developing bonds, offers and personalised communication, adding value through service and peripherals, setting up management and evaluation controls.

Tesco have indeed been extremely successful with their loyalty programme. It demonstrates a number of good practice elements; so follow the general principles that Tesco implemented.

1. It was bold and innovative. The first to market with a genuine proposition often gain several percentage points and tend to keep them. Consumers saw Tesco as a champion, offering something nobody else was offering and forcing the rest of the industry to go in the same direction. Tesco got value as a leader; everyone else was tagged as a follower.

2. The Tesco Clubcard fundamentally changed the relationship dynamic between consumers and the stores. Until then customers were merely baskets. While all supermarkets could analyse baskets at checkout – recording value per hour, per day, the average value and contents – not one store knew how many customers they actually had. They had no detailed or specific knowledge about whether customers were coming in several times or once, or which customers were doing what, or even which customers they had and which they didn't. By offering a reward, Tesco got consumers to put up their hands and say that they were customers. This meant that the reward became a means of generating information, of purchasing information. This is commonly the first purpose of all rewards in loyalty schemes or programmes. Airlines, for example, get the same benefit out of their frequent flyer programmes.

3. Tesco use this information in order to provide incremental value to customers in the form of relevant offers and communication. They have seven different magazines that they send out to different communities of customers, as well as sending a package of specifically targeted benefits.

4. Tesco transformed its brand image, moving from being an impersonal organisation with little or no relationship to their customers, to one in which customers built higher levels of trust and involvement, simply in the process of handing over their names and addresses. As a result, this new positioning has enabled Tesco to widen its range of services, into financial services for example. As I forecast at the time of the launch, this also ideally prepared Tesco for the world of new media.

5. Use your image to extend your channel and product/brand options. Tesco has gone on to become the most successful online grocer in the world, and one of the most profitable, if not the most profitable, online business.

6. Tesco sent a message to customers that said: "We care about you, we appreciate you, we recognise you."

7. Their chairman explicitly stated his belief in the principle that loyalty to customers creates loyalty from customers. 'Loyalty to customers' means engineering the business to provide quality service around useful or desire needs. The Clubcard by itself would not do this, but did succeed as part of a package of service benefits, which included improvements in baby care facilities, point of sales service, and community promotion (Tesco pioneered the idea of saving to provide computers for local schools). For example their One in Front mass and internal advertising campaign was created to promote awareness of a service improvement they had put in place; a service that actually cost several times the advertising cost and delivered the 'meat' of the 'we care' message.

8. To Tesco, their people are the major element of their communication mix.

Exercise:

Contrast this with NatWest credit cards who were one of the pioneer groups to take up the Air Miles promotion scheme. They found that offering Air Miles with their credit cards was highly effective in terms of generating incremental sales and customer retention. Indeed, withdrawing from the scheme showed decisively that there would be significant losses to the brand franchise. However, NatWest make little use of the air miles point programme. They don't advise cardholders of the number of air miles gained other than on a month-by-month transaction basis. All points are then transferred over to the Air Miles pot, leaving someone other than NatWest responsible for all communication. Does this fully exploit the opportunity?

Consider your own strategies. How do you need to improve?

Communicating what the brand means

In the world of customer loyalty, 'The Brand' sums up everything the company means to the customer – the 'being of the brand' as it lives in the soul of the customer. Understanding the brand means understanding its meaning and destiny in the world.

1. The brand must be clearly understood by its own marketers and its positioning promise and personality used as a guideline in all of the marketing activities.

2. This means that everyone must understand: there needs to be a motivating process and document that articulates and communicates what the brand means to the people in the company and the agencies who are going to be involved in customer facing activities.

3. Use this to evaluate ads and marketing campaigns, services (and products), staff and culture – ensuring that they are on-brand.

Many marketers and brand designers seem to like inventing a set of values that the brand should embody. A more useful place to begin is by understanding what a brand's core values really are at their best, then making sure that it stays true to those.

Crafting a brand definition needs to be based on researching what the brand actually means to the customer, usually in the form of intensive focus groups. These are best done with people who know the brand well, although focus groups can also be done with members of the general consuming public. It is the advocates and heavy users who really value what it means to be connected to the brand – and can explain why they are.

Focus groups use qualitative research techniques such as projection, creative exercises and group discussion. These bring out the core values associated with the brand. Such research shows how the brand influences people in their lives, what it means to them, and in what way the brand feels different from other brands or is looked at in a different way.

Once you have understood the essence of what the brand means and stands for, it needs to be fashioned into a precise and evocative formulation that can be used to communicate across the organisation and to agencies.

Case example: The National Trust

THE NATIONAL TRUST

The National Trust is one of Britain's leading brands. As it entered the 21st Century it had questions about what it now meant to its many different customers.

After an extensive process of discussion and consultation, they decided to develop a brand signature. This included understanding not only the essence of the brand that is common to all, but also the 4 core human needs that it meets. These tend to vary with different kinds of members and can be used for community clustering.

After distilling the research, an internal communication tool was created, the National Trust brand signature. Marketing staff across the organisation described how useful, inspiring and empowering they found the result.

Advertising agencies described it as an enormous help.

Senior management felt that it provided a significant steer to strategy and to improving all customer services and communication.

As indicated by the short case study above, a brand definition or brand signature can be applied as a discipline for design and review of all customer interactions (moments of truth).

It is an essential component for internal development and training – clarifying what the organisation needs to do to become ever more 'brand true'. In this sense, it can also be one of the most powerful and accurate of briefing tools for outside agencies.

In crafting a brand definition, there's a set of core standards that need to be met. These include:

- It should bring the brand's true character and values to life

- It should be precise and accurate

- It should be positive

- It should both support strategy-making and reflect it

- It should support operational and cultural benchmarking (standards)

- It should relate the brand to its market context

- It should energise

The six key brand steps

1. Qualitative research to understand the brand

2. Creation of the brand definition (signature)

3. Audit of current status

4. Plan for change

5. Development of internal marketing to communicate

6. Deployment of instruments for training, advertising etc.

Turn your brand promise into a guarantee

As we noted in the previous chapter, a powerful service guarantee works – it produces companies that stand out from the crowd, and, if taken seriously, forces commitment to quality. The result has a double impact:

- Better quality service

- Contented customers willing to pay for assured quality

Some companies are making a positive selling feature of guaranteed standards of customer service. Churchill Insurance, for example, offers a 20% discount off motor policy renewals if any of seven guaranteed standards are not met. Churchill's new business sales of car insurance rose by 25% in 1998, with one of the best operating ratios of the major UK private car insurers in 1998, and a car loss ratio of 85%.

A real commitment to a guarantee conditions the company attitude - as we saw with BBBK in the previous chapter. When Manpower CEO Mitchell Fromstein considered dropping the guarantee it was the *employees* who reacted. They were proud of their standards. A service guarantee gets valuable customer feedback, provides the means to complain, sets standards (Federal Express: absolutely, positively by 10.30 am) and produces great copy focused on relevant customer need.

Consider how you can use the capacity of database marketing/CRM to deliver quality information about product components, to progressively architect your business around a key brand promise and customer commitment and to design and evolve a total service solution. Then like Manpower who grew from $400 million to $4 billion in 10 years by calling every customer when a new person is assigned, you could achieve dramatic results.

Assess the value and relevance of loyalty cards and the club concept

Research shows that promotion schemes are most likely to be of value in situations where the product or service is highly commoditised, ie consumers can see very little difference between alternatives. In such a situation, providing a promotion scheme in the form of 'points generating rewards' gains some advantage. And indeed, reward cards can influence the level of 'price warfare' that is commonplace in certain industries – such as package holidays and petrol. If customers can be induced to stay with one particular brand in order to take advantage of its reward scheme, such as through the GM Card, then that can take the pressure off other competitive elements, such as price.

Creating financial, social and structural value

According to Berry and Parasuraman, value is the glue that binds company and customer together. **Value reflects the total benefit customers receive for the total cost they incur.** Consider how the airline industry used direct marketing disciplines to develop frequent flyer programmes, leading to the establishment of various executive clubs such as the BA Executive Club. Clearly the package of benefits offered goes way beyond those that can be delivered in the mail, though this is frequently the way in which the *communication of the value* is made. Examples include the executive lounge, preferential access to seats when flights are overbooked, online or telephone check-in, points and their benefits, and special offers. Designing such solutions is based on three levels of relationship marketing: the higher the level, the higher the potential pay off. Which do you use?

1. **Financial bonding**

2. **Financial and social bonding**

3. **Financial, social and structural bonding.**

Level 1 relationship marketing, which is often referred to as either frequency or retention marketing, is usually based on pricing incentives to encourage customers. Unfortunately, pricing incentives are the easiest to imitate and the least likely to create enduring loyalty.

Financial incentives for good custom operate as an effective entry-level strategy for loyalty marketing. By themselves, they are not enough.

The advantage of moving to level 2, is the addition of *social bonding*. Use this sample social bonding checklist:

- Creating affinity between the brand values and the customer values
- Personal service to the customer or client
- Making life easier for the customer
- Recognition of the customer, provided it is appropriate and real
- Appreciation of the customer or client; for example, the normal social courtesies of thanking a person for what they are doing for you
- Acknowledgement of the customer; genuinely making explicit their importance
- Increasing their expertise in your products and services so that you become attractive to them
- Increasing your expertise in them so that you can serve them better
- Providing a knowledgeable or dedicated person to look after the relationship on behalf of the customer
- Problem solving and crisis resolution
- Apologising immediately and proactively if things go wrong; trying to make amends
- Seeking out their needs
- Staying in touch with them and reassessing their needs
- Providing personal touches such as gifts, cards and relevant information
- Confiding in clients and getting them to confide back
- Demonstrating a co-operative, responsive, can-do service attitude

These all create social bonding because they enhance trust and appreciation, as well as feelings of affinity and of personally mattering.

The third level of relationship bonding adds *structural* bonding. Once the customer feels positive about the financial package provided and feels a level of affinity, they are more likely to invest in structural commitments with the brand. Structural bonding is based around developing the systems of the brand, in order to deliver value to the customer that is not dependent on the relationship behaviours of individual personnel. Examples of CRM or direct marketing systems that do this include:

- Olympus UK Diagnostics provide high value diagnostic systems to the NHS and other hospitals that make use of various chemical reagents. A system automatically analyses the use of the reagents using an on board computer, and via the Internet automates the reagent supply, thus removing a headache from hospitals as well as improving reliability.

- Amazon patented its so-called one click service. A customer can leave their personal information, including credit card and delivery address, within the Amazon secure systems. A single click of the mouse creates an order that's routinely delivered within a day or two. Here, relationship equity has been translated into structural bonding.

- American Express provides a direct debit service to its charge card customers in order to save them the bother of making separate payments.

- Royal Bank of Scotland offer to automatically sweep up balances from other credit cards each month and transfer them to the preferential Royal Bank of Scotland credit card account.

- Vindis Audi remind you that it is time to service your car (similar services can be provided by opticians, dentists, insurance brokers and so on).

- Amazon analyses customer purchases and preferences to create a recommendations list.

- Inmac has systems that recommend add-on parts such as printer ribbons and cartridges when a customer purchases a relevant item.

- Publishers like Pearson provide university staff with specially designed confidential extranet sites that support their teaching.

- FedEx provides customers with systems to order services and information about the progress of their parcels.

- Computacentre provides systems which enable customers to keep a log of all their computer assets, including the version number, service history and so on.

As you can see, the boundaries of what belongs to product development and what belongs to CRM or direct marketing are blurring. Thomson Holidays, for example, developed systems to recognise high value loyal customers and reward them with upgrades or token benefits in their room when they arrive (such as chocolates, flowers or wine).

Contracts are obviously important structural bonds. When the customer commits to the contract, you have created a formalised method to retain the relationship. However, it's important to recognise that contracts that bind customers against their will, end up being counter productive.

Steps to take in designing value

Designing value for customers therefore requires five process steps:

1. First of all, audit and analyse the current service bundles, researching current customer attitudes and perceptions of these. Make sure that your analysis and research takes into account the different kinds of customers that you have, the brand signature, the financial opportunities of different customers and therefore the amount that you should be investing in them. Also consider the potential to generate more lifetime value by increasing retention or ongoing sales. Use this in order to produce an assessment of current effectiveness and gaps.

2. Then comes a creative process, generating a wide range of thoughts and ideas. It can be very useful to get multi-function teams involved at this point, perhaps involving outside parties such as facilitators or agencies in the process of identifying opportunities. Once the basic ideas have been generated you need to test them for practicability. Leave out anything that's clearly impossible, very difficult or very expensive unless it looks as if it's going to have a very powerful effect on customers.

3. The next stage is to research the customer attitudes to the new proposed solutions, taking into account different customer communities and both rational and emotional aspects, as well as the value versus the cost of each new proposed element.

4. Use this information to design the new value packages that you want to offer customers. Where possible test these in small scale, with a certain group of customers or in one part of the business operations.

5. Implement the new solution and measure the effect.

Design service and contact strategy and applications analysis

Use the moment of truth tool below:

- Start with a customer/client perspective. Where and how do they (want to) interact with you? Which are the moments of truth (MOTs).

- Identify the actual and potential parts of the organisation that could or will need to interact with the customer.

- And the range of different business functions and processes, as well as the different kinds of CRM system that need to be integrated or developed (eg call centre, website, sales force).

- Design communication strategies based on sequences and sequential mixes of communication.

- Repeat this for different customer communities with different needs, so that the final system supports the entire customer base, prioritised according to customer value.

- Apply the learning to database/technology design.

Table 6.4.2   Moment of truth analysis tool, source, valuing your customers

MOT event	Importance to customer	Importance to us	Event trigger	Customer mood	Customer need	Current moment of truth	Cost	Customer cost/worth	Competitor	Changes
What is the moment of truth of event?	How important is our behaviour at this MOT for the customer?	How important is our behaviour at this MOT for us?	What triggers the event? Could be life change, buying mood, client behaviour etc.	What is the customer thinking, feeling, intending, eg 'Unaware' 'angry' 'excited' etc.	What does the customer actually want?	Current interaction/communication between brand and customer. (What is done?)	What is the current financial and brand equity cost to the brand of this?	What is the current cost or value to the customer of this?	What do the leading competitor(s) do that the brand doesn't?	What qualitative or quantitative changes are signalled?

This is a very powerful way of performing customer centred business requirements analysis, rather than the usual technique of simply asking marketers what they think they want.

Identifying defectors and managing complaints

Install systems and practices that proactively or quickly recognise where you will lose customers, and put in place actions to avoid this.

For example:

- Use your database to recognise changes in the pattern of customer behaviour and take avoiding action.

- Provide easy to use and attractive channels to complain.

- Train and empower staff to deal with complaints. Install resources to help them.

- Recognise when customers have had problems and put it in the database. Use this to guide future communications.

- Use your data to discover customers who are affected by problems at your end. Apologise proactively.

Planning integrated marketing communications.

IMC planning has three core stages: planning, doing (or execution) and learning.

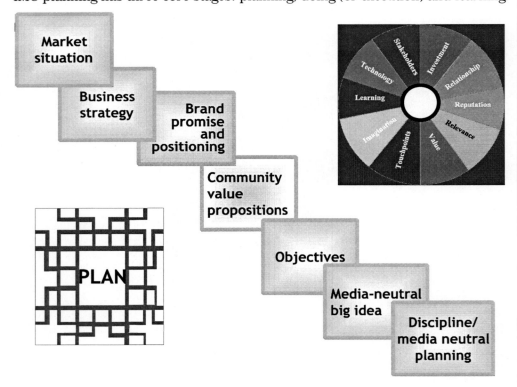

Figure 6.4.5 demonstrates the **planning** phase of IMC:

1.   Begin by understanding the customers and their required value propositions.

2.   Reflect this in your analysis (through research etc.) of the market situation.

3.   Develop a business strategy.

4.   Develop brand promises for each customer market that reflects the brand's core value and positioning.

5.   Develop value propositions as discussed above.

6.   Articulate a set of business objectives for the *marcoms* project. These should also be used as evaluation criteria.

7.   With the help of your agency, develop a media neutral big idea that will overarch all communication and disciplines.

8.   Develop a media and discipline strategy for communication, eg the use of PR and/or direct marketing, and mail and/or e-mail.

The next stage is execution or **doing**. Here the steps to follow are:

Figure 6.4.6

During this stage there are 5 key activities:

1. Planning within each discipline and/or medium (eg radio, telemarketing). Here you are developing the executable concepts, platforms etc. and evaluating how to use them within the medium/discipline.

2. Buying and scheduling within each discipline and/or medium (eg radio, telemarketing).

3. Create the communication pieces with their offers, formats etc.

4. Execute, run or implement these.

5. Project manage, tune and control.

Finally, in stage 3, **learning**, you need to learn and measure across the 7 elements outlined overleaf. The first six represent progressively finer levels of detail, and the seventh is concerned with operational processes.

1. What happened in the market sales, market share, new customers, product launch results etc?

2. What effects were there on customer awareness, perception of relevance, change in consideration set, level of bonding etc?

3. How effective were the customer value propositions/offers? Were some more effective than others? What should be rolled out in future?

4. How effective were the different media and/or the mix of media?

5. Within each medium and/or discipline, how effective were formats, schedules, lists/segments, banners etc. Measurement here corresponds to traditional measures of recall, click-through, response, conversion, offer testing etc.

6. What did you learn about the process of planning, executing and evaluating? What would be a more skilful way in future? How do your technology, systems and processes need to be updated?

Operationalising the programme

Turning the programme into an action; optimising the functional and process elements to achieve success, needs good hard and soft systems as well as skills.

The following description of the steps involved focuses primarily on the 'direct marketing' and interactive part of the process, although of course, integrated campaigns would also need to manage PR and 'advertising' elements.

Taking implementation step by step

1. A **marketing plan for a brand, product or sector** is created which identifies the need for one or more marketing campaigns. Initial work identifies which campaign types are likely to be most successful for the product or sector, and which customers should be targeted in them. In order to do this, the marketers will use data analysis systems on the database; for example data mining or statistical analysis tools as well as counts and cross tabulations and research.

2. An overall IMC **campaign brief** is drawn up at a macro level. (See chapter 7.4 for details on creative briefing.)

3. The brief is used to derive a **campaign specification**, which is entered into a computerised marketing co-ordination system. This co-ordinates the planning, execution and implementation of all marketing campaigns. It ensures that the approach to customers is co-ordinated and prioritised, taking into account the importance of different target markets, budget availability, media and the need to avoid clashes. One of its principal outputs is an agreed schedule of campaigns to be run. Without this, customer management is impossible or at least difficult.

4. Communication elements are **designed** to achieve the marketing objectives within the permitted budgets. The set of briefs plus conference calls or meetings are used to ensure co-ordination. For example when drive to web and web landing pages and functions need to be co-ordinated, or call centre scripts designed.

5. Where possible, test phases are devised to **test the different elements** of the design on statistically significant sample lists extracted from the database. Testing normally covers the main elements of the campaign, ie which customers are targeted, which offers they receive, the timing of contacts with them, how they are to be reached and how their responses are to be handled. A campaign selection system in the marketing database (or data warehouse) will be used to select the customers and allocate them on to various test cells. It will also record on the database which campaign cell the customer was allocated to for use in subsequent analysis. Finally, in an advanced system it will include specifying the criteria for various kinds of response, in order to automate response analysis (eg, an order of product X = a positive response).

6. The test campaigns are **implemented and the results are analysed**, possibly automatically, to determine which campaign elements (eg media, contact strategies) produced the best results.

7. The final design of the **campaign is developed, including the contact and the media schedule**. Depending on the media, appropriate operations are included and briefed. This could, for example, include the call centre, website, sales force, mail and/or print production house, fulfilment centre and so on. As the contact strategy determines a high proportion of the costs of a campaign, contact strategies should be tested very thoroughly and prioritised. The tests provide the basis for prioritising.

8. The operational **details of the campaign** are agreed and implemented. For example, in a database-driven DM or e-mail project, an outbound list or lists are selected from the database. This determines which customers will be contacted. The list is selected by the campaign management system using a formula derived from analysis of tests. Further, customers may be allocated to test cells for the next phase. Each customer would have a promotion record written into the database to show their inclusion in the campaign. Any rules for automated follow-up and response will be specified in the campaign management system. Similarly, each of the other media or channels set up their internal systems, such as telemarketing scripts, landing pages/web functions or production schedules.

9. The **main campaign runs**, eg the customer receives a personalised communication, which is part of the contact strategy. This prompts him to respond eg by coupon or phone, or by going to the website or an event. If the response is to an inbound telemarketing set up, the operator at the latter finds out which campaign or 'offer' the customer is interested in. The operator, cued by a sequence of on-screen displays, asks the customer a series of questions. These include confirmation of the customer's identity (possibly including phone number, address and job title), specific needs concerning the product or service in question, and the customer's needs for further contact. The operator enters the answers into the system. If the enquiry is by mail, the respondent is contacted by an outbound telemarketing call and a similar process takes place. If the response is to a website, eg in reaction to e-mail, a link might be created to its campaign specific web landing page on the site. Again, the website will hopefully collect data.

10. The **enquiry or other information** gathered from the customer is matched to the existing customer file (if any) and merged with other information on the database.

11. The computer uses rules derived from tests and agreed with the campaign originator and project manager, to prioritise and plan follow up according to the likelihood of a customer ordering or other factors. These rules may be based on predetermined campaign profiles (ie the kind of customer the company is trying to attract) and may use **data gathered** during the customer's response. If this is on the web, the activity will take place in real time. It will also determine form the preconfigured rules what should happen next.

12. A particular **sales force or call-centre contact strategy may be triggered**, based on the type of product and customer, and on the priority, and automatically routed or generated to the people or system able to deliver it.

13. **The fulfilment organisation may receive information** indicating, among other things, material to be sent to the customer or, if the product is mail order, what product should be sent.

14. **Local sales offices, sales staff or dealer outlets receive information** about the enquiry on their computers, follow up enquiries, and feed the results of the follow up back to the database.

15. The results of all enquiries and responses are analysed to provide regular reports on the **effectiveness of activities** and to help improve the effectiveness of future campaigns. Detailed performance data plus expenditure data from financial systems are used to evaluate financial performance and plan new campaigns.

The above example shows a range of technologies seamlessly working to help marketers do a better job. This is not a future vision. It is current best practice.

Root cause analysis

Problems happen – customers get lost.
Root cause analysis is the process of identifying why the problem really occurred and involves digging deeper than simply taking what the customer first says. For example, did the problem arise because ...

- the customer didn't understand what was available?

- they did not know how to use it?

- the person concerned wasn't well enough trained?

- the person who did the service didn't have the right resources?

- the data in the database wasn't good enough?

A mailing might be profitable, but are you generating as much profit
and as good results as you could? Are you perhaps generating negative
reactions alongside the positive ones?

Apply technology

The diagram below provides a business checklist for your CRM technology to
accomplish. The starting point for developing CRM systems must be business goals
and these must in turn be led by the customer.

You may not need all of these functions, but it is a good place to start, whether you
are B2C or B2B (or any of the other B2 formulations).

Figure 6.4.7   **What you might want CRM technology to deliver**

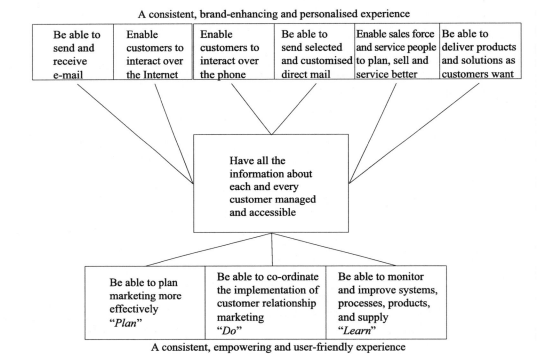

Checklist of customer facing technologies

The following checklist shows a set of applications that might need to be updated or primed for your campaign:

1. **Internet** and e-business applications.

2. **Mailing** applications, including e-mail and direct mail, newsletters, reminders and so on.

3. **Response handling and fulfilment**, using the system to record your customers' responses and manage the next step in the contact strategy.

4. **Phone applications, inbound and outbound,** whether selling to them, doing customer research or providing information services and problem solving.

5. **Dealer, distributor or agent management systems** include providing data to intermediaries to help them meet theirs and your customers' needs better, while monitoring their performance in so doing.

6. **Club or user group marketing** involves creating specialised services for loyal customers who therefore receive special additional benefits in return for their loyalty.

7. **Consumer promotions** (eg coupon distribution and redemption).

8. **Event marketing**, system set up, especially in B2B.

9. **Sales force systems** include diary and contact management applications, helping the sales force to keep in touch at the right time, as well as information collection and distribution about customers.

10. **Sales systems,** that facilitate order taking and customer service, including credit card processing.

11. **Service systems,** the applications that really create customer loyalty. These are described in more detail in Chapter 6.2.

12. **Smart** technologies that connect people, such as electronic tagging and messaging.

Customer website journey

OgilvyInteractive has developed a very useful technique for designing websites. This involves brainstorming and then prototyping desired simulated *journeys* through the website. This entails modelling the customer process or potential processes through the website, looked at from the point of view of what the customer wants and what the brand would find desirable. This is in fact very similar to the kind of process that retailers use when designing store traffic to optimise value for consumers and the brand.

Amazon.com are credited with being the first company to meticulously think through and design every single step in the customer journey, and it is easy to see how this work paid off. Today Amazon.com has one of the highest levels of customer bonding of any brands.

Once you have a clear statement of design requirements based on how customers will journey through the site, including the functional triggers that will attract and facilitate their movement, it is relatively easy to turn this into a functional and visual site design.

Research effectiveness and ROI, loyalty and performance, and improve

Earlier, I described a number of research and evaluation criteria. It may be helpful to make some comment about research and analysis.

The SERVQUAL research instrument (developed by Professor Valerie Zeithaml and others) is one of the most frequently used tools to evaluate customer attitudes. It identifies (in order) 5 key factors that customers evaluate. These are:

1.   Reliability

2.   Responsiveness

3.   Assurance

4.   Empathy

5.   Tangibles

Leonard Berry, an important researcher and professor in the field of customer service, features these five customer criteria as priorities in an article in HBR, 2001:

Relevant (to the customer):

●   Solutions: creatively meeting customer needs

●   Respect: feeling that the whole service, communication, treatment etc. is respectful

●   Emotions: engaging not dry

●   Convenience: for the customer, designed to be easy

●   Fair price: not necessarily the lowest, but fair for what is provided

Both of these (alternative but not inconsistent) schemes emphasise important features of experience that lead to trust and appreciation. It therefore makes very good sense to use such factors in your research.

I have found that the critical incident and sequential incident techniques are very powerful tools for analysing customer experience and improving services effectively. They are more effective than the common satisfaction based attitude questionnaires, because they better mirror the process element of service and get more under the skin of customers to give actionable insight.

In critical incident research, customers are asked to talk about actual moments of truth that made a big difference. Very good learning comes from this.

In the sequential incident technique (as some marketing literature calls it, or servicepoint research, as I call it), customers describe and report on the whole processes (or a major phase) of interacting with the brand. A mixture of unprompted or aided research interviews (in the early phases) and structured questionnaires (with later larger groups) identifies how customers experience the brand and what to improve. The cloverleaf tool (see chapter 6.2) can help with this too. This is the best tool in my opinion.

A major problem of research and analysis is how to measure the relative effectiveness of media and disciplines in the mix. Given the level of test controls in most campaigns, this often comes down to something subjective. However, both these techniques can be surprisingly helpful in providing general guidelines.

Conclusion

In this chapter I have tried – often quite briefly, to illustrate and advise how to implement ideas and principles outlined in earlier chapters.

Creating customer loyalty requires an ongoing and passionate commitment to quality:

- quality of creative communication

- quality of empathy and customer insight

- quality of operational performance

- quality of data

- quality of reward and recognition systems for employees and agencies

- quality and relevance of the value proposition

Marketing is a cultural force, and societal shaper and producer of value (sometimes bad, sometimes hollow, often great). The measure of the value you create is the trust, appreciation and ongoing need you develop in (B2B or B2C) consumers.

Personally, I think there are few things more interesting. This is putting your and the team's inspiration, ethics, passions, skills, intelligence, energy and imagination into action to achieve win-win-win results.

Section 7: Designing your communications

e dealt, in section 4, with the wide variety of communications media that are open to today's direct marketer, and the characteristics of each. In this section we deal with the creative aspects of customer communication: how to put across, whatever the medium, the message that we want to deliver, and how to secure the response that characterises us as direct marketers.

We start with two chapters directed at people themselves employed in creative jobs: one on the principles, and one looking at how to fit the message to the medium. Chapter 3 tackles the designing of websites to maximise interactivity potential. Chapters 4 and 5 are addressed to those who have to deal with creative people – how to get the best out of them, by inspiration, by careful and considerate briefing – the latter accompanied by a heartfelt plea for greater understanding and mutual tolerance between creatives and account executives. Chapter 5 is a collection of checklists for creative work.

Finally, Chapter 6 examines that powerful weapon in the interactive and direct marketer's armoury – the catalogue.

Chapter 7.1

Direct marketing creativity – the principles

This chapter includes:

- ❏ **Rules, objectives and principles**
- ❏ **Awareness and response**
- ❏ **The proposition**
- ❏ **Features and benefits**
- ❏ **Predisposition**
- ❏ **Interactivity**
- ❏ **AIDCA**
- ❏ **Taking the final step**

About this chapter

n this chapter we look at the special function of creative in direct marketing – above all at the drive to produce response. We are not concerned here with the finer points of copy-writing or design, but rather with what constitutes a response-inducing message; how it can be assembled, and, most importantly, how it differs from other forms of advertising.

What are the factors that predispose people to respond to direct marketing messages? How can we create such a predisposition? How can we maximise the chances of our message being seen, read, understood, accepted and acted upon? The principles through which these questions can be answered are, as we shall see, applicable to all direct marketing media.

Author/Consultant: Chris Barraclough

Chris Barraclough
Chairman Proximity London

A law graduate, Chris began his copywriting career at Smith Bundy in 1984 where he learnt his trade at the more traditional end of the direct marketing spectrum.

He then moved on to become Creative Director at DDM Advertising where he met Simon Hall. Between them they turned DDM from being a production agency into the more modern creative and strategic model we recognise throughout the UK today. Their success led to award winning campaigns for British Airways, Barclaycard, Thomas Cook and The Crown Suppliers.

In 1991 Chris became one of the founding partners of BHWG. Starting with just 5 people in an attic in Hammersmith the agency quickly found success and won many large accounts including Alliance & Leicester, Volkswagen, BT, Barclaycard, Eastern Energy, Persil, Pedigree, Pizza Hut, PC World and British Red Cross.

Today BHWG is known as Proximity London and employs around 300 staff and is one of the largest agencies in the UK. In June 1999 Chris was appointed Chairman.

Still one of the agency's most prolific writers, Chris continues to pick up awards for his work including a D&AD nomination for Volkswagen Passat and an international advertising award for a multimillion pound Alliance & Leicester mortgage campaign featuring Snoopy.

Chris is also a noted industry speaker on creative matters and regularly writes articles for the trade press that betray his distinct brand of humour.

Chris Barraclough M IDM

E-mail: barraclough.c@proximitylondon.com
Tel: 0207 298 1440

Bryan Halsey F IDM

We would like to thank Bryan Halsey who has substantially contributed to this chapter.

Chapter 7.1

Direct marketing creativity – the principles

Rules, objectives and principles

For many, the creative part of the direct marketing experience is the most compelling. It is without question, the most frustrating.

It's where science takes a back seat and instinct, experience and a certain degree of luck take over.

The creative is what should be done last. You should only start thinking about the creative once you have decided:

- What you want to say

- To whom you want to say it

- Why should they respond

When a creative project starts going wrong, it's often not because of the creativity. It's simply that the key questions have not been answered.

Another warning before we get into the meat of creative. Occasionally you might hear someone preach that creativity can be approached as you would a mathematical formula. There has been a school of thought that held that the empiric certainty of a response analysis could be extended to the creative idea and execution.

If we could use numbers or algebra to produce the sequence of words and images that are guaranteed to work most effectively every time, many of us would be redundant.

The truth is, there is no guaranteed formula for success. Or we would all be millionaires.

In the past a set of 'rules' emerged. These suggested that a successful creative treatment could almost be guaranteed. These rules were developed in the early days of direct marketing from the results of vast cold mailings for a number of quite sophisticated users who were in a position to analyse response data in a defined and scientific manner. Once the important tests had been exhausted they would turn to more marginal issues such as the difference that a change in envelope colour would make. From findings such as these people started holding daft notions such as *'yellow envelopes always work better than white'* which isn't particularly helpful, even if it were true.

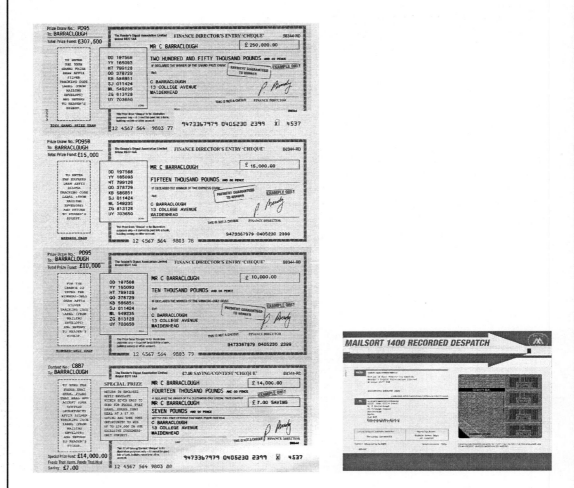

This mailing for Reader's Digest exploits every technique it can to get the reader involved and makes so many offers, that not to respond would seem foolish.

Of course, no one ever really meant the rules to be applied so rigidly. Every brief demands a different answer and judgement of what is appropriate is inevitably subjective (eg your concept of 'upmarket' might not be the same as mine).

The truth is the rules are good for one traditional part of the industry, but these days direct marketing is a broad canvas. Direct marketing is now being used for so many purposes. And most brands that are active in direct marketing have both hard and soft objectives for their response campaigns.

What I term 'hard objectives' might include:

- Direct sales (eg mail order ads).

- Generating traffic (eg store promotions).

- Encouraging trial (eg test driving a car).

- Lead generation (eg life insurance).

- Data collection/cleaning.

- Sales force warm-up (eg business-to-business).

- Web visit/brochure (eg e-mail).

- Conversion (eg incoming telemarketing).

And most campaigns have their own 'soft objectives' which often include:

- Perception shift.

- Information delivery.

- Creating predisposition.

- Relationship building.

Trying to produce a concise guide that outlines an appropriate creative treatment to cover all these eventualities is simply not possible.

There are four major reasons why hard and fast rules no longer work.

1. The presence of major brands in direct marketing, with their own strongly held views on creativity, will inevitably affect the look and style of work more than any test results.

2. Most direct marketing campaigns are now part of a wider integrated campaign usually involving an idea from above the line advertising, which puts additional constraints on the creative product. We will look at the challenge integration poses in greater depth in the next chapter.

AN INTEGRATED CAMPAIGN

Television to build awareness -------------------------------------- ➜

Press to highlight product points ---------------------------------- ➜

Inserts   **Direct mail**

To collect   To encourage

prospects   trial/test drive

                                               Telephone/e-mail

                                             To follow up prospects

Online microsite -------------------------------------- ➜

Provides new product info

To work most effectively, there should be some creative synergy between all the different media used in this simple integrated marketing plan.

---

3.   The growth of the database and new media has demanded far more tailored and relevant communication, as opposed to work that in the past had to fight shrilly for attention. Each database is unique and the work emanating from it should reflect that.

4.   Business-to-business creative doesn't operate to the same rules. Consumers are spending their own money, making decisions (relatively instantly) themselves and basing those decisions on what will benefit them most. They also purchase goods of a relatively low value (with a couple of obvious exceptions such as their house or car).

In business, decision makers are not spending their own money. Benefits are not necessarily personal (the company is usually the beneficiary), the decision making process is more complex (you have to get the MD and Financial Director to agree), and response is often indirect (they get your mailing but contact you via the website weeks later).

Consumer		**Business-to-Business**
Millions of people, in various groups	v.	Smaller defined groups, job titles
Simple decision making process	v.	Multiple decision making process
Generally lower value purchases	v.	High value purchases
Own money	v.	Business' money
Buys for personal benefit	v.	Buys for business' benefit

So throughout, we will try and deal with business-to-business differently from consumer advertising.

Having said all that, there are certain principles that have not changed from the past and that I believe to be universally true. Principles, that when applied with care and craft, will ensure your direct response campaign stands a better chance of success.

But you need to be flexible. The creative work that might be appropriate to sell a collectible porcelain figurine off the page would not be appropriate when attempting to 'warm up' a corporate treasurer before a sales consultant calls regarding a new financial service.

Therefore, the two chapters will attempt to do two things. The first chapter tackles the principles that make for successful direct response (whatever the medium). The second looks at the practice – how those principles can be best applied to different media and objectives.

Direct marketing has come a long way in a relatively short period of time. Major brands are now active users and even the aesthetes of the D&AD now recognise its creative qualities. This mailing from Volkswagen is one of a number that has been featured in the prestigious D&AD Annual.

Awareness and response

Most of us have preconceptions about what constitutes good and bad advertising. But direct response is not similar to traditional awareness advertising. It is worth considering the differences.

Key differences between traditional advertising and direct marketing

- Awareness advertising targets the mind to change behaviour.

- Direct response persuades people to take action directly.

- Direct response presents a proposition to the customer.

- Awareness advertising speaks about the product.

- People who respond are predisposed to your product.

- Predisposed people search for relevant advertising.

- Direct response should be tailored to individual needs.

- Awareness builds over time; direct response works immediately.

- Response needs to overcome inertia and result in some form of action.

- Awareness and response are measured differently.

Direct response creativity gets people to ACT as a direct result of the communication, not just think. That action might be to pick up the phone, to visit a website, to take a coupon down to the supermarket, to complete a survey etc. But ensuring you get action requires a degree of persuasion not apparent in much traditional advertising.

Traditional advertising aims to affect the way you think about something, in the hope that changing your thoughts will eventually lead you to taking a particular course of action.

Now that may not be the most incisive piece of analysis you read today, but it is important to one fact that will underline the difference between direct response creative work and other advertising.

You will be judged by your results

If you are considering producing ANY piece of direct marketing – from an e-mail to a DRTV advert – you will be judged on the response you achieve, the number of phone calls you generate and the number of customers you win.

Everything you will read on the following pages acknowledges that fact. But we do not advocate response at any cost (eg doing a promotion or using language that could harm the investment you've made in the brand). All of the principles we will talk about can be executed within the parameters of any brand.

The proposition

The one thing that will get people to respond is a proposition

All advertising is about propositions. At its simplest, a proposition is why the prospect needs the product. An example would be:"Washes and conditions in one application". John Watson, who has probably forgotten more about propositions than I will ever know says;

Get your proposition right and half your job is done.

Without a motivating proposition you won't get anyone to do anything. So what is a proposition?

The IDM defines a proposition thus: A direct marketing proposition is a **single-minded approach** to an **emotional need** supported by a **rational argument** that **inspires people to act**

Easy to write, very hard to get right.

Single-minded. Most great advertising (of any type) does one thing well. When you think of great ad campaigns from the past, you probably remember a strapline or a thought eg "Volvos are safe", "Persil washes whiter", "Heineken refreshes", "It's good to talk". Really simple, single-minded and effective. But those are examples of awareness advertising where the advertiser is simply making a statement about the brand or product.

A proposition connects directly with the prospect. It speaks to him. A good proposition builds the bridge between the consumer and the product.

Of course, the proposition for the same product may be different for different target markets. The cute little Volkswagen Lupo could be positioned as a fashionable design icon for a young audience but as a solid, safe and secure small car for older drivers.

Testing and research will help determine what the strongest proposition might be. For example, here are two propositions for private healthcare:

Price proposition
"With *Healthcure* you and your family can enjoy the benefits of private health care for just £30 a month".

Security proposition
"With *Healthcure* you can protect your own and your family's health against delays in the NHS".

In these home insurance press ads, it's the same product but with distinct propositions. Some will appeal to those who already know about the benefits of private care but simply need a cheap price. Another specifically targets people renewing during May and June. A third has a specific proposition for the over 50s. The fourth uses an incentive to get people on the phone.

All might work, as they would attract slightly different customers. There's very rarely one answer that's 100% right for everyone.

The detergent market is instructive. Like it or not, the chemical formulae for the brands that clean your clothes are pretty much the same. Brands provide a point of differentiation. So do the formats in which they are offered. We now have standard powder, concentrated powder, liquid, tablets and capsules.

When tablets were launched, direct marketing creative for Persil expressed their benefit in two distinct ways. To people to whom the new technology of tablets would appeal (early adopters) Persil focused on the fact that it was a revolutionary new way to clean clothes.

To others, it could focus on the simplicity and ease of tablets (no messy powders or liquid to spill). And you're guaranteed to use the correct quantity – no wastage.

Differentiated propositions for Persil Tablets:

Early adopters:
The revolutionary new way to clean your clothes.

Persil traditionalists (like my mum):
Try the detergent you trust in an easier-to-use format.

Users of other brands:
Switch to an easier way of cleaning and caring for your clothes.

The same product was expressed in terms of a relevant benefit to different groups. The supports were similar but presented in different ways: the cleverness of tablets working from the middle of the wash to one, group the ease of simply placing them in the drum to another.

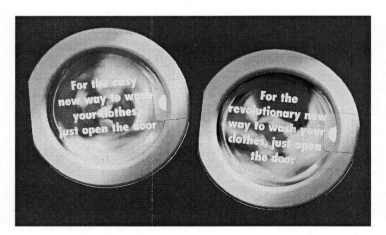

On these two Persil direct mail packs you can see two different propositions aimed very deliberately at two different markets.

Direct marketing allows you to tailor your creative

This is one example of the principle that the more you are able to tailor your communication, the more effective it will be. Some of the media exploited by direct marketers – mail, e-mail, phone – can be personalised and/or tailored to a very high degree. We will look at some examples of this in the next chapter.

The general rule is that the more you can personalise or tailor a communication the more effective it will be. However, personalisation needs to add something. A letter addressed, *"Dear Mr Barraclough,"* is fine. But *"Dear Mr Barraclough, as you sit in your home at 26 Harcourt Place, London ... etc."* while far more personalised is utterly over the top. I don't need reminding where I live.

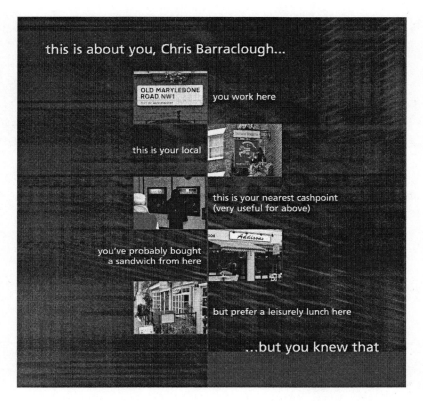

Personalisation can mean more than name and address and customers expect you to use data. This remarkable B2B mailing selling me creative services uses all the power of digital printing to personalise. Not only does it feature my name, address and the name of my production director but to prove how personalisation can grab your attention, it features photographs of my office, nearest cashpoint, restaurant and local pub!

On the other hand, customers expect you to know certain facts about them and to use them in your communications with them. They expect you to know what they last ordered, when they ordered, how much credit they have left, what their phone number is etc ...

There's only one thing more annoying than being asked for information you know the company already has on you. That is for the information to be wrong.

Which means your tailoring will be wrong. Your data must be robust enough to support the level of personalisation you are attempting. If you're not sure, don't do it.

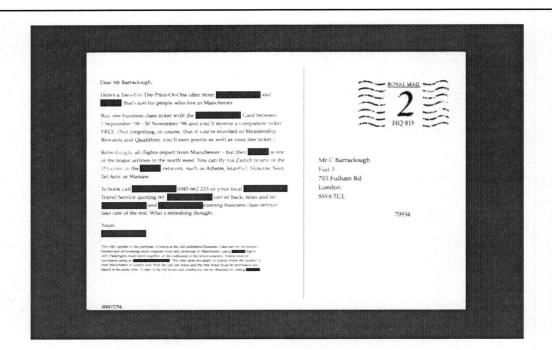

This unfortunate postcard shows the traps data can set. The first line of copy talks about a special offer exclusively for people living in Manchester. It was addressed to me at home in Fulham.

The more you can tailor a proposition and personalise the communication, the better.

Here are a couple of life insurance ads, the same product all with different propositions tailored to different mind-sets. Which do you think would work best? It's not hard.

However, there are still strong and weak propositions. A good proposition comes with the promise of a real benefit to the customer. A weak one is where the customer might respond with a dismissive 'so what'.

Weak proposition
"Why not learn another language?"

Strong proposition
"Speak another language within 3 months".

The first proposition is very broad. It's a big thought but remains too open. Far too big a subject to be tackled in a single responsive execution. It also talks about 'learning' which is a dull, laborious process, not the end benefit.

The second targets those already predisposed to learning a language (who are most likely to respond) and has a clear benefit. People want to *speak* a new language, rather than *learn* one. And they want to do it quickly.

Many propositions are weak because the advertiser is talking about the product or his company (as awareness advertising does), not about how it would benefit the consumer. Or they are just boasting about a feature in a self-centred way. Consider the following examples, and then see how we can turn them into more motivating consumer propositions based on exactly the same facts.

For a credit card:
So what? We have signed up over 1,000,000 merchants worldwide.
Motivating Switch to a card you can use anywhere in the world.

For a bank:
So what? We have the widest range of mortgage products in the UK.
Motivating You can be sure of a mortgage that suits your needs.

For a telecoms company:
So what? We have over 2,000 hard working administrative staff.
Motivating Switch to us for personal service guaranteed 24 hours day.

For a car:
So what? Our People Carrier is made in our brand new Leicester factory.
Motivating There is no correct version. No one really cares where anything is made, just that it delivers on its promise.

Benefits and features merge as markets mature. Then the focus of your proposition will change. 15 years ago mobile phones were originally sold on the basis of "now you can speak to someone wherever you are". Today they are sold on price. Similarly businesses no longer buy broadband on a promise of quicker download times – they know it's quick – they'll get it on how cheaply and quickly you'll install it.

The classic business-to-business proposition

In business-to-business, propositions often distil to a similar claim. And that is "this product/service will save your business time and money (ie help your business become more efficient)". It is very important, when considering what the most motivating thing is to say about your business service, to agree some point of differentiation by way of a support, especially if your proposition is such a generic one.

For example, three companies may all offer businesses an Internet connection, all priced competitively (which will help their customers be more efficient). But only one offers the feature whereby you can create a bespoke e-mail address (ie yourname@yourbusiness.com). The real benefit of this is that it makes your business e-mail easier to remember. Suddenly, this secondary benefit assumes a more important role.

Price is frequently less of a sensitive issue for businesses (price is often positioned in terms of cost-effectiveness and is frequently negotiable or too complex to quote), which is why a good business proposition will focus on how the product will improve efficiency or help control costs. Be careful not to overclaim, though. There are very few business products that will have an immediate and noticeable impact on the bottom line.

Revolutionise your business with our new desktop laser printer is a laughable but all too common headline. Ensure your proposition can be substantiated.

Even a catalogue, while it may contain many products, works most effectively with an overall proposition (eg the latest technical innovations and affordable fashion). Each item's individual proposition should fit within the umbrella proposition.

Where your direct response proposition comes from

Like all good advertising it should come from the product itself. The proposition should highlight some benefit that the product is capable of delivering. It is always worth writing down what elements of the product allow you to make the claim in the proposition. These 'supports' should form the body of your communication – the way you justify your proposition. They might be the product's features and/or something to do with the marketplace that makes the proposition particularly apposite.

Consider this example of a 'flexible mortgage' – one where you can vary your monthly payments, so you can pay more when you're a little flush or take a payment holiday if you've built up some credit.

The proposition might be: "With this mortgage you can save on interest payments".

The headline might be expressed as: "Pay your mortgage off early and save up to £25,000".

The supports are:

1.   It allows you to choose how much you pay each month.

2.   Pay £150 extra every month and you will pay it off 10 years early.

3.   Every year you take off, you save £2,500 in interest.

4.   Our interest rate is very competitive.

5.   We pay your valuation fee.

The proposition came out of the three primary features of the product and have been expressed as a major benefit to the consumer. We don't use every single support to create our proposition, but we will explain them all in the body copy.

Different propositions to maximise the audience – one based on entry price, another on ease of use, one on the joys of limitless online shopping, another on the benefits of being able to surf at length.

Another example could be for a 'one stop' IT package for very small businesses to help them use their PCs more effectively.

Take the supports first – the truths about the product or brand.

1.   PCs and software are cheaper than ever.

2.   This package contains PC, software, Internet connection and training.

3.   It only costs £299 (+VAT).

4.   Word processing software is included.

5.   Price includes 2 year warranty.

6.   We are a trusted supplier.

The proposition might be: "Everything you need to get your business online for just £299", or: "It's never been cheaper or easier to get your business online."

This proposition only works because the online marketplace has matured. A couple of years back we were saying: "Get e-mail and the Internet to improve your business' efficiency". Now we can assume most business people understand the benefits of going online. They just need the 'push' to do something about it.

> Put at its simplest, people will respond to any communication if they think there's something in it for them or their business.

Notice that the six supports for our 'one stop' IT package proposition are all **features** of the package. Features are not the same as benefits.

Features and benefits

The main proposition and preferably the supports need to be expressed in terms of a benefit to a customer or to their business. The more benefits there are, the more reasons people will have to respond.

Put simply, benefits are features seen from the customer's viewpoint.

Example:
Feature: snooze button   **Benefit**: an extra few minutes to doze

Sometimes features become so well recognised that it is not necessary to spell out the benefit. Doing so may even restrict the appeal, because the same feature may benefit different people in different ways. Example:

Feature: 0-60 in 4.9 seconds   **Benefit**: leave traffic cops trailing in your wake

The driver who wants to accelerate from 0-60 in under 5 seconds already knows why. Not all drivers will share the same ambition to outrun the law.

John Watson (*Successful Creativity in Direct Marketing*) advocates the feature/ benefit doublet. This is based on the simple formula: **x has y, which means z.** Example:

There's a snooze button, so you can give yourself an extra few minutes of dozing, safe in the knowledge you won't miss the alarm again.

There will always be exceptions but, as a general rule, it is a good idea to turn features into benefits. Doing so means looking at the product from the customer's angle.

If you think of these benefits in terms of subheads to a brochure, you will typically see lines such as:

Typical consumer benefits		Typical business benefits
Saves you up to 30 minutes a day	v.	Cuts costs by 30%
Costs as little as a pint of milk a day	v.	Discounts for volume
Free gift when you order	v.	Extra guide for business included
Available on a 14 day free trial	v.	Full service and support provided
Post and package included	v.	Experts will install and train your staff
Order via our special hotline	v.	Order via www.ourbusiness.co.uk

> From the important benefits comes your core proposition. Overlay the insights you have for your target market and then differentiate your core proposition accordingly.

Now that we have tackled what it is we can say, we need to consider the people to whom we are saying it. This leads us onto another important principle regarding successful direct marketing creativity.

Predisposition

The people who respond are predisposed to your product

They may even be actively searching for your advertising. Which is nice. The chances are they will have already done a little research and your communication will hit them just at the right time.

> The buying process can be seen in the steps people take when buying a car. When customers are out of the market – perhaps they've recently bought a new car – they are not receptive to communications trying to sell them another one. They will though, be aware of various TV ads trying to build either an image for a brand or introducing them to new models. They might say to themselves, "Yeah, BMWs look nice", but they are unlikely to do anything about it.
>
> However, as the time when they want to replace their car approaches, they begin to take a greater interest. They might start reading a few reviews or press ads. They might draw up a list of suitable brands in their heads. They will begin to acquire knowledge. Which makes, models and formats fit their needs. They might then visit a dealership and finally take a test drive before reducing their shortlist to 1.

It's during these latter stages that they are receptive to direct marketing. They will be sufficiently motivated to act.

Admittedly, not every purchase process is similar to buying a car, but many are and the way you buy items in a supermarket follows a similar pattern, but in a much more condensed form. It is certainly a similar process that you would go through before becoming loyal to a supermarket.

To respond to any piece of direct response usually requires a degree of confidence or knowledge. By the time consumers have come to the point of responding they will, at worst, be in the market and at best be very close to making a decision. Once they have bought, they will probably move out of the market again.

FMCG doesn't work quite like this as you are constantly buying the same products week in week out, but the purchase of many white, brown and other higher ticket products follow this pattern.

That explains why some traditional direct advertisers (language courses, mail order products, music and book clubs etc.) can successfully continue to run the same execution for years and years. Because people come in and out of the market. They won't notice your advert at all while they are out of the market, but as soon as they are interested they will spot it – even if it's small in size.

Adverts like these have run with only a few changes in the same style and format for years. Why do they not tire? Because people continually come in and out of the market.

A good example is financial services. You won't sell a loan to someone who doesn't want to borrow money. But as soon as they have seen the car they want they will avidly devour loan advertising they've been ignoring for the rest of the year. Hopefully this is when your insert will fall out of their Sunday paper.

Why is this important? Because it will have a fundamental affect on your creative work.

Predisposition affects the creative execution in two ways

Firstly, it's important to flag up what the product category is. This again is very true for financial services. People buy financial services on a product by product basis. For example, it is important from a cursory look at an advert to know whether it's for 'Mortgages' or for 'Savings'.

A good technique is to ask yourself whether, without a product flag or name in the headline, the ad could apply to any other product.

To take one example *"act now for our great rates"* could apply to any type of loan (mortgage, unsecured or secured personal loan). On the other hand, the same headline could equally apply to a savings account – a completely different concept. So it's important to make the product category clear. A potential borrower, as well as an investor, will spot the ads aimed at them and hopefully read on.

This principle is the argument for messages on envelopes, subject lines on e-mails and slipping the product category into a DRTV script right at the beginning. People will self-select their mail on the basis of relevance. If the envelope highlights the product category then it stands a better chance of being opened and read. If the envelope promises a benefit, better still.

> If the group you are targeting is tightly defined then you can use their predisposition as your main headline.

This is the basic principle that applies to classified and recruitment advertising.

The headline for an ad in the back pages of a magazine for a homeopathic cure that simply says *"back pain?"* immediately targets those with back problems. *"Turned down for credit"* focuses on one tightly defined group of people who need a loan.

This lead generating advert goes straight for the target market – families who have young children.

Sometimes your advertising needs to accommodate both. *"Need life insurance?"* will probably work well, as will *"Protect your family if you die"*. Which one do you go with? You probably need to try both. The first might appeal to those who understand the need and are 'topping up' their insurance. The latter is more likely to target those without any insurance and who haven't really thought about the concept.

Predisposition doesn't just affect the proposition. It affects the body and style of your communication, too.

People who are predisposed want to know more

This will dictate how much copy you should include and how much detail you should go into. This sometimes leads to tired debates on length of copy and arcane issues such as how many pages a letter should run to. We tackle this and other issues in the next chapter. The principle, for what it's worth, is that copy should only be as long as it needs to be and when you have said what you need to say, stop.

People will read copy if they are predisposed and interested in the subject matter. In the UK, cat owners will lap up everything and anything about their cats. This Whiskas mailing has a long brochure on caring for your new kitten. Every word will be devoured by kitten owners who view their pets very much as small children.

Now, I admit that's not much help and in the next chapter we will give you a better guide than that.

Interactivity

Interactivity is the key to getting online to work

Too many marketers simply adapt their offline work into banner ads, pop-ups, interstitials and transitionals without considering the basic principle upon which online advertising is based. Unlike any other medium, online is directly interactive.

From my PC I can click my mouse on a button and respond directly. That is the way I am used to working with my computer and therefore I have that same expectation when I see your online advertising. In no more than 3 clicks I should be able to get exactly where I want to.

I should then be able to order or enquire and receive an immediate, tailored and personal response. Make it simple for me to submit forms, donations or even make a purchase.

But at the acquisition stage, it is vital that you get me to interact. That's why the most persuasive online work allows me to interact with the message using various techniques and features including games, quizzes, competitions, forums, e-mails etc. Online is not a passive medium. A well-executed campaign will be passed on to friends and family (the direct marketers' dream), producing a viral effect that will rapidly multiply your audience.

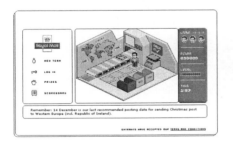

This simple little online game was e-mailed by the Royal Mail to post room managers to help them appreciate the optimum services to use for different types of package.

AIDCA

To sell directly, you need to follow AIDCA

Certainly when you are attempting to sell directly, you will need to apply the full sales pitch following the sales philosophy, AIDCA. This is the principle successfully used by sales forces throughout the world. In direct marketing we simply adapt it to print or broadcast. Attention, Interest, Desire, Conviction, Action.

AIDCA recognises that sales messages are sequential. That there are certain steps you have to go through before someone gets their wallet out. Certainly, when selling directly, there are various criteria that need to be satisfied. And this may take up more space than you think.

You have to get a prospect's Attention first; you then capture their Interest, create a Desire, reassure them that you and your product have Conviction and then ask for Action (closing the sale).

If you've ever been sold to by a good salesman, you'll have been through this from the other side. It is quite possible to complete the same process in a direct marketing communication. Even in a small ad or on one side of a letter.

Effective one-stage sale ads incorporate every AIDCA principle. We can best demonstrate how these elements can be arranged in a single communication by means of an example.

This Innovations ad for silver plate solution may be a few years old now but is still a classic:

- Headline combines news and chief benefit.

- Illustrations show what the product is and what it does. (Products whose benefits are immediately apparent are more likely to succeed in mail order.)

- Text comprises benefits, corroboration and explanation – every possible misunderstanding is soothed away as it arises.

- The copy is honest about what it cannot do, helping to create reassurance.

- A long list of possible uses bolsters value and minimises risk in the prospect's mind.

- The offer is clear to get you to order it now.

- Note the use of features and benefits, eg "non-toxic and odour free, so you can safely use it on cutlery".

- Independent testimonials are prominently sited.

- The technical specification, ie the components of the kit, are spelled out in full in a panel separate from the body copy (top right).

- Conviction is boosted by the 30-day full money refund guarantee; note also the MOPS logo (Mail Order Protection Scheme).

- There is a phone order number as well as the coupon (today there would be website/e-mail details).

This is how Bryan Halsey explains the routing for AIDCA:

Attention	Headline and/or visual Product/service flag Positioning (front page of paper) Format (big, small, different, colours) Online – flash, pop-up etc.
Interest	The proposition Words that suggest news Benefits Features Advantages
Desire	Offers Discounts Exclusivity
Conviction	Tone and empathy Demonstration Comparisons Testimonials/endorsements Guarantees Trial Hot line
Action	Repeating the benefits and offer Response mechanisms Ease of reply Ease of payment

One way to evaluate whether your creative solution abides by the AIDCA principle is to put yourself in the position of the prospect and ask the following 8 questions.

Attention: Are you talking to me?

Interest: Why are you talking to me?
                  What is it you want me to know?

Desire: It's a nice idea but do I really need it?
                  What do you want me to accept?

Conviction: How can I be sure I'm not making a mistake?

Action: What do I have to do?
                  Is it easy to do?

Remember, you are talking to people who are interested. You need to move them into taking an action and that takes persuasive skill. Following AIDCA will help you do that. The principles of AIDCA are sound for both consumer and business marketing when you are trying to open and close the sale in one hit.

Not every piece of direct marketing communication is trying to sell you something directly.

If you are simply trying to elicit a response without a direct monetary commitment you don't need to go into so much detail. If you are targeting a 'money-off' coupon at a segment of your database, the coupon itself with a little explanatory copy should suffice. If you are using relevant data from the database and can tailor your mail quite tightly, it is that relevance that will lead to success.

Amazing what you can win in a raffle these days.

This prospect gathering insert is light on copy, but with an attractive prize draw – win a Volkswagen Golf. The role of the copy and the coupon is to attract the right *quality* of respondent (ie someone who is quite likely to buy a new Volkswagen in the near future). So we ask them what they are currently driving (a good indicator) and when they are planning a replacement.

Quite often you will hear people say "don't write so much copy, no one will ever read it." This, as I hope you now appreciate, is a false argument, and it is not a licence for verbose copywriters to become self-indulgent.

> One exception to this is text e-mails, where however worthy the copy, long chunks of text are very, very hard to read on screen and you cannot rely on people taking the trouble to print them out. However, this affects the style in which the text is presented, more than the volume of text.

In the next chapter on 'Direct marketing creativity in practice' we will talk more about quantity of copy and structure and what formats work best for all media – old and new.

So far we have seen how important the right proposition is to any successful piece of direct response, and also how we must present our proposition in terms of benefits. And we have seen that the type of people who respond are predisposed.

We now move on to the principles that will get people not just to welcome your communication but to take the next step and pick up the phone, visit your website or send in the order form.

Taking the final step

Awareness builds over time, direct response works immediately

This principle has a direct impact on what your communication looks like. But it's worth investigating a little further.

A good brand campaign will build an image or set of values over a period of time. It's not something you can do in one hit, and if you are good at it, like Volkswagen, you will continue expounding the same values over many, many years. A strong TV based campaign may have two or three different executions based on the same idea (eg *Guinness is worth waiting for, The future is Orange, Stella Artois is refreshingly expensive, No FT no comment* etc).

These executions are frequently entertaining, visually exciting and bear repeated watching. Eventually they will sink into your consciousness so the next time you stroll up to a bar, you order a pint of Stella without even thinking about it.

Direct response doesn't work like this. That is not to say there are no examples of direct marketing campaigns that have had a long-term impact on image or values. Land Rover have worked hard to build their brand via direct communications for a number of years, as have First Direct, AOL, Direct Line, Dell and latterly Amazon, as well as other *successful* dot-coms.

Amazon was one of the first examples of a brand being successfully built online through applying solid direct marketing principles.

But when your aim is to get a response from an individual execution, you only have one hit and you have to make it work.

Try this exercise: *List the direct mail packs you received last week: who they were from and what they were about. You will struggle. You probably couldn't even list the e-mails you received at the office today, let alone last week.*

Think of all those direct response TV commercials you see on satellite and cable. The ones with the smiling presenters and the large phone numbers. Without viewing them again, you may find it hard to distinguish one from another.

They follow a formula, certainly, and a none too subtle one. But why? Why is it that you wouldn't get the same levels of response from planting a phone number at the end of a beautifully crafted and entertaining image ad?

The fact is that the direct response execution relies on triggers and a sense of urgency to get people to act there and then. The fact you don't remember the ad the following week is to miss the point.

The even more amazing thing is that even though a company like *'cheap loans direct'* will be using the same execution over and over again, you won't remember it. Probably because you don't need to borrow money. However the style and tone of the piece will be designed to maximise response to that execution, rather than to make it memorable.

When you only have one opportunity of getting a response, you cannot afford to be indulgent, obscure or ponderous. This sometimes causes problems when you are trying to integrate your creative with a very intricate or highly entertaining above the line idea.

Indulgence is a vice that particularly afflicts those who like to 'tease' their customers before revealing either the benefits or the brand. While some commentators applaud their cleverness, most customers couldn't care less.

In the business market I have even seen an eight stage mailing, with each day a postcard revealing (in order) one letter from the advertiser's name. The eighth mailing revealed the brand's name in full. Ingenious or irritating? Being business-to-business it is highly unlikely the recipient would receive the letters in anything like the right order.

The principle of clarity and simplicity applies to branding. A strong brand is always a clear and positive flag and should always be clearly present. Established brands should ensure all work fits comfortably within their values and design guidelines.

Not everyone has a strong brand to reassure consumers. You then have to give them confidence using other techniques such as the advice offered by the US copywriter, Joan Throckmorton:

New marketers

Provide ample *substantiation* – Years in business, awards, premises, people, financial data endorsements, consumer groups.

Testimonials with full names and pictures.

Trial offers, guarantees, refund schemes etc.

Senior management seen to underwrite deal, contact details.

Drayton Bird often and rightly repeats David Ogilvy's mantra 'no one buys from a clown'. That is not to say a good piece of direct marketing cannot have wit and charm, but all-out humour is more likely to get in the way than it is to help explain the message.

There will be exceptions to this, particularly with quirky and youth orientated brands with 'attitude'. But these are small in number and self-defined.

To achieve your response you should be clear and simple

Make absolutely sure the reader or viewer is in no doubt what sector you are in so they can self-select your communication on the basis of their need.

Be clear about the benefits. The customer should be able to look at your communication and instantly assess whether 'it's for them' and 'what's in it for them'. We will study the ways you do this in the different media in the next chapter.

You should apply the principles of simplicity and clarity yourself. This will affect the composition and style of your communication. The experienced FMCG direct marketers, who are usually aiming for targeted product trial, simply mail time-dated coupons (so they encourage weekly usage) with a simple bit of explanatory copy about the brand. 'Money off coupons' inside is written on the envelope and they are strongly branded. Strategically sophisticated, executably simple.

This simple mailing for "I Can't Believe It's Not Butter" brings the product to life and offers a trial coupon. A typical FMCG one piece mailing.

Perhaps the principle of simplicity and clarity comes into its own when it comes to explaining to the recipient what it is you want them to do next.

A simple rule is 'if they can get it wrong, they will get it wrong'. Admittedly, customers are far more aware of what is expected of them than they used to be. But if there is either a lack of clarity as to what the next stage is, or there are too many obstacles in the way, they simply won't bother.

Some customers are more sophisticated than others.

A business audience will normally feel confident responding by phone or via a website/e-mail. They will be used to completing order forms online.

Younger people use the phone, SMS or e-mail.

More elderly, less well-educated consumers will need a coupon as well as a phone number.

Neither business people nor consumers will respond if there are too many seemingly irrelevant questions, or if the terms of payment don't fit within their normal expectations.

Whatever the route is it has to be presented clearly. Viewers do not sit in front of the television with pencil in hand ready to jot down phone numbers. It may surprise you how much more response you'll get by including a pre-addressed reply envelope even when you are offering a *freepost* address.

Bryan Halsey and other leading direct marketing experts believe there are 5 things you should consider:

1. **Plan for a response.** Restate the chief benefit, the offer and any incentives in the vicinity of the order device, if not actually on it. Introduce additional benefits to 'tip' prospects into action, eg a product benefit held back for the purpose, or inducements related only to ordering, eg limited offer, 'early bird' (gift for prompt response), discounts for volume.

2. **Prospects must know a response is expected**. Clarity and simplicity applies to phone numbers; coupons; order/application forms; e-mail addresses; fax numbers; reply-paid devices; and payment options (eg credit card logos, direct debit mandates).

3. **Ask for a response.** Just as the good salesperson will attempt a trial close early in the sales pitch, the good direct marketing creative will introduce a trial close. Some confident marketers bravely open with a 'trial close' before a word about the product. Such an approach requires a very powerful offer.

4. **State response expected.** The response device should be specific as to what response is expected, what commitment (if any) it entails and what will ensue. In the case of charities and financial services, recommended donations/investments will encourage imitation.

5. **Make it easy to respond.** Ease may mean providing sufficient space for writing, holding a phone number on the TV screen long enough for prospects to jot it down, or other physical aids.

People do need a push to respond. Inertia is our worst enemy. That is why we make offers (see point 2 above). No one will decide which car to buy on the basis of whether they get a free travel rug or not. But the offer of a free rug for a test drive will make them act there and then, rather than leave it to another day (which probably means you will lose them).

That's why a good offer will work best in conjunction with an 'offer closes' date.

To summarise the principles of direct response creative:

*   Direct response persuades people to take action directly.

*   Direct response presents a proposition to you, the customer.

*   Direct response needs to meet the demands of predisposed customers.

*   Direct response is tailored to individual needs.

*   Direct response needs to have an immediate effect.

*   Direct response online should be interactive.

*   Direct response demands simplicity and clarity.

*   Direct response needs to overcome inertia.

Chapter 7.2

Direct marketing creativity in practice

This chapter includes:

- ❏ **Working within the parameters of the brand**
- ❏ **Integrating your work with a broader campaign**
- ❏ **Tone and style**
- ❏ **How the use of data defines the creative content**
- ❏ **A basic direct mail pack**
- ❏ **Press advertising demonstrates the techniques in a small space**
- ❏ **Online works best when it's interactive**
- ❏ **The secret life of the insert**
- ❏ **DRTV and interactive TV**
- ❏ **Radio**
- ❏ **Summary**

About this chapter

I n the previous chapter we looked at some of the underlying principles of creative work in direct marketing. Now we get down to some of the nitty-gritty of how these principles might be translated into execution in a wide variety of direct media.

Once again, there are no hard and fast rules: the ultimate question to be asked of any direct creative solution is – does it work? And the joy of direct marketing is that to this question there can always be found a yes/no answer. But the experience of many marketers over many years does suggest that some things are perhaps more likely to work than others; and some of this accumulated wisdom we attempt to share here with readers.

Chris Barraclough author and consultant

Chris's biography appears in chapter 7.1.

I am indebted to Warren Moore, Bryan Halsey, George Smith and Katie Purcer for their help with the chapters where my knowledge is woefully inadequate.

Chapter 7.2

Direct marketing creativity in practice

Introduction

This chapter shows how some of the principles expounded in the previous chapter can be put into practice.

Again, the suggestions we make are not hard and fast rules. No two jobs are the same, but over the years certain things have been found to work well on a consistent basis.

As to new media, there is still much learning to be done. With online communications you have the opportunity to be highly tailored without it being prohibitively expensive. More of that later.

A simple idea, clearly executed with a strong proposition to the consumer is what we are after in almost every case. As we said in the last chapter, the creative work should only be started once all the key elements of the brief are agreed, especially:

- Who we are talking to

- What we are going to say to them

- Why they should respond

- How they should respond

If you are in an agency, working for clients, you'll also want to know how much time you have got and what the budget is.

It is now the creative team's job to take that brief and convert it into something that will gain the attention of the consumer and inspire them to act.

Suffice to say that all the best, most effective work will have been 90% perspiration, attention to detail, crafting and continual reassessment.

In this chapter we will look at how the principles of direct response creativity can be translated into the main direct response media including:

- Direct mail

- Press

- Loose inserts

- Broadcast (including interactive)

- E-mail and online communications

- Others including ambient, radio, door-drops and posters

We will also consider what creative will look like depending on different tasks such as:

- Acquisition

- Direct sale

- Lead generation

- Relationship management

- Fundraising

Along the way we will also see how those principles dictate the creative tone and style for specific sectors, such as:

- Charities

- Mail order

- Financial services

- FMCG

- Business-to-business

Working within the parameters of the brand

Of course, when it comes to considering what your communication should look like, your template will be guided by the brand. If you are working with a major brand, there will inevitably be a set of guidelines covering elements of design such as typography, use and position of logos and other regulations regarding style.

Written or not, there will almost always be a set of guidelines covering 'softer' topics such as language, imagery, tone of voice, and core values etc. Sometimes these are published (often in CD form or online) along with examples and commentary. Sometimes, as in the case of Volkswagen's very individual tone of voice, they reside within the accumulated experience of the client and the agency.

Before embarking on any project, it is worth researching and understanding the parameters of the brand with which you are working. It will save you time and heartache later.

It goes without saying that any direct response creative work should support and bolster the brand. However, all of the direct response principles expounded in the previous chapter can be adapted to fit any brand's values.

For example, a prize draw will stimulate response among an affluent group of jet-setting celebrities as well as low income households in the inner cities. The relaunch of British Airways First Class brand a few years back necessitated the collection of data among passengers flying in the First Class cabin. They represented some of the richest, most urbane people in the world and included minor aristocracy, media celebrities and diplomats among their number.

It was agreed that a prize draw would boost response. Except that the prize was not the usual family car or holiday in the sun. For the same price as either of these classic prizes, BA acquired a small French Impressionist painting. It had a very high perceived value, was unique and perfectly attuned to the aspirations of the First Class passenger.

The tone and language reflected first class values, but it was to all intents a prize draw similar to any other.

This mailing from the Landmark Trust is trying to raise funds to restore the Grange, a house of major importance designed by none other than Pugin. Pugin? He was the architect for the Houses of Parliament. So the mailing recipients are that august body of fine, upstanding men and women – MPs (hence the lofty tone). The purpose is the same as a million other mailings: to get people to part with their money.

Integrating your work with a broader campaign

Ensuring that your creative fits the brand is one thing. Making it integrate into a bigger campaign is another. Now that direct response has become a core marketing activity, rather than some strange sect, it has to take its place within the broader scheme of things.

The creative idea behind the heavyweight campaign will impact on your creative work and you may well be asked to ensure your work reflects that campaign.

The mistake many people fall into at this point is to believe that creative integration equates to slavish copying; that the direct mail pack should simply be the TV ad in a print format. So you will occasionally see print material with poorly reproduced stills from the television advertising.

Yet it is highly likely that your direct response creative work will be performing a different strategic function to other elements of the campaign – it will be turning the general awareness either into leads or sales. It will be operating in its own media – press, inserts, mail and online.

The best rule is to maximise the strengths of the individual medium within the core idea. What works well on television – movement, sound, characterisation etc. – does not work in static media such as mail or press. In mail you can convey information; it is tactile and you can send 'objects' to dramatise what it is you are trying to say. Online you can exploit interactivity and the depth that the Internet gives you.

How you interpret the core campaign idea is a matter of some subjectivity and the chances are you will be obliged to include some common elements – a strapline, campaign design icons etc. You may even be required to include some common campaign phraseology such as 'cares and cleans', 'extraordinary service etc'.

The main point is that you should integrate with the campaign idea, rather than the television execution. Your direct response will prove far more effective if you are able to maximise the strengths of the medium you are working with.

In this example from Volkswagen, the creative idea plays on the fact that everyone likes their new car to stay exactly as it was the day they got it. The television ads that preceded this mailing showed a man hiring a taxi rather than allowing his unkempt dog into the car, and a father refusing to allow his son, whom we see passing his driving test, to drive his new car. The press ads follow this thought and the direct mail pack features pictures of the car with blemishes on them. These marks (including cobwebs and stains) are created via a special printing process and can be wiped off with a cloth that's included in the pack.

Tone and style

If you are working neither with a recognised brand nor within a campaign, you clearly have a much freer rein. But the tone and style of your work should still be governed by the target audience you are addressing, as well as the positioning you want to give your product.

Examples of differing tone, reflected in their copy style:

- Volkswagen: Self-deprecating

- Virgin: Honest

- FCUK: 'Attitude'

- Persil: Caring

- Barclays: Confident

- Audi: Technical

- Easyjet: Eager

- Dixons: Salesy

It is not for us to suggest what may or may not be a suitable tone for your brand, but there a few general points worth considering.

Remember, you can still be hard-hitting, direct and salesy in a sophisticated way if you need to be. John Lewis's famous claim 'Never knowingly undersold' is pretty much the same as, say, Dixons claiming 'You can't beat our prices'. It's just phrased in a way that has proved more appealing to middle class sensitivities.

While it is also true that business people are consumers when they are at home, they do have a different set of priorities when taking decisions that will affect their business lives. For instance, a business decision is one they will have to justify to others and could affect their career, and this is a serious matter. Which is perhaps why humour and entertainment work less well in a business environment than in a consumer one, where the consequences of making a decision are less far reaching.

That does not preclude a little wit, but all-out humour is rarely effective. As discussed in the previous chapter, people don't buy from a clown and in business that is particularly true.

These mortgage adverts use the famous Peanuts visuals to appeal to different attitude types found as a result of research. The cartoons themselves are quite amusing but serve a serious purpose. Research highlighted 3 different types of mortgage buyer. In these ads different features of the product are emphasised, depending on the customer type. For example, one appeals to cautious people who need security and reassurance; another to those who like to weigh up the options from different providers. The Peanuts cartoons are being used to create empathy with these attitudes.

Similarly, charities are almost by definition working with sobering issues and the tone of the creative should respect that.

Tone and style may also change as your relationship with a customer changes and develops. The eager and salesy tone you employed to win them over initially will not be appropriate once they've been with you for a period of time.

To use the correct jargon, the tone and style you adopt for your acquisition creative probably ain't right for your relationship work. Don't talk to people who know you as if you had never met!

Developing a tone for relationship management

I've included a short case history based on some creative research. The principles are as relevant to an online relationship as offline and might help you consider the tone and style of your e-mail communications.

Two agencies were given this brief by a leading building society: Consider the next three years. We will be writing to customers about our range of products including mortgages, loans, savings and insurance. How should we talk to them?

A range of executions were produced by both agencies. As it happened the two agencies were quite distinct in their approaches. To cut a very long researcher's debrief short, the first agency produced direct mail that by and large used the tried and trusted techniques for maximising response to cold mailings. The executions featured flashes, special offers, long letters, PS's etc.

The second agency produced work that was more reserved in its tone. Too reserved, certainly, to generate large volumes of response from 'cold' or even mildly warm prospects. For example, the envelopes were predominantly clean and white with only the logo on the front. The sales messages were discreet. The letters were short (less than a side), yet utilised all the data available on customers right down to exploiting their account information to cross-sell other products.

Customers universally put direct mail into four categories:

1. *Personal mail. (Letters from family and friends, which they read immediately and give them pleasure.)*

2. *Personal business mail. (Letters from their bank, solicitors, estate agents – companies with which they have a strong relationship predominantly giving them information. These they deal with pretty much straight away.)*

3. *Direct mail. (Letters from companies with which they have a relationship and are now trying to cross-sell other products. They look at these when they can find time, probably in the evening or at the weekend.)*

4. *Junk mail. (Hard-hitting mail from companies they either don't know or have no relationship with, selling stuff they are rarely interested in. Either junked or glanced at over the weekend.)*

The client had felt that their work had too often looked and read as though it fitted into category 4 (hence the process). At the very least, they wanted to move it into category 3.

Other findings included the fact that customers were beginning to understand the game. They recognised the Mailsort sign and immediately understood it was a mass mailing unlikely to include anything of immediate personal interest.

Branding on the envelope was important, too. Customers had a strong affinity with brand and felt reassured by its presence.

Contrary to 'pub talk' they appreciated headlines on the envelope and at the top of the letter. It helped them decide whether the information was relevant to them or not – it would prevent them reading about mortgages when they'd just bought a house. And unsurprisingly they wanted letters to be short and to the point, with the main benefits brought out first (English writers have an inherited tendency to beat around the bush).

They also expected all available information to be used. If they had £58.67 in their account they expected an acknowledgement of that. Even if this data was then used to cross-sell something else.

If it was something they were interested in, they wanted more information, which was the role of the leaflet. Again, long copy here proved to be no problem. Customers were intelligent enough to self-select the stuff they wanted. And they wanted visuals to be relevant and to help their understanding.

Customers recognised and recoiled from clichés. 'There's no need to shout at us' they said 'we know you, like you and trust you. Why are you talking at us as if we had never met?' The work was too close to category 4.

The more 'intelligent' creative work became the benchmark for future communications. It came close to acknowledging the relationship that existed between the customer and the brand and understood the harm that too strident an execution might have on people who didn't respond this time but might do next.

This was the best use of creative research I have ever seen in direct marketing. It didn't try to predict which pack would pull the most response, nor try and write the pack. It simply gave a steer on the sort of things the client's customers were looking for and expecting from their relationship and what this meant in terms of creative tone of voice.

Like any creative research, this one comes with a big caveat. Research will tell you what people think, it will not tell you how people will act. For example, customers in research groups will repeatedly tell you that an incentive will make no difference as to whether they respond or not. And yet we all know including an incentive will boost response figures by a massive percentage.

Nor do customers consume creative in the artificial atmosphere of a research group. They will be listening to your radio ad while they are driving or making tea for the kids. They will pick up your mailing as they are rushing out of the door to do the school run or get into work. They will come across your e-mail when they are surfing for something else. They may even be having sex while your TV ad is on.

Of course, the irrefutable way to develop creative is through testing. Yet the opportunities to test in a truly scientific way are limited for most advertisers, which is why research can be a useful aid. Many advertisers simply cannot manage their response handling in a manner that will get them meaningful test results. It is quite simple if a posted coupon is the only form of response, but today response might include a combination of post, phone, online, branch or dealership visit etc. This makes it hard to keep track of exactly which elements are working, as at best you have to rely on customers quoting a reference number when they contact you.

Call now 0845 303 3000
or visit any branch   Please quote ref: XXXX

Mr/Mrs/Ms/Miss   Initial   Surname

Address   Postcode

Home tel No. (inc. STD code)   How much do you want to borrow? £

Now please return to: Alliance & Leicester, Mortgages Dept, Carlton Park, Narborough, Leicester LE9 5XX.

Alliance Leicester

www.alliance-leicester.co.uk

This is the base of a typical financial services ad. You can see there are 4 options to respond. By coupon, by phone, by visiting the website or with a branch visit. Although it makes good sense to offer the customer different options it can make tracking the source of response difficult.

Straight proposition testing is still the best way of finding your most responsive execution, but you might need research to help you find 3 or 4 good candidates to test.

How the use of data defines the creative content

With direct marketing becoming more tightly targeted and tailored, the scope for large scale testing becomes limited – with the exception of mass market acquisition campaigns.

Customer mailing volumes are comparatively small now and it is the data we have on our customers that will dictate creative content. This information will play a more important role in tailoring the communication to make it relevant than lessons learnt at the acquisition stage.

For example, as a famous detergent brand we will have a large group on our database who buy own label liquid detergents. We will lead with our own liquid product (people are very loyal to formats), but the focus of our copy will be the trusted qualities of our brand. To customers who buy liquid from our main competitor (another famous brand), we will give reassurance that our brand is as strong in the areas that concern them as the brand they use (eg it is as effective at low temperatures).

How you use the data is down to you, but inappropriate, irrelevant or mistaken use causes more harm than good. Better not to say anything than to tell the customer he believes something when you don't actually know it to be true.

By now you should be sufficiently prepared to start on your creative project, so let's consider how to get the most from different media and objectives.

In the time and space we have here it is not possible to give you instructions on how to produce a great piece of creative work. That takes experience and not a little skill. What we can do is give you some principles to guide you, that might also help you make some judgements when trying to assess work.

To produce a great piece of creative work, there is one fundamental principle to follow. **That is to exploit all the strengths that the medium offers**. If it is direct mail, then you have a tactile medium that can deliver objects and information that will dramatise your proposition. Television has sound and movement. Online has interactivity etc.

The creative job is to bring your proposition to life. The medium is there to help you do it.

Too many people still equate direct marketing with direct mail. One is a discipline, the other a medium. But direct mail is still the staple ingredient of many direct marketing campaigns. And a good place to start.

A basic direct mail pack

At its simplest, and best in many instances, it may deliver no more than a personal letter or a postcard.

But however simple the format, the cost of direct mail is always relatively high, the most expensive component usually being the postage. For large volume mailings, it is important to work within the restrictions that keep mailing costs low.

If you are a financial advertiser, the rules on VAT should be adhered to; ie the number of personalised pieces should not exceed non personalised (the reply envelope is 'personalised') and the reply form/coupon must be no more than 25% of the total area.

As a consequence, a 'standard' 4/5 piece direct mail package has emerged with each component fulfilling a separate role.

Outer envelope/wrapper. Entices prospect to open but should also induce a receptive mood in recipient. Remember, whatever people might say in the pub, mailings are rarely thrown away unopened.

In business-to-business, the recipient may never get to see the envelope if mail is filtered by a PA. This issue of PAs as gatekeepers is one that is a constant challenge when you are trying to get through to business decision-makers.

In all cases, where you have a strong brand, the logo should feature on the envelope. Not only does it provide reassurance, it primes the recipient as to the product category.

Some clients continue to want to test unbranded outers in the belief these 'Q Ship' mailings will sneak under a customer's radar, yet they can underperform branded equivalents by as much as 1:3.

Letter. The primary communication tool. A good letter can, and often does achieve its objectives unaided. It should encapsulate the proposition, explain the supports and outline exactly what you want the recipient to do next. Obviously, in a one piece mailing (eg FMCG mailings) there will not be a separate letter, but by definition there will be a section that is addressed and you should have a personalised message.

The letter should only be as long as it needs to be. Some commentators have insisted that 4 pages for consumer mail order is the only appropriate length. I don't think you can be quite that didactic, but that you do need to say everything to convince your reader/viewer and answer their objections.

Certainly, in much business marketing, you shouldn't go to much more than a side of text in a letter. People are busy and you should be using a brochure, or other device, to 'sell' your product and position it in a business context.

Brochure. Showcase for the product/service (may also be a video). This is the element that should dramatise your product's benefits. In most cases the brochure will carry your facts, figures and photographs.

This B2B mailing is fairly classic in its structure, except the 'brochure' is not a brochure at all but it performs the same task, carrying the facts and figures. It's a clever piece of cardboard engineering that you keep on your desk and you can't stop playing with! Memorability is important for business mailings.

Reply device. Order form, coupon or card – clarifies offer, provides means of response. Second in importance only to the letter. Where possible this element should be personalised, which is why you will often find it attached to the letter. Personalising the response element will uplift response significantly.

Even if you are seeking a phone or web response, you should give the number and e-mail address separate prominence.

Other elements. One of the problems mentioned in the previous chapter is that much direct mail is quickly forgotten. If your mailing is to be followed up by a sales call you may wish to address this issue by including something that makes the pack more memorable.

For consumers, this may be no more than a press clipping about your product or the market conditions. For business users it may be something they can leave on their desks.

Either way, when the sales call comes, it will be easier for the recipient to recall "the mailing we sent you with the press clipping (or mouse mat) in it" than "the mailing we sent you about investments (or software) etc".

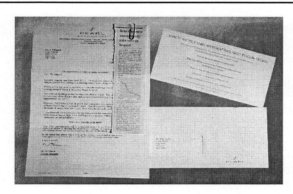

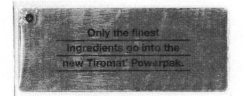

The press clipping on this Pearl Assurance mailing was cheap to produce but memorable and was a great help to the field sales force who were trying to find ways of initiating conversations about savings with customers.

This mailing is generating leads for a huge machine that 'vacuum packs' food in clear plastic. Its USP is that it is made entirely from stainless steel and is therefore easier to clean and more hygienic. To dramatise the point, the mailing is constructed from stainless steel and then sent through the machine to be wrapped! There is no way the recipients would not remember it when the sales manager calls. Not to be dropped on your foot.

Another element to consider adding is the 'lift letter'. This is a secondary letter endorsing the proposition, either from someone else in the client organisation (the chairman) or a customer testimonial or even a celebrity.

At the end of the day, I wouldn't worry too much about the number of pieces in a pack. What you must ensure is that the proposition is clearly understood and supported and it's easy to respond. If you are expecting people to return money as a result of receiving the mailing, you need to have followed and executed all the principles of AIDCA.

Press advertising demonstrates the techniques in a small space

Effective direct response press ads incorporate every principle so far discussed, in a small space.

This advert for Thomas Cook holidays in Canada is a classic example, featuring many response generating techniques. We know we are talking to people who want holidays in Canada; they tend to be older, conservative and keen to know exactly what they'll be doing every day of their holiday.

- Headline flags the targets – all those predisposed to taking a holiday in Canada.

- The central image attracts attention and reinforces their desire.

- Text comprises a full description of a tour's activities.

- The strong Thomas Cook branding reassures the reader, who is risk averse, possibly even nervous about travelling abroad.

- Everything included in the price is listed.

- More confidence instilled by clean layout and elegant typography.

- There is a phone order number as well as the coupon.

- These ads were originally tested without the copy explaining the tours in detail. Though the space cost less, there was a massive decrease in response (because there was insufficient information).

The attached adverts for a fashion catalogue work hard to get customers for their catalogue. The main emphasis, quite rightly, is on the fashion but all the supports are present. A celebrity is used to help stand-out.

In press it is also worth considering how fund-raising advertising works. At its most effective, charity advertising provides an outlet for compassion at times of emergency. Very small ads (20 x 2) positioned on the front page of national newspapers can pull in thousands of pounds worth of donations. The emergency must be well-flagged along with the charity's logo.

This British Red Cross advert is a classic example of a relief appeal press ad. It gets straight to the point, feeding off the news coverage. They have to be capable of fast turnaround, too.

Outside of times when emergency relief is required it can be hard for charities to get fund-raising advertising to work effectively. One exception to this is the child sponsorship programmes run by a number of organisations.

Often, through the use of inserts, they give a lot of detail about the children and the development programmes they are involved in. In fact these charities have been some of the sharpest users of inserts.

Online works best when it's interactive

As we said in the last chapter, online advertising by its very nature is the ultimate interactive medium. A couple of clicks is all it should take to respond.

For direct marketing purposes, online falls into 2 main categories: advertising and e-mail.

Advertising

Websites are cluttered, and being able to cut through can be a challenge. But there are many ways to counter this with pop-ups, banners, interstitials etc. and other methods of getting your advertisement to jump up in front of the customers or even to move across the screen. Economy of message and dynamic use of screen real estate can be very effective. And the more dynamic ads have action and movement. For example, you can roll the mouse over the ad and hidden benefits or pictures can appear using DHTML and Flash animation.

Online ads can now even carry their own response element that pulls down when you roll over the ad, allowing the customer to respond and even transact without having to leave the site.

But don't forget that the space is at a premium (so few words and simple graphics work best) and file size can be limited, so you may not be able to include video clips, complex graphics or photographic images.

E-mail

E-mail is the ultimate direct marketing medium. Or it should be. It is cheap and relatively easy to produce and extremely measurable. It can be tailored like no other and it's fast.

It's easy to pull in data to personalise an e-mail and when a customer does respond, you can instantly 'push' back with a tailored quote or other relevant information.

E-mails can be simple text only messages or more complex HTML versions, containing video and moving graphics. One factor to take into account is the speed with which your customers will be able to download complex e-mails. Until everyone is on Broadband the irritation factor of having to wait for big files to download is a problem. Business users are more likely to be on ISDN or ADSL so you can more safely exploit visual elements; however many servers have protective firewalls preventing complex data from getting through.

E-mails should be clearly branded in the delivery details area. Customers are reluctant even to open 'spam' e-mails (junk e-mails from unknown senders) for fear of receiving viruses or unwanted material such as pornography.

With the proliferation of e-mail, especially among business users, anything that is not instantly recognised will be deleted unseen.

The best e-mails are simple, light on text (long copy is hard to read on screen) with several visible links to relevant websites or microsites.

From: Ticket.Alert@ticketmaster.co.uk
Sent: 27 March 2002 17:40
To: Ticket.Alert@ticketmaster.co.uk
Subject: TICKET ALERT! - 27 March 2002

TICKET ALERT! - 27 March 2002

****

HIGHLIGHTS THIS WEEK:-

Latest News --> Upcoming on sale: WWF, National Trust concerts, New feature: In Town: Robert De Niro, Extra tickets: Santana

New --> V2002, PRIMAL SCREAM, ROD STEWART, DAISY PULLS IT OFF, MASTERS FOOTBALL, SQUASH

Noteworthy --> ISLE OF WIGHT FESTIVAL, TOOL, SINGIN IN THE RAIN, POWERGEN CUP FINAL, MICHAEL BALL

Promotions --> Deals of the week: FAME, FIVE GUYS NAMED MOE, Gift vouchers

Features --> UK Flower Shows, Clubs and Dance Guide Event round-ups: Music Festivals

****

This example from Ticketmaster, while not a work of art, is a fine example of simplicity and clarity. E-mailed once a week it works as an interactive classified ad with direct links to a booking microsite for the events you choose, and which have been prioritised by Ticketmaster according to your known tastes and preferences.

The secret life of the insert

Inserts are the ugly duckling of direct marketing. Due to restrictions on size and weight there can sometimes be little scope for creativity in format and often they are no more than product leaflets. They still struggle against the image they have of being strewn unwanted and unloved across a station platform.

However, there are few easier ways to test different propositions and media than with an insert campaign. They provide space to tell a story, sell product and provide an easy method of response.

Having said that, there are opportunities to use the medium's strengths.

These are inserts promoting a telephony service that makes it cheaper to phone from your hotel room and itemises every call made. By using the 'Do Not Disturb' door hanger and 'Phone Bill' formats they immediately achieve stand out as well as indicating the market for which the product is relevant.

The other execution was targeted at financial controllers in small companies and using the familiar 'internal mail envelope' promised a more efficient way of controlling staff expenses.

Car companies and others use inserts extensively to build names and addresses of prospects, often in conjunction with a prize draw.

You never know how an insert will fall out of a magazine so it's important that there is something to catch the eye on both the back and the front. And if you are running a prize draw, do ensure this is flagged right up front.

Door-drops

Like many people, you may be using your insert as a door-drop. It's worth remembering that without personalisation, door-drops are much colder than direct mail and need to work harder. There are also various rules and agreements on what you can and cannot put through a letterbox. Check with the IDM, ISP or local Trading Standards if you are unsure. For more information on door-drops see chapter 4.7 of this guide.

DRTV and interactive TV

DRTV has proliferated over the past few years. Daytime television and particularly the growth of satellite and cable channels, has lowered cost of the medium and increased its effectiveness as a response generator.

However, with growth comes clutter and it is getting harder for DRTV ads to stand out and be noticed. Which is why you see more and more DRTV commercials featuring celebrities, not just to endorse a product, but to actively present it.

Television has its strengths and weaknesses. To bring your advert to life you should consider how you use people, characters, interviews, sound, animation, music and graphics etc.

When you put words on the screen keep them short and simple. If your TV ends up looking like print ad on screen, you are not using the medium to its full advantage.

Direct sales/fund-raising

Take time (up to 2 minutes) to tell your story. Dwell on benefits and offer – or for fund-raising, the problem and its effects. Make full use of demonstration and follow the AIDCA sequence. The response vehicle – phone number and/or web address – is key and should be prominent in the ad for at least half its running time.

Lead generation

Similar creative execution to direct sales, but usually shorter commercials (30-60 seconds). Sometimes these might feed off another longer commercial in the same break (eg a cheap finance offer on a car).

Product sampling

Important to reflect brand values, coupled to a clear and simple offer. Otherwise as for lead generation.

Support TV

Shorter lengths (10-30 seconds) concentrate attention to the main response vehicle, eg by showing website, ad in newspaper or door-drop falling on prospect's mat.

Direct brands

Short commercials emphasise brand's chief differential, ie its direct-to-customer modus operandi, usually with emphasis on phone or Internet, eg the animated red phone which characterises Direct Line Insurance.

How to get your DRTV to work harder

- Be clear about your objective – which of the above is it?

- Appeal strongly to the predisposed; worry less about other viewers.

- From the start, make it clear what the ad is about.

- Consider people, graphics, characters and sound to sell your message.

- Have a powerful and simple offer and repeat it at the end.

- Consider if music and a celebrity would help.

- Include a clear, preferably memorable response mechanism and have it prominent for at least half the ad.

- Work within brand values.

This DRTV ad for the British Red Cross follows all the principles of AIDCA. It grabs your attention, makes you want to do something (Desire), convinces you that something can be done (aid is getting through) and tells you what to do.

But it is more than a mailing translated into TV. For example, there is a famous voice over (Alan Rickman); there is music to create a mood; the ad changes from mono to colour to represent hope; we see movement and meet characters, none more poignant than the 2 orphaned children walking hand in hand. All these techniques maximise the impact of an advert that is fast and inexpensive to produce.

Interactive TV is still in its infancy in the UK and until we become fully Broadband, interactive TV will remain pretty basic.

The screens can be hosted anywhere but are generally hosted by the platform (Sky, NTL/Telewest/ITV Digital). This is due to bandwidth limitations. Bandwidth also limits the graphics, functionality and response mechanic. People are used to the TV having high production values and it rarely fails, so people get frustrated with how slow DRTV can be.

The platform restrictions are considerable. You have to abide by the Sky, NTL/Telewest etc. structure (for content, navigation etc.)

It is fundamental to give the audience a reason to interact – a prize draw, competition or free incentive. The problem with this is that DRTV is still a very new thing and those that do click tend to be click happy. It's a possibility that you'll end up with lots of data on customers with low value and it could cost a fortune in fulfilment.

Radio

Radio is not a prime medium for direct response. However, what it is very good at is uplifting response to other media. If you are running a door drop campaign, radio support can uplift response levels by as much as 30%.

Radio works best at conveying very simple messages. A local event, a price cut or sale! Phone numbers and web addresses need to be especially memorable. Radio listeners are usually doing something else while listening to the radio (reading, driving, cooking, on the PC) and rarely have pen and paper at the ready.

Summary

Creativity is subjective. That is its beauty. In the end, you can apply all the theories and techniques you like but it is gut instinct and experience that will tell you when you have got it right.

What we have tried to do in these chapters is no more than minimise the chances of getting it desperately wrong.

Simple things work best. But good creativity will have a 'tingle' factor that makes you smile inside. This is an indefinable element when you manage to get all the right words and pictures to work together.

New media are putting new demands on creative people who now have to understand at least some of the technology that brings graphics and interactivity to your screen. But even there, the best ideas are the simple ones.

If someone is taking half an hour to explain to you why their concept will work, it won't. And remember that your target audience has not had the benefit of being able to read the brief in advance. What is obvious to you could be Chinese to them.

Judging your communication

To finish, here are a few simple questions to ask yourself when reviewing a piece of creative:

- Have we dramatised the right proposition?

- Is our proposition clearly and quickly understood?

- Is the execution on or off brand and branded?

- Will it capture our target audience's imagination?

- Have we convinced them to act?

- How easy is it to respond?

Good luck.

Chapter 7.3

Making the web work for you

This chapter includes:

❏ **Making the web work for someone else**

❏ **The practice of simplicity**

❏ **The web production process**

❏ **Pre-production stage in detail**

❏ **Client brief**

❏ **Functional strategy**

❏ **Technical strategy**

❏ **Content strategy**

❏ **Information architecture**

About this chapter

 his chapter covers:
- ✔ Importance of simple web design
- ✔ The emerging discipline of Human Computer Interface practices (HCI)
- ✔ Introduction to the web production process
- ✔ Pre-production stage
  - Client brief
  - Functional strategy
  - Content strategy
  - Technical strategy.
  - Information architectures

This chapter should arm you with all the information you need to be able to brief a web design agency confidently as to your online requirements, and give you an insight into some of the technical and creative issues facing web marketeers.

Author/Consultant: Mark Cripps

Mark Cripps
Head of Digital Communications, Lowe Live Ltd

Mark has been involved in technology marketing since 1984 and has worked with some of the world's best-known brands including IBM, Microsoft, HSBC and General Motors.

In 1995, Mark turned his hand to building and marketing websites – he has successfully led web-build teams for various advertising agencies and has been responsible for launching dozens of websites and online marketing initiatives.

Mark has an MA in marketing and is currently studying for a doctorate – researching the nature of trust in an online relationship marketing context.

Mark Cripps
mark.cripps@lowelive.com

Chapter 7.3

Making the web work for you

Making the web work for someone else

The title of this chapter is 'Making the web work for you', which should be your ultimate aim – but unless your website meets the immediate needs of your audience(s) or customers–ie making the web work for them–then you will fail to make it work for you!

And once your audience hit your website, you don't have long to make it work for them.

For unlike other media or other methods of distribution, the web can bring your audience to very close (intimate sometimes) and immediate proximity of your products, services or brands, before they commit to transacting with you.

> Now, users experience the usability of a site before they have committed to using it and before they have spent any money on potential purchases.
> The equation is simple:
> • In product design and software design, customers pay first and experience later.
> • On the web, users experience usability first and pay later.
> Jakob Nielsen, Designing Web Usability:
> The Practice of Simplicity. New Riders Publishing 2000

I's far too easy for poor interface design, complicated site architectures or overzealous use of technology to get in the way of web usability.

Using simple planning techniques and devoting time to finding out what it is your audience actually wants should enhance the usability of your site and ensure that it works for both you and your audience.

Figure 7.3.1   **Case study 1901 census online – a lesson in how not to do it! (www.pro.gov.uk)**

In January 2002–with much fanfare–the UK Government's Public Record Office announced that they'd managed to digitise the 1901 census and had made it available for all to see.

The first time this had been achieved; information just over 100 years old; memories of people alive at that time were still fresh; offer of very reasonable per search costs (<£1); major announcements in the press; launched when most of the country were on holiday.

Surprise! Demand was huge and the server could not handle the traffic.

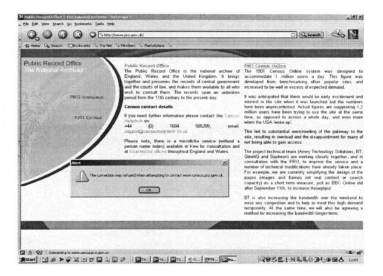

Leaving aside the fact that the navigation design is poor (clicking on the 1901 census text on the left hand side does nothing–to get to the census, the user has to click on the headline top right hand corner–intuitive?); surely they must have realised that demand was going to be exceptionally high.

Two weeks after launch, the site still did not work. Note the apology text on the home page " ... we are currently simplifying the design of the pages (images and frames ...)".

Tip: Always demand that your web designers undertake stress tests on the server to make sure that it can handle the predicted amount of traffic.

Tip: Always ask your web designers to negotiate a scalable bandwidth contract with your hosting provider. In this way, if traffic surges to unpredicted levels, the bandwidth should scale up to meet demand.

The practice of simplicity

Designing with simplicity in mind is a bit of a holy grail – it's extremely difficult to attain.

Two factors in this author's opinion lead to this (they're generalisations admittedly, but truisms too):

1. Technology eggs people on – programmers tend to have large egos and want to show their skills off by adding bells and whistles, which do not necessarily add anything to the user's experience.

2. Designers tend get mesmerised with colours and movement. Their enthusiasm needs to be kept in check.

> Simplicity of life, even the barest, is not a misery, but the very foundation of refinement...
> William Morris (1834–1896), "The Lesser Arts," Hopes and Fears for Art (1882)

So the main task in site design is to design things out ie make the user/computer interface as simple and as intuitive for people to use as is humanly/webly possible.

But there's the problem: people.

It's a fact that it's people and their reactions, or interactions that we're dealing with.

This 'Human Factor' creates an infinite number of unknowns–people mostly react to stimulus in different ways–some of it due to physiology; some of it due to psychology; a lot of it due to cultural socialisation – all problems that human/machine designers have been battling with for decades.

In fact, the study of the human factor, as a discipline, derives from the problems of designing equipment operable by humans during World War II (Sanders, MS and McCormick, EJ, *Human Factors in Engineering and Design*. McGraw-Hill 1987). Many problems faced by those working on human factors at that time had strong sensory motor features (eg, the design of flight displays and controls to allow for easy interaction) and their learnings have been used in computer systems design from the late 40s onwards.

Applied to the Internet, this discipline is known as 'Human-Computer-Interaction' (HCI) and is a growing science.

Human-Computer-Interaction is a discipline concerned with the design, evaluation and implementation of interactive computing systems for human use.

ACM SIGCHI Cirrucula for Human-Computer Interaction

Human-computer interaction arose as a field from intertwined roots in computer graphics, operating systems, human factors, ergonomics, industrial engineering, cognitive psychology, and the systems part of computer science.

As far as the web is concerned, it examines aspects of web design including:

- ✔ Site architecture
- ✔ Navigation methods
- ✔ Functionality
- ✔ Use of copy
- ✔ Use of colour
- ✔ Degree of interactivity
- ✔ Use of symbols/semiotics
- ✔ Recognition and personalisation

Each of these will be covered in turn throughout the chapter, using a web production model as its context.

How not to get lost in the complexities of our own making is still computing's core challenge.

Prof. Edsger Dijkstra, Distinguished Computer Scientist/Mathematician

The web production process

Every web design agency has their own production process. Some are more sophisticated than others.

Tip: Ask your agency to walk you through their production process and to provide you with sample documentation including project scope, functionality and technical documentation, site architectures, issues and deliveries logs at a minimum. Walk away from them if they can't show you evidence of employing any of the above.

All should run through a logical production sequence – passing from stage to stage in a serial fashion.

Figure 7.3.2   **Typical 4-stage website production process**

Pre-production ▶	Production ▶	Testing ▶	Delivery ▶
Activities	**Activities**	**Activities**	**Activities**
Client Brief	Content/creative	Testing	Project Delivery
Project Planning	Prototyping		Project Feedback
Brainstorming	Internal Project Planning		
Functional & Tech planning	Delivery Log		
	Directory Structure		
Deliverables	**Deliverables**	**Deliverables**	**Deliverables**
Client Brief	Content Log	Test Cases	Client Acceptance
Strategic Brief	Jpegs		Project Feedback Sheet
Project Schedule	Prototypes		
Site Architecture	Delivery Timing Plan		
Functional Strategy	Delivery Log		
Technical Strategy	File Structure		
	Development Worksheets		
	Issues Log		
	Change Request		

The client (mainly because they're under considerable pressure themselves to be seen to deliver) will often attempt to fast-track the web design agency into the **production** phase without having undertaken the due diligence necessary in the **pre-production** phase.

Time spent in the pre-production phase is time well spent – for it is here that all parties work together to scope out the project, thus ensuring that everyone is fully up-to-speed with what is envisaged for the site.

The deliverables from this phase are highly important documents (particularly the site architecture, functional strategy and technical strategy) because, together they determine the work undertaken in all subsequent stages and drive the behaviour of the finished item. For major web projects, the pre-production phase has been known to take as long as 18 months – which is a long time to wait, as far as the client is concerned!

During the production phase, the client finally begins to see some real evidence of the work put into the project – page prototypes, colour images, copy, working coded prototypes etc.

At this stage in the production process, the scope of the site is open to change (ie once people can actually see the site working, they're often tempted to revise it). It falls upon the web design agency to capture and document these 'change requests' and to responsibly inform the client of the change's ramifications (in terms of time, budget and technical impact).

Tip: Ask your agency for regular (weekly, if necessary) project status meetings, so that you can go through the change requests and delivery logs to ensure that the project is still on track. Make sure you have access to the place where the change requests and delivery logs are stored.

This section focuses on the pre-production phase.

Pre-production stage in detail

The pre-production phase is a time spent pawing over detail. Some find it an exceptionally boring period. But, like in direct mail, with the web, the devil's in the detail. Mistakes made now are usually incredibly complicated (and therefore expensive) to undo in subsequent stages.

Main elements in the pre-production stage:

✔   Client brief
✔   Functional strategy
✔   Content strategy
✔   Technical strategy
✔   Information architecture

Client brief

It is amazing the number of times that clients brief web design agencies without preparing fully beforehand and without handing over any written brief or documentation. Web design agencies are typically nervous when this happens –it usually means that the project will be harder to manage. In response to the brief (and usually after several consultative meetings), the agency will respond with documents outlining suggested contents, functionality and technical strategies, together with an outlined information architecture.

Table 7.3.1 shows a checklist of items that must be included in a good client brief:

Table 7.3.1 **Client brief checklist**

✔   Background
✔   Target audience
✔   Objectives
✔   Strategy
✔   Competitive site audit
✔   Content overview
✔   Creative parameters
✔   Technical parameters
✔   Budget
✔   Timing
✔   Approvals process

Client brief checklist in more detail

✔ **Background**: Reasons why a site is being built. What's happening in the marketplace? Marketing issues that the client company is facing.

✔ **Target audience**: Design agencies need more than the standard 'ABC1' type profiles. They need to know what it is that client audiences need from the site. Reasons why the current site or competitive sites are not meeting these needs. Ideally, this is supported by research.

✔ **Site communications objectives**: Communications objectives should be expressed in terms of whether or not the client desires the audience's existing perceptions (attitudes and awareness) to be supported or changed – how this is achieved is the role of strategy. Ideally, the objectives should be quantified, eg among the target audience we want to shift awareness that smoking causes cancer from 10% to 25% (perception change). One of the issues with public-facing websites is the fact that people will be coming to your site for different reasons. Try to cluster or segment these into audience typologies and set each group different objectives/priorities.

✔ **Site strategy**: Reasons why the existing site is being redeveloped – include evidence for the reasons where available. How the site fits in with (and is supported by) other activities in the marketing mix. What elements will be employed to support the communications objectives, eg medical proof that smoking causes cancer, testimonials from cancer victims and their families, free check-ups available through the site etc. Site strategy will dictate the type of site it is (see **Table 7.3.2**). Often the agency (or another type of external consultant) will assist the client in articulating the site strategy, as it can call for specialist knowledge.

Table 7.3.2 **Site typologies**

The following list of site typologies is not meant to be exhaustive – sites can defy classification – and very importantly no **one** site these days, conforms to **one** typology!

Type of site	Characteristics
BrochureWare	Passive site Content refresh = key issue
Transactional	Online catalogue of products Security and trust = key issue
Entertainment	Interactive site Display of entertaining content = key issue
Community/portal	Niched or specialised site Keeping community interest = key issue
Relationship	Personalised site Display of relevant contents = key issue

Source: Mark Cripps research

✔ **Competitive site audit**: Although positioned halfway in this particular client briefing template, understanding the competitive space is often a good place to start – it identifies opportunities and illuminates pitfalls. What are your competitors doing? What's best practice in the marketplace? What are your audience's attitudes towards, and use of these sites, if known? See **Figure 7.3.3**.

Figure 7.3.3   **Competitor site audit template**

Competitor:
Site URL:
Target audience description (assumption):

Content breakdown
✔ Home page, content options, functional interface design
✔ Objectives vs. content options/visual hierarchies
✔ User journeys (complexity)
✔ Display of content (brevity, complexity, tone of voice)
✔ Content vs. competitor content
✔ Availability of content (navigation, breakdown per page, personalisation)
✔ Multimedia content and usability (audio, video, streaming, 3D)
✔ Conceptual models

Form breakdown

✔ Information visualisation
✔ Iconic elements/visual language of the www
✔ Visual hierarchies and display of navigation elements
✔ Display of functional objects

Functionality breakdown

✔ Functional objects on the site
✔ Interactivity (general)
✔ Transactional functionality
✔ Direct response functionality
✔ CRM functionality
✔ Personalisation features
✔ 'Bells and whistles' functionality
✔ Help features (FAQ, site maps, contact functions)
✔ Search features and search mechanisms
✔ Forms: layout and usability

Source: Lowe Live internal document

✔ **Content overview**: What contents must be used in the new site? If they already exist – in what format and where? Does the client retain copyright on the contents? If there is a content management process in place – describe it.

✔ **Creative parameters**: Is there a corporate style guide? Does it eg include websafe colours for the logo and corporate colour palette? Are there any copy guides? Are there any regulatory or compliance guidelines/procedures? What does the chairperson like/dislike? Feel free to reference any sites particularly admired/hated. For websafe colour information go to www.lynda.com/hexh.html or www.webmonkey.com.

✔ **Technical parameters**: Does the client have any existing contractual relations with a hosting provider or software vendor (eg content management software)? Describe the corporate or existing site technical architecture. If they exist, describe the site's performance targets (traffic, downloads, page sizes). Describe the audience's browsing environment (browser, bandwidth, viewing machine/device).

✔ **Budget**: Some clients are reticent to include budgetary details in their brief. This is understandable on some levels, but on another, having an indication of the budget does assist the web design agency to formulate a more refined response to the brief. Items to consider in this section include: What is the budgetary period? Are there any budgetary year considerations? Could content generation be paid for out of other budgets (eg literature production)? How much money is there!?

✔ **Timing**: When does the site have to go live? Is there a particular phasing? Are there any particular future events driving the build?

✔ **Approvals process**: Agencies prefer to have a single point of contact for approvals within the client organisation – it tends to clarify and bring a focus to the production process.

Often, however, this is not possible in practice. Because site build requires a multi-disciplinary team (typically involving representatives from all of the departments: IT, legal, security, HR, sales, R&D and marketing etc.), many people are involved. As a client, it pays to clarify in the brief the approvals processes at an early stage – and this means getting buy-in from both the internal organisation and from the agency. Ideally, clients should appoint task specific sub committees reporting to a central steering group, comprising representatives from each of the sub committees. The sub committees should be responsible for scoping, producing, delivering and approving of distinct work packets; while the central steering committee should be responsible for delivery of the final project. One individual on the committee should have ultimate responsibility and final sign-off.

In addition to describing the approvals process, in this section of the brief, client should describe the 'Acceptance Criteria' of the project. Typically, this is dictated by the client's IT and procurement departments and (usually in the guise of a formal contract) details the final delivery specifications and hand-over procedures.

Website typology examples

Figure 7.3.4 **BrochureWare**

Good examples of BrochureWare sites (not necessarily examples of good BrochureWare sites) can usually be sourced from the professional and financial services industries. The main marketing role they fulfil is to reduce the client's customer service overhead, ie customers should turn to the web for their information, rather than contact a call centre or apply for expensive literature to be sent to them.

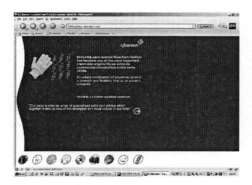

Here is a screengrab from www.sjberwin.co.uk (a large legal firm). Admittedly, the content matter is dry, but they could have made a better attempt with the design – note the big block of reversed out copy (hard to read) and the use of what is known as 'Mystery Meat' navigation (ref: http://www.webpagesthatsuck.com/) – navigation that leaves the viewer guessing what's underneath it!

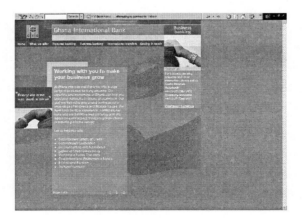

On a more positive note, the screengrab above is taken from www.ghib.com (Ghana International Bank). Although they too are using big blocks of reversed out copy, they have designed it with simple panache and use cultural cues which resonate with the target audience (expatriate Ghanaians).

Figure 7.3.5   **Transactional websites**

The ultimate transactional site example is www.amazon.com – they've got it about right (could be a bit cheaper though). Their marketing role is plain to see: revenue generation.

The navigation is exceptionally clear and intuitive. Great use of a 3-column grid pushes the main contents into the centre of the screen and promotes main navigation to centre top. It *is* a transactional site and so it's laced with 'buy-more' cues – product suggestions, wish lists, offers etc.

This author has noticed that the drinks industry has not been slow to move online with some strong transactional sites. The above screengrab is taken from www.majestic.co.uk (wine merchants). They have successfully used the same techniques as Amazon (3-column grid, buy recommendations, special offers etc.) and have coupled that with a fairly aggressive e-mail marketing campaign. Overall, it presents the target audience with a confident, secure and professional environment in which to transact.

Figure 7.3.6 **Entertainment websites**

Entertainment sites are at their best when they employ interactivity – but that does not have to mean whizzy Flash-based sites. The first example, www.emotioneric.com is one of this author's favourite sites – it's entertaining and yet uses quite basic technology. (Users are asked to send in emotions for 'Eric' to fufil – which he duly does and posts a photo of himself onto the site doing so.) Conclusion: all that's required is engaging contents.

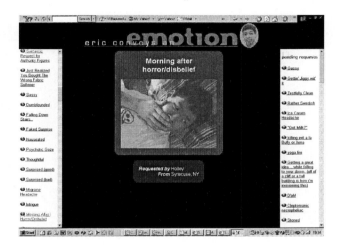

Looking for examples of entertainment sites is fairly easy – there's a rich vein of broadcast media online to turn to. One site which sits outside of any mainstream genre is that of www.joecartoon.com. This site owes its existence purely to the web: it's entertaining (at least to this author), engaging, easy to navigate within and uses superb animations. NB Not only do thick key lines and big solid blocks of colour work well online, they're also an indication that vectorised graphics (eg those produced by Flash) are at play.

Figure 7.3.7   **Community/portal websites**

Community and portal sites tend to be specialist in nature – focusing on one particular topic area. (The exceptions to this are the search engine portals.) For their survival, community sites need approval from the community they're serving – because of this, they often turn to that community for content generation and for site policing/administration duties. In marketing terms, community sites can be very useful – for research purposes, they let the marketer tap into the psyche of the market, for promotions they present a very dedicated audience in an accessible way, and for brand association, they afford good opportunities.

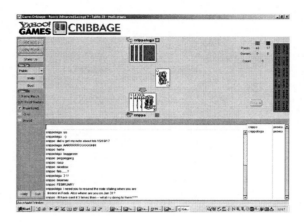

The example above has been taken from www.yahoo.com's gaming areas. On average, this specific crib-dedicated area has nearly 4000 people playing on it at any one time 24 hours per day. And there are approximately 25 other areas – each as active. Apart from having good navigation and great added functionality (eg instant messaging), the site is self-governing, ie the community dictate what contents are on the site, how they interact with it and have the right to kick offenders off. Self-governing sites mean low maintenance overheads, but come with an element of risk ie if the site is not mediated by the site owner, anything goes.

Sports team sites are another good example of a community driven site. Apart from featuring the obvious team and ticketing news, West Ham Football Club's lively site above (www.whufc.co.uk) boasts chat areas, a shop, goods exchange and video arcades and attracts advertisers from a broad range of industries eager to promote to a soccer-mad audience who can prove rather elusive to the advertiser (betting shops, soccer merchandisers, travel agents, motor vehicle manufacturers, alcohol brands and digital TV companies etc.)

Figure 7.3.8   **Relationship websites**

Pure relationship-driven websites are rare because they are normally created with a commercial purpose. To the marketeer, sites boasting high relational bonding with their audience are very useful, because the audience are in a trusting frame of mind, ie they are more likely to trust a message which appears in an environment in which they feel comfortable.

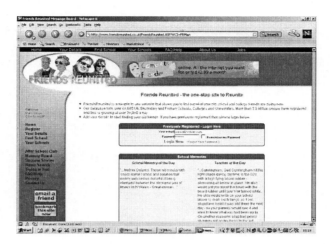

www.friendsreunited.co.uk (above) is quite a phenomenon. Originally designed with no commercial intent, the site allows people to make contact with long lost school friends. Today, the site regularly attracts a daily audience in the hundreds of thousands – many of them returning day after day.

Building relationships with audiences based on their life stage or on life events is an attractive proposition and one frequently used, eg wedding sites, student sites and illness-related sites. www.babycentre.co.uk featured above encourages parents-to-be to register the due date of their expected child. In return, the site pushes relevant (according to foetus'/baby's age) information at the parent to-be and offers the opportunity to talk to parents who are at a similar stage. This is great news for marketers because the parents have volunteered a rich set of information about themselves – the relevant products and services can be promoted to the parents at exactly the right time.

Tip: Encourage your audience to volunteer information about themselves or their business. In return, they will expect a secure environment (ie one where their privacy is not being abused) and should (automatically) be presented with contents reflecting the information that they have divulged.

Functional strategy

Once the client has briefed the web design agency, the agency will begin to work on a functional strategy document. The objective of this document is to detail exactly how the site will behave and to describe which audiences get to see which contents – how they get there and what they can do with the contents once they have arrived.

Functionality strategy examines two main aspects of site behaviour:

1. How do we get the audiences to the contents that they want to get to in the most expedient way?
    - ✔ Searching techniques
    - ✔ Navigation rules
    - ✔ Presenting contents that match viewer profiles

2. How do we get the audiences to engage with the contents?
    - ✔ Interactivity; form design
    - ✔ Movement; sound
    - ✔ Self-selection; personalisation

Researching the audience

The starting point has to be the target audience. Who are they? How can we segment or differentiate them? What do they want from the website? Do they know what they want? Why should they come to our site for that content?

> To help answer these questions, research should be commissioned among the target audience. This can be in the form of traditional desk research, focus groups and questionnaire surveys, or the client could consider undertaking the research online. Examples of online research techniques appear in **Table 7.3.3**.

Table 7.3.3 **Online research techniques**

- ✔ **Site statistics.** Server based statistics describing the existing site's raw traffic data, most frequently requested pages, average page/content view times, user flow (where did they come from – on & off site – and where did they go)? Shows what areas of the site are of most interest to existing users.

- ✔ **V-survey.** A v-survey is a questionnaire that is shown to visitors as they go through the website. The survey appears in a new pop-up window that is superimposed on top of the browser screen. It interrupts the user and ensures that all visitors are encouraged to complete it (or at least positively decline to take part). For this reason they can get very good response rates. What a v-survey tells you: who is visiting your website, how they got there, why they are going there and what they are seeking to do, what they think about your website and how your website compares with aggregated norms of other sites. The questionnaire can be presented randomly during the session, or immediately once the surfer exits the site. Can be presented to all surfers or '1 in x'.

- ✔ **E-mail survey.** E-mail your customer base to find out more detailed information. Respondents are typically given a passworded URL (that only they can access) to fill out the survey.

✔ **Moderated e-mail group.** Particularly relevant for assessing what users think they want from a site. Such groups involve conducting a group discussion over a period of time, with the group communicating by e-mail. They involve sending e-mail messages direct to the group from a moderator (hence the name) and not via a listserv mailing list. The moderator then compiles the day's answers and sends a summary back to the group for comments and with follow up probes. Once these have been answered and summarised the group moves onto another area.

Brainstorming

The results from the research are then employed in brainstorm sessions (client may wish to be present at these) where the ideal blend of – audience – content requirement – functionality – utility – is explored and documented. See the summary in **Figure 7.3.9**.

Figure 7.3.9   **Précis of a functional strategy brainstorm undertaken for www.guinnessworldrecords.com**

Target audience	Contents	Functionality/utility
Fun merchants	Wow	Movies, interactivity Send record to friends
Worthies	Human achievement Raw data	Access to archive Direct navigation Data search
Sports jocks	Sports facts Raw data	Access to archive Games play Data search
Detail freaks	Trivia – all categories	Random button Quiz Data search
Record holders	Their own records Associated records	Site recognition
Aspirant record holders	Records they aspire to Rules and regulations	Download rules and regs

This chart sums up 7 weeks work! The web design agency, working with the client and external consultants, identified 6 types of target audience that could be found on www.guinnessworldrecords.com. Then, the nature of the contents and how the audience should interact with those contents were defined. Each cell in this grid was explored in huge depth – the resulting document was a few hundred pages long.

The functional strategy document

The final output is a functional strategy document. A template for this is shown in **Figure 7.3.10**.

Figure 7.3.10   **Functional strategy document**

L O W E   L I V E™

Digital project
Functional specification
Project title

	Compiled by:	Internal approval:	Client approval:
Name:			
Position			
Signature:			
Date:			
Name:			
Position			
Signature:			
Date:			

LOWE LIVE™

0. Document control

Change record

Date	Author	Version	Change reference

Reviewers

Name	Company

Distribution

Approved versions of this document (ie, where the version is *issue* rather than *draft*) have been distributed to the following:

Copy no.	Name	Location
1		
2		
3		
4		
5		
6		

Table Of Contents

1. Introduction

1.1   Report objective
The objective of this report is to identify *what* is required functionally in order to develop the front end/back end elements of the XXX Internet website.

1.2   Purpose of the project
The purpose of this project is to provide a ...
The XXX website is specified as a breakdown of the main elements that comprise the site. This broadly involves:

- x
- x
- x
- x
- x

1.3   Readership
This document is intended for the project members and business sponsors within ???? This functional specification is one of two reports that should be read in conjunction with the other document referring to the technical specification.

Other reference documents include:
- Site architecture
- Creative brief
- Technical specification

2. Scope

2.1 Build and configuration

Full build and configuration details are referenced in the 'Technical Specification Document'. In summary, the technology to be implemented is an XXX database, providing the information repository, with YYY as the chosen development and web serving technology.

2.2 Language

The site will be English only. If future phases aim to be multilingual, this may involve redevelopment of areas already delivered and must be stressed as an early requirement.

2.3 Definitions

Abbreviation	Meaning

Term	Description
User	Person viewing the website

2.4 Risk and assumptions

Risk management is an ongoing process. New risks appear, that are not anticipated at the start of the project and therefore 'hot' topics need to be highlighted at the point of creating this document.

It is necessary that defined requirements are provided and signed off, 'putting a stake in the ground', releasing it for development as required to sustain development momentum. With every delay, the risk that the site is not ready by the launch date will increase and become more critical.

As new risks appear, they must be aired and managed with the involvement of the project team as a whole. In addition, assumptions may be made at various times and points within a project. When such assumptions are made, they again must be aired and communicated to the project team as a whole.

2.5 Change control

During the continued development of a project, functional change requests and fault reports are likely to result in modifications to specifications and/or modules and/or system documentation.

Management of changes are required in a controlled manner, to ensure that:
- Modifications to the current issue of the site appear in future issues
- Modifications to the current issue of the site do not introduce faults into the system
- All changes to the site are reflected in the documentation
- Errors corrected in one system are communicated to other systems, using the same or related modules, which contain the same error

3. Functional requirements

3.1 Screen xxx

Content strategy

Once the functional strategy has been resolved, work begins on the content strategy document. First, a content audit is undertaken. This determines what (if any) of the contents specified in the functional strategy exist and if so, in what format. In addition, it will identify whether or not the client organisation owns the intellectual property rights to use the content online.

The content strategy document takes the above information and uses it to perform a gap analysis and resulting action plan – if contents described as necessary in the functional strategy are unavailable, a plan to fill those content gaps is made. The plan describes the source of the contents (eg originated vs bought in), who's responsible for sourcing them – by when and how much budget there is to spend.

Figure 7.3.11　　**Content strategy document**

L O W E   L I V E™

Content requirements / gap analysis

Project:

Author:
Job:
Date:

Page ID	Page Name	Description/ Page Type	Content Provider	Can existing content be reused?	Budget available	Content Due Date	Date Rec'd	Priority	Notes

Technical strategy

Drafting the technical strategy document is the next work package. Note that it's slightly artificial to describe this whole production process as a purely serial set of events. There is a very high chance that the technical strategy in particular will be developed simultaneously with the functional strategy. They go hand in hand to some extent.

The technical strategy document describes how the functionality and contents will be delivered – it details the coding standards and practices, it identifies all third party software used, it confirms overall system performance targets (download times, system availability etc.) and recommends the optimum hosting requirements (name of vendor, service level agreement etc.)

Figure 7.3.12   **Technical strategy document**

L O W E   L I V E™

Digital project
Technical specification

Project title

	Compiled by:	Internal approval:	Client approval:
Name:			
Position			
Signature:			
Date:			
Name:			
Position			
Signature:			
Date:			

LOWE LIVE™

0. Document control

Change record

Date	Author	Version	Change reference

Reviewers

Name	Company

Distribution

Approved versions of this document (ie, where the version is *issue* rather than *draft*) have been distributed to the following:

Copy no.	Name	Location
7		
8		
9		
10		
11		
12		

Table Of Contents

1. Introduction

1.1   Overview
This document is intended to specify the coding standards to be adhered to while building the XXX website. This version outlines our preferred way to work. In some cases alternative standards will also be offered which may flow better with proposals put forward by XXX. In these cases our preferred method will be offered first. If, in any cases, our working practices are not compatible with those of XXX, we will put every effort into agreeing a best practice standard for the project.

1.2   HTML responsibility ownership
The responsibility of handing over HTML documents conforming to the following specifications will be handled by the two senior developers and reviewed by the project manager.

2. User platform specification

2.1   Browsers
The site is designed to operate with Internet Explorer and Netscape Navigator version 4 and higher browsers on both a PC and Mac platform.

The site is designed to have a uniform look across all specified browsers and offer identical functionality.

Certain browsers contain bugs in early versions, which can sometimes mean that an area of functionality is not available on some minor versions. For example Internet Explorer version 4.01 (PC) contains a bug, which does not allow JavaScript printing of a page. This bug was fixed in version 4.02; we cannot accept responsibility for these inconsistencies.

Platform	Browser	Version
Windows 95	Internet Explorer	4.01, 4.72, 5.5
Windows 98	Internet Explorer	4.01, 4.72, 5.0, 5.5, 6.0
Windows 2000	Internet Explorer	5.0, 5.5, 6.0
Windows NT	Internet Explorer	4.72, 5.0, 5.5
Windows ME	Internet Explorer	5.5
Windows 95	Netscape Navigator	4.76, 6.0
Windows ME	Netscape Navigator	4.76, 6.0
Mac OS9	Internet Explorer	4.5, 5.0
Mac OS9	Netscape Navigator	4.61, 6.01

Please note: Whenever possible, code is written to W3C HTML, CSS and DOM standards to ensure compatibility with future browser releases.

2.2 Resolution
The site is designed for a screen resolution of 800x600 or greater and as a non-framed site.

2.3 Colour depth
The site will be designed to a 216-colour websafe palette where possible. The many different machines, platforms and settings available mean that different machines can display colours differently, even with the websafe palette.
In particular, some browsers can render HTML backgrounds and images rounded to different colours. The design will minimise these effects by separating areas of image colour and background colour and with the use of transparent image backgrounds. For more information on colour issues, read http://hotwired.lycos.com/webmonkey/00/37/index2a.html. If, for any reason, the design goes beyond the websafe colour palette, it will be fully designed and tested to display in a consistent manner on lower specification machines.

3. Front-end coding standards

3.1   HTML styles
All HTML will be hand coded with no content being produced by WYSIWIG editors.

Each HTML page will have the name of the author embedded at the top of the document along with the date it was created. Subsequent revisions of each page will similarly be documented. Once the page has final go live sign off, revision comments will be removed.

All tag attributes will appear in lower case and be double quoted. Tags will be well formed to assist in any future XHTML compliancy needs.

3.2   Tables
Tables will be coded using the above rules and will be clearly indented as follows – except for where code clarity demands a different format.

```
<TABLE border = "0" cellspacing="2" cellpadding ="2">
<TR>
   <TD>Content></TD>
      <TD>
         Content that is too long for one line and requires wrapping
      </TD>
   </TR>

   <TR>
      <TD>Content</TD>
      <TD>
         Content that is too long for one line and requires wrapping
      </TD>
   </TR>
</TABLE>
```

The code will contain sensible commenting for ease of understanding – particularly when nesting tables.

Care will be taken at each stage of production to produce well formatted, easy to read documentation.

3.3   JavaScript
JavaScript variables will be named descriptively and each word (after the first) will begin with a capital letter, eg exampleFunctionName. The alternative, example_function_name can be adopted if preferred.

All JavaScript commands will be handled in functions, which will conform to the following prototype:

```
function functionName()
   {
command 1
command 2
   }
```

All JavaScript functions will contain the following header information in the form of comments:

Function name
Purpose
Arguments
History
Returns
Author

3.4 StyleSheets

External CSS stylesheets will be used for each document, one for each major browser (IE and Netscape) on each major platform (PC and Mac). These will be accessed by using a standard piece of JavaScript, which detects the browser and platform placed as the first script in each document.

4. Technical architecture diagram

System architecture diagram goes here.

It will include details such as:

- Web server: **Apache with openssl**
- Operating system: **Solaris**
- Database: **Oracle 8i**
- Java servlet environment: **Jserv**
- Firewall: **Firebox**
- CRM application: **Requires investigation into application**
- Call centre: **Requires investigation into phone system**
- Backoffice: **Oracle Financials (accounting, transaction processing, reporting, purchasing, stock/inventory, EDI)**
- SSL Accelerator: **Sun Crypto Accelerator I board**

5. Metrics

5.1   Benchmark metrics

The equation for total page impressions = sessions per hour x 24 x no. of pages

Maximum page weight	35-50k
Execution time on server	Maximum 5 seconds bandwidth average 666Kb per second on an average 10 Mb circuit
Peak page request per hour	100,000 (average ten pages per quiz entry)
Peak users per hour	10,000
Peak database inserts	30,000 (average three per entry)
Peak database reads	50,000 (average five per entry)

6.   Hosting
Recommended hosting arrangements go here.

Information architecture

The information architecture is a diagram (or series of diagrams) which explain the customer journey or flow throughout the site. They are not meant to represent the site interface; they are more there to describe how the contents are categorised and presented to the user.

"You've managed to get the kids into bed by 9 pm. Instead of settling in for an evening of TV, you go online and begin navigating through cyberspace. Following one link to another, you begin to lose yourself ... After what seems like minutes you glance at the clock. It's 2 am. The time warp you've fallen into is 'flow,' a psychological state of high involvement, skill and playfulness."

The Los Angeles Times (July 6, 1998)
http://ecommerce.vanderbilt.edu/html_docs/what is this thing called flow.htm

The work of a good information architect usually goes unnoticed – it means that the information has been presented to the user in a logical and intuitive way. Poor information architecture design leads to website dead ends and lost users!

A number of academics have attempted to apply some science to nature of online customer journeys. For more information:

✔ http://www.ping.be/~ping1339/vect.htm
✔ Novak, TP, and DL Hoffman (1997), "Measuring the Flow Experience Among Web Users," Unpublished Working Paper. http://ecommerce.vanderbilt.edu/flow.html

Figure 7.3.13 **www.guinnessworldrecords.com – simple site architecture example**

Permanent Navigation:

Search
> Display list matching RHP/ Link to RHP
> Advanced Search
> Display list of categories/ geographical location/date record broken drill-down menu/ Link to RHP

Logon
> Displays form

Register
> Displays registration form

Change Profile
> Displays form

Contact Us
> contact us link to forms & FAQ's

Update me
> Capture user details
> User selects content
> GWR message sent
> Option to unsubscribe

Email a friend
> Capture user details
> User selects content
> List of previous addresses displayed for selection

Right Hand panel - Random Rotating icons

Daily Wow
> Link to Daily Wow page

E-card
> Link to E-card form
> E-card form

Screensaver
> Download screensaver

Wallpaper
> Download wallpaper image

Top 5 Favorites
> Content from Favorites page / list of hyperlinks

Permanent Footer

Legals
> Displays static text

Credits
> Displays static text

Site Help
> menu based help

About Us
> History of GWR static text

Other Permanent Links
> Ticker tape / link RHP
> Make GWR my Home Page
> Desktop Shortcut
> Buy the Book

Bookmark It
Rate It
Recommend It

Splash movie (2.1)
1st visit only
Flash sniffer
Skip option to Home Page

Home Page (2.4)
Main page
> Browse capsules / link RHP
> Top Stories / link to feature
> Ticker tape / link to RHP

Top Stories Feature

Favourites (2.10)
Main Page
> Display links for top rated and most hits
Daily Wow/Records/User home pages
> User bookmarks
Daily Wow/Records/User home pages

User Home Pages (2.9)
Main Page
Submit User Page
View User Page
Left-Hand Panel
> as above

Competition

Submit user record page

View user record pages

Display user record pages

Record Categories (2.7)

Category Home Page (2.8)
Main page
> Sub-category menu:
> 4 Browse capsules / link to RHP
> Back/more buttons to cycle capsules
> More - hypertext links / link to RHP
Left-Hand Panel
>12 categories

Record Home Page (2.6)
Main Page
> Record header & capsule
> Biography (optional)
> Rules & regs (optional)
> History (optional)
Page related navigation
> Video button / play video in chat window (optional)
> Rate It button/ options open in pop-up window
> Email Record Holder / link to form (optional)
> View user home page / link to section (optional)
> Send this page to a friend / link to form

View user home pages

Send this page to a friend

Email record holder

Get Involved (2.6)

GWR calendar
> monthly view displayed
> click on calendar item for more detail
> Built as Flash movie /
HTML version to display list view

Do you measure up
> Bespoke section/ built as flash movie

How you can break a record
> Series of bullet points / links to provide more information or option for user to submit information

Notify of us your attempt

Games
Main Page
> 4 icons to launch shockwave games

Daily WOW (2.5)
Main Page
> Featured Article & image
Page related navigation
> Play the Video button / child window (optional)
> Bookmark It button / store reference
> Rate It button / ranking pop-up window
> Go To Record / link to RHP
> Email the Record Holder / link to form (optional)
> Daily wow E-postcard / link to form
Left-Hand Panel
> Recent WOWs/ link to page

Recent WOWs!
Main Page
> Display 6 Wow icons / link to selected Daily Wow
> ability to scroll through all previous Wows

Main section
Sub-Level screen
Child Window
User-input form

Chapter 7.4

Briefing, selling (and buying) the creative solution

This chapter includes:

- ❑ **The four stages of briefing**
  - • **The client brief**
  - • **The pre-brief**
  - • **The written brief**
  - • **The briefing**
- ❑ **Briefing personalisation**
- ❑ **The additional requirements of briefing DRTV**
- ❑ **Briefing for the web/new media**
- ❑ **Briefing for iTV**
- ❑ **Briefing for mobile commerce**
- ❑ **How to brief creatives**
- ❑ **Reviewing creative work**
- ❑ **Selling creative work – 55 presentation pointers**

About this chapter

 o need to dwell on how important are briefing and selling creative work. Everyone with six months' experience in direct marketing will know that good briefing results in cost-effective quality output; poor briefing leads to unworkable or incorrect solutions, wasted time, and lost enthusiasm. So what is a good brief? What questions does it answer – and ask? Who gives it? Who receives it?

In this chapter, Chris Albert sets out his tips and guidelines for creative briefing – not just the who and the what, but the how of good briefing. In particular he answers the age-old question: how much information is too little, and how much too much?

The missing ingredient in many creative briefs, says the author, is enthusiasm. There will be no mistaking the enthusiasm he has for the creative task when you read his spirited advice on this; arguably the most important but often overlooked stage in the communication process.

Author/Consultant: Chris Albert

Chris Albert author and consultant

Chris studied at Kingston School of Art, did National Service in Malaya, worked for 20 years as an art director in several leading agencies of the day with a spell in Singapore as CD.

In London he worked on numerous high profile campaigns and launches, namely Pedigree Chum and The Sun and won Poster, Creative Circle and DADA awards.

In 1978 he joined Trenear-Harvey, Bird and Watson as their first art director and learnt about the world of direct marketing.

In 1981, he broke away with John Watson and Rinalda Ward to co-found WWAV, (the A is for Albert). He pioneered their highly successful

DRTV department creating mould breaking commercials for NSPCC, Oxfam, RSPCA, M&S, Sun Alliance, Chelsea BS and Grattan, as well as winning many more awards than any other direct marketing agency, and grew to become the largest, most successful DM group in the UK. Now WWAV RC is part of Omnicom Worldwide.

Chris was elected to the DMA Roll of Honour in 1996 and is a Fellow of the IDM. He sings bass in a local choir, enjoys walking in Richmond Park, is passionate about skiing, rugby, opera, films and theatre.

Chris Albert F IDM
WWAV Rapp Collins Ltd
1 Riverside
Manbre Road
London W6 9WA
e-mail: albchr@WWAVRC.co.UK

Chapter 7.4

Briefing, selling (and buying) the creative solution

Introduction

It should be a sobering thought that the only product of an agency that the customer (consumer) actually experiences, sees, touches and hears is the advertising they produce.

So, after all the very important groundwork of planning, research, strategy, data analysis, meetings and presentations etc. is completed, getting the right brief, the inspiration to the creative people, is vital both to the final success of the communication and the eventual ROI for the client.

The development of the advertising product within the agency can be described as a 'relay race' – the point where the strategic understanding gleaned by the account team is passed on. It therefore represents the single most important contribution the account team can make towards influencing the power and creativity of the direct marketing product.

Creative people have to generate original ideas on the back of thinking done by other people; they must turn the thinking in the brief into a piece of communication that solves the problem.

The four stages of briefing

Essentially there are four stages in most creative briefing procedures:

1. **The client briefing** – getting the facts

2. **The pre-brief** – whetting the creatives' appetite

3. **The written brief** – passing on the understanding

4. **The briefing** – discussion/inspiration/enthusiasm

Let us first look at the purpose of each briefing stage and note how they differ in content and method.

The client brief

The first stage in any briefing task is for the client (or management) to clarify requirements and objectives.

This initial client brief is usually given to the agency's account team not to creatives. It is their job to glean from the client the requirements and objectives for the task ahead, which will stem directly from corporate objectives, strategies and tactics.

There is always a great deal of debate as to whether it is a good idea for account managers to come between client and creatives. Each side has its adherents. Involvement of account management can be said to have these advantages:

Saves expensive creative time; avoids creative frustration where a brief is incomplete or unsatisfactory.

Ensures a diplomatic exchange between like-minded people at the outset (the managers and administrators).

The client brief may or may not be fulsome in its detail, depending upon the prior knowledge of all the parties involved, and will need adding to and refining for it to be clear for creatives to produce their best work. But it must be strong on OBJECTIVES.

How does the account team manage this?

Client briefs often suffer from two problems: firstly, they are product and sale focused (rather than consumer focused) and thus in and of themselves may not yield insights that encourage great ideas. Secondly, they are often not single minded and will try and get an execution to educate a reader about a whole host of product points, rather than focus on a single proposition; often they are asking to be sales focused, brand building and lead generating all at once.

The account team must guide their client to providing a good client brief, which alone will provide a great execution. Talk to your client outside the briefing session. Clients know more about their business than anyone, they know more about their market and their competition. Get them to open up, and they will often come out with nuggets that can fuel the creatives' imagination.

The pre-brief

Whetting the creatives' appetite, or early warning, is designed to alert creatives to the forthcoming challenge. It enables them to begin thinking along the right lines. The pre-brief may be no more than "Next week we're going to start work on the launch of a new product that costs half as much as any other comparable product on the market, get your thinking caps on!"

Pre-briefs have many benefits:

- Gaining the creative team's buy-in to a project before writing the brief.

- Creative feedback can influence marketing planning before it is set in concrete.

- Alerting the account planners to the project (in a lot of agencies nowadays, the planner may well write the brief); their role is to be the voice of the consumer; they help craft the creative strategy, and the creative concept.

- Other departments can begin preparation, eg production department can begin collecting samples of paper, formats etc. TV can do research into competitive commercials or footage for mood films.

A word of warning on rushing a pre-brief: try to avoid sending the creative team off in the wrong direction. Like supertankers, they will be very difficult to turn around if your marketing thinking was off beam.

These days other departments will be involved: planning, research, business development. To help firm up the brief, different propositions may need to be researched first. So the pre-brief is not an OK to start work.

The written brief

This is the most important document in the agency.

Don't feel that you are on your own. The brief is too important a document for only one contributing author. Employ the help of your planner if the agency has them; if not, 'think like a planner' and remember the consumer. You should also get your director's view and the creative director's contribution.

The briefing form will help to guide you. Every organisation will find the form that works for it, and will be constantly refining and changing it to suit current fashion and their needs. But don't be a slave to it: it's no good if it's full of corporate jargon.

Use ordinary language

It is very important that, as the distillation of the strategic thinking reaches the team whose job it is to 'translate' it into a piece of communication, the language we use changes and is not 'marketing speak'. Creatives do not generally use this kind of language. (Nor does anyone else.)

A common error, especially among inexperienced account handlers, is to delay delivery of the creative brief because a few minor details are incomplete. If the important ingredients are present, better to get the job moving. There is never enough time for the best work.

The full creative brief should contain everything the creatives need to do their jobs properly. Ultimately they are the best judges of how much they need.

Here is a checklist of the main headings that should be covered by the full brief:

- Company/client department.
- Nature of the business.
- Summary job description: e.g. advertisement, mailing.
- Campaign job number (for progress and accounting).
- Objective(s): what are we advertising? What do we want people to do/think?
- Proposition: what are we saying?
- Target market/audience: who are we talking to?
- Product information.

- Features and benefits.

- Offers/incentives.

- Tone of voice/image/positioning.

- Background: What the competition is doing.

- Mandatories: things to avoid; things you must do.

- Tests.

- Other relevant information: eg examples of previous work, results and reports, consumer perceptions, research findings.

- Media specification: eg advertising size(s), publications/schedule, audience, coupon requirements; direct mail mailing quantities, test segments, pack contents, physical requirements, response mechanism, personalisation; other media: radio/TV, phone, door-to-door etc.

- Budget/cost factors.

- Monitoring.

- Contact names, phone/fax numbers.

- Timings, and date of the presentation.

- Types of presentation.

- Approvals.

- Author of the brief.

Let us quickly look at some of the more important headings:

1. **Company/client/department**
    Keep it simple: state simply the name of the company. Confine any further details to the '*background*'.

2. **Nature of the business**
    Again keep it simple: a simple description such as 'medical books', or 'investment bonds', is all that should be necessary.

3. **Summary job description**
    This, again, may be quite straightforward, eg 'new advertisement', or 'renewal cycle mailing' – or it may be a complete new campaign. Brevity and the exclusion of unnecessary detail is the essence of a good brief.

4. **Objective(s)**
    What is the key communication objective: eg **generate immediate action** (sales, lead generation, incentive led sales/leads); **change perceptions** (create awareness, educate/persuade, build relationships).

The brief writer should make a clear decision as to the key task. At times this may seem impossible: you might wish to inform and generate leads at the same time. You should try to have a primary task: if the client will ultimately judge success on how many leads are generated then that is the communication task.

In order to gain leads, the execution may well need to create awareness and inform, but in this case these are a means to an end, not the end in itself.

The different types of execution are:

Sales	A complete ad designed to sell directly from this single piece of communication, e,g, 'off the page' or recruitment.
Lead generation	An ad designed to elicit a response which could be either a request for more information or a register of interest.
Incentive led is *sales/leads*	An action-orientated execution in which the incentive not an added bonus but the core of the idea.
Create awareness	Communicate a new brand or product, or to a new audience.
Educate/persuade	Communicate to a person who is aware of us but is not (known to be) a loyal customer, and change his perceptions.
Build relationship	Communicate to existing customers, and deepen the relationship (not just sell at them).

Be careful not to confuse objectives with technique or offer. At this point it should become clear what end result is expected from the creative product, eg:

Objective   'Get 100 prospects to the site to view the new property and hopefully buy.'

Offer   'Two nights' stay including air fare £150'.

Direct marketing creatives enjoy knowing objectives and trying to beat them. So include such key factors as how many respondents are required to reach breakeven, the allowable cost per order or enquiry, and what production costs have been allowed to achieve these.

5.   Proposition

The central, most important heading in the brief form, the proposition describes the essence of what you want to communicate. It is important that it is single-minded – not containing everything you want to say. It should sum up the consumer benefit and not be mixed up with features.

The proposition should be capable of being summed up in a single line or sentence and be the most persuasive reason for buying or responding (don't try to write a headline). The proposition is usually a feature of the product summed up in a consumer benefit.

Consumer insight/consumer proposition

What is the single most powerful thing we can say to achieve the objective?

We offer...(incentive, product or brand attribute).

Which means you get...........................(rational or emotional consumer benefit).

This is linked to the key objective – sales or lead generation etc.

6.   Target market/audience

The most often quoted saying was David Ogilvy's

The consumer is not a moron. The consumer is your wife

Here more than anywhere it is important not to fall into patronising jargon – eg: Consumer is a C2 housewife, 25-35 living at home, with two kids, living in Acorn areas J-K – household income £20,000 to £25,000 p.a.

Somehow it is difficult to know and like this person you are trying to reach. Think about your personal experiences. If you are in the pub, and find yourself talking to someone you're not interested in, how effective are you at communicating with them?

Try writing using these headings:

- What is the most relevant factor about the target audience that should guide the execution's development?
- What is their relationship with the product/service and brand currently?
- What is their opinion of it? (Positive/negative.)
- Which need/want will it satisfy?
- How do they satisfy that need/want at the moment?
- What are they like as people? (Look for good aspects.)

Or:

Audience

- What is it about them that makes them our target?
- What are they doing now to resolve this need?
- What do they think of us?

Try thinking of the term 'customers' as a term of respect.

Paint word pictures to bring them to life; use tear sheets from magazines to help.

The more you use ordinary language to build up a clear picture of your target audience – their feelings, fears and needs, as well as the basic facts, the better equipped the creative team will be to communicate with them in their advertising.

7.   Features and benefits

In direct marketing we frequently deal with considered purchases, where features can be as important as benefits, eg a long list of desirable features can equate to a benefit or even a USP.

A USP is what is different about the product, its Unique Selling Proposition. Often it is a small difference but one which can be important in the right creative hands.

8.   Offers/incentives

Besides the basic offer, there may also be special offers or incentives, prizes or discounts.

Specify how special offers will be used, eg for enquiry, for buying, for replying early, for repeat buying, for introducing a friend and for volume purchase.

Incentives often play an important part in direct marketing offers, eg free clock radio when you take out a life insurance plan. This can be especially true when the product's advantages over the competition are slight or non-existent.

Remember, in the case of life insurance, the insured doesn't benefit – the dependants do. So a reward for taking out the policy can work well. The point is: think about why the incentive is being offered.

9. Tone of voice/brand image/positioning

Tone: if the communication was a person talking, how would they speak, eg direct, urgent, 'short and sharp' or 'soft and seductive'? Passionate about the offer for a charity? Flowery, upmarket like a Bond Street Gallery for a limited edition collectible? Young, flip and trendy for fashion?

Brand image: what sort of image would the client like to project? Is that image right for the product? Does it match the target market?

What is the brand personality's values and essence? What is the brand experience?

EasyJet build the whole business around being a no frills airline, bringing the cost of flying down by cutting out the middle agent and also using technology to cut costs and to make it all 'easy'.

Their website reflects this brand experience, is simplicity itself and the user can choose flights and book them in under three minutes.

Customers are guided through the sales process almost imperceptibly and at the end are asked: 'Now wasn't that easy'? – a nice little touch.

Brand guidelines: are there any brand issues, eg corporate identity rules, use of logos, house type style/colours, Pantone references etc? Is there a manual? Should one be created?

Integration: are you tying in with an above-the-line image campaign, using the same imagery, photography, copy and layout style?

10. Background/ competition

Find out what the competition is doing in the marketplace. Make a list so that it can be discussed. This will help avoid a me-too execution.

A review of the total marketing environment, including potential sales, current brand shares, competition etc. will be helpful. Also gather background to the company, its aspirations etc.

11. Product information

Include any literature, samples of previous work, competitive examples, research findings and market data.

12.　Tests

Specify any tests required together with the method proposed, eg test quantities or split-runs. Will the product be supplied or will it be a dry test? (See Chapter 4.2 on Testing).

13.　Media specification

The media plan will almost invariably have been determined before the creative brief. But the creatives will have views - another reason for briefing early. In some instances the creatives will determine a media direction, eg unusual space shapes or sizes and use of tip-on enquiry cards.

Direct mail with personalisation requires much more detailed briefing instructions, as the example below demonstrates. Also requiring a very different technique for briefing is direct response TV, also discussed later.

14.　Budget/cost factors

Be honest about how much you can afford – you may be surprised how creatives respond to a low-budget challenge, eg:

Charity insert (£30 per thousand) may permit two-colour printing only but the copy can be no less scintillating. With experience, creatives can make a fair estimate of costs. It is a good idea to provide comparable samples with similar costs.

> It is also a good idea for creatives and production to be briefed together: nothing is more embarrassing, having sold a wonderful new concept, than to find that it cannot be produced – whether for technical or cost reasons.

15.　Mandatories

Not exactly the 'Chairman's wife doesn't like green', but you get the idea. Legal implications are important these days. Certain Financial Services Act copy has to be included, likewise Data Protection details; freephone helpline numbers; tick boxes in the coupon. Authority approval can be quite a headache later if forgotten at the briefing stage, especially for television.

16.　Monitoring

How responses will be handled and reported upon may affect the design of forms, coupons etc.

17.　Contact names

If a creative faced with a brief has a question, who will have the answer? The contact may or may not be the author of the brief. Give names and numbers of any useful contacts, sources of additional information etc.

18. Date of presentation

The most frequently neglected item of all, but very important.

19. Type of presentation

Always conclude a briefing with a firm request. State what it is you expect to see and by when. Is it rough concepts or finished visuals, flat storyboard or a TV animatic with or without recorded voice-over?

20. Timings

Include dates of progress reviews, concepts scamps and of course the presentation date; also timings for artwork and production and media copy dates. All will have a bearing on the creative solution. It's no good having a brilliant idea that needs a couple of months to produce when the copy date is only a week away.

21. Approvals

Include spaces for approval by the appropriate people: creative director, account manager, planner and client.

22. Author of the brief

Briefs should always be owned. It is very helpful to know who wrote it; whom to congratulate, to disagree with, or to chase for more information.

To conclude this section, here is an example of a written brief:

EXAMPLE: A COMPLETED BRIEFING FORM

Client:	Insurance Company
Account Handler:	Andy Jons
Job No:	7358
Job Title:	Personal Accident Upgrade Packs
Date Issued:	September 5th 2000

1. Introduction

The client is planning to mail existing Personal Accident policyholders with an offer to increase their current level of cover.

These mailings will take place on a quarterly basis throughout the year to three files:

File A, File B and File C

Each prospect will be mailed approximately four months prior to the renewal of his existing policy.

2.   The Objective

To upgrade policyholders to a higher level of cover.

3.   Levels of Upgrade

File A
Standard Plan policyholders currently on a maximum fatal accident benefit of £15,000 to be upgraded to current maximum of £25,000 and associated premiums.

Top Plan policyholders currently on a maximum fatal accident benefit of £30,000 to be upgraded to current maximum of £50,000 and associated premiums.

File B
Standard Benefit policyholders currently on a maximum fatal accident benefit of £20,000 and £50,000 for total disability to be upgraded to the Top Benefit of £35,000 and £70,000 respectively.
NB Some policyholders may not have been offered higher benefit plans before.

File C
Standard policyholders currently on a maximum benefit of £30,000 to be upgraded to Standard Plus at a maximum benefit of £70,000.

4.   The Offer

Free cover at the higher rate until the renewal date of the existing policy.

5.   The Pack

Due to the relatively small quantities to be mailed, the packs need to be simple and relatively cost effective to produce. Hence, we suggest using the same format across all three files.

Contents:

> Personalised letter/application form
> A5 brochure
> BRE
> Standard size outer envelope
> Lift letter

6.   Copy Guidelines

General

Prospects should be strongly flagged as existing policyholders, eg important notice/news to existing policyholders.

Technically we cannot describe the upgraded policy as a new policy as they will be retaining their existing policy number. However, we can say that we will be issuing fresh policies.

Offer will be close dated (4 weeks from mail date). Use of the close date should be restricted to the lasered items.

As not all policyholders will currently be paying by direct debit, no DD form required. Payment to be made by their normal method: full details will be sent when renewal is due. Please keep reference to payment methods low key.

Brochures

To be based on existing mailing pack brochures, however, copy stance should be adapted as we are now speaking to existing policyholders.

To include full schedule of benefits and premium table.

Benefits of increased cover should be emphasised.

Q and A section to be included and questions to be related to the upgrade situation, eg
    Why do I need to upgrade?
    Can I add other members of my family?
    When do I start to pay?
    How much extra will it cost?
    How will my 5% inflationary provision be affected?
    Can I change my method of payment?

Personalised Letters

Full use should be made of data already held on policyholder, eg
    Name and address.
    Current premium and cover.
    Type of cover, eg insured only, spouse, family.
    Renewal date.

New cover and premium should also be quoted.

Personalised Application Forms

Space should be allowed to laser in the policyholder's name and address and space allowed on the reverse to amend this, if lasered details incorrect.

Type of cover tick boxes required, ie myself only, myself and spouse, myself and children, my entire family etc.
Spouse details: forename, surname, date of birth.
Signature and date.
Declaration, legal copy etc.
Space should also be allowed for a 25-character reference code.

NB   no direct debit instruction required

Special Notes

On Pack C the personalised letter and application should come from the client, and a lift letter is to be included from AI's Insurance Services.

Please note that on B the letter should come from BI's Insurance Services irrespective of whether they were recruited on to the plan via bank credit card.

7.   The Target Audience

As previously mentioned, the target for these mailings will be existing Personal Accident policyholders recruited in the last five years.

All policyholders have been in operation for a minimum of one year and a maximum of five.

8.   Timing

Full copy and finished visuals to account group

Pack B	Fri	9.09
Packs A and C	Wed	14.09
Initial comments from client	Thu	15.09
Revised copy and visuals to client and third party	Fri	16.09
OK to artwork	Mon	10.10
OK to print	Wed	26.10

9.   Approved by Account Director

10.   Brief Agreed with Client

Briefing personalisation

When briefing a direct mail package, a very important area which needs special attention is the use of personalisation. Technology in the variable text printing arena has advanced so much recently that you should first ask these fundamental questions:

1. What information do we have available to us from the list or database in addition to the target's name and address:

    -   His/her date of birth?

    -   Any renewal dates?

    -   Any affiliations?

    -   Any special interests?

    -   Any order/donation history?

    -   Any financial information/history?

2. Of all the personal information available – which do we want to use? Each piece of data can be used creatively to enhance the effectiveness of the mailing.

3. Which personalisation technique would we like to use from a quality point of view? Does our client have any corporate instructions, such as Xerox laser only? Perhaps they plan to print it in-house.

Run through your thoughts and ideas before firming up the brief with your creative team. Do not despair if you only have name and address details for a cold mailing – a good creative mind can be original with just those few details. (Look how Reader's Digest and Time-Life keep coming up with winning formats.)

Having discussed the use of personalisation with your creative team it is imperative that you and they discuss it with your production team. Gone are the days of having only sheet-fed simplex or 12" drop x 16" wide continuous, or poor quality inkjet. Available today are a wide range of techniques. (See Chapter 8.4.)

The selection of which technique to use will depend upon:

-   Quality of standard required

-   Amount and positioning of personalisation required

-   Print finishing required

-   Cost (ie budgetary constraints)

-   Type of preprint

-   Knowledge and understanding

-   Fitness for purpose

Used well, personalisation is the secret weapon that direct mail has over other media, but that does not mean just slapping a name everywhere. Used with care and, above all, with relevance and originality it can be dynamite! Inspiring the creative team to find original and powerful uses for personalised data is one of the direct marketing creative director's most important roles.

Personalisation on the menu

When WWAV did their first job for Time-Life Books' Good Cook Series, they asked the computing company to programme the name and address so that a unique menu could be created for each recipient to show through a second window in the envelope. Each line of the menu was coupled to an element of the name and address, to create a highly personalised menu for the recipient to savour even before opening the envelope!

DINNER AT THE COYLES

Salade de Coolnasilla Avenue
Terrine de Coyle
Carré d'agneau a la Belfast
Crèpes Co. Antrim

It was a bit of fun that attracted attention, worked well and was taken up in Europe and America. The only data required was the name and address.

The additional requirements of briefing DRTV

Most of the foregoing headings will apply whatever the medium you use. It will always be necessary to have clear objectives, a proposition, an offer etc.

But when briefing TV a few extra considerations are necessary, as follows:

- Generally a direct response commercial will be longer (60, 90 or 120 seconds) than the more familiar 30 seconds, although there are no rules.   (See chapter 4.8 on DRTV in the media section.)

- The budgets are usually smaller than for image television.

- The commercial must impart enough information to persuade the viewer to respond; this includes the phone number (a memorable number if possible) being on screen for a significant part of the whole.

- The proposition and offer must be especially clear; it is very easy for viewers to get a wrong message if the visual does not precisely support the verbal message, and vice-versa.

All of these make DRTV different from brand awareness commercials, and the creative team needs to be fired up to get results in its own field and not to try and win awards in what is sometimes known as the entertainment department.

Controlling TV costs

The costs of TV production can be daunting and there are many factors that affect the budget, eg how the commercial will be shot – 35mm, 16mm, Super 16, Videotape, Hi-Eight etc. And whether it will have a voice-over only (less expensive) or actors talking on screen (sync sound), which is more expensive. Will it be shot on location or in the studio, with one or several scene changes?

Actors, not surprisingly, cost money too. The more actors and scenes you use, the more it will cost. Obvious enough. The real sting in the tail, often forgotten if you haven't done much TV, is that actors and voice artists make their real money from repeat fees and these should be thought about upfront. Clients get understandably upset when the repeat fees come rolling in two months after the commercial was on air and they haven't been warned. Repeat fees are based on the TVRs achieved by each spot and are a minefield for the unwary. It is essential that they are covered in the brief.

It is wise to get the advice of a skilled TV producer on timing and likely costs. They should attend briefings if possible to avoid problems later. They will also help the team consider the choice of director and style of production.

TV rules and regulations

There is also a BACC (Broadcasting Authority Clearance Committee) approval to be obtained first at the script stage before you shoot, and then for the final clocked film before it can go on air. You must build in time for these, about 11 to 14 days in all, unless changes are required – in which case much more. It all adds up to the need for forward planning and an understanding of production requirements to get the most out of this powerful medium.

And radio?

Most of the briefing headings applicable to print and TV apply to radio, although radio is much less expensive in every area. The major costs of radio are music and the use of personalities.

You can afford to experiment, to have fun, and to learn with radio – so it's a chance to give the creative team a bit of real freedom – but remember to get clearance from the Radio Clearance Committee.

Briefing for the web/new media

Again the fundamentals of the creative brief will be the same, adding important elements such as:

- The architecture of the site plan and navigation system to be designed.

- What interaction with the call centre is required – ie: migrate to phone from web.

- How will content be managed? Does the client have a forward publishing plan?

- What customer pathways are needed? What is **each** site visitor looking for – ie existing customers, potential customers, distributors and agents, trade associations, the media, investors, overseas companies seeking alliances.

- What Keywords and Meta tags (page descriptions of hidden information) are needed to help search engines find the site?

- What links to other sites are there or will be needed?

The full technology web brief

This brief is generally worked out by the digital producer and executive along with Account Management and the client's team, where other experts like IT will be needed. The web brief can be broken down into four parts as in **Figure 7.4.1:**

Figure 7.4.1   **The web brief**

1.   Marketing specification

What are we developing?
Who is our audience?
What are they doing at the site?
Why are they here and why now?
What is there to differentiate this product/company/site from its competitors?
User profiles

2.   Web creative brief

Is this an online campaign or integrated campaign?
If integrated specify brief including:

Objective/message
How can it be achieved?
What is the tone of this piece of work?
Brand identity and guidelines specifications?
Are there any specific requests or restrictions? (Phased approach, for example.)
Any navigation notes?
What is the single most persuasive idea we can convey?
Why should they believe it?

Please specify applications:

    1. Flash   yes/no

    2. Shockwave   yes/no

    3. Quicktime   yes/no

    4. Realplayer   yes/no

    5. Others(please specify)

3.   Technical brief

Client technical contact: eg if different from main contact

Hosting requirements, eg client/agency/consultancy

URL to be used

URLs to be registered

Content delivery: eg coldfusion, javascript

Location of databases (if applicable): eg IP numbers

Database version:

Access details of databases, eg user names and passwords

Location of servers: eg IPs, FTP access

Access details of servers eg passwords

Server specification: eg NT, Solaris

Server version:

Screen resolution: eg 640x480, 800x600

Browsers specification: (sizes/versions/types): eg netscape3.x, 4.x

Is security access needed? Yes/No

If yes who should have access:

Continuing maintenance: eg authoring

Frames: Other considerations: eg file sizes, areas currently under development

4.   Functional brief

Please provide a breakdown of each functional aspect to be included in the site.

Title

Objective

Description

Software recommendation: if applicable

Results of function: eg send email, display range, update database

If not sure what functionality is needed please indicate what you would like the site to be able to do, eg sell products. Welcome users personally, e-mail internal staff automatically.

Writing for the web

Good direct marketing copy writing is probably the simplest way to improve any website.

Research shows that people scan text rather than read word for word on the web, so use scannable text:
Highlighted keywords
Meaningful subheadings
Bulleted lists
One idea per paragraph
The inverted pyramid style, starting with the conclusion
Half the word count. Use normal language

What different levels of interest are to be written for?
No interest
Title only
One sentence summary
One paragraph summary
Major points
Minor points
Detail interest
Thirst for more information

Look and evaluate competitive sites and banners.

Briefing for iTV

This is still in its infancy. However, the growth in numbers of digital subscribers (therefore the opportunity to interact) is increasing fast.

The main appeal of interactive TV (iTV) is to turn the television experience from a passive one into an interactive one, unlike traditional advertising where the viewer is passive and is presented with the information in short bursts between 10 and 90 seconds in advertising slots decided by the broadcaster.

iTV allows advertisers to gather accurate information on how viewers are responding to their brands and their advertising. It will allow them to start a simple dialogue with the viewers, to develop a personal one to one relationship with them, to answer their specific questions about a product or service, to find out more about their likes and dislikes to assemble more data and target them more efficiently.

It is the convergence of television and the PC – putting 'the customer in control' – and will eventually be able to link through to the clients' website.

The main purpose of interactive TV must be to complete a transaction, so it is an ideal medium for direct marketers.

What extra instructions are needed for an iTV creative brief?

An interactive TV brief will be radically different from the traditional DRTV brief. It should include the following (in addition to the main proposition, target etc. found in a conventional brief):

- As the iTV advertising spot is likely to be multi-layered the brief must cover the aims and objectives for each layer.

- An idea of the amount of bandwidth that budget will allow must be given, as this will give the creatives a guideline as to how much video, sound etc. they can use in the creative idea.

- What the brand experience inside the interactivity should be – how the interactivity should enhance that experience.

- Where, within the site, response indicators are needed (so that responses can be measured not only by numbers arriving at the site but by which parts of the site have most appeal).

- Which platform(s) is recommended by the media. This is particularly important as each platform has different levels of available interactivity.

As this is a complex new area, no account person should attempt to do this brief on their own; it's a team thing, involving the TV producer, media, web manager, and the interactive channel technical support. All their input will be useful.

Briefing for mobile commerce

The Internet on your mobile phone is becoming an exciting medium, especially to reach the young. It can directly reach the customers wherever they are. Ring them as they pass a store where they've purchased before; their phone rings and on the screen appears an ad offering 20% if you buy now. Just think how creative you could be with such an interactive tool.

How to brief creatives

The most important ingredient of all:

So far we have discussed what should go into a brief, but we have neglected to mention the most important ingredients of all:

ENTHUSIASM / PASSION / INSPIRATION

New executives, who can usually master facts and figures, frequently leave out the magic item that compels and challenges creatives to deliver a better job than the one before – enthusiasm!

Sales managers have a saying: The customer will take out only 80% of the enthusiasm the salesman puts in, so you had better start with 120%! It is equally true of briefing.

Inspiring creative minds is the single most important act in the whole creative process.

Be enthusiastic about the job, the client, the opportunity. Creatives are just like ordinary people really, and your enthusiasm will transfer itself to them. Enthusiastic people do better work.

Verbal or written?

The client brief should almost always be IN WRITING.

Use the checklists in this chapter to create a standard briefing form if you do not already use one. It will greatly simplify and regularise the chore of writing the brief.

The pre-brief may well be entirely verbal, but the full creative brief should be the best of both: written with enthusiastic verbal support and clarification. Just handing over a form and leaving a creative team to get on with it, or relying on a group head or creative director to pass it on, will rarely result in the best work. You will have lost the chance to INSPIRE them in a face-to-face situation.

The best brief should be a two-way communication. Otherwise how will you know the creatives have understood all the points you so painstakingly thrashed out with management, if they do not question and perhaps (God forbid!) disagree with some of the points? So, go through the brief step-by-step. Help the young team members who feel they might look stupid if they admit they do not understand. Ask questions of them. If the creatives fail to understand the brief, who knows what will be produced, or how long the job will take?

A written brief is essential, of course, where the work involves people working at a remote distance from you, eg branch offices, consultants, freelances. Their knowledge of the client or product will be minimal. Wrongly interpreted briefs mean more time spent on the job, which makes it more expensive.

How much information to include?

We have already discussed what should go into the creative brief. We return to it below when we look at an alternative (shorter) briefing checklist.

Generally the more information, background, product samples, reference material, competitive activity, packs, ads and commercials the better – just so long as it is all

RELEVANT and BRIEF

Too many predetermined requirements undoubtedly cramp creativity. A brief to go away and beat the existing pack/ad/commercial may be all that is needed. Working out exactly what needs to be done down to every last detail will get you just that and no more. Leave room for others to think. This doesn't mean you can be slack and leave essential points out – just be brief.

Sometimes it is best to send the creative team off to dig out the information themselves. (They must then write out the brief so that you can judge that they are on the right lines.)

Build up an awareness of costs

Direct marketing works when the figures add up, so the cost of a pack is critical. Targets and ultimate cost per thousand packs should be taken into account in the briefing.

With experience, good creatives can get a good idea of what can be afforded in terms of number of items in a pack, size, paper weight, artwork costs, photography etc. This is where it is important for creatives to work closely with production, or for a pack or format of similar costing to be included with the brief as a guide, but this can be restricting.

Results: the lifeblood of direct marketing

It is vital to share and discuss results with the creative team, backed up with figures for successes and failures. A fascination with results is what normally differentiates a true direct marketing creative from his image-obsessed opposite number in general advertising. A knowledge of results not only inspires creatives to come up with a 'winner', it also points them in fruitful directions.

You may find that experienced creatives do not need or want to plough through a lengthy brief – not to mention the chore of completing it. In some instances it may be preferable to instigate a shorter form of brief such as the example overleaf.

Checklist for a short creative brief

WHAT are we selling?
WHAT do we have to produce?
WHAT are its prime features and benefits?
WHAT is the prime message?
WHERE and WHEN is the message going to appear?
WHAT do we want people to do?

WHAT is in it for them?

WHY should the market do what we want them to do?

WHAT are the creative considerations?

WHAT are the mandatories/legal requirements?

WHAT is the budget?

WHAT are the physical constraints (sizes etc)?

WHAT works/has worked?

WHAT doesn't work/hasn't worked?

WHEN are concepts, scamps, visuals required?

WHO has written the brief?

Example: Charity brief
This is a brief for:
Client: NSPCC – Cold Mail Activity
Brief – Parents

What are we creating?

A direct mail pack that convinces parents to make a regular gift to the NSPCC.

Who are we talking to?

Parents of young families. Those who will understand what the NSPCC is about: this charity's objectives are also their own. (List buying will reflect this.)

How do they feel now?

Aware of the NSPCC Full Stop campaign, but never felt sufficiently emotionally engaged to give.

How do they feel after reading the pack?

- Feels moved to send in a donation immediately.
- Feels a sense of partnership with the NSPCC.

What do we want them to do?

Immediately complete the enclosed donation form to make a regular gift of £2 a month to the NSPCC and return in the BRE provided.

You've got 10 seconds to convince them.

The NSPCC wants for *all* children what I want for mine – but they need my help to achieve this.

Call to action

Give £2 a month to help stop cruelty to children.

Why should they believe you?

Emotion

- Part of this pack's job is to transcend the logical argument ... to move the reader through the combination of copy and design to answer the call to action.
- Look at the *potential* of children – how do you get a child to smile?

Affordability

- £2 a month. Utterly affordable.

Ease

- Regular giving not only makes it easy for you to give, but also allows the Charity to plan ahead and make maximum use of your gift. Just as you plan ahead for your child's future.

Effectiveness

- 'The NSPCC is the leading charity tackling the problem of child abuse – delegate your responsibility to us.'
- We can do this by reassuring the reader that *their* contribution is needed. The NSPCC needs to come across as personal to them.

What tone of voice should the pack convey?

- Very involving – one parent talking to another; establish a partnership.

- This medium works because people *read* it and become emotionally involved – we need to capitalise on this.

- Realistic about the topic of child cruelty, but positive about the NSPCC's vision.

What return do we expect on this idea?

Response rate of 1.48%. ROI of at least one, so involvement with production from an early stage is vital.
Do you want to add any information? Yes ✓ (see attached) ❏ No

Background/other

- The test volume is 50,000
- Uplift items (pen, sticker, window BRE) do uplift response, but do not feel obliged to use them.

The timetable for delivery is:

Brief: Friday, 15 February
Concept by: Wednesday, 27 February
Full copy and visuals: Wednesday, 6 March

This brief has been read and approved by

Creative Director   Date ....   Signature ....

CSD   Date ....   Signature ....

Client   Date ....   Signature ....

Written by   Date ....   Signature ....

When to brief?

The short answer to when to brief is *as soon as possible* ... with one proviso: not so far ahead of the work commencing that the details and mood of the briefing are forgotten before the job starts.

One answer is to deliver the verbal brief first, ahead of the full written brief. A common mistake, already mentioned, is to hold up the briefing process waiting for a written form to be typed or copied, or for some insignificant detail to be completed.

Remember: try not to waste valuable creative time; there is never enough, and good work does take time.

How long to spend on briefing?

Short answer: as long as it takes and no more. There is a moment in all briefing sessions when the creative team will have got the message and want to go away and start work. Let them go if they are raring to create!

Where to brief

Briefs should take place away from your desks in a meeting room.

The advantages of a meeting room include:

A neutral meeting place encourages two-way communication.

Avoids irritating and time-wasting distractions, eg phones and interruptions.

Gives the briefing status; makes it important; heightens the atmosphere.

Greater space facilitates better display of products, competitive materials and previous work (see Synectics sessions).

People subconsciously try to escape from uncomfortable accommodation and lose concentration.

For a really major project it is often a good idea to send the entire briefing team right away from the normal office environment and/or to conduct the proceedings in a totally non-office way, eg:

- Factory visits

- Away days

- Brainstormings

- Synectics sessions

Factory visits encourage creatives to talk to the client, visit the factory, talk to salesmen, even dig into the client's archives. Some of the best propositions and campaigns come out of a visit to the factory by a creative.

Talking to the troops

One direct marketing veteran tells this story from his days as a copywriter. His agency handled the recruitment advertising for one of the armed services. One of his tasks was to recruit engineers who (so the existing ads said) had to have O-level maths. But on a visit to a barracks he asked one young engineer which O-levels he had. 'None,' was the answer. So how did you get in 'I persuaded the local recruitment office that I was keen and that I could do the job.' The writer went back to his agency and rewrote the copy to say: 'O-levels not needed – we will train you'. Recruitment for that much-needed category went up eightfold overnight.

Away days For a major briefing, try working off the premises, at a pleasant hotel or conference centre perhaps with a generous lunch as the reward. Not only do you avoid interruptions but you put gentle pressure on the people present to make it worthwhile ... to come up with the goods. It is amazing how much more creative work can be done out of the office in this way.

Brainstormings There is nothing like a brainstorming session, a greenhouse of concentrated thought to kick-start a job into action, or to revive a flagging project through the injection of additional brains. The essence of a brainstorming is its lack of structure, its freedom to explore all avenues. (For advice on setting up and running a productive brainstorm, see chapter on Market Research.)

Synectics sessions Developed in Harvard, synectics are structured brainstorms with a research director leading the thinking and a senior member of the team suggesting directions to be followed. Synectics groups should include outsiders and every thought or direction is noted on flip charts which are displayed around the walls. Interesting new thinking always emerges, especially valuable when a project needs an injection of fresh ideas. Synectics sessions should be held away from the premises if possible.

It helps if you can make your briefing interesting

Try holding it somewhere unusual to bring it to life, like driving along in a car if you are working on an auto product or in a shop where you can wander around, speak to staff and see how customers act, or at an airport lounge or riding the London Eye. If it's a charity for the homeless, brief huddled in a doorway in sleeping bags.

Bring pictures from magazines of the target audience or any vox pop video of people talking about the product or service. If it's a food or drink product eat or drink it together at the brief.

Who should attend?

Who should attend a major briefing – and why?

Managers, account handlers, marketing executives
Issue brief. Check for understanding. Answer questions. Agree timings. Review progress. Prepare to sell creative product.

Planners/researchers/psychologists
Account planners represent the voice of the consumer and the consumer insight. Interpret and summarise research. Paint pictures of target market. Assist with targeting and selection. Steer general direction.

Creative director/Group head
Control standards/directions. Inspire team. Review creative product. Understand brief (not necessarily in depth). Be objective.

Copywriter
Absorb brief. Ask questions. Agree timings. Liaise with planners/researchers.

Art director
Absorb brief. Ask questions. Liaise with production. Agree timings and budget.

Production manager/assistant
Introduce/suggest formats. Agree timing and budget, especially if tight. Agree technical feasibility. Prepare to progress work.

Database personnel
If major database implications only.

Media
Only if media undecided.

Others, eg consultants, freelances
To cope with exceptional demand.

Designer(s), DTP operators, Visualisers
Only where job has an extra-large or important visual bias, eg involving
corporate identity, new literature, major catalogue etc.

Client
For really massive new departures.

Types of presentation

It is important, at the end of a brief, to be precise about what is expected of the
creative team. There are, generally speaking, three broad types of presentation:

- Concepts

- Scamps

- Finished visuals

Concepts can be very simple black and white layouts comprising headlines and
visual themes. They may or may not be to size. Often several variations are required
or offered at this stage. The concept stage can also reveal any problems with the
brief which might need ironing out.

Concepts have three significant advantages:

- Free-up creative thinking, prevent the intrusion of unnecessary detail.

- Enable work to be reviewed before it has progressed too far (cost too much).

- Allow a quick review of the aptness of the proposition.

Rough scamps are usually one-colour first thoughts, but taken further than
concepts. They will usually be actual size and will show formats, folds, headlines etc.
all in approximate position.

Finished visuals range from marginally improved rough scamps right up to near-
finished items, mostly produced by DTP or Apple Macintosh. Nowadays many art
directors are 'Mac literate' and work straight on the Mac – the rough is virtually the
finished job. Highly finished visuals, however produced, have distinct advantages
and disadvantages:

Highly finished visual

Advantages	Disadvantages

Advantages

- Shows finished look
- Avoids misunderstandings
- Excites interest
- Can be easier to sell
- Easier for non-marketing personnel to comprehend
- Aids final costing

Disadvantages

- Can be expensive and time-consuming
- Can mask a weak idea
- Can lead to acceptance of a weak or wrong idea
- Can rob the creatives of time and money, and stop good ideas developing
- Can limit creativity (if something cannot be done for the presentation it may not be done at all)

Finished visuals are normally composed by visualisers – who are artists skilled in layout, lettering, illustrations, make-up – and often by production and Apple Mac studios. Visualisers allow art directors to concentrate on ideas, design, planning, photographic direction and budgeting control.

The degree of finish you choose for internal and external presentation depends upon the sophistication of the entire marketing team (including top management who may have to approve the scheme), the importance of the task, timing and budget. Finished visuals should be used with care and understanding.

Four questions everybody asks about creative

There are a few questions that regularly arise between the briefing and creative teams, and among creatives. It is worthwhile understanding their significance if the best is to be extracted from creative people.

Q. Whose idea?

A. The team's idea

Direct marketing has tended to follow the creative team route. A team is usually one copywriter and one art director. A team is able to carry out the whole creative task from one briefing. They usually share an office, where they bounce ideas off each other. Often the lines of creation merge: the writer may have the visual ideas, the art director come up with the headlines. This should not be important. What matters is what the team produces. They are, of course, individually responsible for their own craft - the writer for the copy, the art director for the art design and direction of photography, illustration and artwork. Both are responsible for checking the artwork before it is handed to account management and/or client to check.

Q. Should creatives compete?

A. Sometimes

There will be times when more than one creative team is briefed on the same job, usually when it is a more open brief, a pitch for a new account or a new campaign for a long-established product when new thinking is required.

Competition among creatives heightens the tension and generates more lateral thinking. BUT, unless used with sensitivity, it can needlessly depress the incumbent team and become counter-productive. It can also chomp through resources at an alarming rate. So use judgement when requesting more than one team to work on a job.

Q. One idea – or several?

A. Not too many!

At concept stage, there will always be more than one way of meeting the creative brief, perhaps dozens. But too many undeveloped ideas can signify a lack of discipline, uncertainty or fear by those who ask for or proffer them.

Better to restrict the choice than confuse. Revisit the brief to ensure that all ideas meet the objectives (they rarely will). As a rule of thumb: one idea is usually too few in the early stages, six adequate. As the reviewing process proceeds, these will be whittled down to perhaps three, with the favourite clearly identified.

Q. Do creatives produce all the best ideas?

A. No – but they should recognise them

Anyone can have ideas – from clients to tea ladies and janitors. Not everyone can see their value or make them work.

Throughout the creative process it is as well to keep open the possibility that anyone might come up with the winning idea. The mark of experience and success in creativity is often recognising ideas and making them work. Experience also means that mistakes are less likely to be repeated.

Reviewing creative work

Reviewing – not criticising

Reviewing creative work is both essential and inevitable. At various stages in its development, creative work will be reviewed by creatives (group heads, creative director) and non-creatives (account handlers, managers).

The review process fulfils a valuable purpose – if it is done dispassionately, objectively and constructively. The first mistake made by tyro account handlers (or those who never quite succeed) is to regard the review stage as an opportunity to criticise, to get their own way, to show how clever they are, or – worst of all – to deliver missing parts of the creative brief!

The object of the review should be twofold:

1. Make sure the work obeys the brief (or discuss any departures from the brief).

2. Improve and enhance the ideas being developed.

When to hold a review?

Evaluating creative work should be an ongoing process and should be carried out at all the various stages of development: concepts, roughs and final presentation stages, right through to artwork and proofs.

The skilled creative manager will be able to review work while it is being developed, but for most people, looking over the shoulders of creatives at work should carry a safety at work warning.

Nevertheless, one of the more subtle benefits of a sympathetic review is that sometimes creative work which is about to be binned can be seen for the breakthrough it is – and be reinstated.

Who does the reviewing?

Some agencies have formal review boards comprising their most senior people to evaluate briefs and creative work. Certainly this is the case in the larger image advertising agencies. Where large campaigns are concerned, a formal review allows the most experienced people to contribute to the direction of the work, and should be viewed as a benefit. It all comes back to the skill of those doing the reviewing.

Reviews can also be informal. The skilled creative director can literally coax creative work out of inexperienced teams without their noticing that he is involved.

Experienced creatives, on the other hand, will often volunteer to have their work reviewed. One well-known successful copywriter will show a dozen headlines to secretaries and receptionists before deciding which to present. Age and experience in creatives usually breeds humility and a willingness to listen.

So, not only does the review serve to bring out the views of the professionals; it can also be used to sample the reactions of more typical target prospects. The fact is: all of us find ourselves, at times, too close to the problem. One of the major benefits of the review process is to look at the creative solution with a fresh eye.

Most good creatives develop the habit of reviewing their own work, and many apply an 'overnight' test whereby they begin each day by looking at yesterday's work exactly as if they had never seen it before and as if it were not their work.

Regardless of who does the reviewing, or at what stage, the principles of reviewing creative work remain the same.

The golden rule of reviewing creative

There is one piece of advice, above all else, that will help to ensure that reviews are constructive and objective:

REMEMBER THE CUSTOMER

Before you can review or buy advertising (or any other communication for that matter), you must be able to think and react like the intended recipient. Remember who is being targeted. Have a firm picture of the customer in your mind. Don't let anyone change your customer image without good reason.

The two most obvious dangers here are imagining the whole world thinks as the reviewer does – in terms of age, class, needs etc. – and secondly, guessing what the client/chairman is expecting to see. Good advertising communications are very rarely directed at people in advertising!

The first rule of reviewing is to ensure that the message, the language and the style are *ALL* appropriate to the customer or prospect being targeted.

What to look for

A book could be written about what to look for at the creative review. Below is a checklist of some of the more important questions to ask when reviewing creative work, together with some observations on their relevance.

Review creative work with *enthusiasm*

Just as with briefing, it is vital to be enthusiastic when reviewing creative work. Remember a lot of time and hard work has gone into the work you are reviewing. If the work needs adjustment or you adjust the brief in the light of the creative work presented – the creative team must be motivated to work even harder or perhaps to start again.

It is amazing how some managers get consistently good work out of creative teams, while others struggle. Following the guidelines in this chapter will help you to brief and review creative work more successfully.

Step by step: the creative review

Have you read the creative brief?
Reread the brief before reviewing the work. Ask the creative team to do
likewise.

When you have read it – forget it. After all, the customers do not get a brief to
help them understand your communication!

Does the work have initial *impact*?
If an advertisement, does the headline grab you? Can you read it at a
distance? Do you understand it? Does it make you want to know more?
If a mailing, does the envelope invite opening?

Does it feel right for the target market?
Remember the customer!   Will it achieve your objective, ie of persuading the
customer to act in a way you have predetermined?

Does it contain a Big Idea?
Is the big idea readily apparent?
Does it have legs, ie will it translate into other media if need be?

Does it contain a worthwhile and clear *proposition*?
Is the offer clear and upfront?
Does it quickly answer the customer's unspoken question: what's in it for me?

Does the concept promise a clear cut benefit or benefits?
Offers and benefits are what direct marketing is all about.
Both should be present, unmissable and emphasised.

Is the idea original?
You are looking for results, so evolution is often more important than
revolution. When reviewing work that has never been done before, check the
brief again. If it meets the brief, then it is a case of Be Brave or Beware!

Does it project the right image for the product and the company?
When a product/service has been built in a certain image it is a mistake to
seek results at any cost that could do long-term damage to the brand.

Does it project the right values? Does it have the right tone?
Similar to image, but less specific.
Companies and products may, for example, be sure and reliable
(Lloyds TSB) or challenging and exciting (Virgin).
Somehow the direct idea must embrace these less specific aims.

Is there a call to action?
Alongside offers and benefits, calls to action are essential to direct marketing.
Does it ask for/expect action? Is a means provided to act? Is it clear?
Have you TOLD the customer what action you expect?

Does it meet the objectives?
Are the objectives being met? Could the work be better executed?
Has it met the brief?

Reviewing TV and radio commercials

Just as when reviewing a printed message you should put yourself in the place of the reader, when reviewing TV and radio remember to put yourself in the place of the viewer/ listener.

It's not how the script looks that matters; it's how it sounds. The biggest mistake made by inexperienced reviewers is to put themselves in the client's place or to start checking the written script line by line. There will be lots of detail to confuse and get excited about. Don't get caught up in these at this stage; plenty of time for that later!

What is really important: does it grab you?

Remember the viewer will be watching the programme to which your commercial will be an interruption.

Television is a very powerful medium, but its visual power can backfire. Do the script and visual support each other? Are there any visual 'vampires' sucking attention away from the message? Is the phone number on long enough? We are talking about direct response TV, remember.

Will the script fit, or is it over length? A common mistake when direct marketing agencies write commercials is to write 90 seconds of script for a 90 second slot, and often 110 seconds or more! Don't accept an overwritten script, it will be a real problem later on when you have sold the idea. A good rule of thumb is to underwrite by 15%, say 70 seconds of script for a 90-second slot. This allows room for expression, music, pictures, drama ... TV is a visual medium after all.

Remember it's what the viewer gets out that counts – not what you put in. It's no good patting yourself on the back that it all fits, if it isn't recalled, and usually only one thing is remembered. You also want prospects to remember the phone number, and to ring now! So keep it simple.

What works in one medium will often translate to another. A flyer of newspaper cuttings in a mailing for a well-known charity lifted response by over 10%. This was the basic idea for a TV commercial that became the successful control for several seasons.

And radio?

When reviewing radio, make sure your creatives haven't got carried away being too wacky – it's easy to do. Can you remember the phone number? The proposition? The offer, is it correct for the listener? Does it complement the station style, eg Classic FM, Capital, Kiss? Radio media and production are so inexpensive, you can do different commercial styles to suit them all. Radio is a chance to set your creative team really free – why not take it?

Website

The e-commerce acid test – What will be the brand experience online?
Will the site stand the 'Acid Test' – will the experience of purchasing a product online be superior or at least equivalent to the experience of purchasing the same product offline?

Does the brand experience online match the brand position offline?
Will navigation be easy?

Are there clear Meta tags and keywords throughout the site as well on the home page?

Are there too many complex graphics that will take time to appear?

Does the copy allow for scan reading ?

iTV

Is there a clear instruction for the viewer to press their remote control to go from the opening brand element of the commercial to the interactive home page and clear instructions on how to access the different layers?

Will the brand experience inside the interactivity match the brand promise?

Will the interactivity enhance that experience?

Will the response indicators be clear and easy to work, ie just press the remote button to accept? Does the design/idea help this process?

Who should sell the creative work?

Ideally the creative team who developed the work should present and sell it, for several reasons:

- They know the work better than anyone.

- They will ensure the work is to brief if they know they are going to handle questions on it.

- Most recipients of creative work like to meet the team responsible for its development.

Of course, not all creatives are naturally adept at selling, and some account handlers are particularly good at it. But reluctant creatives should be given the chance to try and, if necessary, encouraged to practise and train in presentation skills.

Selling creative work – 55 presentation pointers

- Attend a presentation course if you think you need to. They are good value and will give you the necessary confidence.

- Plan your visual aids – boards, easels, markers – and cue cards to jog your memory. Why risk being tongue-tied?

- If sharing a presentation, practise your hand-over: know who does what, who fields which questions. Don't overlap or talk at once.

- Decide, if you are a team, who is in charge; last-minute decisions may need to be made.

- Before the event ask yourself – am I really the best person to present this work? A less passionate advocate might be preferable. Getting the work accepted is what counts.

- Establish timings. How long do you need? How long are you being given?

- Get housekeeping matters out of the way, eg when/where coffee will be served.

- Set out your agenda: tell them what you are going to tell them.

- Position yourself where everyone can see and hear you.

- Always start by introducing yourself and what you do.

- Introduce the rest of your team.

- Stand up – even for quite small gatherings.

- Begin by restating the main points of the brief; keep it quick and simple to avoid restlessness in your audience.

- Explain if you propose to deviate from the brief – and give your reasons.

- Say how you propose to integrate with other work already produced.

- Introduce any new research findings by way of preparation.

- Remember your first task is to sell yourself – relax, take your time, enjoy yourself without being overconfident.

- Talk to individuals within the group, catch their eye. Don't talk into thin air.

- Warm up your audience, set the scene – it may help to discuss previous work and its performance if it has done well.

- Start the presentation properly by setting out the logic behind what you are about to present, so that your work becomes the obvious answer to the need.

- Allow your audience to enjoy themselves: they are watching a show – everyone loves a good presentation. No need to be shy; your audience will be willing you to succeed.

- Take your time, refuse to be rushed. (It is a good idea to make known your timing requirements when the meeting is first arranged.)

- Remember your audience will be seeing the work for the first time. It may seem foreign, unknown, alien. Expect a certain defensiveness. Don't 'push' at this point: relax! Let each step sink in fully before proceeding to the next.

- Avoid being sidetracked. Hold back questions until you are ready to field them – when the answers help rather than hinder your progress.

- Avoid unnecessary detail. It's dangerous. It's irrelevant. Some people thrive on detail – they are not usually the visionaries you will need to impress.

- If you sense confusion, ask if there are questions. Decide on the question's merit whether to answer it directly or obliquely, immediately or later. Keep your forward movement.

- Begin, slowly, to expose your creative work. Start with it concealed or turned over. Build up the suspense – without being obvious or irritating.

- Slowly unveil the work. You've done your preparation. The logic is accepted. The audience is expectant. Enjoy yourself.

- If it is an advertisement reveal it all at once – the way ads hit readers.

- If it is a mailing, start with the envelope, just as the eventual recipient will receive it.

- Remove the mailing components one at a time; explain the key points of each briefly. Don't linger. Don't rush. Timing is everything.

- Show how the pack tracks.

- Read the important parts of the copy out loud so that they get a feel for the tone of voice and style (without the opportunity to start rewriting there and then as can happen if they have the copy).

- If it is a campaign, begin with the theme – the *Big Idea*.

- If presenting more than one creative approach, explain clearly the difference between each and why you have taken each particular path. Contrast the merits, ie simple, cheap pack needing less response to break even – or expensive that enhances the brand. Leave your preferred approach to last.

- When all the pieces of a mailing have been revealed, put them all back into the envelope and pass the pack round – starting with your most important client or manager.

- If the pack is personalised, use the clients' names and addresses. Corny – but it works. The power of personalisation!

- Sometimes it is a good idea (although a lot of last-minute extra work) to make up a pack for each client at the presentation.

- If a series of advertisements, leave each one on display so that the serial feel – the continuity – are readily apparent.

- If radio, read the script with as much skill and confidence as you can muster. Don't mumble. Never apologise. Better still, have a demo tape pre-recorded by someone good at it, preferably an actor.

- If TV – there are many ways to present a commercial, from simple storyboard and script, to animatics. Incidentally the frames of a storyboard can be revealed with more impact if a projector and slides are used. Create a mood film: 'Steal a matic'.

- Record the TV voice-over but also get the actor to read a narrative description of the scene, to paint a 'picture' in the client's mind before they hear the script. This can be very effective and much nearer to the finished commercial than your own description – unless you're a good actor yourself.

- Show film clips of the style you are recommending, mood boards, location pictures – anything that will help sell the idea. TV is not easy to sell, requires a lot of trust by the client and the agency – an inexperienced client might be nervous in this expensive area.

- Remember, presenting TV is a complex subject: the method you use will depend upon the audience, the task and the budget.

- If a document, try not to hand out copies until you have finished (you will be pressed to do so – it never works).

- Look around – is everybody happy? Take questions if you like (they provide a breather for you and tell you something about your audience).

- Let the questions flow if you choose – questions usually equal interest. The chances are you are already winning.

- Be prepared to go through it all again. You may be halfway there, but you are not home and dry yet.

- When everybody has seen/handled the work, put it up on display. Make sure, before you begin, that facilities exist for displaying work adequately.

- When you've extolled the work and the principles appear to have been accepted, sit down. Let others have their say.

- Criticism may now start to emerge (probably valid). Don't get too excited over small issues – it's the battle you want to win. Accept sensible suggestions on the spot.

- Before it drags on too long, thank everyone for listening and make your exit, having first firmed up the next step.

- Did you have someone present making notes? (You won't have tried to make notes while you were presenting.)

- Did you leave behind a written creative rationale? It is always a good idea when someone else is going to re-present creative work on your behalf for them to have your step by step creative thinking to follow – to ensure nothing important is missed and the development is seen in the correct sequence.

- Finally, be prepared for the unexpected.

  And good luck!

Chapter 7.5

Roger's thesaurus: a creative's checklist

This chapter includes:

■■■■■■■■■■■■■■■■■■■■■■■■■■■■■■■

- ❑ **Twelve ways to get ideas**
- ❑ **Ten ways to get started**
- ❑ **56 ways to make copy work harder**
- ❑ **Using the four leverage points to determine your priorities**
- ❑ **Direct marketing offers – 57 varieties**
- ❑ **Ten ways to beef up reply devices**
- ❑ **A writer's final checklist**

■■■■■■■■■■■■■■■■■■■■■■■■■■■■■■■

About this chapter

 his was one of the most read and enjoyed chapters of our first edition. We called it 'Random Thoughts and Priceless Gems', and that is exactly what it is. With very few amendments, therefore, we are delighted to repeat it for the benefit of yet another generation of new direct marketers.

In a hundred and seventy typically pithy one-liners, Roger Millington shares with you some of the countless tips he has accumulated over a lifetime of squeezing out that last drop of response. Whether you are a beginner or a guru, you will find his advice and ideas a constant source of inspiration.

Much of what you discover here will confirm the advice of other authors in this Guide; some of the ideas contained elsewhere will have been gleaned from Roger's teaching.

Beyond the structure, the psychology and the science of modern direct marketing communications strategies, lies something more fundamental: years of experience of what works and what doesn't. Pour yourself a drink. Put your feet up, and learn with one of the industry's greats.

New in this edition. Nothing – and everything.

Author/Consultant: Roger Millington

Roger Millington, MD
Millington's Direct Marketing

Roger has one of the longest creative pedigrees in British direct marketing, having been creative director of three of the largest and most successful direct agencies: Wunderman, HLY Grey Direct and Ogilvy & Mather Direct. Today, having for several years preferred to exercise his talent as a freelance writer and consultant, he runs his own consultancy, Millington's Direct Marketing. He has clients in the UK, France, US, Australia and New Zealand. He is one of the UK's few internationally renowned direct marketing practitioners and speakers.

He is also a regular lecturer on the IDM diploma course — and one of the most popular, managing to combine fresh jokes and devastating commonsense in what never fails to be a memorable presentation. Recently he co-developed a new IDM course for smaller users called 'Direct Marketing on a Small Budget'.

Roger is credited with a number of 'firsts', including the first edible mailing, the first pictorial bank cheques, the first video rental service and the first radio commercials for contraceptives. His other claims to fame include books on topics as diverse as crosswords, computers, football and murder! He also co-founded DONORS — a computers in fundraising magazine which was later sold to another publisher.

He also once employed Fergie as his secretary about which, for once, he is uncharacteristically silent.

Mr Roger Millington
Proprietor
Millington's Direct Marketing
106 Park Road
Kingston upon Thames
Surrey KT2 5J2

Chapter 7.5

Roger's thesaurus: a creative's checklist

Twelve ways to get ideas

1. Visit prospects and customers with a sales representative.

2. Read the incoming mail from prospects and customers.

3. Get behind a shop counter and listen to the 'silly' questions that people ask.

4. Keep a notepad for random thoughts and ideas.

5. Build a file of ads and mailings. Better still, two files, headed 'Good' and 'Bad'. If you see a good idea, adapt it. There is no copyright on ideas. When you find a well-written piece of text, copy it – preferably in longhand. This way, you get a feel for how the writer composed it.

6. Get your name onto as many mailing lists as you can. Clip coupons. Buy through the post or by phone or the Internet rather than from shops. Get your friends to pass on any mailings they receive.

7. In particular, arrange to receive competitive mailings from your own area of business. It's worth paying people to collect them for you.

8. Find a couple of people in the US who are in the same line of business as yourself. Get them to collect relevant mailings and to send them to you every few months; in return send them batches of UK mailings.

9. Collect mail-order catalogues – particularly from Oxfam, Innovations, Worldwide Fund for Nature. These are masterpieces of concise writing.

10. Get to know suppliers and pick their brains.

11. Use the Royal Mail's splendid advisory service. They are well-informed (especially about local mailing lists) ... they will tell you about tailor-made incentives ... and you get their helpful consultancy service for free!

12. Become one of your own customers. It isn't enough to have your name on your own mailing list; buy something! One managing director of a major company went chalk-white after he was persuaded to phone his own sales office and to pose as a prospective customer.

Ten ways to get started

1. Before you actually begin, go to extreme lengths to research your subject thoroughly. Talk to the production people in the factory ... interview users ... read everything that is remotely associated with your product or service. The unusual facts that you reveal will make a world of difference in developing a good story. The Internet is a wonderful tool for digging up interesting information if you use a search engine such as Google.com.

2. Start by estimating how much time you have to do the job, and how much time you need. Remember to add time for other people's approvals.

3. Write a time schedule for each part of the job. Award yourself a prize (a sweetie or a cigarette) every time you hit each mini-deadline.

4. Discover which are your most productive hours. Reserve your low-creativity hours for fact-finding and boring office tasks.

5. Discover how to psyche yourself into the mood. ("If I get 2.5% response I'll be able to afford that new camera I want!")

6. Discover the tricks that get you going. Look at reference books ... dictionaries of dates, quotations, award-winning ads, DADA annuals ... just leafing through them can spark off an idea.

7. Develop a pattern for working. Always tackle the same bits in the same order. One way is to save the most exciting bits for the last. Do the leaflet, reply device, lift letter, main letter, envelope, in that order.

8. When you are ready to start writing, imagine a typical member of your audience is seated on the other side of the desk. What is going to grab his attention? What offer will turn him on? What sales objections will he raise? Start a dialogue in your head.

9. All copy is improved with a vigorous use of the blue pencil. Few writers get it right first time. If you have a space that requires 500 words, start by writing 800. Then edit down to 500. Even better, edit down to 400 words and increase the size of the typeface.

10. Rather than waste a day searching fruitlessly for a new creative approach, spend your first hour trying to think of a good offer. (See Checklist later in these notes.)

56 ways to make copy work harder

1. Don't be too clever. If readers start admiring your copy, you have failed. They should be drooling over the product. Remember G K Chesterton's advice to writers: "Murder your babies"... if you are proud of an ingenious pun, some smart wordplay, or a brilliant metaphor, strike it out! This is precisely the bit that will halt your readers in their tracks.

2. Remember KISS – Keep it simple, stupid. Aim your text at someone with a reading age of about 14. Yes, even when writing to university professors or to captains of industry. They are too busy to bother unravelling your complicated text or your confused order form.

3. If you are writing to an audience you aren't familiar with (for instance a mailing list you are using for the first time) read the last ten copies of their trade magazine. You'll gain a feel for the concerns that are currently important to them.

4. State facts, not opinions. Puffery – "The best doodah ever" – merely reflects your opinion about your product. Demonstrate every **reason** why your product is better.

5. Don't waste captions. People who skip body copy may just stop to read the picture captions. This is your opportunity to entice them into the main story. The majority of advertisers write dismally dull captions. Even worse, they run photographs without any captions at all. We develop our reading habits from what we read most ... namely, newspapers ... and newspaper editors always accompany their photographs with interesting captions.

6. Don't overclaim. Make one inflated claim – one that you can't prove – and the reader becomes suspicious of all the true things you say.

7. Don't be afraid to repeat. Your best benefits can appear in several places in your text.

8. Keep changing the language. Introduce new wording every time you repeat your benefits. Never let the same words and expressions appear too often – it makes for boredom. Keep using Roger's Thesaurus.

9. If it's new, say what's new about it. A common mistake of many writers is that they highlight new features without explaining what is new about them and why it's important.

10. Use Saxon words (short ones) not Latin words (long ones):

Latin	Saxon
indicate	show
regarding	about
immediately	now, right away
regulations	rules
publication	book
discover	find

11. Use vivid words instead of hackneyed words:

Hackneyed	Vivid
tough	diamond-hard
shiny	glittering
money	cash
dislike	hate

12. Use short sentences ... and vary the lengths. Aim for visual variety. (See Chapter 7.2.)

13. Use short paragraphs... and vary the lengths.

14. Get to the point. Many advertisements and direct mail letters take several paragraphs before they say anything that is relevant to the reader. They risk losing the reader's interest.

15. Use active not passive verbs, and personal words (names, pronouns):
    Instead of: *It will be delivered in seven days.*
    Say: *We'll rush it to you in a week.*

16. Relate the story to the reader:
    Instead of: *Many people must have wondered*
    Say: *I'm sure you have wondered*

17. Use buckets and chains to link paragraphs:
    On the other hand ...
    But there's something else ...
    That's just one example, but ...
    In addition ...
    Now let me explain ...
    ... but do you know the whole story?
    ... so I'll tell you the answer.
    ... and this is how it works.

18. Turn negatives into positives:
    Instead of: *If your hearing isn't improved, we'll refund your money.*
    Say: *You'll hear whispered conversations or we'll refund your money.*

19. Introduce human beings:
    Instead of: *50,000 people have already bought this book.*
    Say: *50,000 wine-lovers and gourmets have already bought this book.*

20. Don't call the reader a ****
    Instead of: *You probably don't know we publish a Serbo-Croat edition.*
    Say: *Many people still haven't heard that we publish a Serbo-Croat edition.*

21. Give authority:
    Instead of: *Widely used by major companies.*
    Say: *Proved in use by IBM and General Motors.*
    Instead of: *The statistics show that ...*
    Say: *The latest figures from the Department of Health state...*
    Instead of: *You'll soon be earning more money.*
    Say: *Our readers gain an average salary increase of £3,873.*
    Instead of: *According to a famous scientist ...*
    Say: *According to the renowned Dr Strabismus of Utrecht ...*

22. Avoid humour ... unless you're a very good writer.

23. Don't allow the reader to stop at the end of the page. Make the copy run over to the next page – in the middle of a particularly interesting sentence. Or print a bold footnote drawing attention to the *special offer* on the next page.

24. Don't believe any nonsense you read about headlines having to be short.

25. Repeat the offer at several places in the text.

26. Keep spacing your benefits throughout the text. Don't crowd them together.

27. Give concrete examples of benefits. Give real figures and statistics instead of being vague:
    Instead of: *This machine saved my office £41 a week!*
    Say: *With the tips I gained from this book, I can now do*
    the *job in 17 minutes instead of one hour!*

28. Don't be pompous. Don't think you have to use *highfalutin'* English when you write to an up-market audience. Imagine you are talking to your prospect in the pub. Pomposity also means droning on about your company and its wonderful achievements. Sensible prospects couldn't care less. They have other priorities on their mind.

29. A sure way to end up with a pompous style is to allow grammar freaks to improve your copy. Rules such as *"You can't end a sentence with a preposition"* or *"You can't start a sentence with the word And"* have no foundation whatever. Unless you are writing to schoolmarms, break these daft rules if it makes for a flowing style. However, avoid split infinitives (as in *"to boldly go"*) – they are a red rag to a bull with many readers.

30. But be sensible: grammar rules can be broken in order to aid readability. But sloppy errors like singular verbs with plural subjects are unforgivable.

31. Don't be too tasteful. It's possibly sad but generally true, that tacky design usually beats restrained design. (Naturally, you need to be aware of the long-term effect of tackiness on your corporate image.)

32. Remember **FAB** (Features, Advantages, Benefits). Most copywriters describe the features of the product; but very few complete the job by explaining the benefits that derive from these features.
    Feature: *Only Snibbo contains new miracle RM97*
    Advantage: *... which cleans your clothes quicker*
    Benefit: *... so you have more time to have fun.*

33. Use interesting subheads. It is a scientific fact that 97% of copywriters' subheads are boring.
    Instead of: *Important new cost-saving ideas.*
    Say: *How a shopkeeper saved £257.*

34. Number all of your significant points. Or use a), b), c) etc.

35. But don't overdo it. Otherwise the reader can't see which are the important points and which are of less importance.

36. Don't be afraid of long copy. How long should copy be? As long as it takes to tell all the interesting facts. If you have a good story to tell, readers will continue reading – until they reach the first boring bit. Test after test has shown that 'busy' executives will read a four-page letter if the information is relevant to them. (The author's personal record is a twelve-page letter. It beat the six-page letter which in turn beat the four-page letter.)

37. Regard the envelope as part of the letter. Put a teaser message on the envelope – something that gets it opened before all the other letters of the day. You need to have a very good reason for using plain envelopes.

38. Don't run a 'PRIVATE and CONFIDENTIAL' overprint on the envelope unless the contents really are private and confidential.

39. Start your story on the envelope. But don't finish it. The reader has to open your envelope to hear the rest of the story.
    Example: *This morning I sold my wedding ring to pay the electric light bill.*

40. On the first page of your letter, start with an underlined headline above the salutation. Or use a Johnson Box to contain the headline.

This is a Johnson Box

41. End by firing a big gun at the end of the letter or in the PS. Use a big benefit early on – but save a huge one for the end. Give a few hints that it is coming.

42. Be mysterious. Promise to reveal some special benefit or some exciting offer, but keep the reader in suspense until the end of the letter.

43. Underline your major benefits. But do it sparingly. DON'T USE CAPITAL LETTERS TO HIGHLIGHT YOUR IMPORTANT POINTS; CAPITALS ARE MUCH HARDER TO READ THAN UPPER AND LOWER CASE.

44. Underline important parts of the text in a second colour. In direct mail letters give the impression of handwritten underlining or of a typewriter ribbon that uses a second colour.

45. Aim for visual interest. To break up long sections of text, use:
    - Italics
    - Box rules around important paragraphs
    - Tables and bar charts
    - Numbered paragraphs
    - Underlining
    - Bullet points (like these in this paragraph)
    - Capital letters – but use them SPARINGLY.

46. Use indented paragraphs to make the text appealing to the eye – so that the eye is directed to the best parts of your story. A specially important paragraph can be made to stand out by being narrower than its neighbours.

47. Consider handwriting to add interest. 'Handwritten' notes in the margin can be effective. It's a question of personal taste. It can make the letter look cluttered. And using such effects to excess will stop your letter from looking like a genuine letter and will turn it into obvious junk mail.

48. Use your reader's name. Today's technology makes it possible to personalise every item in a mailpack.

49. Always include a penalty for not acting now:
    Don't miss this low introductory price.
    The supply is limited.
    You could have an accident tomorrow.
    The longer you delay, the more money you are wasting.

50. The over-50s are a growing percentage of the population. They often have higher disposable income. And they usually wear spectacles. But most direct mail is created by young designers with good eyesight. One of the easiest ways to increase the response rates to your mailings and ads is to increase the size of the typeface!

51. Don't think you can write a letter that will appeal to every segment of the database. Write a version that will appeal to new customers … one for old customers … one for men … one for women. For one client the author ended up writing 29 different versions of a single letter!

52. However, to target your message to specific lists, you can save money by running your winning control package without any alterations. Simply print a targeted message on the outer envelope:
    Now cyclists can save £25.

53. Don't bother altering the entire order form for a specific target group – it isn't necessary. Simply run an overprint on the reply envelope: *Special discount for cyclists.*

54. Another low-cost trick that can help to target a specific group is to run an overprint immediately above the address on the reply envelope: *Cyclist Discount Department.*

55. If you are running a bargain offer, reflect this in the mailing. A badly reproduced leaflet on cheap paper has been known to produce more orders than an expensive leaflet.

56. The ultimate moneysaver is to replace your mailing with a laser-personalised postcard. You can get three of these from a sheet of A4 card. They are wonderfully cheap ... yet unlike mailings within envelopes, postcards are always read by the recipients.

Using the four leverage points to determine your priorities

Marketers who promote products by mail, or who include coupons in press ads and inserts, have a big advantage over traditional advertisers. They can count the coupons and the order forms and analyse the results.

The lesson to be learned is that success or failure depends on only four or five leverage points – in addition, of course, to the product or service being promoted. All these aspects are discussed at length by other authors in this Guide, but there's no harm in including them in this creative's checklist:

1   The audience

How do we characterise the people on the mailing list? Or in the case of a press ad, who are the people who read this newspaper or magazine? Are they predominantly male or female? Young or old? Rich or poor? Protestant or Catholic? And so on ... See Chapter 4.5.

2   The offer

What offer do we make to these people? A price reduction ... a free bonus gift ... a free 10 day trial of the book ... In a moment we shall look at 57 varieties of the offer.

3   The format

Shall we run a glossy multi-piece mailing or a simple one-page letter? Will our catalogue be A5 or A4 in size? Shall we run a large ad in colour or a small one in black and white? See Chapter 4.5.

4   Creative

What words and pictures will appeal to this audience?

The following figures provide a valuable guide to the relative importance of these four factors. These percentage figures are not fixed ... but based on many tests around the world. They are fairly consistent.

1   The audience: 200%

If you test five or six mailing lists at one time, you will frequently find that the best list will outperform the weakest by a ratio of around 3 to 1. Of course, this assumes you make an intelligent selection of tests in the first place; you don't include any wildly inappropriate lists.

You will expect to see a similar spread if you test five similar newspapers or magazines.

If you had been given the powers of foresight you would only have picked the best list and you would have gained a leverage of 200%. But we don't have the gift of foresight which is why we spend so much effort testing lists and media.
The point is that there is a potential leverage of 200% available just from the way you select your audience. Nothing else is as important. See Chapters 4.4.(lists), 6.3 (interactive) and 3.3(segmentation and profiling).

2   The offer: 100%

People in all walks of life respond to offers. Yet there are still companies who don't include a clear cut offer in their mailings and advertisements.

Of the companies who have learned the strength of an attractive offer, only a handful take the trouble to test one offer against another. But offer tests can yield exciting results. Typically, offer A will do twice as well as offer B, or vice versa. The fascination of offer tests is that it is very difficult to predict in advance which will be the winner and which will be the loser.

Consider this: The company that has been running the one offer for ages might well be delighted by its response rates. But what about the offer they never bothered to test? For the same cost they might double their response rates; right now they are getting only half the responses they are entitled to. The potential loss of profits here is worse than it looks at first sight. In retailing if you double your sales you can expect to gain about double the total profit. But because of the highly geared financial dynamics of direct marketing, a doubled response rate doesn't double your profits ... it sends them through the roof! So marketers who don't test offers never know what they are missing.

3   The format: 50%

Big expensive mailings usually bring more replies than little cheap ones. (But not always!) Large colour ads usually generate more coupon replies than small black and white ads. But in both cases it cost you more money to get those extra replies. (See Chapter 4.5.)

Clearly, we can't just count the number of replies. What matters now is the cost per reply and the quality of that reply. However, format tests do show one thing: quite modest changes in format can often yield startling differences in response. Switching to an unusual envelope size ... folding the leaflet in a strange way ... using an expensive paper for the letter ... experiments like these needn't make a major difference to your total costs, yet they can push your responses up by anything from 25% to 50%. Who knows why? Perhaps it's because your audience gets bored by seeing the same old things. Maybe they are intrigued by something different.

4   Creative: 25%

It's a significant achievement to take a currently successful mailing or ad and to improve its response by changing only the words and the pictures.

Give the copywriter and the art director total creative freedom. But tell them that they must go to the same audience, with the same offer, and operate within the same format constraints. If they can push the response of your mailings from, say 2% to 2.5%–a relative increase of 25%–you have a good reason to increase their salaries.

Yes, any experienced copywriter can point to cases where the creative leverage was much more than 25%. Where one headline did ten times better than another. But it doesn't happen all that often. And it's very difficult to improve on creative work that has already proved successful. Rather than waste a day searching fruitlessly for a new creative approach, it is easier and much more profitable to spend time devising a bright new offer. (If the offer is a good one, the headline then magically writes itself!)

As recently as ten years ago, many clients and their agencies probably got the leverage points in the wrong order. They worried overmuch about minor creative details and paid too little attention to the more important factors.

Now, as more clients and agencies embrace direct marketing, things are getting better. But bad news for creative staff? They used to sit at the top of the totem pole. Are they now in charge of the least important part of the advertising mix?

Not necessarily. Sometimes the creative factor is the only leverage point available to you. If, for instance, you are addressing a very restricted audience – perhaps the members of a small profession – there's no opportunity for experimenting with the audience factor. There may be reasons why you can't test new offers with these people. Perhaps the only way to reach them is through a full-page ad in a specialist journal ... no room for format changes there. Suddenly creative improvements are the only ones you can try. The creatives are still paramount in many, many situations.

By the way, there's a fifth leverage point

... and this is the timing of your promotion. But it's utterly impossible to apply a guideline figure here. It depends what business you are in.

For example, one market where timing is important is the schools and colleges market ... budgets are usually allocated at a particular time in the academic year.

Direct marketing offers – 57 varieties

This collection of offers has been drawn from the wide world of direct marketing. Some will adapt readily to your sector; others may be less appropriate.

1   The unique proposition

> If a man can write a better book, preach a better sermon, or make a better mousetrap than his neighbour, though he builds his house in the woods the world will make a beaten path to his door. – Ralph Waldo Emerson, 1803 – 1882.

If you have a better mousetrap (or a guaranteed cure for baldness or for the common cold) the product itself may be the only offer you need to make. Indeed any other offer – such as a free gift or a discount – could even be counter-productive. However, better mousetraps are few and far between. (See discussion on credibility, Chapter 7.1.)

A variant on the Better Mousetrap is to offer a product that no sane person would ever want. 'Pet rocks' made a fortune for their promoter. But don't count on success; one of America's most successful direct marketers advertised a laser operated mousetrap at $1,500. He didn't sell a single one. Which shows that Ralph Waldo Emerson knew nothing about mail order.

2   Discounted price or sale

Be careful – a low price has been known to reduce the number of responses. Don't forget: the Bargain Offers Act requires that your quoted 'original' high price must be a genuine one. Remember, too, that if you are hoping for repeat purchases in the future, the customers who joined you as a result of a price-cut may be reluctant to pay the full price next time you approach them.

3   Privilege price for new customers

But you risk offending earlier customers who paid the full price.

4   Quantity discount

"The more you spend, the more you save". If a £30 discount works, allow the customers to choose a discount of £30, £40 or £50 – depending on the size of the total purchase.

5   Discount voucher

If you give someone an unconditional £30 discount, that's just cost you £30 off your profits. Instead, for example, give a £30 voucher against additional purchases from your product range. That has the same value to the customer – but it only costs you £15 in real terms if you operate on a 100% mark-up.

6   Trade-in discount

A good way to hold on to your existing customer. It's also a way to buy your competitor's customers. The retailing equivalent is "We'll allow you £15 off a new purchase if you bring in your old vacuum cleaner".

Software manufacturers use this offer to persuade you to 'upgrade' from a competitor's software package. One opportunity available to publishers is to allow a trade-in price to the customer who replaces an outdated directory with a new one.

7   Terms of payment

In some markets extended terms of payment are more important than most people realise.

8   Naughty knickers

Customers pay an introduction fee, refundable on their first purchase.

> Example: repliers to press ads pay to receive a sexy-lingerie catalogue. The theory is that catalogue-buyers will become better-quality customers. However, this is an unproven theory: people who pay for a catalogue often buy less than those who receive it free.

9   There will be a price increase soon

This is surprisingly rare. Yet book publishers have done it for decades. (New titles published to catch the pre-Christmas trade often have a reduced prepublication price valid only until 31 December.)

10   As a member ...

... you are entitled to accept this special invitation. It can be very powerful on rented lists: *"Special opportunity for Members of the Institute of Candlestick Makers"*. It is also effective, of course, to your own customers on your house list.

11   Live now, pay later

This can be used to extend a product's normal selling season. *"Take delivery of your coal in summer ... but don't start paying until winter."*

12   Pay now, live later

Give us the money now and receive the product later. The customer gains some special benefit in exchange.

Examples:

"Send £20 in advance and we will credit you with £22."
    Book Club Associates

"Give us £125 ... you receive a book every month for 5 years ... then we return your £125."

An offer from Readers Union in the 1970s. Readers had no choice in the books they received ... so this was a way of clearing the warehouse of unsold stock while earning interest on their payments.

13   Free trial

But consider making a small 'P&P' charge to discourage time-wasters. Magazine publishers have found their most successful offer to be:

"Try our magazine free for 3 months, but pay now with a direct debit which comes into effect after your free issues. If you don't like your free trial copies, just cancel the direct debit".

Many subscribers stay in through sheer inertia. US publishers drool with envy when they hear about direct debits, bankers orders and similar UK payment facilities. One US company makes a similar offer based on sending them a post-dated cheque.

For many years the standard offer from Time-Life Books was, *"Enjoy this book at home FREE for 10 days before you decide whether to buy it."*

14   Free information

Usually a booklet. But it can be a wallchart, a cassette recording, the loan of a video, a 'slide rule' device – or even a free 'consultation' from a salesperson.

15   Free opportunity to get on our mailing list

This is an outrageous adaptation of the previous offer. It is currently being used by at least one mass-market publisher in the UK. You run a press ad offering a "Free Information Pack" ... and you ask coupon-fillers to include £1.50 postage and packing. They then receive your standard cold-mailing! Although they are paying to receive your prospecting mailing, this technique rarely brings complaints. What it does yield is a response rate that is ten, twenty or even thirty times higher than they will receive on the most responsive rented lists!!

16   Free gift for reading this mailing

Include something useful or intriguing as your 'attention getter'. One theory is that the prospect will feel obliged to read your message. It's simpler than that: with so much poorly targeted mail still around, such gimmicks help your mailing to stand out from the crowd.

Examples:

Doctors received a free rose-bush in a mailing to promote a nasal decongestant. One US catalogue always goes out with a free ballpoint pen.

17   Free demonstration

This is ideal for technical products.

18   Free survey of your special needs

This gets the salesperson through the prospect's door.

19   Free gift if you reply to this ad or mailing

Don't make the gift too valuable or you attract people with no interest in the product being promoted. All they really want is the freebie.

20   Free gift if you try the product

The same caution applies as in offer 19.

21   Free gift if you buy the product

Be sure to test different gifts; it makes a great difference. Then see what happens if you offer two gifts ... then three gifts. The record is seven gifts.

22   Free gift with multiple purchases

To get the free gift you have to buy product A **and** product B.

23   Try then buy

A small gift if you try the product, then a super gift if you buy the product.

24   Early bird

Get the prospect to act quickly or he is unlikely to act at all. Offer a gift if he replies within so many days or before a specified closing date. Latecomers are usually given the gift. (Why penalise people who want to do business with you?)

25   Keep on buying

The Green Shield Stamps /Air Miles concept. Collect a token with every purchase – exchange tokens for gifts or for special buying privileges. See Chapter 6.1 on loyalty schemes.

26   Mystery gift

Can be highly effective. Give some indication of its value. And don't oversell its benefits or you might disappoint the customer when it is delivered. The advantage is that you can get rid of old stock.

27   Free delivery

A good way of increasing the order value:

28   Free after-care

This applies to complicated products or services. This offer can be dressed up with certificates, membership cards, and hot line phone numbers.

29   Free sample

Particularly useful if your product is new and unfamiliar. Especially useful if you are hoping to receive regular repeated purchases. 3M launched Post-It notes in the US by giving two free pads of the new product to every office worker in town.

30   Nearly-free sample

"Send £5 for complete range of samples."

31   Get out of jail free

This allows the customer to taste your product or service without being locked in to a long-term commitment.

Example:

"We will refund the unexpired portion of your subscription at any time if you are unsatisfied."

32   Money-back guarantee

Give the most generous guarantee possible. Feature it strongly. Keep it simple and unambiguous.

33   Money-back plus guarantee

"If our product doesn't meet its promise, we will refund your money and give you an extra bonus."

Surprisingly few people take unfair advantage of you.

A computer supplies company which traded on its guaranteed next-day delivery, offered to send a free printout reading rule to every executive in any client company failing to honour its promise.

34   Extended guarantee

If your competitors offer a one-year guarantee, why not give a two-year guarantee? Your customers may be willing to **pay** to have the guarantee extended.

35   Too-good-to-be-true guarantee

Combine the money-back plus guarantee and the extended guarantee. Bargain-space ads in the US sell cheap jewellery with a money-back guarantee if you return the product within 14 days. But one company offers double your money back if you return the product within 10 years! This remarkable offer has given a startling boost to the response rates – but with such a long time available for taking up the guarantee, no one gets around to returning the purchase.

36   Guaranteed buy-back

Offer to buy the product back at a set price after a certain period. This is ideal for products that are likely to be replaced in a year or two.

The concept of car leasing failed in the US until the offer was expressed as: "We will give you a fixed price for your used car in two years time."

37   Deluxe version

In the same way that people will pay over the odds for little extra benefit when they travel first class, a satisfying number will pay extra for a posh version of your product. It's a good opportunity to increase your profits by setting much higher margins on the first class version.

At one time it was quite common for publishers to offer books in standard editions and also in expensive leather-bound editions.

38   Bolt-on goodies

After you sell him the hi-fi, sell him the headphones. Promote these extra sales in the initial promotion or in the delivery pack.

39 Bring a friend

"A special price if you and a friend both buy at the same time." If your product is really special, play hard to get. "This offer is available **only** if you both buy it together."

Example:

"Free meal if you visit our time-share development – but only if you bring your spouse."

40 Limited time

The offer is available **only** if you reply within 7 days. Or if you reply by a specified date.

41 Limited edition

There are numerous variations on this one. Silver and gold editions. Signed and unsigned. Some people sell the non-limited edition at a low price – and a special limited edition at a high price.

42 Charter membership

This allows ordinary people to become special. Buy a product early in its life and you enjoy a special category of membership. Sometimes used in magazine launches. Charter subscribers get a free book, a guaranteed fixed subscription rate in the future, or some other privilege.

43 Test of skill contest

Success is highly dependent on the list being used or on the readership of the medium you are advertising in. You are generally better off with offer 44.

44 Sweepstake or lucky draw

UK law says you must allow non-purchasers an equal chance of winning. It pays to offer an unusual first prize when you address specialist lists:

Win a holiday in Bangladesh

> Third World charity seeking donations

Win a holiday in Nigeria

> Offer to new subscribers from a magazine dealing with the Third World

Win a flight in a Battle of Britain aircraft

> Photocopier company seeking sales force appointments

45   Lucky numbers sweepstake

"Your lucky number may already have won. Reply now to see if it has." This typically does about 30% better than a straightforward lucky draw. It also has the huge advantage that you only have to award the major prize if the person holding the lucky number actually claims it.

46   Lucky draw with a prize for everyone who enters

Everyone gets a free gift for replying, but someone also gets the big prize!

47   Unexpected prize

The prospect has no recollection of having entered any competition and is surprised to learn:

"You have won one of these five prizes ... please come and collect it" – he is then obliged to sit through a sales presentation for his trouble. He usually wins the least valuable of the five prizes, unless .... etc.

This is an example of extremely dubious ethics in this form. However, it should be possible to turn the basic idea of an unexpected prize into something honest and worthwhile by making a few changes. Obviously if the value of the prize is high enough it could become an extremely generous offer.

48   A bribe

Closely related to 47: offer people money or a gift if they are willing to receive a salesperson.

> *"We will pay you for your valuable time."*

A variant on this offer is simply to say that you will bear some expenses incurred by your prospect or customer:

> *"Visit our holiday home development and we will pay for your petrol."*

49   Talent contest

A name-gathering technique used by correspondence colleges.

> Example:
>
> *"Copy this drawing"* or *"Send your short story for free criticism."*

50 Charity link

"Buy this product and we will help this charity."

It makes you look good and also does some good. If you choose the right charity, the results can be spectacular.

The opposite tongue-in-cheek approach yielded a 20% increase in sales when it was featured on a magazine cover:

"Buy this publication or we shoot this dog!"

Most philanthropic offers up to now have been tied to children's charities or animal charities. Environmental, Third World, and human rights organisations are worth a try.

51 Someone else's offer

If you are renting someone else's list, gain from the loyalty he gets from his customers: make it look as if **he** is making the offer. Such endorsements are occasionally used by suppliers of financial services.

52 Auction

Let the customer decide the price: the highest bid received by post will get the product. In conventional direct marketing circles the first known example was in 1981. But dealers in rare jazz records have advertised this way since the 1950s. Several jazz record dealers now run e-mail auctions over the Internet.

53 Lower the price

Return to your failed enquiries and reduce the price of the product ... or merely the first payment. The publisher of the Charles Atlas body-building course used to go back again and again with steadily reducing prices, as do several other correspondence (distance learning) courses today.

54 Utility version

Return to your failed enquiries with a cheaper version of your publication.

55 Dare me

Promise to do something outrageous.

"Bring this invitation and if you are not impressed by our product demonstration, I will eat the invitation card."

"I will sit on the church roof until I receive enough money to repair the steeple" – a vicar who thus raised £7,000 in seven days.

56   Sell a second premium

Establish the value of your free gift by allowing the customer to buy a second copy of the gift. You can make a decent profit on this extra sale.

57   Count on the customer's dishonesty

Let the customer think he has caught you out – an arithmetical error in your order form that allows him to pull a fast one on you. (A neat trick to apply in the fourth letter in the bad-debt collection cycle!)

There are several highly effective variations on this theme, all of them disreputable.

WARNING!!!

These 57 offers are mostly legal in the UK, Ireland and the US. But be aware that many offers are severely restricted if you direct a promotion to other countries in Europe.

For instance, in Germany you can give samples away only if your product is 'new'. Low-value gifts are generally permissible in Germany if they are seen to be 'attention-getters' but not if they are regarded as an 'inducement to make a purchase.' Member-get-Member offers are not allowed in Switzerland. And so on.

Be sure to get local advice before mailing into Europe. See Chapter 4.4.

Ten ways to beef up reply devices

1   Give your reply devices a good title. Something more exciting than *Order Form*.

2   Repeat the offer at the top of the reply device.

3   Repeat all of your bonus incentives on the reply device. Include a new incentive if you can, exclusive to the reply device.

4   Include your address elsewhere in the mailing in case the reader loses your reply envelope.

5   Put your phone number in large print and point out that it's quicker to order by phone. Stress that it's an 0800 number or a Freephone number.

6   Encourage readers to fax the reply form to you. Use an 0800 number for your fax reply service.

7   At the beginning of the form write in a sample order in handwriting.

8   Add a 'handwritten' thank-you at the end of the form.

9   Print the reply device on coloured stock.

10   Ask your granny if she understands how to use the order form.

Five tips for editing your own work

1   When you've finished your copy read it aloud. Does it sound like you talking? Or is it stilted?

2   Even better, get someone else to read it aloud to you. Preferably, someone you don't get along with too well. Then if there's anything that is clumsy, they'll unwittingly highlight it for you.

3   Sleep on copy overnight before going to print. Ideally, wait a week. This is the surest way to spot those literary allusions you thought were so clever when you came up with them the other day.

4   Be merciless at removing adjectives and adverbs. Most of them add nothing to your copy except to slow it down. Pretend that your typesetter charges you £20 for each adjective. On this basis, an adjective will get into print only if it really pays its way.

5   Employ the £50 test: "If someone offers me £50 as a challenge, can I remove any of this copy without losing essential facts?"

A writer's final checklist

1	Is my opening sentence gripping?
2	Do I take too long to get to the benefits?
3	Does it talk features or benefits?
4	Have I included proof of what I promise?
5	Did I ask for the order?
6	Have I made it easy to order?
7	Does my order form correspond to the main text?
8	Have I used the word 'you' often enough?
9	Have I made the text chatty or pompous?
10	Does it track?
11	Did I use short words, short sentences, short paragraphs?
12	Am I repeating words and expressions unintentionally?
13	Does my company name appear too often?
14	Am I using active or passive verbs?
15	Does my text have a dull visual appearance?
16	Any split infinitives ... wandering verbs?
17	Is it believable? Have I used such tired words as 'amazing'?
18	Why should the reader act now? Have I given enough good reasons?
19	Have I included testimonials?
20	Can I cut the text by a quarter without losing any of the vital sales points?

Chapter 7.6

Creating a successful catalogue

This chapter includes:

- The changing catalogue market
- Planning a catalogue
- The four main success factors of a catalogue:

    Success factor one: finding the right product

    Success factor two: who is your target customer?

    Success factor three: your catalogue needs a brand image

    Success factor four: effective format and design – the selling catalogue

- How catalogues work
- Taking competitive catalogues apart
- Analysing catalogue performance
- Example: outline catalogue launch plan

About this chapter

Catalogue marketing in the UK has undergone a revolution in the past twenty-five years – and is still changing fast.

Initially, the advent of the Internet seemed to herald the death of the paper catalogue, as a brave new era of ordering online and the paperless transaction dawned. The reality is that the paper catalogue is still as powerful and important a tool in the direct and interactive marketer's armoury as ever – if not more so.

However, it still remains one of the costliest things you can reasonably create in direct marketing – here we give invaluable advice and step by step guidance on how not to have an expensive disaster.

Author/Consultant: Graeme McCorkell

Graeme McCorkell consultant and writer

Graeme founded MSW, one of the first UK direct marketing agencies. It grew from three to 103 people between 1976 and 1987 and introduced clients such as Volvo, Abbey National and P&O to direct marketing as well as serving past masters such as the AA, IBM and GUS. In 1983, MSW became the first UK direct marketing agency to be acquired by an American advertising group and was renamed MSW Rapp & Collins. After Graeme left it was merged by new owners, Omnicom, with WWAV to form WWAV Rapp Collins.

Working as a consultant and occasional copywriter since 1988, his clients have included The AA, Alliance & Leicester, Barnardos, Boots, The Consumers' Association, GE Capital, GUS, Holiday Property Bond, National Savings, Royal Mail and many more.

Graeme served as a director of the Institute of Direct Marketing, of which he is also a Fellow, until May 2000. From 1990 to 1995 he acted as chairman. Between these years, the IDM grew by over 300%, opened its doors to membership and was awarded institute status by the DTI. Graeme also acted as non-executive chairman of Australia's fastest growing direct marketing agency, Lavender Direct, from its formation in 1997 to 2000.

In 1990, his first book *Advertising That Pulls Response* was published by McGraw-Hill, selling all over the world. This was followed by the standard Institute of Direct Marketing work, *Direct and Database Marketing,* published by Kogan Page in 1997.

Graeme McCorkell F IDM,
The Gables, Wistanstow, Craven Arms, Shropshire
SY7 8DG, England. Telephone 01588 672900.

Chapter 7.6

Creating a successful catalogue

The changing catalogue market

atalogue marketing in the UK has undergone a revolution in the past twenty years - and is still changing fast. For over fifty years the giant 1,000-page catalogues of GUS, Grattan, Freeman, Littlewoods and Empire dominated the scene.

Then, in the 1970s, along came Scotcade and Kaleidoscope, quickly followed by Innovations and Next. At first the catalogue establishment took little notice - but then the implications began to dawn. In America, legends like Montgomery Ward and Sears, pioneers of the big catalogues, closed their doors. J C Penney, the largest of them all, reduced its book by over 50 per cent and introduced seventy specialist catalogues to compensate.

While the 1970s saw the first stirrings of modern catalogue development in the UK, led by industry visionaries Bob Scott (Scotcade) and Nigel Swabey (Kaleidoscope and Innovations), the most important and far-reaching breakthrough came in 1987 with the launch of the Next Directory, the Next store group's first catalogue venture.

Next changed not only catalogue design but also cataloguers' whole approach to customers, with 48-hour deliveries, elegant packaging and, of course, an established brand built up through the successful chain of High Street stores.

Next's classy High Street image brought instant credibility – a vital mail order ingredient – and earned it a loyal following of young, middle-class customers who had little or no previous propensity to buy by mail. It brought panache to a scene which had been synonymous with poor quality merchandise, out-of-date style, and a working-class dependence on extended credit.

Enter Racing Green and Lands' End

The change had begun. In 1991, two clothing catalogues were launched on to the market that were as radically different from Next as Next was from GUS. Racing Green and Lands' End pushed the boundaries of the mail order market even wider.

UK-based Racing Green emulated successful US lifestyle catalogues such as J Crew. It appealed to an affluent, young, busy market and traded only on cash-with-order (cheques, credit cards etc.) and from a catalogue of fewer than 100 pages. Lands' End, on the other hand, brought a highly successful formula to the UK by simply anglicising its US marketing.

Both catalogues overcame the fact that their products were more expensive than those in other catalogues through the use of superior photography and excellent copy. This skill was born out of the owners' genuine love of their products, their total involvement with every aspect of the catalogue process, and their merchandising and marketing skills.

The scene was now set and newcomers to the market arrived in numbers, from Bob Scott's new catalogue Scotts of Stow, to Divertimenti aimed at cooks, and Kingshill and Elegance aimed at the highest of fashion markets.

All these new catalogues had one thing in common. They were aimed at specific segments of the market. They were targeted at socio-economic groups qualified by interests, special needs or other identifying characteristics.

The rules for successful catalogue marketing in this environment differ totally from the skills required in the old days, as we now explore.

Planning a catalogue

We now look at the process of producing a new catalogue and making it successful. Where should we begin?

As with all forms of marketing, planning is the key to success. Without a detailed strategic plan any catalogue operation will struggle. Every activity should be carried out with the plan as the road map, and the outputs of each step matched against it.

A catalogue plan is not just theory but must very soon be made real. It is a good idea to have a dummy catalogue in your hands at the earliest possible stage. No doubt, if you are diligent, you will have other people's catalogues in front of you, too.

It also helps to appoint a custodian of the plan who can remain objective about every decision. This guarantees that product, pricing, creative and marketing decisions are not overly influenced by personal feelings and experience.

Short-term profit – or long-term customer?

The way you approach the plan will be governed by the objectives and expectations of the business and the market you are entering. It takes a far different strategy to enter a mature crowded market than it does to start up in a totally new niche. Equally, if the proprietor is in it for a quick buck, then customer acquisition strategies are poles apart from those required for a long-term project.

For the purposes of this Guide we shall look at the processes involved in developing a long-term business with real profits coming down the line from a retained customer base. We will, however, touch upon some of the techniques required for those with a shorter term view.

The four main success factors of a catalogue

Whether you are starting your catalogue from the beginning, or repositioning an existing business, the main factors in building your catalogue will always be:

1. **Product**
2. **Target market**
3. **Branding and positioning**
4. **Format and design**

We have deliberately put product first as this is the factor that will determine the market you enter. Defining the target audience will then form the basis for your product selection, pricing strategy and subsequently the overall positioning of your catalogue. In turn, the positioning will guide you towards the best trading terms, eg the need for credit etc. Finally comes the design and copy, which should reflect all of these.

Getting three other factors right will be vital to your success and you are recommended to refer to the appropriate chapters in this Guide:

- **Finding customers**   - see particularly Section 5

- **Developing customers**   - see particularly Section 6

- **Logistics and fulfilment**   - see particularly Chapter 8.6

We now begin our closer look at each of the above, beginning with the product.

Success factor one: Finding the right product

Earlier in this chapter we highlighted the common denominator of all successful new catalogues. It is worth repeating here with some additional underlining:

The new catalogues
They are aimed at specific segments of the market. They are targeted at socio-economic groups qualified by interests, special needs or other identifying characteristics.

In the brave new world of direct response catalogues it is unlikely that you will be a generalist with no particular theme for your catalogue range. To really stand apart you need to differentiate your product range, or at least make your customers think your offering is different by treating it in a unique way.

Ideally, your products should be selected around a theme, for example, a room in the house, the source of the products, a time period, a fabric or a hobby. This approach is vital for positioning your catalogue and defining the target audience. Developing a golf catalogue, for instance, ostensibly makes targeting very easy - although even here there are new golfers and experienced club golfers with possibly different aspirations and different needs.

Branded or own label?

For your first catalogue it may be beneficial to include products with well-known brand names as this lends instant credibility. This is not essential. However, without well-known brands you will need to increase the branding of your catalogue and put more pressure on the promotion people to 'get your catalogue across'. Good examples are Racing Green and Scotts of Stow respectively.

Racing Green launched to an unsuspecting market with a catalogue that contained only own-brand products (even though some of it was rebadged from the manufacturer's label). Scotts, on the other hand, contained a mix of well-known brands and unnamed products. This mix was strengthened by the inclusion of 'exclusive' products with the added bonus of being very competitively priced.

Of course, if you are already blessed with a well-known corporate brand, such as Next, then your product should be truly representative of all the values normally associated with that brand. This applies whether your catalogue is another way of reaching your target audience, as in the case of the Harrods catalogue, or a new range diversification, as in the case of Mini Boden.

We will return to the issue of branding in a moment.

The catalogue warning triangle

Let us say you have chosen the general theme for your products. Before you embark on your product scouring trips, there are three other issues and strategies that you need to address and finalise, each of which will directly impinge on your product selection. These are target audience, pricing policy and offer and terms.

Figure 7.6.1

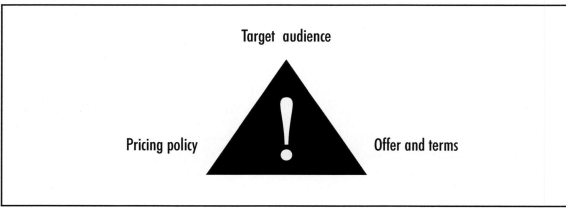

It is absolutely vital that these three elements are in congruency. If any one is out of line, then product selection and subsequent marketing will become exceptionally difficult, if not impossible.

Success factor two: Who is your target customer?

Your next step, then, is to define the target audience. As with most direct marketing in the 1990s, simple age, gender and socio-economic groupings are not enough. To be really successful you need to get inside the minds of your typical prospects. You need to totally empathise with their needs, aspirations, expectations and circumstances.

Data analysis will help, but it cannot replace intimate knowledge of the product and the likely customer. This is one of the major reasons why retailers, even if they have only one outlet, start with a major advantage. They know what sells, having carried out intensive qualitative research through continuously seeing, and talking to, their customers.

Try and draw up a clear mental picture of your customer and carry it with you when you are looking at a product.

How about your pricing strategy?

Your pricing strategy will more or less be determined by the choice of target audience. Again Racing Green provides an excellent example:

"You pays your money ... "

In 1991 many cut-price or discount cataloguers were selling men's 'Lacoste' style shirts for around £7. David Krantz knew intuitively that his customer would immediately perceive a product at this price as being of poor quality. He developed a product that was of near equal quality to well-known branded products and priced it at £16. The rest of his range was developed and priced in the same way.

But never mislead your audience by promising more than you can deliver. Everybody knows that a 20-piece towel bale is likely to be of modest quality with sizes on the small side. Do not try to pretend that they are St. Michael quality and the bath towel is the size of a door. You may get away with it - but only once.

Credit or cash-with-order?

The definition of your target audience and pricing strategy, combined with your product categories, will influence your terms of trade. If you are working with low value items, at almost any socio-economic level, then simply asking for payment by cheque or credit card will be sufficient.

If, however, you are selling products of higher value, say £50 and upwards, then it may be necessary to think about offering credit terms. This will be vital at the lower end of the market and good to have at the upper end. Credit will increase response (though this may be counter-balanced by credit-rejected orders) and average order values. More importantly, it helps to cement customer relationships.

If you do not wish to get involved with any kind of credit offer then choose your product, target audience and pricing strategy with care.

Your catalogue starts to take shape

Back to your overall plan. Quite early on you will need some idea of how your catalogue will look and feel - it is, after all, an important aspect of your philosophy.

Now is the time to decide how many pages you will have in the catalogue, how many products will be on each page, how many ranges you will have, and how much space you will allocate to each range.

It may only be a start but if you do this now you will have taken one more important step on the road to success.

Product density, ie how many products per page, is a key issue. Here the best rule of thumb is to use the pricing guide. The lower the prices of your products the more you should put on a page. For higher priced items, lower the density.

Remember, though, that eye fatigue will set in if the pages are too busy, too densely packed - and you also have to fit in some copy. The technical term for this part of catalogue marketing is pagination, which we return to shortly.

Shopping for products

Sooner or later it will be time to go shopping for products. And when you set off, remember every product must meet the stringent selection criteria laid down in your planning and positioning phase. Ideally, try to find more products than you need, then let them fight it out for inclusion in your final range. Never select products that do not match your criteria just to fill up the space - reduce the number of pages in the catalogue instead.

Product scouring could be the subject of a book in its own right, but for now we will stick to the basics. Here are three simple rules worth abiding by:

- Start by looking around the shops and at other catalogues to get a feel for the kind of products, designs, styles and colours that you think you want in your catalogue.

- Visit as many trade exhibitions as you can and meet as many suppliers as possible.

- Sample sparingly and do not try to make a supplier happy by sampling for the sake of it. It will only clutter your mind and build up the supplier's hopes.

Later on, when you are an established cataloguer, suppliers (some) will come to you. But there is still no substitute for getting out and about if you want to be first in the queue for any innovative product.

Success factor three: Your catalogue needs a brand image

Branding a catalogue is no different from branding any other product - except that here the 'product' is the catalogue in its entirety. There are no hard and fast rules but a number of elements, individually or in combination, help build a catalogue's image or personality. First, of course, comes the product selection, quality, and pricing which, as we have mentioned, help to define your target audience.

Close behind in terms of importance, come the name, format, design, copy and illustrative style. We now look at each of these in terms of image. Later, we will look at some of them again in terms of their persuasive effect.

The all-important name

Naming your catalogue goes a long way to creating your brand, and there are several routes you can follow. The three main ones are: naming it after the owner or the location of the business, eg Boden (after Johnny Boden), Scotts of Stow, Kingshill Collection; using the range of products as a guide, eg Hold Everything, The Museum Collection, Past Times, Long Tall Sally; or choosing a generic or abstract title with appropriate connotations.

If you elect for a generic title, it is advisable to be evocative and to encapsulate one or two of the brand values in the name, eg Victoria's Secret (lingerie), Aspirations (housestyle), Racing Green (traditional casual clothing).

Your name may have the advantage of being unusual and memorable without describing your product or positioning it, in which case it may be useful to develop a strapline or positioning statement to support the brand, eg Divertimenti's "For people who love to cook."

Format

Before deciding on the format, it is worth considering how the catalogue will be distributed. If inserting the whole catalogue in newspapers or magazines, your page size and number of pages will be critical. The same can be said of direct mail to cold lists. Here, postage is a key element and therefore weight is very important.

Another restriction is that many catalogues are based on economical print formats and become uniform in size. Nevertheless, the paper can play a major role in differentiation and it may be worthwhile thinking about paper types, textures and colour.

Restrictions apart, it is as well to remember that the format is probably the first thing recipients will notice about your catalogue. Good examples of format differentiation include Kingshill Collection's and Next Directory's hardbacked books, Rediscovered Originals' brown paper stock, and the A3 page size favoured by Breck's Bulbs in the US.

Format changes and unusual formats can be costly, even prohibitive. The best advice is to test. And before testing, rehearse your Profit and Loss calculations to see whether your ideas stand a chance of being viable. (See Chapter 1.4.)

Design

The layout is the next opportunity to create individuality. But this too should follow as many of the golden rules as possible. The elements that can be mixed and matched for effect are photography versus illustrations, models versus still life, colour versus black and white, and also typography and style of graphics.

Remember we are talking here about design as an image ingredient. Sometimes the requirements of a stylish design clash with the 'rules' of selling, which calls for a delicate balancing act by the creative team.

Copy

Lands' End, still one of the finest examples of all that is good in cataloguing, has developed a copy style and tone which is the envy of many a writer. Not only does it sell the benefits of the product, but it accomplishes the task in a way that creates its own unique positioning.

J Peterman, another fine catalogue out of the US, features the owner's idiosyncratic copywriting. A similar US catalogue was the late lamented Banana Republic. Our own Rediscovered Originals combines the best of both these books to stamp an indelible mark on the catalogue (which goes to show that you don't have to re-invent the wheel to create a successful design).

Models

Johnny Boden has used his friends (and pets!) as models in his catalogue to great effect, whilst Charles Tyrwhitt takes the opposite extreme using well-known professional sports personalities to model its Jermyn Street shirts.

Whatever tools you employ to differentiate your catalogue, be consistent, and make sure that each element plays a role in building the brand values that you want to communicate to your chosen target audience.

Examples of good catalogue design and pagination

The more offer-driven the catalogue the busier the front cover should be

The lower the prices of your products the more you should put on a page

Source: Dean Lindell, Divertimenti (Mail Order) Ltd, 14.11.97

A strapline or positioning statement to support the brand

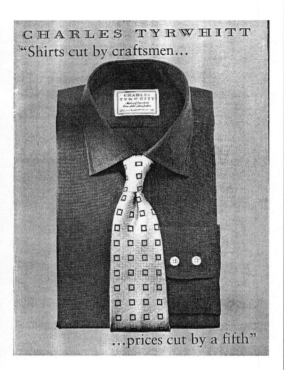

Source: Peter Higgins, Charles Tyrwhitt, 20.11.97

The more upmarket your positioning the more stylised the cover will be

Source: Karen Patterson, Racing Green, 3.11.97

For higher priced items lower the density

Source: Patti Millard, Historical Collections, 14.11.97

Naming the catalogue by using the range of products as a guide

Success factor four: Effective format and design – the selling catalogue

So far we have looked at aspects of your catalogue that will help it to develop a personality of its own - its brand character.

Now we must revisit some of those elements - only this time we are concerned with their influence on getting a response and increasing order values. What makes one catalogue sell and another fail?

Here the catalogue creator is engaged in a delicate and skilled balancing act. Not every design feature that lends distinction to a catalogue will be effective in terms of its selling power - in fact, 'too much' design can be seriously detrimental. Before we go on to look at elements which induce customers to buy rather than just admire, look at the examples on the foregoing pages and see if you can deduce what it is that makes them all powerful sales channels.

Pagination - making every page work harder

Before you can start the creative process you must 'construct' your catalogue page by page. We call this process 'pagination' (although it is sometimes called merchandising). In effect, we need a blueprint for the catalogue.

Pagination is the process of deciding several key factors that will affect the overall density, layout and pace of your catalogue, chiefly:

?   Which product goes on which page?

?   How much space should be allocated to each product?

?   The sequence or position of each page in the catalogue.

The term pagination is obviously derived from 'page' and we have used the word page in referring to each of the three main elements above. However, you are strongly advised to paginate in spreads (ie two facing pages). Pages are viewed as spreads by your customers and eye tracking research has proved categorically that the eye traverses the two pages as a single entity. It is even possible to view the front and back covers as a spread to get maximum consistency in the creative approach.

After product selection, pagination is the most important part of putting a successful catalogue together. Sadly it is also one of the least developed and most underrated of skills. The pagination will ultimately determine the overall performance of the catalogue, especially with new or recently acquired customers.

Every catalogue has its 'Hot spots'

One of the first and most important steps in the pagination is to decide which products are to occupy the *hot spots*. These are the most important parts of your catalogue. The hot spots are the same for all catalogues and are as follows:

- **Outside front cover**

- **Outside back cover**

- **First inside spread**

- **Inside back spread**

- **The middle spread (if the catalogue is stapled)**

- **Opposite the order form**

You should also consider the second and third spreads of larger catalogues, although their role is more educational, in that they describe at a glance the range your catalogue contains.

The rule for hot spots is very simple. They must contain the products that are your best sellers and match your brand and its positioning. A possible exception is the front cover which you may reserve for branding.

'Hot spots'
Products allocated to hot spots in your catalogue must be best sellers and they must reflect and reinforce your brand and its positioning.

For established cataloguers, following the above advice is easy - they can use their previous sales history as a guide to which products are the best sellers.

But what about you, a new cataloguer? The best advice is again simple: be bold! Even if the products you allocate to hot spots do not turn out to be your best sellers, hopefully you will have interested your readers and helped to establish your position in the market.

The only hot spot where the above rules may not apply is opposite the order form. The ideal use for this space is to include low-value products that are relative impulse purchases, can be considered treats, or are 'stock' items (eg batteries). These products will help build order values. (Take a look at the checkout of your local M&S or B&Q for good examples of how retailers use the same technique, ie placing low-value treats close to the point of sale.)

How much space per product?

Again, deciding how much space to allocate to a product is easier if you have a detailed sales history. The simplest technique is to calculate the sales-to-space ratio for each product. This is a comparison of the percentage space a product has of the entire catalogue, compared to its percentage of sales.

$$\frac{\text{per cent of sales}}{\text{per cent of catalogue space}} = \text{sales:space ratio}$$

For example, if a product attracts 7 per cent of the revenue for a catalogue from only 3.5 per cent of the space, the sales:space ratio is 2.

Any product where the result is one or greater has 'taken its space'. For products with a ratio of less than one the decision must be either to reduce the amount of space allocated to it or drop the product from the range altogether.

Of course, if you have no sales history, you will not be able to carry out this step. However, we have included it so that you will be in a position to calculate your own sales:space ratios at the first opportunity.

Q. If my product reaches the heady heights of a sales:space ratio of TWO or more, should I give it more space and prominence-because it is successful-or leave well alone because it is already doing more than its fair share?

A. On the surface, leaving well alone is a sound argument, but it is wiser overall to exploit your successes to the full - possibly giving them even more space. This is especially effective if you are seeking new customers or trying to reactivate lapsed or dormant names.

If you increase the space allocated to a successful product to match its previous sales, the sales will usually grow at least in line with the increased space but, will often do even better. A prominently featured product is 'recommended' and will be the first item to gain attention on a spread.

One factor that may modify your use of the sales:space formula in relation to hot spots is seasonality. You will naturally increase or reduce the space allocated to exceptionally seasonal products, eg lawnmowers, in line with the period in which the catalogue is issued. In such cases your sales:space calculations should refer to comparable seasons.

The need for a change of pace

Changing the space/product allocation helps to introduce a change of pace, and pace is synonymous with heightened interest. We use the term 'pace' although we are literally trying to slow readers down.

Certain pages should be given the job of stopping the customer's eye flow and making him or her refocus. Without these 'stopper' pages it has been proved that a person can flip through an entire catalogue without the eye coming to rest.

One of the best ways to achieve pace is to dedicate entire pages to one product or photograph. Strong headlines, graphics or price points can achieve the same result. Your catalogue should contain a number of these pages spread evenly throughout.

Left-hand or right-hand pages? Despite some recommendations to the contrary, your stopper pages should be left-hand *and* right-hand pages. Many people, particularly those who are left-handed, start to browse from the back of the book and so see left-hand pages first. So use both sides of the spread for maximum effect.

'Heroes' are essential

Closely related to pace is the need for a 'hero' on every spread. The hero is not a male model! It is a dominant product that will provide a focal point for the eye, achieved by either the space given to it or its treatment.

A spread may feature a single hero or it may feature two, so positioned as to guide the eye around the spread. Looking at well-designed catalogues you will see that heroes are often placed top left or bottom right on the spread, to direct your eye into the spread, rather than allow it to wander off the page. However, variety is the name of the game and, when you turn over the page, you are likely to see a hero near the optical centre (just above halfway up the page). This is especially effective when the 'satellite' items are accessories, or otherwise go with the recommended item. Variety is also achieved by mixing squared-up pictures with cut-out pictures.

Looking at a small format (A5) catalogue, such as one from Hawkshead, you will see that spreads are simplified and hero items may even occupy more than a whole page.

Make it easy!

While you are striving to achieve maximum impact and interest, do not overlook the need for the copy and order information to be accessible. Put obstacles in the way of prospective customers and you will reduce the overall response.

Remember, many people use catalogues for convenience, ie they save time. Do not reduce this power by making any part difficult to understand. Make it easy to select and order - that is another golden rule.

Front cover: Sales counter or picture window?

Now, at last, we are ready to start the final design. We start, logically enough, with the front cover: Hot spot No 1.

There are endless arguments about the cover. Should you sell from it? Should it contain products? Should it reflect the season? Only one rule applies: the cover must get your customer, or prospective customer, to look inside. If your cover does not achieve this simple objective you do not have a chance.

Above all, the cover should reflect the overall positioning of your business. If you are in the discount market then perhaps use a very strong offer backed by a graphic suggesting more savings inside. Scotts of Stow, on the other hand, settles for a mood shot which encapsulates its brand positioning and aspirational range. Variations in set design and accessorising can set the seasonal tone.

The cover should get your message across as quickly and as relevantly as possible, not misleading your customer in any way. The more offer-driven the catalogue the busier the front cover should be. Alternatively, the more upmarket your positioning the more stylised the cover will be, with clear but understated messages. Good examples are Racing Green and Viking Direct, both successful despite their opposite styles.

And do not ignore the back cover. It is also a hot spot, remember. A good idea, as we have said, is to design it as if it were part of a spread along with the front cover.

The inside front cover - Hot spot No 2

Use the inside front cover to introduce yourself and your catalogue. Start the process of building a relationship with your customer by stating your principles, benefits and levels of service. Tell your customer how to order and, equally as important, how to return goods. Surprisingly, an open returns policy will have little effect on return rates but it will help build confidence and generate more orders.

The rest of the first spread should provide a real guide of what the customer can expect from the remainder of the catalogue. Remember the rules for hot spots!

Is an index necessary?

If you have a large number of pages and a wide range of products then include at least one index. This can be an informal table of contents in the front of the book or a fully detailed index at the back.

There is no hard and fast rule but 64 pages and above would seem to be the point where you should consider this full indexing approach. Obviously, if your catalogue is also a reference work, as in the case of some horticultural catalogues, indexing and cross-referencing are vital. There is no need to put the index in a hot spot, but it is a good idea to tell readers on the front cover (or inside front cover) where they can find the index and, of course, the order form.

Creating the body of your catalogue

Designing the pages and spreads of a catalogue obeys most of the principles of designing good direct response advertisements. One of the features of a modern catalogue is that every product is treated as a mini-ad in its own right.

Although the principles discussed in Chapters 2.1 and 4.5 apply, it is worth highlighting some important guidelines for designing and writing pages that sell. It is also important to pinpoint differences in the ways that ads and catalogues are prepared, so here we go.

How catalogues work

We start this section right away with a difference between advertisements and catalogues.

Whereas an advertisement is usually geared to persuading the prospect to agree to a single 'yes', success for a catalogue depends on obtaining a large number of smaller 'yeses'. Together these add up to the one big 'yes' - the order.

But in most other respects your reader is simply browsing through a series of ads - each with its own headline, illustration, proposition, benefits and price information.

Each entry works like an ad:

- **The picture/headline stops the eye**

- **The headline/picture confirms the first interest**

- **The copy convinces with features and benefits**

- **The terms/offer close the sale**

Of course, designing catalogue pages (and ads) is more complex than that. Every product poses a different problem. But there are some universal Do's and Don'ts as shown in the checklist in Table 7.6.1.

Table 7.6.1

	Dos and don'ts of catalogue design
✔	Do vary the size of each shot and mix cut-outs with squared-ups; start the process when planning your pagination, then use this as your guide.
✗	Don't have all your shots the same size or your catalogue will quickly become boring – you will have failed to introduce "pace".
✔	Do use words to sell your product. The picture tells only half the story, make the copy do the rest.
✗	Don't assume that your customers know more than they do. Get across all the features and benefits as well as the technical details.
✔	Do use benefit headlines for either individual products or the range of products on a spread.
✔	Do start each copy block with the main benefit of the product.
✔	Do use an appropriate tone of voice for the target audience, from street cred for kids to plain English for adults. Correctly used, tone will add authority to your proposition.
✔	Do choose typefaces and sizes that are easy to read. Consider the age of your customer when making these decisions.
✔	Do make sure that copy is adjacent to the picture or use indexing to help your customer match pictures to copy.
✔	Do consider putting picture and copy in a self-contained box if you have a high product density.
✗	Don't skimp on photography. It is easy to look at photography as a commodity but the most successful cataloguers take every shot seriously. Use lighting and props to best advantage.
✔	Do use models liberally (even if they are just friends, relations or colleagues). People add interest to a book.
✔	Do keep restating and reinforcing your service benefits and calls to action, but vary the words and layout from spread to spread.

In general, the following hierarchy exists in the way photographs are viewed:

> Colour before black and white
> Large before small
> People before things
> Children before adults
> Portraits before figure shots

So a large colour portrait of a child will gain far more attention than a small black and white shot of a widget.

Make sure it is enjoyable

Reading a catalogue should be an enjoyable and relaxing experience. Browsing in the comfort of the home is one of the real pleasures of catalogue shopping and the final product of your creative process should fulfil this expectation.

And when the customers have found themselves interested in a product, remember to make it easy for them to order.

Enjoyment plus ease are two more keys to successful catalogues.

Taking competitive catalogues apart

It is instructive to analyse catalogues you admire – to take them apart and see what makes them tick. The format, pagination, page density, theming of sections, use of heroes, price pointing and so on.

Let us look at a few pages of the first edition of *La Maison* from Scotts of Stow (as used for inserting in weekend magazines).

Size and layout. 32 pages, 270mm x 205mm. 3-column layout with 10mm outside borders and 10mm gutter. Glued, not stapled.

Design features. Full colour throughout. All photography. Mix of squared up and cut out pictures. Bled off as appropriate. Borders feature catalogue brand, telephone number and 24-hour service. Average page density: 7 items. Themed by room/garden.

Front cover
Mood shot.
Abbreviated
contents list.

First spread: style setting

Column 1: Policy letter. Incentive £1000+with any order.

Columns 2/3: Lamp and bust, under £60. Hero: chest £499.95

Columns 4-6: Hero: Sofa bed/ armchair suite Others: Lantern, rug, easel, mag. rack.

Second spread: the hall *(grand entrance)*

Columns 1/2: table, shelf, wall sconce, rug c. £17 - £100.

Column 3: vase, baker's rack c. £20 -£150.

Columns 4/5: Hero: table. Mat, topiary, shelf, c. £8 - £150.

Column 6: chair. coat/hat stand, c. £100 - £130.

Inside back (final spread): summer treats and order form

Column 1: picnic back-pack and rug, c. £30 -£40

Column 2: folding stool and lantern c. £13 - £35.

Column 3: loveseat, picnic basket and boules, c. £30 - £80.

Columns 4-6:
order form, £3 off
next purchase offer.

Our study of this and other catalogues can provide much useful information. Over time, we will be able to deduce which items were winners and which were not. However, the example we have been looking at is a summer catalogue and many outdoor items will be rested until next spring, even if they were runaway successes.

Of particular interest is the page density, the amount of descriptive copy, the number of branded items and the mix of prices on each spread. These aspects can be compared with other catalogues offering similar merchandise or aimed at people with similar tastes and lifestyles.

Equally important is the information that can be extracted from the order form. In this case orders are accepted 24 hours a day by phone, fax, post and e-mail. There is a separate enquiry line, a 90-day guarantee and returns are free. There is a delivery charge and all major cards are accepted. No credit terms are offered.

Finally, a catalogue reflects an overall mood. In this case it is rather cool. Few words are wasted in description and the pages are not populated by models - amateur or professional. The designers believe their customer is quite style conscious but with little time to read loving descriptions of painstaking craftsmanship or searches across the seven seas for rare exotica. Similarly, items are not heavily 'propped' to suggest a particular ambience. The merchandise is allowed to speak for itself.

Analysing catalogue performance

We can use the example of *La Maison* to consider how you might analyse your own catalogue's performance. In earlier chapters (for example, chapter 1.4) we have considered the overall contribution of the catalogue in provoking orders from both new and previous customers. At the other end of the spectrum lies the minute investigation of the contribution made by every single item we sourced for the catalogue.

Of course, this is important - crucial, in fact. However, to maximise our learning from experience we need to organise our analysis. Even a catalogue designed for one-stage selling (in this case loose inserting in magazines) will include perhaps 200 - 250 items. If we are smart we may have grouped some related items into special price 'bundles' that can be purchased at a special price. In this way our 250 items could become 270 or more. With so many pieces of sales information, it is all too easy to lose the thread.

Let us therefore consider various ways we could serve up the information:

Size: We observed that *La Maison* used a three column layout; the maximum number of products per column was three. Thus the basic unit of space was a ninth of a page. Some items used one unit, others two, three or four units. One way of looking at contributions is to compare the results of small and large space featurings. As we get better at picking winners, we might find that the smallest size is not the most cost-effective and we might reduce page density slightly.

Page/spread: How hot were the hot spots? Looking at the contributions of each page and spread, we can see if we put cool items in hot spots or, perhaps, if we wasted too much hot spot space on policy or index copy. Pagination analysis gives us a better appreciation of the pulling power of an item than merely looking at its raw contribution. An item that pulled well on a bad page will pull superbly in a hot spot.

Theme: Still taking the example of *La Maison,* we could compare the hall with the bathroom, the study, the garden and so on. Which themes have worked well and which not? Does the hall deserve to be near the front, should the bathroom take over the centre spread?

Merchandise category: How good are we at picking winners in soft furnishings, decorative items, furniture, garden ornaments, crockery and so on? Do they all merit the space they have received?

Price bracket: What business have we done within various price bands?
You will appreciate that this analysis could (should) consider sales volume (most usefully the sales:space ratio), profit contribution and number of item orders. The number of items ordered from any spread give some indication of the interest the spread has aroused. Lower ticket items can be disproportionately valuable in securing new customers who might uptrade later.

Contribution analysis

To undertake contribution analysis on an item-by-item basis, it is necessary to know the gross margin, the returns rate, associated costs and stock write-downs.

This task is too important to be left entirely to your accountant. The fact is that problems such as out-of-stocks and returns may be the cause of customer frustration and dissatisfaction respectively. As marketers, we are vitally interested (or should be) in the by-products of these failures to complete sales. It may be smart to drop a product (or product category) that keeps coming back to us on the basis of soft data about customer dissatisfaction - even if our hard profit data tells us we can afford the high returns ratio.

Systematic planning

A virtue of analysing the results in the ways suggested is that it fosters the use of systematic planning; that is, planning which takes account of the carefully organised and recorded learnings from each catalogue issued.

By serving up and looking at each set of item-by-item results along five different dimensions, we learn five times as quickly. These dimensions are then considered in planning the next catalogue.

Example: outline catalogue launch plan

Our example is based on a real life plan. A few adjustments have been made to respect the confidentiality of the real life calculations but the figures used are broadly realistic.

The launch is on a very large scale test basis and might have followed *either* a small scale test *or* extensive research/experience of the potential demand for key catalogue lines *and* concept testing.

Tests to be carried out
1. one-stage full catalogue mailing to selected segments of own customer database.
2. one-stage full catalogue mailing to selected outside lists.
3. one-stage insert-size catalogue in selected media.
4. two-stage insert cards.
5. two-stage space ads.

Catalogue sizes and runs
*   Full catalogue - 48pp A4 Polywrapped - 700,000
*   Insert catalogue - 24pp A5 - 2,500,000

NB Full catalogue will be used for one-stage mailings and for fulfilment of two-stage requests. Also sent to orderers from one-stage inserts and reissued to 'hot' database segments. See the schedule outline in **Table 7.6.2.**

Table 7.6.2

Outline acquisition schedule			
Activity	Lists/media	circulation	cost
one-stage full catalogue	7 database segments	210,000	£189,000
one-stage full catalogue	7 outside list tests	140,000	£147,000
one-stage insert catalogue	5 selected media	2,500,000	£161,000
two-stage insert cards.	7 selected media	3,300,000	£ 95,000
two-stage space ads.	15 ads/10 media	17,000,000	£133,000
Total direct cost			£725,000

NB   (a) Additional expenses would include two-stage fulfilment and order incentives.
       (b) Full rollout potential on outside lists is 1,600,000 pre-deduplication.
           Rollout potential for one-stage inserts is 10,250,000.
       (c) Tests may include use of/type of order incentives, ad space sizes etc.

Table 7.6.3

Outline P & L statement	£	
Customer demand	1,650,000	
Less service losses (stock-outs)	(165,000)	10 per cent
Gross despatches	1,485,000	
Returns	(223,000)	15 per cent
Net sales	1,262,000	
Distribution charges less costs	52,000	
Product cost	(631,000)	
Mark downs on returns	(51,000)	
Marketing expense	(840,000)	
Profit (Loss)	(208,000)	

From the outline P&L statement (**Table 7.6.3**) we see the test plan shows a projected loss of £208,000, which is considered to be acceptable against the estimate of potential and repeat sales from subsequent catalogue issues.

Note the use of all types of high-potential media. It is a mistake to make too many assumptions about what will work best. The larger the scale of the test, the more the risk should be spread between reasonable alternatives.

How often should you mail a customer segment?

In the real life example we have just looked at in **Tables 7.6.2** and **7.6.3**, the marketer is betting that the revenue stream from established customers will recover any losses made on customer acquisition. Once established, active buyers are the source of most, if not all, the profits of any home shopping business. It is therefore essential that they are mailed as frequently as possible to generate profit. **If it is not cost-effective to keep producing new catalogues, the same material can be mailed more than once**. Another alternative is to change a small number of pages, eg the covers, and to change the sequence of the remainder to give the catalogue a fresh look.

It may well not be right to mail each segment of the database with equal frequency. That will depend on profitability. The way to measure the profitability of each segment is to identify one factor that eliminates variables and gives an accurate, unweighted comparison. Typically, you can use a marketing cost-to-sales ratio. Or, ideally, use a return-on-investment index that reflects the marketing cost as a factor of the gross contribution from each segment. The latter gives you a guide to the actual profits being generated and the contribution to fixed overheads etc. (see chapter 2.4).

The best way to assess the optimum mailing frequency is to identify cells where the actual performance of the mailing is at least twice as good as the 'breakeven measure', eg an ROI index of 200 plus, or a marketing cost-to-sales ratio of less than 10 per cent. **As a rule of thumb, a re-mail will only produce about 50 per cent of the original mailing, so any segment that did not achieve better than twice the target will not be profitable if mailed again.** On the other hand, if the original mailing index was, for example, over 400, then this group can be mailed twice more with the same material, allowing for a 50 per cent drop-off with each mailing.

This simple methodology, plus constant testing of pack elements and offers, will ensure that you are mailing the file for optimum profits.

What about non-actives?

Non-active buyers, those who have not ordered for about twelve months, should be viewed as a recruitment source. Almost certainly you will be able to reactivate a large number of these at a far lower cost than recruiting totally new customers from outside. Always mail as deeply as you can into the dormant part of your database before spending money on external recruitment.

Compare your decision-making criteria, eg ROI, with that of outside sources to decide where best to deploy your recruitment budget.

Summing up

We have given a brief guide to the strategies and components that make up a successful operation.

The ten main guidelines are these:

1. **Decide your target audience and product niche.**

2. **Develop your strategic plan and stick to it.**

3. **Do not select products to fill space; reduce the amount of space instead.**

4. **Use every creative technique to develop your unique proposition and build a hard-working catalogue.**

5. **Do not put any obstacle in the way of ordering.**

6. **Recruit as cost-effectively as possible and use lapsed customers as much as possible.**

7. **Set exactly the right expectation in your recruitment programme, one-stage or two-stage, or you will generate instant customer attrition.**

8. **Treat one-stage media buyers as prospects, not customers.**

9. **Mail your active buyer file as often as possible.**

10. **Incentivise to achieve specific segment marketing objectives.**

Section 8: Production and fulfilment

I t is inevitable that this subject should appear towards the end of any direct marketing manual – because in any direct marketing campaign these are the last tasks to be undertaken prior to the message reaching its target. Unfortunately, this too often means that these two subjects are the last to be considered, and mistakes built into earlier stages of the process must be expensively rectified at the latter end.

So, in this section we deal with tasks which, although implemented only late on in the process, must be included in the proper planning of a campaign from the beginning. A brilliant creative idea which can't be printed, or, once printed, can't be enveloped; a splendid customer offer which has not been communicated to the contact centre to whom response is directed; a mailing piece that fails to take advantage of postal discounts – these are great wasters of time and money.

Here are the criteria which govern the practical problems of turning strategic plans, tactical approaches and creative solutions into reality: planners, media people and creatives all need to know and understand the limitations – and the opportunities – offered by these functions.

Chapter 8.1

Managing the production process

This chapter includes:

- [ ] **The extra contribution a production manager can make**
- [ ] **The proactive production manager**
- [ ] **Managing your suppliers**
- [ ] **The six key control documents**
- [ ] **Key strategies in campaign execution**
- [ ] **The twelve things which no one else will look after**
- [ ] **Saving VAT for financial services and charities**
- [ ] **Considerations about paper**
- [ ] **The importance of price**
- [ ] **How to decide whether to do it yourself, or hand it all over to someone else**

About this chapter:

roduction is complex, time-consuming, and fraught with risk. Managing production is like being a goalkeeper: whilst you can occasionally make a spectacular save, it is the least glamorous position, and any mistake you make is likely to result in disaster.

Yet a proactive, commercially aware production manager can make a massive contribution to the success of a campaign. The aim of this chapter is to show you how.

There are separate chapters in this Guide about the specifics of data processing, personalisation, enclosing and fulfilment. This chapter concentrates on managing the whole campaign, whether it is an e-mail broadcast, a point-of-sale brochure, a door-drop, or a personalised mailing.

Nick Pride-Hearn
Direct Marketing Consultant

Nick has been involved in direct marketing ever since he found himself managing direct mail campaigns for Sadler's Wells Theatre nearly twenty years ago. Since then he has worked as client, production buyer, account director, and marketing services director in a number of direct marketing organisations. After four years in Australia and two in the Netherlands, he returned to the UK and took over as managing director of TCG Production House, where he remained until the end of 2000. He currently works as a direct marketing consultant.

Nick Pride-Hearn M IDM
North Fording
St Mary in the Marsh
Romney Marsh
Kent TN29 0DF

E-mail nick.pride-hearn@talk.21.com

Chapter 8.1

Managing the production process

The extra contribution a production manager can make

 good production 'executive' carries out the necessary tasks to complete a campaign on time and on budget. A good production 'manager' makes a contribution much earlier on. The difference between the two is best illustrated by their involvement in the design and budgeting stages of campaign development.

Design

Many people do not involve their production staff at this stage, and there are some production people who do not see why they should have anything to do with design.

Here's what a production person can contribute at the design stage:

- Knowledge of machinery and production techniques that can prompt new creative approaches from the design team, while keeping within the realms of the possible.

- Understanding the implications for cost and time of certain complex formats or printing requirements.

- Understanding of risk (if for instance, a particular piece can only be produced at one factory in Germany).

- Alternative options to achieve the same or similar result.

It is crucial for the production manager to understand just what everyone is trying to achieve. If it is important to use a special colour (for instance, for a credit card logo), then far better for the production manager to know in advance, than to find out only when the artwork arrives (or worse, when the proof comes back from the printer).

A fantastic design, and the client loves it ...

The designer of an insurance acquisition mailing asked me a question in passing, about a particular way of folding and trimming a personalised letter to create a nested personalised voucher. A week later, the account manager briefed me on the job: "The designer said he had checked this with you, and we showed it to the client who loved it, so can we get some prices now?" The piece the client had seen and loved was a letter with three personalised pieces nested inside. The designer had made an understandable assumption about the way the machinery worked, and I had not taken the time to understand exactly why he was asking the question.

Budgeting

Even if you had no involvement in the design process, there is still a great deal to contribute at the budgeting stage.

Make sure there are at least three days in every campaign schedule to get prices and budgets together – more if you know it involves anything new, clever or complex.

What you can expect from a budget compiled in a hurry:

● A quotation for the exact specification – no alternatives, enhancements or recommendations.

● A higher price than necessary (everyone will be playing safe).

● A potentially costly mistake or two.

The ideal budget will include suggestions about alternatives which may be quicker or more cost-effective, such as:

● If I can have another few days in the schedule, I can print this overseas and take advantage of a favourable exchange rate.

● If we were to change some of the sizes a little, then there are two suppliers who could produce it at a better price.

● This pack could be produced in another way which would make it machine-enclosable.

The ideal budgeting process will include a conversation between production manager and designer to come up with the best solution for the task in hand.

For this to be possible, the production manager needs to be:

- Knowledgeable about his suppliers and their capability.

- Willing and able to call on his suppliers to discuss the best solutions.

This has implications on the supplier relationship which we will look at a little later.

Your suppliers will naturally want to find good reasons for you to place work with them. So, get them involved, tell them what you are trying to achieve, and they will be happy to help.

The proactive production manager

If you want to become a manager of the production process, then aim for the following:

- Keep in touch with your colleagues in the creative department, not just when you are working on a '*live*' campaign.

- Keep your designers up-to-date with new technology and the results it can achieve.

- Keep samples of interesting packs, find out who produced them and how.

- Show them to your colleagues in production and creative.

- Stay abreast of changes in your suppliers' capabilities.

- Let your current and prospective suppliers know of your interest – they will be more than happy to keep you up-to-date.

- Don't just become an expert, become *known* as an expert.

Order quantities

When quoting and ordering, you need to allow for the inevitable wastage of material at each stage of the production process. Here is a rough guide to the number of '*overs*' to add to your mailing quantities.

Table 8.1.1 **Calculating order quantities**

Component	Additional quantity for overs (%)	Minimum overs	Notes
Outer envelope	5%	2000	
Reply envelope	2%	1000	
Preprinted stationery for personalisation	5%	2000	Increase to 7% for duplex (two-sided) jobs, or for reel-to-reel applications
Other items	2%	1000	

Add more for complex processes, and where there are many versions. Do not be afraid to print plenty of overs – it will always be cheaper than a reprint.

Managing your suppliers

How do you refer to your suppliers? Do you '*use*' them? Or do you '*work with*' them? Which attitude is more likely to get a better result for you?

The way in which a production manager runs relationships with suppliers can make all the difference between a smooth, well-ordered campaign delivered on time and on budget, and a fraught succession of firefights followed by angry disagreements over the invoice.

A loyal supplier ...

I had recently moved companies, to a better job in a smaller organisation. I had placed a large and important piece of work with one of my '*best*' suppliers, and suddenly there was a problem: we were late, and it was our fault, but we still wanted to mail on time. I fully expected my supplier to help me out in the way they frequently had before. They did not. I realised, too late, that I had always relied on the buying power of my previous company, and not spent enough time cultivating my personal relationships. I resolved to take a different approach to my supplier companies.

There are three key elements to supplier relationship management:

1. Selection

2. Developing the relationship

3. Management

Selection

Supplier selection is not just a case of looking at a plant list. Here is a checklist for selecting your roster of suppliers:

- Equipment and capability (of course).

- Location (is it important to you that they are close by for proofing or sign-offs or impromptu visits?)

- Credibility (membership of industry bodies, references).

- Financial strength (paying for a financial check on a new supplier will be _much_ cheaper than trying to get your material out of a printer that has gone into receivership halfway through your job).

- Do they understand direct marketing/direct mail? (if they do not you will have a lot of work to do to avoid misunderstandings on things like overs, stationery requirements for laser printing, and bundling of material for machine enclosing).

- Do they understand the importance of samples (see separate section later for more on sample packs).

- Have you been to see them? Does it look and feel as if they know their business? (You can tell a great deal by just walking round.)

- Do you understand their quality control procedures?

- Do you know who to talk to when your normal contact is unavailable?

- Do you like them?

You will notice that it could be difficult to get good answers to these questions just by sending out a request for quotation.

Check your terms and conditions (*Ts and Cs*) of business. Make sure they accompany your purchase order, and that they cover your expectations regarding overs, delivery times, and ownership of material and artwork. Remember that in the absence of a specific set of agreed terms between two businesses, the terms and conditions in force for a particular project can be held to be those most recently distributed.

Developing the relationship

Some production managers I have met believe it is up to suppliers to build relationships with their clients. That is one way of doing it. Most successful relationships I have come across are two-way.

This means simply that the better you each understand one another, the more likely you are to come up with good solutions to a particular problem, and the more likely you are to develop new ideas that can be taken back to your designers, product managers or clients.

Keep in mind the following guidelines:

- There will be no long-term relationship if your suppliers cannot make a profit too.

- With a longer-term relationship you will have more flexibility when you really need it.

- A long-term relationship takes effort from both parties.

Managing your suppliers

Even if you are not a specialist, there are some simple guidelines to getting the best result from your suppliers:

1. Give full, accurate, early briefs

It is easy when you get absorbed in a job to forget that others do not know as much about it as you. Make sure that you give a full, accurate brief, as early as possible. When a printer's representative collects the artwork, make sure you go through it with him to ensure understanding of exactly what you want.

2. Spread your risk

Select a 'core' group of preferred suppliers for the majority of your work, and a 'reserve' list of alternatives who are willing to work with you. Deliberately place some of your work with the reserves to keep them interested in your business.

3. Visit

Go and see your job being produced. Call in at short notice on occasion. Not only do you give a clear message about the importance of your job, you may also learn something.

4. Be clear about overs

Many printers' normal terms include an allowance to deliver plus or minus 10 per cent of the quantity ordered. Most who work in direct mail understand why this is inappropriate. Nevertheless, be explicit: be clear that the quantity you order is a *minimum*, and that short delivery is unacceptable (see Table 8.1.1 above for a guide to calculating the number of overs you need).

5. Put it in writing

You have gone to a great deal of trouble to brief the job accurately and thoroughly. Make sure you go the extra mile to *document* your briefs, and especially the changes you agree. It will prevent messy arguments afterwards. And if you have ever tried to pick up someone else's job halfway through, you will know how helpful it can be for everyone to work with the same thorough, organised approach to documentation.

6. Trust your instinct

Now and again, you may detect a nagging feeling in the back of your head that there is something not quite right about a job. Trust that instinct. Go back to your brief, and to your supplier, and talk it through. The worst anyone will think is that you are being 'fussy' (and there is not much harm in that); the best is that you may just catch the snag before it becomes a disaster.

Oh, it will be OK ...

The personalised piece was to be trimmed, folded, glued, bound - in to a cover with a window, and then enclosed into an envelope with another window. I had checked the positioning of the address many times. Shortly after the personalisation began, I had a feeling that something was not right. I reminded myself of the number of times I had already checked and rechecked everything, and told myself not to worry. Wrong. I had to reprint and re-laser a substantial portion of the job. I should have followed my instinct.

If you have to book a specific time for your managers or clients to check and approve proofs, make sure your supplier knows how important the proof supply date is.

The six key control documents

There are guides and checklists throughout this Guide for all the specialist stages of production. The following six key documents will help you marshal the whole production process. There are examples of each on the following pages:

1.   Print production checklist
When every job is different, there can never be a comprehensive checklist. So the best way to work is with a good 'aide memoire' which prompts you to make sure you have covered the key areas.

Once you have completed a checklist for each component, save it and use it as the basis for quotation requests and purchase orders.

2.   Master schedule
The schedule in the example might be a reasonable one for a mailing pack of, say 100,000. The dates are shown as numbers of working days, so the example job takes nearly six working weeks from start to finish. The important variables in any schedule are:

- Total quantity

- Number of versions

- Whether there are any business forms or web printing required

- Complexity of data work

- Complexity of personalisation

- Method of enclosing

The construction of a good, workable schedule is one of the important attributes of a successful campaign. If you are in any doubt, talk to your suppliers before you circulate it.

Make it part of your procedures to get explicit approval of your schedule internally (and where appropriate from your client) as well as from your suppliers.

3. Mailing plan

The mailing plan summarises the requirements for different versions. It is also the best place to identify your requirements for samples.

If you use a spreadsheet to create the mailing plan, it is then relatively simple to create a summary of the quantities of each component you will require, and this can be a useful cross-check against the data and print quantities.

When allocating codes to different printed items, make it easy for everyone, and use the *end* of the code to distinguish between different versions of the same item (for instance OE/2001/C for Control Outer Envelope, and OE/2001/T for the Test)

4. Quotation summary

The quotation summary allows you to compare quotations and identify discrepancies. It helps you make decisions about budgets and about where to place the work. The example shown is based on a simple spreadsheet.

5. Order

It is unrealistic to expect the purchase order to contain every relevant detail. It is also unnecessary. However the order should include:

- Supplier name

- Job name and number

- Quantities

- Summary of the requirement

- Reference to other documents which form part of the brief (such as a mailing plan, product specification, or table of quantities)

- Key dates

- Sample requirements

- Cost per thousand where quantities may vary

- Maximum value of purchase order

- Reference to your own terms of business

6.   Weights and sizes

Most direct mail designers in the UK are aware of the extra postage cost incurred by going over the 60 grams threshold. Yet it is still possible to be caught out by a mailing which is heavier than anyone expected. And if you are working on an overseas mailing (usually a 30 grams threshold, sometimes 20 grams), or something to qualify for Mailsort Light (20 grams), then you need to pay close attention to the weights.

If you are working on an insert, make sure you know each publisher's requirements on size, weight and delivery. The same applies if you are working on any form of door-drop.

Figure 8.1.1   **Key control document 1: Print production checklist**

Client:
Campaign:
Job number:
Component:
Date of issue:

Quantities
Total quantity (allow for overs)
Number of versions
Quantities per version (allow for overs)

Sizes
Flat size
Finished size
Number of folds
Sequence/type of folds
Special finishing (die-cuts, perforations, glueing, lamination, saddle stitching)

Colours
Number of colours front
Number of colours back
Special colours?
Varnish, seal?
Printing to bleed?
Number of colours changing per version

Substrate (paper)
Stock
Weight

Origination
Artwork supplied how? (board, film, digital)
Number of transparencies, illustrations, scans
Cut-outs, retouching required?

Proofing
Type of proof required (Cromalin, digital, wet, running-sheet)

Delivery
Additional coding
Packing instructions
Delivery address
Delivery instructions

Dates
Date of artwork
Proof supply date
Proof approval date
First delivery
Completion delivery

Samples
Samples required – number, version

Figure 8.1.2   **Key control document 2: Master schedule**

Client: AV Marketing
Campaign: Autumn mailing
Job number: 123/321
Date of issue: 20 November 2001
Total quantity: 100,000
Number of versions: 3

Key Stage	Data/laser	Print/enclose
Input data available	day 1	
Data brief	day 1	
Fixed text for personalisation		day 1
Text proof		day 2
Text approved		day 3
Artwork approved		day 4
Proofs due		day 7
Output data for approval	day 6	
Proofs approved		day 10
Data approved	day 7*	
Personalisation brief supplied	day 8	
Preprint for personalisation delivered		day 17
Personalisation proofs	day 18*	
Approval of personalisation	day 20	
Personalisation commences	day 21	
Trim and fold guide issued	day 21	
Other print deliveries commence		➜➜day 19
Trim and fold commences	day 22	
Enclosing commences		day 23
Samples supplied		day 24
Mailing commences		day 25
Mailing completes		day 28

(➜➜ = change since last issue)

*You can see from this schedule that the data work could be started later without affecting the completion date. However, you will often want to complete the data work before you start printing, in case the quantities need to be amended.

When you amend or reissue a key document, change the date of issue, and indicate clearly what has changed. Do not rely on highlight colours – use something which will show when printed in black and white.

Figure 8.1.3   **Key control document 3: Mailing plan**

Client	AV Marketing				
Job title	Autumn mailing	Posting			
Job number	123/321	Postage rate			Mailsort 3
Total quantity	100,000	Postage account			Client
Number of merges	3	Mailsort reports sent on			

SAMPLES					
Merge name	Merge no.	A B	Dupe lives	Text only	Others*
Control	1	250	50	200	0
Incentive test	2	100	0	0	0
Offer test	3	100	0	0	0

* specify 'other' samples

Enclosures listed from window (front) of envelope	Facing (F)ront or (B)ack	Merge no	1	2
		Merge name	Control	Incentive test
		Quantity	50,000	25,000
Outer		Codes	AVM/01/OE/C	AVM/01/OE/T1
Personalised letter	F		AVM/01/L 1234	AVM/01/L 1235
Terms and conditions	F		AVM/01/T	AVM/01/T
Reply envelope	B		AVM/01/RE	AVM/01/RE
Brochure	B		AVM/01/B	AVM/01/B
Incentive flyer	B			AFM/01/IF

Enclosures listed from window (front) of envelope	Facing (F)ront or (B)ack	Merge no	3	
		Merge name	Offer test	
		Quantity	25,000	
Outer		Codes	AVM/01/OE/T2	
Personalised letter	F		AVM/01/L 1234	
Terms and conditions	F		AVM/01/T	
Reply envelope	B		AVM/01/RE	
Brochure	B		AVM/01/B	

Figure 8.1.4   Key control document 4: Quotation summary

Client: AV Marketing
Campaign: Autumn mailing
Job number: 123/321
Date: 20 November 2001

Component	Quantity (k)	Suppliers									Cheapest	Most expensive
		London Envelopes	Complex Envelopes	Business Forms	Central Continuous	Media Print	Chameleon Litho	The DP Group	Postal Marketing	QP Communications		
Outer	107	2,839	2,336								2,336	2,839
BRE	105	1,471	1,046								1,046	1,471
Continuous stationery	110			4,755	4,358						4,358	4,755
Brochure	105					2,930	2,240				2,240	2,930
Ts & Cs	105					1,849	1,612				1,612	1,849
Incentive flyer	28					575	688				575	688
Data processing	150							2,210			2,210	2,210
Personalisation	100								1,757	1,882	1,757	1,882
Enclosing	100								1,505	1,400	1,400	1,505
											17,534	**20,129**
Mailing quantity	100,000									Cost / k per pack excl postage	175.34	201.29
											0.175	0.201

If you set up this form in a spreadsheet, then you can use a simple formula to calculate the lowest and highest prices. This can help your decisions about budgets and where to place the work. In the above example, for the outer envelope in row 3, the Microsoft® Excel formula to place in the 'cheapest' column is "=MIN(B3:K3)"; in the 'most expensive' column the formula is "=MAX(B3:K3)". These formulae can then be copied for each row. The totals, and costs per thousand are then easy to set up.

Figure 8.1.5 **Key control document 5: Purchase order**

Order number:	2001/1456
Date:	20 November 2001
Job number:	123/321
Job name:	Autumn Mailing

Invoices must be accompanied by a copy of this purchase order
Invoices in excess of the amount signified by 'value of order' below will not
be paid without additional purchase order cover.

To:	Postal Marketing, Printanden Close,
	Yourtown, YR1 1AA
Total quantity:	100,000
Description:	Receive 12" drop x 405mm continuous stationery in three merges. Trim merge and fold to A5 as per trim and fold guide to follow. Machine enclose with four other items (2 merges, 75,000) or five items (1 merge, 25,000) to C5 window as per sample enclosing pack to follow, seal and mail.
Samples:	See mailing plan for sample requirements. Samples must be supplied and approved before mailing is released.
Postage:	Mailsort 3 on our account
Delivery:	
Schedule:	Personalised stationery 3/12 Other materials 5/12 Mailing commences 7/12 Mailing completes 10/12
Price:	Finish and enclose four items: 75,000 @ £27 per thousand Finish and enclose five items: 25,000 @ £28.50 per thousand
Value of order:	£2,737.50
Signed:	

Figure 8.1.6   **Key control document 6: Weight schedule**

Client:	AV Marketing		
Campaign:	Autumn Mailing		
Job number:	123/321		
Date:	20 November 2001		
Component	Flat size in square metres*	Paper weight in grams per square metre (gsm)	Component weight in grams (g)
Outer envelope	0.364 x 0.229 = 0.084	90	7.5
Reply envelope	0.244 x 0.214 = 0.053	80	4.3
Personalised letter	0.380 x 0.300 = 0.114	100	11.4
Brochure	0.297 x 0.210 = 0.063	100	6.3
Incentive flyer	0.100 x 0.210 = 0.021	90	1.9
Ts and Cs	0.200 x 0.210 = 0.042	90	3.8
		Total	35.2
		Add 5% allowance for ink, humidity	1.8
		Pack weight	**37.0**

*To reach the flat size in square metres, first convert the dimensions from mm by dividing by 1000 (eg an A4 letter is 297x210mm = 0.297m x 0.210m = 0.06237m² (round up to 0.063)

For special formats such as in-line or 3D products, ask your supplier to confirm the weight of the item.

Key strategies in campaign execution

There are four stages in the execution of a campaign where the production manager has a special role to play:

1. Artwork

2. Proofing

3. Keeping track

4. Samples

Artwork

The production manager's role with artwork is to:

1. Check that it corresponds to the brief, and to the specifications already issued to your suppliers:

   - Check flat size
   - Check finished size
   - Check folds
   - Check markings for perforation, die-cut, glueing or other special finishing
   - Check colour mark-up
   - Check transparencies, illustrations
   - Check guide prints are correctly sized and positioned
   - Check window positions
   - Check anything else you have not already checked
   - **Take your time**

2. Make up dummies:

   - If the designer has not already done so, copy the artwork, and make up a full-size dummy of each component.
   - Check that each item works properly – page 3 follows page 2, the inside is the same way up as the outside, the reply envelope will fit inside the outer, the reply device will fit inside the reply envelope.
   - Send one of the dummies with the artwork to your supplier.
   - Keep a set of copies and dummies for yourself.
   - Where the job involves a special format, such as an in-line web product, your supplier will normally work with you to prepare the dummy. You will almost certainly need a plain paper dummy from them as a guide for creating your artwork in the first place.

3. Obtain any outstanding approvals:

   - Make sure that every '*stakeholder*' in the project has approved the artwork, and documented their approval (it can save heartaches later).
   - Keep copies of any amendments marked on the artwork.

4. Ensure it is delivered safely to your suppliers:

   Make sure you know how each supplier needs to receive artwork for each process. Brief your studio accordingly.

If you are sending digital artwork, whether on disk or over the Internet, make sure that you send something which clearly identifies the files to the recipient. '*Brochure*' as a file name is not much help to your printer when they are receiving dozens of different files every day. And do not forget you still need to send a made-up dummy anyway.

5.   Know where the artwork is:

Artwork can be expensive and hard to replace. It is also infuriating trying to find artwork when you need it for the next job (everyone always assumes that someone else knows where it is). Keep a record of where artwork goes.

6.   Match the appearance of preprinted letter text with subsequent personalisation:

When you are producing a personalised letter, you may often have a non-personalised text on the reverse, or on following pages. It is usually the responsibility of the production manager to get the closest possible match between the two. Here is how to achieve just that:

- Get a brief from the designer on the fonts and layouts they require.

- Send a copy of this brief, along with a fair copy of the approved letter text, to your supplier.

- Ensure that your supplier uses the correct machinery to produce the text:

  - Ask for your letter text to be run on a production printer.

  - Make sure that they use the same dot resolution as the printer which will run the 'live' job.

- Get proofs of the whole text, including the portion which you will be personalising. That way, you can check that you have given yourself enough room to fit everything you need to on the first page.

- Check copy, and paste up the laser setting in the correct position.

- Pass on to your litho printer with instructions to replicate the colour, weight and density of the text.

- Keep a copy of the text as printed by your supplier.

- At proof stage, compare the letter text with the copy you kept, and use this to highlight any changes you need to make to match the text quality

If the preprinted letter text looks too dark or solid on the proof, try printing the text as a 95 per cent or 90 per cent tint of black; it may be just enough to tone down the density of tone, and replicate the slight unevenness of the 'live' personalisation.

Proofing

The role of the production manager at the proofing stage is:

1.   Ensure that everyone knows what their responsibility is:

      Be specific with everyone involved in the approval of proofs, and make sure
      everyone understands who is checking what. For example, a supplier should
      never be asked to take sole responsibility for variable data – a marketing or
      database person must take responsibility for verifying that the correct data
      processing has been carried out.

2.   Ensure that everyone understands the limitations of the proofing process:

      The details of different proofing processes for litho print are covered
      elsewhere in this Guide. Make sure that everyone knows what they are looking
      at – for example, the designer needs to be aware that his job will never look
      exactly like the glossy Cromalin proof.

3.   Get comments on proofs, on photocopies, not the real proofs.

4.   Make the final marking of proofs the responsibility of one person:

      Even if you do not use the British Standard correction marks yourself, you
      will work with a number of people who do, so you may find the '*dictionary*' of
      correction marks overleaf useful.

      Each correction needs to be clear, in ink, and in the margin nearest the
      correction. Show the end of a correction by using a forward slash or solidus
      ("/"). If you are not sure about using one of these marks, then simply write the
      correction out in full clear English.

Figure 8.1.7   British standard proof correction marks

Meaning	Mark in margin	Mark in text
INSERT		
words	is /	Direct Mail effective advertising.
comma	, /	Direct Mail is effective advertising
full stop	⊙ /	Direct Mail is effective advertising
semi-colon	; /	Direct Mail is effective advertising
colon	: /	Direct Mail is effective advertising
interrogation mark	? /	Is Direct Mail effective advertising
exclamation mark	! /	Direct Mail is powerful advertising
apostrophe	✓ /	Direct Mails effective advertising.
dash (long)	⊢—⊣ /	Direct Mail effective advertising.
hyphen (short)	⊢-⊣ /	Direct Mail is cost efficient.
parenthesis	(/) /	Direct Mail 1990/91 is effective.
quotation marks	❝ / ❞ /	Direct Mail is effective advertising
ellipsis	... /	Direct Mail is effective advertising
oblique	⊘ /	Direct Mail 1990 91 is effective.
DELETE		
through character(s)	ग /	Direct Mail is effective advertising.
through word(s)	ग /	Direct Mail is effective is advertising.
delete and close up	ग /	Direct Mail is effective advertising
MOVE		
close up	◠ /	Direct Mail is ef fective advertising.
move left	⊏ /	Direct Mail is effective advertising.
move right	⊐ /	Direct Mail is effective advertising.
move up	⊓ /	Direct Mail is effective advertising.
move down	⊔ /	Direct Mail is effective advertising.
indent	⊏ /	Direct Mail is effective advertising.
centre	⊏ ⊐ /	Direct Mail is effective advertising
SPACE		
equalise space	Ɏ /	Direct Mail is effective advertising.
insert space	Ɏ /	Direct Mail is effective advertising.
insert space between lines	⊃ /	Direct Mail is effective advertising.
reduce space between lines	⟵ /	Direct Mail is effective advertising.
CHANGE		
to capitals	≡ /	direct mail is effective advertising.
to small capitals	≡ /	direct mail is effective advertising.
to lower case	≢ /	Direct Mail is effective advertising.
to upright type	⊔ /	Direct Mail is effective advertising.
to italics	⊔ /	Direct Mail is effective advertising.
to bold type	⌇⌇ /	Direct Mail is effective advertising.
wrong font	⊗ /	Direct Mail is effective advertising.
bad letter	× /	Direct Mail is effective advertising.
TRANSPOSE	⊔ /	Mail Direct is effective advertising.
INVERT TYPE	↺ /	Direct Mail is effective advertising.
STRAIGHTEN LINE	⹀ /	Direct Mail is effective advertising.
STRAIGHTEN MARGIN	‖ /	Direct Mail is effective advertising.
NO PARAGRAPH	⌒ /	Direct Mail is effective advertising.
NEW PARAGRAPH	⌐ /	Direct Mail is effective advertising.
UNDERLINE	underline /	Direct Mail is effective advertising.

Based on data from B.S. 5261C: 1976, published by British Standard with additional inclusion of dash/hyphen. For advice on using these marks see previous page.

Keeping track

Nobody wants their mailing to be late, but it is always better to be correct and late, than on time and wrong.

The good production manager plays an important role in keeping a campaign on track. Here is what you need to do:

- Find out what is happening at every stage of the campaign, even if it is not explicitly your responsibility:

    - If you know a few days in advance that the artwork is going to be late, you have time to talk to your suppliers and work out a new schedule.
    - Even if you are not looking after the data processing, you can still find out whether the data has arrived, and if the processing reports will be ready in time.
    - Speak to your suppliers a day or so in advance of their receiving your artwork, and make sure they are still ready for your job. If not, you have still got time to activate plan B. (You do have a plan B, don't you?)

- Remind people about approvals which are due in a day or so. Where will they be when the proofs come in? Will there be any unusual difficulty if the proofs are late?

- Find out if your campaign is part of any other activity. Is it supporting advertising in other media such as TV or radio? If so, then keep in touch with the media buyers now and again – you may get early warning from them if the other media schedules are about to be put back.

- Get a good idea of the current workloads at your suppliers, and not just the ones you have appointed to work on this campaign. It will give you a better insight into consequences and options of any delays.

- Naturally, once your job is '*live*' with your suppliers, it is up to you to make sure they do what they promised:

    - Where any process takes more than a day or two, insist on knowing progress to date.
    - As soon as you can, put together a sample pack using samples of all completed components. Check:
        - that it all fits
        - compare it to the dummies you made at artwork stage
        - compare it to the briefs you have issued

        If there is a problem, or something which does not look right, now is the time to act.

    - Staple together an example of your sample pack and use it as your '*master*' copy.

- In any case, and at all times, *keep people informed*. Even if there is absolutely nothing you can do about it, *tell the people who need to know*. You may not get much gratitude at the time, but it is a lot easier conversation than the one which starts: "What do you mean, it hasn't mailed yet?"

Repetitive stress . . .

A long time ago I was one of the first people to use a continuous laser printer to produce Cheshire labels. The mailing quantity was nearly two million. Fortunately I had asked for daily reports of the quantities lasered and enclosed. I became concerned when the reported quantity of packs enclosed did not seem to match the quantities which were still left to laser. Eventually it became clear that almost half of the names to be mailed had been duplicated. The record counter used in the laser printing programme contained six digits. Once the lasers had printed the first 999,999 records, they had started again at record 000,001. Without the daily progress check, we would not have known there was a problem until it was too late.

Samples

Here's where a production manager can make everyone look good (and avoid a lot of unnecessary pain):

- Understand everyone's requirements for samples in advance; the usual types are:
  - AB sample packs (the most common samples, with multiple copies addressed to a made-up name). Find out if your manager or client has a particular address they use.
  - *'duplicate live'* – samples created using live data, usually the first from the start of the job, and sometimes from a *'proofing file'* which contains at least one of every permutation of variable data.
  - *'blanks'* – usually where the only items missing from the pack are the name and address; these packs are often used by a call centre to send out on request.

- Help your colleagues to understand that a later request for samples is likely to involve additional cost.

- Establish the number required for each version.

- Adjust your print volumes if necessary.

- Speak to the people handling the data processing, and ask them to produce specific *'sample'* output files.

- Identify the sample requirements as part of your supplier briefs.

- Include the samples in your schedules.

- Make it clear to your suppliers that samples must be run first, that they are at least as important as the *'live'* job, and that *'no samples'* = *'job incomplete'*.

- Recognise that samples will not always be produced in the same way as the *'live'* job – check the samples yourself before distributing to your managers and clients.

The twelve things which no one else will look after:

Transport

Have you allowed for all the transport costs, especially if you are moving different elements of a pack? Have you allowed for split deliveries so that you can start the next process before the previous one is complete?

Storage

When the quantities are large, make sure that your suppliers will be able to hold your stock, especially if you have printed additional quantities for use in later campaigns. Do not assume that everyone will have space to store your materials forever, for nothing.

Postage

Make sure you know whose postage account is to be used. Do you have mailing dockets? Do you have enough (remember that Royal Mail insists on a docket for every day that part of a mailing goes in)? If you are mailing on your supplier's account, make sure that your finance department is geared up to have cleared postage funds with your supplier before the mailing is due to release

Overs

After most mailings there will be a surplus of some materials. Your supplier will usually hold them for a short while before they ask for your instructions, and may charge you for holding material beyond then. Get clear instructions internally about whether to keep or destroy overs. Always keep copies of instructions to destroy (often referred to as '*destructions*'). You might want to create a simple spreadsheet or database to keep track of the various materials being held at your suppliers.

Overseas production

Apart from the usual considerations about time and communications with an overseas company, it may be important to consider the exchange risk. Talk to your finance department before you issue your purchase order. You may find a supplier who is willing to take the exchange risk and allow you to order in sterling, but this is unusual. Your finance team will often be able to '*hedge*' against movements in exchange rates to minimise possible losses. In some cases you may simply choose to take a conservative position, regarding the exchange rate you use for budgeting, and recognise any savings at the point of payment.

100% mailings

There is a growing demand for 100% mailings, where it is important that every single communication is actually produced and despatched (for instance bills, or annual statements, or legal communications). This means that your suppliers need to keep hold of anything which is spoilt or wrecked in the production processes, and re-make them. There is significant additional work involved, and you must expect to pay a premium for it. Most importantly, you must be able to tell your suppliers in advance of the requirement.

Conversely, it can be important to ensure that your colleagues are aware that the conventional production methods for printed output are *not* 100% mailings.

International posting

There is more detail on this subject elsewhere in the Guide. Be aware that the requirements for address formats, envelope design, window position, sortation for postage discounts, bagging and bundling can all be very different depending on the destination of your mailing. Make sure you are working with experts.

Window show-through

So how do you know that the name and address will show through the window? One thing is for sure, everyone will be assuming that you have checked this.

If you already have examples of all the stationery, use them. *Never* use an envelope from a different campaign unless you are *absolutely certain* that it is identical in every respect to the one you will be using in the current campaign.

Otherwise, follow the guide shown on page 24, and this will allow you to draw two boxes on your address carrier. The smaller box will outline the area which will always show through the window; anything appearing in the larger box may show through depending on movement within the envelope.

Sometimes it can be just as important that some elements <u>do not</u> show through the window (some brand guidelines insist that headlines and letter text must not show). Check this.

Table 8.1.2   **Window show-through calculations**

all dimensions in mm	Bold shows data entry required	
Envelope height	A	162
Envelope width	B	229
Window height	C	35
Window width	D	95
Window start position from left	E	50
Window start position from bottom	F	35
Folded Address carrier height*	G	149
Folded Address carrier width*	H	210
*address carrier measures are for piece after trimming and folding		
'Always shows' box - position on address carrier		
Box start position from left	= E	50
Box start postion from bottom	= F	35
Box height	= C-A+G	22
Box width	= D-B+H	76
'May show' box - position on address carrier		
Box start position from left	= E-B+H	31
Box start postion from bottom	= F-A+G	22
Box height	= C+A-G	48
Box width	= D+B-H	114

In practice, the weight and bulk of the printed components will reduce the amount of movement within the envelope, and this calculation takes no account of that. So the actual size of both boxes will usually be a little smaller than that calculated here.

Figure 8.1.8   **How window show-through calculations work**

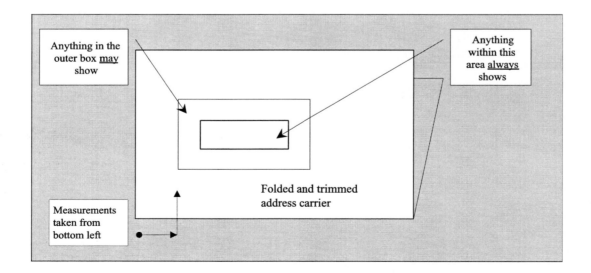

Bar-codes

Bar-codes and other special marks are used for a number of applications, including:

- Qualification for extra postage discount (Royal Mail CBC code).

- Faster response handling (scanning a code instead of keying a name and address).

- Matching with other personalised pieces on machine.

If you are using such codes in your job, make sure that they are checked as part of the proof approval. Are they read, accurately, by the appropriate machinery (check live names, not just the AB samples)?

Pull-outs

It's quite common to have to extract particular individuals from a mailing just before it is released. Find out from your colleagues whether this is likely to be a requirement. If it is, find out from your suppliers the best way of doing this, and then make sure your people understand the latest point at which they can request a pull-out. Include this date in your schedule. Anything later than this date may incur substantial delay or cost or both.

Component codes

Never let anything be produced which does not carry a unique identification code. You will regret it if you do.

Dockets

Ask for copies of the mailing dockets as the mailing starts to release. There should be no problem in getting them, and you will need them as part of your reconciliation of the job. They can be tougher to locate after the event.

Saving VAT for financial services and charities

Under regulations in force at the time of compiling this Guide, financial services and charities cannot reclaim VAT charged on design and production of printed matter. However, it may be possible for them legally to avoid paying VAT in the first place by meeting certain criteria set by HM Customs and Excise.

The following general guidelines should help:

- Non-personalised and non-returnable items such as leaflets, brochures and flyers are generally zero-rated.

- Personalised items, and returnable response devices are standard-rated (this includes reply envelopes, and application forms where the returnable element is 25 per cent or more of the surface area of the item).

- If the pack contains a majority of zero-rated items, the pack can be regarded as VAT-free (the outer envelope is regarded as neutral for the purposes of this comparison).

- If there are equal numbers of standard- and zero-rated items (again ignoring the outer envelope), then the pack can be regarded as VAT-free if the production cost of the zero-rated pieces exceeds that of the standard-rated items.

- Paper heavier than 180 grams per square metre (gsm) will render an item standard-rated.

- Laminating will also render an item standard-rated.

- Including a non-paper item will render the pack standard-rated.

- Where a pack is VAT-free, the savings can be extended to include preparatory and post-production processes as well.

It is *essential* to bear in mind that the exact interpretation of VAT regulations is a matter for each local VAT (Customs and Excise) office, and can vary. The above guidelines are not guaranteed to work in every situation. The savings are obviously worth making, so seek advice from your local office, or talk to your supplier about their experience.

Considerations about paper

Other parts of this Guide give detailed information on the selection of stock. For the purposes of the production management process, then take account of the following:

Know your sizes

The number of copies of a component which can be printed in a single pass is a major factor in the price. If you can make a small change to dimensions to fit more copies per impression, you will make a significant difference to the cost. Be aware of the sizes and print areas available from your suppliers.

A rough guide to paper weights

Assume the following typical uses for various paper weights:

60 to 70 gsm – light, inexpensive, often used for simple two-page flyers

80 to 100 gsm – '*standard*' medium, ordinary, usually specified for letterheads, order forms

110 to 130 gsm – heavier, generally better quality paper

If you are printing a postcard, remember that the Royal Mail is more interested in the bulk (width and flexibility) of the item (230 microns minimum) than its actual weight.

What is it for?

If you are printing an item which is going to be personalised, you need to take account of the different requirements for inks, toners, drying or fusing. Take particular care if your designers want to personalise on any kind of coated or glossy substrate, and talk to your suppliers if you are in any doubt.

A common mistake when producing reply devices and order forms is to use a type of stock which will not readily accept normal handwriting. It is easy to check.

The importance of price

Good buying comes from knowledge and understanding of:

- The result you are trying to achieve

- The range of possibilities available to you

- The capabilities and limitations of your suppliers

To buy well, you must know what is possible, so that you can negotiate sensibly. In this way you will end up paying the best price for the job. The cheapest price is not necessarily the best. It is extremely rare to make a good buying decision based on price alone.

How to decide whether to do it yourself, or hand it all over to someone else

There are many service companies who will offer to manage the entire production process for you. Some of them offer an excellent service. How do you decide between DIY (do it yourself) and GSI (get someone in)? Here are some advantages and disadvantages that might influence your decision:

Advantages

- If one company is to produce everything for a campaign, then that may remove any concerns about transport and storage of stock — either it will all be produced on one site, or the logistics will be taken care of.

- If one company is responsible for everything, then you may be able to relax about the management of the schedule, since they will have no one to blame but themselves if they start to run late and have to work overtime to catch up.

- If one company is printing all the items, then they will be responsible for ensuring that the colours match across the job.

- The company you are dealing with may have greater buying power than you, and so be able to offer a more competitive price on some aspects of the campaign.

- Your supplier may be more knowledgeable and expert than you.

- The overall price could be the same or less than you would pay by separating the job and running it yourself.

Disadvantages

- Your job is very unlikely to be as important to your supplier as it is to you, and you may believe that is a problem.

- If the supplier you are considering does not have all the right equipment in-house, then they will be buying in some services, which you might just as easily do yourself.

- It is unusual (although not impossible) to find one supplier who is an expert in every aspect of production; they often have a core business to which they have added other services to 'feed' the core.

- If your job is all in one place and starts to go wrong, it may be harder to rectify than if you were running it yourself across a number of different suppliers.

- Although the financial risk may be no worse than with any other supplier, your maximum loss could be much greater if there is a problem.

Making the choice

The decision is yours. The most important factors are probably:

- How much time and expertise you have to manage the project.

- How important the project is to you.

- How well you know and trust your suppliers.

And that last factor takes us right back to the beginning. It is the knowledge, relationship, and management of your suppliers that makes the difference between someone who is a good production manager, and someone who just produces the job they have been given.

Chapter 8.2

Data processing for interactive and direct communications

This chapter includes:

■■■■■■■■■■■■■■■■■■■■■■■■■■■■■■■■■■

- ❏ **What is data processing**
- ❏ **The stages in data processing**
- ❏ **Step one: collecting the data**
- ❏ **Step two: processing data for output**
- ❏ **Making and outputting selections**
- ❏ **Choosing and briefing your data processing supplier**
- ❏ **How to avoid data processing troubles**

■■■■■■■■■■■■■■■■■■■■■■■■■■■■■■■■■■

About this chapter

Sooner or later, in any direct marketing campaign, data must be understood and utilised by non-data processing specialists. This simplified data processing user's guide explains simply and clearly how that list of names and addresses should be handled and what the pitfalls and important issues to consider are.

Author/Consultant: John Wallinger

John Wallinger, Database Planner, Craik Jones Watson Mitchell & Voelkel

John Wallinger has worked in the database business for two decades. He began his career with Rank Xerox (UK) Ltd, where he was responsible for setting up their lead-handling and fulfilment systems. He then started a computer bureau, Response Analysis and Mailing Ltd, where he handled work for Rank Xerox, Coca-Cola, Peugeot-Talbot and BAT.

His next move was to Ogilvy & Mather Direct where, as Database Director, he set up the agency's database department and associated services. This led him to form his own consultancy, BMP Database (part of BMP Young Clark Craig), where his clients included Woolwich Equitable, Marks & Spencer and British Telecom Mobile Communications.

In 1990, after a successful spell as an independent consultant, he joined Impact Targeting Communications where he was Strategic Planning Director assisting the agency group's many large database clients.

In 1994, John joined Datascope Marketing Ltd as Managing Director where he is also responsible for product development and account management. His skills bridge marketing and technical delivery and cover database design, statistical analysis and data processing for such clients as: Land Rover, Orange, Virgin Trains, Association of Train Operating Companies, UDV — Gordon's, Bell's and Baileys, HealthNow, COI and comdirect.

He has published many articles on database marketing, and has been a member of the DMA List & Database Council, the DMA Brussels Group, and the IDM Faculty of Speakers. He is a frequent speaker at courses and seminars (including the Diploma in Direct Marketing) and is also a Founder Member of the Institute of Direct Marketing.

John Wallinger M IDM
Database Planner
Craik Jones Watson Mitchell & Voelkel
120 Regent Street
London W1B 5RY
020 7734 1650

Chapter 8.2

Data processing for interactive and direct communications

What is data processing?

Data processing is one of the most important areas in the production of a direct marketing campaign. It is, however, often seen as a very unglamorous task compared with creative and strategic planning.

But the bottom line is, no matter how good the concept and strategy behind your campaign, the whole exercise can be totally undermined by poor selection, mistargeting, incorrect addressing and unwanted duplication.

To avoid such catastrophes, many organisations committed to direct marketing employ database managers who have computing skills and a detailed knowledge of the business environment. But such people are still comparatively in short supply.

Other organisations, the majority, rely on computer service bureaux. In most respects this is an ideal solution — although some bureaux lack sufficient marketing skills to interpret their clients' requirements into workable computer runs, hence the need for this Guide and this chapter.

> **At its simplest, data processing for direct marketing involves preparing lists of customers or prospects, analysing their records in order to make selections, and then outputting these selections in a usable format, eg for laser printing, address labels or listings.**

Before we look at the steps in data processing in more detail, let us remind ourselves of some of the more important definitions, most of which you will already have come across in the earlier chapters on database applications. In this brief chapter we shall be concentrating on data usage from the producer's viewpoint.

Table 8.2.1

Data processing: A producer's dictionary	
Data element	Individual piece of information, eg initial or birth date.
Field	A group of data elements that together create a logical string of information, eg full name (title, initial, surname).
Record	Group of fields, logical piece of information, eg address.
File	A group of identical records held together in one file, eg a mailing file split down to individual test cells.
List	A group of files or a single file used for a specific application, eg a mailing list.
Database	A collection of records retained permanently on computer, constantly updated and supporting a range of applications. Data may be added from purchasing behaviour, telemarketing reports, questionnaires etc.
Data processing	Creating a single output (tape, labels etc.) using one or more sources of data; cleaning and refining data for particular applications, eg mailing.
Database management	Storing and maintaining a high volume of information on customers and prospects, which is constantly updated and used for a range of applications.
Table	A group of fields holding information relating to a specific entity, eg address and sales area code and local store.

The stages in data processing

The stages in data processing we cover here are:

- Data capture: collecting and inputting data

- Data transfer, eg from list broker to computer bureau

- Deduplication

- Making selections

- Outputting

These can be represented by the flow chart below:

Figure 8.2.1

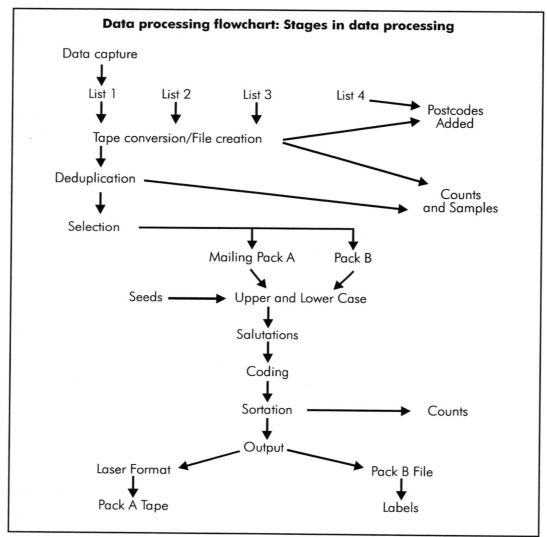

Step One : Collecting the data

The first stage in building and using a database is collecting data and converting it from paper-based records onto computer. Records from other computer systems are also incorporated at this stage.

Data can be collected from a variety of sources.

Typical sources of data for direct marketing include the following:

Table 8.2.2

Sources of database data	
Administrative systems	Accounting systems Prospect files Customer files Business partners (i.e. exchange data)
Paper-based records	Letters, eg complaints Enquiries, eg from press advertisements Sales force records Phone reports Questionnaires Guarantee certificates Sales promotion responses Competition entries Coupon redemptions
External systems	Market research databases Rented lists Compiled lists Lifestyle databases Geodemographic databases
E-based	E-mail Microsites Websites SMS Interactive TV Viral e-mail Personal organisers Interactive kiosks Call centres Banners

Recognising new sources of data is one of the creative aspects of good database management, but data must be kept up-to-date – for reasons we are about to examine.

Why data is never permanent

Data is rarely permanent or 'static'. In direct marketing data is **never** regarded as static, but only ever as either 'semi-static' or 'volatile'. Semi-static refers to data that sometimes changes or changes periodically on a regular basis. Volatile means always changing or unpredictable.

One look at the example below will demonstrate why a database must be kept up-to-date.

Table 8.2.3

Semi-static data	
Surname	Can change, eg when a woman marries.
Address	Until recently around 10 per cent of the population moved annually.
Employees	Numbers and individuals are affected by growth and decline of the economy generally.
Job title	An individual may change titles; likewise a title may be occupied by a new individual.
Age	Age records need amending annually (whereas date of birth is permanent).
E-mail addresses	Business and personal e-mail addresses can change on a regular basis.
Volatile data	
Status	An enquiry may develop from "cold" to "warm" or from "hot" to "convert"; parents of a teenage family may rapidly turn into "empty-nesters".
Behaviour	A gardening customer may, for example, complete the stocking of his new garden and settle down to become a regular customer — or never buy again.
Contacts	In a company, these may alter for a variety of reasons, eg a fundraising task may rotate annually among employees.

Capturing data — still largely a manual operation

Despite sweeping technological developments, data is normally converted to computer by hand-keying. This is a labour-intensive task which is inevitably expensive although costs have fallen in recent years. Typical (1996) costs for transcribing 1,000 paper-based records to computer, depending on volume, can be as low as £50 for consumer name and address and around £100 for a company record including name, job title, company name, address, phone number, industry sector etc. More use is made now of rapid address keying. Inputting the postcode and house number brings the full address from the postal address file (PAF).

Optical scanners (OCR), which read data direct from the page, and bar-codes, have sped up the process in some cases. More recently swipe cards with magnetic strips, smart cards with chips embedded, text readers and the Internet have all been used for collecting data. However, to date there is no foolproof means of automatically reading handwriting, so that reply cards and self-completed questionnaires can still lead to unacceptable error levels.

> **Yet, as many other authors in this Guide have stressed, accuracy is imperative.**

For recipients of direct mail, there is nothing more annoying than receiving communications that are incorrectly addressed or contain information which has no relevance to them. To the mailing company the result is inevitably wasted expenditure all down the line: not merely the cost of processing but of print and postage, too.

Names and addresses spelt, or formatted incorrectly, also lead to problems in identifying duplicates, a further cause of waste and customer annoyance.

Furthermore, if the name and address—the basic building block onto which all other items of information are attached—are incorrect, the whole database structure or file is undermined.

How to overcome data capture problems

Fortunately, there are several ways by which database professionals have learnt to overcome the problems inherent in capturing names, addresses and other vital data. Chief among these are:

✔   Structured input forms

✔   Punch and verify procedures

✔   Data tables

✔   Unique Reference Numbers (URN)

✔   Mandatory fields

✔   Intelligent software

✔   Keying directly against the Postal Address File (PAF)

We now spend a few moments looking at each of these in turn:

1.   Structured input forms – 'a place for everything'

The ideal input form, i.e. one designed to have '*a place for everything — and everything in its place*', is the first bastion against incorrect inputting.

Wherever possible use a structured form at the point where information is collected, for example in the sales department or phone reception. The form should emulate the design of the input screen, breaking down every piece of information into its constituent parts as in the examples below:

Table 8.2.4

Title	(10 characters)	Mr
Christian name	(10 characters)	John
Initials	(5 characters)	J G
Surname	(30 characters)	Wallinger
Job title	(30 characters)	Database Planner
Company name	(40 characters)	Craik Jones Watson Mitchell Voelkel
Street	(40 characters)	8–10 Lower James Street
Town	(40 characters)	London
Postcode	(8 characters)	W1R 3PL

One simple way to ensure a vast improvement in your data collection procedure is to use a structured form which is large enough to allow operators to write in the data clearly and legibly. Be generous.

2. Punch and verify – two heads better than one

One of the oldest methods of ensuring accuracy in record keeping is one that pre-dates computers, i.e. a form of double-entry system.

In data processing data is input twice, usually by two different individuals. Sometimes only a part of the data, eg account number, is subjected to double-input. The two entries (fields) are then compared and if there is not 100 per cent match the record is rejected and checked.

3. Data tables – shorthand for longer data

Data tables are used to simplify data that is common to all/most records. The principle is that a simple character or code is used in place of a frequently used phrase or title. The computer 'looks up' the character on the table before printing out the full description.

Table 8.2.5

Example of data table	
Code	**Description**
Titles	
0	Unknown
1	Managing Director
2	Sales Manager
3	Financial Director
4	Chief Purchasing Officer
Gender/title	
0	Unknown
1	Mr
2	Mrs
3	Miss
4	Ms

The use of data tables ensures a common spelling for regularly used pieces of data, which could include title, post-nominal qualifications (eg BSc, OBE), departments etc. Data tables cut down on input time and also allow you to select and analyse records more readily, eg pull out all records coded '1' to select managing directors.

4.   Unique Reference Number – the customer's fingerprint

One of the simplest and most effective of all data capture techniques is the allocation, by the computer, of a unique number to each record. This enables immediate location of a record and further reduces the risk of errors.

A Unique Reference Number (URN) is especially useful when updating records or bringing together a customer's data held on separate files. A URN might be a customer account number.

Applied to labels or lasered letters, where it may appear as an element of the address, the URN has many other benefits. For example, it assists operators when collating matching items for hand-enclosure. Another benefit is as an easily identifiable start/stop point for the print room – very useful if printing stops unexpectedly for any reason.

Unique reference numbers can be further 'individualised' by the addition of suffixes, eg:

The ACME Company:		12345-0
The ACME Company:	Managing Director	12345-1
The ACME Company:	Sales Manager	12345-2

5.   Mandatory fields – the computer's own check

Another way of ensuring accuracy is where the computer is required to accept data in specific fields. If key input data is missing or inaccurate, the faulty record can be rejected or highlighted for close attention. Examples of mandatory data may include date of initial contact, postcode, date of birth etc.

Programs can also be set up so that fields will only accept certain values, eg telephone number will accept only numeric values; *name* will accept only alpha values – further safeguards against error.

6.   Intelligent software – knowing the answers in advance

When data reaches the processing bureau, most have software programs that can correctly identify elements of a name and address from knowledge already built into it by the software producers.

For example some intelligent software can identify whether company XYZ is Ltd or Plc, or whether Acacia Drive, Guildford, should read Acacia Avenue, and so on. It may even be able to identify whether a certain Hilary Smith is '*Mr*' or '*Mrs*' Hilary Smith or, more typically, whether Jatundra Patel is Mr or Mrs, and even whether or not the name is spelt correctly.

7.   Keying directly against PAF

The Postal Address File (PAF) is used to verify and enhance address data and to add correct postcodes. Many operators now begin their dialogue with prospects by asking for the postcode so that they can be sure of the address even before taking any further instructions. While administratively effective, it is perhaps not always wise to begin a customer care conversation by interrogating the customer in this way.

Data capture and the web

Most of you will have registered with sites or ordered products and services across the web. You will have had to enter your personal details, credit card data, and delivery address and maybe some personal information.

These data capture pages range from excellent to shabby and with little thought put into them.

> The first rule is that you have to think like a consumer.
> Is it necessary to collect all this information?
> Do they feel that you will handle their data securely?
> Is the data relevant?
> Is there a natural sequence to the layout of the data capture fields?

Like many websites, funky graphics and spinning logos seem to have taken priority over a functional and user-friendly design. If your web page takes forever to load, the consumer is likely to move off your site (especially as most of the country still only has access via 56k modem).

Many companies store your data so that you do not have to enter it again (you can amend it online); this is protected using user-ID and passwords.

Data collected through registration to a site or ordering can also be used to tailor specific content to your interests and put forward buying suggestions based on your profile or ordering habits.

All the rules for capturing data on forms, reply devices or the phone are relevant for the web:

- Rapid addressing software is available.

- Use well-designed forms.

- Make sure fields are long enough (for example for double-barrelled surnames).

- Use radio buttons for multiple-choice questions.

- Use look-up tables for dates of birth, country of origin, products and services.

- Use rules to verify data (does that date of birth make the person 134 years old?)

- Be careful about the use of mandatory fields (the consumer might take great exception to having to provide certain pieces of information, and will take their business elsewhere).

Step two: Processing data for output

How data is transferred

Data for direct marketing is invariably computer-processed, as we have seen. Thus it will exist as either tapes (normally) or disks. CDs are used by most list suppliers, while e-mail is used for smaller files. Frequently as a direct marketing producer you will find yourself ordering data from one source (eg list broker) for onward transmission to another service (eg computer bureau).

Data transfer presents few problems, as most direct marketing data owners and brokers supply and use tapes of a common format, as follows:

Table 8.2.6

Magnetic tape format	
1600/6250	Speed of the tape (1600 bits of data, or bytes, per inch)
EBCDIC/ASCII	Tape format
9-track	9 tracks of data on the tape
Fixed record format	Pre-specified fields of a fixed length
Fixed field format	Fixed fields where each field is predefined, eg 1st field, 30 bytes (the name)
Delimiters	Where fields are not fixed format, a character is used to define the end of one field and the beginning of another; this may be a comma or a carriage-return character.

Files can also be supplied as CSU and .xls formats. When ordering list data from one supplier or department for use by another, always ask for a **file dump** (a printed copy of a selection of the records) and a **record layout**. These will enable the recipient to understand the data that has been received and check for any obvious errors or omissions.

On receipt of the tape, the processing house or department then loads it onto their computer. Files usually arrive in different formats and therefore have to be restructured, so that data is in the correct place for efficient deduplication and processing. If file dumps and records layouts are not supplied it is difficult for the file handlers to be totally sure of the structure.

Always ask for a file dump and a records layout so that file handlers can be totally sure of the structure.

Deduplication – essential success factor

Deduplication (or deduping) is the process of detecting duplicated pieces of information within a database. This can be done manually with very small files, but with anything over a few hundred records it is a laborious job if a computer program is not employed.

When processing large volumes of data, deduplication is undertaken in batch mode, eg deduplicating rented lists against a customer file.

All data processing systems should contain some deduplication facility. This may be at the point where new records are entered onto the system, when the computer will automatically search for records with similar sounding names or addresses. Deduplication software works within tolerance levels, so that addresses that are slightly different can be compared, eg whether Road is Rd, and Hilary Smith is H Smith.

In business-to-business data processing there is a particular problem in trying to match abbreviated company names. If Datascope Marketing Ltd is also held as Datascope, most systems will have a problem matching these two records. In this case the duplicate may be at the address level.

But what if Datascope shares an office address with twenty other companies? The duplicate can then be defined as the same address plus the same individual's name (or job title). Thus the following comprehensive record below (left) is unlikely to be confused with any other. However, by the same token, it will not be recognised as necessarily matching that on the right.

John Wallinger	The Database Planner
Database Planner	Data Division
Craik Jones Watson Mitchell & Voelkel	CJWM&V
120 Regent St	Regent St
London	London
W1B 5RY	W1B 5RY

The fact is deduplication software simply cannot match all the available name and address details, as the volume of data would slow the system down considerably and render costs totally prohibitive.

How deduplication works – a quick recap

Successful deduplication requires all addresses within a file or files to be presented in the same format, otherwise you will not be matching like with like. The computer must be able to recognise roads as Roads, towns as Towns, and postcodes as Postcodes, in order to restructure data into a common format. Hence the importance of structured data capture at the collection stage. This, of course, is especially critical (and difficult) in the case of international direct mail where names are unfamiliar and address formats often quite different from one country to another.

In operation, deduplication software derives a matchkey based on elements of the address. This may include the postcode, street number and name and company name etc.

Another method of deduplication which is gaining ground is 'Soundex' and phonetic deduplication, whereby the software looks for words that sound similar.

When you brief in deduplication, you have first to decide what **you** would consider to be a duplicate. The permutations are legion and only you can decide.

Table 8.2.7

Duplicates or not?
✔ Multiple decision-makers within a company at the same address
✔ Multiple decision-makers within the same company name at multiple addresses
✔ One decision-maker per company per address
✔ A single person in a household with male title taking preference over female, or vice versa (probably depending upon product category)

Remember always to include *stop files* and/or the MPS file and TPS file into deduplication to ensure that anyone who does not want to receive direct mail is taken out. Stop files may include poor credit risks, persistent rejectors of certain products, or regular free-gift takers, as well as existing customers. Additional industry suppression files include:
> national change of address(NCOA)
> deceased files
> national suppression file
> gone-away and suppression file (GAS)

MPS stands for Mail Preference Service and TPS for Telephone Preference Service, details of which can be found in the information section of this Guide.

The importance of 'hierarchy' in deduplication

Clearly, if you are removing duplicate records it is important to retain the record which is preferable, eg more up-to-date, or more important to your activities for any other reason. Thus you must devise and implement a strict system for deciding hierarchy within your files.

A good example of applied hierarchy is where your own customer file becomes a stop list, so that a matching record from any other list is automatically dropped. Other examples of hierarchy include where you stipulate your prospect file being elevated above rented lists, or your best performing list being elevated above lesser lists – thus ensuring the best prospects are mailed the most appropriate offers.

Intra- and Inter-file duplicates

Intra-file duplicates are duplicates *within* a list or file. Inter-file duplicates are duplicates *against* other lists or files.

Your data processing department or bureau should supply you with a '*dedupe*' matrix showing all the matches list by list, the percentage drop, and the net output file by file. If you get a large number of duplicates within a rented list you should take this up with the list broker/owner and negotiate a discount.

Making and outputting selections

Making selections for mailing or listing

One of the major benefits of a well-kept database is its ability to provide you with selections of names and addresses for specific purposes. Selections can be based on simple variations of data, eg geographical, job title, customer type (recency, frequency, value).

Selections are basically one of two types:

✔   Eligibility selections

✔   Rule-based selections.

Eligibility selections are where records should not be ignored when they are selected, eg **absence** of a bad debt indicator, gone-away. In other words where there is no reason NOT to admit a given name once selected.

Rule-based selections are used when you can define all the reasons why a record SHOULD be selected, eg all records **in London** where **no bad debt indicator** is set, who enquired about **product X** in the **last 2 months**.

Be very careful in deciding your selection needs, or you could select totally the wrong data set. Selection is another creative aspect of data processing and should not be left to data processing personnel, especially if they have no knowledge of marketing or of the company's detailed objectives.

Outputting selections for the mail

A few more pointers to watch out for when preparing name and address selections for laser printing, labelling or listing:

Upper or lower case?

Output programs are geared to produce upper and lower case letters *'in all the right places'* – providing the data itself are standardised as discussed.

Thus:

MR HILARY SMITH	becomes	Mr Hilary Smith
12 ALBERT ROAD		12 Albert Road
LONDON		London
SW12 9NN		SW12 9NN

Problem names?

Problems can occur with names, and it is surprising how many names fit into the non-standard category.

Examples include:

✔ Double-barrelled names with hyphens

✔ Post nominal qualifications, eg BSc

✔ European names, eg De Costa or DE Costa?

✔ Account numbers appearing as '*names*'

If errors are made at the inputting stage, expect the computer to print out obediently such mirthful and wrath-inducing salutations as 'Dear Mr OBE', 'Dear 3971', 'Dear De' or 'Dear Jonesy' for Mr Jonesy-Featherstone-Haugh!

If no title can be identified you can use a *default* title, eg 'Dear Customer'. You could also overlay a default title if you are unsure of the individual's name, eg The Managing Director or The Occupier.

Too clever by half?

Personalisation can, of course, go beyond the salutation and you may want to add pieces of individual data to other elements of the communication, eg account numbers on the reply device, or recognition of the last product a customer bought.

However, remember each new piece of data employed, **unless your inputting procedures and internal disciplines are immaculate**, is an opportunity to impress the recipient not with your brilliance but with your potential ignorance. So be warned!

The need to identify mailpacks

It is always advisable to allocate mailpack codes to individual selections or test cells. Pack codes may be needed to determine which offers a customer or prospect has received, and will certainly be needed to assess the outcome of tests.

A good pack code should identify the list, the creative, the offer and any other elements being tested, as in the example below.

Table 8.2.8

Pack Code 101	List 1	Control	Unknown sex
Pack Code 1A2	List 1	Creative A	Male
Pack Code 1B3	List 1	Creative B	Female
1 = List; 0, A or B = Creative test; 1, 2 or 3 = Sex			

How sorted?

An output file can be sorted by a range of elements, eg alphabetical within post town, Mailsort, account number. (For further information on sorting for Mailsort refer to Chapter 8.7.)

Seeds and sleepers?

> *'Sleepers'* are names and addresses purposely seeded into an output list to enable the performance of a mailing to be checked.

Sleepers can be used to carry out spot-checks on a wide range of services and at several stages within a campaign, e.g:

✔ Printing quality

✔ Output data, use and presentation

✔ Make-up of mailing packs

✔ Condition of mailings on arrival

✔ Postal delivery times

✔ Abuse of rented lists

Perhaps the best-known use of sleepers is as a security measure, i.e. to ensure that lists are not used without prior permission and are used in accordance with any conditions stipulated by the list owner.

How names and addresses are output

The final destination of a data processed record is invariably one of the following:

✔ Laser printing (via a magnetic tape) or CD

✔ Disk, cartridge or CD

✔ Labels (especially Cheshire labels)

✔ Listing (eg for sales calls or telemarketing follow-up)

✔ Analyses (for research purposes)

✔ Via e-mail to another computer

✔ Via the Internet

A magnetic (laser image) tape or CD destined for laser printing will include information on the precise positioning of the output data on the printed page. For example, you will almost certainly require the name and address in the usual format for addressing purposes. But in the case of a personalised reply device the name and address may be separated from each other, or may be spaced in an entirely different pattern.

For how to instruct the laser printer to make use of personal data in exactly the way you intend, refer also to Chapter 8.3 of this Guide. An example of a simple instruction follows:

Table 8.2.9

Example of instruction to laser printer	
P1	Mr Hilary Smith
A1	12 Albert Road
A1	London
A1	SW12 9NN
P2	Dear Mr Smith
P3	Unique Reference Number (URN)
P4	Pack code

("P" is the instruction to move to the next print co-ordinate and "A" is the instruction to print and move down a line. In this example, the name and address appear at the top of the letter, the salutation four lines down and the URN and pack code on the bottom left and right of the page respectively.)

Checking and counting – do not leave them until last

Experience shows it is unsatisfactory to leave checking and counting until a mailing is enclosed and possibly mailed. Samples and counts should be supplied at key stages throughout the processing run. Most problems with data processing can be overcome by spotting problems early in the process. This is the responsibility of the data processing department and the individual responsible for the management of the job.

Typical counts and checks should include:

✔ Gross input counts list by list

✔ Samples of records from the input files

✔ Data population counts, eg number of Mr, number of addresses without postcodes

✔ Examples of records before and after enhancement

✔ Dedupe matrix, samples of 'dupe' record (after deduplication)

✔ Breakdown by pack code (after selections)

✔ The number of salutation defaults (after salutation)

✔ Image formatting (after printing)

Choosing and briefing your data processing supplier

Making your shortlist

There are many types of data processing supplier offering a range of services from simple file processing to sophisticated database management. Some bureaux specialise in processing business names and others consumer names. Currently there are some 200 bureaux able to carry out data processing work for direct marketing spread throughout the country.

At the present time there is no regulatory body or trade association able to offer unbiased guidance, although lists of suppliers can be obtained from the industry's recognised trade associations, eg The UK Direct Marketing Association or DMA (UK).

You will need to get any third party company which is processing your data to sign a contract. This is stipulated under the data protection act. A model contract can be obtained from the DMA.

However, there is no substitute for 'asking around' and meeting your prospective suppliers face-to-face. Advice given throughout this Guide on the selection of suppliers applies here also.

In particular:

?   Have you received a personal recommendation?

?   Does the bureau regularly handle your type of business?

?   Are they a member of an industry trade body, eg DMA (UK)?

?   Are they registered with MPS, or DMARC (Direct Marketing Accreditation and Recognition Centre)?

?   Are they registered with the Data Protection Registrar?

?   Are they willing to undertake a test on your data, eg deduplication, salutations?

?   What reports can they provide?

?   Can their reports be easily understood?

?   Have you compared quotes and costing structure?

?   Was your brief clearly understood?

?   Did they ask questions and volunteer constructive suggestions?

Ultimately the successful appointment of a supplier will be down to the relationship that you build with them – there must be a mutual trust – and the quality of brief.

The all-important brief

In order for your data processing suppliers to undertake the work competently, they must fully understand your needs. The majority of mistakes occur because of fundamental misunderstandings before or at the briefing stage. If you do not understand the technical areas, make sure your bureau explains what they mean.

Above all, make sure you are totally clear on what you want to achieve. A good supplier will be able to fill in the gaps.

On pages 20 to 21 will be found a useful data processing briefing document which will be applicable in virtually every instance. Copy it and use it with the author's blessing. On pages 22 to 23 will be found an example of a completed data processing brief, covering a consumer mailing of 136,000 names.

Sample data processing briefing document

Date: _____   Account handler/contact: _____

Client: _____   Campaign: _____   Job no: _____

Start date: _____   Completion date: _____

1.   Brief campaign description: _____

_____

_____

2.   Data sources

List	Quantity	Disc/tape/paper
1. _____	_____	_____
2. _____	_____	_____
3. _____	_____	_____
4. _____	_____	_____
5. _____	_____	_____
6. _____	_____	_____
7. _____	_____	_____
8. _____	_____	_____
9. _____	_____	_____
10. _____	_____	_____
11. _____	_____	_____
12. _____	_____	_____

3.   Output requirements
(Brief description including quantities and lists)

Test cells: Creative: _____
_____

List: _____
_____

Offer: _____
_____

Other: _____
_____

4.   File processing
Deduplication
List hierarchy: _____ Stop list
_____
_____

☐   ☐

Include: MPS
Stop lists
Gone-aways

Deduplication level (ie 1 per household)
_____
_____
_____

5. Output processing

☐ ☐

Upper and lower casing

Salutations: _____

Default title: _____

Default salutation: _____

(Specific to list)
Other personalisation: _____
_____

☐ ☐

Pack codes: Comments: _____
URN: _____
SRN: _____
Sortation: _____
Mailsort:
Pack weight:
Other: _____

_____
_____

Seeds: Agency   ☐   ☐
        Client

Output formats:

Laser tape: Data to include: _____
                          _____
Comments: _____   _____
          _____   _____
          _____   _____
          _____   _____

Listings/labels (S/A, Cheshire)
        Data to include:
Comments: _____   _____
          _____   _____
          _____   _____
          _____
          _____
          _____

Other:
          _____
          _____
          _____

Issued by: (Contact)   _____
            Organisation   _____
            Contact telephone number _____
            Contact fax number _____

Table 8.2.10

Example of a completed data processing brief

1. Lists

List		Quantity	Pack code	Disk/tape/paper
0.	MPS Stop file	120,000	0	Tape
1.	List 1	10,000	A	Tape
2.	List 2	2,000	B	Tape
3.	List 3	1,000	C	Tape
4.	List 4	3,000	D	Tape
	Total	**136,000**		

2. Input/file processing

a) Load and convert to system and provide gross input counts by list identification ID.

b) Drop records where neither identifiable individual and/or job title exists. Supply counts by list ID.

c) Undertake inter- and intra-file dedupe to multiple contact per address (hierarchy as lists above). Provide net counts.

d) All records in the net dedupe file to be selected for the mailing. Split out by list ID as the mailing will not use merged files.

3. Output processing

a) Upper and lower case the file. Do not derive salutations.

b) Apply pack codes to records in each file.

c) Apply one seed to each pack code as follows:
Mr Hilary Smith
12 Albert Road
London
SW12 9NN

d) Provide 100 cased records from each file for approval *prior* to output.

e) Apply Mailsort 2 to the file. Pack weight 50 grams.

f) Apply SRN starting at 1 to each list.

g) Add 100 sample records to the front of each file.

h)   Output will be for self-adhesive labels (list by list) To aid set-up of the
      machinery, add 100 records at the front of each output cell:
      XXXXXXXXXXXX
      XXXXXXXXXXXX
      XXXXXXXXXXXX
      XXXXXXXXXXXX
      XXXXXXXXXXXX
      XXXXXXXXXXXX
      XXXXXXXXXXXX
      XXXXXXXX

      XX   XXXX

i)   Output records in the following format:
          Name
          Job title
          Company name
          Address line 1
          Address line 2
          Address line 3
          Address line 4
          Postcode
          Pack code   SRN
          Label size 1.5 inches by 4 inches

j)   Close up fields where blanks occur.

How to avoid data processing troubles

Some likely problems

!   Unwanted duplication (identical mailpacks reach same customer).

!   Incorrect salutations (Dear Mr BSc).

!   Un-postcoded records (lose postal discounts).

!   Poor quality data.

!   Bad casing (deaR mR joneS).

!   Mailing existing customers with new-customer communications.

Some possible causes

?   The list owner supplies poor lists.

?   The data processing bureau is not properly briefed.

?   The client/agency does not understand data processing mechanics.

?   Client/agency fails to supply a stop list.

?   Bureau fails to ask for stop list.

?   Bureau neglects to ask key questions.

?   Bureau using unproven software.

Signs of improvement

✔   List owners are cleaning and updating lists.

✔   More users/buyers understanding data processing.

✔   Users/agencies are writing better briefs.

✔   Bureau staff begin to understand marketing.

✔   All parties are committed to training.

Ten rules for healthier data processing

- Have a clear idea what your selection and output needs are.

- Remember how flexible you can be.

- Personalise reply devices wherever possible; cut down data capture by using Unique Reference Numbers.

- Allow sufficient time to deal with problems; at least two clear weeks.

- Brief data processor as early as possible to get the job booked and scheduled (availability may have an impact on creative and production).

- Be creative; try to move away from straight dedupe and output.

- Ask questions whenever you are unsure.

- Keep changes to a minimum once the job has started, as changes cause delay and increase costs.

- Above all, do not be put off by the computer. It is there to carry out your demands, and it can be made to talk **your** language.

- If you realise that data processing is not your forte, bring in someone who can help, **now**!

Chapter 8.3

Personalisation: the safe and effective use of a power tool

This chapter includes:

- ❏ **Introduction**
- ❏ **Advantages and disadvantages of the different technologies**
- ❏ **Choosing your preferred technology**
- ❏ **The printers in detail**
- ❏ **The importance of your supplier**
- ❏ **Creating the brief**
- ❏ **Making proofing simple**
- ❏ **Finishing the job**

About this chapter

Personalisation can be an immensely powerful tool; and like most tools, it can do a fair amount of damage when used inappropriately.

This chapter is in two sections: first, the options available for personalisation on paper, their advantages and disadvantages; and second, how to prepare a brief, and how to be sure that everything is correct before a project goes 'live' (which applies to all forms of output, whether on paper or on-screen).

Our ability to gather, interpret and use large volumes of personal data has grown beyond recognition since this Guide was first produced in 1992. The technology which allows us to create unique, highly personalised, high quality communications on paper and on-screen, is young and still developing rapidly. However, the best way to brief the work, and to check the proofs, remains the same.

Author/Consultant: Nick Pride-Hearn

Nick Pride-Hearn consultant and writer

Nick's biography appears in chapter 8.1

Chapter 8.3.

Personalisation: the safe and effective use of a power tool

Introduction

 o start with, it may be helpful to define the less familiar technical terms we will meet throughout this chapter:

Table 8.3.1:   **Glossary of terms**

Bowe (usu. pronounced 'Bow-ee')	From German manufacturer Böwe (pronounced Burr-vuh in German), most common source in the UK for machines which cut continuous stationery into single sheets, removing sprockets, and taking a horizontal double cut either side of the (fanfold) perforation; now generic term for this finishing process. NB term not recognised outside UK.
Burst	Process which converts continuous stationery into separate sheets; originally described a specific process which separated fanfolded stationery at the perforation leaving a ragged edge; process rarely used now, and 'burst' usually used to mean the same as 'Bowe' and 'guillotine' overleaf.
Default	Variable to use instead of missing or invalid data, eg default salutation 'Dear Sir or Madam' if no salutation can be generated.
Digital print(er)	'Digital print(er)' is used as shorthand for four-colour process printing where the image is formed digitally. It often implies the use of variable data.
Dot resolution	A measure of print quality; the higher the number, the smaller the dot and the better quality of image.
DPI	Dots per inch, see dot resolution.
Drop	The vertical measure of a continuous stationery form, usually in inches (while all other measures are usually in mm).
Duplex	Printing (personalising) on both sides of the paper.

Embedded variable	Variable which is embedded in the middle of fixed text, usually requiring changes to the positioning of subsequent fixed text.
Fanfold	Continuous stationery which is supplied concertina- or z-folded on a horizontal perforation, usually boxed in 1-2,000.
File layout	Description of data fields and their location within a data record – an essential 'map' of the data without which processing cannot start.
Fixed (text)	Element which does not vary, yet which is printed as part of the personalisation process.
Fusing	Process of fixing the personalised image on the paper; fusing usually refers to a combination of heat and pressure used to force toner-based inks into the fibre of paper.
Guillotine	When used in connection with continuous stationery, usually used to mean the same as 'Bowe' above. This term easily confused in this context, and best avoided.
Laser	Originally a description of the light-source used to create the variable image; 'lasers' hardly used in current personalisation technology (most use LED arrays), but the name has stuck as a generic description of toner-based printers.
Live proof	Proof of personalisation using live data.
OCR	'Optical Character Recognition' – used in this chapter for a combination of cameras and software which drive multiple personalised pieces and/or selective enclosing requirements.
OMR mark	'Optical Mark Recognition' variable, usually a series of short horizontal lines read by enclosing machinery to match multiple personalised pieces and/or selective enclosing requirements.
Pinless	Continuous stationery and/or continuous lasers without sprockets.
Preprint	Printed stationery before it has been personalised.
Print image tape	The finished compiled job ready to drive the personalisation engine. In many cases the printers are networked, although some installations do still use a physical tape.
Print image area	The maximum area which can be personalised.
Proofing tape	Set of data selected from the live file(s) to include examples of all possible permutations.
Rotated	Describes a form which has been printed at 90 degrees from vertical, either to achieve a particular finishing format, or to reduce cost.
Simplex	Printing (personalising) on one side of the paper.
Sprockets	Holes at either side of stationery used by continuous lasers to drive the paper through the machine.
Stitching	Linking two or more inkjet heads to create a wider print image width.
Variable	An element of data to be personalised which may vary from one record to another.
Variable colour	Generally used to refer to personalisation on a digital printer (see above).
White proof	Proof of personalisation on plain paper.

Advantages and disadvantages of the key technologies

The different technologies used in personalisation are closely linked with both the creative and the printing process. The formats, types of paper, amount and location of personalisation can all affect the personalisation process available.

The key paper-based technologies are:

- Sheet-fed laser

- Continuous laser

- Inkjet

- Digital colour

The following section looks at the significant advantages and disadvantages of each. Immediately afterwards follows a simple decision 'map' to help select the most appropriate process.

> If the personalisation required has a complex combination of text, tables, large fonts and columns, then brief your designer to keep the variables falling at equal increments of 1/6" or 1/8" down the page. Although any personalisation process can print at any co-ordinate on the page down to the smallest dot, a layout which keeps to these increments will be quicker to set up, easier to adjust, and more likely to be correct on the first or second attempt.

Sheet-fed laser

- Preprint readily obtainable from sheet-fed printers.

- Likely to be more cost-effective for runs up to 50,000.

- Sheet-fed litho preprint and high resolution laser image combine to produce high quality finished product.

- Multiple input bins allow for use of more than one stationery type on one job (sometimes used for separator sheets to highlight changes in record, code or Mailsort).

- Plentiful capacity available – many suppliers, robust technology, well understood.

- Intolerant of paper outside specifications, eg with coating, or incorrect inks (supplier of preprint must understand requirements for laser printing).

- Heavy coverage of ink on preprint can cause problems in the fusing process.

- Perforations must be 'micro-perfs' – tight and smooth, with substantial ties at the edges of the paper (again, make sure your stationery supplier has experience with personalisation).

- Fusing process limits possibilities for peel-off labels or pseudo-cards (specialist stationery supplier required, and test with your laser supplier in advance).

- Quality control easy to perform.

Continuous laser

- Generally more cost-effective than sheet-fed above 50,000 records.

- Continuous paper allows for more complex finishing and folding (for example to create multiple nested personalised pieces without the need for special enclosing).

- Quality of some preprint from 'business forms' printers can be poorer than equivalent products from sheet-fed litho printer; when combined with 240dpi laser, the finished product can suffer by comparison.

- Very fast production.

- Proofing can be a slow process, especially when stationery is on reels, and even more so for duplex work.

- Quality control is difficult, especially for duplex.

Keep stationery width for a sprocket-fed continuous laser a few millimetres below the maximum; then the machine will always be able to exert some horizontal 'pull' on the stationery to keep it flat; otherwise, if the paper picks up a little extra moisture and expands, the laser image can move out of position and focus.

Inkjet

- Versatile and flexible.

- Capable of personalising wide range of material.

- Can be very cost effective for high volumes and small amounts of personalisation.

- Only option for some special formats, especially in-line finishing from web presses.

- Almost every installation has slightly different characteristics, so some jobs are locked in to a particular supplier.

- Personalisation may need to be approved at the same time as the print.

- Where personalisation is separate from printing, proofing is usually on the live machine, and a quick sign-off will be required.

- Successful ink-jet personalisation requires very close collaboration *in advance* with your supplier.

- Quality of the personalised image depends as much on the skill and experience of the supplier as on the theoretical capability of the machine.

Digital colour

- Huge scope for creativity.

- Images can be varied as well as text.

- Colours within images can be varied.

- The item printed for record two can be utterly different to that printed for record one; if it's produced on a reel-fed printer, it need not even be the same size.

- Digital printers demand the combined skills of data specialists and four-colour process printers – a combination not always readily to hand.

- Set-up and proofing, particularly where images are varying as well as text, can be very time-consuming.

- Complex applications can still create unpredictable hold-ups in the preprocessor (the 'rip').

- Not all printers offer 'special' colours.

- Although costs are expected to reduce significantly during the lifetime of this Guide, cost per page is likely to remain an issue: currently the successful applications of digital printing share some of the following characteristics:

    - High margin product (eg automotive)
    - Complex data (eg Red Letter Days, the 'experience' retailer)
    - High perceived value (eg investment portfolio statement)
    - Time-sensitive
    - Replaces very costly analogue alternative (eg the IBM catalogue)

- Different page sizes or numbers of pages within a single printing run can make subsequent processes difficult to manage.

Choosing your preferred technology

Figure 8.3.1 shows a simplified decision 'tree' to help determine the most effective technology to apply based on the type of result you are looking for, and the quantities involved.

Figure 8.3.1   **Determining the most appropriate technology for paper-based personalisation**

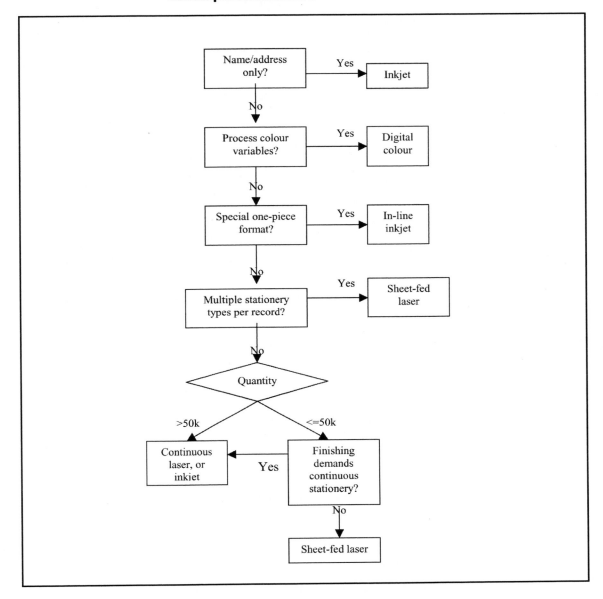

The printers in detail

In this section we look in a little more detail at the different printer technologies, the options they offer, and the way your supplier is likely to charge you.

Sheet-fed laser

This is toner-based printing – similar to most office printers. An image is created by an array of LEDs on a photosensitive drum. Toner is applied to the drum and transferred to paper, which then passes through a fuser station where the toner is heated and forced into the fibres of the paper. Most of these printers have multiple input trays, which means it is possible to mix different paper stocks within a single print run.

- Most printers are Xerox machines, usually 'Manhattan', 4635, or more recently DP180. The main differences are running speeds. Older machines like the 9700 or its predecessor the 8700, are unusual now and have stricter limits on paper size.

- Accepts sheets from 210x210 millimetres to a little over A3. See Table 8.3.2 for a guide on stationery supply.

- Most machines print at 600dpi, which is good quality. Some older machines still print 'interpolated' 600 dots, which is an enhanced version of 300. The differences are only visible when printing large graphics or under a magnifying glass.

- In duplex printing, the sheet is held momentarily after the first image is printed, then turned, and sent back to the printing cycle for personalising the reverse. Therefore duplex printing requires two passes through the machine, and reduces the effective speed.

- Most manufacturers charge on a combination of a fixed charge and then a 'click' charge. A 'click' is a pass of a sheet through the printing process. The click for an A3 piece is the same as for an A4; duplex printing incurs two clicks. So your supplier will charge you based on a combination of the speed at which the job will run, and the number of 'clicks' it will incur.

- Colour option is available. 'Sienna' printers offer a second colour–red, blue or green–along with black. The second colour must be constant (you cannot print one page black and red, the next black and blue). You pay a second click for the second colour. Can sometimes get you out of jail with a missing signature, or lift response with a colour headline.

Table 8.3.2   **Supply of stationery for sheet-fed personalisation**

Stationery for sheet-fed personalisation should be supplied as follows:
- Packed flat in boxes
- Consistently cut (no difference in position of image on finished sheet)
- Crisply cut (no ragged edges)
- In boxes the right size for the paper
- Facing the same way (no turning or alternating)
- Not banded or taped inside the boxes
- Long-grain (the grain of the paper running parallel with the long sides of an A4 page)
- No mixed versions in boxes
- Boxes stacked flat on a pallet, one version per pallet
- Versions clearly marked on boxes
- Distinguishing codes clearly visible on stationery for different versions

Sometimes stationery will fail to run on a sheet-fed laser, despite meeting every element of the specification. First, try a sample at another supplier. Otherwise, leave the stationery in the laser room for 48 hours before trying again, and you will be surprised how often this makes the difference.

If you're producing A4 lasered letters, consider lasering them as A3 and separating afterwards – this could be both quicker and cheaper.

Continuous laser

Toner-based technology, very similar to sheet-fed laser above, in the way that the image is created on the paper. However, the fusing process is cooler and with less pressure. The paper path is also relatively flatter. Standard configuration is for fanfolded stationery; as faster machines are installed, many are being configured to run reel-to-reel.

- Most machines are supplied and serviced by Océ, although some carry the original Siemens badge. The primary differences are in speed and duplex capability; the older machines (NDX and NDZ) may have a lower dot resolution.

- See Figure 8.3.2 for general layout of stationery. The drop sizes are measured in inches, and are usually up to 28" maximum, although this is obviously dependent on your stationery supplier. The width can start from as little as 165 millemetres up to 18"/457 millemetres. Allow ½" either side for sprockets; normally you will not be able to laser in this area (it is usual to keep the left side sprocket area clear of preprint as well, as this is where most machines print the mark used to check and control the density of the toner).

- Most print at 300dpi; some newer machines are being installed with 600dpi, while a few older survive which print at 240 dots. Whilst 240dpi can still be acceptable, it is often possible to tell the difference between 240 and 300 dots in smaller serif fonts.

Figure 8.3.2   **Continuous stationery layout**

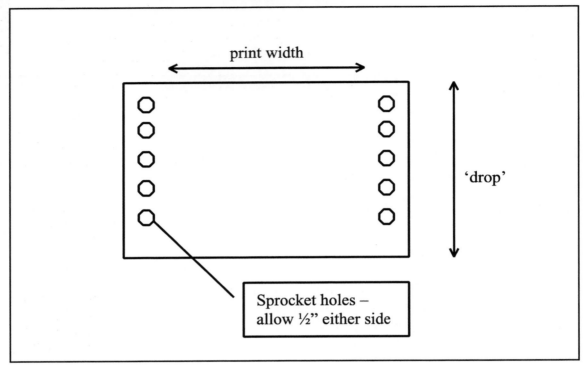

- Most manufacturers charge a combination of a fixed fee plus 'clicks'. For continuous printers, 'clicks' are based on footage of paper passed through the machine.

- Duplex printing is achieved by linking two machines to run in tandem, and they must then run reel-to-reel. Run-speed is unaffected, although set-up takes longer, and two 'clicks' are charged.

- Where two printers are running in tandem, it is usually possible to use the second machine to laser a second colour, most often a standard blue.

- 'Pinless' machines are becoming more prevalent, where the paper is driven without the need for sprocket holes at either side of the page. This can give you a larger sheet size, and you may also be able to personalise from edge to edge.

Inkjet

Inkjet is similar to most office colour printers. Ink is passed through a printing 'head' with many tiny holes (the number and size determine the dot resolution); the head creates a very precise stream of ink dots which are fired from the head down (always down, never up or across) towards the substrate; complex electronics scavenge most of the dots and prevent them reaching the substrate, allowing through only those which will make up the required image. The ink must then dry on the surface of the substrate. One head will print one colour.

Inkjet heads can be attached to all sorts of other machinery such as printing presses, folders, and polythene enclosing machines, as well as being set up as standalone machines. It can be an immensely versatile and fast method of personalisation.

There are important differences in inkjet technologies, and you need to be sure of the version you are using. The key variables are the type of ink, type of controller and head size. Talk to your supplier before you commit yourself.

Inks: Solvent-based inks will dry on almost any surface, and are often found in industrial applications (such as printing the item code on a piece of plastic guttering, or a drug identity code on a bottle of pills); water-based inks normally require some mechanical assistance (heat or ultraviolet (UV) light) to dry, and will usually need a porous substrate such as an uncoated cartridge paper.

Controllers: Line-printers will print a set number of lines of text and are incapable of printing even simple graphics like a PPI (postage paid indicia); graphics-capable printers can print any font or graphic.

Head-size: Many simple inkjet applications, such as those which apply a name and address on the plastic wrapper of a magazine, use a printing head which is 1" wide, allowing a maximum of 6 (sometimes 8) lines of addressing. Some applications will allow two or more heads to be used simultaneously to increase the amount of personalisation available. Many direct mail installations make use of the Scitex 4¼" head, and a 9" Scitex head is just becoming available in the UK at the time of writing. Two 4¼" heads 'stitched' together can personalise an A4 width of paper, as can a single 9" head. Where multiple heads are 'stitched' in this way, it requires considerable skill from the machine operators to avoid some slight but perceptible misalignment between the outputs of each head.

- The size and format of substrate for inkjet printing is determined by the type of machine on which the inkjet head is mounted.

- At the 'industrial' end the quality can be as low as 110 dpi, which looks like a 'join-the-dots' colouring book. However, this can be ample for a simple addressing application. Most direct marketing applications vary between 240 and 300dpi. The newer Scitex heads offer 600dpi.

- The amount of personalisation is determined by the number of print heads available. Duplex printing is straightforward as long as the machine in question is able to turn the item over before passing the second heads.

- One colour can be printed by one print head at a time. The usual colour is black. Other standard colours are available, and some 'special' colours are possible (with plenty of advance notice, and usually additional cost). At the end of 2001, four-colour process printing with inkjet started to become available. Currently this is only available on very high speed Scitex web printers, which are aimed at the transactional market (for example, printing BT phone bills); however it is likely that this technology will become available to direct marketers in the course of 2002.

- Usually charged at a simple cost per thousand records; where the personalisation is an integral part of a complex print and finishing job, the separate cost of personalisation is unimportant.

A note on dot resolution/dpi

The comparison of dot resolution can be misleading. While a dot resolution of 600dpi will give a higher quality image than a dot resolution of 300dpi produced on the same technology, the same comparison is much less meaningful when the technologies are different. So although 240dpi on a Scitex head may sound 'worse' than 300dpi on a laser, the difference in the technology is probably more important. Look at examples before you get too hung up on the numbers, and make your decision based on the quality of the finished product.

Never allow yourself to be persuaded that your supplier can produce a duplex job by running it twice through a simplex machine; even camera-matching systems are not perfect. Either find a duplex machine, or change the specification of the job.

Digital colour

'Digital colour' is the usual shorthand for four-colour process printers where the image is formed electronically. These print engines were first seen in any numbers in the late 1990s. Early on in their development it became clear that they had the very interesting potential to use variable data to personalise in full colour. In practice there are many glorious samples, but still only a small number of companies using the technology successfully. There is no question that variable digital colour will become an established tool for personalisation.

- Until 2001 there were two basic versions of digital colour printer capable of incorporating variable data: the Xeikon (pronounced Zy-kon) engine, which uses coloured toners; and the Indigo, which uses inks. The Indigo generally produces results that are closer to offset litho quality, and usually produces a better quality print where there is heavy or intense colour in the original.

- At the time of writing, the future of both manufacturers looks uncertain.

- During 2001, Xerox installed a number of its own '2060' sheet-fed, toner-based printers. The quality is a significant advance over the Xeikons, and the front-end software looks promising. The next generation of these printers, which may be launched as early as 2002, promise higher productivity, and perhaps this will see the breakthrough in costs per page.

- 2002 will also see the first installation of the NexPress from Heidelberg. It is significant that Heidelberg, the doyen of litho printers, believes it should be involved in digital print; and their history and market position suggest it is likely to offer a first-rate product.

- There are sheet-fed and reel-fed printers. The sheet-fed are usually A3 or a little larger to allow for bleed. The reel-fed printers incorporate a cutter which automatically cuts to the correct size before dropping in the output tray. They require special papers, although the range is expanding rapidly. Check with your supplier.

- All digital colour printers are capable of printing duplex.

- Most manufacturers charge a combination of a fixed rental, a 'click' charge based per thousand sheets (or footage if reel-fed), plus ink (the ink usage can vary dramatically depending on the colours used, the intensity and the coverage). Most suppliers will also need to account for set-up and processing time.

Designing a job with variable images: if you plan to use images as variables, create a template for the images, and edit each image so that it neatly fits the template; this makes it possible to control all the possible combinations. For the same reason, avoid having variable images butting up to one another, as it will be difficult to ensure that there is no unattractive or inappropriate combination.

The importance of your supplier

If you are at all uncertain about your ability to look after the personalisation of a direct mail campaign, then it is essential that you are working with an expert, someone you trust. If you are comfortable working with a supplier who does not offer the whole range of personalisation, you are better working with the technology he offers, than looking for a new supplier when you are unsure of yourself. Consider any additional cost an 'insurance premium'.

Selecting a supplier

In addition to all the usual criteria you would use in selecting a supplier (see 'Selection of suppliers' in 'Managing the Production Process' Chapter 8.1), add the following:

- Appropriate software for turning data and texts into personalised pages. The industry standard applications are PrintNet by GMC, PReS from Program Products, DocOne from Group One, and Isis Papyrus.

- Quality control procedures specifically for personalisation which include:

  - Detailed hand-over briefing to production.

  - Proof sign-off sheets for each merge, indicating variables and fixed texts, and relevant stationery codes

  - Periodic checks by machine operators for quality and position of personalisation

  - Clear method of identifying bad copy or restarts when printing on reels

  - Clear labelling of finished job showing reel or box number, and sequence start and stop numbers

  - Audit trail which demonstrates that whole job is complete, with volumes reconciled to data quantities

Creating the brief

This is a checklist for briefing personalisation, which covers all forms of output media.

General

- Total number of records expected:
- How will incoming data be identified? (eg file name, source, ID number):
- Number of versions of stationery:
- Number of discrete merges expected at end of job:
- Method of personalisation (eg inkjet, continuous laser):
- Simplex or duplex:
- Document size:
- Number of records per document:
- If more than one record per page, what sequence required? (if you need to maintain a sequence, for instance for Mailsort discounts, then your supplier will need to know whether to run records across or down the page – see Figure 8.3.3; talk to your finishing and mailing house, as the answer will depend not just on the format of the pack but also on the way they work).
- Look up tables required? (Yes or No):
- Images for scanning (such as signatures): number, type.

Data

- File layout supplied? (NB – make sure that the sender of the data includes a file layout, even if it is 'the same as before'; your supplier will be unable to start work without it, and if they use a layout from a previous job which turns out to be wrong, you will be in trouble).
- Correspondence table to show which data files to be used on which stationery (see example in Table 8.3.4).

Texts

- Copy for all fixed text(s). If sending soft copies on disk, include a printed version to show exactly the font and layout you require.
- Correspondence table to show which texts to use on which stationery, and with which data.
- Clearly mark embedded variables (see glossary) and refer to them in the detailed brief.
- Mark texts clearly to show where the different lengths of embedded variables may demand changes to line-endings, and possibly to the starting positions for subsequent paragraphs.

Look-up tables

Where your job requires the use of look-up tables, have them checked by your colleagues before you send them to the supplier. Make sure the tables are very clearly marked to indicate which values are the criteria, the data field to which they refer, and which are the resulting variables to be personalised (see example in Table 8.3.3)

Table 8.3.3   **Example look-up table**

Look-up table for item 14, 'New Loan Amount'

Input field	Criteria	Output variable
Outstanding Loan Amount, position 42, 8 characters	<= 1,000.00	2,500
	1,000.01 – 2,000.00	3,000
	2,000.01 – 4,500.00	5,000
	> 4,500.00	7,500

'Position' relates to the location within the data record, as specified in the file layout

Note precision concerning the figures; if the decimals were present in the data, and not included in the table, then an outstanding amount of 1,000.55 would show a zero or blank in the output

Window position

- Sample envelope supplied?:

- If no sample envelope, then dimensions as follows:

  - Window size, window position

- Trim guide and fold guide supplied? (unless in-line web finishing, in which case it's part of the personalisation process).

Table 8.3.4   **A correspondence table for data and stationery**

Merge no	Description	Dataset name/File ID	Quantity	Stationery code
1	Control	AVM001	75,000	AVM/CS/C
2	Incentive test	AVM002	25,000	AVM/CS/T
3	Offer test	AVM003	25,000	AVM/CS/C

Figure 8.3.3 **Data sequencing when more than one record per page**

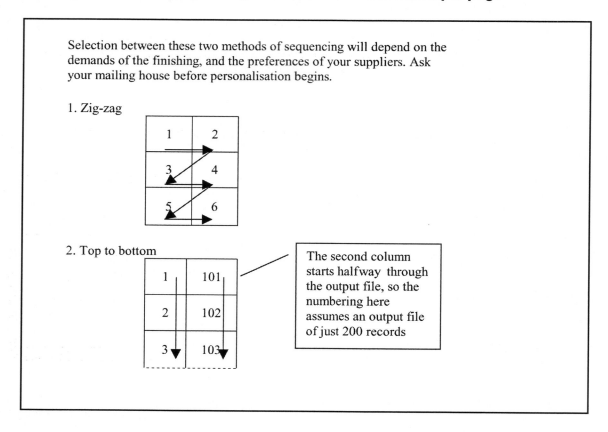

Selection between these two methods of sequencing will depend on the demands of the finishing, and the preferences of your suppliers. Ask your mailing house before personalisation begins.

1. Zig-zag

2. Top to bottom

The second column starts halfway through the output file, so the numbering here assumes an output file of just 200 records

Images

Often you will require just a digitised (scanned) signature, or sometimes a simple black and white map. Digital colour applications, however, are likely to involve substantial amounts of four-colour images, which are themselves variable depending on the data. The brief for variable images follows exactly the format of the detailed brief shown below.

If you are personalising tables, with values dropping in to boxes, leave the boxes off the preprint, and have them lasered – that way they will always fit neatly.

Detailed brief

Your brief should include specific detail on each piece of text, and each variable, which shows:

- The source of the relevant data (for example, 'name field')

- The position in which it appears on the personalised piece (usually easiest to show by marking a copy of the artwork); take special care with embedded variables to ensure that the fixed text will work with all permutations

- The font type, case, size, and style (eg Times Roman, mixed case, italic, 12pt, left justified)

- Colour, if appropriate

- Calculations or look-up tables to apply

- Correspondence between data and texts (for example, 'If 'customer type' = A, B or C, use text 1, otherwise use text 2')

- Where you want the customer number or URN to show

- Where you want the sequence number to be printed (used by printers for controlling the job, especially restarts)

This requires a considerable amount of detail, even for a relatively simple job. There are two things worth remembering here:

1. If your brief can be misinterpreted, it will. Be as clear and precise and thorough as you can (use numbered points and cross-references throughout).

2. Most other people involved in this campaign will not realise the importance of your brief, and will rely on you to get it right.

See section **'What to do if you are not happy writing the brief'** overleaf if you are not comfortable about doing this yourself.

Defaults

However good the data processing, however high the standard of data collection, there will always be data that is ambiguous or missing. Assigning defaults to any variable where this could create a problem, is a powerful and much overlooked solution.

The following defaults should always be specified in the brief:

- Salutation (eg Dear Sir or Madam)

- Valediction (if the sign-off is to be printed as part of the personalisation, then you may wish to change 'Yours sincerely' to 'Yours faithfully' when the default salutation is used)

Where there is restricted space for names and addresses, such as when there is a box into which the name is dropped, check whether the longest name on the file will fit (look at the number of characters specified for the field in the file layout; if in doubt, ask your supplier to do a report on the actual data). If not, then specify a smaller (default) font, for instance: 'If name line >20 characters, print in 10pt'.

For each variable, consider the implication if the data is missing, or is not one of your expected criteria (for instance you expect the field 'customer type' to contain A, B, or C; what do you want the personalisation process to do if the customer type is missing, or is some other value?). Either specify a default value (in the above example, 'if 'customer type' is blank or other, treat as C'), or ask for the record to be dropped so that it is not included in the output. Get a report on the number of records dropped before proceeding – you may discover that there is a category that someone forgets to tell you about.

> The data field which your client and colleagues assure you will always be filled and correct, is the one most likely to cause problems!

Samples

Specify the number and type of samples you require:

- Which merge(s) will you want samples from (eg control and incentive test).

- How many 'AB Samples' do you want?

- If you have a particular name and address to use for samples, specify it.

- How many 'duplicate live' samples do you want (where the whole pack is a replica of a live record)?

- Do you want any 'text only' samples (often for use by call centres who will fill in the name and address as required).

What to do if you are not happy writing the brief

Most briefs for personalisation require nothing more than a methodical, logical approach. However, there may be times when you are not convinced that this is enough, either because of the complexity of the job, its importance, or your own confidence. In which case, arrange a meeting with your supplier at which you will write the brief together. If you need to include other colleagues, then do so. If your supplier is unhappy to work with you on this, find one who will. Please do not ever go ahead without a written brief in place, because regret is a terrible thing.

Making proofing simple

Proofing file

The most efficient way of checking a personalisation job is to set up a 'proofing file'. A proofing file contains one example of every permutation that is possible from the 'live' output file. Running proofs from this file will make it easier for you and your colleagues to check that the job is correct in every respect. A proofing file will be especially important for digital colour work, where you want to see that each permutation of colour images is working properly.

Checking proofs

- Be clear with everyone involved about their responsibilities, and what each of you is checking. Put it in writing. See Table 8.3.5 for a suggestion.

- Make sure that a hard copy of the data accompanies the proofs so that you can check that the correct variables are being generated.

- Ask for a printout of the look-up tables your supplier is using in their programmes to check against the original you supplied.

- Insist on at least one set of proofs being produced on the 'live' stationery.

- Keep a copy of each set of proofs, and identify them by date, time or number.

- Put all amendments and corrections in writing.

- As a final check, look at the errors identified on previous sets of proofs, and ensure they have not crept back in (shouldn't happen, but it does, and it's tempting to concentrate only on the items which were wrong in the previous proofs).

Table 8.3.5   **Suggested allocation of responsibilities at proof stage**

Proofing check	Responsibility
Data compared to original database	Database Administrator
Calculations, look-up tables	Project Sponsor
Layouts, fonts, colours	Designer
Window position	Project Manager
Defaults working	Project Manager
Texts	Copywriter
Wrap-arounds	Project Manager

Some 'expert' checks

Here are some extra checks which, once every dozen jobs or so, will catch a snag before it becomes a disaster:

- On duplex work, check that the back and the front match (sounds obvious, but it's surprising how easy it is to miss a problem here).

- Cut and fold an example and make sure it works the way you expect, and that the address will show through the window (time-consuming, but essential).

- Find a proof where default values are being used, and check them.

- Where there are bar-codes, check them with a bar-code reader.

- Find a record with a long address; now look at the record immediately after it, just in case the last line of the long address has been carried forward to the next record. (I see this happen about once every couple of years.)

- Find a record with a long name, or a long single line of address, and check that all of it is being printed (occasionally a field can be set too short, and the data gets truncated).

- Where you have embedded variables, check the text immediately after the variable (sometimes this may have changed since you saw the text-only proofs).

- Also with embedded variables, check line breaks for different values of the variable.

- When proofing an in-line web job, where you are checking the offset print as well as the personalisation, try to treat the personalisation as a separate process, and allow yourself sufficient time to check it thoroughly. If you can, check the personalisation while waiting for a change to the offset print. Once you are content with the print quality, beware the temptation (and often the subtle pressure from the printer) to press ahead before you have properly checked the personalisation.

Finishing the job

Once your job has been signed off to run, you should now:

- Prepare the trim and fold guides

- Prepare the enclosing sample

- Check that the samples have been produced

- Ask for daily reports on the quantities and versions produced

- Reconcile the reports against the quantities you expect

Then carry on with all your other work!

Successful management of personalisation demands close attention to detail, and a careful, logical approach. Work with experts, and take your time.

Chapter 8.4

Essentials of the printing process

This chapter includes:

- ❏ **The 8 essential steps of print production**
- ❏ **Information your printer will need**
- ❏ **Preparing the artwork correctly**
- ❏ **The 6 main types of paper used in direct mail**
- ❏ **Proofing: the four types of proof**
- ❏ **The 6 printing methods**
- ❏ **Printing technology**
- ❏ **Why use digital printing?**
- ❏ **Envelopes for direct mail**
- ❏ **Choosing your print supplier**

About this chapter

s many authors have noted elsewhere in this Guide, there are few areas of direct marketing which do not involve direct mail. One of the chief differences between marketers in the conventional sphere and those in direct marketing is the knowledge required to implement complex print campaigns. These may well involve dozens of different items of print, each produced in a different quantity, using different printing processes, different paper stocks and different finishing techniques.

In this brief but essential introduction to printing and print buying, Philip Moreland throws light on some of the terms you will encounter and the sequence of events to be followed when translating finished artwork into mailing packages ready for the mail.

Printing, like every other area of the business, is undergoing constant technological change and a knowledge of the principles will help you to keep pace with them.

Author/Consultant: Philip Moreland

Philip Moreland
Print Consultant, Marketing Specialists

Philip joined the printing industry as an apprentice in 1964 with John Waddington Ltd where he worked for five years gaining practical experience of all the printing processes. At 21 he joined Petty & Sons, one of the original 'pioneers' of web offset, in the estimating department. He then joined Quadrimetal, a French printing plate manufacturer, as a demonstrator and troubleshooter.

He gave his first technical presentation, at PIRA, the printing industries research and development organisation, on developments in printing plate technology and has since been a regular speaker on print technology for IDM.

In 1978 he joined Waddington & Ledger as a salesman and was appointed Marketing Director five years later. W & L was one of the first UK companies involved in the production of direct response products using 'in-line' finishing.

In 1989 he joined the Hunterprint Group, then Europe's largest direct mail producer, as Special Products Development Director, becoming involved in laser/inkjet personalisation. After a short period at St Ives Direct he rejoined Waddington & Ledger as Managing Director in April 1990. In 1994 he and a colleague set up Marketing Specialists to run alongside W & L. This company offers technical consultancy and print management services.

Philip has four children and six grandchildren, is a keen sailor and spends as much time as possible cruising the Mediterranean. He enjoys playing squash and in quieter moments paints and still plays the guitar ... badly!

Mr Philip Moreland M IDM
Managing Director
Waddington & Ledger Ltd
Lowfields Business Park
Elland
West Yorkshire HX5 9DA

Chapter 8.4

Essentials of the printing process

The 8 essential steps of print production

All printed work, no matter what the process or volume, should follow a set procedure if your work is to be produced exactly to your specification, on time, and to your budget.

Let us first set out the procedure, and then look at each of the stages in more detail.

The sequence you should follow is always the same. The timings, where given, are recommended minimums. Where no timing is given this is, of course, dependent on the nature of the work and will be advised at time of estimate.

1.   Estimate – 2 weeks prior to delivery

2.   Paper order – 4 weeks prior to delivery (If a making)

3.   Origination – Allow 2 working days

4.   Platemaking – Allow 1 day

5.   Ozalid proof – Allow 1 day

6.   Printing – Will be advised

7.   Finishing – Will be advised

8.   Delivery – Your due date

Factors affecting mailpack timing

The overall timings above are for a typical mailing pack comprising brochure, letter, order form, envelope etc. Special timing arrangements must be negotiated in the case of catalogues which, with perhaps 48 pages or more, are the equivalent of several regular mailings.

Factors which will affect your general timing for direct mail will include:

?   Special papers – 'makings'

?   2nd and 3rd colour proofs

?   Late specification changes

Remember printers' estimates assume **no further corrections** to your copy or art. Changes during production can potentially jeopardise your mailing date, although any reputable printer will lean over backwards to accommodate you. Remember to consult your mailing house regarding delivery dates needed to meet proposed mailing dates. Your start date should always be calculated backwards from the proposed mailing date.

Step 1 : The estimate – start early

It is always advisable to contact your printer as soon as you have a rough visual, some ideas of your proposed mailing quantity, and, if possible, desired mailing date. Ideally you should ask for a printer's estimate prior to beginning artwork production.

There are many reasons for this: for example, your printer may suggest minor changes (eg of fold or size) which can save significant amounts of money. These may require artwork to be prepared in a slightly different way. Sometimes your printer will be aware of new techniques which, if employed, can give your mailing a competitive edge. Just occasionally your designer may create a superlative package on paper which technically cannot be executed, or only at inordinate cost – all good reasons for calling in your printer as early as possible.

With large-scale direct mail campaigns, or in the case of small quantity tests which may become large-scale rollouts if successful, getting an early printer's estimate is paramount, since even a small price differential multiplied by millions can amount to tens of thousands of pounds. And, of course, a large-scale plan that is held up due to an avoidable technical hitch can lead to massive shortfalls of revenue for the advertiser.

Here are some of the ways in which your printer can often show you significant savings if consulted early in the process:

✔ Changes in format size

✔ Modifications to the format, e.g. inbuilt envelopes

✔ Alternative paper stocks

✔ Rationalised production methods – pre-inserted flyers and order forms

✔ Inkjet coding rather than plate changes

✔ Inbuilt involvement devices, eg scratch-off panels

Information your printer will need

All printers and production managers require certain standard information in order to provide costings and to plan for a job. It is a good idea, since you may find yourself using several printers, to use your own standard Print Enquiry Form.

An example of the items to be covered on a typical print enquiry/estimate form is shown on the facing page, from which you can readily create your own form. **It may be necessary to prepare a separate enquiry form for each item in your mailing or campaign** as virtually every item will be different, eg envelope, order form, leaflet, price list, letter, reply envelope, and so on. In some cases they will be handled by different printers.

Cover

Remember to note whether a brochure or booklet is self-covered (ie same paper as text) or whether a different paper stock is required for the outside pages.

Bleed

The amount of bleed (where ink 'runs off' the edges of the pages) can affect the cost of a print job noticeably. Your direct mail designer will be aware of the significance of bleed, but may not be aware of its true impact on costs.

Figure 8.4.1

Suggested print enquiry/estimate form		
Job title:		
☐ Quantity		☐ Run on
☐ Flat size	☐ Saddle stitch	☐ Ink-jet coding
☐ Finished size	☐ Spine glue	☐ Scratch 'n' sniff
☐ No. of pages	☐ Remoistenable glue	☐ Fragrance burst
☐ Colours	☐ Wet pattern glue	☐ Silver/gold latex
☐ Paper (cover)	☐ Perforations	☐ Silk-screen inks
☐ Paper (text)	☐ Die cutting	☐
☐ Packaging	☐ Coin react ink	☐
☐ Delivery	☐ Numbering	☐
☐ Artwork/film date	☐ Delivery date	

☐ Additional
information

_____

_____

_____

_____

☐ Repro

_____

_____

_____

Type of proof ☐ Machine ☐ Cromalin ☐ Ozalid

Diagram

Quantity

Printers will normally print a larger quantity than you request to allow for spoils, although every printer's 'overs' policy is different.

Transparencies

It is often not realised how the cost of a full-colour print job increases in direct proportion to the number of transparencies used, and whether they are to be reproduced actual size ('s/s' or same size), enlarged or reduced.

Paper

The weight of paper is a major factor in the weight, and therefore the postage cost, of a mailing – as well as the cost of print.

Finishing

This is a printers' term for a variety of processes that include folding, stapling, glueing and varnishing etc.

Size

Most direct-mail designers are fully au fait with standard paper sizes and how to get the best from them. Generally speaking, the advantages of having a non-standard print size (eg extra impact or awareness) are heavily outweighed by the disproportionate costs due to ordering non-standard paper and having it 'cut to waste'.

Delivery

State all relevant details concerning delivery: quantities, destinations, method of packing (if appropriate) and so on.

Dates

Remember to state the date at which you plan for artwork or films to be ready, if being prepared by a specialist supplier and not the printer. Invariably your printer will be able to carry out the stages known as origination on your behalf.

Preparing the artwork correctly

Artwork is the image used for reproduction and is the province of the art director. However, here are a few thoughts on artwork preparation as seen from the printer's perspective:

- Always supply some form of colour proof with disk (positional guide only) – it can be low resolution.

- Make sure trim/tick marks are shown and base artwork is correct to size.

- Check against printers laydown sheet if appropriate. (Complex finishing jobs.)

- Make sure transparencies are all together and are in focus. Check with glass.

- Check that the colour mark-up is complete with no areas of doubt, ie tint panels, headlines, key lines and whether they print or not.

- Watch out for type reversals in very small type – no less than 8pt.

- Check for 'special colours' ie those that cannot be achieved with the four colour process.

- Make sure the disk provided is compatible with the repro house/printer.

- Ensure the repro house/printer carries the fonts specified on the disk.

- If any type corrections are made on or after the first proof, make sure the original disk is also corrected at some stage.

Check with your printer that he is happy with the disk and format of artwork you propose to supply.

Digital artwork is now the norm as most companies have desktop publishing and design systems. It is imperative that some form of colour proof is presented with the relevant artwork disk. This proof will act as the positional guide and colour mark-up. It is not necessary for this proof to be of high resolution for this particular purpose.

Check that the printer/repro house can handle the system disk selected.

Step 2: Ordering the paper

Most printing paper is bought through specialist paper merchants and each merchant will give the paper a brand name. This brand name will be different from merchant to merchant even though the paper is the same and may have been manufactured by the same mill. Only very large printers are able to buy paper directly from the mills.

If a job requires in excess of two tonnes of paper then a 'making' is normally bought. A 'making' is paper of a specific size, whether in reel or sheet form, and of the required weight. Such paper can take 4-6 weeks to manufacture and deliver. Stock paper can be bought for almost immediate delivery. However, stock paper may be the wrong size and weight for the job, possibly resulting in excessive waste. Stock papers are also more expensive per tonne to buy.

In practice, very large regular mailers (eg financial service organisations, publishers, mail-order catalogues) buy paper by the making, whereas most business-to-business mailers are generally forced to rely on stock papers. If you're a business mail, therefore, create your designs with stock sizes in mind. Smaller mailers should not concern themselves unnecessarily with early ordering of paper unless a very rare paper is being contemplated, eg antique finish or 'laid' paper (watermarked).

The 6 main types of paper

There are six generic types of paper in common use for direct mail. Each has specific advantages and disadvantages of which weight and price are two – although by no means the only two.

The chart below sets out the six grades of paper, together with the chief features and uses of each.

Table 8.4.1

The 6 grades of paper	
Type	**Uses**
W.S.O.P. (Web-sized offset paper)	Bottom of the range Low-cost, high-volume work Long-run weekly magazines, eg TV Times
Blade coated mechanical (BCM)	Off-white, mid-range, coated For run-of-the-mill colour work Magazine inserts, brochures, broadsheets etc
Matt coated part mechanical	Off-white matt coated (cartridge) Semi-high quality work Letters, application forms, brochures
Near woodfree	Whiter than above Better quality, better colour reproduction Brochures, inserts
Woodfree matt coated	Top-of-the-range Extra white, high quality Application forms, letters, brochures etc
Woodfree art	High gloss/high reflection Prestige reproduction Quality brochures, prospectuses, company reports etc

The effect of paper weight

Most papers used in direct mail can be bought in a wide range of weights, ranging from as low as 45 grams per square metre (gsm) to 200gsm, or more.

Weight, generally speaking, is synonymous in the recipient's mind with quality. The heavier the weight the better it resists unwanted creasing and spoiling due to handling. But weight, of course, equals cost in postage and print terms.

The most commonly used weights of paper in direct mail are as follows:

65gsm	High volume brochures, magazines, catalogues
90gsm	Volume letters, application forms
115-135gsm	Prestige leaflets, brochures, certificates etc.

International paper sizes

Everyone connected with direct mail should be familiar with the international 'A' sizes for paper and printed goods. The principle is that all stock paper sizes can be cut from a standard A1 or A0 sheet.

However, your designer will know that some paper is lost during trimming and folding and you should be certain of whether your sizes are for flat (opened out) size or trimmed and folded size.

In the case of booklets of 8pp (8 printed pages) and 16pp, many print machines will print, fold and finish them in one pass – so that special sizes apply, as there may be no trimming.

On rare occasions you might be involved in printing items for use in the US, in which case be aware that international 'A' sizes have not been universally adopted there. This can lead to mistakes and misunderstandings and is worth a special check.

Figure 8.4.2   **International 'A' paper sizes**

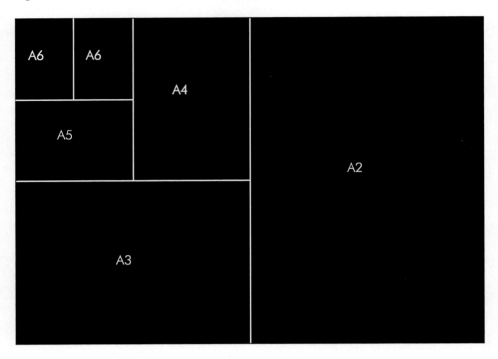

Table 8.4.2

International A-sizes of paper				
Trimmed		**Untrimmed**		
A1 =	840 x 594 mm	SRA1 =	640 x 900 mm – 16pp booklets	
A2 =	594 x 420 mm	SRA2 =	450 x 640 mm – 8pp booklets	
A3 =	420 x 297 mm			
A4 =	297 x 210 mm			
A5 =	210 x 148 mm			
A6 =	148 x 105 mm			

Step 3: Origination – colour separations and proofing

Origination is the first stage in the print process proper, after the designer has completed his artwork and the photographer has supplied the transparencies.

Origination is the point at which artwork is separated into the four printing colours for what is called the 4-colour process or full-colour work.

The four printers' colours are:

- Black

- Yellow

- Cyan (blue)

- Magenta (red)

Figure 8.4.3

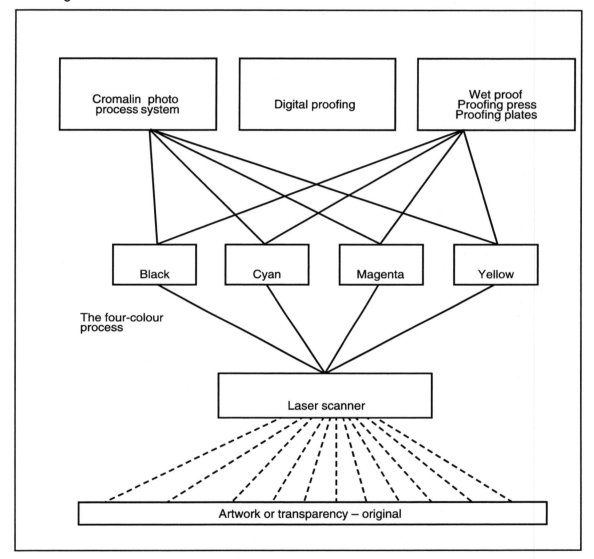

Every full-colour picture in a printed piece comprises arrangements of tiny colour dots in the four so-called process colours. To reach this stage, original artwork is usually scanned electronically by laser beam. The scanner views the originals through a series of filters which allow only one colour to register at a time. The result is four separate **positive** films, one for each of the process colours.

Step 4: Platemaking – fixing the image in metal

In order to transfer the separated and screened images to the paper it is necessary first to produce a printing plate or cylinder.

The different types of plate are described later under printing methods. Plates are generally of flexible metal and are bolted or clipped around a cylinder.

3 types of screening

Conventional screening is a process in which the positive films are broken down into a series of dots. Each colour is screened at a different angle and the dots vary in size according to the depth of colour and detail present in the original.

Geometric screening is the same in principle, except the dots are elongated and bumped against each other to form lines, appearing as a sharp, fine-line screen.

Fulltone is a random (stochastic) screening that excels in handling text and linework and provides outstanding rendition of fine detail.

Step 5: Proofing —— the four types of proof

To check the quality and accuracy of the positive films, they must be 'proofed'. For most colour work there are four types of proof which you need be aware of:

✔ Wet proofs

✔ Cromalins

✔ Ozalids

✔ Digital proofs

Proof checking

Wet proofs — These are produced on a small single colour printing press, specifically designed for this purpose. Each colour is printed separately and has to dry before the next one is printed down. As a general statement the wet proof is the closest we can get to the actual printing process to be used. An added advantage of the wet-proof system is the ability to proof on the actual paper stock to be used for the print run itself. Needless to say wet-proofing is a costly and time-consuming process.

Wet-proofing is often preferred by non-experienced print buyers, especially for quality work, because of its closer approximation to the finished job.

Wet-proofing is used when multiple proofs are required, eg twelve or more. In most circumstances proofs can be 'backed' up (printed on reverse) so that dummies can be made up exactly as the finished item.

Cromalin proofs – The word 'Cromalin' is a trade name but is now commonly used to describe methods of photomechanical proofing. In short, a light sensitive laminate is applied to a base material. A film positive is laid on it and exposed to a bright light. The laminate is dusted with a powder dye (one for each process colour) and the excess is removed. This is repeated for each process colour. The final result is an accurate representation of the positives used.

Cromalins are quicker and cheaper than wet proofs provided that only one or two proofs are required. The nature of the proof itself, being on heavy duty paper, makes it very difficult for realistic dummies to be made up to show what the job will look like. Cromalins cannot be double-sided.

Ozalid proofs – In some respects ozalids are the most important proofs of all. They are taken at the platemaking stage and are a black and white representation of the images on the printing films. If any type of alterations have been made after the first proof, this is the last opportunity to examine corrections before the job goes to press. Corrections after this stage can prove very costly, particularly if a press is left to stand while the alteration is made and a new plate is made.

Digital proofs — These are now the preferred method of checking documents for the positioning and content of text, images and tints throughout the creative process.

The choice of proofing technology for a particular job can be made from a list which includes laser printer (or colour laser), liquid inkjet, solid inkjet, thermal wax, dye-sublimation and hybrid electro-photographic techniques.

In the professional desktop publishing market the technologies of dye-sublimation, inkjet and thermal wax provide the basis for mid-range proofing solutions. 3M have developed the Rainbow Proof (brand name), a dye-sublimation process meant to simulate the offset printing process with continuous tone output.

However, digital proofs still have some way to go before they become accepted as a 'proof to work to' by most commercial colour printers. But proofing technologies are constantly being developed and improved by the various manufacturers. It should not be too long before they become accepted as 'contract quality proofs'.

Things to check when passing a proof include:

- Register or fit

- Colour against transparency/illustration/colour artwork

- Read the copy

- Tint panels and headings

- Spotting

- Trim lines

- Make up a dummy and trim to size

The most important point about proofing is to stipulate the type of proofing you require, at the outset, as it can considerably affect the cost and time required for a job.

Step 6: Ready to run – the six printing methods

There are six printing processes in commercial use today, all of them employed in the direct mail business. They are:

1. Letterpress, including flexography (impact printing)

2. Photogravure

3. Silk-screen

2. Lithography: sheet-fed or web offset

3. Laser and inkjet

6. Digital offset colour

We now look briefly at each of the above: the differences and their chief applications.

Letterpress – Caxton's method

Letterpress is the oldest of the printing processes and is used nowadays exclusively for very short-run work such as business cards and formal invitations. The image is in relief, the ink is applied directly onto the plate ('forme' as it is called) and the print is taken from the forme itself. This is a classic example of impact printing.

Letterpress gives printing a particularly 'crisp' look which can enhance the 'olde worlde' prestige of very short-run productions. But for all other intents and purposes you will not be concerned with it in direct mail production.

Figure 8.4.4 **Letterpress – impact printing**

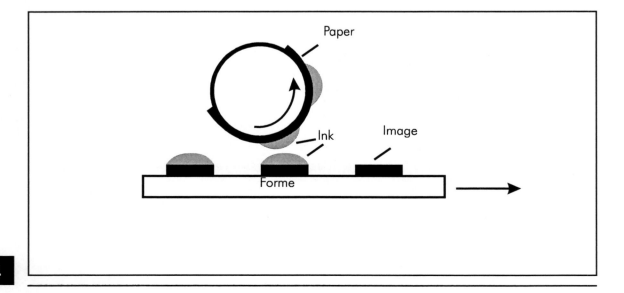

Flexography – modern impact printing

Flexography is the modern equivalent of the Dickensian letterpress process and is used for high volume packaging. The image is in relief on the printing forme which is inked by a roller. The paper passes between the inked forme and an impression cylinder and so picks up the image.

Figure 8.4.5 **Flexography – for volume packaging**

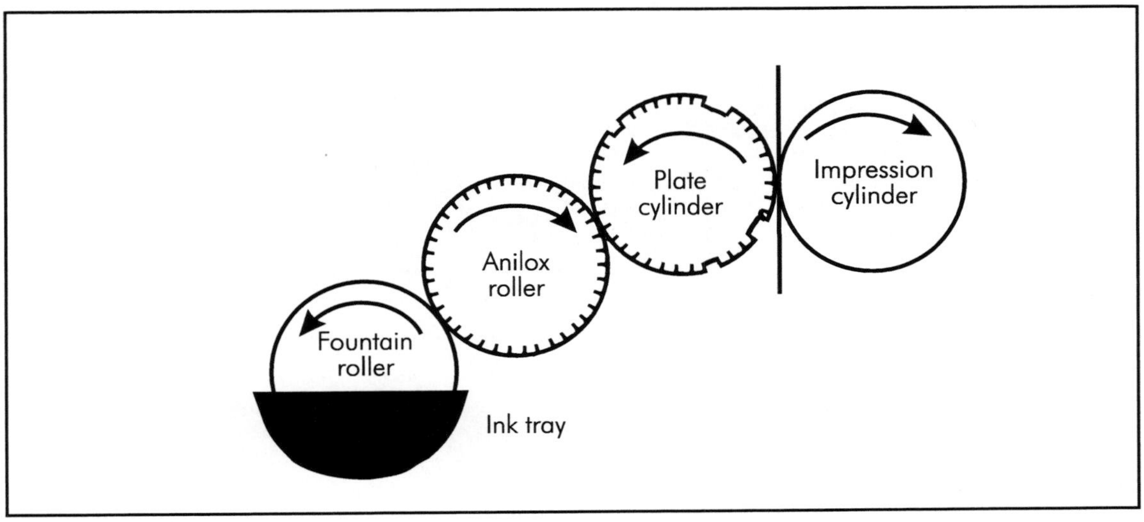

Photogravure – the multi-million method

Like all printing processes, photogravure is very simple in principle. The image areas are engraved into the surface of huge printing cylinders. The cylinders rotate in reservoirs of ink and surplus ink from the surface (non-image) areas of the cylinders is removed with a 'doctor blade'. This leaves ink in the 'cells' of the engraved cylinders, rather like honey in a bee's honeycomb, which has been rolled up with the open cells outwards.

As the paper comes into direct contact with the cylinders the ink is transferred. This takes place at extremely high speeds for each of the four colours, all colours being printed simultaneously.

Photogravure is mainly used for large volume magazine and catalogue production and can prove expensive on all but the very longest runs, as the cost of cylinder preparation is high.

Figure 8.4.6   **Photogravure – like a honeycomb**

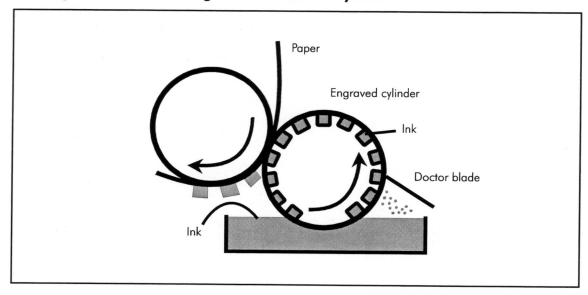

Silk-screen – a specialist technique

Silk-screen is another simple printing process and is based on the stencil method of printing. A material with a fine open weave (screen) is stretched across a frame. On top of that frame is a stencil which blocks out areas not required to print. Ink is poured into the frame and the frame is lowered onto the material to be printed. The ink is squeezed across the screen forcing the ink through the open weave not protected by the stencil. This is repeated for each colour.

In recent years rotary silk-screen machines have been developed. Silk-screen is used for short runs on virtually any material, eg plastic and glass. It is commonly used for posters and any work requiring a high density of solid colour, such as portfolio covers, gifts and novelties.

Figure 8.4.7   **Silk-screen – the stencil method**

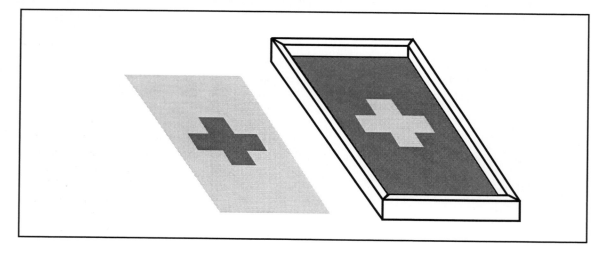

Lithography – the direct mailers' choice

Lithography is undoubtedly the most widely used printing process and the one with which all direct marketers should be familiar. Depending on volume there is a choice of two lithographic systems: sheet-fed and web offset. How they differ can be seen in the diagram overleaf.

Both systems are based on the principle that grease and water do not mix. The image on the plate surface is grease receptive, while the non-image area (background) is water receptive. To begin with, a film of moisture is applied to the plate surface and is attracted to the non-image areas and repelled by the greasy image area. This is immediately followed by a film of ink which is greasy in nature. The ink is attracted to the image area and is repelled by the non-image area covered in moisture.

The moisture evaporates to leave the ink behind to form the image. This is then transferred onto a rubber blanket and then onto the paper. This process is repeated for each of the printing colours. The plate is totally smooth, with the image neither raised nor engraved. Because the actual printing is via an intermediary 'blanket' and not direct from the plate – it is called offset litho.

Figure 8.4.8 **Litho – the principle**

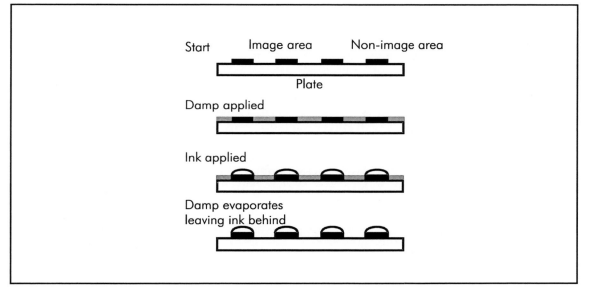

Sheet-fed litho – one sheet at a time

Sheet-fed presses print from flat-cut sheets and deliver flat-cut sheets. Such presses are capable of printing speeds up to 18,000 sheets per hour. They are most suitable for runs of up to 50,000 impressions but this very much depends on the sheet size of the press. Presses designed for packaging applications may well produce several hundred thousand impressions. Most sheet-fed machines print from 1 to 4 colours, one side only. Specialist machines can print more colours with varnishes and some can print both sides. Sheet-fed machines can also print the board weights used in packaging, an advantage over web offset which would otherwise prove to be cheaper.

Figure 8.4.9   **Sheet-fed litho**

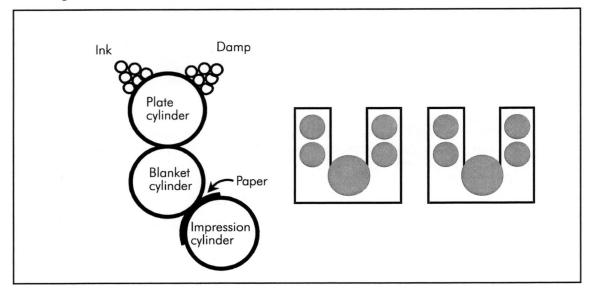

Web offset litho – from a continuous reel

Web offset presses print from a continuous reel of paper, usually in 4 colours and on both sides of the paper simultaneously. The ink is dried with hot air which tends to give a high gloss finish. Quick drying enables the web to be folded on press if, for example, 8 or 16 page sections are required. Some presses are fitted with in-line finishing which allows them to glue and perforate, make envelopes, and produce completely finished products at the end of the machine. Most of the novelty one-piece formats associated with direct mail are produced by this method.

Web presses can run at speeds approaching 40,000 impressions per hour and are suitable for runs of 50,000 up to several million.

Figure 8.4.10   **Web offset litho (printing on both sides)**

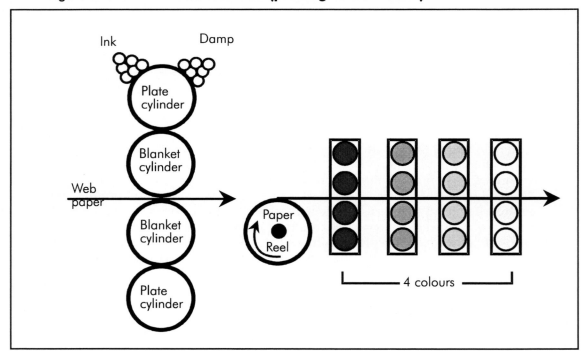

Sheet-fed and web – paper differences

The table below summarises the important differences between sheet-fed and web presses. Note that each type of press calls for its own paper sizes for maximum efficiency – one clear reason for consulting your print estimator before finalising your design and artwork.

Table 8.4.3

Litho printing presses – sizes and specifications		
	Size	**Specification**
SRA1 4-col sheet-fed	640 x 900	4 colours one side only
SRA2 4-col sheet-fed	450 x 640	4 colours one side only
8pp mini web	Cut off web width 630 x 505	4 colours both sides
16pp web	Cut off web width 630 x 965	4 colours both sides

There are several important points of difference between sheet-fed and web, as follows:

Sheet-fed

- Usually prints one side only

- Prints from flat-cut sheets

- Delivers flat sheets

- Ink has to dry before backing up, ie printing reverse

- Paper stocks from 70gsm to220gsm

Web offset

- Prints both sides simultaneously

- Prints from a reel of paper

- Delivers flat sheets or folded sections

- Ink is dried by hot air, ie heat-set

- Paper stocks from 52gsm – 180gsm

- Some presses can produce continuous stationery

Printing technology

Laser printing – the 21st Century method

Laser printing is an electronic printing process, but is closer to being a high speed computer process. Its use in direct mail is primarily to print letters by means of an online computer which 'tells' it specific information such as recipient's name and address. This feature is used for personalising letters, order forms etc.

Laser printing (and other forms of computer-directed printing such as inkjet) is frequently employed to in-fill data on preprinted items that have been produced by one of the conventional print methods described above. The production of print for subsequent laser printing comes within the scope of any printer geared towards direct mail.

Until recently personalised printing was confined to black and white reproduction achieved almost always by the dry toner method, similar to that used in photocopiers.

Note: Laser personalisation is covered in more detail in the previous chapter of this Guide.

Inkjet printing – spray printing dots of ink

Inkjet printing is the original electronic printing process. It differs from all the others in as much as it is a non-impact printing system. Electronically charged ink particles are sprayed onto the paper.

The simplest systems apply sell-by dates on foodstuff packaging and codes on inserts, while high-end versions produce fully personalised mailings at a quality that matches many laser printers. They key strengths of inkjet in this application are speed, versatility and cost, particularly when combined with in-line finishing technology.

Over the last few years inkjet has also developed as a colour imaging system for designers, desktop publishers and repro companies. Costs for these systems vary greatly depending on the intended application. Low-end colour printers used with Apple-Mac design stations can cost a few hundred pounds. High-end printers as used by a repro house to produce colour proofs can cost several thousand pounds. Similar high-end systems are used by some companies to produce short-run posters.

Digital offset – colour plus personalisation

Two key issues have influenced the development of printing technology over the last decade:

- The need for more targeted communications

- Shorter lead times and lower costs from design to print

Targeted communications

It is well-documented that personalised communications deliver higher response rates than non-personalised. Laser printers have been used to personalise mailings for many years. Laser printing technology for direct mail applications, though proven, only offers personalised text in one or two colours. The base stationery has to be preprinted by some other process before it is passed through the laser printer.

The ultimate concept is one-to-one marketing, which requires us to reach an individual customer with a personalised message. This quest is fast becoming a reality with digital printing technology – albeit at a price. However, with some users claiming response rates of between 10% and 20%, it is worth a closer examination.

As far as printed communications are concerned, digital technologies were first introduced in the early 90s.

One of the first digital colour presses was the Indigo E-Print 1000 launched in 1993. There are now seven or more manufacturers of digital printing presses, some of which have up to five models in their range.

The digitisation of printed communications

Over the last two decades, most organisations have invested in some form of desktop computers and or publishing equipment. These systems now allow users to send electronic files to other parts of their organisation or to printers. Today most printers receive well over 50% of their jobs in electronic form.

Digital technology enables images to be stored as digital files ('dots on disc') rather than film. Photographic images can be electronically scanned or downloaded onto a computer from digital cameras or photo CDs. Other images are created on the computer using various software packages. Once the data is loaded onto a computer it can be manipulated. After correction or modification, it can than be transmitted to a printing machine in another room or even in another country if an ISDN line is used.

In experienced hands this technology has the potential to provide a much quicker and cheaper route to market than the more traditional film based methods.

How a printer then converts the data into images on paper or other substrate depends entirely on what the communication is to be used for. Different machines have been developed for different types of printed products.

Digital printing presses

It would be quite wrong to view digital printing as a generic process. To be specific, digital printing is any printing completed via digital files. Digital printing machines can have very different methods of applying images to paper. Manufacturers each have their own view on the technological way forward.

Some are based on a process technology called xerography. Xerographic printing uses an electrostatic image that attracts powder toner. The toner is then transferred to the paper by electrostatic or direct physical means.

Others use a development of this process and use electrostatic inks rather than toner. The imaging cylinder is exposed with a laser beam, so establishing an image that attracts the liquid ink. The image is then transferred to a 'printing' cylinder and from there directly to the paper. The image is created from digital data that has been transferred from a computer. For each subsequent copy the imaging cylinder has to be 're-exposed' by the laser.

The computer can be programmed to create a different image for each copy to be printed. It could be argued that this notion is not new since laser printers have for many years offered this facility for personalised text.

The fundamental difference with this new technology is that it can also combine pictures and words. Some presses are designed to print in one colour only, others can print up to six colours.

Why use digital printing?

One-to-One

There are clear benefits in producing direct mail pieces with words and pictures that are relevant to the recipient only. However, few companies are likely to have a database that is individualised to such an extent. Even if it were, there are certain practical problems to consider:

- The creative costs for producing totally individual communications are likely to prove prohibitive, unless a very high-ticket item is being sold.

- Each mailpack would have to be checked and effectively signed off prior to printing.

- The cost and time implications of data preparation need to be considered.

Test marketing

There could be a case for using digital printing for testing different creative ideas. Quantities of 1,000 or less could be printed and mailed in order to establish which creative to adopt for the rollout – subject to the minimum required for statistical validity. However, if it were simply a question of testing different propositions, then digital printing would not show any particular cost advantages.

Fulfilment packs

In a two-stage campaign where fulfilment packs are mailed in response to off-the-page advertising, DRTV or inserts, digital printing may offer some advantages.

As digital printing also offers print on demand in very small quantities, it may be possible to print fulfilment packs at short notice when response levels to the advertising are known. The packs could be printed and mailed as necessary, so avoiding potential wastage.

For large ticket items, such as cars, totally unique mailings could be beneficial. If a consumer has shown interest in a specific model and colour/trim combination, it is possible to print a single brochure for that particular customer.

On the other hand, it is most unlikely that a catalogue of 'hand-picked' products targeted at one person would ever cover its costs, whereas to a group of 500, it may do.

As in all aspects of direct marketing, a cost/benefit analysis should be carefully undertaken to avoid using technology just because it's there!

Figure 8.4.11 **Digital printing**

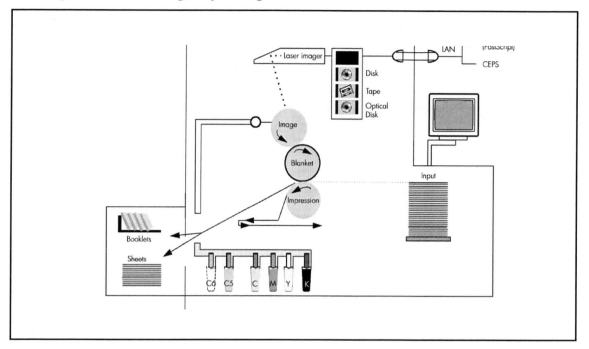

Step 7: Finishing

Once items have been printed they have to be cut and folded for end use. On certain products re-moist gumming and perforations may be added. In many instances this forms part of the finishing process, although these features can be incorporated while printing on specialist machines designed for volume production. Ask your printer for details of his finishing capacity when making your initial enquiry.

Table 8.4.4

Some everyday print finishing terms	
Saddle stitching	Wire staples used to hold multi-page sections together
Spine glueing	Multiple pages glued together rather than saddle stitched
Re-moist glue	Applied glue for self-seal application forms or envelope flaps
Impact glue	Applied glue for making up envelopes or glueing two sheets together to form postcards
Pattern perforating	Perforating in any direction or shape
Trimming	Cutting leaflets or brochures to a finished size
Die-cutting	Cutting leaflets or pages of a brochure into an irregular shape
In-line finishing	Products that are folded and trimmed on press – very sophisticated formats can be produced this way (see following page for examples)
Off-line finishing	Similar features as above but produced from flat sheets after printing

Step 8 : Delivery

Unless specified otherwise a printer will quote ex works. It is important to be specific about your delivery address and number of 'drops' if you want an accurate costing. Note, with insert campaigns (where delivery may be direct from printer to publisher), delivery can prove to be quite an expensive item with quantities of print being despatched to various magazines around the country. It is not uncommon for such a campaign to be spread across 30 or more destinations.

Figure 8.4.12

Examples of finished formats

The examples below cover almost all formats in everyday use. In the case of high-volume print runs using web offset presses, these formats can be produced on the machine, ie in one "pass" and can include glueing and perforation etc.

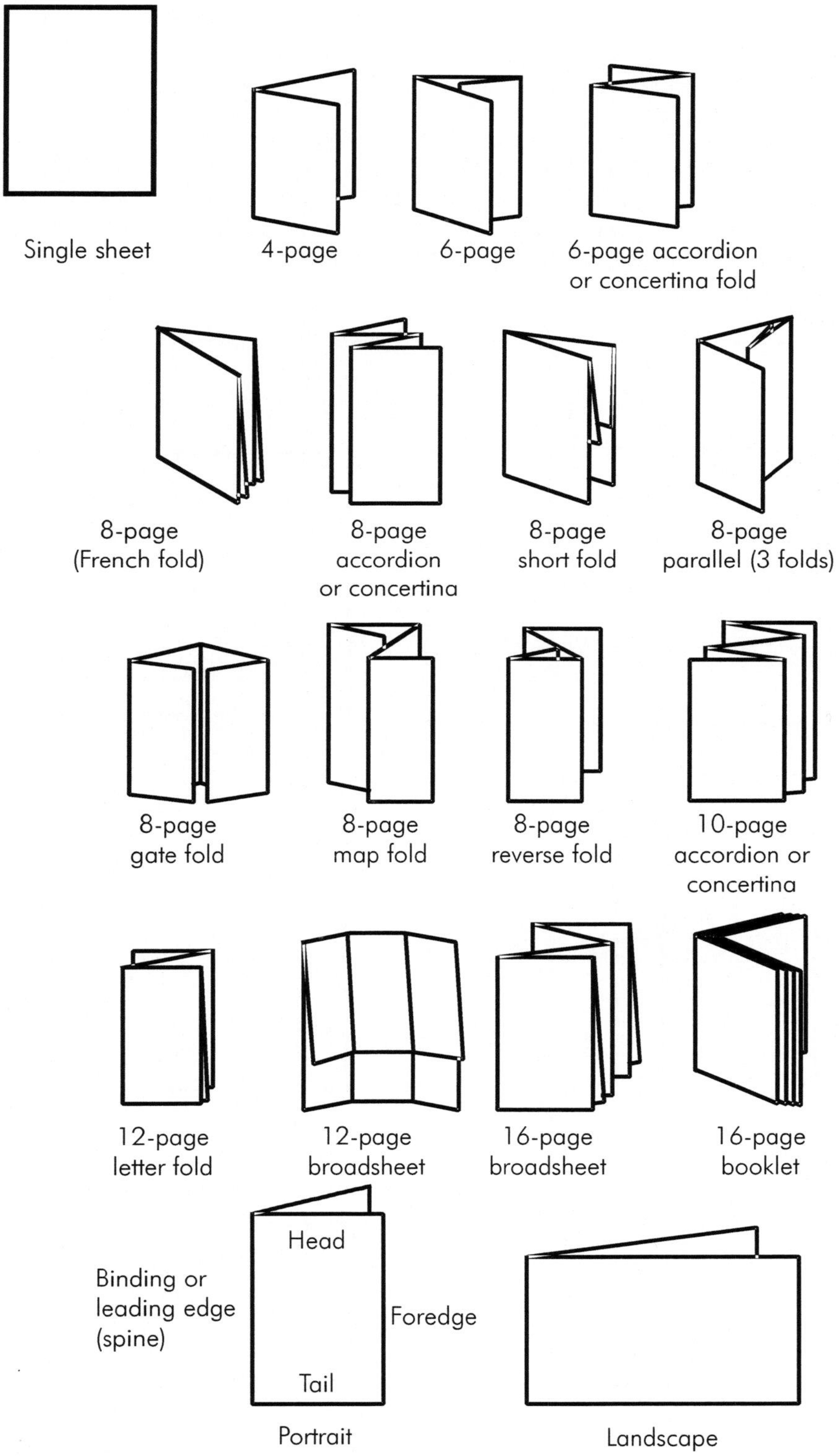

Single sheet	4-page	6-page	6-page accordion or concertina fold

8-page (French fold)	8-page accordion or concertina	8-page short fold	8-page parallel (3 folds)

8-page gate fold	8-page map fold	8-page reverse fold	10-page accordion or concertina

12-page letter fold	12-page broadsheet	16-page broadsheet	16-page booklet

Binding or leading edge (spine)

Head

Foredge

Tail

Portrait

Landscape

Envelopes for direct mail

The most common envelopes in use in direct marketing are DL (to fit A4 folded twice) and C5 (A4 folded once). C4 (to fit A4 flat) envelopes are used on occasion. Outside of those stock sizes are bespoke envelopes, made to whatever size you require.

Envelopes can be printed in up to 4 colours. With large volume, production envelopes are printed and manufactured on a machine that accepts reels of white paper and delivers finished printed envelopes. Smaller quantities are produced by either overprinting stock envelopes or printing in flat sheets and making them up as a separate operation.

A special making of envelopes can take 6-8 weeks to deliver. Overprinted stock envelopes can be produced in 10-14 days but are more expensive. When envelopes are filled at a mailing house they are often filled by machine. These machines require 'machine insertable' envelopes if they are to run at maximum speed. This should be borne in mind when envelopes are being ordered.

Figure 8.4.13

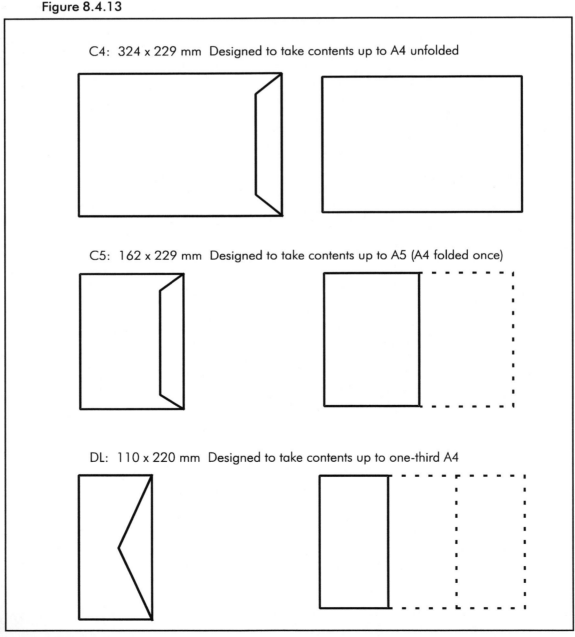

C4: 324 x 229 mm Designed to take contents up to A4 unfolded

C5: 162 x 229 mm Designed to take contents up to A5 (A4 folded once)

DL: 110 x 220 mm Designed to take contents up to one-third A4

Table 8.4.5

Leaflets – 50,000 +		
Important: In the majority of instances, due to the size and quantity required, paper is rarely available from stock. Therefore we have to order the requirement direct from the manufacturers. Much of the UK's paper is made in Scandinavia, which requires approximately four weeks lead time.		
Day 1	Receipt of artwork.	Required by midday.
Day 2		Proofs sent out overnight.
Day 3	Proofs to client 10am.	Approval/Amends required 4pm.
Day 4	am we to amend.	Proofs sent out overnight.
Day 5	Reproof to client 10am.	Approval required 4pm.
Day 6	Film to printer.	Final Ozalid proof sent out overnight.
Day 7	Final Ozalid proof to client 10am.	Final Ozalid proof approved.
Day 8	Commence printing and folding/finishing.	On most products we would expect to complete approx. 500,000 copies per day.
Day 9/10	Commence delivery.	Dependent on quantity we will notify quantity available.

Table 8.4.6

Direct mailpack schedule (simple)		
Simple mail pack i.e. C5 outer, A4 or A3 stationery, t's & c's, BRE + flyer, simple laser up to four versions/letter variants per nationality.		
Day 1	Receipt of artwork (With sample pack mock up).	Required by midday.
Day 1	Receipt of letter text.	Required by midday.
Day 1	Complete DATA required.	Required by midday.
Day 2		Colour proofs sent out overnight.
Day 2		Data dumps sent out overnight.
Day 3	Colour proofs to client 10am.	Approval required 4pm.
Day 3	Data dumps to client 10am.	Approval required 4pm.
Day 4	We to make any colour proof amends.	Proofs sent out overnight.
Day 5	Reproof to client 10am.	Approval required 4pm.
Day 6	Film to printer.	
Day 7	Commence printing.	
Day 7	Produce live lasers.	Sent out overnight.
Day 8	Live lasers to client 10am.	Comments required 3pm.
Day 8/9	Corrections made to laser proofs, this can take up to 24 hours.	Whenever possible we will fax the corrections but often this is not possible due to size of font i.e. caveats, in which case we will send overnight.
Day 10	Revised laser proofs to client 10am. Delivery of all additional inserts and envelopes required.	Final approval required 2pm. Note; If we receive further corrections this will result in delay.
Day 11	Commence lasering	
Day 12	Commence enclosing.	
Day 13	Commence mailing	Commence mailing. Quantity TBA dependent on complexity of product.**
** Mailing schedule subject to total quantity and complexity of product.		

Print buying – the three key issues

There are several thousand printers in the UK without looking to Europe. Apart from a few specialist printers they all do much the same thing – put ink on paper.

However, some do it on a larger scale than others, some do it cheaper, some do it faster. Your choice of printer should be based on three considerations:

1. Quality of service

2. Quality of product

3. Price

Price should always be the last of your three considerations. The cheapest quote can easily become the most expensive job if it does not arrive on time and to the required standard.

It is important to develop a close working relationship with your suppliers. There is a trend towards 'partner' relationships between client and supplier which began in the early 1990s, with organisations working with 'preferred' suppliers only.

Good communication is the key to a good working relationship. Poor communications between parties will lead to jobs being produced inefficiently.

Every job should begin with a well specified request for a quotation. If the job changes in specification or timing (as is often the case), then this should be re-evaluated by both parties, with revised costs and schedules submitted. This will ensure that the job is produced to specification, on time, and most importantly – to budget.

A good supplier should also act as an adviser and suggest alternative production approaches when appropriate.

Choosing your print supplier

We said earlier that not all jobs are suitable for the same printer. It is important to establish at the outset what each potential supplier is capable of.

Below is a checklist of questions to ask yourself and your short-listed printer before you hand over the job:

Table 8.6.7

Ten questions to ask about a printer:
Are they recognised by the appropriate trade bodies, ie BPIF or DMA?
Do they have appropriate equipment and capacity for your work?
What are their materials handling and storage facilities like?
Is there a general air of tidiness and efficiency about their works?
What experience do the sales and estimating staff have?
Who would be the day-to-day account handlers?
How do they handle production supervision and quality control?
Do they understand your product and its uses?
Are they financially stable?
Are there any client references and samples of previous work available to be seen?
Are they ISO 9000 accredited? (For a description of ISO 9000 see chapter on Fulfilment.)

Chapter 8.5

Using mailing shops

This chapter includes:

- ❑ **Typical mailing house services**
- ❑ **Case study introduction**
- ❑ **Planning your mailing campaign**
- ❑ **Printing**
- ❑ **Data processing**
- ❑ **Formatting**
- ❑ **Variable printing**
- ❑ **Finishing**
- ❑ **Enclosing**
- ❑ **And so to recap**

About this chapter

n the long process of planning, creating and executing a campaign, the mailing shop is at the end of the line. If the project is running behindhand in the planning or creative stage, it will be the mailing shop that will be expected to pick up the pieces and ensure that the original schedule is nonetheless met. Mailing shops are well accustomed to this – but if they are to be effective they require proper advance briefing on just what is required of them. Such briefing can only be adequately given by client (or agency) personnel who understand the mailing shop's potential, as well as the client's needs. This understanding is the aim of the present chapter to impart.

Author/Consultant: Mike Hughes

Mike Hughes, Chief Executive, Mail Marketing International

Mike joined Mail Marketing in 1989 having studied Electrical, Electronic and Mechanical Engineering, Computer Sciences and enjoying a spell in the IT industry. Mike has subsequently trained at the London College Of Print.

Today Mail Marketing can produce in excess of 8 million mailpacks per week from its state of the art facilities in Bristol and Weston-Super-Mare.

Direct mail has seen huge innovation over the last 50 years since Vera Hughes founded the business and, with the introduction of digital colour personalisation, the opening up of the postal distribution market and ever increasing levels of data processing power, the next 50 years promises to be just as innovative as the last. Direct mail continues to re-invent itself as a leading communication media.

Mike is also very active in a number of trade associations and is the Chairman of the Bristol District Association of the British Printing Industries Federation.

When Mike isn't producing mail he loves nothing more than spending time with his wife Sue and his two young children, Jack and Rebekah, enjoying the Somerset countryside where they live.

Mike Hughes M IDM
Chief Executive
Mail Marketing International Limited
Springfield House
West Street
Bedminster
Bristol
BS3 3NX

Tel: 0117 9666900
E-mail: mike.hughes@mailmarketinginternational.co.uk

Chapter 8.5

Using mailing shops

Typical mailing house services

In the 1950s mailing houses employed typists and handworkers to produce the mail from customers' paper sales ledgers and lists.

The mailing industry is almost unrecognisable from these humble beginnings as it rides the wave of IT innovation and automation. Many of the processes have been fully automated enabling reduced unit costs, fast turnaround, high volumes, and sophisticated personalisation. As a result mailing houses bring together print, paper handling and IT skills and bind these disciplines together through skilled project managers.

Many mailing houses can provide a 'full service' to organisations wishing to communicate with their customer (or potential customer) base.

The following list gives a summary of the types of services on offer from a modern mailing house.

Pre Production Services

✔ Strategic planning

✔ Pack design

✔ List acquisition and management

✔ Data processing

✔ Artwork production

Production Services

✔ Project management

✔ Stationery printing

✔ Personalisation

✔ Finishing

✔ Addressing

✔ Plastic cards production

✔ Self mailer production

✔ Tipping

✔ Envelope enclosing

✔ Polythene enclosing

Distribution Services

✔ Receipt and quality inspection of goods

✔ Storage

✔ Sortation

✔ Consolidation

✔ Postal despatch and management

✔ Product despatch (parcels)

Many mailing houses can also provide response handling and product fulfilment services in addition to the lettershop services.

Case study introduction

The following example campaign will be referred to throughout this chapter to illustrate how each activity within the production process will be managed.

Speedy Direct Cars is a car dealership exclusively marketing cars direct. The campaign is intended to promote their range of vehicles to names obtained from various lifestyle databases. Recipients can apply for a written quotation by using an application form and reply envelope included with the mailing. Applicants will also be entered into a prize draw with a chance of winning a new car.

In order to make the campaign more personal and relevant to each recipient, Speedy Direct has decided to mail out 5 different pack types dependent on the recipients' presumed preferences. The database will therefore be profiled to categorise each recipient with a preference of sports, cruiser, economy, 4x4 or family vehicles.

Each pack will contain the following:

- *Personalised A4 letter*

- *Personalised A4 application form*

- *8pp A5 Colour leaflet*

- *C6 Business Reply Envelope*

- *C5 Window outer envelope*

The letter and application form preprint will be similar for the entire campaign with letter text varied according to the category of the recipient, ie 'You could be a winner of a new sports car' or 'Your family could enjoy the luxury of a new family car'.

There will also be a version of the brochure for each category.

Planning your mailing campaign

For all but the smallest and simplest mailings it is useful to produce a production process map, also referred to as a critical path analysis, detailing all the processes to be undertaken. In this way you can ensure that nothing is forgotten.

The use of planning tools, such as Microsoft Project, can assist in the process and allow you to communicate your plans to your chosen mailing house, printers and other suppliers.

The diagram below shows the production process map for the Speedy Cars example detailed earlier in this chapter.

Figure 8.5.1   **Example of a critical path for a mailing campaign**

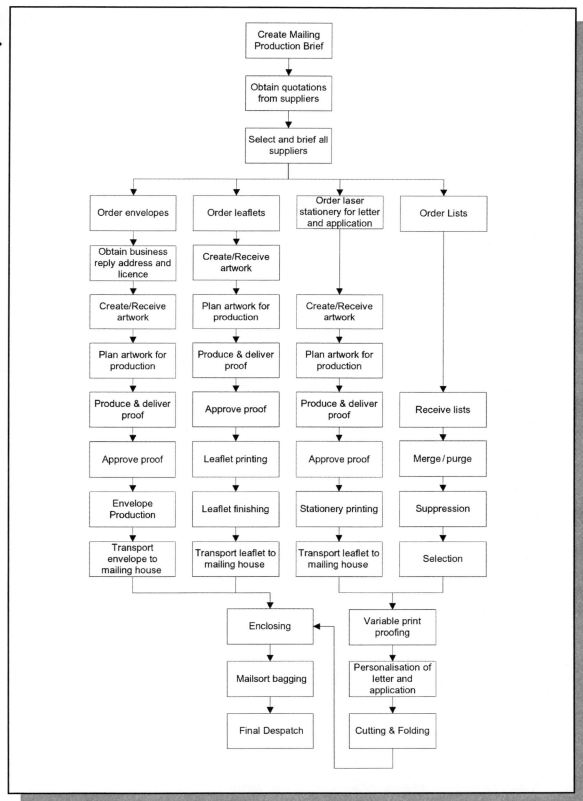

Consider carefully how much time will be required for each task within the production process and consult with suppliers when you are uncertain.

Always allow adequate time for transportation of materials between the various suppliers. Proofs will also need to be sent for your approval and returned to the mailing house or printers.

Mailing campaign briefs should also contain a Mailing Matrix and Printing Matrix which are discussed later in this chapter.

REMEMBER GOOD PLANNING AND COMMUNICATION IS THE KEY TO SUCCESSFUL DELIVERY OF A MAILING CAMPAIGN

Printing

Most printing for mailing purposes is produced using offset lithography, with some envelope printing using flexography. Lithography offers the highest quality results required to make the best of the highly graphical content of leaflets, letters, envelopes, brochures, flyers and self-mailers.

Shorter runs are produced on sheet fed presses and longer runs (250,000 plus) using web and continuous presses. Drying systems can also be employed on the presses to accelerate the drying process. Heat-set presses use gas fired ovens which

can reduce the humidity of the paper to levels lower than that acceptable to laser printers. In order to overcome this problem UV drying is used instead; this technology minimises the amount of heat in the drying process and is recommended for printing laser stationery.

The picture shows a continuous stationery press.

Colour

Colour can be reproduced using spot colours or process colours or a combination of both.

Spot colours are produced by pre-mixing inks to the exact colour required. Some colours can only be produced this way, such as metallics. Spot colours guarantee consistency of colour and are therefore also used for corporate colour schemes.

Combining cyan, magenta, yellow and black in varying amounts can be used to reproduce a wide spectrum of colours. The use of these four colours is commonly referred to as *process printing*. Process printing is used to reproduce photographs and illustrations.

As process printing is used extensively for the production of highly graphical direct mail literature, most other items to be printed are also produced from process colours; however, if a particular colour is highly sensitive, such as a corporate logo, then spot colour and process colour printing can be combined.

The printing industry has adopted the Pantone system for specifying colours. Pantone colour books are published with examples of a whole spectrum of colours, each with is own individual Pantone, or PMS reference.

The picture shows a Pantone book.

Not all colours published in a Pantone book can be reproduced using process printing, requiring additional spot colour to be printed. Where possible select a colour scheme that can be reproduced using process colours.

Paper

Many paper merchants and printers work to standard sheet sizes based on a system devised by the International Organisation for Standardisation (ISO). Wherever practical it makes economic sense to conform to these sizes. Paper mills will produce bespoke sizes for very large orders.

Figure 8.5.2   **ISO paper sizes**

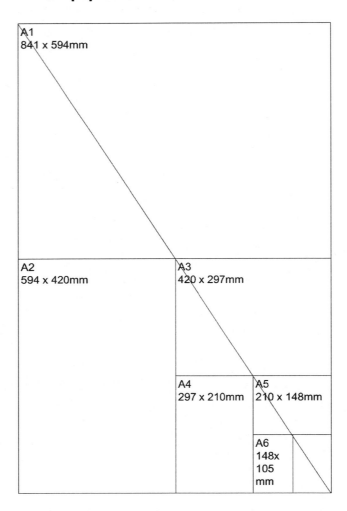

There are many different types of paper reflecting the wide variety of printed products. The following are the most common papers used in direct mail:

Banks, bonds and cartridge -   These have matt surfaces and are often used for letterheads and order forms

Coated art papers -   These have glossy surfaces, used for leaflet, catalogue and brochure production

Boards -   Used for reply cards, brochure covers etc.

Each of these can be supplied in many different grades, with textured surfaces, watermarks and colour tints, so that marketers have a large variety of materials to choose from.

The most cost effective papers are those held as stock papers by your printer; over papers are available at additional cost. Some specialist papers can be more than twice the cost of stock grades. Ask your printer which stock papers they have on offer.

Laser printers can only use compatible paper and therefore it will be necessary to produce letterheads and application forms from suitable papers. A wide range of laser compatible papers are available.

Envelopes

There is a range of envelope sizes to match ISO paper sizes. A C5 envelope will carry an A5 insert for instance. The following diagram shows standard envelope sizes:

Figure 8.5.3

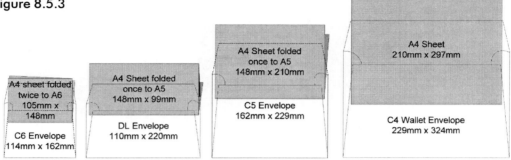

Envelopes can be supplied as wallets where the flap is on the long edge, or pockets where the flap is on the short edge as illustrated below. High speed enclosing machines generally can only enclose into wallet envelopes!

Figure 8.5.4

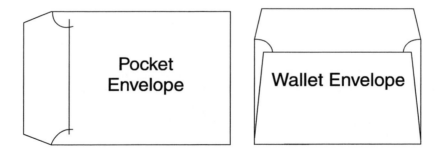

Envelopes can also be supplied as self-seal or with gummed flaps. Self-seal is preferable for hand enclosing, but if you are machine enclosing, then you *must* specify gummed flaps.

If you are unsure whether envelopes are being used for hand or machine enclosing then always specify a wallet envelope with gummed flap as this can be used for both.

Envelopes will need to be overprinted with the Postage Paid Impression (PPI) and return address and can also include much more extensive artwork to include marketing messages, pictures and illustrations.

Overprinting can take place prior to, during, or after the envelopes have been made. Long runs of more than 100,000 are usually printed prior to or during the envelope making process, while short runs are achieved by overprinting stock envelopes.

The following diagram is a guide to be used when choosing and specifying envelopes:

Figure 8.5.5

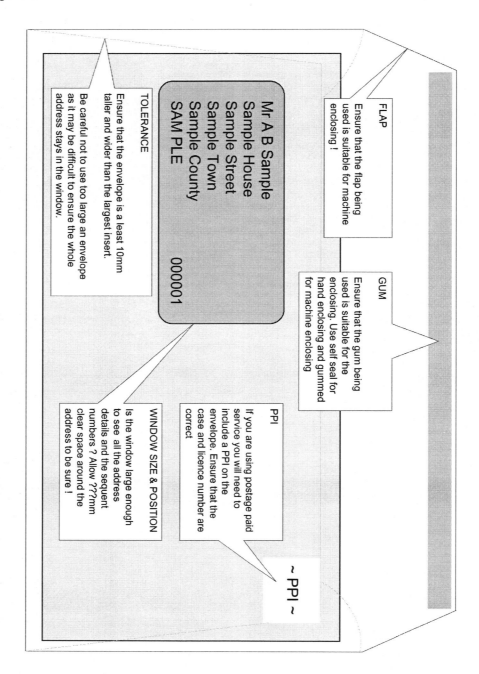

Weight

Postage costs are directly affected by the weight of the finished mailpack and therefore it is critical that these are estimated at the planning stage. The following formulae can be used to calculate the weight of each printed item:

Finished size (m²) * Extent * Paper weight (gsm) = weight in grams

The extent of the item is measured in leaves of paper. For example, an 8pp brochure contains 4 leaves of paper. For envelopes allow the equivalent of 2 leaves + 15% for flaps and seams, giving an equivalent of 2.3 leaves.

The table below shows a worked example for calculating the pack weight for the Speedy Cars campaign detailed earlier in this chapter:

Table 8.5.1

Item	Size (metres)	Leaves	Paper weight	Item weight (rounded up to the nearest gram)
Letterhead	A4 = 0.297x0.21	1	100gsm	7 grams
Application form	A4 = 0.297x0.21	1	100gsm	7 grams
Colour leaflet	A5 = 0.21x0.1485	4	135gsm	17 grams
Outer envelope	C5 = 0.299x0.162	2.3	90gsm	10 grams
BRE envelope	C6 = 0.114x0.162	2.3	80gsm	4 grams
			TOTAL PACK WEIGHT	45 grams

Make-ready and overs

All production processes incur an amount of waste and scrap in the set-up and running of every job. It is critical that an allowance is made for this waste when ordering stationery, in order that there is enough good product to fulfil the full mailing requirement.

The following table can be used as a guide for calculating the additional quantity required when ordering stationery for a mailing campaign:

Table 8.5.2

Mailing quantity	Personalised inserts	Over inserts	Envelopes
<10k	10% + 1,500	5% + 1,000	5% + 1000
>10k	7.5% + 1,500	4% + 1,000	5% + 1000
>50k	7.5%	7.5%	5%
>100k	5%	5%	5%
>500k	3.5%	3%	5%
>1m+	3%	3%	5%

Where there is complex finishing required then additional make-ready and overs will be needed; always consult with your mailing house to ensure that there is a large enough allowance.

Reprints are very expensive, even for short volumes, due to the additional make-ready costs associated with rerunning a job. Furthermore, there may not be adequate time to print additional stationery, so always be as generous as is economically possible with make-ready and overs.

Artwork

Artwork typically contains a mixture of copy (text), photographs, illustrations, lines and tints which are all assembled together in the desktop publishing system, such as Quark Express, Corel Draw and Pagemaker, to form final artwork.

Electronic artwork is very easy to copy and transport via tape, disk, ISDN and Internet. Make sure that all elements are sent to the printer, including pictures, fonts, DTP files etc.

The printing industry has adopted Quark Express using Apple computers as the standard for receipt and manipulation of artwork. If you use any other system then you must check with the printer to ensure that your requirements can be handled.

Remember to include all pictures, fonts and DTP files and a low-resolution print when sending artwork to the printer.

Print proofing

Proofing is a critical part of the production process; it confirms that the artwork sent to the mailing house/printer has been received and interpreted correctly.

The following proofing methods can be used:

Soft	Soft proofs are files which can be displayed and inspected on a computer. PDF and XML file formats are commonly used for soft proofing.
Digital	Digital proofs are produced on digital printers calibrated to give similar results to the final production process.
Film	Film proofs are produced from the film that will be produced to make the plates. Cromalin and Matchprint proofs are both examples of film proofs.
Wet	Wet proofs are produced using the same plates, ink and paper that will be used in the final production process, but use a proofing press specially designed to produce very short runs at low cost, compared to the live production equipment.
Machine	Machine proofs are produced on the same equipment as the final job and will therefore give the most accurate depiction of the final product.

Not so many years ago machine and wet proofing were the only sure way of producing a proof that accurately depicted the final product. They are expensive and time consuming as both film and plates must be produced prior to proofing. This is compounded further if corrections are subsequently required, as film and plates will need to be reproduced again, adding hundreds of pounds of additional cost to a job.

Produce a soft or digital proof as the first proof; this can then be checked to ensure that the copy, pictures, lines, tints and page layout are correct. These proofs are cheap and quick to produce, so alterations and reproofing is cost effective.

When satisfied that the soft or digital proof is correct then produce a film, or wet proof to check the colour and materials. Wet proofs are more expensive and will take longer to produce, however they do have the added benefit of allowing multiple copies to be easily produced, while film proofing does not. This may be necessary if a large number of people need to be consulted in order to obtain production approval.

Machine proofing is very uncommon as it is very expensive and can only be produced when a production slot becomes available on the live production equipment.

The final approved proof is a legal document, and is sometimes referred to as a Contract Proof. It will be used should a dispute arise, due to the quality of the final product. Therefore, pay particular attention to the final proof, checking every detail prior to approving it. Use the check list below to help you:

✔ Spelling and grammar

✔ Correct dates are being used (especially offer begin and end dates)

✔ Cropping and position of photographs and illustrations

✔ Colours match 'corporate standards' where these apply

✔ Correct fonts being used

✔ The finished item fits inside the outer envelope being used

✔ A stationery code has been included on every printed item

Allow enough time in the campaign schedule for proofs to be produced, corrections to be made and final approval to be obtained. For a typical direct mail campaign allow at least one week.

Printing matrix

A mailing matrix is a useful tool for identifying and keeping track of all the printed items required for a mailing campaign. To follow is an example printing matrix for Speedy Direct Cars.

Table 8.5.3 **Printing matrix for Speedy Direct Cars**

Item code	Description	Mailing qty	Overs	Print qty	Paper	Printer	Progress
LEAFLETS							
LSPO	6pp A4 Sports car colour brochure	25,000	2,000+5%	28,250	CELESTIAL -100 GSM	MM	Approved
LCRU	6pp A4 Cruising car colour brochure	25,000	2,000+5%	28,250	CELESTIAL -100 GSM	MM	Approved
LECO	8pp A4 Economy car colour brochure	25,000	2,000+5%	28,250	CELESTIAL -100 GSM	AQUA	Approved
L44	8pp A4 4x4 car colour brochure	25,000	2,000+5%	28,250	CELESTIAL -100 GSM	AQUA	Approved
LFAM	8pp A4 Family car colour brochure	25,000	2,000+5%	28,250	CELESTIAL -100 GSM	MM	Approved
ENVELOPES							
E01	C5 Window wallet outer	150,000	1,000+5%	157,500	BRANDIA 90gsm	COMPACT	Approved
B01	C6 BRE with standard return address	150,000	1,000+5%	157,500	BRANDIA 70gsm	COMPACT	Awaiting proof
LASER STATIONERY							
FLET	Combined A4 letter + A4 application form	300,000	3,000+5%	318,000	LUMIART 115 GSM	MM	Awaiting proof

Printing check list

✔ Set up a printing matrix identifying all items required for the mailing campaign

✔ Specify the paper types and weights to be used

✔ Check the overall pack weight

✔ Ensure all stationery to be laser overprinted has been specified to be laser compatible

✔ Ensure that all inserts fit within the outer envelope specified

✔ Include a unique stationery code on each item of stationery

✔ Increase printing quantities to allow for make-ready and overs

✔ Remember to include all pictures, fonts and DTP files and a low-resolution print when sending artwork

✔ Use the envelope guide to check envelopes

✔ Include the correct PPI on the envelope as required

✔ Allow enough time in the production schedules for proofing and corrections

✔ Discuss your requirements with the chosen printers and keep them up to date with any changes

Data processing

The flow chart below shows the data processing activities required for Speedy Direct Cars detailed earlier in this chapter. Two lists are purchased and then various data processing tasks are carried out until, finally a live data file is out-put for sports, cruiser, economy, 4x4 or family vehicle promotions. This will be necessary, as a different brochure and personalised letter text will be used dependent on the promotion type.

The following are more detailed descriptions of each data processing activity.

Loading and converting data

Mailing houses receive data from many different customers using many different systems. All data must be loaded into the mailing house data processing system and, as there are few standards which apply to the data being received, the data is converted to a standard format for subsequent processing. In order to ensure the data received is interpreted correctly a data layout guide should accompany every data file.

An example of the Speedy Direct Cars data layout guide is shown overleaf:

Table 8.5.4

Structure for table:	E:\DATAIN\SPEEDY_DIRECT
Number of records:	150,000
Last update:	12:52

Field number	Field name	Type	Width
1	MMSENQNO	Character	7
2	ACCOUNT_NO	Character	8
3	TITLE	Character	4
4	FORENAME	Character	25
5	SURNAME	Character	30
6	ADDRESS1	Character	40
7	ADDRESS2	Character	40
8	ADDRESS3	Character	40
9	TOWN	Character	40
10	CITY	Character	40
11	POSTCODE	Character	8
12	CONTACT	Character	50
13	SALUTATION	Character	50
14	CATEGORY	Character	1

Example data processing flowchart

Figure 8.5.6

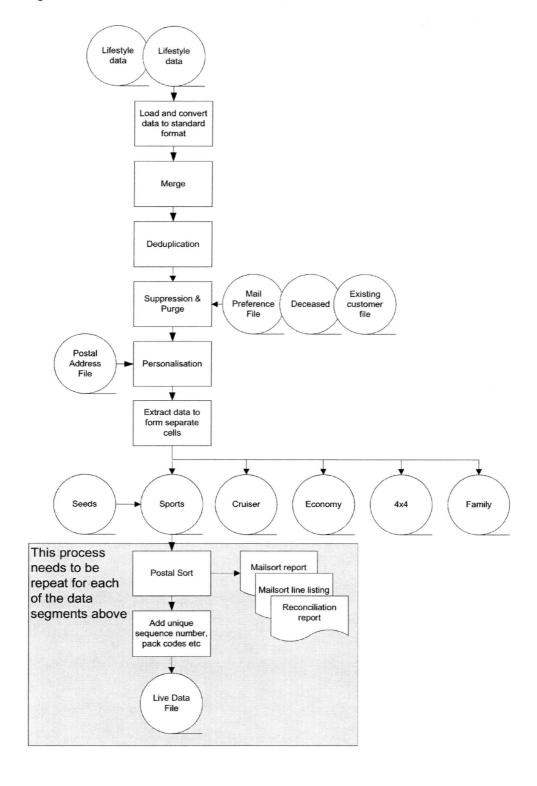

Merging and deduplication

A number of databases may be combined to form one database used for the campaign, such as an in-house customer database and a rented list from a 3rd party. The process of combining the database together is referred to as merging.

Names and addresses may well be duplicated on the various databases being merged and therefore an additional process of deduplication is recommended. Deduplication can be very sophisticated due to the various ways in which names and address can be expressed.

The addresses below are example duplicates:

Mr. M Smith
The Barrows
12 Burtle Road
Edgetown
Somerset
BS22 6DY

Mike Smith
12 Burtle Road
Edgetown
Bristol
BS22 6DY

Both these addresses are correct and would result in two mailings being sent to Mr Smith; however, they are not exactly the same and therefore require sophisticated logic to recognise the same addressee.

Sending duplicate mailings is, at best, a waste of stationery, production and postage cost and at worst can cause insult to your target audience and result in your mailing being thrown away unopened. It has been known for there to be in excess of 50% duplication of names and addresses when a number of databases are merged.

Suppression

Industry guidelines require some names and addresses to be excluded from direct mail campaigns. It will be necessary to suppress any excluded address from your database in order that you comply.

The following table lists databases available for suppressing names and addresses:

Table 8.5.5

MPS	Mailing Preference Service scheme. People on this database have specifically asked not to receive direct mail.
Read GAS	The Gone Away Database available from the ReaD Group contains names and addresses of people who no longer live at the addresses listed.
Mortascreen	Contains details of all deceased persons in England, Wales, and Scotland whose estates have gone to probate.
The Bereavement Register	A register of people who have died, available from ReaD Group.

As with deduplication, suppression names and addresses are not always exact matches so 'fuzzy logic' is used to increase the suppression rates.

People who have specifically asked not to receive direct mail, and bereaved relatives will take offence when receiving direct mail. This may result as adverse publicity so always instruct the mailing house to suppress these names from your mailing.

In the Speedy Direct Cars example both the Mailing Preference Service and deceased suppression files are used. In addition however, Speedy Direct want to ensure that existing customers' names are also suppressed from the list, as they have a different range of promotions which will apply to them.

Personalisation

Personalisation is the creation of new personalised fields within the database by the manipulation of existing data. This is best demonstrated by the creation of a salutation from the given name and address. For example "Mr M Smith" could be manipulated to create the salutation, "Dear Mr Smith."

A database is available of 8 million people who have moved addresses. Using this database and comparing it to the existing data supplied, it is possible to update the existing data where the name and address is out of date, with the new name and address.

Data cleansing

There are a number of processes which can be used to clean up data files, ensuring that addresses are correct with full postal town and postcodes. This may be required when using discounted prepaid postal products such as Mailsort where most addresses must be postcoded in order for discounts to be claimed.

It is common for people to alter their address to give the impression that they live in a more affluent area than they actually do, or to add house names where they are not officially registered. Using data cleansing techniques may well correct these addresses but may cause offence to the addressee.

Extracting/splitting data

Data can be split into separate files, referred to as cells, segments or batches. This is often used to segregate data that will have different inserts, base stationery or delivery dates.

The Speedy Direct Cars campaign uses different brochures and letter text for each category of promotion (ie sport, 4x4 etc.) and therefore it will be necessary to segregate the file accordingly, in order that each promotion can be managed separately in the subsequent production processes.

Postal sort

Maximum postal discounts are obtained by sorting the post according to its postal destination. Postal distributors, such as the Royal Mail, offer a number of discounted direct mail products such as Mailsort, Walksort and Packetsort. Each scheme has specific rules that apply and you should refer to your postal provider for fuller details of the schemes they have to offer.

Sortation routines produce a number of reports that will be required by the postal provider to give evidence that the sort has been carried out correctly. Mailsort requires a Mailsort statistics report, line listing and postal dockets to be produced and submitted with the mail, and for the mail to be batched according to postal delivery points and banded, bagged and caged in accordance with the Mailsort requirements.

Unique sequence numbers

The addition of unique sequence numbers to each record within the files produced is the only sure way to guarantee accurate reconciliation of the final personalised piece and its corresponding database record.

Formatting

Formatting brings together variable data with fixed text and graphics to produce final print stream to print the variable letter text.

Word processors incorporate simple mail merge applications that can be used for relatively small and simple campaigns with limited personalisation requirements. However, for large volumes or complex personalisation requirements, far more sophisticated tools are used such as DOC1 (from Group One), PReS (from PrintSoft) or PrintNet (from GMC).

These tools use a preparatory programming language specifically designed for creating a highly personalised print stream. The set of instructions used by these systems is commonly referred to as a script.

Should the mailing requirement be even more sophisticated than it can be produced using DOC1, PReS or PrintNet, then a bespoke program will need to be produced to format the data. This is costly and usually only undertaken for mailings that are produced on a regular basis.

The Speedy Direct Cars campaign will require a script for each of the different letter types being used.

Variable printing

Variable printing techniques will depend on the level of personalisation required within a document, the size of the document, the size of the mailing, whether printing is required on one side only, or duplex, and the number of colours which will be variably printed.

The following list summarises the variable printing techniques available.

Inkjet Addressing	The most efficient method of addressing is to use an inkjet printer with a 2 ½"-4" head. These are capable of addressing between 20 and 40 thousand items an hour and can be mounted in-line with other production processes such as printing, finishing or enclosing.
Labels	Labels are overprinted using the methods below and then attached using a labelling machine. Label addressing is more expensive than inkjet addressing and therefore has largely been replaced with inkjet addressing. Piggyback, or peelable labels are used where the recipient can reuse the label on application forms, to save them having to rewrite their address details.
Page overprinting	Preprinted stationery such as letter text or application forms, is overprinted with black text, similar to that produced by a standard black and white office printer. This allows any part of the text, tables and simple black graphics to be varied.
Highlight colour	As above but with the addition of one or more overprinting highlight colours. This is used to enhance special offers within the copy, to print blue signatures.
Full colour page	Digital colour printing technology enables an entire document to be produced in a single process. The entire content of the document can be varied using this method.

As a rule of thumb, the cost and turnaround times increase as the level of personalisation increases. Check with the mailing house to determine how much time must be allowed for personalisation.

Mailing over 250,000 is usually personalised in-line during the printing, finishing or enclosing process, or on continuous laser printers that accept reels containing 30,000 A4 letters. Output speeds in excess of 50,000 A4s per hour can be achieved.

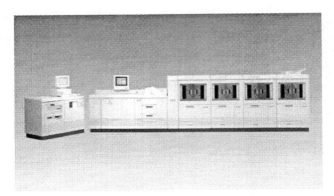

Xerox DocuPrint Cut Sheet Laser Printer

Cut sheet printers can also offer a facility to dynamically select different stationery types from various feeders, similar to those on an office photocopier. In this way the preprinted form can also be varied.

The Speedy Direct Cars campaign has a personalised letterhead and application form which are printed together on A3 sheets. The campaign totals 150,000 packs and has 5 segments and therefore cut sheet laser printing will be more efficient for the personalisation of the letters and application forms.

Variable print proofs

Complex mailing campaigns utilising many different preprinted form types and a high level of personalisation can be very challenging to proof, due to the number of combinations to be produced and checked.

Careful consideration must be given to produce test data that will enable all the different combinations of variable output to be checked.

The following proofing methods are available:

Plain paper	Plain paper proofs can be produced if the preprinted stationery is still in production. The personalised element of the form is printed on the plain paper for checking. This should be checked in conjunction with a copy of the printer's proof for the preprinted stationery to check position and content of the personalised text. This can be made easier by photocopying the printer's proofs onto an acetate in order that it can be overlaid onto the plain paper personalised proofs.
Soft proofing	Soft proofing enables the personalised print to be produced in proofing file format such as PDF or XML that can be inspected on computer-based viewing applications such as Adobe Acrobat. More recent methods have enabled both the printer's soft proof and the personalisation soft proof to be combined and viewed together.
Production proof	The final laser proof should be produced using the pre-proof printed stationery and the same machine which will carry out the personalisation.

I would advise that you begin with soft proofs, or where they are not available, plain paper proofs. Only when you are satisfied that the soft proof is correct should you produce a final personalised proof.

Data processing checklist

✔ Produce a data processing flowchart

✔ Ensure a data layout is supplied with files sent

✔ Deduplicate data

✔ Use the Mail Preference Service and a gone-aways and bereavement list to suppress names from the mailing list, to ensure compliance with legal and industry best practice

✔ Include a unique number with each mailpiece to enable later reconciliation and regeneration as required

✔ Take care when selecting test data to ensure that each output combination can be checked

✔ Allow adequate time for proofs to be checked and corrections to be made

Finishing

Having printed and personalised the example letterhead and application form, it is now necessary to undertake various cutting and folding operations to prepare the piece ready for final enclosing. These processes are referred to as finishing.

The following finishing processes are commonly available:

✔ Cutting

✔ Sheeting of continuous stationery to cut sheets

✔ Folding

✔ Perforating

✔ Scoring

✔ Stitching

✔ Glueing to seal items

✔ Adding remoist glue strips to produce response mechanisms

✔ Die Cutting

The above finishing processes can be undertaken by a number of different machines in stages, or by a combined finishing line.

In order to ensure that the finished product meets with expectations it is critical to have a finishing guide supplied to the mail house, or produced by the mail house for approval in a similar way to a print or variable print proof.

The easiest method of producing a finishing guide is to cut and fold by hand stationery which has been produced and approved from the printing and personalisation process. Any part of the finishing which cannot by easily replicated by hand, such as the application of glue, scoring and perforating, should be clearly indicated on the guide by use of a highlighter pen.

The way inserts are folded can cause problems in the subsequent enclosing process. Most inserting machines need to be able to grip the leading edge of an insert cleanly when pulling it from the feeders into the collating track, so the items must present only a single fold, or closed edge. The diagram below demonstrates correct and incorrect folding:

Figure 8.5.7

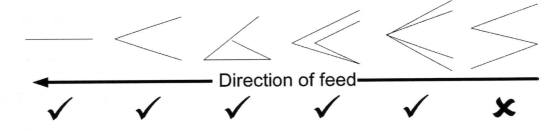

The enclosing speeds can be significantly enhanced if the finished inserts are ram bundled. Although this increases finishing cost, cost savings due to faster enclosing may well more than compensate.

Pay particular attention to the address carrier. Once enclosed in the outer envelope the address should show through the window of the envelope. To ensure that this actually does happen a sample of the envelope must be made available during finishing, and regular checks made by enclosing samples of the finished personalised insert in the envelope.

The following checklist will help to ensure that finishing is undertaken correctly:

✔   Produce a finishing guide/mock-up

✔   Ensure that an outer envelope is used to check that all items fit and the address of the personalised letter is positioned in the window of the envelope

✔   Ram bundle inserts

✔   Clearly mark finished items with item codes and quantity per box and pallet

The Speedy Direct Cars campaign includes a personalised letter and application form which are printed and personalised together on A3 sheets. They will require folding to A5 in order that they can be enclosed in the envelope; furthermore, a slitting wheel is used in the folding process to separate the letter from the application form.

Enclosing

Enclosing can either be carried out by hand or mechanically. The type of enclosing required will depend on the size and complexity of the pack and the volume to be mailed.

Very complex, or short run mailings of less than 10,000 packs will be produced by hand.

The automated enclosing equipment used will also depend on the size and complexity of the pack to be produced. There is no one machine that is a 'master of all trades'. Some machines are designed to enclose to C4 packs, while others can only enclose to C5 but considerably outperform the former.

Consult with your mailing house during the design process in order that they can advise what designs will be most efficient to enclose. Negligible differences in pack design can cause large difference in performance and therefore price.

The inserts and the outer envelopes are loaded into hoppers on the machine. Each time the machine cycles, an insert is taken from each feeder and placed into a collating track, then moved along to the next position. Once all the inserts have been collated they are finally place in the outer envelope.

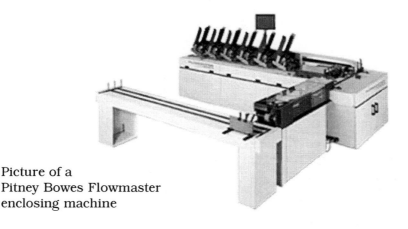

Picture of a
Pitney Bowes Flowmaster
enclosing machine

Lettershops are very busy environments producing many jobs for many customers at the same time; it is therefore critical that all stationery is clearly marked to ensure that it can be easily identified.

Prior to enclosing, the following documents will be required by a lettershop:

✔ Mailing matrix

✔ Sample enclosing pack

✔ Mailsort summary report

✔ Mailsort line listing

✔ Postal dockets (or payment of postage if using the mail house's own mail account)

An example of a mailing matrix is shown below:

Table 8.5.6

MAIL DATE	CELL CODE	MAIL PACK DESCRIPTION	MAILING QUANTITY	PACK CODE	OUTER ENV	BRE ENV	INSERT CODE
FRI 25 JAN	002	**Sports**	**25,000**	PSPO	E01	B01	LSPO+LAPP+LT&C
	003	**Cruiser**	**25,000**	PCRU	"	"	LCRU+LAPP+LT&C
	004	**Economy**	**25,000**	PECO	"	"	LECO+LAPP+LT&C
	005	**4x4**	**25,000**	P44	"	"	L44+LAPP+LT&C
	006	**Family**	**25,000**	PFAM	"	"	LFAM+LAPP+LT&C

A sample of each mailing pack to be produced will be made up by hand in order that the following checks can be made:

✔ Inserts fit within the outer envelope

✔ Correct stationery is being used and has been received

✔ Orientation and order of each insert is checked

✔ Address is clearly visible through the window

A copy of the Sample Enclosing Pack (SEP) is sent for approval to the client.

It is particularly important that this is carefully checked. Mail houses have the capacity to produce mailings as large as 500,000 in 24 hours, so subsequent alterations are likely to be too late.

The enclosed mail will then be decollated into presorted Mailsort order, bagged, tagged and caged in accordance with the postal service providers' requirements. Reconciliation can be made against the Mailsort line listing, confirming which mail districts have been completed. This will be required in order to produce the postal dockets.

The postal service provider will be responsible for checking the receipt of mail and signing a postal docket and receipt evidencing that mail has been despatched.

Finishing and mailing check list

✔   Consult with the mailing house to determine the most effective pack design which meets your requirements

✔   Ensure that all printed materials, and packing used to transport them are clearly marked with the description, stationery code and quantity

✔   Produce a mailing matrix identifying all the pack types, contents and quantities.

✔   Check all inserts fit within the outer envelope

✔   Check that the address is clearly visible through the window (where used)

And so to recap

As this chapter draws to an end you should have a good overview of the direct mail production process and be able to put together a production mailing and manage a campaign for yourself.

The following checklist may come in useful when planning and executing mailing campaigns.

Planning

✔ Produce a production process chart

✔ Produce a mailing matrix

✔ Produce a stationery matrix

✔ Consult the mailing house and printers to determine how much time will be required for each activity

✔ Remember to allow time for proofs and goods to be transported

Printing

✔ Set up a printing matrix identifying all items required for the mailing campaign

✔ Specify the paper types and weights to be used

✔ Check the overall pack weight

✔ Ensure all stationery to be laser overprinted has been specified to be laser compatible

✔ Ensure that all inserts fit within the outer envelope specified

✔ Include a unique stationery code on each item of stationery

✔ Increase printing quantities to allow for make-ready and overs

✔ Remember to include all pictures, fonts and DTP files and a low-resolution print when sending artwork

✔ Use the envelope guide to check envelopes

✔ Include the correct PPI on the envelope as required

✔ Allow enough time in the production schedules for proofing and corrections

✔ Discuss your requirements with the chosen printers and keep them up to date with any changes

Proofing

✔ Spelling and grammar

✔ Correct dates are being used (especially offer begin and end dates)

✔ Cropping and position of photographs and illustrations

✔ Colours match 'corporate standards' where these apply

✔ Correct fonts being used

✔ The finished item fits inside the outer envelope being used

✔ A stationery code has been included on every printed item

Data processing

✔ Produce a data processing flowchart

✔ Ensure a data layout is supplied with files sent

✔ Deduplicate data

✔ Use the Mail Preference Services and a gone-aways and bereavement list to suppress names from the mailing list, to ensure compliance with legal and industry best practice

✔ Include a unique number with each mail piece to enable later reconciliation and regeneration as required

✔ Take care when selecting test data to ensure that each output combination can be checked

Finishing and enclosing

✔ Consult with the mailing house to determine the most effective pack design which meets your requirements

✔ Ensure that all printed materials, and packing used to transport them are clearly marked with the description, stationery code and quantity

✔ Produce a mailing matrix identifying all the pack types, contents and quantities.

✔ Check all inserts fit within the outer envelope

✔ Check

Don't forget to consult with your suppliers - they are there to assist you. In my experience most problems arise due to poor communications and can be most easily overcome by ensuring that all the parties involved in a mailing campaign are fully informed.

REMEMBER GOOD PLANNING AND COMMUNICATION IS THE KEY TO SUCCESSFUL DELIVERY OF A MAILING CAMPAIGN

Chapter 8.6

Fulfilment – delivering the promise

This chapter includes:

- Where promise meets delivery
- Response handling and fulfilment
- Cases: 2D, 3D and virtual fulfilment
- The basic steps of response and fulfilment
- Ten things to consider
- Selecting a fulfilment house
- Summary – and a benchmarking checklist

About this chapter

To most customers, nothing has happened until their enquiries or orders are fulfilled. Yet fulfilment can so easily be the Achilles heel of direct and interactive marketing. The fact is that fulfilment rarely receives the management attention that it merits, particularly in companies where direct response handling is a sideline. The car manufacturer that is slow to mail out requested brochures, the dot-com retailer who fails to respond to e-mailed queries, the gift supplier who delivers too late for that anniversary: they are all committing suicide by degrees.

In this chapter we examine the fulfilment process and give mini case history examples of the three main types of fulfilment: **2D, 3D** and **Virtual.** We discuss the alternatives of **in-house** and **contracted out** fulfilment, provide a 10-point checklist of planning considerations and portray **the 8 stages of a fulfilment operation**. We supply guidance on selecting a fulfilment house and, most importantly, suggest that every marketer must continuously monitor and benchmark fulfilment performance against competition. What is often described as back-end marketing should always remain a front-of-mind preoccupation. **It is fulfilment that delivers customer satisfaction**.

Author/Consultant: Stephanie Rouse

Stephanie Rouse author and consultant

This chapter was prepared by Stephanie Rouse, Operations Director of MM Group with contributions from other senior managers at MM Group. Stephanie is a regular contributor to industry press features and a regular speaker at conferences having spoken at events throughout the UK, Eire, and the US.

MM Group is an award winning, customer communications specialist with a nationwide network of multimedia contact centres and specialist fulfilment operations.

MM Group work with many of the world's leading organisations providing outsourced business solutions involving communication via phone, internet, e-mail, fax and post, database management and analysis and the latest in e-commerce and fulfilment services.

MM Group was named "Telemarketing Agency of the Year 2001" by Marketing Magazine and awarded "European Call Centre of the Year: Best Multi-service Call Centre", and has achieved numerous accolades for inspiring work in providing innovative database management and fulfilment solutions.

Full ISO accredited and a member of the DMA, they have been an approved government roster agency since 1993.

Stephanie Rouse
MM Group
Contact House
Feeder Road
Bristol
BS2 OEE

Tel 0117 916 8000
Fax 0117 916 8268
www.mmgroup.co.uk
Stephanie.rouse@mmgroup.co.uk

Chapter 8.6

Fulfilment – delivering the promise

Where promise meets delivery

The best-planned campaign, backed up by the most brilliant offer and the most exciting presentation will add up to nothing unless what you promise is actually delivered. Where you stop promising and start delivering is in the fulfilment area.

Response handling and fulfilment are the last steps in your marketing cycle – the final moment of truth in the dialogue between you and your customer. At the same time a good experience at this stage sows the seeds for the next cycle and a long-term relationship.

What is fulfilment?

fulfil /ful'fil/ *v.tr.* *(US* fulfil) (fulfilled, fulfilling) 1. bring to consummation, carry out (a prophecy or promise). 2a. satisfy (a desire or prayer). b. (as fulfilled adj.) completely happy. 3a. execute, obey (a command or law). b. perform, carry out (a task). 4. comply with (conditions). 5. answer (a purpose). 6. bring to an end, finish, complete (a period of piece of work). • fulfil oneself develop one's gifts and character to the full.
fulfillable *adj.* fulfiller *n.* fulfilment *n. (US* fulfilment). [1]

Source — The Concise Oxford Dictionary ninth edition

Or to summarise: carry out a promise, satisfy a desire, (make) completely happy, execute a command, perform or carry out a task, comply, answer, bring to an end, finish and complete.

The term fulfilment originally referred to 'fulfilling the order', which meant opening the mail, typing a label, keeping track of the orders and payments and finally mailing out the merchandise. In today's world the process is much more complex and the terminology more extensive.

Today the response might be a coupon, a phone call, an e-mail message or an online request (or other form of electronic media response). The 'label' is likely to be the input onto a computer record (besides the contact information and delivery address, there may also be detailed answers to a questionnaire). The response may include a payment, it may be a subscription, a request for further information, a membership application or, of course, an order for a variety of products or services.

Meeting customer expectations

Fulfilling a customer's enquiry or order today involves so much more than rows of people sitting at benches in draughty warehouses packing glossy brochures into 4-colour envelopes with beautifully printed personalised letters. Just as customers increasingly use different communications channels to make their enquiry or place their order, so their expectations of fulfilment become ever more sophisticated and demanding.

Think of the last time you requested information from, or placed an order with an organisation – how long were you prepared to wait to receive it? **Increasingly people want companies to deliver goods while they are at home and they want information quickly.** If you are working Monday to Friday you would probably choose a company who would deliver on a Saturday morning. When sending a gift to someone else, you want it to arrive on their special day **and** you would want it gift wrapped with a personalised message from you.

While there is still a place for the glossy 'coffee table' brochure, you will also need to present your brochure on the Internet or make it available in an electronic format, so that people can access the information they want immediately. Companies which are listening to their customers are finding their methods of fulfilment are constantly diversifying and the speed and accuracy at which they need to fulfil is quicker than ever.

Some typical fulfilment tasks

- **Catalogue redemption**: ie handling and recording enquiries; despatching catalogues; recording and analysing response data.

- **Information and brochure despatch**: including quotations; reader/listener/viewer information services; travel brochures; government services.

- **Customer care communications**: two-way communications, eg between retailer and customer; building and maintaining customer data.

- **Subscription services**: receiving orders and payments; reminders; organising despatch; renewal programmes.

- **Promotions**: processing prize draw or other competition entries; taking orders for free gifts or other incentives.

- **Home shopping orders**: receipt of orders; banking; statistics; despatch of a wide variety of merchandise.

- **Quotations:** providing quotations by phone or on the Internet and confirming by post or e-mail.

- **Data capture, reporting and analysis:** in respect of all the above functions.

Response handling and fulfilment

Fulfilment includes not only information and goods, but care and service too.

In theory, fulfilment is the whole operation, encompassing what happens from the receipt of an order to the shipment of goods and subsequent customer service procedures. In practice, the industry uses two different terms for two separate stages of the process, as follows:

Response handling covers the receipt and processing of orders, requests etc. including the computer and paperwork.

Fulfilment means the despatch of goods and services, which further breaks down into:

- **2D** – normally something flat that goes in an envelope (see **Case 1** – Go)
- **3D** – products that come in a parcel (see **Case 2** – ITV Digital)
- **Virtual** or E-fulfilment – eg SMS texting and e-mail (see **Case 3** – Encyclopaedia Britannica)

Either or both of these tasks—response handling and fulfilment—can be contracted out. The whole process is sometimes called 'back-end marketing'. However, as we will demonstrate, it should always be considered and planned at the front end. Not only can it influence the response rate and average order value of a campaign, early planning can have a profound influence on the success and even the survival of your business.

Case 1: 2D fulfilment

- *Letters, quotations, catalogues, brochures, vouchers – typically items which can be packed into an envelope and sent through the post.*

- *May be complex multipart, multi combination packs or may be simple and machine enclosable.*

Go case history

The Go Service Centre at MM Group provides mail, fax and e-mail fulfilment of travel itineraries for all Go bookings made via the web or phone.

Sophisticated generic database software, specifically built from software developed in-house at MM Group, provides highly personalised itineraries which include customer information and sales messages that vary according to the booking data received.

Examples of these sales messages are:

- *Customers who have not taken out insurance are reminded of insurance offers from Go.*

- *Travellers who have not booked train tickets are provided with the most appropriate train to catch to make their flights.*

MM Group has developed vigorous manipulation and processing techniques which allow the use of over 600 text variants, producing thousands of possible text permutations. A typical itinerary contains between 50 and 60 elements which are personalised and can be provided in up to seven different languages. Over 4,000 bookings are processed daily, seven days a week.

This programme was the winner of Gold Direct Response SMART Award 2001.

Case 2: 3D fulfilment

- Sending products, samples etc. Typically items which go in a parcel and cannot be sent by Royal Mail, but by another distribution channel.

- Are less likely to be machine enclosable than 2D fulfilment.

ITV Digital case history

One of the selling points of ITV Digital, which rebranded from ONdigital in July 2001, is its plug and play ease of use. But while customers don't have to call in an engineer to install a satellite dish, they do require items such as smart cards, keyboards and special remote controls.

In February of last year, ITV digital began working with MM Group to improve its fulfilment operation to strike the balance between 3D fulfilment of items such as smart cards, remote control units and keyboards, and traditional paper based skills in laser personalisation and data manipulation.

To keep people supplied with parts or instructions needed to keep their system up and running, all requests come into ITV Digital's two main UK call centres and are tagged with an appropriate pack code, which is embedded with all the instructions needed to generated the correct pack.

This is the vital tool – between the various welcome packs, payment letters and prospect communications, there are 200-300 different texts involved, with variants among these.

The data is collected overnight and fed to MM Group over an FTP (File Transfer Protocol) link early the following morning. Then a series of automated processes filter the data according to the material that needs to be generated. In addition, deduplication, or address checking, is done automatically so that, by 8 am, all the data is ready for lasering, needing minimum human intervention until it gets to the printer.

MM Group supported ITV Digital's much acclaimed Monkey campaign, through the despatch and tracking of individually boxed monkey puppets. Over a five week period, MM Group despatched tens of thousands of toys under tight security. All items were tracked to the point of hand-over to the customer. MM Group also operated an enquiry line for customers asking about the status of their order. Agents had live access to tracking information directly from the distribution firm, allowing agents to inform customers about the expected delivery time.

Case 3: Virtual or e-fulfilment

- *E-mails, SMS text messages, confirmation of Internet orders. Items for which no paper/hard copy is produced. Typically, virtual fulfilment is an automated or computerised process.*

Encyclopaedia Britannica case history

Encyclopaedia Britannica have been able to completely change the way they do business using Internet and e-fulfilment technology, replacing the traditional direct sales approach with a swift online operation.

All products are available for purchase over the Internet using an 'intershop' solution. Through sophisticated software, purchases can be made online by credit/debit cards. MM Group handles the merchant banking as well as the 3D (product) fulfilment, which is despatched within 48 hours.

The site has most recently been developed to handle multiple campaigns, which involve code entry points to deliver promotional prices across selected products. A high proportion of traffic is generated by targeted e-mail campaigns, which MM Group manages using Lyris software. E-mailings are presented to customers in HTML or plain text versions.

In addition to e-commerce services MM Group also processes orders via phone and coupons and offers and online technical support service.

The website can be found at http://britannicashop.britannica.co.uk.

Contract out or do it yourself?

If fulfilment of requests and orders is so vital, should these tasks ever be delegated? In the first instance, at least, the answer may well be 'yes'. The logistics of maintaining stocks, handling response and fulfilling orders are not necessarily straightforward and the capital cost in setting up is often considerable. For example, when **Lands' End** first landed in the UK, their fulfilment was contracted out and won considerable praise from users.

All 3 cases illustrating 2D, 3D and Virtual fulfilment were contracted out.

> We used to process the order internally and then give it to someone else to fulfil. Now we focus on sales and marketing. *Jane Helps, Encyclopaedia Britannica*
>
> *MM Group lets us use fulfilment as a marketing tool..* Valerie Maguire, Go
>
> Both quotes are from *Marketing Direct (September 2001)*

However, some firms set out to develop their own logistics capability, seeing this as a competitive advantage. A well known and respected example is provided by **Viking Direct.** The facts in **Case 4** are as reported in *The Daily Telegraph* in 1997. Since then, Viking have also opened an online sales channel.

Case 4: In-house fulfilment: Viking Direct Limited

Viking Direct supply office products to about 500,000 customers, many of them very small businesses or homeworkers. Orders are generated mainly from monthly supplements and frequent themed supplements to the main catalogue. Average value of a customer's business is about £400 a year. Inventory numbers some 10,000 items. Almost all orders are received by phone or fax and despatched from three central warehouses (employing some 850 people) on the same day. 'Stock outs' number less than 0.5% . Goods are invoiced with despatch on 30 days' credit. Orders worth £30 or more (ex-VAT) are delivered free.

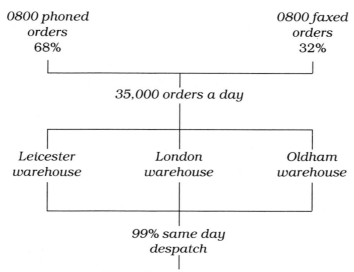

0800 phoned orders 68%   *0800 faxed orders 32%*

35,000 orders a day

Leicester warehouse   *London warehouse*   *Oldham warehouse*

99% same day despatch

same day delivery in 30-mile radius

1. *Customer's phone number recognised by Magic software.*

2. *Customer details and transaction history appear on VDU screen.*

3. *Consignment labels generated as order details are keyed in; simultaneously number of items, size and weight are calculated by system.*

4. *System identifies most efficient picking route and correct number of cartons.*

5. *Bar-coded laser label and picking list for picking by hand.*

6. *Checks on consignment details and weight made while goods are on conveyor.*

7. *Automatic loading and shrink-wrapping within cartons.*

8. *Cartons are lidded, labelled and chuted into carrier's waiting vans.*

Data entry for database is integrated within process and complete customer histories are maintained. These are used to prompt personalised offers which are inkjetted onto catalogue covers and order forms.

                                   Facts from Daily Telegraph, 18/9/97.

The basic steps of response handling and fulfilment

Figure 8.6.1 shows the eight basic stages through which a customer's response must proceed.

Figure 8.6.1   **The 8 basic steps of response handling and fulfilment**

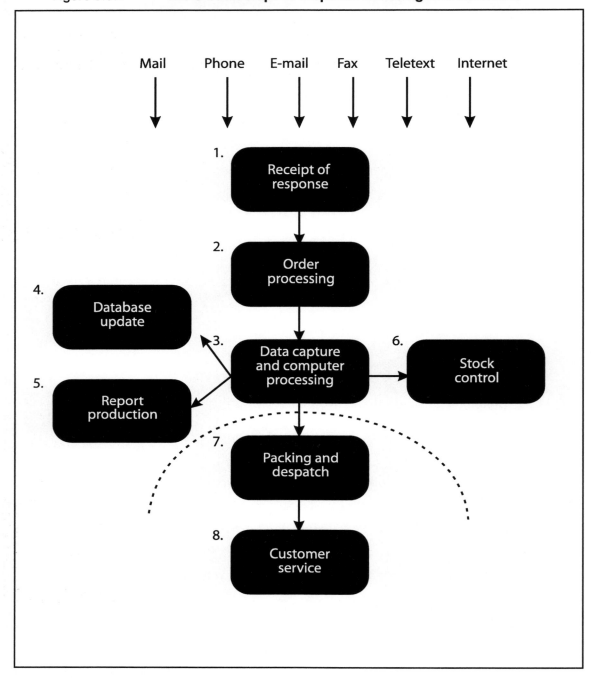

The media carrying responses can be very varied although most responses are still by mail and phone in B2C marketing.

... by mail

Orders are received, counted, sorted into types, eg payments, orders, correspondence, returns. Initial sorting, preparation and, if necessary, annotation of the data maximises speed and throughput of data entry operators. The aim here is to eliminate queries, to avoid recycling of rejected orders/requests, and to ensure quality at the data capture stage.

If handling cheques, these are vetted to ensure they are signed and dated, and words and figures agree. With credit card handling, the signature must be on the response piece. If the home shopping company is itself extending credit, orders will have to go through a credit clearance procedure (usually automated).

Receiving money: Cheques, credit card details etc. should be handled under tightly controlled supervision within a secure area; payments should be deposited at the banks and/or credit card retailers on a daily basis. Where customers' orders, cash handling and banking are entailed, it is important that total accountability is built into the system.

The above refers to an offline system where computer processing will update all transactions. An online system has the benefit of directly inputting the information on to the customer database.

... by telephone

Whether you use your own phones or an outside call centre, phone contact is an opportunity for your company to make a positive impression by the way the call is handled. With credit card orders using an online system, the entire transaction can be confirmed and entered, and customer details updated while the customer is still on the phone.

In best practice call centres, agents (operators) have on-screen access to the entire inventory with any out-of-stocks or stock delays noted and suggested substitutes. Further, a record of the customer's most recent transactions can be accessed instantly and, perhaps, a note of any unresolved query.

... online

However well designed your website, it makes sense to offer human help. Some 75% of online orders are aborted by the potential customer. Many could be saved by offering the facility to click onto an immediate phone call back service.

Amazon offer repeat customers one-click shopping. This uses the system's memory of the customer's credit card and delivery address details to save the customer the labour of re-keying the data. A special advantage of online order receipt is the ability to personalise the site to meet the customer's interests, and to offer access to additional information. Amazon's customer book reviews are an interesting example.

Designing coupons and order forms

When designing the coupon or order form, think about its ultimate objective, which is to give you precise and complete information about who your customer is and what that customer wants. It is important to provide enough room for the customer to fill in the relevant information. The physical size, shape and general layout of the response piece are crucial in ensuring data capture errors are kept to a minimum, a point to establish in the minds of art directors and catalogue designers.

In any area involving many pieces of paper, it is beneficial to have the printed materials the same size and of a quadrilateral shape. It is essential that coupons are rectangular and that the spacing is generous for filling in name, address and other details. Circular or triangular coupons are especially difficult to handle at every stage, and should be avoided no matter how much the designer wants to do 'something different'.

The importance of a clear offer

Making the coupon area physically easy to complete is only one of the ways of rendering response easier. Another is to make sure that the offer is clear and unambiguous. To underline the importance of a clear offer, consider the following as seen from a fulfilment perspective:

What's 7.5% of £38.39, Ethel?

When a company launched its thermal underwear via mail order in the UK, the launch took place during one of the warmest winters on record. That, however, was not the only misfortune ... the major setback was that the company gave customers the facility to discount the first item purchased by 7.5%.

This resulted in having to return most of the orders because of incorrect payment (albeit some tolerance had been built into the order value). The problem was that the UK audience, en masse, had difficulty with the arithmetic associated with the offer.

Database update

The heart of any direct marketing operation is its customer data – information comes largely from marketing campaigns that ask for responses, each response containing fresh items of customer information. It is important to maximise the management information potential and design systems that will embrace response handling and database requirements working closely with your fulfilment team. (Step 4 in Figure 8.6.1.)

Response handling and fulfilment play a major role in the development and maintenance of your database – when you contract work out to a fulfilment team you are appointing a guardian of your most valuable marketing asset.

Producing reports

Although the trend is towards providing accessible 'look-up' data rather than formal reports, regular reports on routine matters (step 5 in Figure 8.6.1) provide useful alerts. For example:

- **Banking** – credit and billing information, cash books, credit cards, cheques etc.

- **Campaign analysis** – response by source, response by offer, cost per enquiry, order statistics, eg average order value.

- **Inventory data/stock maintenance** – stock levels in numbers and days (at current depletion rate) etc.

- **Customer service** – tabulations of complaints and outcomes, enquiries, unfilled orders, returns etc.

- **Continuity** – subscriber or club membership levels, lapsed members, renewals.

Reports generated within the fulfilment process enable you to evaluate the quality of customers generated by the promotion; the value of the customer base as a whole; the acceptability of the company's product, and the health of the entire business.

Stock control

In a warehouse several important functions must be performed, among them receiving merchandise and keeping track of it, quality checking, verifying quantities and storing the merchandise in an appropriate section of the warehouse, clearly identified with location codes. (Step 6 in Figure 8.6.1.)

Stock control should keep track of not only what actually arrives, but also what is supposed to arrive and when. Marketers will want to know exactly how much is in stock at any time and when reordering should take place. A strict control of stock is critical as customers must be promptly notified if an item is not available. There are legal and regulatory, as well as customer care, implications of non-supply.

'Stock-outs' may also mean lost business and can lead to stock wastage. It is important to carry out regular physical stock checks to validate the theoretical stock figures. Where returns are recycled into the warehouse, these must be accurately monitored and documented (including the update of the financial records and audit trails).

NB It is also crucial to maintain control of the stocks of promotional and informational materials, such as brochures and instruction manuals.

Despatch

The response handling phase may be complete but, as far as the customer is concerned, nothing much has happened until delivery is completed. We now move onto 'the moment of truth' (Step 7 in Figure 8.6.1) – when promises must be turned into efficient delivery ... or else. We are into 'fulfilment' in the traditional industry meaning of the word.

Once the order has been assembled, it goes to a packer. The packer checks each item against the despatch note/packing slip and places it in an envelope or carton. Labels (or other address carriers) are affixed, cartons sealed and weighed, and handed over to the carrier.

At this late stage, quality is still paramount. Obviously, the right goods must be picked, and double-checked, in the right quantity, colour, style etc. Boxes must be packed neatly, labels stuck on with care, sealing tape applied in a professional manner. There is scope, even now, to impress a customer ... or to lose his confidence. In a good fulfilment house or operation everyone knows that they have an important role in the big scheme of things, ie satisfying the customer and winning them over to a further purchase.

Customer service

In theory, there should be no need for a customer service function. (Step 8 in Figure 8.6.1.) If everything went right all the time, there would be no need for handling complaints, replacements and enquiries. But, of course, it isn't always like that. You may have little 'live' contact with the customer, but the customer service function of your fulfilment house can provide you with valuable feedback on your campaign and your products.

Speed is of the essence. Long delays in despatch may lead to cancelled orders and undermine the customer's confidence in your entire organisation. It is difficult enough and very expensive finding customers – service them effectively and you are more likely to retain them.

In a well-run business, customer mail – complaints, enquiries etc. – are handled within one or two days of receipt. Badly managed customer service generates complaints and to service one complaint may be very time consuming.

With more and more enquiries coming in via the phone or e-mail, the customer expects problems and queries to be resolved faster. This means that customer service must have instant access to the customer's account record and preferably online enquiry access should be available for every campaign. If you, as the marketer, are not in a position to answer customers instantly, you need to ensure that your fulfilment people are – and do. This may entail empowering the customer service unit to compensate customers on the spot to resolve complaints.

Ten things to consider

1)   Plan, plan, plan!

The planning of any fulfilment activity is critical to the success of achieving the required customer service levels. Therefore information up front is essential.

The general information required is:

✔   Expected daily volumes

✔   Required turnaround times

✔   Complexity of pack (eg does it contain personalised items, is it hand enclosing or can it go through a machine)

✔   Paper type/size/weight for any personalised document to be enclosed

✔   Special recording information at point of despatch (ie product serial number)

✔   Packaging requirements; envelope, large padded envelope, carton, pallet

✔   Delivery requirements; Royal Mail, Carriers, UK, European, International

The above information assists in the planning process, which will determine the correct staffing levels, hours required to complete the operation, (ongoing or one-off's) equipment types and usage, and despatch vehicle types, quantity and frequency.

2)   Make sure you have sufficient stock of accessible materials

Another critical area is the accessibility of your warehouse – it is essential you have easy access to any products or materials. A few days' delay on a print run of brochures can build into a huge backlog very quickly and be costly to clear.

Warehouse layouts vary, but generally the materials and products in daily use should be within reasonable distance of the fulfilment area, with the bulk quantities stored in racking locations. Having the daily usage items close to the fulfilment area reduces the need for equipment ie forklift trucks, and so speeds up the process by taking a link out of the chain of product flow.

Deadlines are increasingly being reduced and any process that reduces the number of elements within the supply chain is a benefit, enabling the fulfilment to get there quicker.

3)   Know your capacity and tailor your response to meet it

It is pointless to generate thousands of orders for product you do not have in stock, a thousand requests for brochures when you can only pack five hundred a day, three thousand phone calls when you have too few staff to answer the phone, more coupons than you are able to data capture – you will just disappoint your customers and cause yourself an (expensive) administrative nightmare.

4) Manage your customers' expectations

Try and give the customer an idea of when to expect to receive their fulfilment, eg 'Delivery within 7 days', 'next day service', 'Thank you for calling, we'll post that brochure to you later today and you should receive it by tomorrow'.

5) Test the system and processes

Make sure you leave plenty of time to test your fulfilment processes from end to end. If you have a failure early on in the programme or campaign the resulting backlog will have ramifications which seem endless.

6) Quality control

Get it right first time. Handling returned mail can be expensive and unwieldy. Exchanging incorrect or damaged products or sending a second fulfilment pack (or worst of all losing a potential customer) means you double your workload and your cost.

7) Can you do it in-house or should you outsource?

As with any outsourcing decision the main considerations will be the level of service to the customer and cost of undertaking the work in-house as opposed to outsourcing it.

In addition, this cost should be weighed up against how well the work fits into your 'core business'; is it something that can be done without too much disruption to your daily business.

If the requirement is likely to be longer term then it may well be that it justifies the cost of investment into technology and people within the in-house operation. Experience shows, however that the majority of fulfilment requirements are best suited to the skills, experience and services which can be offered by an outsourced supplier.

When selecting a supplier, you will need to consider the size of their operation and whether it 'fits' the business you wish to outsource. For example, if your requirement needs a large amount of storage space then the supplier should clearly have adequate warehousing facilities to accommodate both current and future storage requirements. The warehousing system in operation should be demonstrated in order to ascertain whether it has all the functionality that you require.

Dependent on the coverage you require, verification should be sought on which postage carrier is utilised and what % of UK addresses they cover. It is important that the supplier has experience in the fulfilment requirement you are wishing to outsource and can prove success in this area. References should be sought from other clients for whom they currently provide this service.

8) Collecting money

Where a financial transaction forms part of the process you should ensure you are complying with MOPS (The Mail Order Protection Scheme) or other appropriate best practice. Also, if using an outsourcer, consider how fast the monies will be transferred to your business and what methods of payment you need to offer customers.

9) Reporting and analysing

You don't just need to know what response you have from specific advertisements or activities. Analyse how people are paying, what the peak times are in response (these traffic patterns help you to plan your next campaign). Analyse the returns, too, to see if that gives you any pointers for improving any part of the process.

10) Delivery and return methods

Agree delivery method and tracking; understand the distribution when it has left you. (If a package has to be delivered to a person's home but is too big to get through the average letterbox your return mail will be massive).

Delivery method will be dependent on whether the goods are 2D or 3D. Therefore it is essential to arrange the appropriate carrier; Royal Mail, Parcel Carriers, General Hauliers (pallet deliveries) or dedicated couriers.

The ability to link into the carriers' systems is paramount to the speed and tracking of despatched goods.

Royal Mail offer a web enabled docked system called E-pro, which links directly into their systems, thereby enabling the despatching company to send the correct information via the web, eliminating the use of paper (except for a delivery note for the collecting driver). This also assists the Royal Mail in managing their workloads easier, which means faster and more efficient sorting of mail.

The use of carriers is on a similar basis to the Royal Mail E-pro system, except it is by individual package or consignment, rather than docket number.

Linking directly from the order system into the carrier systems gives the ability to produce the despatch/consignment address label with it's unique number, thereby reducing multiple keying in of the same data and increasing the audit trail for tracking the products through the complete supply chain.

Tracking the goods is again via web-enabled processes, and inputting the consignment number can show the user exactly where the goods are, such as:

- Left collection point
- Arrived at main sorting terminal
- Left terminal
- Arrived at delivery depot
- Out on delivery vehicle
- Delivered

This line on most carriers' systems gives the time, signature, delivery address and consignment number.

Several of the advanced carriers have HHT whereby the recipients sign on a miniature screen. When the drivers return to their vehicles, they insert the HHT into a cradle fixed to the dashboard and the data is then downloaded directly to the central system. In several cases, this gives the ability to get 'real time' proof of deliveries.

Selecting a fulfilment house

If, after careful analysis, you choose an external fulfilment house, you will need to be confident that they (a) can perform the required tasks and (b) understand the importance of delivering what you have promised – at the right time and within the agreed budget. They will, after all, be responsible for helping you deliver and, at the end of the day, establish your credentials and build a long-term relationship with each valued customer.

To help you decide between possible suppliers we now outline some of the key selection criteria:

Size and capacity

Initially, ask fulfilment houses for their brochures. These should tell you a little about their company status; nature of business; project and capacity indicators – eg how many items are mailed per week, whether they have built databases for clients, how many records they hold etc; and how many orders have been received and responses processed in one day. The brochures will also tell you about the services they provide and perhaps even mention their customer bases.

Next, visit your short listed fulfilment houses, and ask to be shown around. What are
the storage facilities? Do they look efficient and well organised? Are they capable of immediately reporting deliveries and controlling and monitoring stock?

Equipment and software

Ask for a list of equipment used in handling and the specifications of their machinery - check this against your list of requirements. Equipment on site could be a major factor in your final decision:

✔ Data capture facility enabling response data to be captured from all channels and transferred to storage

✔ Computer processor, storage, software etc. – for processing the information keyed in and matching it (where appropriate) to existing files

✔ Data output machinery – printers (inkjet and laser); card embossing/thermal imaging machines

✔ Print machinery

✔ Telemarketing systems

✔ Storage and materials moving equipment

✔   Addressing and labelling equipment

✔   Finishing, packing and wrapping equipment

Experience and performance

Make sure that your short listed fulfilment house has a good track record of delivering projects on time, to high quality standards and on budget. Use any business contacts you have to check their reputation in the marketplace – good companies have good reputations.

Quality control

Quality is a major issue. Some useful questions to ask are:

?   Is the fulfilment house a member of, or recognised by, any trade associations?

?   Do they have clear processes and systems for handling jobs, from quotation through to agreement to a schedule, and signing off work as it goes through the different stages?

?   For home shopping fulfilment projects, check that the fulfilment house is recognised by MOPS (The Mail Order Protection Scheme).

?   Check also that they are registered as a bureau under the Data Protection Act – and, of course, they will seek a similar assurance from you.

?   Does the fulfilment house conform to any Quality Assurance Scheme or Policy? Many large organisations will do business only with organisations that are certified under ISO 9002.

What is ISO 9002?

ISO 9002 is the international standard signifying that organisations provide the quality their customers and clients expect. It describes a system that organisations can adapt to ensure quality in their services and is a continuous commitment to quality. It gives customers and clients confidence and helps avoid mistakes and misunderstandings, which in turn lead to fewer customer complaints and therefore greater satisfaction.

The strength of a system such as ISO 9002 is that it is 'alive'. When mistakes happen, the system changes in order to improve procedures and ensure that the same mistakes will not recur, thereby constantly improving quality.

Organisations certified under ISO 9002 have their own quality representative, who monitors the quality system and ensures that everyone within the organisation works together — for quality.

Service and account management

You will be working closely with your supplier. Their quality of service and account management will considerably affect your opinion of them. A useful question to ask is: "What is your philosophy of service in relation to control, timing etc?"

An account manager with the support team should be assigned to you and work with you to ensure that your instructions are accurately translated into a course of action. The account manager will also assist you in determining what services you need and what the procedures and timing criteria should be, before the response handling and fulfilment process begins. Look for fast turnaround on quotation requests, speedy responses to enquiries and the general quality of their correspondence – all the hallmarks of a professional, service-minded operation.

Tidiness and efficiency

When visiting the site, check to see if the premises are clean and well maintained. Tidiness can tell you about the company's culture and give you an insight into how your merchandise will be handled. This is particularly important as the customer will blame you, the marketer, if they receive soiled or damaged products.

How does the fulfilment house control security systems? What about fire safety?

Location

Consider the importance of logistics. Is it important that the fulfilment house is located close at hand, or is distance of no great importance?

Cost

Big fulfilment houses may be more expensive, but may be better managed and pay more attention to quality than some smaller, less well-resourced organisations – although smaller operations can be good, too.

Ask competing fulfilment houses for quotations, but be careful not to compromise on quality, control and performance.

Reputation

Ask for references from companies that operate in a similar market to you. Make sure that you follow up the references – are they real?

It is also advisable to develop a relationship with the fulfilment house to gain an in-depth knowledge of their capabilities and procedures.

Finally, before you sign the contract, make these six final quick checks:

Checking out possible suppliers

✔ Meet the client service contact – you will be putting your reputation in their hands: make sure that you have confidence in them.

✔ Discuss the project timetable and mailing schedule and see if you agree.

✔ Specify checking and approval procedures and ensure that procedure controls and quality checks are in place at every stage.

✔ Establish reporting requirements and compare them with established procedures.

✔ Discuss Royal Mail considerations (eg postal response method, First Class Business Reply, Second Class, Freepost, standard tariff).

✔ Discuss material coding and identification.

Summary – and a benchmarking checklist

Whatever the future of direct marketing, and of fulfilment, the three keys to efficiency will always be:

✔ **Control**

✔ **Speed**

✔ **Accuracy**

To the question: "What is fulfilment?" the answer will always be: "A satisfied customer". We finish this part with a competitive benchmarking checklist.

Table 8.6.1   **Best practice checklist**

Benchmark against the competition – promises and performance

Enquiry handling

Phone:	0800, 0345 or equivalent? 24 hrs/7 days or less?
Mail:	Freepost or Business Reply? Or paid by customer?
Online:	Human assistance available? Within 5 minutes? 24/7?
Brochure delivery:	48 hours?
Reply incentive:	Yes/No

Order handling

Phone:	0800, 0345 or equivalent? Orders and enquiries on same line?
	Opening hours for live operator order handling?
Other electronic:	IVR out of hours? Fax? E-mail? Website?
Mail:	Freepost or BR?
Monitoring:	Contact centre efficiency, manner, product knowledge?
	Speed of response to non-phone requests?
Offers etc:	First order incentives? Surprise gifts?
	Price promises? Free approval?
	Bundled offers or other promotions via website/contact centre?
	Query handling
Phone:	Can orders and queries be handled by one person/within same call? Are there dedicated advice or suggestion lines or product information lines?
Other media:	Is it clear how to raise queries or complain and who to?
Monitoring:	Contact centre efficiency, manner, knowledge?
	Empowerment of operator to make amends?
	Speed of accessing information from other departments?
	Speed of response to non-phone requests?
	Promises kept? Checks made (eg outbound satisfaction calls)?

Terms of business

Guarantees:	Free approval? Money back? Approval period?
	Performance guarantees on goods – 1-year? Indefinite?
Credit terms:	Free credit period? Longer term credit? Interest rates?
Payments accepted:	Cheques? Credit cards? Debit cards? Bank Giro? Direct debit?

Delivery

Free delivery:	Any order? Orders over £...? No orders?
Delivery charges:	Per item? Per order? Insurance included?
Guarantees:	24 hours? 48 hours? Extra charge for guaranteed delivery?
Returns:	Collected? Prepaid label supplied? Prepaid label offered?
Packaging:	Added value – eg hanging garments, goods shrink-wrapped in carton?

Stocks

Stock outs/delays:	First time service level? Notification and substitute procedures?

It is essential to set up 'seed' customer relationships with your own company and your competitors to keep benchmarking your service. It is also a good idea to set up customer relationships with admired non-competitive companies. Often, you can learn more from other market sectors where there may be outstanding service providers.

Chapter 8.7

Interactive and direct marketing and the mail

This chapter includes:

- ❏ **Defining your market with postcode data**
- ❏ **Outward mailing – delivering your message**
- ❏ **Reply services to boost response**
- ❏ **Despatching your goods**
- ❏ **International direct marketing using the mail**
- ❏ **Despatching the goods internationally**
- ❏ **Contact details for all Royal Mail Services**

About this chapter

This chapter tells you about the key services which Royal Mail offers and how they can help you at every stage of the marketing process. Royal Mail offers a wide range of services, many of which have been specifically developed for marketers. Whether you are prospecting, managing the relationship with your customers or distance selling, getting the most from the mail is an important part of marketing.

Author/Consultant: Tim Rivett

Tim Rivett Director, Mail Media Centre

Tim is Director, Mail Media Centre, for Royal Mail Media Markets, the team in Royal Mail dedicated to the needs of the advertising, publishing and data markets.

After graduating in Psychology from Exeter University Tim worked in television production, moving on to the burgeoning world of corporate television in the eighties. (At that time, doing a video seemed to be a panacea for all communications needs - sounds familiar?) He then joined Spafax TV as Senior Production Manager.

In 1989, Tim joined Aspen Corporate Communications, an internal marketing agency, as Production Services Manager. From here he progressed within the Aspen Group, becoming Managing Director of Aspen's new integrated agency, Aspen Business Communications. Mergers with Aspen Internet (1995) and Aspen Direct (1997) created the Aspen Agency, where Tim was Client Services Director. In 1999 Tim joined Summerfield Wilmot Keen as Director, Direct Marketing, and in May 2000 joined Royal Mail.

Tim's role at Royal Mail is to promote the effective use of the mail medium, and to overcome the barriers to its use. This includes the provision of information about the medium and the development of leading edge media tools. The Mail Media Centre also works with top advertising clients, media, advertising and direct marketing agencies to optimise their use of the medium and use mail as part of an integrated marketing solution.

The IDM Guide is a valuable source of practical, value added information, with which Royal Mail is delighted to be involved.

Tim Rivett M IDM
mmcinfo@royalmail.co.uk

Chapter 8.7

Interactive and direct marketing and the mail

ail is remarkable in being able to contribute to every phase of a marketing campaign – from the start of a campaign through to the delivery of your product. The strengths of mail in targeting, relationship-building and goods delivery make it an indispensable marketing tool across all business sectors. Mail is the perfect advertising medium for delivering your message and your brand image to individuals in your target audience.

The strengths of mail in outbound communication are matched by its abilities to receive incoming information from your customers. Prospects use mail more than any other medium to respond - through a postal coupon or a reply-paid service. And with the sale made, Royal Mail and Parcelforce Worldwide services can close the loop and deliver the goods. Mail works with electronic media to get real goods to real customers.

It is no surprise then, that the latest figures from the Direct Mail Information Service (November 2001) show that the mail medium continues to grow. Expenditure is up 5.9% year on year at £510 million, and volume has increased by 4.5% year on year. It is taking a more central role in the media mix, becoming increasingly used as a brand building medium and as an integral part of multimedia campaigns.

In this chapter we tell you about the services that can help you:

- Find prospects with our address management products.

- Communicate with individual customers and prospects.

- Maximise response.

- Deliver goods or fulfilment materials to your customers.

- Use the mail in international marketing.

The diagram below is a guide to which products apply to different parts of the marketing process, each of which we describe below:

Table 8.7.1

Marketing activity	Mail service	
	Inland	International
Defining your market with postcode data	• Postcode Address File • National Change of Address database	
Outward mailing - delivering your message	**Low volume mailings** • Stamp rolls • Stamped/Prepaid envelopes • Prepaid in Cash • Franking machines • Printed Postage Impressions • **mail**media™ **Higher volume mailings** • **mail**media™ • Mailsort • Mailsort Light • Cleanmail • Walksort • Door to Door • Direct to You • Presstream	**Low volume mailings** • Airmail Letters, Small Packets, Printed Papers. • Airpacks • International Signature Services and Swiftair • International Zone and Format on Demand • International Mailing Options **Higher volume mailings** • International Zone and Format Services • International Country Sort • International Mailing Options
Reply services to boost response	• Response Services • FREEPOST NAME • Admail • PO Box • **mail**media™	• International Response Services
Despatching the goods	• Guaranteed and Signature Services • Packetpost • Packetsort 12 • Flatsort 12 • Local Collect • Parcelforce by 9:00am, by 10:00am, by Noon • Parcelforce 24 and Parcelforce 48 • Parcelforce Worldwide Select	• Airmail Letters, Small Packets, Printed Papers • Airpacks • International Signature Services and Swiftair Parcelforce Worldwide • International Datapost • Euro 48 • International Scheduled • International Standard and Economy

The information in this chapter is subject to change, as existing products and services are developed and new products are launched. You can keep up to date with the latest developments at Royal Mail by visiting www.royalmail.com/insight, or calling your local Royal Mail Sales Centre on 08457 950950, and Parcelforce Worldwide at www.parcelforce.com or on 0800 22 44 66.

Defining your market with postcode data

Estimates vary but most analysts agree that in excess of £100 million of marketing budget is being wasted each year because businesses use data that is out of date. Clearly it is in nobody's best interests for this to continue. Every effort should be made to remove from your lists any names that aren't relevant - duplicates, people who have moved on, gone-aways, deceased people etc. By doing so you reduce costs and improve the profitability of your mailing. It also means you maximise return on investment and maintain or enhance your brand's reputation.

Following the introduction of the Data Protection Act 1998 there is also an obligation on businesses to regularly clean and update their databases. Under the 4th principle 'all reasonable efforts' must be made to ensure that data is accurate (and that includes the address).

Data cleansing can be linked to permission marketing and there is clear evidence of the benefits of ensuring your marketing activity is driven by a recognition of your customers' increasing sophistication. Already in the US, response rates are on average 15% ahead of conventional campaigns, when mail is targeted at prospects or customers who have in some way consented to receive it, or expressed an interest in the product or service. Indeed this appears to mirror response figures seen by permission based marketers in the UK.

The postcode is perhaps the single most important piece of information about your customers and prospects. Most obviously, it is essential for fast and reliable deliveries - the quality of address data will impact directly on the success of mailing activity. But postcodes are also vital for targeting and profiling.

Using Royal Mail's Postcode Address File (PAF) and National Change of Address (NCOA) data is the best way to ensure accuracy. PAF contains some 27 million UK addresses, including 1.7 million business addresses, and 1.7 million postcodes, which are constantly updated to ensure accuracy. NCOA uses information on individuals who have subscribed to Royal Mail's Redirection Service.

Postcode data is used in many different market sectors, and for a variety of applications:

- Rapid addressing (within phone ordering or reservation systems).

- Credit checking.

- Route planning (sales and territory distribution).

- Addressing mail (business or social).

- Database management.

- Improved profiling and targeting.

A number of products are based on PAF and NCOA data. These are produced either by Royal Mail or indirectly through Licensed Resellers of Royal Mail data. You can access the information in a variety of formats, as a data solution from Licensed Resellers, Royal Mail UK Addresses on CD and raw data.

Licensed Resellers

We work with a number of independent companies who are licensed to use PAF and NCOA data. You can buy a wide range of address management products from them (many off the shelf) and expert advice. Many will also take your mailing list and use their software to correct errors.

NCOA

The NCOA service uses information on the names and addresses of private individuals who have subscribed to Royal Mail's Redirection Service. Access to the service is available through Licensed Resellers.

Royal Mail UK addresses

This CD contains all known UK addresses, including Jersey, Guernsey and the Isle of Man. There are two ways you can use it:

- **Address finder** uses software to locate address data quickly for reference purposes.

- **Address manager** can be used for reference like Address Finder but also enables you to compile , maintain and sort mailing lists or databases. It includes grid references, Mailsort codes, NHS codes and local authority codes.

- **PAF data** is available in raw data formats which can be processed to suit your own IT applications on a variety of media, DAT and 3490E cartridges.

To find out more or for a list of Licensed Resellers, contact Royal Mail Address Management Products, Freepost SCO5731, EDINBURGH, EH12 9PG; call 0845 603 9038; fax 0131 316 7392; www.royalmail.com/atwork/amc or e-mail address.management@consignia.co.uk.

The Postal Preference Service (PPS)

Launched in October 2000, PPS delivers a step change in the way advertising mail is targeted, by creating a national database of detailed mailing preferences from consumers throughout the country. The purpose is to provide advertisers with information on the kind of advertising mail that consumers do and do not want to receive.

For more information you can contact the Postal Preference Service on www.thepreferenceservice.com.

Outward mailing – delivering your message

How to save time and money

If you are sending out any more than a few dozen items of mail a day, you probably won't want to stick a stamp on each one. Happily, Royal Mail offers a number of labour-saving and money-saving alternatives. The volumes indicated are just a guide to help you find the best service for your needs.

Low volume mailings

If you are doing a low volume mailing, these are the services that are likely to be most useful to you:

- Stamp rolls 500+ items.

- Stamped/Prepaid envelopes for weekly volumes of 100-500 items.

- Prepaid in cash 500+ items.

- Franking machines 500+ items.

- Printed Postage Impressions (PPIs) 1,000+ items.

- **mail**media™ 1,000 + items.

1. **Stamp rolls**
   If you prefer to use stamps for a mailing, but do not have time to stick them on your envelopes by hand, stamp rolls of gummed 1st and 2nd class stamps can be applied by machine. Rolls of 500, 1,000 and 10,000 are available for next day delivery, and other sizes or formats such as self-adhesive stamps can be ordered.

   For more information, contact Royal Mail Direct, 21 South Gyle Crescent, EDINBURGH EH12 9PB, phone 08457 782677 or visit www.royalmail.com/shop.

2. **Prepaid envelopes**
   Standard prepaid envelopes can be purchased from Royal Mail Direct on 08457 782 677 or by visiting the website at www.royalmail.com/shop. However if you need a large number, it may make sense to print your own envelopes. This allows you to have them made to your own specification and improve corporate branding by printing your logo or message. There is no need to store all the envelopes, you can call them off as they are needed. Orders can be placed with Royal Mail Direct by phone on 0845 076 2000, or by fax on 0131 316 7118.

3. **Prepaid in cash**
   Most main Post Offices and some delivery offices will frank your mail for you through our Prepaid in Cash service. You simply hand your unstamped items over the counter and pay the standard postage for each item, in a lump sum. Royal Mail then franks each item before delivering it as usual. There is a minimum number of 500 items or a minimum cost of £95.

4. **Franking machines**
    Franking is a fast and convenient alternative to stamps. Instead of putting a stamp on the envelope by hand, the value of the postage paid and the date is printed by machine.

    When you use a franking machine you have a contract with us that allows you to purchase your postage in advance. The franking machine postmarks any number of your letters or parcels up to your prepaid total. You can use franking to pay for all types of mail to any destination worldwide, including 1st and 2nd class, Packets, Recorded Signed for, Special Delivery and Swiftair. It is particularly suitable for low-volume direct mail, eg: local retail or small business-to-business applications, but is sometimes used for higher volume mailings too.

    Franking machines can be either bought, leased or rented from a number of companies authorised by Royal Mail (see Useful Addresses section in Volume 3).

5. **Printed Postage Impressions (PPIs)**
    If you despatch large quantities of identical inland or international mail, letters or packets, the Printed Postage Impression (PPI) facility may prove to be the most time and cost efficient option for you.

    To use PPI you print your envelopes with a unique licence number incorporated into a Printed Postage Impression. So that you can choose a design appropriate to your corporate identity, we offer a number of different PPI designs.

    Your company must spend more than £5,000 on postage each year to qualify for the PPI service. There are three approved designs which are shown in the illustration below.

6. **PPI designs to suit your corporate look**
    Here are three examples of approved PPI designs from which you can choose:

Figure 8.7.1

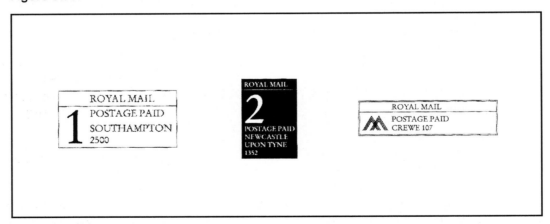

Some companies design their own PPI to reinforce a corporate look.

7. **mail**media™
    Please refer to the section on higher volume mailings for details of this service.

Higher volume mailings

For larger mailings, there are a number of purpose-designed Royal Mail services:

- **mail**media™
- Mailsort
- Mailsort Light
- Cleanmail
- Walksort
- Door to Door
- Direct to You
- Presstream

1. mailmedia™

Launched in April 2002, **mail**media™ is the new mail service designed exclusively for advertising mail. The product can be used to send all forms of mail from a letter to a large packet. **mail**media™ combines a range of mailing options along with an inclusive response element covering postal responses of up to 10% of the original mailed volume. The product options are based on two core criteria:

1. The speed with which you require delivery
2. The level of sortation that you are able to provide prior to us receiving your mailing

Delivery options are:
mailmedia™ premier	Targeted for delivery the next working day
mailmedia™ standard	Targeted for delivery within three working days
mailmedia™ economy	Targeted for delivery within seven working days

Sortation and entry options are:
Clean	requires items to be read by our sorting machinery minimum 1,000 items
1400	requires you to sort to around 1400 selections minimum 4,000 items
Flat and packet12	requires you to sort to 12 selections minimum 1,000 items

mailmedia™ has an initial weight step of 100 grams and can be used for items up to 2kg. The product also has an initial entry level of 1,000 items for all items, making it easier to set up test cells or run smaller mailings. **mail**media™ offers a unit price for the outward mail item that includes postal responses of up to 10% of the original mailed volume.

For more information or to book a mailing using **mail**media™ please contact the **mail**media™ booking centre on 0845 60 90 500.

mailmedia™ is only available to customers who hold a contract and deal directly with Royal Mail, or use an agency or mailing house with its own **mail**media™ contract. To arrange a contract please contact your account handler or your local Sales Centre on 08457 950 950

2. Mailsort

Mailsort is an important range of services for large-volume mailings. It offers you a discount in return for doing some of the sorting work yourself. You sort your mailing items, usually by computer, into postcode groups before handing them over in bags and bundles to Royal Mail for delivery. Your mailing must comprise at least 4,000 letters, 2,000 letters within the same postcode area (eg OX, CV, B etc.) or 1,000 packets of the same size and weight.

Mailsort prices offer a discount of up to 36% off public tariff. The exact figure will depend on the weight of your mailpack, the volume sent, time of posting and the type of Mailsort service you use. Delivery options available are:

Mailsort 1   Targeted for delivery the next working day
Mailsort 2   Targeted for delivery within three working days
Mailsort 3   Targeted for delivery within seven working days

To use Mailsort, you can either become a Mailsort contract holder and deal directly with Royal Mail, or use a mailing house with its own Mailsort contract. All contract holders have free access to the Mailsort Database which contains the Mailsort sortation plan. Together with the Mailsort User Guide (also provided free) the database will help you plan the computer programming and handling operations necessary for Mailsort.

3.   Mailsort Light

Adding an extra stage to a mailing can be a powerful way to boost response, either by building expectation through a 'teaser' mailing or providing a final prompt through a 'reminder' mailing. Royal Mail has introduced Mailsort Light to let direct mail users take full advantage of this by offering a further discount on multi-stage advertising mailings where at least one stage of the mailing is a lightweight piece.

To qualify for Mailsort Light your multi-stage mailing must amount to 40,000 items in total, consist of a main stage and at least one lightweight stage which must be sent using Mailsort 3. The mailings must be clearly linked as part of the same campaign and the lightweight element must weigh less than 15 gm.

For the latest information about Mailsort, and a rates calculator, go to www.royalmail.com/mailsort.

4.   Cleanmail

Cleanmail provides mailers with the opportunity to benefit from a work-share discount by providing correctly addressed machineable mail bearing either an OCR readable font or a bar-code. However, the Cleanmail service is for **unsorted machinable mail**.
Your mail needs to be faced, trayed (to a maximum weight of 10 kg), labelled and segregated into 1st or 2nd class.

5.   Walksort

Walksort is a value-added version of Mailsort that provides a discount of between 36% and 42% on postage for mailers who sort and bundle mail by individual postal delivery walk. The service is ideal for organisations such as local authorities or utilities that post to a high proportion of addresses within a specific area since, in order to qualify, the mailing must be sent to at least 10% of households within the coverage area.

There are two service options:

– Walksort 1 – delivery next working day after posting

– Walksort 2 – delivery within three working days of posting

6. Royal Mail Door to Door

Royal Mail Door to Door provides the hand delivery of unaddressed mail, leaflets, special offers and other promotional material. With this service, your items are delivered reliably and safely by our postmen and women operating nationwide. It is the only door-to-door service that delivers with the morning post, improving credibility and the chances of your messages being read. Royal Mail Door to Door is also the only unaddressed service that delivers to all 25 million delivery addresses across the UK. Deliveries can be as small as a postcode sector (on average 2,500 delivery points) or on a nationwide scale, and can take place any time during a specified one-week period. Items in any given distribution must be identical in size and weight. A weight limit of 100 gms applies and there is a minimum distribution charge of £500.

Royal Mail Door to Door has many valuable uses which include lead generation, increasing store traffic, new product test marketing and market research. It can also be used to deliver multimedia advertising and sales promotion campaigns. Door to Door is an excellent means of obtaining names and addresses for subsequent follow-up by addressed direct mail. (For a general introduction to the benefits of door-to-door distribution see also Chapter 4.7 of this Guide.)

Targeting of household distributions can be arranged in a variety of ways, eg by TV region, drive time, geodemographic breakdown or lifestyle selection. For further details on Royal Mail Door to Door contact the National Booking Centre on 01865 780400 or your local Sales Centre on 08457 950 950.

7. Direct to You

Direct to You gives you the benefits of Door to Door operations while sharing the costs of the campaign with other advertisers. Your message is inserted with up to seven other non-conflicting messages, in a specially designed envelope delivered by our own professional postmen and postwomen with the morning post.

Distribution can be targeted, so you can be sure that your message will reach those postcode sectors most likely to contain the types of people who will be interested in your product. You can currently choose from three Direct to You packs: Kids/Family, 50+ and Home and Garden.

To find out more about Direct to You call 01761 233 122.

8. Presstream

Presstream is designed for organisations that regularly produce newsletters, journals or periodicals (but not catalogues). Presstream works much like Mailsort, so each batch must be at least 1,000 packets or 4,000 letters.

Presstream offers two levels of delivery timing - next day and within three days - with discounts of up to 40% available.

Reply services to boost response

Research shows that the easier you make it for a customer to respond, the more responses you will receive. Putting effective response channels in place is one of the most important parts of campaign planning. Royal Mail offers a number of services to help you strike the right balance between convenience for your prospects, and for you. These are:

- Response Services (Business Reply and Freepost)

- FREEPOST NAME

- Admail

- Private box

- **mail**media™

1. Response Services (Business Reply and Freepost)

Business Reply and Freepost allow your customers and prospects to reply to you without having to pay for the postage. They encourage customers to respond and show your business to be helpful and customer orientated.

The Response Services licence, costing £60 annually, allows you to use either service. You pay the postage only on the items sent back – not on any unused cards or envelopes.

In addition to the postage, which may be 1st or 2nd class, there is a handling fee of 0.5p per item, or 1p when used with priority delivery. Although if you use the bar-coded service you will not be charged a handling fee.

The key difference between Business Reply and Freepost is style of presentation.

With **Business Reply**, favoured for business-to-business communications, all your reply cards and envelopes are preprinted with your address and the symbols identifying the service. This means Business Reply is an option when you are placing inserts in magazines or mailings to your customers. Business Reply can operate at either 1st or 2nd class postage rates.

Freepost can be used in this way too, and is especially good for a 'consumer-friendly' image. The extra advantage with Freepost is that respondents can use their own stationery to contact you, which means you can advertise easily on TV, radio or in the press. This latter option travels at, and is charged at, 2nd class rate.

The design specifications for Business Reply and Freepost are shown on pages 14 and 15:

2. FREEPOST NAME

FREEPOST NAME is a postal response mechanism from Royal Mail Response Services, developed for use in media where fast communication is imperative, eg TV, radio, cinema, posters, Teletext and on vehicles. It allows advertisers to use a one-line address, eg FREEPOST NICKELODEON. No full address or stamp is required.

FREEPOST NAME offers many benefits: it is memorable and helps reinforce the brand. The service is available through a 12 month licence fee (£150) plus premium rate postage per item. FREEPOST NAME can carry either a registered company, product or brand name. Generic names are allowed on a first come, first served basis.

3. Admail

Admail is a redirection service which redirects incoming responses to a different address. As a result you can offer customers one address to reply to, while actually processing the replies somewhere else.

You might, for example, wish to give a prestigious address or a local address for customer replies but redirect their responses to your fulfilment house or a processing centre. In effect you can appear to be located anywhere you choose, but still process replies at the most efficient location. You can choose a short, memorable address as a proven response aid, and combine the service with Freepost to increase responses further. The cost of Admail varies with the length of the contract required. Details of fixed period contract rates are available from your local Royal Mail Sales Centre.

An example of an Admail address is:
Quality Cutlery Direct, Admail 123, SHEFFIELD, S99 9XX

4. PO Box

PO Boxes enable you to quote a box number instead of a return address. As with Admail, this reduces the length of your address and makes it easier for customers to remember.

Replies go directly to your local Royal Mail delivery office. You can collect your replies yourself, or have them delivered to you.

Mail order regulations prohibit the use of abbreviated addresses such as PO Box numbers for cash-with-order advertisements. If customers are sending you cash, you must ensure your full trading address is displayed.

There is a six-month or annual fee for a PO Box with further charges for additional services. You might, for example, opt to pay a small additional charge and have your items delivered to you, rather than having to collect them yourself.

Business Reply

DESIGN SPE

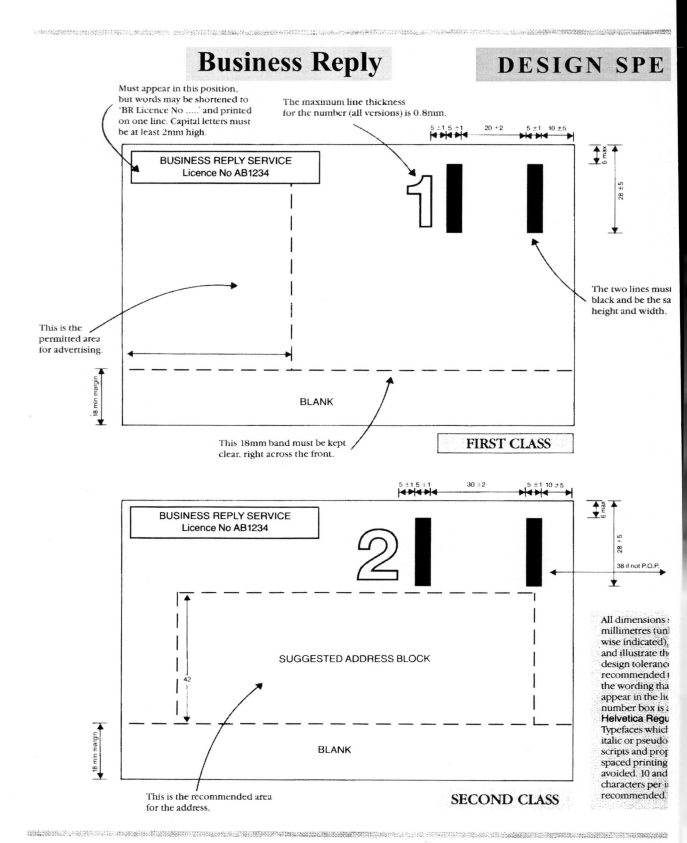

Must appear in this position, but words may be shortened to 'BR Licence No .....' and printed on one line. Capital letters must be at least 2mm high.

The maximum line thickness for the number (all versions) is 0.8mm.

BUSINESS REPLY SERVICE
Licence No AB1234

This is the permitted area for advertising.

This is the recommended area for the address.

The two lines must black and be the sa height and width.

BLANK

This 18mm band must be kept clear, right across the front.

FIRST CLASS

BUSINESS REPLY SERVICE
Licence No AB1234

SUGGESTED ADDRESS BLOCK

BLANK

SECOND CLASS

All dimensions : millimetres (unl wise indicated), and illustrate th design toleranc recommended the wording tha appear in the li number box is Helvetica Regu Typefaces which italic or pseudo scripts and prop spaced printing avoided. 10 and characters per i recommended.

IFICATIONS

Freepost

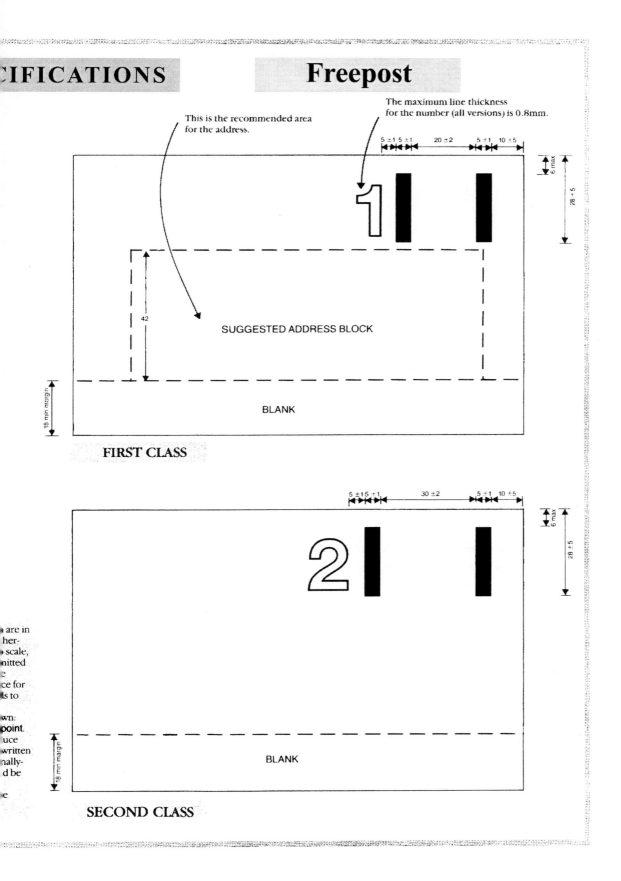

This is the recommended area for the address.

The maximum line thickness for the number (all versions) is 0.8mm.

5 ±1 5 ±1   20 ±2   5 ±1 10 ±5

6 max

28 ±5

42

SUGGESTED ADDRESS BLOCK

18 min margin

BLANK

FIRST CLASS

5 ±15 ±1   30 ±2   5 ±1 10 +5

6 max

28 ±5

18 min margin

BLANK

SECOND CLASS

are in
her-
scale,
nitted
e
ce for
s to

wn:
point.
uce
written
nally-
d be

e

PO Box charges

Standard annual fee £52   Standard six month fee £42

Additional facilities/fees (all subject to local availability)

Delivery to your normal address   £52/year
                                                   £42/6months

Transferred items(transferring normally
addressed mail to your PO Box)   £52/year
                                                   £42/6months

5.   mailmedia™

Please refer to the section on higher volume mailings for details of this service.

Despatching the goods

The increasing popularity of remote shopping, both through mail order and the
Internet, has placed fresh emphasis on delivering the goods. A virtual purchase
cannot represent real income until real goods are delivered to a real address. The
quality and timing of delivery services are essential in establishing good customer
relations and turning first-time buyers into long term customers. Royal Mail and
Parcelforce Worldwide, the UK's largest express parcel carrier, have developed the
following range of delivery services especially for the direct marketing industry:

Guaranteed and Signature Services

There are two signature services, one of which is guaranteed: **Special Delivery** and
Recorded Signed For.

1.   Special Delivery

Guarantees delivery of your items by 12 noon the next working day to 99% of UK
addresses with a money-back guarantee for delay. Special Delivery uses its own
dedicated, secure overnight delivery network. In the unlikely event that your item is
lost or damaged, you can receive compensation of up to £250. The cost of this cover
is included in the price. For a higher level of compensation, you can increase cover
to either £1000 or £2500 for a small additional payment. As part of the Special
Delivery service, we offer a Confirmation of Delivery. By calling 0845 700 1200 after
1pm you can confirm that your item has been delivered that day. Or you can check
online at www.royalmail.com/trackandtrace.

Prepaid, durable Special Delivery envelopes can be ordered through Royal Mail
Direct, 21 South Gyle Crescent, EDINBURGH, EH12 9PB, tel: 08457 782677 or
www.royalmail.com/shop.

2.   Recorded Signed For

Although Recorded Signed For does not offer a guaranteed delivery time, we only
deliver if we can obtain a signature from the delivery address. Proof of posting is
given in the form of a receipt. Delivery can be confirmed via the track trace facility on

the Internet or by phoning the Confirmation of Delivery helpline; by calling after 2pm you can confirm that your item has been delivered that day.

All Guaranteed and Signature Services labels can be obtained by phoning your local Royal Mail Sales Centre on 08457 950 950. You can pay by postage stamp, franking machine or on account.

Packetpost

Packetpost is a convenient and simple method of posting medium-to-large numbers of packets, eliminating the need to weigh and stamp each packet individually. It applies to any item over 60 gm, with no weight limit on 1st class postings and a 1 kg weight limit on 2nd class postings. There is no set minimum daily quota and Packetpost delivers to all UK addresses.

The service is offered at two levels:

- Daily Rate for organisations that post medium numbers of packets daily and more than 5,000 packets a year, or about 100 packets each week. The weight of each day's packets is divided by the number of items. This gives an average weight from which a price can be calculated for that day's despatch.

- Flat Rate for organisations that post more than 10,000 packets a year, or about 200 packets each week, and whose packets have a stable average weight. Price is simply calculated by counting the number of items charged at a prearranged flat rate, based on the average weight of each packet.

Packetpost items use a Printed Postage Impression and payment will be set up on account. The service can be used for an additional fee with Recorded Signed For. A return service allows customers to send goods back to you at your expense.

Packetsort 12

This new service is for organisations sending out 1,000 packets in a single posting. It simply allows us to share the work in despatching packets over 100g. Before handing it to us, you sort your mailing into 12 geographical areas and in return we offer a lower price than for Packetpost. Options include Daily Rate or Flat Rate and 1st or 2nd class.

Flatsort 12

Another new service, Flatsort 12 offers further price reductions if your packets are of a particular size. They need to be no bigger than 353mm x 250mm with uniform thickness of 10mm or less. As with Packetsort 12, mailings need to be sorted into 12 selections.

Further inforamation can be found on the packets website www.royalmail.com/packets.

Local Collect

As more and more people shop from home, Royal Mail has devised a service that solves the problem of being out when the postman arrives. If the parcel needs a signature or is too big for the letterbox, Local Collect allows your customers to pick up the delivery from a local Post Office which will usually be nearer and more convenient for them than their Royal Mail delivery office or Parcelforce Worldwide depot.

Parcelforce Worldwide Services

Parcelforce by 9:00am, by 10:00am, by noon

Parcelforce Worldwide offer guaranteed next-morning delivery - by 9am, 10am or noon to 95% of UK business addresses - with confirmation of delivery on request. Individual items can weigh up to 30 kg, with no limit for multi-item consignments.

Parcelforce Worldwide services are fully documented, offering a proportionate money-back guarantee for delay and a regular Customer Service Report for contract customers. In addition, every item is automatically covered up to £250 against loss and damage at no extra cost. Saturday delivery and Enhanced Compensation up to £2500 are available. Packages can be tracked via www.parcelforce.com. Call 0800 884422 for a free collection.

Parcelforce 24 and Parcelforce 48

Two **guaranteed** services for either next-day (to arrive by close of business) or two-day delivery to over 95% of all UK business addresses.

Computerised tracking allows you to confirm delivery with a free phone call, while regular Customer Service Reports allow you to keep in touch with your deliveries. Collection times can be arranged to suit your particular needs or you can hand in parcels at any Parcelforce Worldwide depot or at selected Post Office branches. Both services are supported by easy to use, simple documentation.

All despatches carry inclusive compensation for loss or damage and the service is covered by a proportionate money-back guarantee for delay. Individual items can weigh up to 30 kg and there is no weight limit for multi-item consignments. Saturday delivery is available for both Parcelforce 24 and Parcelforce 48. Call 0800 884422 for a free collection. Enhanced Compensation up to £2500 is available. Packages can be tracked via www.parcelforce.com.

Parcelforce Worldwide Select

Parcelforce Worldwide Select has been developed to meet the growing demand from consumers for flexible delivery times. Convenient time windows can be selected to ensure that your customer is at home to receive their goods.

Parcelforce Worldwide Select is available on the Parcelforce 24 and Parcelforce 48 services, offering guaranteed delivery within the following time windows:

PF24 and PF48 services	Mon to Fri	18.00 to 21.00
	Saturday	07.00 to 12.00
PF 48 service	Mon to Fri	07.00 to 12.00

International direct marketing using the mail

Overseas mailing services

One way to tackle the important but complex business of marketing overseas is by international direct marketing - using the mail to find and locate prospects, generate sales leads, sell direct, and deliver the goods. As customs and tariff barriers have relaxed, international direct marketing provides real opportunities for British businesses. Royal Mail offers a complete package of international services, many of which are recent additions especially developed for the international marketer:

- Airmail Letters, Small Packets, Printed Papers

- International Zone and Format

- International Country Sort

- International Mailing Options

- International Response Services

- International Signature Services and Swiftair

Outward mailing - delivering your message internationally

Low volume mailings

1. Airmail Letters

The Airmail Letters service gives you a complete, fast, reliable worldwide coverage for business or personal mail. We aim to deliver to Western Europe within two days of posting, to Eastern Europe within three days of posting and to destinations outside Europe within four days. (Surface mail letters can be sent to destinations outside Europe.) Airmail letters have a weight limit of 2 kg. Items should carry a special airmail label or you should write 'PAR AVION - BY AIRMAIL' in the top left-hand corner.

2. Airmail Printed Papers

A special, economical service for sending printed matter, such as books, newspapers and brochures abroad. You benefit from savings against Airmail Letter rates. As with Airmail Letters, we aim to deliver within two to four days depending on global region. The maximum weight is 2kg but packages containing only books or pamphlets may weigh up to 5kg (with exceptions for certain countries). A surface mail service is available.

You might want to consider using our Airmail Small Packets and prepaid Airpack services, International Signature services and Swiftair products for your low volume mailings – please refer to **Despatching the goods internationally** for more information.

3. International Zone and Format on Demand

If you do not have enough mail to qualify for International Zone and Format Services (see below on higher volume mailings) but wish to send one-off international mailings, try International Zone and Format on Demand. To qualify for the service, mailings must total £100 or more in value and payment must be made seven days prior to posting.

4. International Mailing Options

International Mailing Options gives you the benefit of access to discounted domestic rates and/or local look services in a wide range of countries in Europe and North America, as well as other destinations. These are shown in the table below. International Mailing Options is an exciting option for international direct marketing, providing cost and service advantages for mailing publications and mail order goods. Your mail is delivered by the postal service of the destination country. It arrives complete with local printed postmark and return address, making your targeted mailings indistinguishable from local mailings. This offers the potential for improved response rates which can be further enhanced by using International Response Services.

Contract facilities are available, so the service is easy to use for nearly all companies conducting high or low volume mailings.

Table 8.7.2   International Mailing Options – countries and services (Dec 2001)

	Direct Mail and catalogues	Publications	Packages
Canada	✗	✗	
USA	✗	✗	✗*
Austria	✗	✗	✗
Belgium	✗		✗
Denmark	✗		✗
Finland	✗		✗
France	✗	✗	✗
Germany	✗	✗	✗
Ireland	✗	✗	✗
Italy	✗		✗
Luxembourg	✗		✗
Netherlands	✗	✗**	✗
Norway	✗		
Spain	✗		✗
Sweden	✗		
Switzerland	✗		✗*
Australia	✗	✗	
New Zealand	✗		

* Printed matter only
** Letters and packages

Higher volume mailings

1. International Zone and Format Services

International Zone and Format Services is the Royal Mail international contract service developed with the needs of the business customer in mind. Reliable, cost-effective and with account facilities, International Zone and Format Services are especially suitable for businesses sending regular volumes of international mail.

You can use the service to mail up to 2kg including letters, statements, invoices, reports and mailshots. It is useful for sending books, newspapers, magazines and personalised printed items, because the maximum weight limit increases to 5kg for books and pamphlets. Little or no presorting is needed, depending on which service you choose.

We will return to you, at no extra charge, any items that cannot be delivered. This occasionally happens when a recipient moves and leaves no forwarding address, or if a company ceases trading. Receiving these items will help you to maintain up-to-date mailing lists and retain greater control of future activity. All Royal Mail international delivery times are measured by an independent auditor to ensure quality of service is maintained. Key benefits are:

- The only UK based carrier to deliver direct to 280 destinations worldwide.

- Direct delivery – no re-mail centres – for accuracy and speed.

- Cost-effective service at highly competitive rates.

- No rounding up of weights; no 'hidden charges'.

- Everything supplied for your mailroom: documentation, bags and labels.

- Free collections.

- Uses PPI (Printed Postage Impressions); no stamp or franking necessary.

- Billed on account.

2. International Country Sort

If you are able to presort your mail to the international sort criteria, you will obtain larger cost savings with International Country Sort, which is a worldwide distribution service for large mailings. International Country Sort offers three service options, allowing contract customers to select the best combination of speed and economy for their individual requirements:

Priority – when speed is the prime consideration International Country Sort, Priority delivers print items by airmail directly to over 280 destinations throughout the world.

Standard – International Country Sort Standard offers a combination of speed and economy. Direct flights to 90 countries outside Europe, followed by economic handling in the country of destination, means the service combines reliability with value for money.

Economy – International Country Sort Economy uses the Royal Mail global surface network to ensure secure and reliable distribution with economy.

There is a set of seven pricing zones across all three speeds offering a range of competitive prices. Choose the speed and work-share option that suits your needs.

3. International Country Sort M-Bags

When sending a consignment of printed matter to a single address overseas you can make additional cost savings on all International Country Sort service streams by using International Country Sort M-Bags. Each M-Bag can carry a consignment of printed matter weighing up to 11 kg to a single address. Your mailing is bagged in the UK and reaches its final destination without the need for any re-sorting or processing on the way. This means that M-Bags simplify handling both in the UK and abroad which, in turn, leads to significant reductions in postage costs for your company.

Bags, address labels and documentation are all supplied by Royal Mail International. Pack your consignment in the bags, then complete and affix the relevant labels.

4. International Mailing Options

This service is suitable for both high and low volume mailings. See above on low volume mailings for a description of International Mailing Options.

International reply services to boost response

International Response Services

Royal Mail offers you a number of different international response options:

- International Business Reply Service

- International Admail

- International Freepost Response

- International Stamped Response

1.   International Business Reply Service (IBRS)

Not long ago it was necessary to arrange reply services with the various local post offices all over the world. Today, however, it can be done simply and quickly from the UK using International Response Services.

International Business Reply Service (IBRS) works in the same way as Business Reply in the UK: you send your customers a prepaid envelope or reply card, allowing them to reply free of charge to a UK address. With IBRS all reply devices have the same address and design no matter where your customer is based. Replies are returned to you direct by airmail. IBRS is simple to arrange with a one-off fee covering an annual service licence and a standard worldwide charge for each item returned.

2.   International Admail

International Admail works in much the same way as the UK Admail service. You offer a local address for customer responses while having your replies forwarded to another global address for efficient processing. Royal Mail supplies the local design specification to ensure it matches local postal designs. Available in 16 key international markets, with new countries being added all the time, International Admail's direct route gives greater control over responses and can keep costs down by bypassing local agents. Details of countries participating in International Admail are available through your local Sales Centre on 08457 950 950.

3.   International Freepost Response

Currently only available in Ireland, the service works in a similar way to International Admail. We give you a local address to which your customers can reply. You can choose to supply preprinted reply devices, or invite your customers to put the Freepost address on their own packaging. Items of up to 2kg can be carried.

4.   International Stamped Response

If you wish to offer your customers a local address, but prefer them to pay their own postage, you can opt for International Stamped Response. You offer your customer a printed reply device or simply tell them the address to write back to. Either way, they apply the stamp but pay only local rate postage. The service is available in 14 countries, including the US and the main European markets.

Despatching the goods internationally

Airmail Small Packets and Prepaid Airpacks

This convenient and economical service for goods, gifts and commercial samples offers savings against Airmail Letter rates with worldwide coverage, (a surface mail service is also available). Maximum weight is 2kg (apart from Saudi Arabia, 1kg). A letter, invoice or other document can be enclosed if it relates to the contents of the packet. We aim to deliver within the same timescales as those for Airmail Letters.

Alternatively, you can purchase prepaid Airpacks, especially designed for use with the Small Packet Service, at any Post Office or by mail order from Royal Mail, Tallents House, 21 South Gyle Crescent, EDINBURGH, EH12 9PB, or by phoning us on 08457 782677.

Airpacks come in two sizes (C3 and C4) and prepaid up to 500 gm and 300 gm respectively. If you wish to send heavier items in an Airpack, you will have to pay an extra charge. Please check with your Post Office branch.

International Signature Services and Swiftair

1.   International Recorded

You can use International Recorded for items which are low in value but need a signature on delivery. Your item can be sent worldwide by Airmail or surface mail using the Letter, Small Packet and Printed Papers services. All you have to do to use the service is stick special labels to your item.

2.   International Registered

If you need a signature on delivery and compensation for loss or damage to valuables, use International Registered. The service is easy to use with special labels, and your item can be sent using the Airmail or surface mail Letters and Small Packet services. Maximum compensation is either £500 or £2200 - depending on the fee paid and availability to individual countries. The service is not available to some countries and maximum compensation is lower for some destinations. For country availability, please check with your Post Office branch or by contacting us on 08457 950 950.

3.   Swiftair

Swiftair is an express airmail service for important letters, papers or documents. The payment of a premium over normal airmail secures despatch on the first available flight to a destination country. Your item can be sent using the Letters, Small Packets and Printed Papers services (weight limits are 2 kg for letters, small packets and printed papers and 5 kg for books and pamphlets). The service is easily accessed by special labels or prepaid Swiftpacks (see below).

Travelling alongside the normal mail, Swiftair items are immediately transferred and separately processed on arrival at each of the five international sorting offices, speeding their sorting and onward despatch. They are then expressed to their destination on the first available flight - on the day of posting where possible. Items are bar-coded for tracking up to the point of departure from the UK postal system. Swiftair is ideal for priority letters, documents and packages. However, delivery times are not guaranteed because internal delivery standards vary from country to country.

4.   Swiftair labels

Simply affix a Swiftair label to each piece of international mail, add standard airmail postage for the destination, plus the fixed Swiftair item fee, then post at any Post Office branch or have the items collected with your company collection.

5.　Prepaid Swiftpacks

Alternatively, you can purchase prepaid Swiftpacks at any Post Office or by mail order from Royal Mail, Tallents House, 21 South Gyle Crescent, EDINBURGH, EH12 9PB, or by phoning us on 08457 782677.

Swiftpacks come in three sizes (DL, C5 and C4) and prepaid up to 50 gm, 100 gm and 300 gm respectively. Each one is distinctly identifiable as a priority item. If you wish to send heavier items in a Swiftpack, you will have to pay an extra charge. Please check with your Post Office branch.

6.　Swiftair plus Recorded

Available worldwide, Swiftair plus Recorded combines express Airmail with a signature on delivery for low value items. Special labels make it easy to use and your item can be sent using the Letters, Small Packet and Printed Papers services. We cannot guarantee delivery times because internal delivery standards vary from country to country.

7.　Swiftair plus Registered

If you are sending valuable items by express Airmail and need a signature on delivery, use Swiftair plus Registered. You simply stick special labels to your item which can be sent using the Letters and Small Packets services. We cannot guarantee delivery times because internal delivery standards vary from country to country. Maximum compensation is either £500 or £2200 depending on the fee paid and availability to individual countries. The service is not available to some countries and maximum compensation is lower for some destinations. For country availability, please check with your Post Office Branch or contact us on 08457 950 950.

For more information on all Royal Mail's international services call your local Sales Centre on 08457 950 950.

Parcelforce Worldwide International Services

Perhaps even more critical than at home, fast, reliable delivery of goods is essential when opening up overseas accounts by direct marketing.

Parcelforce Worldwide offers the following services, with differing speeds and rates:

- International Datapost

- Euro 48

- International Scheduled

- International Standard and Economy Services

1.　International Datapost

International Datapost is a guaranteed, timetabled express delivery service for documents and parcels to 225 countries and territories worldwide. It includes next-day delivery of documents to many European destinations and New York. Long-haul destinations such as the Far East are reached within two to three working days. For Contract customers International Datapost offers by 9am, by 10am and by noon options for many major destinations within Europe.

You have the reassurance of a proportionate money-back guarantee and enhanced compensation of up to £2,500 for loss or damage. Call **0800 884422** for a free collection.

2. Euro 48

Euro 48 is a highly reliable, guaranteed parcel service for door-to-door delivery from two working days to many European cities and towns. The service is supported by a computerised tracking system, which provides customers with prompt confirmation or proof of delivery on request.

Euro 48 is available to contract customers by calling 0800 884422, through selected Post Offices and all Parcelforce Worldwide depots.

3. International Scheduled

This service complements the Euro 48 service, providing guaranteed deliveries to countries outside Europe from three days, and is available to contract customers only.

4. International Standard and Economy Services (only available from Post Office branches.)

Parcelforce Worldwide serves 239 countries and territories, with straightforward zonal pricing. International Standard Service offers delivery to Europe from three working days and the rest of the world from five working days. Compensation cover for actual loss or damage up to £150 per parcel is included.

When cost is paramount, Parcelforce International Economy Service offers a very competitive option, with expected delivery times to European destinations from ten working days and to the rest of the world from 20 working days.

For more information on all Parcelforce Worldwide services visit www.parcelforce.com or contact the Parcelforce Worldwide Enquiry Centre on 0800 224466. Alternatively, write to Parcelforce Worldwide Commercial, FREEPOST, Solaris Court, Davy Avenue, MILTON KEYNES, MK5 8PP.

Chapter 8.8

Contact centres

This chapter includes:

- ❏ **Call versus contact centre: what's the difference?**
- ❏ **Growth of contact centres**
- ❏ **Contact centre performance management**
- ❏ **Contact centre operations**
- ❏ **Successful outsourcing**
- ❏ **Identifying a well managed contact centre**
- ❏ **The future of the contact centre**

About this chapter

hapter 4.6 dealt with the use of the phone for outbound telemarketing. Here we concentrate on its function as an incoming communication channel.

As consumers' use of the phone grew in the 1990s, companies developed dedicated call centres – either in-house or outsourced. But it gradually became clear that a call centre divorced from other channels of communication, and often without access to historical customer data, was inadequate.

This realisation was reinforced with the arrival of new communications media in the shape of the Internet and e-mail, redoubling the need for the integration of communication channels: hence the rise of the contact centre.

We look at the way contact centres work–or should work–at questions of work measurement and performance evaluation, and outsourcing versus in-house.

This chapter has been compiled for direct marketers wanting to know how to deal with customer contact problems, rather than for those wanting to know how to run a contact centre.

It has been written by Steve Pink, who has also used a quantity of material provided by Liz Fry.

Steve Pink Managing Consultant
Telecommerce Consultancy

Steve is a contact centre consultant and customer service professional — experienced in the provision and operation of customer interaction centres. Steve specialises in combining people, processes and technology to deliver profitable customer relationships. With over 15 years experience managing call centres and contact centre projects, Steve has a significant record of success managing telesales channels, direct marketing operations, e-commerce channels and customer-focused call centres.

Steve has worked on projects with organisations large and small in the private and public sector including BUPA, Forte Hotels, P&O, The Post Office, Demon Internet, Thus plc, Fleming Premier Banking and Vizzavi.

In addition to presenting contact centre training workshops, contributing articles to contact centre magazines, participating in Direct Marketing Association and Communications Managers Association forums, Steve is the chair of the examination board for the IDM Certificate in Contact Centre Management.

Steve Pink M IDM
Telecommerce Consultancy
PO Box 385, Aylesbury HP22 6XL
Tel: +44 (0)1296 69 68 61
Fax: +44 (0)1296 69 65 89
E-mail: steve@telecommerce.co.uk
Website: www.telecommerce.co.uk

Chapter 8.8

Contact centres

Call versus contact centre: What's the difference?

The current topical debate focuses around call centre versus contact centre. The public in general are just about getting used to the term call centre when we throw another one at them. So what is the debate and what is the difference? Quite simply:

Call centre =

Contact centre =

> A call centre — a work environment in which the main business is conducted via the phone while simultaneously using display screen equipment (DSE). This includes parts of companies dedicated to this activity such as internal helplines as well as the whole company.
>
> A contact centre — a place where customers and prospects interact with the business though various media channels. Typically phone and e-mail communications are prevalent; however written contact (ie direct mail and correspondence) is also common, and communication via the Internet is a growing feature.

Deciding to set up a call centre or contact centre goes back to strategy:

?   What are you trying to achieve?

?   How do you want to communicate with or contact your customers?

?   How do they want to contact you?

?   What percentage of your 'traffic' is phone/e-mail/Internet-based, and how will the volumes of each change?

?   What technology could you use?

?   What will it cost? What savings will you make by combining operations?

?   What is the competition doing?

?   What skills do your people have or will they need? How can you support that with training and coaching?

Growth of contact centres

✔   At the end of 2000, there were around 15,000 call centres in Europe.

✔   The number of call centres in the UK is predicted to be 5,720 by the end of 2002, an increase of approximately 1,500 call centres since 1998.

✔   The European growth rates have slowed down from 22% in 1998 to around 9% in 2001.

✔   The UK accounts for more than one third of the European call centre market.

✔   On average, 55% of call centre budgets are spent on salaries.

✔   UK call centres will spend a total of $2.5 billion on CRM-based technologies from 1998-2003.

Source: *Datamonitor*

The 1990s saw the evolution of the call centre – large operational units, some with up to a thousand operators, supported by state-of-the-art technology. At the start of the 21st Century, we have seen the emergence of the contact centre -the marriage of the phone with e-mail and the Internet, enabling a centre to deal with various customer communications in one place.

Current estimates state that some 2% of the working population (around 500,000 people) work in the industry. Growth rates for call and contact centre development have slowed down within the UK from around 40% in 1997 to an estimate of 9% by the end of 2001.

The huge growth in contact centres over the last three years has primarily been driven by the advancement and cost reduction of technology. Added to the emergence of the Internet and web presence, customers demand choice. They are no longer content to 'phone'; they want to 'contact' us via e-mail, fax, web-chat, text messaging and whatever else they choose (see more in the chapters on new media). Companies need to set themselves up to handle that.

Call centres truly realised the need to handle web-based enquiries during the last five years. In 1998 there were less than 120 European call centres with Internet functionality (Datamonitor). Germany was at the forefront with 38% of the European web-enabled call centre market. It will take until 2003 for the UK and German market shares to be approximately equal, which means that both markets will be important for sales and marketing. **Figure 8.8.1** illustrates the European growth

Figure 8.8.1   **Web-enabled call centre European country splits**

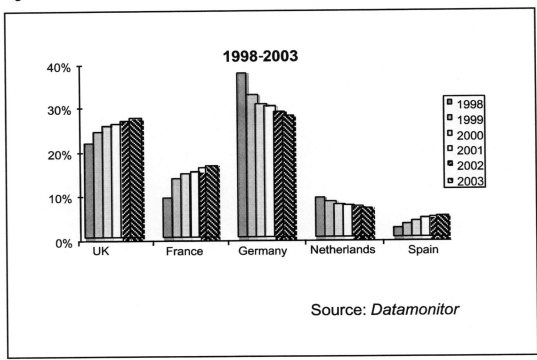

Source: *Datamonitor*

The UK centres will not experience the levels of web penetration of the other major national markets, possibly due to the fact that many UK call centres are older than the European average – growth rates are slowing down dramatically (9% in 2000 compared to an average of 22% in 1998 -Datamonitor).

So what does this mean?

✔ Companies are investing in e-technology now.

✔ Marketing communications are now referencing web and e-mail addresses.

✔ Service levels are being set, not only for calls but also for all customers 'traffic'.

✔ Operators are required to have a higher level of technical ability and be able to multi-task.

From a marketing perspective, it means we too have more choice -we can integrate marketing methods and use not only the call centre for response, but the Internet too.

The customer is in charge

Very quickly, having a web presence meant that customers who liked what they saw wanted to get in touch. The traditional route was to pick up the phone or write, but technology has given customers more choice. Now a customer can do any of the following that are shown in **Table 8.8.1**

Table 8.8.1   **Actions a customer can take**

Contact media	Activity	Success/speed of answer
Pick up the phone	✔ Usually connected to a call centre	✔ Should get an immediate response ✘ Opening hours dependent ✔ Average 80% calls answered in 20 secs.
Fax a request	✔ Traditionally received by a head office administration department ✔ Could now go through to a contact centre.	✔ Service levels should be set by the company ✘ Can 'get lost' if received on paper.
Send a letter	✔ Traditionally received by a head office administration dept ✔ Could now go through to a *contact centre*	✔ Service levels average 48 hours to reply ✘ Again, can get lost
Search for answers on the company website	✔ Search through pages of information ✔ Some sites have FAQs (frequently asked questions)	✔ Immediate ✔ Customer can access anytime at their leisure ✘ Can lack specific answers
Send an e-mail	✔ Send an e-mail to a specified company e-mail address ✔ Could now go through to a *contact centre*	✔ The company should have specific service levels ✘ Can wait days for a reply ✘ Difficult to follow up if no reply has been received
Click on a 'call me' button on the web page	✔ Company website -call me button requests a call back from the *call/contact centre*	✔ Should get an immediate reply depending on service levels and opening hours ✔ Operator and customer can view the same data at the same time

But it works two ways -it also means we can direct prospects or customers to a particular response channel. The customer is in charge – but customer choice must not undermine the commercial objectives of the organisation. So it is important we have a customer contact strategy.

Contact media strategy

Once integrated marketing, sales and service strategic principles are agreed between client (managing director / marketing manager) and contact centre (in-house contact centre manager or outsource supplier), it is important to define – and regularly review – a contact media strategy.

First – agree which media are to be supported:

The main media that need supporting (in rough order of priority) are:
Live voice, Interactive Voice Response (IVR), fax, white mail, e-mail, web interaction (including static pages/self-help/call me buttons/web-chat/page shadowing).
Developing media that need consideration are: interactive TV, mobile services (SMS and WAP) and public kiosk.

Second – a management discipline to ensure a unified approach:

This starts with centralised management to ensure that the controllers of the different media all report to one manager/director. This ensures unified purpose and intention, which should result in customers receiving a similar response to common issues, irrespective of which medium the customer chooses to use.

Third – introduce common scripting control:

To ensure 'ultimate' unified response irrespective of medium chosen by the customer, all scripting and content should be brought under common control. This will result in call centre agents being provided with scripting guides that use similar phrases to the IVR scripts. These will complement (not conflict with) announcements on the website that flow logically from the web-based self help pages etc.

Fourth – match media options to customer segmentation:

Now that a robust contact media approach is in place it is time to decide 'who gets what'. By analysing the lifetime value of a customer and comparing this with the allocated 'cost to serve' we can select the appropriate media that should be used to provide a service for the customer. For example, low value customers may be restricted to web and IVR services. High value customers should be given a choice of which media they prefer and always receive priority transfer to a suitably qualified live agent at any stage of their call (or indeed to answer the call, if that is what the customer chooses). Exceptions to the preplanned media should be allowed for – for example in an organisation with CTI (Computer Telephony Integration) and CRM (Customer Relationship Management) capabilities, it will be possible to identify a customer, using web or IVR channels, who is being chased for outstanding debts. The customer can be 'intercepted' by a live operator (live call transfer or web page 'push') so that the customer is confronted with unpaid bills, rather than continuing to use services while in debt management.

Fifth – survey and review the contact media strategy:

The organisation's contact media strategy ought to be the subject of regular customer satisfaction surveying to ensure it is fit for purpose and meets with the needs of customers.

Key users of contact centres

As expected, the early adopters of web-enabled call centre technology became the first developers of contact centres. Two key vertical markets at the forefront were **financial services** and **IT**. Financial services, typically, have high value products that justify the spend on web technology, while IT prospects and customers would expect businesses to lead the way with contact centre applications.

Other markets now developing contact centres include:

✔ Remote shopping

✔ Telecommunications

✔ Utilities

✔ Travel

✔ Manufacturing and distribution

✔ Entertainment

There are potentially great benefits to be had from integrating the web and call centre for business-to-business operations within distribution:

✔ Centralisation of information.

✔ Centralised order placing online or over the phone.

✔ Simple tracking of goods via the web.

✔ Complex queries handled by the call centre.

✔ Up-selling or revenue generating queries handled by phone.

✔ Consistency of message across all customer communication channels.

Parcelforce

Parcelforce allows customers to track and enquire about deliveries through various channels:

✔ *Phone Us* – 0800 number through to its enquiry call centre.

✔ *Phone Me* – 'Phone Me' button on the website [www.parcelforce.com] where Parcelforce call you back at a time you specify.

✔ *Online tracking option* – track and enquire about an order online.

✔ *E-mail* – customer services/ business/ logistical enquiries via e-mail.

✔ *FAQs* – online frequently asked questions which try to help solve your query immediately.

A 'Customer Interaction centre' -a place where all interactions and communications with our customers take place, surely has to be the ultimate operation. Seamless from the outside, it requires clever technology, highly skilled staff, key measures and service levels that satisfy customer and business needs.

Contact centre performance management

Whether we are talking about management appraisal of a contact centre's performance or a call centre's appraisal of an operative, how do we relate efficiency and effectiveness?

Efficiency – for example:

- The volume and/or speed of contacts handled.

- The volume and/or speed of fulfilment packs despatched.

- Cost per unit of work undertaken (call handled/pack despatched).

Effectiveness – for example:

- Campaign ROI. (How did the actual revenue compare to our plan?)

- Prescribed successful outcomes relative to successful customer contacts. (When we established contact did customer and organisation achieve a satisfactory or desired outcome?)

- Customer loyalty. (Is customer churn lower?)

- Brand awareness over time. (How do customers perceive the organisation?)

- Customer satisfaction. (Were customers satisfied with the service received from the contact centre?)

The quality challenge

How does quantity stack up against quality?

What do we mean by quality anyway?

How do we measure quality?

What is quality worth?

For example:

Operative A: Handles **a** calls per hour at a cost of **£b**
Derives revenue (by cross- or up-selling) of **£c**
Receives a customer satisfaction rating of **d** units

Operative B: Handles **a-x** calls per hour at the same cost (of **£b**)
Derives revenue of **£1.1c**
Receives a customer satisfaction rating of **10d** units

Which of these is better?

1)   from the point of view of the contact centre?

2)   from the point of view of the contact centre's client?

Of course there isn't an answer: the point is that client and call centre (or marketing management and in-house call centre management) need to be clear about the real everyday situations of which this is typical.

Both call centre and client must have clear expectations in these situations – otherwise any void will encourage management accountants (in the call centre or the client) to squeeze quantity out of the operatives in a bid to reduce today's costs with no concern for tomorrow's consequences.

This issue is at the heart of the in/outsourcing debate (see later in this chapter). An in-house call centre manager has to keep the financial controller at bay, but it is more difficult for an external bureau that has to deal with its own accountants, the client's accountants, and the competition.

It is essential that marketing managers responsible for managing relationships with a contact centre understand the terms on which the balance between quantity and quality has been agreed.

Suggested performance indicators

- Abandoned rate – those calls where the caller gives up before the centre answers, expressed as a percentage of the total call attempts. *Clients should expect a maximum 5% of calls to be abandoned.*

- Average speed of answer – the delay between the customer dialling the number and the start of the resolution conversation (could be a live operator or a managed, interactive voice response). *Clients should expect 5 – 15 secs.*

- Percentage of calls answered within service level – *such an indicator might be set at 80% of calls to be answered within 20 secs.*

- Average work time – the time to handle the customer conversation and any 'after call' work resulting from it. *This has to be piloted to ensure the customer satisfaction scores and call outcomes are balanced* Also look to 'remove' after call work to a specialist area to improve efficiency.

- Average talk time – the time to handle the customer conversation. *This has to be piloted to ensure the customer satisfaction scores and call outcomes are balanced.*

- Cross-selling conversion (in a selling environment) – to sell additional products to the calling customer.

- Conversion rate (in a selling environment) – to sell campaign products to the calling customer – *might be 15% for a European Travel campaign.*

- Error rate – if it can be measured (eg a brochure fulfilment campaign).

- Cost per sale (in a selling environment).

- Monitoring evaluation – to establish and maintain quality standards .

Contact centre service levels

Studies confirm that customer satisfaction with call centres has been showing a downward trend, despite the industry's fixation on customer relationship management, customer lifetime value and the drive for call centres to become contact centres.

A recent survey of 579 call centre managers showed that only 23% of the respondents stated that they regularly meet their inbound service level goals. If we can't get around to answering the phone or responding to e-mail in a timely fashion, we are not going to fulfil the promises of the things that really matter: building relationships with our customers and earning their loyalty. We need to learn some new rules of service level management:

The rules of service level management

- Service level must be in parity across all channels.

- Service level must be supported by multi-channel workload planning.

- The terms and tools must be appropriate for the application.

- Improving quality is the sure way to improve service level.

- Budgets must reflect today's workload dynamics.

Service level must be in parity across contact channels, although being in parity in this context doesn't necessarily mean being equal. That is, it doesn't mean you can respond to e-mail as fast as you can respond to a phone call. Rather, it means you are operating within customer expectations across contact channels.

The customer who expects a reply to an e-mail within a few hours but doesn't get it may pick up the phone and call. Now you have two contacts going, which sends the call centre productivity down the drain.

Keeping customers informed

Similarly, if a customer ends up in an eternal phone queue they may send an e-mail, try alternative numbers or work through a different set of voice response unit options. If you want to know what your customers' expectations are, then ask them, and then observe their behaviour. Also, tell them what to expect in terms of response times. E-mail response management systems have the capability to send automated replies sending a response to the customer, acknowledging that the e-mail they sent was received and informing them of when to expect a response from an agent.

The most successful contact centres have an established systematic planning process. They understand how the contact centre supports the organisation's mission and they ensure that everyone in the contact centre and those with key supporting roles outside the contact centre, have a basic understanding of how contact centres operate.

Service level versus quality?

On the surface it appears that service level and quality are at odds. You can have an excellent service level but your agents may still misunderstand callers' requests, enter or relay the wrong information, make callers angry and miss opportunities to capture valuable feedback. The list goes on.

But service level is an enabler – it means that contacts are getting in the door and to the places they need to go. For example, as service level deteriorates, more and more callers are likely to verbalise their criticisms when their calls are finally answered. Call handling time will go up. Occupancy will increase. If this condition continues then agent morale is bound to sink. Turnover and burn-out will go up, as will recruitment and training costs.

In truth, there is no such thing as quality versus service level or response time. These objectives work hand in hand.

The components of a quality contact

- Customer is satisfied.

- All data entry is correct.

- Agent provides correct response.

- Customer receives correct information.

- Agent captures all requisite or useful information.

- Customer is not transferred around.

- Customer doesn't get rushed.

- Customer is assured that contact was effective.

- Call centre mission is accomplished.

- Unsolicited marketplace feedback is detected and documented.

- Customer doesn't feel it necessary to check up, verify or repeat.

- People 'down the line' can correctly interpret the information.

- Agent has pride in workmanship.

- Customer doesn't get a 'busy' signal when using the phone or a 'no response' from web page.

- Customer is not placed 'in queue' for too long.

We must do everything possible to prevent unnecessary contacts at the source by improving quality and customer information, and we should encourage customers to use automated support alternatives – improving web-based self-service systems, teaching customers how to use those alternatives and building customer communities so they can assist each other.

We must be realistic about total demand in the operational budgets. Contact centres are more necessary than ever. In the end, service levels must be viewed in the context of a much larger objective: customer loyalty. Service level does not guarantee a satisfying customer experience, but it cannot be minimised either: it is an enabler.

Building a performance management framework

Performance management is a means for evaluating and improving individual, team and organisational performance against predefined strategies and objectives. Performance management places emphasis on the need to:

- Set key accountabilities.

- Agree future objectives in each of those key accountability areas.

- Agree measures and standards of performance.

- Assign timescales and priorities.

Performance management of the contact centre should become a formal documented system for the periodic review of performance against predefined strategies and objectives.

Contact centre operations

Planning

The first link begins at marketing director/contact centre director level, with a shared understanding of how the organisation's marketing communications strategy will impact on customer contacts. The next challenge is to convert this strategy into a detailed marketing plan with clear dates and media volumes against each campaign event. From here the contact centre can start to plan media volumes over time and convert this data into resource requirements.

Building an integrated self-service model

An organisation trying to cut cost and improve service will focus on staff costs, automating previously labour intensive processes and reducing cycle times (get quicker). Re-engineering the business to provide more (or even all) services online will be seen as a primary solution.

It is important that organisations providing more self-service functions also provide more online self-help. Even if this is done the customer will expect additional 'live' help whenever they require it and will expect the contact centre adviser to know exactly where they had got to in the self-help process. It is, therefore, important to develop an integrated multimedia contact centre that can see the customer's latest status, whichever communications method the customer has chosen to use.

Briefing an inbound phone campaign

There are five key questions to ask before embarking on an inbound phone campaign:

? What will stimulate the call?

? What do you want to happen during the call?

? What do you want to happen after the call?

? How should the activity be measured?

? What do you want to be analysed?

Crucial to an inbound phone operation is to have the right number of people available when the calls come in. This is not easy. One solution is to use a bureau – particularly for TV responses (see outsourcing section). If you are using internal resources, you will need to develop a model to forecast the number of calls you anticipate.

If the planned resources cannot handle your predicted number of calls you may need to spread your advertising. There is nothing worse than generating priceless leads that you cannot capture because your contact centre is overloaded.

Table 8.8.2 shows a basic checklist for use with inbound phone campaigns. Undoubtedly you will find more to put in your brief, but whatever you put in it -make sure it is in writing. As somebody once said: "A verbal brief isn't worth the paper it's printed on".

Table 8.8.2   **Briefing checklist for operators**

What is the creative message?

What am I offering callers?

What is the product/service?

What are the product's key features?

What benefits do the features give the customers?

What is its price?

What discounts are available?

What phone number types do I require (0800/STD etc)?

What questions might be asked?

How do I want questions answered?

Is a fulfilment package available?

Is the fulfilment package to be personalised?

When and where does advertising appear?

Volume of response anticipated?

Are coupons involved?

Ratio of coupons/calls expected?

How frequently are reports wanted?

What is to be reported?

Does information have to be sent to others (branch offices etc)?

Start date and likely duration of campaign (allow four weeks to get campaign up and running)

Measuring performance

The phone has to be operationally controlled from start to finish. Increasingly this is being done by users in-house. Getting operational procedures right is crucial. Here is a sample phone report form for an in-house call centre.

Suggested phone report form (inbound)

Calls handled ....

Calls lost
(Abandoned calls) ....

Average call duration ....

Calls per hour ....

Calls per hour per operator (average) ....

Media source(s) ....

Coupon/e-mail/phone ratio ....

Tabulated responses
to customer scripted questions ....

Volumes of business generated, in terms of:

   customers ....

   income ....

   leads ....

   appointments etc ....

Labour hours ....

Call charges ....

The costs

Using a bureau, you can expect to pay £4,500-£7,500 to set up even a simple campaign, with cost per call being £0.80-£1.20 per call handled. To this you must add 0800 phone charges and any fulfilment costs.

Handling calls yourself can cost you even more. Unless you have a very large unit where calls are absorbed into other phone traffic, the risk is that you will have a lot of people sitting around doing not much for most of the day. These inefficiencies cost money. But once you are past a certain critical mass, the cost savings of managing your own inbound phone services can be dramatic.

Beware! Undertaking inbound services is a little like signing a blank cheque. You have only limited control over the volume of calls you will generate. The more calls, the more it will cost you. Think carefully about the cost and budget allocation before setting up a contact centre/customer service operation.

Successful outsourcing

Outsourcing telemarketing has become big business. In 2000, the global outsourcing market was worth $21 billion with a growth rate of 70-80%. (Source: *Call Centre Outsourcing, The Guide* –CallCraft). That is a lot of business, so why are businesses choosing to give it to someone else?

Why outsource?

✔ **High volume** – insufficient resources internally to handle the response.

✔ **Timescales** – too short a deadline to set up internal call centre.

✔ **Campaign driven** – not cost-effective to have a 'full time' unit.

✔ **Lack of experience** – operational experience weak.

✔ **Cost savings** – avoid the operation costs and overheads of a call centre.

✔ **Piloting** – test new ideas before heavily investing in-house.

✔ **Specialist services** – certain outsourcing companies are market specialists.

✔ **Improve company focus** – open up a new customer communication channel.

✔ **Free internal resources** – to focus on core business/services.

In-house call centre or outsourced bureau?

Most of the functions and requirements described in this chapter relate to a properly equipped and manned call/contact centre. What is the difference between that and an outsourced bureau?

The comparison following in **Table 8.8.3** outlines where there may be differences between the two types of centre, although the distinction is clearly not a rigid one in every case:

Table 8.8.3 **Comparison of call centre and bureau capability**

Call or contact centre	Outsourced bureau
Dedicated operators trained to a very high standard; in-depth knowledge of products, client and market	Non-dedicated operators answer calls for a wide range of clients. Operators have limited knowledge of clients and customers
Comprehensive service embracing all aspects of phone/e-mail marketing	Volume call handling, mostly simple requests for information
Involved in strategic applications of phone, e-mail and contact strategy	Confined to straightforward call handling/e-mail handling
Ongoing role in terms of customer service and satisfaction; performance not always so easy to measure	Clearly defined response; output usually easily measured, eg response rates, conversion rates

Who and what is being outsourced?

Table 8.8.4 **Who and what is being outsourced?**

Who (% of UK market 2000)	What
Telecommunications (21%)	Field sales support
Financial services (20%)	Technical help desks
Utilities (20%)	Customer support
Manufacturing and distribution (10%)	Outbound cold campaigns
Government (7%)	Inbound direct response (eg DRTV)
Technology (5%)	Outbound list and database cleaning
Travel and leisure (3%)	Customer care lines
Other (14%)	Retail ordering

Source: *Datamonitor*

Outsourcing options

Outsourcing will continue to grow in the UK with around 27% of the European market being based here -equivalent to 27,000 agent positions by the end of 2002.

What and how much to outsource can be a difficult marketing decision to make. Finding the right outsourcing operation will help, but ultimately, there are five main options to consider, as shown in **Table 8.8.5**.

Table 8.8.5 **Outsourcing options**

1. In-sourcing	Infrastructure is retained by the client. Activities are sourced individually by suppliers.
2. Selective outsourcing	Certain activities are retained by the client. Certain activities are outsourced to suppliers.
3. Alliancing	Two companies working together to share resources. Non-competing companies minimise peaks/troughs.
4. Co-sourcing	Stronger degree of partnership. Can include client management teams operating at the outsourcing company premises.

According to Brann Contact, the majority of interest is around **selective outsourcing**.

Choosing an outsourced agency

There are many phone agencies in the UK varying from *'one-man bands'* to large companies turning over several million pounds. If you are planning an outbound campaign there is ample choice. But with inbound the choice is more limited.

Getting advice as to how to choose your supplier is always advisable. Help can be offered by:

✔ The DMA.

✔ Direct Response Magazine.

✔ Independent management consultancies who specialise in acting as a 'mediator' between client and supplier.

Whoever you talk to, the following checklist in **Table 8.8.6** provides a useful guide to evaluating and choosing a phone agency, once you have arrived at a short list.

Table 8.8.6 **Checklist for choosing a phone agency**

✔ Visit the agency with the brief. Have a good look around. Don't be frightened to ask difficult questions. Remember: the agency's people will be talking to your customers, not theirs.

✔ Check how they propose to manage the campaign. Meet the people responsible for the campaign. Remember: the agency's salesman's job is to relieve you of your money! The account handler is responsible for the quality aspects of your campaign.

✔ Ask for a written response to your brief and specify that all the costs be detailed in their proposal. Phone agencies have a habit of coming up with a long list of hidden extras.

✔ Ask for contact names that you can use as referees. Check their references. That way you can build up confidence in the agency's ability to complete your task successfully.

✔ Ask the referee what has gone wrong with their campaign as well as what is right. Ask if they believe they get value for money.

✔ Use your instincts. Do you like the agency?

✔ Are you confident that they can handle your campaign (and your customers!) in the way you want? Will they reflect the image that your company wants to portray? Broken reputations are far more expensive than failed campaigns.

✔ Stipulate when reviews are to be held, and what the financial ceilings are to be. They are managing your money too.

✔ If they are in competition for the job, tell them. Tell them who they are up against; it will sharpen their resolve —particularly when it comes to costs.

✔ Does their response to your brief display an understanding of your objectives? Does it indicate that they can 'get behind' your project and produce the results?

✔ Do you have confidence in the company and the management? Do the account handlers have the level of experience needed to manage your campaign?

✔ (If inbound) Make some test calls into them on their other clients. Is what you hear how you want your prospects addressed?

✔ Test vs. rollout. If you are starting with a test, can they handle the rollout? When your test is successful, you do not want to go through the selection process all over again!

✔ Cost. It is usually unwise to take the lowest quote. Usually it means your campaign has either been under-costed or is likely to be under-resourced. Do not be frightened of the agency earning a profit. Profitable suppliers are important to continuity.

✔ Last, probably most important, do you 'get on' with them? Is it an open relationship? You are looking for a business partner, somebody with whom you will want to develop a relationship.

Below in **Table 8.8.7** is a useful checklist for managing your phone supplier, or in-house call centre:

Table 8.8.7   **Managing your phone supplier**
                        (or in-house call centre resource)

✔   Keep an eye on such data as time to answer, percentage of calls answered in service level, cost of abandoned traffic and the quality of the information gathered.

✔   Run test calls and check the quality of information you receive. If a fulfilment pack is sent, make sure the spelling is accurate, the correct pieces are in the envelope, and the information is what was asked for.

✔   Keep a record of the date the call was made and the date the information was received. Is this elapsed time acceptable?

✔   If there are problems, keep records that are as accurate as possible -and keep them in perspective. Five bad calls out of a thousand is not a failure!

A few final points about outsourcing:

✔   Be available and respond when they ask for your help.

✔   Ensure you meet your deadlines for them.

✔   Attend all briefing and feedback sessions to get qualitative input -they will always need your input too.

✔   Check, double check and triple check the costings before going ahead.

Identifying a well managed contact centre

If you are a marketing manager liaising with an in-house contact centre manager or taking the role of client with an outsourcer, it is important to manage the relationship from a position of knowledge and understanding. In this section we attempt to point out some of the elements that ought to be present in a well-managed contact centre.

The contact centre has evolved from the call centre in response to customer demand. Contact centres are about more than phone calls. They are communication centres, offering customers a range of options: e-mail, fax, website call-back facilities, face-to-face and video contact. A contact centre is open 24-hours a day, seven days a week. It offers customers more flexibility, more choice and more control – they can contact you when and how they want. So, if you have management responsibility for setting up a relationship with an in house call centre or the contracting of an outsourced contact centre–or just liaising with your chosen contact centre–it is important to meet customer needs comprehensively, both now and in the future.

Contact centre strategy

The most successful contact centres are an integral part of their overall organisation. Begin by clarifying the aims and intentions of your contact centre. Is it there to generate revenue, or to provide customer service? The contact centre of the future will do both and provide its customers with an efficient, effective, convenient way of dealing with its organisation.

Planning

Good planning is essential, along with a genuine commitment from everyone within your organisation. Without it there cannot be full, shared understanding of all the likely implications and benefits of setting up and running a contact centre.

Modelling

Simulation and modelling can be a useful tool. It enables you to scope your business requirements; try 'what if' scenarios and establish:

- The volume of tasks (how many transactions there are and how long they take).

- How many teams you need, and how many people in each team.

- The impact of technology, such as interactive voice response, on your service.

- The benefit of blending and predictive dialling technology.

- The amount of resource allocated to e-mail and web handling.

- The arrival flow of the tasks and service standards in terms of immediate response and task completion (phone, fax and e-commerce transactions).

- Whether or not you need to be open for 24 hours a day.

- Financial data on projected costing.

- AND ... Remember to plan for the unexpected too.

The well-run contact centre

You will not, of course, make the mistake of simply choosing the cheapest contact centre on offer: an operation that will competently meet your long-term needs must, of necessity, be stable, well-run, profitable and pleasant to work in. Here is a list of questions you might ask of any centre you are considering. Does it have:

- Light and airy office?

- Large open plan floor area?

- Wide column spacing? Flexibility of layout?

- High ceiling clearance? Air is a great absorber of sound.

- Plenty of natural light and absence of screen glare?

- Category two lighting?

- Good air conditioning?

- Absence of traffic and other noise?

- Raised floors to enable concealed (and flexible) wiring?

- Good quality seating and an ergonomic desk layout?

- Good IT and telephony infrastructure?

- Plants and pictures?

- Correctly sized workstations? 50 sq ft per person?

- Space for personal storage? Especially in a 'hot desk' centre

- Training/interview room?

- Break/coffee/rest area?

- Drinking water available?

- Ample parking or proximity to public transport?

- Good security (for after-hours operations)?

- Easy communication between operators, supervisors and managers?

- Wall space for motivation boards?

- Leisure activities encouraged ie social clubs, reduced leisure memberships, team fun events?

The future of the contact centre

The call centre or contact centre market is firmly divided between those who have and those who haven't. In the next five years, the trend will be towards existing call centres converting to contact centres in order to maximise efficiency and offer choice.

Businesses that aren't yet using the phone significantly will look to do so. These will tend to be small to medium-sized organisations that realise the importance of excellent service. Here we shall see significant growth in new call/contact centres.

Rapid development of a number of factors is likely to change the way the phone is used in business. These include technology and its reduction in cost: labour and its increasing cost; and the increasing use of tools, such as the Internet via contact centres. Of these, the factor which is driving companies' decision-taking is the increase in labour cost. We are already seeing a decrease in growth rates of the more established call centre countries.

But there will be continued change. Volumes are growing so rapidly that we shall see the Internet taking simple functions such as renewals and applications away from the phone. Responses to advertisements will continue to be handled by voice technology. The same can be predicted for situations such as checking the balance of a bank account. Simple or 'commodity' transactions are likely to be handled by a computer. This should free up resources to handle the more complex transactions using highly skilled people.

The Internet will continue to be a key support tool. Today the technology is more commonplace, that allows a consumer to be viewing a web page and talking to an operator at the same time. Indeed, contact or customer interaction centres will provide a seamless front for our customers.

Finally, operator skill sets will continue to change -technical ability as well as voice skills allow companies to multi-skill between phone and e-mail, and operators who fit the bill will be hotly sought after by businesses.

Whatever happens next we can guarantee that the phone will continue to play an integral part of it. Customers will demand it of us.

Chapter 9.1

Legal, decent, honest and truthful. Are you sure?

This chapter includes:

■ ■

❏ **Introduction**

❏ **General legal framework**

Intellectual Property – Defamation – Trade descriptions –

Pricing – Misleading and comparative advertisements -

Sales promotions

❏ **Difficult areas**

Distance selling

E-Commerce

Lotteries, competitions and prize draws

Data Protection – collecting data – cookies – spam - privacy

policies – using a data processor – transfers outside the EEA

❏ **Codes of Practice and Sanctions**

■ ■

About this chapter

his chapter deals both with the law, as it affects direct marketing, and with best practice, as catered for in industry Codes of Practice. The law, of course, is constantly liable to change, and at the time of writing there are even more areas of uncertainty than usual – particularly in the field of e-commerce and in relation to such things as cookies, country of origin and spam, etc. The aim, therefore, is not to give the last word on legal issues – there is, in any case, no substitute for person-to-person qualified advice in particular circumstances – but to indicate the general condition of the law, and of the voluntary codes which support and supplement it, at the time of writing. We deal first with the general legal framework that applies across the whole range of marketing enterprise; we then look at those areas that are particularly relevant to direct marketing. In all cases we attempt to elucidate the *principles* on which the law, or a code of practice, is based, since these are always less transitory than the precise provisions of changeable legal texts.

Authors/Consultants: Christine Reid, Lesley Tadgell-Foster

Christine Reid

Christine, an expert in information technology law, has been advising national and multi-national companies and institutions on a wide range of IT related matters since the early 1980s. She now concentrates on e-business related contracts. Christine read Classics at St Hilda's College, Oxford. After Oxford, in 1979, she joined Morrell, Peel & Gamlen and went on to become a partner in that firm in 1986. Then, in 1997, when Morrell, Peel & Gamlen merged with Manches, Christine became a partner in Manches — and started to develop the interest in data protection that she has today.

Christine Reid
e-mail: Christine.reid@manches.co.uk
Tel: 01865 722106
3 Worcester Street, Oxford OX1 2PZ

Lesley Tadgell-Foster, Shelfline Consultancy

Lesley began her sales career in copier sales, pounding the streets in the hope of making successful cold calls. Recognising that it would be a more efficient use of her time to introduce herself first, she developed a personal mailing campaign using a Petite typewriter and a copy of the local Kompass Directory. This tactic proved more successful than door-knocking and made life infinitely more pleasurable. She was smitten by the direct response bug although her employers remained uninterested.

After several increasingly senior posts in sales management, she joined her first agency, The Sales Machine, where she worked on a number of classic sales promotion accounts. In 1982 she set up the Shelfline Promotional Consultancy, initially still concentrating on consumer incentive programmes. However, she soon became embroiled in direct response again. This was timely, for clients such as English Tourist Board, Rowenta UK and the London Museums & Galleries Association, were all discussing direct marketing at about this time, and became her clients.

She is now building distribution for The London White Card, the museums passcard, using a good old-fashioned letter-writing campaign to tour operators to fix sales meetings around the world.

Lesley tutors the IDM Diploma at Imperial College and lectures widely on topics such as campaign management and data protection. Her varied experience has given her a very broad appreciation of the legal and regulatory aspects of all sides of the business.

Lesley Tadgell-Foster M IDM
Managing Director
Shelfline Promotional Consultancy Ltd
155 Felsham Road
Putney
London SW15 1BB
Fax: 020 8780 2024

Chapter 9.1

Legal, decent, honest and truthful. Are you sure?

Introduction

Every day the law is becoming more complicated. Not only do we have to respect the rules and regulations that apply to the more traditional areas of our commercial activities, but the advent of new technologies and the move to harmonise laws within Europe mean that there is constant change. We ignore these changes at our peril. Mention topics such as privacy or permission marketing in polite circles and people change the subject, but members of the public are increasingly aware of their rights. To win their business, we need to gain their confidence and meet their expectations. That means understanding what the law requires of us, complying with the letter of the law, and building trust through compliance.

Take, for example, the Data Protection Act. It regulates how we collect, use and disclose information about individuals. It affects many aspects of direct marketing and our relations with the public, but it is not all negative. If we ignore complaints about the use of personal data for marketing purposes, not only do we break the law, we damage our relationships and counter the effect that our marketing activities were intended to have. On the other hand, we can use privacy policies and give information to data subjects in a way that instils confidence. It is up to us to make the most of that sort of opportunity.

As the European Commission goes further down the road towards the harmonisation of laws throughout the community, we can expect Directives on subject matters as diverse as intellectual property, telecommunications and sales promotion in the not too distant future. All of these will affect how we communicate with, and get our message across to, people. But the European legislative process is long and cumbersome, and there is much negotiation and 'politicking' before a European Directive reaches the British statute books; it's essential in the meantime, to keep abreast of developments if we are to plan and implement effective marketing campaigns.

Warnings:

Take proper advice: Where possible this chapter refers you to useful sources of information but, with the best will in the world, it can give you no more than a taster of some of the legal issues. There will be other issues and this chapter is no substitute for taking proper legal advice.

The law changes and is different in different countries: This chapter deals with UK law, as it now stands, and with some existing and proposed European legislation that has a bearing on UK law. Remember that the law changes and, if you are marketing in other territories (even within the European Union), that different laws, regulations and codes may apply to your activities.

Sector specific regulations: This chapter attempts to cover the law that is relevant to marketers in general. Those working within specific sectors will also have to be aware of and comply with the rules appropriate to those sectors, be they television, charities, financial services, professional services, pharmaceuticals, food or whatever.

General legal framework

Most laws are not formulated with direct marketing in mind, but they have an important bearing on day to day business activities, such as the content of advertisements, the material used in promotions, what is said about competitors, how contracts are formed and the terms of those contracts, and how marketing lists and databases are compiled and used.

Ignorance of the law may have serious consequences: you may be committing a crime, punishable by a fine or even imprisonment; you may be liable to compensate someone financially; your campaign may have to come to a sudden halt; or you may find that you cannot legally do whatever it is you want to do.

Not only must you consider legislation and case law, you must think about the terms of any contracts or undertakings that might have a bearing on your activities. Are you free to use that great idea for a new campaign, or is its use restricted by a non-disclosure undertaking? If you intend using e-mail for your next mailshot, does your contract with your ISP prohibit this? Could your ISP terminate your access to the Internet and sue for breach of contract? Considerations such as these need to be addressed in addition to the law on spam discussed below, and may be just as important.

Intellectual Property Rights (IPR)

There are two sides to this coin. It's likely that every campaign will generate some intellectual property that you might consider protecting, such as a new logo or format, or a database of information or other materials. It's even more likely that you will want to use some existing material in that campaign. If that is the case, you need to take care that you are not misusing someone else's intellectual property. In general the owner of IPR is able to stop you using his property without his permission (licence) to do so. Below you will find a very brief explanation of the key types of intellectual property rights of relevance to marketers.

Trade marks

Trade marks may be names, logos, slogans, designs, packaging, shapes, sounds, colours and even smells. Registering a trade mark under the Trade Marks Act 1994 gives the owner of that mark the sole right to use it in connection with certain categories of goods and services. Trade marks protect the brand image of the owner, and the owner's rights may be infringed if you use an identical or a similar mark in connection with the same or similar goods or services.

Trade marks work geographically and there are various trade mark registries throughout the world and a European Registry based in Spain. If your activities cover several countries, you will need to check the position in each registry.

Not all trade marks are registered; it's possible to give another business grounds for suing you for passing off if you damage it or its goodwill by misrepresenting that your business and it are associated in some way, and by doing so confuse customers or potential customers. It's not uncommon for this sort of confusion to arise from the use of hypertext links from one website to another.

Domain names

Strictly speaking these are not property rights at all, but in the world of the Internet, they are just as important. Normally they are registered on a first come, first served basis, but there are a multitude of registries with different country codes (.uk, .de, .fr etc.), and you will need to register in different parts of the world if you want to stop someone else using your name with a different suffix or country code.

In general they are cheap and easy to register, but different registries have different rules. In the long run it's usually cheaper to register a domain name early to avoid finding that someone else has already taken the name you would like to use.

Copyright

Text, graphics, images, films, plays, photographs, artistic works, sound recordings, computer programs, music, lyrics, tables and the layout and appearance of websites are all protected by copyright. It is an infringement of copyright to copy, adapt or publish any of these without the permission of the copyright owner.

We have no system of registering copyright in the UK, so you cannot check to see whether or not any material you intend to use is protected. In practice, if you see the copyright symbol ©, assume that you need the owner's permission before using the material. Even if the symbol does not appear, as a rule of thumb, assume that any material that is less than 70 years old will be protected by copyright and that even older material may be. (In most cases copyright protection expires 70 years after the year in which the author or maker died. The period is 50 years for sound recordings and computer generated works.)

There is no copyright in an idea as such, but a developed concept, such as the plot of a play or the details of a marketing campaign, may be protected. A marketing slogan, or the title or name of a product will not be protected by copyright, but beware of falling foul of a trademark or of passing off if you use a similar name, title or slogan to one that is already in use.

A common mistake is to assume that because someone has commissioned a freelancer to produce some material, the copyright is owned by the commissioner; in the UK that is not the case. If you do commission someone to produce marketing material, make sure that you take an assignment or transfer of the rights in that material, and that the assignment is made in writing and signed by the freelancer. If you do not, you will not have the freedom to use that material in any way you choose. The copyright in material written by an employee in the course of his employment will belong to the employer, so there is no need for an assignment.

Moral rights

Even if you have secured the copyright, you still need to think about the author's moral rights; that is his right to be credited as the author, the right not to have his work subjected to derogatory treatment, the right not to have work falsely attributed to him, and the right to privacy for photographs and films taken for private purposes.

If you want to be sure that your activities are not hampered by someone's moral rights, you need to take an unconditional and irrevocable written waiver of those rights.

With the advent of the Human Rights Act 2000, you also need to respect the right to privacy if you are using any material, such as photographs or a storyline, that relates to someone's private life.

Database rights

Collections of works, data or other materials are protected by database rights. Many web pages contain databases and most websites are themselves databases. The owner may prevent anyone else extracting and reutilising all or a substantial part of the database without his permission, and the repeated extraction of small parts of a database may be enough to infringe database rights.

When you collect data for your campaigns, do not take data from existing databases without first obtaining a licence to do so, and abide by the terms of that licence. It's likely that deep-linking from one website to another (bypassing the second site's homepage) will be an infringement of database rights. When buying in lists, try to obtain a warranty from the seller that it has the right to make the database available to you, and you have the right to use it as you wish.

Rights of confidence

You can use the law of confidence to protect ideas, concepts and formats that may not be protected by copyright. *Before* you disclose an idea etc. make sure that you take a written undertaking from the recipient not to disclose your idea to anyone else, to use the information disclosed only for a specific purpose, and not to use it for his own benefit.

Summary of key points:

✔ If you commission a freelance designer to develop material for your campaign, take a written assignment of IPR.

✔ If you are developing a brand:
 – check that a conflicting trademark isn't already registered
 – register trademarks in the countries where the branding will be used
 – check at Companies House to see whether there is already a business with the same or a similar name
 – register appropriate domain names

✔ If you want to use existing copyright material that you do not own, obtain a licence from the owner.

✔ If you are willing to let someone else use your intellectual property, make sure that you have a written agreement that gives you control over how it is used and the ability to terminate their right to use your intellectual property.

✔ The fact that material has appeared on the Internet does not mean that it is not protected by IPR or that you may use it without a licence.

✔ When compiling mailing and other lists, don't extract data from directories or other sources without permission.

✔ When publishing your material, alert others to the fact that it is protected – use a copyright, database or trademark notice where appropriate, and let people know exactly what they may or may not do.

✔ Use non-disclosure/confidentiality agreements to protect ideas and concepts.

Defamation and trade libel

The law of defamation protects a business against false statements that damage its reputation, whereas the law of trade libel protects businesses against untrue and malicious statements that disparage goods or services (as opposed to reputation). If you publish a statement knowing it to be untrue, or not caring whether or not it is true, you are acting maliciously.

The key to avoiding being sued is not to say anything derogatory, unless it is true and you can prove it to be true.

Trade descriptions

The Trade Descriptions Act 1968 outlaws the misdescription of goods and services, including misdescriptions in advertising and promotional material. It is the overall impression that counts, so it is dangerous to give a false impression, for instance in visual material, even though that impression is corrected by the small print (should anyone read it).

If you describe something in an advertisement for any goods, all goods in that class must comply with the description, and using a disclaimer is no defence to having applied the misdescription in the first place, although a mere publisher of an advertisement, who had no reason to suspect that an offence was being committed, may have a defence.

The Trade Descriptions Act has a different set of rules for services, accommodation and facilities. In those cases the law prohibits making a false statement knowingly or recklessly; that is without regard to whether or not it is true.

Pricing

To give a misleading indication of price to a consumer (someone acting in their private, not business capacity) is a criminal offence under the Consumer Protection Act 1987.

Even though a price indication may be correct at the time of going to press, if it later becomes misleading, you will still have committed an offence, unless you have taken reasonable steps to prevent consumers relying on it.

Steps you might take to avoid trouble are: include the VAT in any price quoted when you are targeting consumers; make sure the conditions relating to any offer (eg time limits) are clear; and avoid any misunderstandings by using unambiguous language.

You may find the Code of Practice issued by the Department of Trade and Industry useful – courts will take account of whether you have followed the code, although compliance with it doesn't ensure that you have complied with the Act.

Misleading and comparative advertisements

An advert is misleading if it deceives someone and affects their economic behaviour and, as a result, harms competitors of the advertiser. Initially, complaints about misleading adverts are dealt with by the appropriate authority – the Advertising Standards Authority, the Independent Television Commission, the Radio Authority, ICTIS, or Trading Standards. Once they have had a reasonable opportunity to deal with the matter, the advert may be referred to the Director General of Fair Trading under the Misleading Advertisements Regulations 1988, and it's not unknown for the authorities themselves to refer an advertiser who refuses to comply with their decision to the Director General.

Under the Control of Misleading Advertisements (Comparative Advertisements) (Amendment) Regulations 2000 you may use comparative advertising provided it is not misleading; a competitor is not discredited or denigrated; unfair advantage is not taken of a competitor's reputation, branding or products; the comparison is objective; like is compared with like; and businesses and their trademarks and products are not confused.

A misleading advert may also be unlawful under the Trade Descriptions Act and/or the Consumer Protection Act (see above), but there are other possible consequences – the customer may be able to claim damages for misrepresentation and/or may be able to rescind (cancel) the contract for the purchase of goods or services.

Draft Regulation on Sales Promotions

The European Regulation on Sales Promotions was first proposed over 4 years ago in order to harmonise the rules for pan-European campaigns; the rules as they stand at the moment vary radically from one European country to the next, with what is common practice in one country being outlawed in another.

The draft Regulation covers premia, free gifts, below cost sales, promotional competitions and games and discounts, both online and in more traditional media. The main thrust of the Regulation is to achieve transparency in promotions and prevent member states restricting or limiting certain activities that may be perfectly acceptable in other European countries. Like the e-Commerce Directive the Regulation contains requirements about the information promoters are to give, such as a geographical address. It also seeks to protect children (defined as people under 14), so that promotional games don't encourage them to give personal data without their guardian's consent.

Unfortunately the Regulation has been postponed pending the results of the European Green Paper on Consumer Protection.

Difficult areas

Distance selling

The Consumer Protection (Distance Selling) Regulations 2000 apply to B2C contracts formed by some distance selling means – mail order, press advertising with an order form, the Internet, phone sales, telesales etc. (The distance marketing of financial services is the subject of a separate European Directive currently in draft.) Some sorts of transaction such as vending machine sales, the supply of accommodation, transport, catering and leisure services, the sale of land or construction of a building, and auctions, are not subject to the Regulations.

Information

As a general rule, you need to ensure that the following information has been given to consumers *before* they decide to buy:

✔ The supplier's name.

✔ The supplier's address, if money is to be paid up front.

✔ The main characteristics of the goods or services.

✔ The price (including taxes).

✔ Any delivery costs.

✔ Any communication costs, eg if phone calls are to be at premium rates.

✔ The arrangements for payment, and for delivery or performance.

✔ The period of any offer.

✔ The customer's right to cancel.

✔ The minimum duration of the contract and how indefinite contracts, or those lasting more than a year, are to be terminated.

✔ Any proposals to provide substitute goods or services if those ordered are unavailable.

✔ That the cost of returning substitute goods will be paid by the supplier.

Further information must be given at least by the time the goods are delivered or while the services are being performed:

✔ Conditions and procedures for cancelling, including returning goods.

✔ The supplier's geographical business address to which complaints may be directed.

✔ After-sales services and guarantees.

✔ Conditions for terminating any contract that is of unspecified duration or longer than a year.

Information must be given in writing or some other durable medium (including e-mail), and it must be given in a clear and comprehensible manner.

Cooling off

Consumers have a cooling off period of 7 *clear* working days in which they may cancel. This period starts the day after the consumer receives the goods or the day on which the contract for services is concluded, *but* if the supplier doesn't tell the consumer about the cooling off period, the 7 working days is extended by up to 3 months. Once a contract is cancelled it is as though it never existed.

There are circumstances where the cooling off period doesn't apply:

✗ If the supplier of services has informed the consumer in writing **before** concluding the contract that the consumer may not cancel once performance has begun with the consumer's agreement.

✗ Where the price depends on fluctuations in financial markets which the supplier can't control.

✗ Where goods are made to the consumer's specification, or can't be returned or deteriorate, or expire rapidly.

✗ Audio and video recordings and software if the seal has been broken *by the consumer*.

✗ Newspapers, periodicals, magazines (but *not* books).

✗ Gaming, betting, lottery services.

If the consumer cancels, all payments must be refunded within 30 days, and the supplier must collect the goods unless the contract clearly places this responsibility on the consumer.

e-Commerce Directive

The European e-Commerce Directive was adopted in June 2000 and was supposed to become law in the UK by 17 January 2002, but it hasn't yet been implemented. The draft UK Regulations were published in March 2002. They cover both B2B and B2C activities.

Country of origin

One of the most important provisions of the Directive is that information society service providers (which includes advertisers) are subject to the law of the country in which they are established. This is known as the country of origin principle. It's obviously helpful to anyone doing business over the Internet to know which system of law applies and, in particular, not to have to comply with a multitude of different laws. One critical stumbling block is that the country of origin principle does not apply to areas such as consumer contracts, IPR and unsolicited commercial e-mails (spam), so someone using e-mail as a marketing tool has the difficulty of having to comply with rules in one country that impose an opt-in regime and rules in another being satisfied by an opt-out. Add to this the fact that different countries interpret 'consent' for data protection purposes differently and the marketer is faced with a minefield.

The Directive and Regulations regulate online trade and advertising including:

any form of communication designed to promote directly or indirectly the goods, services or image of any person pursuing a commercial, industrial or craft activity or exercising a regulated profession.

Under the draft UK Regulations:

- All providers of information services (including advertisers) must give: their name; geographic address; and contact details (including e-mail). These are to be made easily, directly and permanently accessible, so that if someone doesn't want to receive e-mails in future, they can do something about it.

- Providers of VAT-able goods/services must give their VAT number.

- Members of regulated professions must give details of their professional body.

- References to prices must be clear and unambiguous, and indicate whether they are inclusive of tax and delivery charges.

- All commercial communications must be identifiable as such.

- Senders of commercial communications must identify the person on whose behalf the e-mail was sent.

- Promotional offers – discounts, premia and gifts – and promotional games and competitions must be clearly identified as such, and any conditions must be clear, unambiguous and easily accessible.

- *Unsolicited* commercial communications must be clearly identified as such, as soon as received – so they can be deleted without being read.

The Directive requires senders of *unsolicited* commercial communications to consult regularly and respect opt-out registers, available to individuals ('natural persons'). This is not reflected in the draft UK Regulations because the government thinks that existing codes of conduct give recipients of e-mails sufficient protection. The DTI's Guidance Notes acknowledge that this may need to be revisited in the light of negotiations on the proposed Communications Data Protection Directive. (See below under Data Protection.)

Lotteries, competitions and prize draws

Some of the most popular promotions are prize draws and competitions. Although there are moves in the UK and Europe to revise the law that governs prize draws, competitions and games, for the moment it is important not to fall foul of the Lotteries and Amusements Act 1976. Under that Act most commercial lotteries are illegal. Commercial competitions that are run in the course of trade promotions may also be illegal.

How the Act works in practice

An illegal lottery is where players pay or make some contribution for the opportunity to win a prize that is awarded by chance. The golden rule is that if all of the following are present you will be running an illegal lottery:

✗ Payment/contribution

✗ Prize

✗ Chance

Remove any one or more of the above elements, and you are likely to be within the law. So, for instance, it is legal to charge someone to enter a competition where the winner has to use his skill and the prize is not awarded by chance. However, if success does not depend to a substantial degree on skill, it may be an illegal competition.

Key Issues:

- **Is there more than one distinct stage involved in the promotion?** If 500,000 mailings are sent out, but only 10,000 contain competition entry forms, there is a two stage promotion - the first stage depends on luck; the second on skill. Check whether each stage (including any tie breaker) is an illegal lottery.

- **Does success depend on skill or chance?** To avoid running an illegal competition, skill must play a substantial part in determining success; answering a very easy question is not enough.

- **Does the skill involve forecasting the result of an event?** Predicting things like the winner of the Grand National is not regarded as skill for these purposes.

- **Is there any purchase or payment?** This might be something like an entry fee, or a purchase such as a journal subscription. Payments to third parties and premium rate phone calls count as payment. Promotions where entry is via a standard rate call or ordinary postage are not considered as involving payment. If entry requires completing a lengthy questionnaire online, any payment made for Internet access could turn the prize draw into a lottery.

- **Are you operating only in the UK?** Other countries may have stricter rules, particularly southern US states and Arab countries. It's wise to state that the competition is only open to UK residents.

- **Are you falling foul of the Prevention of Corruption Act?** This may be the case if you are running a competition for customer employees who are civil or public servants, or where the employee is a procurement officer choosing between competing products or bids, or where incentives are given for orders over a certain value.

- **Do you have clear and unambiguous rules?** (See the British Code of Sales Promotion – www.asa.org.uk.) The rules must be made available to entrants.

Overleaf you'll find a diagram. Use it to check whether any competition or prize draw you are running is an illegal lottery or competition.

Figure 9.1.1

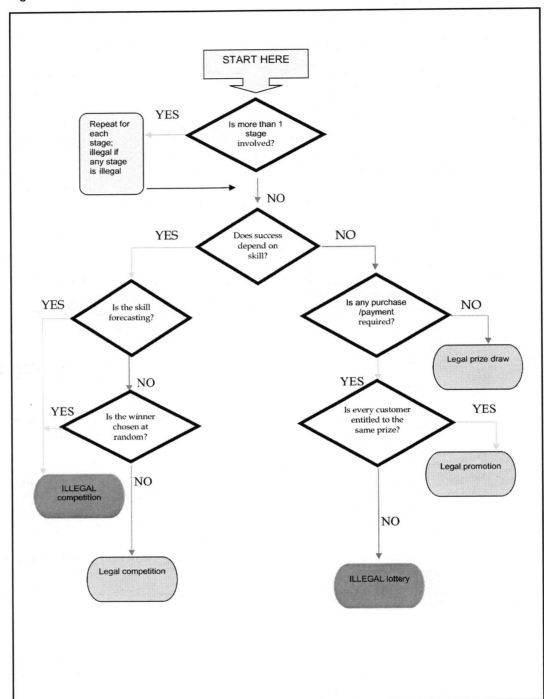

Data Protection

Are your activities caught by the Data Protection Act?

You need to ask two preliminary questions:

? Does my organisation process personal data?

The Act applies only to the processing of data that relates to a living individual. It doesn't apply to information about companies. If you are processing data about companies, you can forget about the Act, but be careful about data relating to individuals within a company. That is personal data caught by the Act.

? Is my organisation a data controller?

Responsibility for complying with the Act rests largely with the person (that includes a company) who decides the purpose for which the processing takes place and how the personal data is processed – that is the data controller. In a typical marketing context, a mailing house is a data processor, but the company hiring the mailing house is a data controller.

If the answer to both questions is 'yes', your organisation needs to be registered under the Act and to comply with the Data Protection Principles and other requirements of the Act.

Don't worry about whether what you are doing with personal data is processing – it almost certainly is. Processing covers almost any activity you can think of – collecting personal data, storing it, consulting it, transferring it, disclosing it, deleting it, in addition to what most of us would think of as data processing.

For guidance on the Act generally, your first port of call should be the Information Commissioner's website – www.dataprotection.gov.uk.

Collecting personal data and The Fair Processing Code

Whenever you collect personal data you must comply with the Fair Processing Code set out in the First Data Protection Principle. This involves informing the data subject of:

✔ The identity of the data controller (or its representative)

✔ The purpose(s) for which the data is intended to be processed

✔ Any other information which is necessary to enable processing to be fair. (To all intents and purposes this means telling the data subject about any likely disclosures.)

Signpost

You can use the Signpost symbol to alert the public to the fact that personal data is being collected. It should be accompanied by an explanation of the reason for collection and how and by whom the data will be used, or by an indication of where that information can be found. You may download a copy of Signpost from the Information Commissioner's website.

Cookies

The UK Information Commissioner is not sympathetic to the undisclosed use of cookies to obtain personal data and, if you use cookies without informing a visitor to your website you are likely to be in breach of the First Data Protection Principle.

When considering the proposed **Communications Personal Data Protection Directive**, the European Council of Telecommunications Ministers rejected the European Parliament's suggestion that cookies should not be used without consent (to the undoubted relief of many website owners) and has taken the view that cookies should be permitted, but only if individuals receive clear and comprehensive information in advance about the purposes of the processing and are given the right to refuse to allow that processing. In other words, there is to be an opt-out for cookies.

Direct Marketing

Any individual may, at any time, require you to stop using their personal data for direct marketing purposes. If you receive that sort of request, you *must* comply with it. It's important that your complaints and customer care procedures allow you to deal with this sort of request, and that you keep your marketing databases up to date.

Unsolicited commercial e-mail or spam

The law doesn't distinguish between marketing e-mails sent by legitimate businesses and those sent by more dubious concerns, or between indiscriminate unsolicited e-mailings and selected mailings or even isolated mailings. An e-mail address is personal data and you may not use it unless you comply with the Data Protection Act.

> Under the **Distance Selling Directive** methods of distance communication (except faxes and automated calling machines) may only be used where there is no clear objection from the consumer (opt-out); faxes and automated calling machines may only be used with the consumer's consent (opt-in). Bear in mind that the Directive is only concerned with protecting consumers.

The UK government hasn't carried the provision about distance communications into the Regulations. Austria, Italy, Germany and Sweden have, or are likely to go for, an opt-in regime when implementing the Distance Selling Directive.

In July 2000 the European Commission adopted the proposed **Communications Personal Data Protection Directive**, with the intention of replacing the 1997 Telecoms Data Protection Directive. There has been debate about whether or not the 1997 Directive applies to e-mails, and the Commission wanted to apply the rules in the 1997 Directive that apply to faxes. In short, unsolicited e-mails would be prohibited unless the recipient had given his or her consent (opt-in).

The European Parliament later decided to let Member States decide whether unsolicited commercial e-mails should be subject to an opt-in or opt-out regime, and in December 2001, after much disagreement between the Commission, the European Parliament and the Council of Ministers, it was decided that e-mails should not be used for direct marketing unless the recipient had given his or her prior consent, but with one exception – opt-out should be allowed for businesses marketing their own products and services, similar to those purchased by the recipient in the past. Still things are not settled.

The UK government favours an opt-out scheme for unsolicited commercial e-mail, and the draft UK Regulations implementing the e-Commerce Directive do not include the European requirement that senders of unsolicited commercial e-mails consult opt-out registers. The DTI recognises that the issue may have to be revisited. For the moment the DMA is supporting opt-out as the best practice.

e-MPS

The e-Mail Preference Service is a worldwide service, run from the US and sponsored by the DMA. It allows individuals to register if they don't want to receive spam, and for a small charge you can purge your e-mailing lists. (Visit www.e-mps.org.)

If you use this service, you have to send your list electronically to the e-MPS. Remember that that will be a transfer caught by the Eighth Data Protection Principle. (See under Exporting Personal Data below.)

The DMA and the ASA Codes favour the use of preference services.

Privacy policies

There is nothing in the Data Protection Act that obliges anyone to use a privacy policy or statement. Originally they appeared because many UK businesses were modelling their sites on US examples but, since the advent of the Data Protection Act 1998, privacy policies have assumed an increasing importance; used properly they can play an important part in assisting you to meet your obligations under the Act.

They may be used to give anyone visiting a website the information required by the Fair Processing Code, to obtain consent to processing or for transferring data outside the EEA, and to help you to keep personal data accurate and up to date (Fourth Data Protection Principle), and to help you process in accordance with the rights of Data Subjects (Sixth Data Protection Principle). You might use a privacy policy to invite your visitors to update their personal data when they visit your site, and to give them contact details if they don't want their data to be used for direct marketing purposes. If you have the right systems in place you will save a lot of time and effort and your customer and contact data will be that much more useful and valuable.

Practical steps:

✔ Whenever you collect personal data about visitors to a website (including taking orders online) give the fair processing information by including it in your privacy policy, and directing visitors to the policy.

✔ Don't hide it away, or make it look unimportant.

✔ *Before* a data subject sends you personal data, make it clear that by doing so he is consenting to its use in accordance with the privacy policy.

✔ Give individuals a real opportunity to read the privacy policy, and make sure the policy sets out clearly what use of the data may be made.

✔ Follow this procedure *every* time any personal data is collected via the site.

Warnings:

• **Abide by your self-imposed policy and don't overstate your case** – Otherwise you may be guilty of misrepresentation, or even breach of contract if the privacy policy forms part of the contract with the customer.

• **Check that the privacy policy reflects your entry in the Data Protection Register** – It is an offence for a data controller to process personal data unless certain details appear on the Data Protection Register. (Those details include the purposes for which the personal data is processed, a description of the personal data being processed, and a list of recipients, ie the sorts of organisation and individuals to whom the data may be disclosed.)

• **Don't mislead or confuse visitors where sites are linked** – Sometimes it's not apparent to the visitor that he has left one site and has entered another, where a different organisation is collecting his personal data and using it for a different purpose.

• **Remember that the data subject's consent must be explicit if sensitive data is involved** – Sensitive personal data is information about racial or ethnic origin, political opinions, religious beliefs, trade union membership, physical or mental health, sexual life, the commission or alleged commission of a criminal offence and any criminal court proceedings.

Checklist

A good privacy policy should include:

> ✔ **The identity of the data controller** – Many sites contain a logo or a trading name, but often forget to include the full corporate title and registered office of the site owner.
>
> ✔ **The sort of personal data that is collected** – For instance, alert users of a bulletin board that their data will be available to visitors to that board.
>
> ✔ **Whether you are using cookies** – And how to disable them.
>
> ✔ **The purposes for which you will use personal data** – Mention direct marketing specifically.
>
> ✔ **The sorts of people to whom you may disclose personal data** – Mention that they may be transferred outside the EEA if that is the case.
>
> ✔ **Contact details** – So the data subject knows to whom he should direct requests/enquiries.
>
> ✔ **A warning about links** to other sites.
>
> ✔ **What security steps are taken** – In broad terms so as not to help anyone to breach your security.

Using a data processor

If you engage someone to process personal data on your behalf, for instance a mailing house, or someone analysing visitors to your website or carrying out market research, you need a *written* contract with the data processor and, to comply with the Seventh Principle, that contract must contain the following provisions:

✔ The data processor must act only on the controller's instructions.

✔ The data processor must take appropriate technical and organisational measures to protect the data from unlawful processing and against accidental loss or destruction or damage.

✔ Reasonable steps must be taken to ensure the reliability of employees.

✔ You must be allowed to take reasonable steps to ensure compliance, eg by monitoring the data processor's procedures.

Exporting personal data

The Eighth Data Protection Principle prohibits the transfer of personal data to a country outside the EEA, unless that country gives adequate protection for the rights and freedoms of data subjects. Major trading partners such as the US do not give that level of protection, and it was always known that this Principle would cause serious difficulties.

The Data Protection Act doesn't define a transfer, but the Information Commissioner has stated that it means "to convey from one place, person, ownership, object, group etc. to another". This is broad enough to cover sending data to a sister company; releasing data about customers to a prospective purchaser; or forwarding an e-mail to a colleague.

It may not be immediately obvious that a transfer is taking place. For instance, someone in the US may access a UK database without anyone in the UK actively sending any data; the data may be transferred during a phone conversation; or an employee may remotely access a UK database while abroad on business. Publishing personal data on a website is a transfer of that data outside the EEA.

Every data controller should assess whether the country to which the data is to be transferred adequately protects the rights of data subjects whenever personal data is transferred outside the EEA. This is a difficult assessment to make, but to help data controllers the European Commission decided that it would designate some countries as having adequate protection, would work with the US government on some safe harbour principles for US businesses to adopt, and produce some clauses which, if used in contracts, would protect the rights of data subjects. Unfortunately few countries have been designated – only Switzerland, Hungary and, to a limited extent, Canada; the Safe Harbour has not proved popular with US businesses or the Bush administration; and the model clauses are widely thought to be unworkable.

What should a data controller do?

- Check whether you have the data subject's consent for the transfer, or whether you can obtain it.

- If not, check whether the recipient is in the US <u>and</u> has subscribed to the Safe Harbour. (View the list at www.export.gov/safeharbor.)

- If not, check whether the recipient is in a designated country.

- If not, assess whether there is still adequate protection. (NB It's dangerous to assume there might be if the Commission hasn't recognised this.)

- If not, put in place a contract with the recipient that meets the standards imposed by the European Commission. (Check the clauses via www.dataprotection.gov.uk.)

Codes of Practice

DMA

The Direct Marketing Association maintains a Code of Practice for direct marketing. Members of the DMA must adhere to this Code. The Code covers areas such as the use of personal data, the use of lists, information to be included in offers, targeting minors (those under 18), customer service, debt collection, phone marketing, and promotions and prizes.

The Direct Marketing Authority hears complaints. If a member is in breach of the Code, the Authority's sanctions include publishing a formal admonition and the suspension of the member or the termination of its membership.

The DMA publishes a Code of Practice for Commercial Communications to Children Online and a Code of Practice for e-Commerce. Both can be obtained at www.dma.org.uk, together with a useful list of legislation affecting direct marketers.

The DMA operates the e-mail, mailing, phone and fax preference services. Details of these are also on the DMA website.

Codes of Advertising and Sales Promotion

The British Codes of Advertising and Sales Promotion (which you can obtain from www.asa.org.uk) contain the self-regulatory regime administered by the Committee for Advertising Practice (CAP) and the Advertising Standards Authority (ASA) to ensure that advertisements are legal, decent, honest and truthful.

The CAP (made up of representatives from trade and professional bodies) draws up the Codes while the ASA oversees them by investigating complaints from the public and spot-checking to ensure that adverts comply with the Codes. The ASA operates a free prepublication advice service for anyone who wants to check that their advert doesn't breach the Codes.

The Codes cover advertisements and promotions in all media apart from broadcast media.

Key requirements:

- ✔ Adverts must be legal, decent, honest and truthful. The detailed rules of the Code on Advertising are interpreted to give effect to this fundamental principle.

- ✔ Advertisers must be able to prove any claims that are capable of being substantiated objectively.

- ✔ Advertising must be clearly identifiable – and distinguishable from editorial material.

- ✔ Advertising must not unfairly attack or unfairly use the goodwill (including that attaching to a trademark) of others.

- ✔ Advertisers are urged to get permission from people used in campaigns for the use of their image or name, and before implying any endorsement.

- ✔ Adverts should not cause fear or distress without good reason, or condone or provoke violence.

- ✔ Prices should be clear and normally should include VAT.

- ✔ Comparisons should be clear and fair.

- ✔ Adverts should not mislead or cause confusion because of their resemblance to another.

The Sales Promotion Code contains, among other things, rules on charity-linked promotions, addressing adverts or promotions to children (someone under 16), motoring, medicines, and health and beauty. The Code also contains rules relating to distance selling, list/database practice, and the use of incentives.

Although the Codes do not have the force of law, they complement the law; the sanctions available are serious, and they may be used against anyone. Not only may the media decide not to carry any advert that doesn't comply with the Codes, the ASA may refer misleading adverts or promotions to the Director General of Fair Trading, who may apply for a court order (injunction) to prevent the advert being published. Failure to comply with that order is a contempt of court.

Other member states of the EU operate similar systems and the European Advertising Standards Alliance co-ordinates cross border complaints from consumers.

Also available from the ASA website is a list of statutes and regulations relating to advertising and promotions. This covers all sorts of areas from Accommodation Agencies, through Charities, Competition, Consumer Protection, Honey, Local Government, Road Traffic and Vagrancy to Wildlife and Wireless Telegraphy!

TrustUK

This is a not for profit organisation, backed by the UK government, whose aim is to allow consumers to buy online with confidence. Accredited websites display the TrustUK symbol or hallmark and must comply with codes of practice approved by TrustUK. Aggrieved consumers may appeal to the TrustUK Approvals Committee if they are not satisfied with the result of any complaint to the organisation that usually enforces the code.

TrustUK recommendations cover areas such as privacy, online secure payments, clear pre-contract information and the protection of children (someone under 12). Details can be found at: www.trustuk.org.uk.

Index

D

R

Helpline

If you require further assistance on how to use this CD-ROM, please call: +44 (0) 1993 880223, during UK office hours or e-mail: help@chameleonhh.co.uk.

Please note:

- This CD-ROM should autorun – if it does not please run the setup.exe file on the CD-ROM in your CD drive

- This CD-ROM will run on Win 98+ operating systems

- This CD-ROM is intended for single-user installation only it may require that you keep it in the CD drive whilst it is in use.